The Edinburgh History of the Greeks, c. 500 to 1050

The Edinburgh History of the Greeks
Series Editor: Thomas W. Gallant

Titles available
The Edinburgh History of the Greeks, c. 500 to 1050: The Early Middle Ages
Florin Curta

Forthcoming titles
The Edinburgh History of the Greeks, 323 to 30 BC
Joseph G. Manning

The Edinburgh History of the Greeks, 1453 to 1774: The Ottoman Empire
Molly Greene

The Edinburgh History of the Greeks, 1774 to 1909: The Long Nineteenth Century
Thomas W. Gallant

The Edinburgh History of the Greeks, c. 500 to 1050
The Early Middle Ages

Florin Curta

EDINBURGH UNIVERSITY PRESS

© Florin Curta, 2011, 2014

Edinburgh University Press Ltd
The Tun – Holyrood Road, 12(2f) Jackson's Entry,
Edinburgh EH8 8PJ

www.euppublishing.com

First published in hardback by
Edinburgh University Press 2011

Typeset in 11/13pt Adobe Sabon
by Servis Filmsetting Ltd, Stockport, Cheshire

A CIP record for this book is available from the British Library

ISBN 978 0 7486 3809 3 (hardback)
ISBN 978 0 7486 9432 7 (paperback)
ISBN 978 0 7486 9537 9 (epub)

The right of Florin Curta
to be identified as author of this work
has been asserted in accordance with the
Copyright, Designs and Patents Act 1988, and
the Copyright and Related Rights Regulations 2003
(SI No. 2498).

Contents

List of Illustrations	vi
List of Tables	viii
Acknowledgements	ix
Series Editor's Preface	x

	Introduction	1
1.	The last century of Roman power (c. 500 to c. 620): army, church, and countryside	13
2.	Collapse or adaptation? The problem of the urban decline in late antique Greece	48
3.	Invasion or inflation? Hoards and barbarians in sixth- and early seventh-century Greece	68
4.	Dark-Age Greece (c. 620 to c. 800)	97
5.	Revival and expansion (c. 800 to c. 900)	135
6.	The beginning of prosperity (c. 900 to c. 1050)	166
7.	Early medieval Greece and the Middle Byzantine economy	209
8.	Social structures and Byzantine administration in early medieval Greece	230
9.	Christianity in early medieval Greece	249
10.	Conclusion: the people of early medieval Greece	276

Bibliography	298
Index	354

Illustrations

1.1	The distribution of late fifth- and sixth-century fortifications in Greece.	22
1.2	Sixth-century fortifications in Greece.	25
1.3	The distribution of late fifth- to sixth-century basilicas in Greece.	30
1.4	Reconstructions of wine presses in sixth-century rural houses.	36
3.1	The distribution of hoards of sixth- and seventh-century Byzantine coins in Greece.	76
3.2	The value of thirty-five hoard collections from Greece.	83
4.1	The distribution in Greece of single finds of coins struck after 630 and before 711.	98
4.2	Nea Anchialos, burial chamber: plan and associated artefacts.	102
4.3	Corinth, the 'wandering soldier' grave.	104
4.4	Anonymous seal of the imperial *kommerkia* of Hellas, 736/7.	111
4.5	The distribution in Greece of single coins struck between 711 and 811.	113
5.1	The Church of the Dormition of the Holy Virgin, Skripou (Orchomenos), Boeotia (873/4).	148
6.1	The distribution in Greece of hoard, single, and stray finds of coins struck between 913 and 959 and between 963 and 969.	182
6.2	The distribution in Greece of hoard, single, and stray finds of coins struck between 970 and 1050.	183
6.3	The distribution in Greece of churches dated to the tenth or tenth-to-eleventh century and early eleventh century, respectively.	192
7.1	The distribution of estates of the Athonite monasteries of the Great Lavra and Iviron during the late tenth and the first half of the eleventh century.	214

8.1 The distribution in Greece of tenth- and early eleventh-century cemeteries and isolated graves. 238
9.1 St Nikon *Metanoiete*, mosaic on the northern side of the nave in the *katholikon* of the Monastery of St Luke the Younger near Distomo. 264

Tables

1.1	Sixth- to seventh-century raids into Greece.	21
1.2	Marble capitals from sixth-century Greece.	29
3.1	Sixth- to seventh-century hoards of early Byzantine coins in Greece, in the order of their latest coins.	70
3.2	Sixth-century hoards with minimi from Greece.	78
3.3	Sixth-century hoards with heavy folles struck between 538 and 550.	80
3.4	The value in fractions of solidus of sixth- and early seventh-century hoards from Greece, calculated on the basis of the solidus–follis ratio at the time of each coin's minting and at the time of the latest coin.	82
3.5	Sixth- to seventh-century hoards of gold from Greece.	89
4.1	Seventh- to early ninth-century seals of officers and officials associated with the Byzantine themes of Greece.	114
6.1	Tenth- and early eleventh-century coins from continental Greece.	179
6.2	Churches built in Greece between c. 900 and c. 1050.	189

Acknowledgements

The origins of this book are to be found in discussions I had over the years with the editor of the series, Thomas Gallant. It is only right, therefore, that he heads my list of acknowledgements. I thank him for the invitation to participate in this series. A Dumbarton Oaks fellowship in Byzantine studies provided time and resources for the preliminary research, as well as a most congenial atmosphere in which to plan the volume during the academic year 2006/2007. I wish to thank Alice-Mary Talbot and Edward Keenan for encouragement and helpful suggestions. Alan Walmsley, Pagona Papadopoulou, Suna Çagaptay-Arikan, Dmitri Korobeinikov, Arietta Papaconstantinou, and Christos Simelidis have all discussed earlier variants of the chapters in this book and helped me locate facts and figures. I have learned much from their insights and suggestions. Both conceptually and substantively I owe a great deal to conversations and communications with Paul Arthur, Joanita Vroom, Alan Stahl, and John Haldon. I warmly thank Dimitri Gondicas for the opportunity offered to present a preliminary version of Chapter 4 in the colloquium of the Program in Hellenic Studies at Princeton University. Back in Gainesville, George Agrios and Mary Price supplied invaluable assistance with the translation of Greek texts. I owe a considerable debt of gratitude to them. I am also indebted to several institutions and publishers, who have generously given their permission to print their work: the Swedish Institute, the American School of Classical Studies, and the German Archaeological Institute in Athens, as well as the Archaeological Receipts Fund. I would like to express special appreciation to Euterpi Marki and Berit Wells for allowing me to use their drawings.

The time spent on writing this book has been a particularly unhappy phase of my professional life at the University of Florida. I was able to bring this volume to its completion only because of the understanding, the unwavering support, and the resilience of my family. I therefore dedicate this book to Lucia and Ana, my two compasses pointing at the important things in life.

Series Editor's Preface

The Edinburgh History of the Greeks is a multi-volume, chronological series covering the history of the Greek people from Antiquity to the present. Each volume combines political history with social and cultural history in order to tell the story of the Greek people over the course of recorded history in an exciting, novel, and innovatory way. Drawing on resources from anthropology, archaeology, and history, as well as political science, philology, art, literature, and law, the books will be rich and diverse in their coverage.

The Greeks suffer from too much history, some have said. Indeed, library bookshelves sag under the weight of the massive number of tomes devoted to the history of Greece during the ancient, medieval, and modern periods. This series differs from them by focusing on the history of a people, the Greeks, and not a place, Greece. The story will reflect the fluctuating dynamics of change while primary sources and accounts of the lives of individuals and communities will give life to the text.

The history of the Greeks over the long durée must be told on a vast and at times even global scale, and so the Greek world is not just taken to include the area traditionally associated with ancient Greece or the territory of the modern Greek state, but encompasses all areas where Greeks have settled, including the diaspora of modern times.

Thomas W. Gallant

Introduction

Few are the periods in the history of Greece for which continuity is a more sensitive issue than the early Middle Ages. For none is ethnic (as opposed to any other kind of) continuity more important for writing the history of Greece and the Greek nation. Discontinuity was first proposed by the German journalist Jakob Philipp Fallmerayer (1790–1861), who in the early nineteenth century claimed that modern Greeks were descendants not of ancient Greeks, but of Slavs and Albanians, whose ancestors had settled in Greece during the Middle Ages and had learned to speak Greek from the Byzantine authorities. Writing in the political climate created by the treaties of Adrianople (1829) and Constantinople (1832), which placed the newly created Greek state under the protection of the Great Powers, including Russia, and vouchsafed its independence from the Ottoman Empire, Fallmerayer was not as concerned with the Slavs *per se* as he was with what he viewed as the catastrophic consequences of their migration into Greece (Fallmerayer 1830, 1835, and 1845; see also Lauer 1993: 140). Driven both by the political liberalism of the *Vormärz* years and by apprehensions about Russia's increasing influence in the Balkans, Fallmerayer saw the proclamation of an independent Greek state as a weakening of the Ottoman Empire and a strengthening of Russia. He was therefore enraged by the political naiveté of the European Philhellenes and attempted to prove that the Greeks and the Russians shared not only the same religion, but also the same ethnic origin (Fallmerayer 1830: iii–iv; see Thurnher 1995; Skopetea 1997: 99–132). His 'Slavs' were therefore primarily Russians, which may explain the extraordinary popularity of his views at the time of the Crimean War (Lauer 1996).

In Greece, those views had by then already stirred interest in the Slavs, if only to combat Fallmerayer's increasingly pernicious influence. It was in reply to Fallmerayer that the Greek historian Konstantinos Paparrigopoulos (1815–1891), then only 28 years old, published the first Greek refutation of Fallmerayer's theories, which was also the first study published in Greek and dedicated to the problem of the early Slavs in Greece (Paparrigopoulos 1843 and 1858: 261–370; see also Nystazopoulou-Pelekidou 1999: 98–101). To Fallmerayer's racist theory, Paparrigopoulos opposed the idea of an immutable and timeless social organism, the Greek nation. The Slavs were neither sufficiently numerous nor culturally superior enough to be able to break the continuous progress through history of the *hellenikon ethnos* (Kitromilides 1998: 29). Against Fallmerayer's emphasis on such late sources as the *Chronicle of Monemvasia*, Paparrigopoulos brought forward the evidence of earlier authors, such as Theophylact Simocatta; against the idea of an early destruction of Greece by Slavic barbarians in the late sixth century, he cited Constantine Porphyrogenitus, whose testimony he interpreted as evidence for Slavs moving to Greece peacefully only after the plague of 746, when the Byzantine authorities allowed them to settle on deserted lands (Paparrigopoulos 1843: 77–89 and 1858: 105–12).

Paparrigopoulos' arguments set the course for the subsequent generations of Greek historians dealing with the early medieval history of Greece, especially with the problem of ethnic continuity. The canon established by him remains essentially unchanged to this day, with one or the other argument being simply refined or expanded, but not substantially modified. As Peter Charanis once noted, following Paparrigopoulos' lead, no Greek scholar writing in Greece has ever acknowledged that the Slavs settled in Greece during the sixth century (Charanis 1970: 26). By contrast, the first work dedicated to the problem of the Slavs in Greece, and written outside Greece, rejected one by one all the arguments which Paparrigopoulos had put forward. Alexander Vasiliev believed that the Slavs had already begun to settle in Greece at the end of the sixth century. That few Byzantine sources mentioned them after c. 600 did not mean in any way that they had entered Greece peacefully. After the plague of 746, a second wave of Slavic colonists arrived, who, in order to distinguish them from the native population of Greece, were now called *Helladikoi* (Vasil'ev 1898: 669–70).[1] Much, if not all, of the subsequent literature on the Slavs in Greece may be divided into two groups of studies: those that follow Paparrigopoulos, and those that follow Vasiliev. Almost all studies published in Greek fall into the former category. Like Paparrigopoulos, Greek historians for a long time maintained that the presence of the Slavs in Peloponnesos cannot be dated earlier than 700, and that the Slavs came to Greece not as invaders or hordes of barbarians to attack the country, but in family groups that sought out deserted areas in which to settle peacefully (Zakythinos 1945; Karagiannopoulos 1971: 460 and 1996: 189; Stratos 1975: 180; Nystazopoulou-Pelekidou 1986: 348; Anagnostakis 2000: 25). Most other historians dealing with the early history of the Slavs followed Vasiliev's lead (rarely, if ever, citing him) and argued instead that the earliest Slavic settlements in Greece must be dated back to the 580s (Niederle 1906: 51 and 1910: 212, 215, and 444; Charanis 1959: 40; Herrin 1973: 115; Zasterová 1976: 62; Dunn 1977: 72; Haldon 1997: 45). In Greece proper, Paparrigopoulos' arguments were further reinforced during and especially in the aftermath of World War II and the subsequent Civil War. By then, Fallmerayer had been demonised to the point where, although actually an enemy of Russia, he came to be regarded as a Panslavist and an agent of the tsar. Long before its first translation into Greek, Fallmerayer's work was stigmatised as 'anti-Greek' (Zakythinos 1945: 101).

But during and after the Civil War, the 'Slavs' themselves became a national enemy. Throughout the Civil War, the Slav Macedonians of northern Greece made an important contribution to the Communist cause. A strong link was thus established between national identity and political orientation, as the Civil War and the subsequent defeat of the left-wing movement turned Slav Macedonians into the Sudetens of Greece (Augustinos 1989: 23). By 1950, those embracing the ideology of the right saw their political rivals as the embodiment of everything that was anti-national, Communist, and Slavic. To hold Fallmerayeran views thus became a *crimen laesae maiestatis*. Dionysios A. Zakythinos, the author of the first monograph on medieval Slavs in Greece, wrote of the Dark Ages separating Antiquity from the Middle Ages as an era of decline and ruin brought by Slavic invaders (Zakythinos 1945: 72 and 1966: 300, 302 and 316). In the United States, Peter Charanis regarded Emperor Nikephoros I as the hero who saved Greece from Slavonicisation (Charanis 1946). The early medieval Slavs thus became a historiographic problem, *to slavikon zētēma*.

What caused this outburst of interest was a radical shift in emphasis, from historical sources to linguistics. The publication of Max Vasmer's study of place names of Slavic origin in Greece not only set a new course for the study of the Slavs in Greece, but also brought the scholarly research closer to the politics of the day. In his work, published shortly after the Nazi occupation of Greece, Vasmer claimed that the Slavs in Greece spoke a dialect closer to modern Bulgarian, given that several place names in Greece displayed linguistic features most typical of that language (Vasmer 1941: 295; for the first Greek reaction, see Amantos 1939–1943). However, his arguments resonated even more deeply with Greek scholars of the mid-twentieth century. In order for the influence of Slavic on Greek to have been as important as Vasmer suggested, relations between native Greeks and speakers of Slavic in the past must have been largely peaceful and quite close. Historians in post-war Greece therefore insisted upon Paparrigopoulos' old idea that the Slavs had entered Greece peacefully. There had never been any such thing as a Slavic conquest of Greece. 'The Slavs came, but they did not conquer' (Setton 1950: 511; see also Bon 1951: 56; Avramea 1997: 80). Instead of outright invasion, some now wrote of an insidious, yet peaceful infiltration of the Slavs into Greece (Setton 1950: 510; Bon 1950: 14; Lemerle 1963a: 35; Dunn 1977: 73; Hendy 1985: 619; see also Papoulia 1995). Advancing with women, children, and livestock in tow, often in small bands, the Slavs established themselves in Greece, but were quickly 'domesticated' as a consequence of the beneficial, yet irresistible influence constantly exercised upon them by native Greeks and the Byzantine administration, which forced them to abandon their previous life of nomadic bandits (Bon 1951: 56; Yannopoulos 1980: 353; Nystazopoulou–Pelekidou 1993: 23; see also Malingoudis 1988: 15–18).

The obsessive preoccupation with the problem of ethnic continuity may be partially responsible for the lack of interest in any other aspect of the history of early medieval Greece. Another reason is the extraordinary influence which Paparrigopoulos' idea of the 'Hellenic nation' had on the scholarly and popular perception of the Middle Ages in Greece. In both historiography and school textbook production, medieval Greece is understood as the Byzantine Empire in its entirety, and not as just one of its parts (for school textbooks, see Kolias 2003: 68). Developments in Greece proper, if treated at all, are regarded as of less importance than those in Constantinople. Because the Byzantine past is seen as a core element of national identity, in Greece 'early medieval' translates as 'Middle Byzantine' and the periodisation employs dates which have more relevance for the history of the Empire as a whole. In this context, political and military events such as the restoration of the cult of the icons in 843 or the recapture of Constantinople by Michael VIII Palaiologos in 1261 may serve historical or national agendas, but their significance for developments in early medieval Greece may be less apparent and they may call undue attention to the 'joins' between periods.

The emergence of the early Middle Ages (c. 500 to c. 1050) as an object of study in its own right has been a slow process. For a relatively long while after Paparrigopoulos' monumental history of the 'Hellenic nation', the publication of source material was mostly the work of non-Greek scholars. The first foreign school established in Greece was the Ecole Française d'Athènes (1846), and the French were the first to take an interest in the Byzantine monuments of Greece. Salomon Reinach (1858–1932) brought to light the inscription of Christoupolis regarding the rebuilding of the town's ramparts in 926 by the *strategos* of Strymon (Reinach 1882), while the author of the first monograph on the Monastery of St Luke the Younger in Phokis was the renowned Byzantinist Charles Diehl (Diehl 1889). The first modern study of the problem of dating the churches of St Demetrios and Hagia Sophia in Thessaloniki is that of Joseph Laurent (Laurent 1895). An early French interest in such written sources as the *vitae* of St Euthymios the Younger and St Athanasios the Athonite is associated with the name of Paul Petit, who also published the list of early medieval archbishops of Thessalonike (Petit 1900–1901, 1903, and 1906). Saints' lives and the history of Athonite monasticism remained the domain of French scholars well into the twentieth century (Binon 1942; Leroy 1953, 1963, and 1964; Lemerle 1963b). In fact, the idea of a critical edition of all documents available in the archives at Mount Athos was first put into practice in the 1930s at the Collège de France in Paris, under the direction of Paul Lemerle (1903–1989).[2] French scholars were also the first to write on settlements and settlement patterns (Antoniadis-Bibicou 1965; Lefort 1979).

Equally important has been the Imperial (later German) Institute in Athens, which was founded in 1874. Andreas David Mordtmann, the envoy of Hamburg, Bremen, Lübeck, and Oldenburg to the High Porte, published the first seals of Hellas and Peloponnesos (Mordtmann 1877), while Adolf Hermann Struck (1877–1911) wrote the first study dedicated to John Kaminiates' account of the conquest of Thessalonike (Struck 1905). Following the discovery in Olympia of the first 'Byzantine village' in Greece (Völling 1996 and 2001; see also Eiwanger 1981), German scholars affiliated with the German Institute conducted the first systematic excavations of early medieval sites in Greece (Bulle 1934; Grundmann 1937), while Hans Zeiss (1895–1944) first raised doubts about the ethnic attribution of archaeological finds dated to the 'Dark Ages' (Zeiss 1940). Gustav Meyer authored the first study of Slavic loans in Greek (Meyer

1894), and, as mentioned above, the publication of Max Vasmer's monograph on place names of Slavic origin in Greece set a new course for linguistic studies on early medieval Greece (Vasmer 1941).

The American School of Classical Studies opened in Athens in 1881. The School's excavations in Corinth began in 1896, but medieval remains began to be recorded only after 1920 (Finley 1932; Brooner 1935; Waage 1935; Davidson 1937; Scranton 1957). Despite the fact that the first early medieval coins to be published were from Athens, the coin finds from Corinth quickly became the standard monetary sequence for Greece, with which all other finds were to be compared in the future (Svoronos 1904 and 1909; Edwards 1933 and 1937). The earliest study of the Byzantine pottery from Greece was also based on finds from Corinth (Morgan 1942). Alison Frantz (1903–1995) and John Travlos (1908–1985) are the most important names associated with the late antique and early medieval finds from the American excavations in the Agora of Athens (Frantz 1988; Travlos and Frantz 1965; for the coins see Thompson 1954). The American School of Classical Studies also sponsored the publication of Otto Demus' stylistic analysis of the mosaics in the Monastery of St Luke the Younger (Diez and Demus 1931).

Although the first history of medieval Greece to be written by a European Philhellene was that of George Finlay, a participant in the War of Independence (Finlay 1877), the British School of Archaeology at Athens opened only in 1886. Two of its resident students, Robert Weir Schultz and Sidney Howard Barnsley, made some of the first architectural drawings, coloured copies of mosaics, and photographs of churches in Athens and Thessaloniki. They also published the first work in English dedicated to the Monastery of St Luke the Younger (Schultz and Barnsley 1901). A few years later, when he first joined the British School, Ramsay Traquair (1874–1952) began working on the churches of western Mani (Traquair 1908), while the School was also funding the excavations in Sparta, which produced medieval remains (Dawkins and Droop 1910–1911). His work was then continued by Arthur H. S. Megaw, who first attempted to establish a chronology of the 'Middle Byzantine' churches of Greece (Megaw 1931–1932 and 1932–1933).

The first Greek contributions to the study of early medieval Greece were in the fields of sigillography and numismatics (Konstantopoulos 1902, 1906, and 1930; Veis 1914; Kyriakidis 1941; Svoronos 1904 and 1909). However, Greek scholars became interested relatively early in Traquair's work on churches, as well as Dawkins and Droop's study of pottery (Giamalidis 1913; Sotiriou 1924; Philadelpheus 1924). A native of Lakonia, Sokrates Kougeas, first drew attention to the parallel between the *Chronicle of Monemvasia* and a scholium in the margin of a manuscript belonging to Arethas of Kaisareia and dated to the early tenth century (Kougeas 1912; see also Veis 1928). Greek historians were more receptive than non-Greek Byzantinists to the use of hagiographic sources, such as the *Life of St. Nikon* (Galanopoulos 1933; Papadopoulos 1935a; see also Oikonomides 1967; Kyriakopoulos 1976). They were also much more interested in the history of Byzantine monasticism (Papadopoulos 1935b), daily life (Koukoules 1936), and economic and social issues (Xanalatos 1937). The first Greek excavations of any medieval site in Greece were those of Edessa and Thebes (Pelekides 1923; Keramopoulos 1926). Excavations on the latter site started in 1924 under the direction of Giorgios A. Sotiriou (1880–1965), the director of the Byzantine Museum in Athens, which had been founded in 1914 (Sotiriou 1929a, 1929b, 1935, 1939; for the museum, see Voutsaki 2003: 250). He was also the first to draw attention to pieces of early medieval sculpture in the Byzantine Museum in Athens and in other museum collections (Sotiriou 1937; Megaw 1966; Pallas 1970; Drandakis 1972; Grabar 1975; Boura 1980). During World War II, Apostolos Vakalopoulos excavated the Byzantine fort at Platamon in northern Greece (Vakalopoulos 1940 and 1968). Many more forts were explored in the 1960s and 1970s through archaeological excavations, the most famous of which are Nikolaos Moutsopoulos' at Rendina (Moutsopoulos 2001).

After the war, however, the interest shifted back to ethnic issues, mostly under the influence of the political polarisation created by the Civil War. The tendency now was to deny any presence of the Slavs in the medieval past and to stress the idea of 'Hellenic nation' first put forward by Paparrigoupolos (Zakythinos 1945; Kyriakidis 1947; Georgakas 1950; Pallas 1955a; Chrysanthopoulos 1957). Replies came initially from the United States (Charanis 1946, 1949, 1950, 1952, and 1953; Setton 1950 and 1952), France (Bon 1950 and 1951; Maricq 1952; Grégoire 1952b), and Germany (Dölger 1952; Werner 1953), and only later from Slavic countries on the other side of the Iron Curtain (Nasledova 1956; Tăpkova-Zaimova 1964; Zaimov 1967 and 1968). The post-war years also witnessed the first attempts to study the history of Greece as part of that of the Byzantine Empire (Vogiatzidis 1949; Lemerle 1951; Ostrogorski 1952; Charanis 1955a; Zakythinos 1965). The idea of an *early medieval* history of Greece, or even of 'Dark Ages', did not, however, appear before the 1970s (Charanis 1970; Huxley 1977). During those years, the first attempts were made to assess the historiographic production in response to Fallmerayer's ideas (Veloudis 1970), but the concern with denying, or at least minimising, the Slavic presence in Greece continued unabated (Karagiannopoulos 1971; Liakos 1971 and 1977; Tsaras 1971; Thavoris 1975; Kordosi 1981a). New models of interpretation were not introduced before the late 1980s (Anagnostakis 1989 and 1996; Koutrakou 1993). A new direction in the study of place names of Slavic studies was taken by Phaedon Malingoudis' microregional research in the Outer Mani (Malingoudis 1981). Much of the archaeological research carried out between 1950 and 1980 and pertaining to the period covered in this book focused on churches, often divorced from their context. Less attention has been paid to civilian architecture (Bouras 1974; Sodini 1984). Only in the 1980s did the agenda change, and archaeologists began to concentrate not just on churches but on the sites on which they were found, as in the case of Synaxis near Maroneia (Bakirtzis 1985, 1987, and 1996). Since the 1980s there has been an increasing interest in dress accessories – mainly buckles and fibulae found in burial assemblages of the 'Dark Ages' (Gounaris 1984; Poulou-Papadimitriou 2002 and 2005). The 1960s and 1970s witnessed an explosion of numismatic studies (Metcalf 1962a, 1962b, 1963, and 1966; Vryonis 1963; Adelson and Kustas 1964; MacDowall 1965; Oikonomidou-Karamesini 1966; Weller and Metcalf 1969; Hohlfelder 1970 and 1973). Another area of considerable growth since the 1960s is art history, particularly studies of frescoes and mosaics (Papadopoulos 1966; Cormack 1968; Skawran 1982). Attempts at collecting the medieval inscriptions of Greece scattered in various museum collections resulted in the publication in the 1980s of the first regional corpora (Asdracha and Bakirtzis 1980; Feissel 1983; Feissel and Philippidis-Braat 1985; Avramea and Feissel 1987).

With so much data now available, the time is ripe for a historical synthesis. However, this book is not a survey of the earlier and recent research on Greece in the early Middle Ages. Its aim, instead, is to examine the emergence of the economic and social structures in Greece between c. 500 and c. 1050. The book utilises the archaeological evidence, as well as that of coins, seals, and written sources, mainly narrative, to describe changes in the economy and society of early medieval Greece and the power structures associated with them. Several themes provide the foundation for the volume and run through several constitutive chapters. The first is the Balkan context, which is particularly prominent in Chapters 1 and 4. Instead of a polar opposition between the Byzantine Empire and the 'barbarians' (Slavs or Avars), the history of early medieval Greece must be understood within a larger Balkan context shaped fundamentally by complex economic and social phenomena. There are several reasons for adopting a general view of the Balkans when dealing with the Byzantine presence in Greece during this period. The withdrawal of the Byzantine troops from the Balkans in c. 620 was followed by the creation of the first land themes in the region, first Thrace, and then Hellas. It has also been long noted that in terms of archaeological and numismatic evidence for the 'Dark Ages', Greece has much more in common with the coastal areas of the Balkan Peninsula than with Anatolia.

Another important theme is the economic and social role of the army. Any discussion of continuity, either cultural or ethnic, cannot avoid tackling the problem of the nature of the Byzantine power in eastern and northern Greece between the seventh and the ninth century. The number of known seals of military officials referring to Hellas is almost as large as that of seals of *strategoi* and officers of Thrace. The continuing use of coins, mostly small denominations, in Corinth, Athens, and a few other places cannot be explained in the absence of the navy, which was responsible for the maintenance of local markets supplying basic means of subsistence to soldiers and sailors. The army is also the institution associated with the repopulation of Peloponnesos in the early ninth century. Shortly after 900, local *stratiotai* seem to have been given the option of commuting their military obligations into cash. By then, the representation of social rank employed the hierarchy of so-called 'imperial titles', the most important of which, *protospatharios*, was normally reserved for the local *strategos*.

Similar but more modest titles were granted to the Byzantine clients on the borders of the first theme (Hellas) established in Dark-Age Greece. The *archontes* of the Slavs are mentioned throughout the eighth century, but by 750 their seals began referring to individual tribal groups, such as Drugubites, Belegezites, and Evidites. The distinction mattered, apparently, because some of those groups were seriously involved in the political struggles inside the theme of Hellas. No such clients existed on the western frontier of the theme, although the Milingoi and Ezeritai appear to have enjoyed a great degree of autonomy inside the theme of Peloponnesos during the tenth and, in the case of the Milingoi, the eleventh century.

Considering the early medieval history of Greece from an economic and social perspective is of course no novel idea; the novelty of this book resides in bringing together existing strands of work, which have until now failed to recognise one another. The traditional interpretation has been that changes taking place in Greece between c. 500 and c. 1050 were the result of exclusively political factors, mainly related to the revival of Byzantine military power under the Macedonian dynasty and the desire to convert the Slavs to Christianity and to 'hellenise' them. Nonetheless, a careful examination of the evidence now available suggests a different view. My contention is that both the political and the ethnic factors have been much exaggerated. The book is divided into two parts, the first being a synchronic, the second a diachronic examination. Chapter 1 discusses the sources pertaining to military developments, the role of the church, and the changes taking place in the countryside of sixth-century Greece. Having introduced the idea of the relative prosperity of Greece during the last century of Roman power, my study turns to cities as the hallmark of that prosperity. Chapter 2 focuses on the 'decline' of the urban centres and the lack of evidence of devastation, either by barbarians or by such natural catastrophes as earthquakes or the plague. I contend that many cities were abandoned when their well-to-do inhabitants began seeking opportunities for positions in the state elsewhere, the long-distance trade networks collapsed, and the Roman armies were withdrawn from the Balkans, c. 620.

Chapter 3 discusses a single category of sources, hoards of sixth- to seventh-century coins, which have long been associated with barbarian invasions and the end of Roman occupation on several sites in Greece. The analysis focuses most prominently on the role of the army in the distribution of specific denominations, as well as its association with the hoarding phenomenon. This chapter shows the multi-faceted implications of moving away from the interpretation of hoards as signs of political or military instability. As will become apparent, a new interpretation emphasising the role of the army is needed not only because it fits better the sixth- and seventh-century evidence, but also because in the early Middle Ages irregular injections of coins into local markets have demonstrably been associated with the presence of the military.

Chapter 4 concentrates on the articulation of the archaeological, numismatic, and sigillographic evidence with that of the written sources. My analysis highlights the ways in which the economic and social structures of Dark-Age Greece reflected the military organisation of the territories under Byzantine control. The discussion here emphasises the buffer role of the eighth-century Slavic clients and the intrusive character of the group, which buried its dead in the cremation cemetery in Olympia. The army and military developments are also given much attention in Chapter 5, which covers the ninth century. My analysis brings out the important divergences between the instability caused by Arab raiding and Slavic revolts in Peloponnesos and in the islands, on one hand, and the recovery and burgeoning prosperity of northern and central Greece. Chapter 6 focuses on the last 150 years of the period covered in this book. The explosion of church building, most visible in southern Peloponnesos, signals the spread of prosperity to that region of Greece as well, which is otherwise reflected in such sources as the *Life of St. Nikon*.

The second part of the book examines economic and social developments in early medieval Greece, as well as religious and ethnic phenomena. Chapter 7 focuses on economy, the historical aspect most neglected so far in the study of the early Middle Ages in Greece. Chapter 8 is dedicated to social structures in relation to the Byzantine administration. Chapter 9 looks at church organisation and religious practice, while Chapter 10 discusses the construction of ethnic identities. The conclusion in Chapter 10 is something of an epilogue, for it suggests that if there was continuity in the history of early medieval Greece, that was the continuity of the concept of Roman-ness defined in terms of Christianity and loyalty to the Emperor.

Notes

1. The idea that the medieval Greeks were called Helladikoi goes back to Finlay 1877: 405. According to Finlay, 'in Greece itself the Hellenic race had been driven from many fertile districts by Sclavonian settlers, who established themselves in large bodies in Greece and Peloponnesus', while the 'European Greeks' occupied 'the maritime districts of Greece, Macedonia, Thrace, as far as Constantinople' (Finlay 1877: 403).
2. As detailed in Lemerle et al. 1970: 3–6, Lemerle continued an idea initiated by Gabriel Millet (1867–1953).

CHAPTER 1

The last century of Roman power (c. 500 to c. 620): army, church, and countryside

'The outpost at Thermopylae had from early times been under the care of the farmers of that region, and they used to take turns in guarding the wall there, whenever it was expected that some barbarians or other would make a descent upon Peloponnesus' (Prokopios of Kaisareia, *Secret History* 26.31–4).[1] So writes Prokopios of Kaisareia in one of the last chapters of his *Secret History*, a work written in direct response to Emperor Justinian's legislation and financial reforms initiated by the imperial agents in the provinces. At this point, Prokopios' *bête noire* is the *discussor* (*logethetes*) Alexander, nicknamed 'Snips' because of his ability to clip coins. In 540 or 541, Alexander apparently introduced a series of changes concerning the defence of Thermopylae, which, although not appearing in any surviving edict of Justinian, were apparently sufficiently outrageous to incriminate the regime:

> But when Alexander visited the place on the occasion in question, he, pretending that he was acting in the interests of the Peloponnesians, refused to entrust the outpost there to the farmers. So he stationed troops there to the number of two thousand and ordained that their pay should not be provided from the imperial Treasury, but instead he transferred to the Treasury the entire civic funds and the funds for the spectacles of all the cities of Greece, on the pretext that these soldiers were to be maintained there from, and consequently in all Greece, and not least in Athens itself, no public building was restored nor could any other needful thing be done. Justinian, however, without any hesitation confirmed these measures of 'Snips'.

There are many reasons for not taking this story literally. For example, in his *Buildings*, a work composed a few years after the *Secret History*, Prokopios notes that Justinian 'rendered secure all the cities of Hellas, which are inside the walls at Thermopylae . . . For they had fallen into ruin long before, at Corinth because of terrible earthquakes, which had visited the city; and at Athens and Plataea and the towns of Boeotia they had suffered from the long passage of time' (Prokopios of Kaisareia, *Buildings* 4.2).² In Corinth and its hinterland, at least, a number of 'needful things' were done under the reign of Justinian, including walling 'the whole Isthmus securely'. The evidence of inscriptions substantiates Prokopios' interpretation of events given in the *Buildings* and warns against taking his alternative views in the *Secret History* at face value. However, on other accounts, he was much more consistent. For example, the idea that instead of a garrison of regular troops, the 'outpost at Thermopylae' was manned by farmers from the area, who would take turns as guards and, if needed, soldiers, is confirmed and not contradicted by the evidence of the *Buildings*. According to Prokopios, the walls at Thermopylae were 'entirely unguarded from early times' even to his own lifetime, 'and some peasants from the neighborhood, when the enemy came down, would suddenly change their mode of life, and becoming makeshift soldiers for the occasion, would keep guard there in turn' (*Buildings* 4.2).³ There are therefore sufficient reasons to believe that in general lines Prokopios' story of the *discussor* Alexander's replacement of the local peasant militia at Thermopylae with regular troops is true. The general point of the story – that soldiers needed from then on to be paid and supplied from local resources, rather than from the imperial treasury – may well have been one that Prokopios was hoping to score against Emperor Justinian. However, and irrespective of his bias, Prokopios would not have been able to convince anyone, had that practice not have been perceived, rightly or wrongly, as particularly outrageous. In other words, the expectations of Prokopios' audience for his *Secret History* – a select group of classically educated readers – seems to have been that regular troops stationed in Thermopylae would not be paid and maintained by locals.⁴ In any case, they, together with Prokopios, must have regarded it as abnormal that the costs of such troops would be covered from civic funds and 'funds for the spectacles in all the cities of Greece'. What then was the expected, normal way, and just how was the military defence of Greece organised during Prokopios' lifetime? Irrespective of the government's niggardliness, why did 'peasants from the neighborhood' accept becoming 'makeshift soldiers for the occasion' at the risk of turning themselves, 'together with Greece itself', into an 'easy prey for the enemy'?⁵

Part of the answer, of course, is in Prokopios' own work: during the sixth century, Greece was attacked so many times by so many enemies that local militias appeared as a better or prompter response than regular troops. There is much truth in this explanation. In 517, marauders for whom Comes Marcellinus employed the archaistic name Getae devastated 'both Macedonias and Thessaly' and 'plundered as far as Thermopylae and Epirus Vetus' (Comes Marcellinus, *Chronicle* s.a. 517).[6] In 533 and 537, regular Roman troops on their way to Africa and Italy, respectively, had to stop for a while in the Greek lands before embarking for their final destination from ports on the northwestern and southern coasts (Prokopios of Kaisareia, *Wars* 3.11.24 and 3.13.9 [Peloponnesos] and 5.24.20 [Aitolia and Akarnania]).[7] Prokopios claims that in 539 or 540, the 'Huns' (most probably Cutrigurs) 'plundered Illyricum and Thessaly and attempted to storm the wall at Thermopylae; and since the guards on the walls defended them valiantly, they sought out the ways around and unexpectedly found the path which leads up the mountain which rises there'. As a consequence, they devastated Achaia, but could not reach Peloponnesos, no doubt because of being stopped at the wall across the Isthmus of Corinth (Prokopios of Kaisareia, *Wars* 2.4.11). However, since this scenario is suspiciously similar to that of the Cutrigur invasion of 558/9, Ewald Kislinger advanced the idea that Prokopios was confused or deliberately invented a second invasion, which in fact never took place (Kislinger 1998: 55–6).[8] If so, his reason may have been an attempt to paint the background for the measures taken in 540 by the imperial *discussor* (*logothetos*) Alexander. In any case, Greece does not seem to have been the target of any one of the subsequent raids into the Balkan provinces of the Empire, which Prokopios attributed either to the Huns (in 544/5) or to the Sclavenes (in 545, 548, 549, 550, and 551).[9] The only attack on Greek lands mentioned during this period is the seaborne Gothic expedition of 551, which plundered Kerkyra together with 'the other islands called Sybotae which lie near it'. The Goths then crossed over to the mainland and plundered the hinterland of Dodona, 'and particularly Nicopolis and Anchialus' (Prokopios of Kaisareia, *Wars* 8.22.30–2).[10] They captured a number of Roman ships, including those 'which were carrying provisions from Greece for the army of Narses', an indication that the northwestern region of Greece may have served at that time as a gathering point for supplies to be sent to the armies engaged in the war with the Goths in Italy.

In 558, the Cutrigur chieftain Zabergan, on his way to the Chersonesos of Thrace, sent a part of his army to Greece. The Cutrigurs reached Thermopylae, where they were initially met with stiff resistance. After bypassing Thermopylae, perhaps using a path across the mountains, they were probably stopped at Isthmia, and returned (Agathias of Myrina, *Histories* 5.11–12; see Kislinger 1998: 50).[11] It took twenty more years before Greece experienced anything similar. According to Menander the Guardsman, in 578, 100,000 Sclavene warriors 'devastated Thrace and many areas', and were still plundering Greece, when the qagan of the Avars organised an expedition against the Sclavenes north of the Danube River (Menander the Guardsman, fr. 21).[12] The expedition does not seem to have fulfilled the expectations of Emperor Tiberius II, who intended to force the return of those Sclavenes raiding the Balkans as far south as Greece. According to John of Ephesus, two years later, 'the accursed people of the Sclavenes' set out and plundered all of Greece, the regions surrounding Thessalonica, and Thrace, taking many towns and castles, laying waste, burning, pillaging, and seizing the whole country (John of Ephesus, *Ecclesiastical History* 6.6.25).[13] Judging from the evidence of Book I of the *Miracles of St. Demetrios*, the attack on Thessalonica seems to have been organised by 'professional' warriors coming from afar, whom Archbishop John of Thessalonica, the author of Book I, called 'elite and experienced soldiers' (*Miracles of St. Demetrios* 1.12.107–8).[14] There is no mention of any regular troops having been garrisoned inside the city walls. Instead, when an official of the prefecture sounded the alarm, the citizens rushed home to get their weapons and then took their previously assigned positions on the walls. The attack was therefore easily repelled. According to Archbishop John, the Thessalonicans were already prepared for the attack, which they seem to have expected at any moment (*Miracles of St. Demetrios* 1.12.107).[15] This seems to indicate a serious and continuous threat to the city, of a kind that may indeed be associated with the invasion referred to by John of Ephesus. The attack of the 5,000 Sclavene warriors must have taken place at a time of intense raiding, when the citizens of Thessalonica had become accustomed to barbarian onslaughts. Indeed, John of Ephesus, to whom the 'accursed Sclavenes' represented an instrument of God for punishing the persecutors of the Monophysites, claims that in 584, they were still occupying Roman territory, perhaps including Greece, 'as if it belonged to them'. The Sclavenes had 'become rich and possessed gold and silver, herds of horses and a lot of weapons, and learned to make war better than the Romans' (John of Ephesus, *Ecclesiastical History* 6.6.25; see Olajos 2000: 394–6). However, in distant Spain, John of Biclar knew that in 581, those who had occupied parts of Greece were Avars, not Sclavenes (John of Biclar, *Chronicle*, p. 216; see Kollautz 1983: 466; Pohl 1988: 76 with n. 40). But at that time, the major Avar forces were concentrated in the northern Balkans, at Sirmium, which in fact fell in 582. It is of course possible that John of Biclar muddled Avars with Slavs, but the same cannot be true for Evagrius, according to whom, under Emperor Maurice, the Avars conquered and plundered cities and strongholds in Greece (Evagrius, *Ecclesiastical History* 6.10; see Curta 2004a: 518–19). The twelfth-century chronicle of the Jacobite patriarch Michael the Syrian, who relied heavily on the now lost parts of John of Ephesus' *Ecclesiastical History*, mentions an attack of the Sclavenes on Greece, during which they carried off on carts the holy vessels and *ciboria* from devastated churches. In Corinth, their leader, who is referred to as qagan, took the great *ciborium* from one of the city's churches and, using it as a tent, made it his dwelling. The chronicler then attributes the attack on Anchialos on the Black Sea coast to Sclavenes, not Avars (Michael the Syrian, *Chronicle* 10.2; see Niederle 1906; Guseinov 1969; Yannopoulos 1980: 366). The reference to Anchialos could be used for dating the attack on Corinth in or shortly before 584.[16] But it is very difficult to disentangle Michael's narrative and decide who exactly was raiding Greece in 584. He may have muddled Avars and Sclavenes, but the evidence of Evagrius cannot be dismissed on such grounds. There are therefore good reasons to suspect that in the early 580s, Greece was raided by both Avars and Sclavenes. Some of the latter may have been under the orders of the former, while other Sclavenes, such as the 5,000 warriors storming Thessalonica, operated on their own.

While the war with the Avars continued in Thrace, an army of 100,000 Sclavenes and other barbarians obeying the orders of the qagan appeared under the walls of Thessalonica. According to Archbishop John of Thessalonica, the attack took place on a Sunday, 22 September, in the reign of Emperor Maurice. This could have been in either 586 or 597, and historians have been divided on this issue ever since the publication of the *Miracles of St. Demetrios* by Paul Lemerle. Lemerle supported the earlier date on the basis of a better fit of the event into the general picture of Avar–Byzantine relations in the 580s (Lemerle 1981: 49–69).[17] Others argued that 597 should be preferred, because the poliorcetic technology and the siege machines which the army of Sclavenes and other barbarians brought under the walls of Thessalonica could not have been acquired before 587. In that year, according to Theophylact Simokatta, the Avar army besieged and conquered Appiaria, a town in Moesia Inferior, after being instructed by a Roman defector as to how to build a siege machine (Theophylact Simokatta, *History* 2.15; see Vryonis 1981a; Korres 1998: 172 and 176–7; Vryonis' arguments have now been refuted by Kardaras 2005). In 586, as well as in 597, the bulk of the Avar forces led by the qagan were far from Thessalonica. But in the 590s, most, if not all, of the operations of the Avar–Byzantine war took place in the northern Balkans. The 580s are the only period in which the Avars are known to have reached the southern regions of the Balkans.

When attacked by Sclavenes and other barbarians in 586, the city of Thessalonica had just recovered from a particularly devastating bout of plague. In addition, the 'young elite soldiers of the army' and 'those who serve in the great praetorium' had left under the command of the city prefect to the 'land of the Hellenes' (*Miracles of St. Demetrios* 1 13.128).[18] This has rightly been interpreted as referring to regular troops garrisoned in the city, a good number of which were on a special mission somewhere in Greece, probably to reinforce the local troops' battle against some barbarian attack. Despite such considerable handicaps, the Thessalonicans took advantage of the fact that the enemy had mistakenly attacked the fortified *martyrium* of Matrona located outside the city walls, believing that they were storming Thessalonica. This allowed the Thessalonicans to prepare for the assault. According to Archbishop John of Thessalonica, the news of the barbarian attack on the *martyrium* was brought by older soldiers left behind by the city prefect, who, together with members of the city militia, had been busy harvesting their fields outside the walls (*Miracles of St. Demetrios* 1.13.127).[19] Quickly withdrawing behind the walls of the city, those soldiers and the members of the city militia organised the defence, and a few days later, the barbarians withdrew without accomplishing anything.

Attacks on the southern regions resumed only during Emperor Herakleios' early regnal years. In Spain, Isidore of Seville learned that at the beginning of the reign, the Persians had conquered Syria and Egypt, while the Slavs had taken Greece from the Romans (Isidore of Seville, *Chronicon*, p. 479).[20] Peter Charanis has insisted that Isidore's notion of *Graecia* was too vague and could have referred to the whole of Illyricum, and not just to Greece (Charanis 1971). Whether or not Isidore had Greece in mind, the unknown author of Book II of the *Miracles of St. Demetrios* clearly referred to the southern regions of the Balkans. He knew that before attacking Thessalonica, the Slavs had devastated Thessaly and its islands, the islands of Greece, the Cyclades, Achaia, Epirus, and most of

Illyricum, in addition to parts of Asia (*Miracles of St. Demetrios* 2 1.179; see Koder 1986: 530–1; Iliadi 2003: 62–6).[21] The reference to both Illyricum and Greece makes it clear that there was no confusion. The date of the third attack on Thessalonica cannot be dated with any precision. We are only told that it occurred under the episcopate of John, the author of Book I. The description of the territories ravaged by Sclavenes before they turned against Thessalonica was interpreted by many as referring to the troubles of the first years of Herakleios' reign, snapshots of which are given by George of Pisidia or Isidore of Seville. In particular, the fact that the author of Book II specifically refers to maritime raids on canoes reminds one of what George of Pisidia has to say about the 'Sclavene wolves' moving quickly on land and water (*Miracles of St. Demetrios* 2.1.179; see also 2.4.253–4; George of Pisidia, *Bellum Avaricum* 197–201; see also Ivanov 1995: 66–7). Frano Barišić has therefore dated the siege to 616, and Paul Lemerle to 615 (Barišić 1953: 86–95; Lemerle 1981: 91–4; see also Korres 1998: 180, who advances an even earlier date, namely 614). Unlike in all previous attacks, this time the Sclavenes had brought with them their families, for 'they had promised to establish themselves in the city after its conquest' (*Miracles of St. Demetrios* 2.1.180). This suggests that they were coming from the surrounding countryside, for the author of Book II used 'Sclavenes' as an umbrella term for a multitude of tribes, some of which he knew by name: Drugubites, Sagudates, Baiunetes, Berzetes, and Belegezites.[22] There are several cross-references to most of those tribes in Book II. It is hard to believe, however, that they were responsible for the devastation of the islands of Thessaly, the Cyclades, Illyricum, and parts of Asia. There are two other 'lists of provinces' in Book II, one of which betrays an administrative source (*Miracles of St. Demetrios* 2.2.197 and 2.5.284). In other words, in describing a local event – the attack of the Drugubites, the Sagudates, the Belegezites, the Baiunetes, and the Berzetes on Thessalonica – of relatively minor significance, the author of Book II framed it against a broader historical and administrative background, in order to make it appear as of greater importance. When all the other provinces and cities were falling, Thessalonica alone, under the protection of St Demetrios, was capable of resistance. In fact, the attack, although for the first time organised from both land and sea, was short and easily repelled (*Miracles of St. Demetrios* 2.2.197–8; see also Iliadi 2003: 66–7).[23] With their fleet of canoes destroyed by the storm, the Sclavenes nonetheless did not give up their idea of establishing themselves in Thessalonica after its conquest. More important, they now called upon the qagan for assistance. They offered rich presents and promised him much more provided that he would help them capture the city.

Two years later, the qagan sent to Thessalonica an army of Bulgars, Sclavenes, and other barbarians, which he commanded in person. The siege must have taken place in 617 or 618, at the latest (*Miracles of St. Demetrios* 2.2.198; see Lemerle 1981: 99–100; Pohl 1988: 242–3). The Avar horsemen attacked by surprise the Thessalonicans who were out of the city to tend to their fields. At the time, there were many refugees inside Thessalonica, who had come from cities in the northern and central Balkans, such as Naissus and Serdica. Again, there is no mention of regular troops in the city. Instead, Archbishop John, the author of Book I, is said to have encouraged the local militia and to have toured the battlements in order to inspect the position of every armed citizen. Although the Avar army now appears as equipped with siege machines, not only an earthquake but also the constant supply of food and, one may presume, weapons, which kept coming to Thessalonica by sea, eventually prevented the Avars from accomplishing anything and convinced the qagan to abandon the siege after thirty-three days (*Miracles of St. Demetrios* 2.2.213). The siege of Thessalonica was definitely not an event of major importance. The author of Book II specifically mentions that no one knew about it, not even the Emperor (*Miracles of St. Demetrios* 2.2.210). We are not told who that emperor was, but he must have been Herakleios, for the siege occurred not long after the one described in the first homily of Book II.

A quick examination of a list of recorded barbarian attacks on Greece during the sixth century (Table 1.1) shows that no serious barbarian problem existed before the middle of that century. Leaving aside the invasion of the Huns, reported by Prokopios of Kaisareia and generally dated to 539 and 540, the only military developments taking place in Greece during the first fifty years or so of the sixth century are the invasion of the 'Getae' in 517 and the Ostrogothic expedition to Kerkyra and Epirus, which is commonly dated to 551 (Heather 1996: 269). Moreover, twenty years separate the 558/9 invasion of the Cutrigurs from the earliest invasion of the Sclavenes into Greece. Most military developments affecting the Greek mainland can thus be dated to the last twenty-five years of the sixth century. This may explain why regular troops are rarely, if ever, mentioned in Greece during the first half of that century. Besides

Table 1.1 Sixth- to seventh-century raids into Greece.

Year of raid	Target	Marauders	Source
517	Macedonia, Thessaly	*Getae*	Comes Marcellinus
551	Kerkyra, Epirus	Ostrogoths	Prokopios
558/9	Greece, Thermopylae	Cutrigurs	Agathias
578	Greece	Sclavenes	Menander the Guardsman
581	Greece, Thessalonica	Sclavenes	John of Ephesus
581	Greece	Avars	John of Biclar
580–590	Thessalonica	Sclavenes	*Miracles of St. Demetrius* I
580–590	Greece	Avars	Evagrius
584	Greece, Corinth	Sclavenes	Michael the Syrian
586	Thessalonica	Sclavenes	*Miracles of St. Demetrius* I
614/16	Greece	Sclavenes	Isidore of Seville
615/16	Islands of Greece, Cyclades, Achaia, Epirus, Thessalonica	Sclavenes	*Miracles of St. Demetrius* II
618	Thessalonica	Avars	*Miracles of St. Demetrius* II

the 2,000 soldiers moved to Thermopylae by *discussor* Alexander in 540 – an event which Prokopios and his audience seem to have perceived as extraordinary – regular troops appear only as crossing Greece on their way to Africa or Italy. The first regular troops are mentioned in relation to the events of the early 580s. While no such troops were in view during the surprise attack on Thessalonica by 5,000 Sclavene warriors, regulars in the garrison of that city are at least mentioned, if not actually present in Thessalonica, on the occasion of the siege of 586. It is important to note that Archbishop John of Thessalonica explains the absence of the regular troops from the city by means of what appears to be a mission to bring reinforcements to cities elsewhere in Greece, which were most probably under barbarian attacks. Throughout much of the first half of the sixth century, key fortifications, such as Thermopylae, seem to have been manned by local militias, peasants turned into 'makeshift soldiers for the occasion'. This is by no means contradicted by the evidence of archaeology. Until the mid-sixth century, there were proportionately fewer troops and military installations in Greece than in any other Balkan province of the Empire. To be sure, there were proportionately more fortifications in northern and western than in

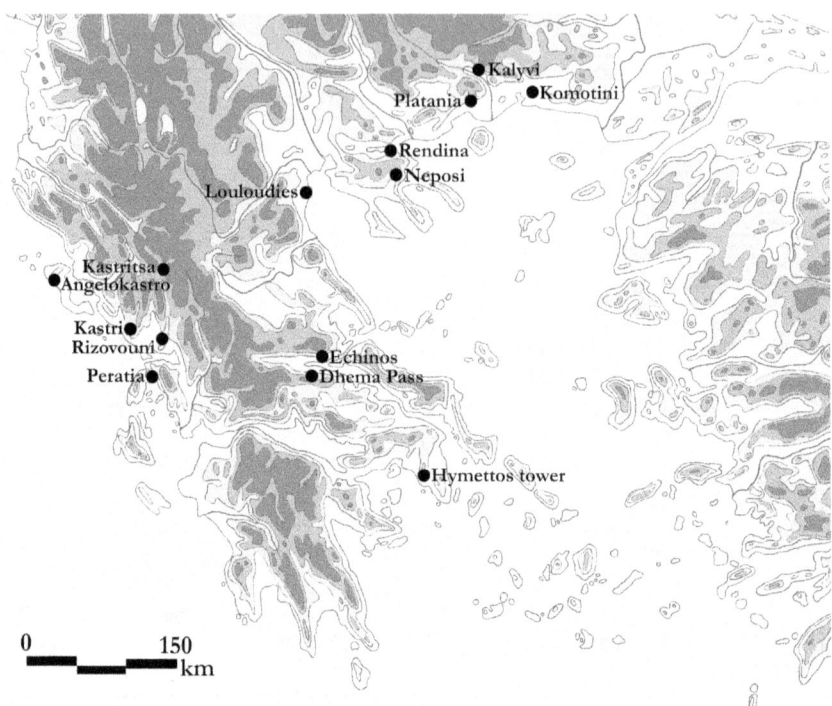

Figure 1.1 The distribution of late fifth- and sixth-century fortifications in Greece.

central Greece, and practically none in the Peloponnesos (Fig. 1.1).[24] In western Greece, such forts were built either close to the coast or along the roads linking cities such as Dodona and Photike with the coast.[25] Similarly, most sixth-century forts in northern Greece were along the Via Egnatia. The fortification at Komotini, which was coin-dated to the reigns of Emperors Justinian and Justin II, may have been a *mutatio* ('station'), while the forts at Rendina (on the eastern shore of Lake Volvi, in the prefecture of Thessaloniki) and at Neposi near Palaiochorion (prefecture of Chalkidiki) may have simply been garrison posts along or next to the segment of the Via Egnatia closest to Thessalonica. That much follows from the fact that most coin finds from Rendina are sixth-century issues struck within the mint in that city (Moutsopoulos 1987 and 1989; see also Dunn 2002: 707 and 709).[26] There were similar forts farther away from the Via Egnatia to the north, arresting access from across the Rhodopes, along the valley of the Nestos River. Many such sites were not built anew in the sixth century, but consisted of a new occupation and restoration of much earlier fortifications, which had been erected in the early Iron Age or at some point between the third and the fourth century.[27] The fort built on the shore of Lake Kastoria at Longas (prefecture of Kastoria) has been dated to the sixth century on the basis of iron fibulae with bent stems, which are otherwise typical of contemporary military sites in Bulgaria (Moutsopoulos 1992a: 9–10 with 9 figs 7–8). The fort at Setina near Achlada (prefecture of Florina) produced a coin of 16 nummia struck in Thessalonica during Justinian's reign (Moutsopoulos 1992a: 17). A sixth-century re-occupation of ancient fortifications has also been documented on several sites in Attica.[28] None of them seems to have been very large, nor was occupation probably permanent. By contrast, a permanent occupation is suggested for the strategically located sixth-century forts behind Thermopylae at the Dhema Pass, and, on the other side of the Malian Gulf, at a site tentatively identified with Echinos mentioned by Prokopios (Prokopios of Kaisareia, *Wars* 8.25.18; see also Daly 1942).[29] The most impressive fort built for the permanent stationing of troops is nonetheless Isthmia, a comparatively large site, without any analogue in Greece, which could have easily accommodated one or two legions (Kardulias 2005: 31–46 and 107–24; see also Gregory and Kardulias 1990: 505).[30] The size of the Isthmia fort can be explained only in terms of its being adjacent to the wall across the Isthmus of Corinth, the building of which Prokopios attributed to Justinian, even though the archaeological evidence points to an early fifth-century construction (Prokopios of Kaisareia, *Buildings* 4.2; for the date of the Hexamilion (the name later given to the wall across the Isthmus), see Gregory 2000: 111–12). Unlike most other forts in Greece, Isthmia was very probably built at the initiative of and with funds from the government in Constantinople. The fort must therefore have been manned by regular troops, for 'it would not have made much sense for the state to undertake expensive projects such as the construction of the Hexamilion and Fortress, only to leave defence in the hands of local militias' (Gregory and Kardulias 1990: 505). However, the presence of regular troops is also attested for some of the forts in northern Greece guarding the Via Egnatia. Seven out of eight grave inscriptions found in Macedonia before 1983 may be dated to the fifth and sixth century and specifically mention names of such regular units as the *Germaniciani*, the *Secundani*, the *Ascarii iuniores*, and the *Atecotti* (Feissel 1983: 44–5 [from Edessa] and 175 [from Thessaloniki]).[31] Except at Isthmia, no other regular troops appear anywhere else in Greece.[32] A graffito on a pavement marble slab found in Corinth mentions two *buccellarii* named

Boudios and John, both personal bodyguards in the service of the prefect of Illyricum. The two men were certainly not unlike 'those who serve in the great praetorium', who, at the time of the 586 siege of Thessalonica, are said to have been on a mission in Greece under the command of the prefect (Feissel and Philippidis-Braat 1985: 361; *Miracles of St. Demetrios* 1.13.128).[33] The two *buccellarii* from Corinth were therefore not members of the local garrison of troops. Whether or not forts in western and central Greece were manned by 'makeshift soldiers for the occasion', a conspicuous feature of the archaeology of sixth-century fortifications in Greece is that, in sharp contrast to similar sites in the northern and central Balkans, those in Greece produced very few weapons. One single spear head is known from the fortification at the Dhema Pass (Rosser 2001: 40 and pl. 4.4a), while most other spear and arrow heads were found either in urban centres or in burial assemblages.[34] Equally significant is the relatively small number of Greek finds of belt buckles of the Sucidava class, which are otherwise one of the most typical dress accessories on military sites in the northern Balkans.[35]

Not all fortified sites may have been associated with the military. The fortification at Louloudies near Pydna (prefecture of Pieria) had four square towers, but inside the ramparts there were no military installations and no barracks. Instead, archaeologists found a basilica, olive oil presses, and storage facilities, as well as a large building interpreted as an episcopal palace (Fig. 1.2). The basilica was destroyed by fire at some point in the mid-sixth century, and a cemetery appeared around the much diminished church. After destruction, a kiln was installed in the area, together with glass- and metalworking facilities, in addition to a marble-carving workshop. The site, which has been coin-dated to the reigns of Justin I and Justinian, has produced numerous finds of amphorae of the Late Roman 1 and Late Roman 2, as well as *spatheia*, all of which bespeak the long-distance trade contacts between the site at Louloudies and production centres in the Eastern and Southern Mediterranean region (Marki 1997a; Marki and Polychronaki 2000; Marki and Cheimonopoulou 2003).[36] Despite the presence of ramparts and towers, Louloudies was clearly a site very different, in terms of both size and function, from the garrison fort at Isthmia. On the other hand, it reminds one of similarly fortified churches of the northern Balkans, such as Pirdop, in western Bulgaria, the function of which remains unclear (Chaneva-Dechevska 1999: 303–9; Curta 2001b: 162).[37] As different as the fortification in Louloudies may be from any other in Greece,

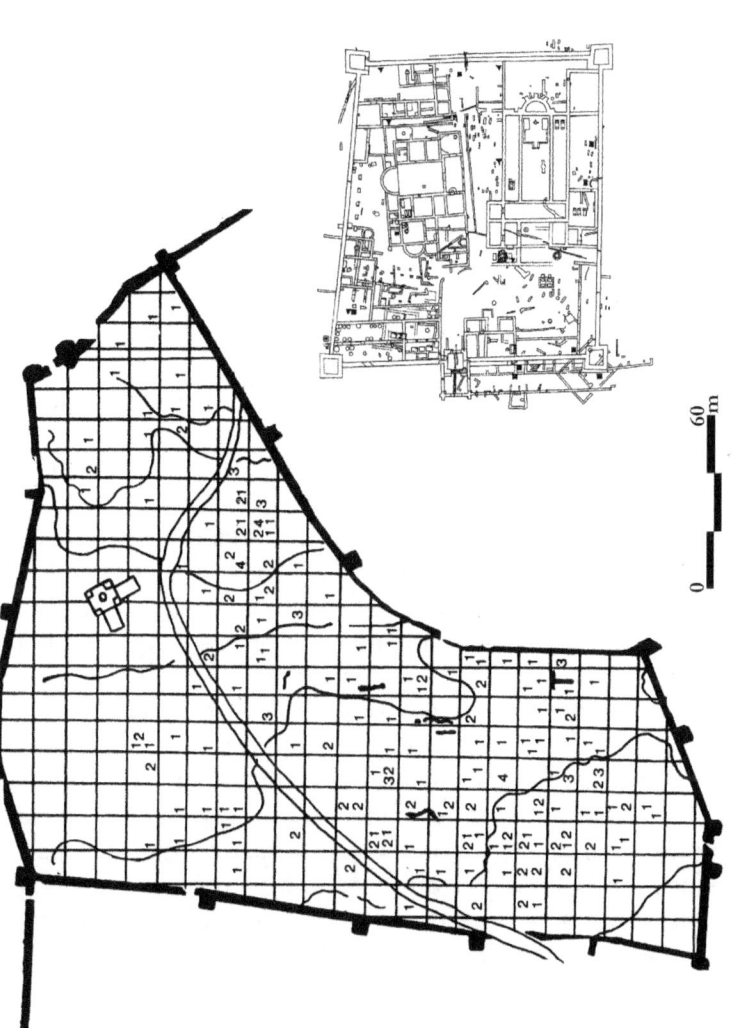

Figure 1.2 Sixth-century fortifications in Greece. On the left, Isthmia with the distribution of Late Byzantine pottery. On the right, Louloudies with the distribution of coarse ware pottery (marked by squares) and amphora finds (marked by triangles) (after Gregory and Kardulias 1990: 494 fig. 19; Marki and Cheimonopoulou 2003: 711 fig. 19). *Reproduced courtesy of the Trustees of the American School of Classical Studies at Athens and the Archaeological Receipts Fund.*

its three-aisled basilica, most probably built at some point during the second quarter of the sixth century, still shares a number of common features with other churches erected at that time in the Greek lands. For example, the excavators of the Louloudies basilica stumbled upon a vaulted tomb to the southwest of the narthex. On each of the long walls of the tomb, there were murals depicting large foliate Latin crosses (Marki 1997a; for the accompanying inscription, see Kiourtzian 1997: 31–2). A barrel-vaulted tomb was also found on the southern side of a room built next to the baptistery of the basilica excavated in Bgadoudi near Epanomi (prefecture of Thessaloniki). Much like the tomb in Louloudies, the one in Bgadoudi had walls covered with frescoes depicting large Latin crosses (Pazaras 2001a: 293–4).[38] This is also true for the vaulted tomb at the eastern end of the northern aisle in the basilica at Kastro, in Larissa, as well as for a vaulted tomb near the basilica on the Zoodochos Pigi Hill in Kilkis (Laskaris 2000: 60–1 and 63). A vaulted tomb was also found in the southern apse of the transept of the sixth-century basilica in Synaxis, near Maroneia (Laskaris 2000: 66). Another such tomb was found just outside a fifth- to sixth-century basilica excavated in Pilaia, a suburb of Thessaloniki, and was decorated with murals showing, among other things, an image of the Scriptures (Marki 2001a: 274 and 276 fig. 3). But examples of vaulted tombs next to sixth-century basilicas are not restricted to northern Greece. A vaulted tomb has also been found on the northern side of the basilica of Agia Sophia in Mytikas (Aitoloakarnania) (Paliouras 2004: 58–9). Two other examples are known from Stamata (Attica). One of the two tombs found there had large murals depicting Latin crosses, a bird, and a fish, as well as an inscription. Unlike other vaulted tombs in Greece, those in Stamata were not outside, but inside a three-aisled, fifth- to sixth-century basilica. The tomb with murals produced a pair of gold earrings and a gold clasp, in addition to bronze and silver spatulas and a lekythos, all dated to the sixth century and betraying the presence of a female burial (Gkini-Tsophopoulou 1990; Touchais et al. 1996: 1130; Laskaris 2000: 78–9; for the basilica, see also Gkini-Tsophopoulou 1980).[39] Vaulted tombs with murals found in Greece may be interpreted in terms similar to those applying to the episcopal basilica in Stobi, which was restored during the first half of the sixth century, when a vaulted tomb appeared at the eastern end of the southern aisle. Inside the tomb, there was a skeleton of a man, 40 or 50 years of age, who was buried dressed in a robe and wearing leather shoes, but without any grave goods

(Veljanovska 1987). Whether or not this was the tomb of Bishop Philip of Stobi, who is known to have paid for the building of the episcopal basilica, burying important persons in vaulted tombs inside or close to the church was a practice which seem to have existed in sixth-century Greece, but which may have begun in the fifth century. On the basis of a few surviving inscriptions, the idea has been put forward that burial in (urban) churches was a prerogative of the clergy (Snively 1998: 494–5; Laskaris 2000: 74). This may indeed be true for Louloudies, Bgadoudi, and Pilaia, but the grave goods found in one of the two vaulted tombs in Stamata strongly suggest that wealthy female donors could also have been given such a treatment in death. After all, the early sixth-century inscriptions of the deaconesses Agrippianis from Patras (Feissel and Philippidis-Braat 1985: 374; Moutzali 2002: 179) and Theoprepeia from Vonitsa-Drymos (Paliouras 2004: 56) show that female patronage must be taken into consideration for the interpretation of the vaulted tombs.[40]

Basilicas with privileged inhumations in vaulted tombs must be distinguished from cemetery churches, which appear in the late fifth and especially during the sixth century in areas where concentrations of tombs, presumably Christian, were located. This is the case, for example, with the cemetery basilica found in Dion (Litochoron, prefecture of Pieria), which received a mosaic pavement in the nave c. 500 and brick pavements in the aisles in the mid-sixth century (Gounaris 1989: 2699; Laskaris 2000: 39).[41] Both the decoration and the existence of a second building phase in the mid-sixth century are otherwise typical of churches with no burials. The late fifth-century basilica built in Tithorea (Phthiotis) was repaired after c. 550, when a new pavement was installed, together with a new altar table (Gialouri 2004: 98). A fifth- or early sixth-century church with mosaic pavements excavated in Paliambela near Arethousa (prefecture of Thessaloniki) was destroyed in the late sixth or early seventh century (Karivieri 2001). Two fifth-century basilicas in Varvara (prefecture of Chalkidiki) received walls during the second half of the sixth century, which replaced the stylobates, thus effectively separating the nave from the aisles and considerably diminishing the size of the repaired churches (Tavlakis et al. 2003: 399–400). In Agia Kyriaki near Filiatra (Messinia) a five-aisled basilica was built shortly after 500 with stone brought from Attica and decorated with a mosaic pavement in the sanctuary. After its destruction, a much smaller, three-aisled basilica was built on top of the other in the late 500s (Gerstel 1998: 214). By contrast, a three-aisled basilica built in the fifth century was repaired and enlarged in the mid-sixth century in Palioklisi near Elasson (prefecture of Larissa) (Deriziotis and Kougioumtzoglu 2004: 66). The earlier building phase dated c. 500 often involved the setting of mosaic pavements, as in Kephalari in the prefecture of Argos (Oikonomou-Laniadou 2003: 15–16), Aigion in Achaia (Gounaris 1989: 2693), Andikira in Voiotia (Kourenta-Raptaki et al. 1994; Kourenta-Raptaki 2004: 113–15 and 116 fig. 4), Koromilia in the prefecture of Kilkis (Makropoulou 2002: 361–2), or Agia Kyriaki in Messinia (Gerstel 1998: 213).[42] In Nikopolis, the mosaic workshop responsible for the splendid decoration of four basilicas in the city, the mosaic in the bema area of basilica B on the island of Kephalos, and the narthex mosaic at Palaiopolis in Kerkyra operated during the last decades of the fifth and the first half of the sixth century. Similarly, most, if not all of the few imported column capitals of Epirus cannot be dated later than the first half of the sixth century. The two largest groups of imported or high-quality capital columns found in Greece – double zone and Kautzsch's types V/VI – are also to be dated primarily to the first half of the sixth century (Table 1.2; data after Sodini 1984 and 1989; for Epirus, see also Bowden 2003: 116 and 150). It is interesting to note that the largest number of capitals from Achaia, either composite Ionic or double zone, are also to be dated between the fifth century and the third quarter of the sixth century. It has long been established that master carvers from Constantinople must have worked at Lechaion, at St Demetrios in Thessalonica, at Philippi, Amphipolis, and Nea Anchialos. Their work was immediately imitated locally, with local workshops developing in Thessalonica, Attika, and Magnesia (Sodini 1984: 211 and 296–7; Sythiakaki 2004). However, Table 1.2 shows that no basket-shaped capitals have so far been found in Epirus, while the largest number of such capitals is known from Macedonia. Similarly, three different sites in Macedonia have produced capitals of Kautzsch's types III and IV, with one of them known for no fewer than twelve specimens. By contrast, such capitals are rare in neighbouring Thessaly, with only one specimen known from Lamia. This strongly suggests that networks of patronage in adjacent provinces may have not have been interconnected, a conclusion further substantiated by the comparison of basilica types. Of all fifth- to sixth-century churches so far known from Greece (Fig. 1.3), the largest is the great basilica in Lechaion, the building of which has recently been redated on archaeological grounds to c. 525 (Warner Slane and Sanders 2005: 292; for an earlier dating of this basilica,

Table 1.2 Marble capitals from sixth-century Greece.

	Kautzsch III/IV	Composite Ionic	Double zone	Kautzsch VII	Kautzsch V/VI	Basket
Amphipolis (M)	12		4		1	
Nikopolis (E)	1		1		3	
Philippi (M)	3	3	3	1	1	13
Argos (A)	1			1		
Samos (I)	3			1	5	
Maximianoupolis (R)	1					4
Kavalla (M)	1					
Lamia (Th)	1					
Maroneia (R)	1					
Rhodes (I)	1					
Thessalonica (M)		12	15	3	11	3
Arta (E)		4			1	
Nea Anchialos (Th)		4	2		2	4
Corinth (A)		3	1	5	11	
Chalkis (A)		3			2	
Stomion (Th)		1			1	1
Sikyon (A)		1	2		1	
Edessa (M)		1	3			
Volos (Th)		3		2	1	
Delphi (A)		1			1	
Athens (A)		1			2	1
H. Loukas (A)		1				1
Aigina (A)		1				
Kato Lipochori (M)		1				
Vassilika (M)		1				
Thasos (M)			10			
Kalyvia Kouvara (A)			2		1	
Patmos (I)			1		1	
Mount Athos (M)			2			1
Brauron (A)			1			
Nisi (A)			1			
Plemeniana Selinou (C)			1			
Preveza (E)			1			
Rhodes (I)			1			
Syia (C)			1			
Veroia (M)			1			
Philippias (E)				1	1	
Komotini (R)				2		
Drymos (M)				1		
Kos (I)					6	
Nisyros (I)					3	
Gytheion (A)					1	

Table 1.2 (continued)

	Kautzsch III/IV	Composite Ionic	Double zone	Kautzsch VII	Kautzsch V/VI	Basket
Merbaka (A)					1	
Nauplio (A)					1	
Olympos (A)					1	
Panormos (C)					1	
Photike (E)					1	
Veran Episkopi (C)					1	
Paliani (C)					1	1
Megara (A)						3
Pherrai (R)						1
TOTAL	25	41	53	17	63	33

Notes: A – Achaia; C – Crete; E – Epirus; I – islands; M – Macedonia; R – Rhodope; Th - Thessaly

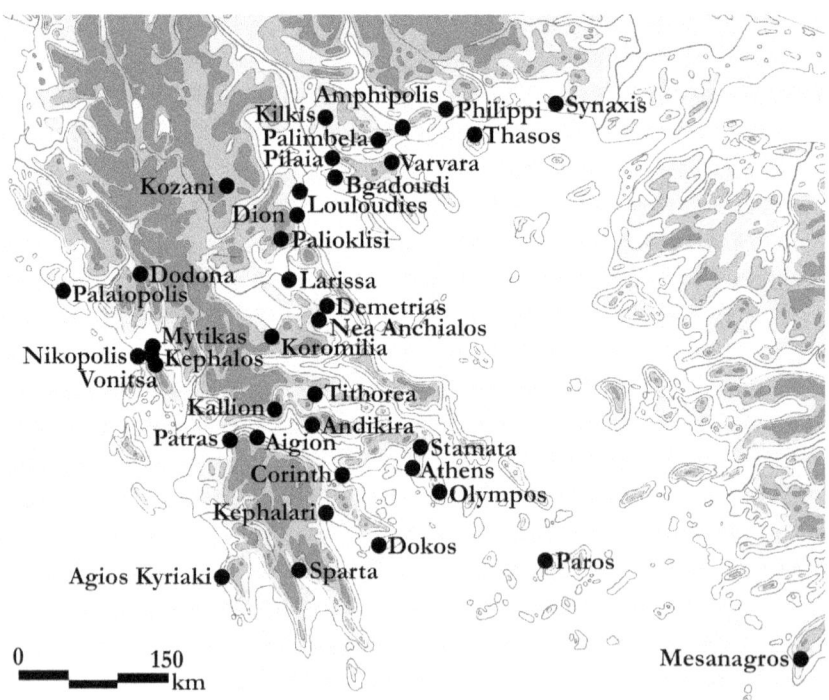

Figure 1.3 The distribution of late fifth- to sixth-century basilicas in Greece.

see Pallas 1957, 1960: 166–7, 1961, 1962, 1965: 168 and 161). With its 171.7m-long west–east axis, Lechaion is perhaps the largest basilica in the Balkan provinces of the Empire, and may well have been associated with an important pilgrimage site (Pallas 1979: 96; Bouras 2006: 42). It appears to have served as the model reproduced or imitated by builders of several transept basilicas in Epirus, at Nikopolis, Dodona, Phoinike, Palaiopolis (Kerkyra), and on the island of Kephalos in the Ambrakian Bay (Bowden 2003: 121–7). By contrast, no transept basilicas are so far known from Thessaly (Ulbert 1984: 170).

Some have argued that such stylistically contrastive choices reflect an economic situation. According to such views, the bishops of Nikopolis or the wealthy donors in their diocese could not afford the same standard of decoration as their counterparts in Corinth, Philippi, or Nea Anchialos (Bowden 2003: 150). However, Corinthian capitals most probably carved by Constantinopolitan masters have been found in Photike, Philippias, and Arta (all three in Epirus), while excavations on sites closer to Constantinople, such as Synaxis (Maroneia) and Thasos, have so far produced only cheap imitations (Sodini 1984: 213 and 219). On one hand, a praetorian prefect is said to have been depicted as donor on one of the exterior mosaics of the basilica of St Demetrios in Thessalonica (*Miracles of St. Demetrios* 1.1.24; Iliadi 2003: 44).[43] On the other hand, a lay donor is known for having created the mosaic in the basilica at Palaiopolis 'on behalf of his soul', which has been interpreted to mean that he received no payment for his work.[44] When a fire destroyed the silver *ciborium* of the basilica of St Demetrios in Thessalonica, and the archbishop was complaining about not having enough money to repair it, a certain citizen named Menas donated 75 pounds of silver (*Miracles of St. Demetrios* 1.6.60).[45] However, at Kallion near Lidorikion (Phokis), three lay donors gave only half a solidus each for the mosaic pavement, while a fourth one paid a solidus (Caillet 1987: 35). When considering prices and salaries in the early 500s, such amounts appear very small, indeed no larger than necessary for the paying of a small team of mosaicists working for a couple of days or so.[46] Mosaic pavements were one of the cheapest forms of decoration available at the time, and pavements in Greece appear to have been considerably cheaper than those in the other parts of the Empire (Caillet 1987: 35–6; Bowden 2003: 141).

Nonetheless, it is perhaps no accident that the donors most commonly acknowledged by mosaic inscriptions are local bishops, at

Nikopolis, Palaiopolis (Kerkyra), Thebes, Sparta, and Hermione.[47] Inscriptions carved in stone and brick stamps praise local bishops, primarily for their generosity, as in Nikopolis, Larissa, and Paros.[48] In other cases, it is not just the generosity of the local bishop that stands out, but his political status. In Palaiopolis, for example, the inscription on the tribelon describes Bishop Jovianus demolishing the 'temples of the Hellenes' and building instead the basilica (Bowden 2001: 63). Bishop Alkison of Nikopolis is credited for the mosaic in the annex of basilica B in that city (Bowden 2003: 110). However, it is quite possible that Alkison's act of generosity was at the same time a bold statement of independence and self-reliance. At the time, Alkison was well known for his fierce opposition both to the imperial policies of promoting Monophysitism and to Archbishop Dorotheos of Thessalonica, Emperor Anastasius' loyal supporter in the Balkans. Alkison was the central figure in the revolt of forty bishops of the Dacian and Macedonian dioceses, who in 515 withdrew from communion with the archbishop of Thessalonica and declared themselves on the side of Pope Hormisdas (Zeiller 1926: 223–4; Pietri 1984: 45). In addition, it was Alkison whom a group of monks in Palestine approached to assist them in obtaining papal support for defending Chalcedonian Orthodoxy and resisting the imperial pressure to accept Monophysitism (Evagrius, *Ecclesiastical History* 3.21; see Bowden 2003: 155). In 516, Emperor Anastasius ordered that Alkison be arrested and brought, together with other rebels, to Constantinople, where the bishop eventually died in captivity. His death provoked outrage, and, as a consequence, all bishops in Epirus Vetus declared their loyalty to the pope, who, in turn, recognised Bishop John as Alkison's successor in Nikopolis (*Collectio avellana* 119; Pietri 1984: 45). The reaction of the archbishop of Thessalonica was immediate: he apparently sought the support of the imperial administration in Epirus Vetus for bringing John to justice. Although Chalcedonian Orthodoxy was restored in 519, when a papal legate arrived in Thessalonica to obtain Dorotheos' renunciation of Monophysites beliefs, he was attacked by a mob, while the leader of the Chalcedonian faction in Thessalonica was assassinated. Dorotheos was summoned to the court in Constantinople, but because he was a protégé of Justinian, he managed to keep his see, despite Pope Hormisdas' protestations (*Collectio avellana* 107 and 225; Pietri 1984: 47–8).

By the mid-sixth century, the influence of the archbishop of Thessalonica in Greece seems to have been considerably diminished.

In the face of increasing pressure from Constantinople, the bishops of Thessaly turned to Rome, not to Thessalonica. In 531, most bishops of Thessaly voted for Stephen of Larissa, an old official, to be elected metropolitan of that see. However, three bishops who did not agree with the choice complained to the patriarch of Constantinople, who ordered Stephen to be deposed. Stephen was eventually arrested and taken to Constantinople, where he appealed to the pope for assistance. His case was presented in Rome in December 531 by Theodosius, bishop of Echinos (Pietri 1984: 51). Nothing else is known about the outcome of this issue, but in 536, Pope Agapetus welcomed the decision of a bishop of Larissa named Achilles to opt for the Roman and not Constantinopolitan jurisdiction over his see. Other prelates of Greece found themselves closer to the interests of the imperial court. For example, in 533, the bishop of Philippi, Demetrios, participated in a series of talks with the Monophysites. A bishop of Crete, another of an Epirote see, and delegates from Corinth participated in the 536 synod of Constantinople meant to condemn the deposed patriarch Anthimus. In 553, five bishops from Rhodope, four from Achaia, three from Macedonia, and one from Crete participated in the Fifth Ecumenical Council, which condemned the Three Chapters and the teachings of Origen according to the wishes of Emperor Justinian (Pietri 1984: 52; for Rhodope, see Soustal 1991: 126).[49]

Pope Gregory the Great's correspondence shows that even in the late sixth century, bishops in Greece felt closer to Rome than to Constantinople.[50] Some letters concerned the appointment of new bishops in Corinth and Nikopolis (Gregory the Great, *epp.* 5.62–3 and 6.7, both dated to 595). In another, the pope took up a position against the illegal actions of the metropolitan of Nikopolis on behalf of one of his suffragans (*ep.* 14.7–8 and 13). He also wrote in defence of the bishop of Thebes, Hadrian, who had been deposed by the archbishop of Justiniana Prima, a decision which Pope Gregory annulled. He scolded the bishops of Achaia for having endorsed the election of Kyriakos, patriarch of Constantinople, and invited the metropolitans to reject John IV the Faster's claims to the title of ecumenical patriarch (*epp.* 7.7 and 9.156). In 599, the pope asked the bishop of Thessalonica, Eusebios, to take action against the Monophysite clergy in his city (*epp.* 9.196 and 10.55, both of 601). The same bishop was scolded for having interfered in the affairs of the bishopric of Kerkyra (*ep.* 9.55; see also Waldmüller 1976: 200–1). There is no sign any more of the influence which Thessalonica previously had over church affairs in Greece. On the contrary, what Pope Gregory the Great's letters show is an increasing regionalisation of the church organisation, with various metropolitans now usurping the power which the archbishop of the Macedonian metropolis once had in the Balkans. By 600, Corinth, Larissa, and Nikopolis appear to have been more important in their respective provinces than Thessalonica, Rome, or indeed Constantinople.

This local particularism is best illustrated by the development of baptisteries. It has long been noted that, starting with Justinian's reign, there is an increasing number of baptisteries, often built next to older basilicas. Indeed, the addition of baptisteries is demonstrably associated with a second building phase in such diverse cases as Olympos near Laurion (Kotzias 1952), Stamata (Pallas 1988: 221), Agia Paraskevi in Kozani (Kourkoutidou-Nikolaidou and Michailidis 2002: 9), Kephalos (Barla 1965, 1966, and 1967; Paliouras 2004: 58), Agia Varvara in Mesanagros, on the island of Rhodes (Gounaris 1989: 2701), and Paros (Pallas 1988: 217). Canon law required that the baptismal sacrament be administered by bishops only. However, by 500, perhaps due to the bishop's increasing administrative tasks, his presence at the baptismal ceremony was no longer a requirement (Pallas 1989: 2490; Chevalier 1988; Zavadskaia 2002; for bishops taking on administrative tasks, see Liebeschuetz 2001: 145–55). The presence of baptisteries next to churches built in the countryside, outside the walls of cities and the area of direct episcopal involvement, suggests the performance of baptism by clergy other than bishops. In Greece, most churches built in the countryside received baptisteries in the course of the sixth century, especially after c. 550 (Pallas 1988: 217–18, 1989: 2486).[51] However, much as in cities, not all basilicas excavated in rural areas turned out to have baptisteries. In some cases, this may simply be the result of a faulty strategy of excavation (as in Soulinari, near Pylos, in Korinthia, for which see Kavvadia-Spondyle 2002). In others, it is quite clear that a second building phase for the basilica did not in fact involve the addition of a baptistery. For example, the three-aisled basilica built at some point during the second half of the fifth century on top of the former workshop of Phidias in Olympia was destroyed in the mid-sixth century together with the surrounding settlement. The basilica was rebuilt after c. 550, but as in Varvara (Chalkidiki), the restoration was on a much smaller scale, the new church using only the nave and the choir of the previous building. No baptistery was added to what may have by now been just a cemeterial church (Völling 2001: 304–5 and 307–8).

The settlement associated with the first building phase of the basilica in Olympia has been called a 'Byzantine village', despite the fact that most artefacts pointing to agricultural occupations found on the site may be attributed to the new settlement which appeared to the east from the Temple of Zeus, in the ruins of the Altis and of the Heraion, at the same time as the basilica was restored. Much as in the first settlement, houses were built of spolia from older buildings, marble rubble, and daub, and had multiple rooms, each with a simple hearth, built-in *pithoi*, and a raised area serving as kitchen. Unlike the previous settlement, however, houses clustered on either side of narrow alleys in what appears to have been a compact occupation. Most importantly, the agricultural occupations of the new inhabitants are revealed by a large hoard of coins and agricultural implements found in 1877. The two iron spades found in the hoard were most suitable for work in viticulture, arboriculture, and horticulture. The Olympia hoard dated with coins struck for Justinian and Justin II includes twelve harvesting tools (five billknives and seven sickles), but only six tilling tools (two mattocks and four pickaxes). It is important to note that none of those tilling tools may be associated with any form of large-scale cultivation, and all formed part of the typical tool-kit required for work in orchards or vegetable gardens. Neither tools connected with husbandry (scythes, shears, brand irons, castration forceps) nor oil presses have so far been found in the sixth-century 'village' in Olympia. However, the growing of cereals is indirectly attested by numerous quern stones from several houses within the settlement (Völling 1995 and 2002: 196–9). One of them has been found, together with fragments of a bronze scale and various other implements and tools, in the westernmost room of a house excavated in 1878 between the northeastern corner of the palaestra and the gate to the Gymnasium (Fig. 1.4). This was one of three rooms of the house, and may have well served as kitchen or at least as food preparation area. The easternmost room was reserved for a small-size wine press, either of the beam or of the screw type. The house may have already been built at the time of the first, early sixth-century settlement, but the last occupation phase is clearly coin-dated to the reign of Tiberius II (578–582) (Völling 1996: 404). The wine press, the scale, and the coins bespeak the commercial character of the occupation: the house may well have served as a shop for the small-scale production and sale of wine and other goods.

A similar situation has been documented in Pyrgouthi near Prosimna (Argolis). At some point after 550, a farmstead was

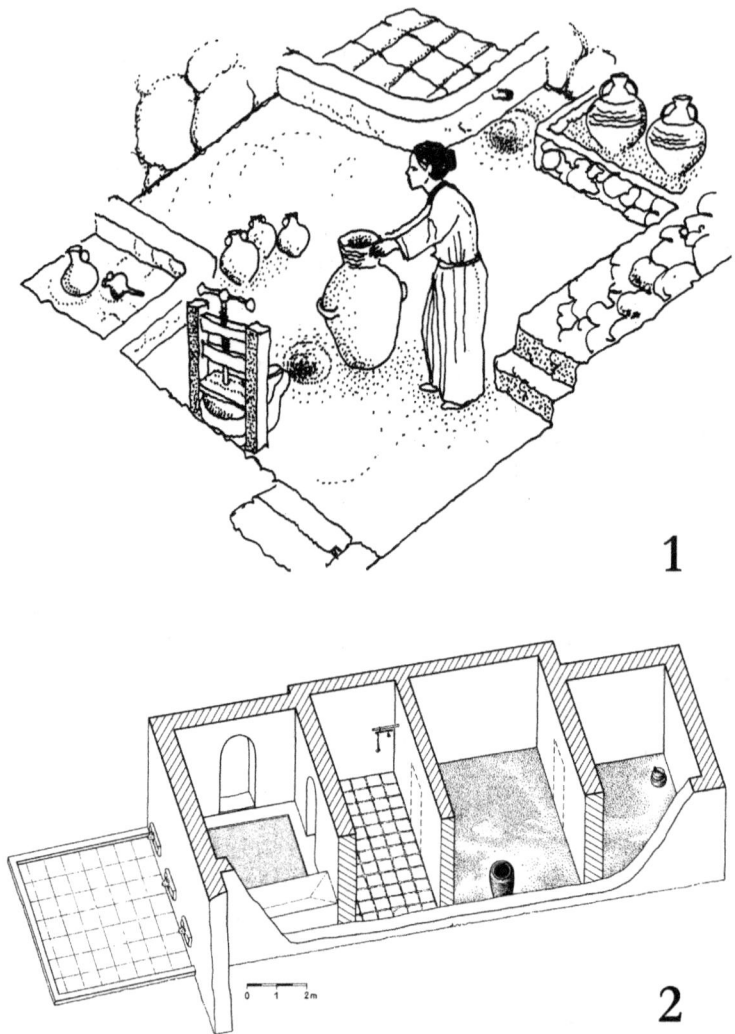

Figure 1.4 *Reconstructions of wine presses in sixth-century rural houses: (1) the room inside the refurbished tower in Pyrgouthi; (2) the house excavated in 1878 between the northeastern corner of the palaestra and the gate to the Gymnasium of Olympia. Drawings by Attila Thoth (first published in Hjohlman et al. 2005: 247 fig. 104) and S. Sutt (first published in Völling 1996: 409 fig. 9).*

installed in the ruins of a tower dating back to the early Hellenistic period. The refurbishing of the ancient tower involved building a treading floor, a rectangular trough, a wine press, and a structure in the southeastern corner of the tower which may have been used for storage. Outside the tower, several structures with stone foundations and mud-brick walls indicate the existence of a compound with at least six rooms, some of which may have been used as living quarters, others for storage, for food preparation, or as stables. There were open courtyards and corridors between the rooms, the configuration of which led the excavator to the conclusion that the farmhouse had living quarters on the western and agricultural quarters on the eastern side. The agricultural quarters were associated with the production of wine, as indicated by a large amphora found in a pit to the north of the treading floor inside the tower (Fig. 1.4). The interior of the amphora was blackened by fire, probably as a result of pitch coating, which the excavator interpreted as evidence for the amphora being used to store must for fermentation. The wine production in Pyrgouthi was small-scale, with no indication of a surplus for trade. That potsherds of household and cooking vessels covered the treading floor suggests that wine production was abandoned some time before the destruction of the site and its subsequent abandonment in the early 600s. At that time, the room inside the tower had long been turned into a kitchen. Palaeobotanical studies of samples from the ash stratum revealed that besides wine production, the inhabitants of the farmhouse in Pyrgouthi ate barley, wheat, rye, millet, and oats. An ardshare and a sickle suggest that at least some of those crops were grown locally. However, the presence of seeds of Persian wheat (durum) requires a different explanation: perhaps Persian wheat was imported from the Black Sea area and cleaned on site. At any rate, the economic profile of the Pyrgouthi farmstead may be best described as mixed farming. In addition to cereals, a number of pulse crops have been identified, some of which (chickling, bitter vetch, and carob) were commonly used as animal fodder. Unlike Olympia, where no sign of animal husbandry has been found, in Pyrgouthi the most common domesticated animals were sheep, goat, pig, and cattle. The zoo-archaeological study of the faunal remains showed that most animals died old, an indication that sheep and goats were kept for secondary products (wool, milk, hides, and dairy products) and not for meat. Only pigs seem to have been bred for meat, but the quantity of meat in the diet was supplemented with game, especially rabbits (or hares) and birds. Fragments of figs, walnuts, and pomegranates show that those fruits were consumed, and possibly obtained locally (Hjohlman et al. 2005: 244–52). By contrast, despite the presence of olive trees in the area (which is betrayed by fragments of charred olive tree wood) the olive fragments found in the tower do not seem to have been processed in any way.

The results of the field survey in the Berbati Valley where Pyrgouthi is located suggest that many sites appeared in the sixth century in locations without any continuity from earlier periods (Hahn 1996: 438; Hjohlman et al. 2005: 257; for a sceptical view of what field surveys can tell about sixth-century rural settlements, see Sanders 2004: 163–8). No villa or larger estate was found and the survey indicates only small farmsteads, like that in Pyrgouthi. This is true for other parts of Greece as well (see, for example, Bowden and Gill 1997: 90). By 500, most rural villas or estates established in the fourth century had already been deserted. It is important to note that all cases known so far of rural villas dated to the sixth century are in fact earlier foundations with a sixth-century occupation, for which no indication exists of a similar function. For example, a fortified villa, with a walled enclosure with a tower, a bath, a peristyled courtyard, rooms on either side of a triclinium, and a storeroom with a wine vat or cistern, was built in the early fifth century in Paliokastro, near Oraiokastro (prefecture of Thessaloniki). The site was still occupied in the sixth century, as evidenced by coins struck for Justinian and Justin II, the latest of which is from 572/3 (Marki and Akrivopoulou 2003). Nothing indicates, however, that the situation in Paliokastro was any different from that at Findspot 500 in the Berbati Valley, where occupation of the site of a Roman villa continued on a much reduced scale after its abandonment (Hahn 1996: 438). In other words, a sixth-century occupation on the site of a *villa rustica* does not necessarily mean that the site was still a *villa rustica* in the 500s. Much has been made of the existence of a bath on the rural site at Portochelion (ancient Halieis, near Kranidhion in Argolis). Although no precise dates exist for the 'early Byzantine' occupation of the bath and, consequently, 'the specific nature and size of the establishment at Halieis is difficult to determine', the excavator nonetheless concluded that the site may have been 'a villa for a wealthy landowner with a bath near it' (Rudolph 1979: 296 and 304; Konti 1997: 337).[52] The only argument in support of that conclusion is that the excavation produced a relatively large quantity of fine ware (African Red Slip and Late Roman C wares). Similarly, the site at Akra Sophia was identified by means of a field survey, which resulted in the collection of mosaic tesserae. The site was therefore hastily interpreted as a 'large and sumptuous villa of early Byzantine date' (Gregory 1985: 418).[53] The tendency to associate the presence of fine ware pottery, amphorae, or fragments of mosaic floors with 'villas', and their absence with 'small farmsteads', has been recently criticised as too simplistic (Hjohlman et al. 2005: 258 with n. 472). Although self-sufficient, the inhabitants of the Pyrgouthi farmstead, for example, were not completely isolated. However little, the evidence of trade on that site points to Corinth as a source of regionally made household ware, amphorae, lamps, and very small quantities of fine ware pottery produced outside the Greek mainland (Hjohlman et al. 2005: 259). The multi-roomed house found in 1982 in Nemea (prefecture of Korinthia) during the excavation of the Temple of Zeus, which has been interpreted as a farm, produced sixth-century lamps and two coins struck for Emperor Justin II (Miller 1983: 84 and 86). Similarly, in the environs of Patras, finds of sixth-century coins are known from rural sites with ruins of a few buildings, sometimes associated with presses, possibly for the production of olive oil (Callegher 2005: 228). In short, the rural landscape of sixth-century Greece seems to be much more complex than previously assumed.

To be sure, no solid evidence exists so far for a survival into the sixth century of any rural villas or estates.[54] In that respect, Greece was no different from the rest of the Balkan provinces of the Empire, in which *villae rusticae* were completely abandoned c. 450 (Henning 1987: 22–35; Curta 2001a: 205). What distinguishes Greece from other provinces in the central and northern Balkans, however, is the presence of peasant settlements. By 500, the settlement pattern in Greece was clearly a highly dispersed one, with small rural sites like Pyrgouthi in Argolis. This was a landscape of isolated, single-family farmsteads, making more intensive use of their agricultural land, a pattern conspicuously absent from the more northerly regions of the Balkan Peninsula (Kosso 1993: 130–1; for the relative lack of any rural, open settlements in the Balkans, see Curta 2001a: 205–6). Unlike in those regions, the rural economy of Greece changed between the mid-fifth and the late sixth century beyond recognition, but did not collapse. In fact, the existing evidence points to the contrary. Greece certainly produced an agricultural surplus, which was exported outside Greece. That much follows from a brief mention of imperial granaries in Prokopios of Kaisareia's *Buildings* 4.2.[55] Moreover, in his *Wars*, Prokopios mentions that in 533, in order to prevent heavy losses among his troops, because of food poisoning from the rotten bread they had brought with them from Constantinople, Belisarius ordered the 'bread of the country' around Methone to be furnished to his army (*Wars* 3.13.20; see also Anagnostakis et al. 2002: 157–8). In 551, the Ostrogoths captured on the coast of Epirus 'some of the ships which were carrying provisions from Greece from the army of Narses' (*Wars* 8.22.32).[56] That oil and wine were exported is also indicated by the local production of Late Roman 2 amphorae, which were used for the transportation of such commodities. Kilns for the production of Late Roman 2 amphorae have been identified between Ermioni and Portochelion, and a shipwreck with a cargo of the same type of amphorae is known from the vicinity of Portochelion. Given that Late Roman 2 amphorae produced in the Aegean and used for transporting either wine or olive oil have been found in large quantities on military sites in Bulgaria and Serbia, they may well have served as the main container for *annona*-type distributions to the army stationed in forts in the northern Balkans (Curta 2001b: 186–8; Karagiorgou 2001b: 145).[57]

That the agricultural surplus from Greece was shipped either to the troops engaged in war against the Ostrogoths in Italy or to those stationed in forts in the northern and central Balkans is a clear indication of the still thriving agricultural economy of Greece. Whether that agricultural surplus was siphoned outside Greece through trade or simply exacted as tax by the state and then redistributed through the *annona* system remains unclear. Nor is it possible to establish whether the occupants of small farmsteads, like that in Pyrgouthi, were independent freeholders or tenants. What is clear, however, is that during the sixth century, Greece 'went through the last flourishing period of the Late Antique Roman civilization' (Laiou and Morrisson 2007: 23). The relatively small number of regular troops stationed in Greece, which were not therefore an unbearable burden on local taxpayers, the longer resilience of the agricultural economy, and the inclusion of the Greek lands in the larger network of exchange across the Mediterranean set Greece apart from other provinces in the Balkans, which at the same time experienced much decline and crisis. The prosperity of the upper classes in sixth-century Greece is well documented by inscriptions revealing patronage of church decoration; by the impressive burials *ad sanctos* in large, single- or multi-room vaulted tombs with murals; and by the associated gold dress accessories. While that prosperity may well have derived primarily from the thriving agriculture in the countryside, its material expression is more often than not associated with cities. Cities, rather than the countryside, have been regarded as a hallmark of the ancient, Graeco-Roman civilisation, and it is to urban centres that we need now to turn in order to approach the problem of how the short-lived prosperity of sixth-century Greece came to an end.

Notes

1. For chapter 26 as part of the *Secret History*'s plan to respond to Justinian's legislation and financial measures taken on his behalf by imperial agents, specifically by Alexander 'Snips', see Kaldellis 2004: 227. The *Secret History* was completed in 550 or 551, probably at the same time as Books I–VII of the *Wars*. See Greatrex 1994: 102.
2. The wall across the Isthmus is what would later be known as Hexamilion. For inscriptions attesting the sixth-century restoration of the Hexamilion, see Feissel and Philippidis-Braat 1985: 279–81. For the archaeology of the Justinianic restoration of the Hexamilion, see Avramea 1997: 65–6. For the date of the *Buildings*, see Greatrex 1994: 113, 1995; Kaldellis 2004: 46.
3. For the interpretation of this passage as evidence of peasants abandoning agricultural occupations, see Curta 2001a: 205.
4. For the audience of the *Secret History*, see Kaldellis 2004: 115–17 and 50, who believes John Lydus, Tribonian, and Agathias to have been among those able to reach the deeper levels of the text and to read the *Secret History* as 'an esoteric commentary on the *Wars*'.
5. Prokopios of Kaisareia, *Buildings* 4.2, blames the inexperienced peasants turning into 'makeshift soldiers for the occasion' for the fact that 'the country through its whole extent lay open to the oncoming barbarians'. This stands in direct contradiction to Prokopios' own account of the events in the *Wars* 2.4.11. According to that account, during the Hunnic invasion of 539 or 540, the guards on the walls at Thermopylae 'defended them most valiantly', although the barbarians were nonetheless able to bypass them through a side path across the mountains and to destroy 'almost all the Greeks except the Peloponnesians'. Given that the measures taken by the *discussor* Alexander post-date his trip to Ravenna, and assuming that a Hunnic invasion truly reached Greece at that time, then it must have pre-dated Alexander's visit to Thermopylae. The guards who had valiantly defended the walls must then have been the 'makeshift soldiers for the occasion'.
6. The identity of the marauders is hidden behind Comes Marcellinus' use of a Biblical quotation (Jeremiah 6.22) to refer to them as 'the people from the north country'.
7. The port of call in 533 was Methone, which the Roman fleet reached after safely passing by Cape Malea and Cape Matapan (Irmscher 1992: 77–8). In both 533 and 537, the troops were under the command of Valerian and Martinus, who in 537 began their trip to Italy too close to the end of the sailing season to reach their destination. For the events of 533, see Anagnostakis et al. 2002: 155–8.
8. For the invasion of 558/9, see Agathias, *Histories* 5.11–12. The invasions of both 539/40 and 558/9 targeted also the Chersonesos of

Thrace, and the account of the one in Prokopios is strikingly similar to the account of the other in Agathias.
9. The only exception is the Sclavene attack on Topeiros (now Xanthi) in 549, for which see Prokopios of Kaisareia, *Wars* 7.38.11–23.
10. The Sybota islands are located in the southern part of the channel between Kerkyra and the mainland. The location of Anchialus is unknown. For the date of the expedition, see Soustal and Koder 1981: 267. Bon 1951: 14 and Anagnostakis et al. 2002: 137 wrongly dated it to 549.
11. No Slavs were associated with the Cutrigurs raiding Greece, *pace* Yannopoulos 1980: 332.
12. Yannopoulos 1990–1993: 32 has advanced a slightly later date (early 579) for this Sclavene raid, but see Živković 1997 (English version in Živković 2008: 7–16) for serious arguments against that.
13. Olajos 1985: 514–15 proposed an emendation of the text, replacing Thessalonica with Thessaly, but none of her arguments can stand criticism. Moreover, the attack on Thessalonica by 5,000 Sclavene warriors, which is mentioned in the *Miracles of St. Demetrios* 1.12, may have been associated with the events to which John of Ephesus referred in his *History*. See Curta 2004a: 516 with n. 11.
14. Speck 1993: 275, 512, and 528 has argued that Archbishop John, who wrote during Emperor Herakleios' early regnal years (see *Miracles of St. Demetrios* 1.10.82), was not the author of Book I, which was a much later compilation of the ninth century. Speck's arguments are not very convincing, especially his idea that the John mentioned by the author of Book II as responsible for the collection in Book I was not a bishop, but an abbot. In fact, John is specifically mentioned as bishop (*Miracles of St. Demetrios* 2.2.201). See also Skedros 1999: 111–14.
15. For the date of the attack, see Barišić 1953: 49–55; Ivanova 1995a: 182. For the city militia defending the walls of Thessalonica against the 5,000 Sclavenes, see Liebeschuetz 2000: 123.
16. There is no basis for the emendation of Corinth into Perinthos proposed by Zakythinos 1945: 37 and endorsed by Karagiannopoulos 1990. For John of Ephesus as the source employed at this point by Michael the Syrian, see Ginkel 1998.
17. An earlier date has been also proposed by Barišić 1953: 57–67, and is now endorsed by most historians. See Skedros 1999: 129; Iliadi 2003: 57–60; Živković 2008: 20–1. According to Archbishop John of Thessalonica, the attack had been ordered by the qagan, who wanted to take revenge on Emperor Maurice's refusal to meet his demands. This most probably refers to the events of 585, when an Avar envoy coming to Constantinople was arrested and thrown into jail by Emperor Maurice, for boldly demanding 100,000 solidi as annual subsidies to be paid to the qagan (Theophylact Simokatta, *Histories* 1.8.7–10). See

Whitby 1988: 117–18; Ivanova 1995a: 186–7. For the *Miracles of St. Demetrios* as a historical source on barbarian attacks on Greece, see now Iliadi 2003: 23–4.
18. 'Those who serve in the great *praetorium*' were most probably the *scholae* of the city prefect. By contrast, the 'young elite soldiers' were *iuvenes*, i.e., soldiers of regular troops, aged 18 to 40, who were the first to be called in case of emergency (Pillon 2005: 57).
19. Those soldiers do not appear to have resided in separate quarters, but like many others in the city, they must have had their own houses and land plots.
20. The author of the *Continuatio hispana* written in 754 dated the raid to the fourth year of Herakleios' reign (614). However, Isidore does not seem to have been among the sources he used for this bit of information. See Charanis 1971; Szádeczky-Kardoss 1986: 53–54; Marín 1991–1992: 225 and 228; Ivanova 1995b: 355–7. Isidore employed the word 'Sclavi' (instead of 'Sclavini') for the Slavs, which may indicate that his informant was from Constantinople. See Curta 2001b: 45–6.
21. Moniaros 1995–1996 argued that the Slavs could not have possibly reached the Cyclades on their canoes. However, a seaborne Slavic attack on Crete is mentioned in the *Chronicon Miscellaneum* (also known as *Liber Chalifarum*), a compilation of various sources with different authors, which was preserved in an eighth-century Syriac manuscript. The attack is dated to the year 934 of the Seleucid era (AD 623). See Krivov 1995. No evidence exists, however, to substantiate the idea advanced by Bon 1950: 13, according to which the Slavs raiding Crete came from Peloponnesos.
22. For the multitude of tribes, see *Miracles of St. Demetrios* 2.1.179. For the location of the various tribes, see Lemerle 1981: 89–90; Panov 2001: 26–7.
23. The Sclavenes attacked on the fourth day (*Miracles of St. Demetrios* 2.1.185) and the decisive confrontation took place on that same day.
24. According to Prokopios, *Buildings* 4.3–4, Justinian built or restored thirty-six forts in Epirus Vetus and forty-six in Macedonia. By contrast, Prokopios knew of only nine forts in Thessaly.
25. Such as Peratia (across the strait from Levkas) and Angelokastron, on the northwestern coast of Kerkyra. See Bowden 2003: 181–2, with further examples from Rizovouni, Kastri (both in the prefecture of Preveza), and Kastritsa (prefecture of Ioannina).
26. For coin finds from Komotini and Rendina, see Georganteli 2005: 310, who believes Rendina to be Artemision mentioned by Prokopios, *Buildings* 4.3. The last coin so far found in Rendina was struck for Emperor Maurice in 583/4 (Galani-Krikou and Tsourti 2000: 350).
27. For a restored Iron-Age fort in Platania, near Drama, see Peristeri 1990.

For the third-century fort at Kalyvi in the valley of the Nestos, which was re-occupied in the 500s, see Georganteli 2005: 313.
28. Hymettos Tower, Beletsi, Kantili round tower, Phyle, and Kerata Tower, all of which have been dated to the sixth century on the basis of fragments of sixth-century lamps found on the surface during field surveys (Ober 1987).
29. A sixth-century date for the latest occupation phase within the fort at the Dhema Pass was established on the basis of ceramic remains of Central Greek Painted Ware. See Rosser 2001. For an attempt to locate the fortification mentioned by Prokopios as guarding the Thermopylae Pass, see MacKay 1963.
30. The total area enclosed by ramparts is 2.71 hectares. For an estimated military population within the ramparts, see Kardulias 1992 and 1993.
31. All those units were under the command of the *magister militum per Illyricum*. See Dunn 2002: 708–9. The *Notitia Dignitatum* has no evidence of regular units stationed in southern Greece (Gregory 1992: 248).
32. An inscription from Amorgos mentions an *actuarius* (official associated with a *numerus*) named Kyriakos. Two graffiti on the cliff at Grammata on the island of Syris mention a soldier named Synetos and an *optio* (official who distributed the wages to the soldiers) in the service of the governor of Bithynia. See Kiourtzian 2000: 40–2, 192, and 193–4. However, nothing indicates that any of those individuals was actually stationed in the place where the inscriptions have been found. Given the circumstances, they may have simply stopped in either Amorgos or Syris on their trip by sea to some other destination. At least one of them – Kyriakos – died before reaching that destination.
33. Wozniak 1982: 204 and 1987: 265 argued that *buccellarii* (private armies) played a key role in the provincial defence in Western Illyricum. There is very little evidence to support the idea that *buccellarii* manned sixth-century forts, especially in Greece. At any rate, the two *buccellarii* from Corinth were most probably not residents of the city.
34. Several other spear heads are known from excavations in Nea Anchialos (Sotiriou 1939: 38 and 69 fig. 28; Lazaridis 1965: 327–34). Another was associated with a fragmentary dagger blade in the assemblage from a tile-grave accidentally found in Ladochorion near Igoumenitsa (prefecture of Thesprotia). See Agallopoulou 1975: 239. Two arrow heads are known from the 1922 excavations in Edessa (Pelekides 1923: 262).
35. Louloudies near Pydna, in the prefecture of Pieria (Marki 1997a: 293 and 296 fig. 5); Eleutherna, in Crete (Poulou-Papadimitriou 2005: 697 and 706 fig. 2); Olympia (Völling 1992: 491 and 494 fig. 4); and Nea Anchialos, burial chamber (Sotiriou 1956: 113–15 and pl. 41β). The Eleutherna and Nea Anchialos buckles are specimens of the Sucidava-Beroe II variant, which may be dated as late as 600. For belt buckles of

the Sucidava class as typical dress accessories expected to be found on military sites of Justinian's age, see Vinski 1967: 38; Varsik 1992: 78 and 1993: 208–9. The presence of 'barbarian' troops of (ir)regulars has been also associated with such exotica as the bird-shaped fibula from Corinth or the equal-armed fibula from Daskaleio, in the Argolid Bay. See Davidson 1952: pl. 113.2170; Schulze-Dörrlamm 2003: 437 and 438 fig. 1.1.

36. Nothing indicates that Louloudies was a site of 'unquestionably imperial (public) origin', as Dunn 2002: 708 would have it.
37. As in Louloudies, the fortification has only four square towers. However, the area enclosed by ramparts in Pirdop is much smaller and no traces of any other buildings have been found except the basilica. Another fifth- or sixth-century basilica surrounded by ramparts was found on the island of Dokos in the Argolid Bay, but no details have so far been published on the excavations (Touchais et al. 1998: 764).
38. The Bgadoudi tomb has been dated to the late fifth or sixth century, but the church, which was most probably built in the fifth century, was still in use during the reign of Justin II (Pazaras 1998 and 1999).
39. The vaulted tombs belonged to a cemetery extending outside the basilica, which is dated between the mid-sixth and the early seventh century on the basis of the associated pottery (Gkini-Tsophopoulou and Chalkia 2003).
40. Another, un-named deaconess may have been a patron of the basilica built in the fifth century on the northern side of the agora of Thasos (Feissel 1983: 214). A female burial inside the church, dated to 559, is also known from Olympos near Laurion (Gkini-Tsophopoulou 2001: 152). Had the tombstone been found in the vicinity of any known church in Corinth, a similar interpretation would have applied to the grave of Euphrasia, who died in 533, during Emperor Justinian's third consulate (Feissel and Philippidis-Braat 1985: 277–9).
41. Also cemeterial were the Ilissos Basilica in Athens, the Basilica of Kodratos in Corinth, basilica D in Nea Anchialos, basilica B in Demetrias, the basilica on the 3 Septemvriou Street in Thessaloniki, and no fewer than three basilicas in Philippi and another two in Knossos (Crete) (Laskaris 2000: 32–51). There were also sixth-century cemeteries in Greece, which had no churches (Loverdou-Tsigarida et al. 2001; Ziota 1998).
42. A few mosaic pavements have been dated to the second half of the sixth century or even the late sixth century. However, in such cases, the stylistic criteria used for establishing the date of the mosaic pavement and, by default, of the building are contradicted by coin finds clearly pointing to the first half of the sixth century. Such is the case of Agia Paraskevi in Kozani, the mosaic pavement of which was dated on stylistic grounds to the third quarter of the sixth century, despite the

presence in the baptistery of a coin struck for Justinian between 527 and 538 (Kourkoutidou-Nikolaidou and Michailidis 2002: 19).
43. The praetorian prefect Marianos is said to have donated many gold and silver artefacts, as well as a large sum of gold coins, to the basilica. Two other wealthy citizens of Thessalonica, Menas and John, donated money for the reconstruction of the wooden roof and the *ciborium* of that same church (*Miracles of St. Demetrios* 1.6.60–1).
44. Bowden 2003: 133 believes that the donor may have been a professional mosaicist.
45. At an exchange rate of 1:18 between gold and silver, the amount donated by Menas was the equivalent of 300 solidi, which is about as much as a merchant at that time needed to get a ship ready for sail (Spieser 1984: 20–1). Menas may have been a rich merchant (*naukleros*).
46. For fifth- to seventh-century prices and salaries, see Morrisson 1989. One solidus was the cost of a military mantle in c. 534, while half a solidus was the ransom price which the Avars demanded in 598 for every one of their prisoners.
47. For Bishops Alkison, Dometius I, and Dometius II in Nikopolis, as well as for Jovian in Palaiopolis, see Chevalier 2005: 76; Bowden 2003: 108 and 112–13. For Bishop Peter of Thebes, see Avramea and Feissel 1987: 363–4. For Bishop Stephen of Sparta, see Laskaris 2000: 58. For Bishop Epiphanios of Hermione, see Feissel and Philippidis-Braat 1985: 297–8.
48. For the inscription and the stamped bricks found in the basilica at Kastro in Larissa, which mention Archbishop Achilleios, see Laskaris 2000: 60–1. For the inscriptions in the narthex and atrium of basilica A in Nikopolis, which mention two different bishops named Dometios, see Bowden 2003: 111. For the inscriptions and monograms carved on column capitals found in the Katopoliani basilica in Paros, which mention two bishops named Hylaios and George, see Kiourtzian 2000: 120–5. Members of the lower clergy may have also been donors. A privileged inhumation inside the basilica in Panormos (Crete) was the tomb of a singer (*psaltis*) named Theodore, who may have been responsible for the decoration of that church (Laskaris 2000: 70).
49. It must be noted that the number of participants from Greece was modest, quite in tune with the conspicuous absence of the western bishops.
50. The collection of Pope Gregory's correspondence contains fifteen letters addressed to bishops in Greece. Of all Balkan provinces, only Dalmatia is better represented in that collection.
51. The conclusion that the phenomenon must have been associated with Justinian's reign follows from the analysis of specimens found in Dalmatia, all built or otherwise modified in the period immediately

following the Byzantine occupation of that region during the war in Italy (Cambi 1978: 615).

52. That the burials found in Portochelion had few, if any, grave goods has been wrongly interpreted as evidence of slaves working on the rural estate (Kaplan 1992: 159; Avramea 2005: 216).
53. Gregory's interpretation of the site has been uncritically reproduced by Avramea 1997: 127, who lists several other similar sites in the Peloponnese, none of which can be securely dated to the sixth century (Avramea 2005: 217).
54. Nor is there any evidence for anything similar to the 'early modern Sicilian agro-town', a comparison advanced by Bintliff 2007: 670. According to him, the large estates were simply emptied, with only a small number of permanent personnel on site, and the labour force of tied or paid workers now living in greatly shrunken cities. While occupation on a much reduced scale on the sites of former estate centres cannot be denied, all other evidence of rural settlements in sixth-century Greece points to a few independent farmers or tenants residing in the countryside, not 'tied or paid workers' living in neighbouring cities.
55. That grain levies may have been an important part of the regular taxation in Achaia is an indication of production beyond subsistence levels (see also Kosso 1993: 148).
56. The first to have noted that the remark implies the production of an agricultural surplus in sixth-century Greece was Gregory 2000: 114.
57. The site excavated in Portochelion may therefore have been neither a *villa rustica*, nor a simple rural occupation of an abandoned estate centre, but a town involved in the local production and export of amphorae. This is further substantiated by the presence of African Red Slip and Late Roman C wares, all of which could have been obtained only by means of trade.

CHAPTER 2

Collapse or adaptation? The problem of the urban decline in late antique Greece

According to the *Synekdemos* of Hierokles, by 500 there were about eighty cities in the province of Achaia, apparently one of the most highly urbanised regions of the eastern Mediterranean (Honigman 1939: 7 and 16–19; see also Bon 1951: 21 and 23–4).[1] Most of them had no appropriate defence. Prokopios mentions fortifications being renewed for all cities south of the Thermopylae Pass, and specifically mentions Corinth, the walls of which had been ruined by 'terrible earthquakes which had visited the city', Athens, Plataea, and 'the towns of Boeotia' (*Buildings* 4.2). But he also claims that the fortifications of cities in central Greece and Peloponnesos had fallen into ruin long before Justinian's reign. The Emperor's intention was apparently to rebuild the walls of all the cities south of the Thermopylae Pass, but realising that the operation would take too long, he decided 'to wall the whole Isthmus securely'. The implication is that most, if not all cities south of the Hexamilion remained unfortified. North of the Thermopylae Pass, Prokopios mentions the rebuilding of fortifications at Echinos, Thebes, Pharsalos, Demetrias, Metropolis, Gomphi, and Trika (Trikala), with only Kassandria (Potidaea) mentioned in Macedonia (*Buildings* 4.2).[2] Conspicuously absent from this list is the great Macedonian metropolis of Thessalonica, the largest city in the Balkans and the second city of the Empire after Constantinople.[3] Indeed, the evidence available so far suggests that although Emperor Justinian certainly contributed to the decoration or endowment of the basilica of St Demetrios in Thessalonica, the repair or extension of the city fortifications is a much earlier work, some of which at least was paid for by private citizens.[4] However, Thessalonica is mentioned in the *Secret History* as having, like Constantinople, a hippodrome in which both the father and grandfather of Belisarius' wife Antonina demonstrated their skills as charioteers (Prokopios of Kaisareia, *Secret History* 1.11).[5] The author of the first book of the *Miracles of St. Demetrios* mentions both the city's stadium and the theatre. During the plague, shortly before the siege of 586, the sick who had taken refuge in the basilica of St Demetrios were making their way every morning to the baths. The city had also a praetorium, to which the praetorian prefect Marianos was going from the basilica.[6] After 600, Thessalonica had numerous two-storeyed buildings, for during the civil strife at the centre of one of the homilies of Book I in the *Miracles of St. Demetrios* 'women and children, the old and the young' were thrown to their death from the windows (*Miracles of St. Demetrios* 1.112–13; Skedros 1999: 126; for civil unrest in Thessalonica, see Ditten 1991).

The only church in Thessalonica the building of which may be dated to the sixth century is the basilica of St Demetrios (for the basilica of St Demetrios as an early sixth-century building erected c. 510/20, see Spieser 1984: 212–13). The church benefited from imperial patronage, as evidence by a mutilated inscription found on the ground near the basilica's northern wall. The inscription may have been an edict issued by Justinian I (Feissel 1983: 81–2).[7] The many churches of Thessalonica coexisted with elements of the ancient city, such as the agora, which retained its commercial significance (Hattersley-Smith 1988: 269, 304, 310, and 319). The extramural cemeteries continued to be used through the early seventh century, as attested by a barrel-vaulted tomb found to the west of the city walls, at the junction of the Agathonos and Leonida Spartiati streets in Ambelokipi (Marki 2001b: 325–6).[8] There were also intramural burials, such as the fifteen tile graves found in the Agora (Laskaris 2000: 236). However, until recently, very little was known about the urban habitat of sixth-century Thessalonica, for research had typically focused on either city walls or churches.[9] So far, the only *villa urbana* known from Thessalonica is that discovered at 90 Kassandrou Street, which, though first built in the third century, was apparently still in use in the 500s (Makropoulou and Tzitzimpase 1993).

Similarly, in neighbouring Thasos, the Roman villa built in the third century at Tokatlis was repaired in the late fifth or early sixth century, when a courtyard was added together with a second storey around it. The villa thus received a *nymphaeum* with a rectangular pool, which was supplied with water in abundance coming through lead pipelines. The villa was destroyed in the late sixth or early seventh century, as shown by two coins struck for Emperor Tiberius II (578–582) found in the debris. A second villa was found at Valma-Delkos, which in the sixth century received a bath with pavement in *opus sectile*. By the end of the century, the building was robbed of most of its marble revetments, then abandoned. A second occupation of an ephemeral character is coin-dated between 603 and 619 (Sodini 1995: 289 and 291). Much like contemporary Thessalonica and Philippi, sixth-century Thasos preserved its ancient street grid. The city harbour was rebuilt in the sixth century, and a few churches were added to the already existing ones: the cruciform church next to the Hellenistic rampart (perhaps a pilgrimage site), the three-aisled basilica on the northern side of the agora, and the church in the ruins of the Herakleion (Sodini 1995: 279–82 and 285).[10]

Who were the inhabitants of the rich urban villas in Thessalonica and Thasos? The information provided by the *Miracles of St. Demetrios* about generous donors to the basilica dedicated to that saint suggests the existence in Thessalonica of a group of rich merchants, possibly owners of ships and shipyards, as well as of storage facilities and several houses within the city walls (*Miracles of St. Demetrios* 1.1.24 and 1.6.60–1). In Thasos, the wealth of the local aristocrats was most probably based on trade with wine, silver, and marble (Sodini 1995: 294). None of the neighbouring cities of Amphipolis and Philippi produced any such evidence of the prosperity of the local aristocracy. In Philippi, new alterations were brought to the Octagon in the first quarter of the sixth century, while basilica C was restored in the second quarter of that century, when the church apparently received stained glass windows (Hattersley-Smith 1988: 133, 149, and 155).[11] The glass may have been produced locally, as suggested by a glass- and metalworking shop found on top of a Roman building in the southern range of the city. More workshops existed at that time in the ruins of the theatre (Koukouli-Chryssanthaki and Karadedos 1999: 80–1). Basilica B (Direkler) had a cross-domed unit in addition to vaults over the aisles, galleries, nave, and transept wings. The combination of a transept and a cross dome is a clear indication that the source of inspiration for this building was the Justinianic architecture of Constantinople. Corinthian capitals from the excavations of the Philippi basilicas also indicate that masters from Constantinople worked in the city. It remains unclear, however, whether the situation should be interpreted as imperial patronage of the city's many churches or, perhaps, as a sign of the loyalty of the city's bishop and elites to the Emperor.

Amphipolis too had several basilicas, five of which (including a hexagonal church) were built at different times in the course of the sixth century. By the end of that century, the acropolis was surrounded by a new wall, the west side of which cut through the atrium of basilica A, erected in the first half of the sixth century. The area now enclosed was less than ten acres and included only three churches. Basilica C was left outside the encircled area. Its lavish decoration appears to have been paid for by a group of donors, as evidenced by a mosaic inscription. A small, single-nave chapel was erected in the late 500s or slightly later on the basilica's eastern side. The latest coin found in Amphipolis was struck for Emperor Maurice, and no occupation can be dated later than c. 620 (Hattersley-Smith 1988: 202 and 207–8; Dunn 1999: 402).

In northwestern Greece, the largest late antique city was Nikopolis. The early Byzantine walls, which were probably built after the sack of the city by the Vandals in 474, enclosed only a small area (some seventy-four acres) within the northeastern corner of the early Roman city, which represents only a sixth of its entire territory. The new enclosure left out many public buildings and sanctuaries, which were most probably in ruins at that time. The towers at the west gate were similar in size to those of the large wall at Constantinople and to the larger towers at Resafa, which has been interpreted as an indication that the walls of early Byzantine Nikopolis were built by an imperial architect, being sponsored by the urban community and by the provincial authorities, with some imperial assistance (Gregory 1987: 260; Hellenkemper 1987: 250; see also Konstantios 1992: 64–6). Within the new enclosure, the street grid of early Roman Nikopolis was maintained well into the late sixth century. In a manner reminiscent of Thessalonica, all three churches built in the sixth century – basilicas A, B, and D – were aligned with the street pattern of the older town. The earliest of them is basilica B, which was built at some point during the second half of the fifth century in the middle of the new enclosure by Bishop Alkison, who is mentioned in the inscription of the mosaic pavement. Basilica A, which was built between 550 and 575, is a three-aisled church with a mosaic pavement inside the atrium, which mentions St Demetrios as the saint to whom that church was dedicated and Bishop Dometios (II) as donor. Another mosaic in the northern *pastophorion* mentions Bishop Dometios I, who appears again in the inscriptions of the mosaic pavement between the narthex and the nave, on the one hand, and the sacristy on the other hand (Dimitriadis 2001: 22–3 and 25–6). Only the builders of basilica C, the last one to be built in early Byzantine Nikopolis, were more concerned with a west–east orientation than with the alignment to the street grid (Bowden 2003: 163). Basilica C seems to have been built at some point during the last quarter of the century, at which time the orthogonal street grid in Nikopolis had begun to lose its coherence in certain areas (Dimitriadis 2001: 27–8; Bowden 2003: 163). During the second half of the sixth century, a number of houses with walls built of limestone rubble and spolia bonded with earth were built to the southeast of basilica A. It is not known at what point the city was abandoned.

By contrast, it is quite clear that the city of Demetrias was abandoned in the early sixth century, together with the basilica of Damokratia, which had been built in the early 400s in the northern harbour quarter of the city. The population appears to have moved to the nearby hill of Iolkos, at the western end of the modern city of Volos (Karagiorgou 2001a: 203). In neighbouring Thebes, however, occupation seems to have continued after 600. Basilica B, which was built in the centre of the city in the late fifth century, was repaired in the early sixth century, and then destroyed by fire at some point during the second half of that century. Basilica A, which was built in the mid-fifth century and dedicated to St Demetrios, was equally restored in the sixth century, after being destroyed by fire. As a result of that restoration, a new, but much smaller church continued to be used, the space for which was obtained by walling off the nave with rubble masonry, and abandoning the aisles. The most impressive church in Thebes, however, was basilica C, which probably served as cathedral. It too may have been built in the fifth century, when a baptistery was also added, together with mosaic and *opus sectile* floors of exceptional quality. Of a similar date may be a group of six rooms at the southwestern corner of the southern stoa, which have been interpreted as an episcopal palace (Karagiorgou 2001: 189). A second baptistery was added in the sixth century, when a room previously created on the southern side of the southern stoa received a mosaic pavement with an inscription mentioning a teacher from Pergamon named Moschos Ippokratou. The room has therefore been interpreted as a school. Like the other two churches, basilica C was destroyed by fire, but only in the late 600s, an indication that at least some parts of Thebes were still occupied in the seventh century. An aristocratic house with sculptural decoration existed in the immediate vicinity of basilica A, but nothing is known about the exact dates of its building and abandonment.

By contrast, a relatively large number of sixth-century aristocratic houses are known from Delphi, besides the city's two churches (Petridis 1997: 686–7, 2005). A house between the Lesche of the Knidians, the ex-voto of Daochos, and the northeastern angle of the

Peribolos was most probably a *triclinium* with a large central room with walls painted in red and white (Petridis 2005: 196).[12] Another house, to the southeast of the Peribolos, was built in the late fourth century on two terraces. It was a two-storeyed building with three *triclinia* and a bath complex. The house was restored and slightly modified in the course of the sixth century, before being abandoned by the end of that century. By that time, many of the houses still in use in Delphi had been subdivided into smaller rooms, with corridors and passages blocked, a phenomenon interpreted as a sign that the place of the rich was now taken by the less well-off. However, since many of the rooms created by means of the subdivision of previous villas operated as workshops, it is clear that around 600 Delphi was not a city of squatters. A pottery workshop was found next to the precinct of the sanctuary in Delphi, where potters gradually moved shortly after 590. The workshop comprised six, perhaps as many as seven kilns, which produced amphorae, pitchers, bowls, beehives, and lamps (Petridis 2003). I will return to the significance of the Delphi kilns for an assessment of the economic situation in Greece c. 600. For the moment, however, it is important to note that at Delphi, the abandonment of the city in c. 610–620 followed a dramatic transformation which brought forward the economic role of a much diminished community (for the date of abandonment, see Petridis 1997: 688).

A five-aisled basilica built in the early sixth century, an episcopal palace, a villa complex, ordinary houses, shops, and bathhouses have been found in an urban settlement established in Andikira, away from the ruins of the ancient city, much as in Demetrias. It is not, however, clear when the move from ancient Antikyra to the new locale took place. Nor is it known when the new settlement was abandoned, if at all (Kourenta-Raptaki 2004).

In Athens, the so-called 'post-Herulian' wall included the Acropolis, but not the Agora, since at that time the political and commercial centre of the late antique city appears to have shifted eastward to the less damaged Library of Hadrian and the Roman Market. In the early 500s, a bath was built on top of an older fountain on the southern side of a Late Roman house on the Areopagus. A collection of antique marble sculptures was found in a courtyard north of the bath, which was interpreted as evidence of Emperor Justinian's anti-pagan legislation of 529. A mosaic floor in the room south of the bath was replaced in the course of the sixth century with *opus sectile* in a cruciform pattern. Another *villa urbana* was found in the southern corner of the Acropolis and was attributed to Proclus. A large *triclinium*, a relief representing the goddess Cybele, and an altar are viewed as sufficient evidence for this attribution (Sodini 1984: 348–52 and 359; see also Gregory 1984: 273; Hattersley-Smith 1988: 367 and 374). A third villa was excavated on the eastern side of the Library of Pantainos. The earlier stoa was converted into an elegant suite of small rooms belonging to a two-storeyed building, no doubt similar to that in Delphi. On the first floor, there was a large peristyled courtyard and a *triclinium*. At least one room on the first floor had a barrel vault, and the walls of the neighbouring rooms had niches for statues. Very different houses coexisted in Athens with those villas. A sixth-century building with eight rooms and two courtyards, all built in stone, including spolia, bonded with mortar, was excavated in the southeastern quadrant of the Tholos. The building was erected c. 500 and damaged by fire at some point after the reign of Tiberius II (578–582) (Frantz 1988: 83). The many rooms of a large structure overlying the east end of the South Stoa II may have served as shops or workshops. Lamp production in sixth-century Athens was based on the imitation of African specimens imported into local markets. However, no evidence exists of the organisation in large workshops of earlier centuries, and it is quite possible that lamps were produced in rooms not very different from those excavated at the eastern end of the South Stoa II (Karivieri 1998: 424). During the sixth century, two industrial establishments were set up on either side of the Panathenaic Way, near the southeastern corner of the Agora: a flour mill driven by a water wheel, which was active between c. 450 and c. 580 (the water coming from the newly restored Aqueduct of Hadrian), and a small olive press (Hattersley-Smith 1988: 377). Small houses, each with two or three rooms, have also been found around the Palace of the Giants. One of them produced a large quantity of stamped unguent flasks (ampullae) of Palestinian origin, which may have contained holy oil and were dated to the late sixth or early seventh century. The finds have hastily been attributed to a monastery, although no church has so far been found in or around the Palace of the Giants (Frantz 1988: 84 and 91).

By 500, there were already prominent churches in Athens. The earliest were built around the middle of the fifth century: the tetraconch in the Library of Hadrian and the basilica on the Ilissos, to the southeast from the Olympieion (Frantz 1988: 72–3).[13] Two other churches, one between the *peribolos* wall of the Temple of Olympian Zeus and a second-century bath, the other in the Agora, are of a later date, but it is not clear whether any of them may be attributed to the sixth century. Of a Justinianic date may be a three-aisled basilica built on the southern slope of the Acropolis, on the site of the Asklepieion (Frantz 1988: 92; Kazanaki-Lappa 2000: 200). Contrary to some divergent opinions, the Parthenon was converted into a church dedicated to Our Lady only in the second half of the sixth century (Tanoulas 1997: 270; Kazanaki-Lappa 2000: 200; for a much earlier, fifth-century date, see Koder and Hild 1976: 128; Mango 1995–1996).[14] Burials were introduced into the urban area shortly after 500, especially on the southern side of the Acropolis and the area between the Odeion of Pericles and the Theatre of Dionysos (Gregory 1984: 273; Hattersley-Smith 1988: 381). Two vaulted tombs with lekythoi and late sixth- or early seventh-century pottery were found on Kallirois Street, another at Galatsi (Kumothois Street). An ossuary on the northeastern slope of the Areopagus was used in the sixth and early seventh century, while another found at Sophroniskou-Mouson produced eight gold coins, the latest of which was struck for Emperor Maurice (Laskaris 2000: 147–8, 150–3, and 156).

The situation in Corinth was not much different. Any use of the forum as a public square or for private housing had ceased by 500. This is not surprising, for the late antique wall, while enclosing a much reduced area of the early Roman city (less than 100 acres), seems to have left out the forum area (Sanders 2004: 179; Warner Slane and Sanders 2005: 245). Inside the new walls, only a few buildings are known to have been erected in the sixth century. A structure interpreted as either a *martyrium* or part of a baptistery has recently been discovered to the east of the forum on the road to the Kraneion basilica close to the amphitheatre (Sanders 2004: 185). Excavations in the Panagia Field at Corinth revealed that in the sixth century a bathhouse was built in the ruins of a third- to fourth-century urban villa. The bath was coin-dated to the mid-sixth century, but an additional, larger structure of unknown function was found to the south, which may also have been built in the 500s. By that time, burials had already been introduced within the urban area, as demonstrated by a number of them found just outside that structure. Some of them were tile-graves, others graves of infants buried in amphorae (Sanders 2004: 178). The forum area just outside the late antique wall also became a burial ground, with graves in the ruins of fourth-century shops and baths to the rear of the Southern Stoa, or in the court of the Peirene fountain (Ivison 1996: 104; Laskaris 2000: 161–3).

Funerary inscriptions are known from the cemetery on the edges of the Asklepieion court, north of the Theatre. Many of them mention not just the occupant, but often the purchaser or the seller, and sometimes even the price for which the tomb had been purchased. For example, a miller named Artemon purchased the tomb in which was buried a woman named Photine, who died in 559 (Feissel and Philippidis-Braat 1985: 359).[15] Similarly, a woman named Noumenis was buried in a tomb which a certain shoe and clothing merchant named Eusebios purchased from a fuller named Leonidios (Feissel and Philippidis-Braat 1985: 362).[16]

Despite being left out of the late antique wall, many areas of the early Roman city witnessed dramatic rebuilding. An inscription found in 1931 north of the amphitheatre records the restoration of some structures done by a certain *patrikios* named Ianouarios and a *domestikos* named Paul (Feissel and Philippidis-Braat 1985: 294). The corridors along the eastern and northern side of the peristyled courtyard known as the Peribolos of Apollo were transformed in the early 500s into small rooms, which belonged to a glass-working workshop (Hattersley-Smith 1988: 403; Ivison 1996: 104; Avramea 1997: 113). A house was built in the sixth century in the northern half of the Great Bath on the Lechaion Road. The walls were partially built with re-used material. A coin struck for Justin II gives a *terminus post quem* for the fireplace in the southeastern corner of the house (Biers 1985: 12). Several large churches existed outside the late antique wall, the most important of which was the Lechaion basilica, built over a relatively long period between the mid-fifth and the early sixth century (Sanders 2004: 184; Warner Slane and Sanders 2005: 292). The basilica was still in use c. 600, as indicated by red-slipped pottery found in two brick-built graves placed outside and immediately south of the apse, which pre-date the destruction of the church. To the east of the late antique wall, the Kraneion basilica was a three-aisled cemeterial basilica built c. 500 and abandoned at some point during the second half of the sixth century (Pallas 1976; Snively 1984: 119–20). Also cemeterial were the basilica excavated by the Kenchreian Gate, probably of a sixth-century date, and the basilica of St Kodratos, to the east of the Lerna Hollow (Shelley 1943; Stikas 1964 and 1966).[17]

There were many churches in neighbouring Argos as well. The basilica on the Hill of Prophet Elias, which was built in the sixth century in the ruins of the Temple of Apollo, had a baptistery coin-dated to 575, and may have served as a cathedral

(Oikonomou-Laniadou 2003: 11–13; Piérart and Touchais 1996: 89–90).[18] Another baptistery was found next to the basilica in Florou, which was built in the late fifth century, and then abandoned after destruction by fire in the mid-sixth century (Oikonomou-Laniadou 2003: 21). Five more churches are known to have operated during that century in Lymberi, Gonei, Doutsou, Gargassoula, and Liapi. Only the former three appear to have been cemeterial basilicas (Oikonomou-Laniadou 2003: 13–17 and 79).[19] By 500, most cemeteries were still outside the city walls, to the north, south, and east of the city. By 600, besides Lymberi and Gonei, another cemetery appeared next to the basilica in Florou (Oikonomou-Laniadou 2003: 78). Much as in Corinth, many tombs had stones with inscriptions, and some of them were precisely dated, such as that of Stephanis, a ten-year-old girl who died on 19 June 536. Another funerary inscription mentions a bishop of Kephalodion (Cefalù in Sicily) who died in Argos at some point during the sixth century (Oikonomou-Laniadou 2003: 52; Gerolymou 1999: 51–6). During the late fifth and sixth century, the centre of the city moved to the east, between the modern streets Agiou Konstantinou and Danaou, in an area until then only sporadically inhabited. A number of urban villas appeared during the sixth century in that area. Two *triclinia*, one of which had a mosaic pavement dated to the early sixth century, were discovered on the Athanassopoulou and Koutroumbi properties, respectively. A third was found outside the city walls, in Paliopyrga. A large villa with a bathhouse built in the fifth century on the OTE property was abandoned in the mid-sixth century. A large building with a mosaic pavement, possibly another urban villa, which had been built in the mid-fourth century, then restored in the course of the fifth century, was turned into a workshop after c. 500, as demonstrated by the oven, well, and water tank, all coin-dated to the reign of Emperor Justin II (565–578) (Oikonomou-Laniadou 2003: 61). Two bathhouses (A and B) were abandoned before 500, but their ruins were quickly turned into workshops. That in bathhouse B appears to have been a glass-working shop (Oikonomou-Laniadou 2003: 6–7).

Very little is known about other cities in Peloponnesos. The acropolis of Patras appears to have been fortified at some point during the sixth century. Two sixth-century churches, both with mosaic pavements, have been identified at 283 Korinthou Street and 46–52 Kanakari Street, respectively. In addition, the bath excavated at 1 Vyronos Street appears to have been still in use in the early sixth century (Moutzali 1991: 261–3, 2002: 179–81).[20] Five vaulted tombs found at 116 Karaiskaki were coin-dated to the reign of Justin I, while a single tile-grave found at 26–30 Nikita Street produced a coin struck for Emperor Justinian. Another group of eleven tile-graves and two vaulted tombs discovered at 73 Hellinou Stratiotou Street was coin-dated to the reign of Justin II (Laskaris 2000: 182–4). Olympia was clearly not a city any more, and the rural character of the settlement surrounding the basilica erected not far from the Temple of Zeus was described in Chapter 1. In Messenia, a group of houses built in stones bonded with clay appeared after c. 500 in the ruins of the Theatre, as well as in the portico of the Asklepieion. The new buildings are coin-dated to the reigns of Anastasius and Justin I, as well as to the early regnal years of Justinian, and, as in Olympia, they seem to have surrounded a three-aisled basilica built in the Theatre (for the church, see Themelis 2000: 82–4; for the houses, see Themelis 2002: 36–7, 53 fig. 16, 54 fig. 17).[21] Whether the sixth-century occupation of Messenia may still be regarded as urban remains unclear. As in Olympia, houses with walls built of stone bonded with clay may have been associated with a purely rural settlement, but no contextual information exists to confirm this interpretation.

There are several conclusions to be drawn from this survey of the urban centres in Greece. First, cities in Greece such as Thessalonica or Nikopolis are the only ones in the Balkans for which we have information about the survival of the ancient urban layout and street grid beyond AD 500. No other city in the region is known to have still had a hippodrome, a praetorium, or public baths in the sixth century. Everywhere else, the dominant pattern is one of shrinking urban occupation, often of a fortified acropolis, and encroachment into formerly grand buildings. The hallmark of the early sixth-century urban landscape is the urban villas with mosaic or *opus sectile* floors, of which there are many more in Greece than in any other part of the Balkans. Both before and after the middle of the century, the urban landscape was invaded by houses and shops with walls built in stone, sometimes with spolia from dilapidated ancient buildings, all bonded with clay. Another parallel phenomenon is that of intramural burials, often right in the agora, as in Thessalonica. It is important to note that in Delphi, the last phase of occupation is associated with a pottery production centre. Industrial establishments also appeared in Athens (a flour mill), Argos, and Philippi (glass-working shops). Elsewhere, the building of churches, the only form of monumental architecture known in the sixth century, stopped almost everywhere before 600. All cities in Greece whose layout and internal organisation has been studied archaeologically produced evidence of more than one intramural church. In Thebes, there were two baptisteries associated with one and the same church (basilica C, probably the cathedral), while in Argos two different baptisteries were associated with different churches, a sign that baptism was now administered not just in the cathedral and perhaps not just by the bishop alone.

Why did the population in some cities revert to a rural mode of life, while in other cities the settlement contracted and regrouped around a defensible acropolis, often dominated by churches? The traditional interpretation blames it all on barbarian invasions and earthquakes. To be sure, Prokopios specifically mentions Corinth in a list of cities destroyed by earthquakes in the series of 'calamities which fell upon all mankind during the reign of the demon who had become incarnate in Justinian' (Prokopios of Kaisareia, *Secret History* 18.36 and 41–3; see also *Buildings* 4.2). Despite the fact that Prokopios gives no date for the event (except to say that the earthquake was followed by the plague, known to have taken place in 542), many have dated the earthquake to 522, 524, or 525.[22] Emperor Justin I is said to have intervened in person and used money from the imperial treasury to help with the recovery of the city. No layer of destruction on the level implied by Prokopios' account has so far been identified in Corinth which could be dated to the 520s, and, *pace* Dimitrios Pallas, the last building phase in the Lechaion basilica in fact post-dates the reign of Justin I (518–527) (Pallas 1960: 159 and 166–7; Warner Slane and Sanders 2005: 291–2). Equally difficult to spot in the archaeological record is the other, much more devastating series of earthquakes which, according to Prokopios, rolled through 'both Boeotia and Achaea and the country on the Crisaean Gulf' (Prokopios of Kaisareia, *Wars* 8.25.16–23). He listed eight cities being levelled to the ground, among them 'Chaeronea and Coronea and Patrae and all of Naupactus, where there was also great loss of life'. Following that, his account then insists on extraordinary phenomena, such as a tsunami levelling to the ground another two cities, Echinos and Scarphea in Boeotia.

> And for a long time the sea thus visited the mainland, so that for a very considerable period it was possible for men on foot to walk to the islands which are inside this gulf, since the water of the sea, obviously, had abandoned its proper place, and strange to say, spread over the land as far as the mountains which rise there. But when the sea returned to its proper place, fish were left on the ground, and

since their appearance was altogether unfamiliar to the people of the country, they seemed as a kind of prodigy. And thinking them edible they picked them up to boil them, but when the heat of the fire touched them the whole body was reduced to a liquid putrefaction of an unbearable sort. But in that locality where the so-called Cleft is located there was a tremendous earthquake which caused more loss of life than in all the rest of Greece, particularly on account of a certain festival, which they happened to be celebrating there and for which many had gathered in that place from all Greece.

Historians have not yet decided what to do with this particular account. On the surface, it looks like an authentic report of strange natural phenomena taking place at the time of or shortly after a major earthquake. But there are several problems and contradictions which are not easy to resolve. The fish turning into 'a liquid putrefaction of an unbearable sort' looks suspiciously like a fantastic creature. The description of the tsunami appears to have been influenced by the tradition of linking earthquakes – specifically those in Greece – with key events, such as the deaths of emperors (Sanders 2004: 170–1). The reference to a perhaps religious festival being celebrated in a place called Cleft may also be a pastiche of ancient ethnography, although no such place is known to have existed in ancient Greece. The hardest nut to crack, though, is the image of the sea moving from its bed onto the mainland 'as far as the mountains'. It is hard to escape the impression that, far from being an objective report from the field, Prokopios' account serves a particularly ironic goal, but it is not at all clear what that goal might be. Meanwhile, archaeologists do not seem aware either of the problems with this text or of the fact that no evidence exists that any of the cities mentioned by Prokopios was levelled to the ground. Patras, as we have seen, was most probably still occupied during the second half of the sixth century. None of the so far occasional excavations in the city have produced any evidence of large-scale destruction. Attempts to attribute the cemetery excavated on the Nikita Street to the earthquake of 552, only because spolia (closure slabs, thresholds, and impost blocks) were used as tombstones (Koumousi-Vgenopoulou 1996), simply ignores the widespread recycling of architectural elements from ancient monuments in sixth-century Greece, as well as almost everywhere else in the Mediterranean region. There have been attempts to attribute the destruction of a number of houses on the southwestern side of the forum in Corinth to the earthquake of 552, on the basis of a hoard of minimi found there in 1933, the latest coins of which cannot be dated with any more precision than the reign of Emperor Justinian (527–565). This, however, is simply circular reasoning: the last coins – nummia struck for Justinian – are dated to the late 540s on the basis of Prokopios' account, which is used to explain the layer of destruction in which the hoard was found (Edwards 1937: 249, a conclusion uncritically adopted by Morrisson et al. 2006: 236). Similarly, the date of burial for the hoard of thirty-six minimi found in the bath-fountain complex in the Gymnasium Area has been established before 551, on the dubious basis of two nummia struck for Justinian whose dating actually covers the entire reign of that Emperor (i.e., they could just as well have post-dated the earthquake) (Dengate 1981: 176; Morrisson et al. 2006: 238). It is important to note, moreover, that there is no mention of Corinth in Prokopios' account of the 552 earthquake. Conversely, the earthquake postulated as an explanation for seventy-six bronze coins found in 1925 with two skeletons in the room of a building to the west of the Lechaion Road is not mentioned in any source (Dengate 1981: 160–1; Morrisson et al. 2006: 239). As Guy Sanders correctly points out, the epicentre of the earthquake of 552 must have been hundreds of kilometres away from Corinth, and the earthquake could therefore not have been responsible for either the shrinking or any other changes taking place in the mid-sixth century in Corinth (Sanders 2004: 172).

Could then the plague of 542 be blamed for the decline of cities in Greece? Neither Prokopios, nor any other contemporary source, specifically mentioned Greece among the regions in the Mediterranean which were affected by the plague. According to Comes Marcellinus, 'a great pestilence' ravaged Illyricum in 543 (Comes Marcellinus, *Chronicle* s.a. 543). 'Illyricum' is of course a much too broad a notion to narrow down this bit of information to events affecting the Greek lands. Nonetheless, according to Dionysios Stathakopoulos, those responsible for the spreading of the plague to Illyricum must have been the troops coming by sea from Constantinople, which in 542 reached Epirus (Prokopios of Kaisareia, *Wars* 7.6.11; Stathakopoulos 2004: 291).[23] If so, Prokopios had no knowledge of it, and no traces have so far been found of plague devastation in Epirus. In Corinth, a funerary inscription from the cemetery around the Kraneion basilica, which mentions one Peter, son of Sergios, who died at the age of 21 because of the plague, is so far the only hard piece of evidence for the pestilence, although nothing indicates that of 542 (Feissel and Philippidis-Braat 1985: 368).[24] The mass burial of over 100 adults and children in Reservoir IV at Lerna, which was believed to be an illustration of the effects of the plague of 542, is in fact of a later date (Sanders 2004: 182, who points to a coin of Justin II recently identified in the assemblage from that mass burial; for the wrong interpretation of the mass burial as evidence of the plague of 542, see Curta 2001b: 142). On the other hand, where the plague is clearly documented in detail, neither the written nor the archaeological evidence seems to indicate any changes in the urban infrastructure that could be attributed to the pestilence. For example, the plague said to have hit Thessalonica a few weeks before the siege of 586, although devastating in terms of the number of deaths, does not seem to have diminished in any way the ability of the surviving community to organise the military resistance against the large army of Sclavenes and other barbarians sent against Thessalonica by the qagan of the Avars (*Miracles of St. Demetrios* 1.29–45, 1.147 and 155).[25] As mentioned above, the baths remained in use at least for those who had taken refuge in the basilica of St Demetrios. According to Archbishop John, the author of Book I of the *Miracles of St. Demetrios*, many corpses were tossed into whatever tombs were vacant, but no archaeological evidence of crowded cemeteries has so far been found in any of the cemeteries excavated inside or outside the city walls (*Miracles of St. Demetrius* 1.36; for cemeteries in Thessalonica, see above in this chapter). At any rate, Thessalonica, like Corinth and Athens, was never abandoned, and the area enclosed by the late antique walls does not seem to have shrunk or changed at all as a result of the plague.

In the absence of a satisfactory explanation based on such catastrophes as the plague or earthquakes, one needs to look for more systemic reasons for the urban decline in Greece shortly before or after 600. It has long been noted that the phenomenon must have been connected to economic and administrative factors, particularly to the relation of urban centres to the central administration. Whereas in Thessalonica and, perhaps to a lesser degree, in Corinth and Athens, the formal hierarchy of the central government was maintained, as evidenced by the presence of the eparch and of other notables, in many other cities the absence of any opportunities for positions in the state may have driven out the local elites in search of self-betterment (Brubaker 2004: 87–90; Wickham 2005: 601). In other words, when the formal hierarchy of the central government withdrew completely from a city, no incentive existed any more for the local urban elites to remain there. It is no accident that in several cities in Greece

– Thasos, Amphipolis, and Delphi – the last phase of occupation ends at the same time, namely around AD 620, as Emperor Herakleios withdrew most troops and, probably, the imperial administration from the Balkans (Curta 2001b: 189). In Demetrias, Olympia, and perhaps Messenia, the urban centre appears to have been abandoned earlier, with a final phase of occupation in the latter two cases which cannot be described as urban any more.

Moreover, the evidence of long-distance trade and local production of pottery confirms this picture of rapid decline shortly before and after 600. African Red Slip (ARS) and Phocaean Red Slip (PRS, also known as Late Roman C) wares appear everywhere in late fifth- and early sixth-century Greece.[26] Catherine Abadie-Reynal has suggested that while ARS was linked to the kind of long-distance trade that moved the grain *annona* to the regions of greater concentrations of troops, PRS may have been more of a local commodity, which moved from harbour to harbour in what may have been a regional network of trade covering both coasts and the islands of the Aegean Sea (Abadie-Reynal 1989b: 157). That the demand for red-slipped wares increased during the sixth century is clearly attested by pottery assemblages from Argos and Athens. At Demetrias, during the last phase of occupation, 80 per cent of all fine, red-slipped wares were PRS. No ARS or PRS forms were found in Demetrias that could be dated after c. 550, while in Corinth not only does the quantity of both ARS and PRS increase during the second half of the sixth century, but ARS wares of later forms (Hayes 104, 105, 107, and 109) have been found in deposits dated as late as the middle or third quarter of the seventh century (Warner Slane and Sanders 2005: 274; see also Sodini 2000: 181–2; Bonifay 2005: 570). Red-slipped wares imitating ARS or PRS were also produced locally, in Athens during the first decades of the sixth century, or in Boeotia, perhaps around Askra, during the second half of that century (Hayes and Petridis 2003: 533; for red-slipped wares from Boeotia, known as Askra Ware, see Vroom 2005: 40–1).[27] In the early sixth century, Athens also produced imitations of African lamps or of third- and fourth-century specimens of local production (Karivieri 1998: 424). Other centres of lamp production have been recently identified in Argos and in Samos (Oikonomou 1988: 499; Poulou-Papadimitriou 1986: 594–8). Although no indication exists of a mass production in large workshops, what all this shows is that there was a relatively high demand in the 500s for fine pottery and lamps. Cheaper wares without red slip, both fine and semi-fine, were also produced in

Greece. The centre of production for Central Greek Painted Ware, first identified in ceramic assemblages from Argos and Delphi, may have been in Nea Anchialos (Petridis 1997: 693, 2003: 445; Vroom 2005: 42–3).[28] In Delphi, half-slipped wares, as well as lamps, were still produced shortly before 600 (Petridis 1997: 692–3).

Equally revealing is the evidence of amphorae. Late Roman 1 specimens produced in Cilicia, near Antioch, in Cyprus, as well as in Rhodes were a familiar presence in Argos (Abadie-Reynal 1989a: 51–6). Late Roman 2 amphorae, which appear on many sites in Greece, at Argos, as well as in Thasos, may, however, have been produced locally, in the southern Argolid, not far from Portochelion (Arthur 1998: 168; Karagiorgou 2001b: 145; Vroom 2003: 143). Imitations of Late Roman 2 amphorae have also been found in sixth-century ceramic assemblages in Corinth and Pyrgouthi (Warner Slane and Sanders 2005: 287). Types produced in Palestine (Late Roman 4–6), which were common in the western Mediterranean area and in Gaul, appear in Argos in much large numbers than either Late Roman 1 or Late Roman 2 amphorae. Palestinian amphorae and Late Roman 2 amphorae were still in use in Corinth in the mid-seventh century (Warner Slane and Sanders 2005: 278; for a so-called Gaza amphora [Late Roman 4] from Corinth, see also Touchais 1982: 542 fig. 25). Catherine Abadie-Reynal explained this situation in terms of different distribution networks. Like ARS, amphorae of the Late Roman 1 and Late Roman 2 types transported *annona* commodities primarily for the army, while the Palestinian amphorae indicate 'free-market commerce' (Abadie-Reynal 1989b: 159). The association between the state-run distribution of the *annona* and Late Roman 2 amphorae follows also from a comparison of Late Roman's relative significance in ceramic assemblages in mainland Greece and in Crete. In Argos, 30 per cent of all sixth-century amphorae are of the Late Roman 2 type, which is otherwise absent from ceramic assemblage in Gortyna, where the most important amphorae are Late Roman 1 and Late Roman 6 (Sodini 2000: 192; see also Karagiorgou 2001). Late Roman 1 and Late Roman 2 amphorae were still in use in Corinth in the mid-seventh century (Warner Slane and Sanders 2005: 274–6). However, both amphora types and red-slipped wares completely disappeared by the end of that century. By that time, many of the urban sites in which such ceramic categories had appeared during the sixth century had long been abandoned. In Corinth and Athens, two sites on which occupation continued uninterrupted, the late antique amphorae and the red-slipped wares made room for new ceramic categories, such as Glazed White Ware and globular amphorae, which will be discussed in Chapter 4. That both globular amphorae and Glazed White Ware have a much more restricted distribution than older amphora types and red-slipped wares is an indication that by 700 the trade networks which had underpinned and supported late antique urbanism in Greece were gone (Wickham 2005: 785). In other words, there is a strong connection between the collapse of the long-distance and regional commercial networks during the seventh century and the abandonment of urban centres in Greece. The evidence is still not sufficient to draw a more general conclusion, but the fact that in at least three cases – Amphipolis, Thasos, and Delphi – no evidence exists of abandonment being caused by violent destruction (i.e., barbarian invasion) strongly suggests planned evacuation. It remains unclear whether such a measure may have been associated with the withdrawal of troops from the Balkans in c. 620 or was a more or less private initiative only indirectly inspired by the withdrawal of troops. In any case, this interpretation of the archaeological evidence from urban centres is confirmed by the analysis of coin finds, to which we now need to turn.

Notes

1. The *Synekdemos* was compiled between 528 and 535, but reflects the situation at the time of Theodosius II (Avramea 1997: 35). According to the *Synekdemos*, there were forty cities in Macedonia, seventeen in Thessaly, twelve in Epirus Vetus, and twenty-two in Crete (Koder and Hild 1976: 52).
2. Six other cities north of the Thermopylae Pass not yet identified (Sakkos, Hypate, Korakia, Unnon, Baleai, and Leontarion) had their walls strengthened.
3. Thessalonica is also absent from the *Wars*, which contains no reference to the fortifications of this important city of the Empire. The city is mentioned in the *Buildings* 4.3, but only in relation to the river Rhechios, at the mouth of which Justinian is said to have built the Artemision fort.
4. Such as Paul, son of Vivianos, the consul of 512 (Feissel 1983: 90–1). For the fifth-century fortifications, see Vickers 1974: 251 and 254; Crow 2001.
5. Nothing is known about the exact location of the hippodrome of Thessalonica (Vickers 1971).
6. The only other sixth-century praetorium known from the southern Balkans is that mentioned in an inscription from Ainos as having been

built by the vicar of Thrace, Flavius Marcianus, and the *praeses provinciae* Flavius Valerius Stephanios in c. 600 (Asdracha 1994–1995: 287 and 288–9).
7. Two other edicts dated after 569 may also refer to the basilica of St Demetrios (Feissel 1983: 82–3).
8. Twelve vaulted tombs have also been found on the Langada Street at the intersection with Galanaki and Ivanof. More graves, some of which were vaulted tombs, were discovered on Xirokrini and produced coins struck for Emperor Justinian (Laskaris 2000: 233–4).
9. For an example of a monograph on Byzantine Thessaloniki with an exclusive coverage of churches, see Mauropoulou-Tsioumi 1992.
10. A cemeterial church existed outside the city walls, at Cape Evraiokastro. It, too, had been built on top of a pagan sanctuary. Finally, a monastery dedicated to the Archangel Michael and located near Rachoni is mentioned in an inscription, for which see Feissel 1983: 212–13.
11. Pieces of coloured glass were also associated with the second building phase of the extramural basilica, which was remodelled under Emperor Justinian (Pelekanidis 1955).
12. The house is dated to the second half of the sixth century by means of a fragment of a Central Greek Painted Ware bowl, but its initial building date is unknown.
13. The building of the first churches in Athens is traditionally associated with the Empress Eudokia, said to have been the daughter of an Athenian sophist who converted to Christianity before marrying Theodosius II (Kazanaki-Lappa 2000: 200; Živkov 2003).
14. Graves found on the southern side of the Parthenon produced a sixth-century coin (Laskaris 2000: 51–2).
15. The death is dated on the inscription to Thursday 29 May, seventh indiction, which could have fallen in 424, 469, 514, or 559. However, the dating by indiction was made compulsory for all legal documents only under the reign of Justinian (Sanders 2004: 183).
16. The grave contained four skeletons. The associated lamps may be dated to the late sixth or early seventh century (Sanders 2004: 183).
17. For the funerary inscription of one Eugenios, born in Nikopolis (perhaps that of Epirus) and buried in the basilica of St Kodratos, see Feissel and Philippidis-Braat 1985: 367.
18. A cemetery existed around the church, which produced coins struck for Emperors Justinian and Justin II (Laskaris 2000: 56).
19. For the basilica at Aspis, which was destroyed in the mid-sixth century and turned into a cemetery, see Piérart and Touchais 1996: 89–90.
20. For the fort on the acropolis, see also Georgopoulou-Verra 2002.
21. The occupation is also dated by means of a hoard of Ostrogothic and Vandalic coins (Sidiropoulos 2002).
22. This is often believed to be the same earthquake as that mentioned by

John Malalas, *Chronographia*, pp. 417–18, and Evagrius, *Ecclesiastical History* 4.8. Koder and Hild 1976: 53 and Soustal and Koder 1981: 49 chose 522; Finley 1932: 478 dated the earthquake to 542, the year of the plague. Perhaps influenced by Finley, Avramea 1997: 45–6 refers to another earthquake of 543 mentioned by Elias of Nisibis as having destroyed the walls of Corinth.
23. The expedition of 542 consisted of Thracian and Armenian recruits under the command of the praetorian prefect of Italy, Maximinus.
24. The inscription has initially been dated much earlier, but Dennis Feissel argued for a sixth-century date.
25. For the date of the plague, most probably the late spring or early summer of 586, see *Miracles of St. Demetrios* 1.127; Lemerle 1981: 79; Iliadi 2003: 55. That the epidemic in question was indeed the plague follows from the description of its symptoms in the *Miracles of St. Demetrios* 1.38. See also Stathakopoulos 2004: 291, according to whom the plague had previously visited Constantinople in 585 or early 586.
26. E.g., at Argos, for which see Abadie-Reynal 1989b: 155–6. For definitions of African Red Slip and Phocaean Red Slip Ware, see Vroom 2005: 32–8.
27. Boeotian red-slipped wares have also been found in Corinth (Warner Slane and Sanders 2005: 284), while local red-slipped wares are known from Argos (Aupert 1980: 417–18).
28. At Gortyna, in Crete, local production of painted wares survived well into the eighth century (Poulou-Papadimitriou 2001: 236 and 250–1 with figs 3–5).

CHAPTER 3

Invasion or inflation? Hoards and barbarians in sixth- and early seventh-century Greece

Despite being often accused of having brought the ancient civilisation of Greece to an abrupt end, the Avars and the Slavs have rarely been associated with the destruction of specific cities or monuments (for Avars and Slavs responsible for a wave of destruction throughout Greece, see Weithmann 1985: 103). Shortly after World War II, the Greek historian Dionysios Zakythinos wrote of the Dark Ages separating Antiquity from the Middle Ages as an era of devastation and ruin brought about by the Slavic invaders (Zakythinos 1945: 72 and 1966: 300, 302, and 316; see also Lemerle 1951: 343). Georgios Sotiriou believed that the destruction of basilica A in Thebes was the result of a barbarian invasion, an event ultimately responsible for the settlement in the region of Thebes and Demetrias, around the Bay of Volos, of the Slavic Belegezites (Sotiriou 1929a: 8–9).[1] A French archaeologist attributed the destruction of Corinth and Argos to the Slavic invasion of 586, despite the fact that neither has any such destruction been documented for Corinth, nor is Argos mentioned in any source pertaining to the Slavic and Avar attacks of the 580s (Aupert 1989: 418–19).[2] The absence of any solid evidence of destruction to be attributed to any sixth-century invasion is in sharp contrast to the interest historians have shown in the numismatic evidence, particularly hoards of sixth-century coins. The first to treat coin hoards as a class of evidence pertaining to barbarian invasions was the French numismatist Adrien Blanchet (Blanchet 1900). His approach was based on the idea of associating each individual hoard with a corresponding historical event known from the written sources (Blanchet 1936: 246–7). For sixth-century Greece, this approach was first employed (without any reference to Blanchet) by Michael Metcalf, who argued that several hoards found in Athens indicated devastating Slavic raids into Greece in 582/3, while blaming Slavic invasions into the Balkans at the beginning of Emperor Herakleios' reign for the deposition of such later hoards as Thasos, Nea Anchialos, Politika-Psachna, Solomos, and Athens (Metcalf

1962a: 14 and 20, 1962b: 147). His conclusions were quickly embraced by others who associated the concealment and loss of specific hoards of early Byzantine coins with the disturbances caused by the Slavic invasions (MacDowall 1965: 264; Hohlfelder 1973: 99; Athanassopoulou-Penna 1979: 203; Oikonomidou-Karamesini and Touratsoglou 1979: 63; Oikonomidou-Karamesini 1991: 1290). Some began to draw up lists of coin hoards with latest coins struck at the same time, which could then be plotted on a map in order to trace the routes of the invasion (Nystazopoulou-Pelekidou 1986: 348–9; Galani-Krikou et al. 2002: 17; Morrisson et al. 2006: 79–82 and 98).[3] Others went as far as to claim that such hoards were never retrieved, because of the sudden death of their owners, who were killed by the Slavs (Kroll et al. 1973: 304). Without excluding other possible explanations, Robert Hohlfelder nonetheless believed that not only the burial (and subsequent non-retrieval) but also the 'formation' of a specific hoard could be associated with the 'onslaught of the Avars and Slavs' (Hohlfelder 1975: 273 and 1976: 337).

A comparison between the general list of hoards of sixth- to seventh-century Byzantine coins found in Greece (Table 3.1) and the lists of hoards associated by various scholars with particular invasions or raids shows that a significant number of early and later hoards, including seven assemblages from Corinth, have no associated invasion and, therefore, no historical explanation. No hoard with the latest coin struck earlier than 538 can be attributed to any invasion, for none is known to have reached Greece at that time.[4] That, with one exception, no hoards with latest coins struck between 585 and 607 have so far been found in Greece has been interpreted as a sign that, while military operations moved to the northern Balkans, 'conditions in Greece improved' (Nystazopoulou-Pelekidou 1986: 350). According to the historical sources, Epirus was under attack by the 'Getae' in 517, the Ostrogoths in 551, and the Sclavenes in the 610s and 620s. One would expect to find a large number of hoards within an area under such a serious and continuous threat. However, the distribution map of all hoards found in Greece shows no hoards in the entire central and northwestern area of present-day Greece (Fig. 3.1). By contrast, most finds cluster in southern Greece, and the Sclavene attacks of 578 and 581–584 have indeed been blamed for the burial of hoards found in that region which have the latest coins struck between 575/6 (Agios Nikolaos) and 584/5 (Pellene 1936; Morrisson et al. 2006: 81–2). However, the *Miracles of St. Demetrios* clearly show that it was Macedonia, specifically Thessalonica and its

Table 3.1 Sixth- to seventh-century hoards of early Byzantine coins in Greece, in the order of their latest coins.

	Latest ('closing') coin	Find place	Metal (other than AE)	Bibliography	Container	Other artefacts	Ancient coins (before 498)	Archaeological context	Incomplete
1	491–518	Corinth 1960		Morrisson et al. et al. 2006: 231–2			x		x
2		Eleusis 1992.I		Morrisson et al. et al. 2006: 243			x		
3		Zogeria 1992. II		Galami-Krikou 1992: 71			x		
4	518–27	'Greece'		Bendall 1977: 22			x		
5		Porto Rafti		Morrisson et al. et al. 2006: 270					
6		Thasos 1977		Picard 1979: 430–2			x		
7	527–65	Ano Voula		Morrisson et al. 2006: 213–14			x	x	
8		Athens 1963		Morrisson et al. 2006: 216–17			x		
9		Chersonissos		Morrisson et al. 2006: 290					
10		Corinth1971a		Morrisson et al. 2006: 232–3			x		
11		Corinth 1930		Adelson and Kustas 1964: 162–163			x		
12		Corinth 1933		Adelson and Kustas 1964: 163			x	x	
13		Corinth 1937		Morrisson et al. 2006: 236–7	x		x	x	

#	Date	Location		Reference					
14		Corinth 1971b		Dengate 1981: 175–8		x	x		
15		Corinth		Mattingly 1931: 229–33		x	x		
16		Megara 1979		Morrisson et al. 2006: 257	x	x	x		
17		Patras 1938		Morrisson et al. 2006: 264	x	x	x		
18		Trypi		Morrisson et al. 2006: 286–7					
19		Zacha		Adelson and Kustas 1964: 159–205		x			
20	533–8	Megara 1884		Morrisson et al. 2006: 257		x			
21	537/8	Petrochorion		Morrisson et al. 2006: 122–3					
22	538–62	Bocotia		Bendall 1993					x
23	542–62	Amphipolis	AV	Morrisson et al. 2006: 184–5					x
24	548/9	Thira		Galani-Krikou et al. 2002: 27					
25	542–65	Nestani	AV	Morrisson et al. 2006: 261				x	x
26	552–62	Adam Zagliveriou		Morrisson et al. 2006: 183 and 228–9				x	x
27		Athens		Weller and Metcalf 1969: 311–14					
28	565/6	Corinth 1965		Morrisson et al. 2006: 238		x	x		
29	565–78	Argos 1892–5		Morrisson et al. 2006: 214–15		x	x		
30		Athens 1933a		Morrisson et al. 2006: 218–19		x	x		
31		Athens 1933b		Morrisson et al. 2006: 220					
32		Corinth 1971c		Dengate 1981: 153–75		x	x		

Table 3.1 (continued)

	Latest ('closing') coin	Find place	Metal (other than AE)	Bibliography	Container	Other artefacts	Ancient coins (before 498)	Archaeological context	Incomplete
33		Eleusis 1992.II		Morrisson et al. 2006: 244			x		
34		Eleusis		Morrisson et al. 2006: 244–5					
35		Kenchreai 1963.II		Hohlfelder 1973: 89–101		x	x		
36		Olympia 1876/7		Morrisson et al. 2006: 261–2		x	x		
37		'Peloponnese'	AV	Metcalf 1988: 107					
38		Pinios	AV	Avramea 1983: 66					x
39		Thebes 1932		Morrisson et al. 2006: 285–6			x		
40		Thessaloniki		Morrisson et al. 2006: 199					
41		Zogeria 1979	AV	Morrisson et al. 2006: 278					
42	569/70	Laurion		Morrisson et al. 2006: 254–5					
43		Spata		Morrisson et al. 2006: 276					
44	571/2	Orchomenos		Morrisson et al. 2006: 262					
45		Thasos 1957		Picard 1979: 450 and 453					x
46	573/4	Bozikas		Avramea 1983: 60				x	
47	575/6	Agios Nikolaos		Morrisson et al. 2006: 248–9			x		
48		Kenchreai 1963.I		Hohlfelder 1970: 68–72			x		

49		Mantinea			x	Morrisson et al. 2006: 256
50	576/7	Nemea 1979			x	Morrisson et al. 2006: 259
51		Thebes 1995.IV		x		Galani-Krikou 1998: 166
52		Zogeria 1992.II		x		Galani-Krikou 1992: 70–1
53	577/8	Koutsi				Oikonomidou-Karamessini 1991
54		Megara				Morrisson et al. 2006: 258
55	578–82	Thessaloniki	AV			Oikonomidou-Karamesini and Touratsoglou 1979: 294–310
56		Zogeria 1995				Morrisson et al. 2006: 279–80
57	579–582	Athens 1971		x	x	Kroll et al. 1973: 301–11
58	c. 580	Argos				Morrisson et al. 2006: 215–16
59	581/2	Athens 1936			x	Metcalf 1962b: 144
61	582/3	Agia Kyriaki		x		Morrisson et al. 2006: 268–9
62		Argos 1983		x	x	Morrisson et al. 2006: 216
63	582–600	Apidea	AV			Morrisson et al. 2006: 214
64		Patras 1986	AV	x		Moutzali 2002: 183
65		Zogeria	AV			Galani-Krikou 1992: 69
66	583/4	Athens 1908		x		Morrisson et al. 2006: 225–6
67		Eleusis 1893				Morrisson et al. 2006: 246–7
68		Isthmia 1954			x	Morrisson et al. 2006: 249–50

Table 3.1 (continued)

	Latest ('closing') coin	Find place	Metal (other than AE)	Bibliography	Container	Other artefacts	Ancient coins (before 498)	Archaeological context	Incomplete
69		Kleitoria		Morrisson et al. 2006: 253–4			x		
70		Priolithos Kalavryton		Morrisson et al. 2006: 271–2			x		
71	584/5	Pellene 1936		Morrisson et al. 2006: 266			x		
72	584–602	Eleusis 1885	AV	Morrisson et al. 2006: 245	x				
73	607/8	Chalkis		Morrisson et al. 2006: 231					
74	607–609	Malaisina	AV	Morrisson et al. 2006: 255					x
75		Paiania	AV	Morrisson et al. 2006: 263					
76	609/10	Patras 1987	AV	Morrisson et al. 2006: 265					
77	602–610	Pellene 1982		Morrisson et al. 2006: 267				x	
78		Vasaras	AV	Morrisson et al. 2006: 287					x
79	613–616	Sane	AV	Morrisson et al. 2006: 192–3					
80	615/16	Nea Anchialos		Metcalf 1962a: 21–2					
81		Politika-Psachna		Metcalf 1962a: 22					
82	617/18?	Thasos		Picard 1979: 451–2					
83	619/20	Solomos 1938		Morrisson et al. 2006: 274–5					x
84	615–624	Thasos 1979		Morrisson et al. 2006: 198				x	

85	616–625	Kratigos	AV	Morrisson et al. 2006: 386–7	x
86		Polichnitos	AV	Morrisson et al. 2006: 387	
87		Solomos 1956	AV	Morrisson et al. 2006: 274	
88	622–627	Samos 1983	AV	Oikonomidou-Karamesini and Drosogianni 1989: 147	x
89	624–629	Delos		Galani-Krikou et al. 2002: 72–3	x
90	633/4	Athens 1972		Morrisson et al. 2006: 227	
91	c. 668	Athens 1876	AV	Morrisson et al. 2006: 227–8	x
92	669–674	Kalymnos		Galani-Krikou et al. 2002: 76–7	
93	669–680	Arkessini	AV	Morrisson et al. 2006: 385	

Notes: AE – copper; AV – gold

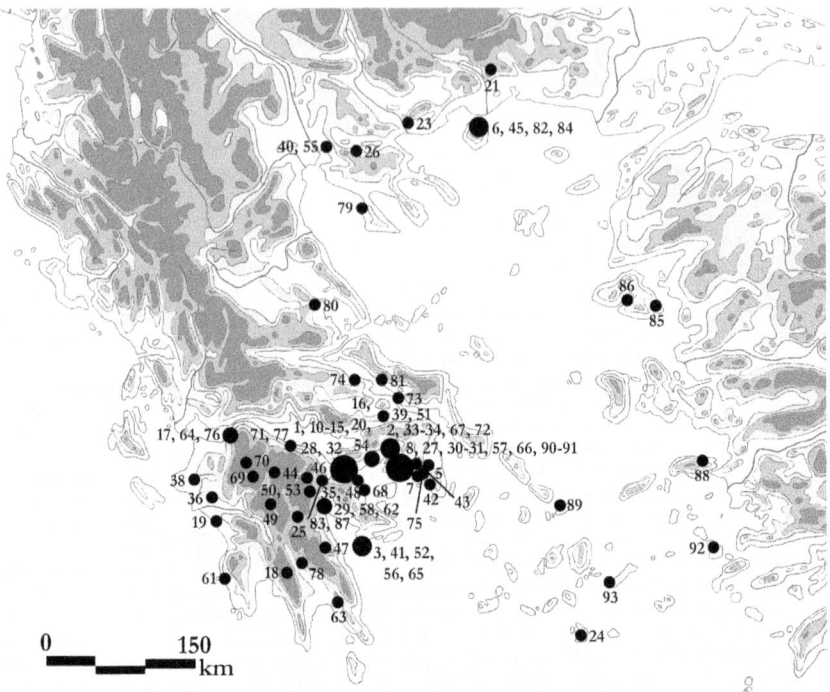

Figure 3.1 The distribution of hoards of sixth- and seventh-century Byzantine coins in Greece. Smallest circle for single hoards, thereafter up to three, five, and nine hoards. Numbers refer to the list in Table 3.1.

hinterland, and not Achaia, which was most often and hardest hit by the Slavic and Avar attacks of the late sixth and seventh century. To date, no hoards of copper are known from Macedonia which could be associated with the 584 surprise attack on Thessalonica by 5,000 Sclavene warriors; with the siege of that city, two years later, by an army of 100,000 warriors under the command of the qagan of the Avars; or with the siege of 25 July 677 by a coalition of Sagudates, Rynchines, and Drugubites (*Miracles of St. Demetrios* 1.12.107–13, 1.13, 2.4.271–6).

There is in fact no consistent correlation between the chronology offered by written sources and the dates of the latest coins in hoards (Karagiannopoulos 1996: 200–1). Moreover, an obstinate preoccupation with linking physical remains such as coins to particular moments in history known from the written sources obscures the complexity of the questions raised by the analysis of coin hoards. Before being buried for whatever reasons, hoards were first and foremost collections of coins, and as such they should be treated as indicating the hoarding behaviour or the 'currency habits' of the population in sixth- and early seventh-century Greece.[5] It has long been noted, that unlike most other contemporary hoards of copper in the Balkans, many of those found in Greece include relatively large numbers of small or very small denominations. For example, the largest number of sixth-century five-nummia pieces struck in Constantinople appear in Greek hoards (Morrisson et al. 2006: 67 fig. 12).[6] Even more compelling is the evidence of minimi – small coins of AE4 module struck from the last years of the fourth to the early decades of the sixth century. The Corinth hoard (no. 15 in Table 3.1), for example, included a few coins struck for Claudius II, Tetricus, Constans, Constantius II, and Julian, but also a large number of coins minted under the fifth-century emperors, from Arcadius to Leo I. Recent studies have shown a great number of the fifth- and early sixth-century minimi from Greek hoards to be of African origin, which dovetails nicely with the archaeological evidence of a contemporary increase in the quantity of African Red Slip wares from Greek sites (Morrisson 1998: 922–3; see Chapter 2). Most fourth- and fifth-century coins seem to have been cut up into fractions or clipped down to an average weight of 0.7 to 0.8 grams, in order to render them equal to the standard nummion (the smallest copper denomination) in circulation after 498. If they were indeed treated as nummia, then those clipped coins must have circulated at an over-rated value, for most if not all of them are heavier than the theoretical nummia. In other words, the weight of forty minimi is in fact larger than the weight of a corresponding follis (the highest copper denomination, which was worth forty nummia). The over-rated value of the minimi may thus have been based on weight, which could easily be increased by adding lead to the alloy employed for their production. This may have been a deliberate policy designed to promote the coin on the market and inspire the confidence of the population. If so, then that was also the reason for the hoarding of large numbers of such minimi (Morrisson 1996: 192; Hahn 2000: 13; Callegher 2005: 232; see also Adelson and Kustas 1964: 178).[7] During the first half of the sixth century, several hoard assemblages included only minimi, often with large quantities of more recent specimens struck under Emperors Zeno, Leo I, and Anastasius. The latest coins in minimi-only assemblages with over 500 specimens were struck under Emperor Justinian (Table 3.2).[8] Hoards with the latest coins struck after 565 typically combine a

Table 3.2 Sixth-century hoards with minimi from Greece.

	Hoard	Date of latest coin	Other denominations	Number of minimi
36	Olympia 1876/7	565–578	yes	at least 20,300
9	Chersonissos	527–565	no	1,786
19	Zacha	527–565	no	1,179
11	Corinth 1930	527–565	no	742
10	Corinth 1971a	527–565	no	626
32	Corinth 1971c	565–578	yes	549
15	Corinth	527–565	no	478
12	Corinth 1933	527–565	no	at least 460
66	Athens 1908	583/4	yes	447
13	Corinth 1937	527–565	no	387
30	Athens 1933a	565–578	yes	374
57	Athens 1971	579–582	yes	249
71	Pellene 1936	584/5	yes	233
61	Agia Kyriaki	582/3	yes	226
4	'Greece'	518–527	no	224
35	Kenchreai 1963.II	565–578	yes	97
1	Corinth 1960	491–518	no	85
28	Corinth 1965	565/6	yes	85
18	Trypi	527–565	no	82
47	Agios Nikolaos	575/6	yes	82
7	Ano Voula	527–565	no	77
29	Argos 1892–5	565–578	no	73
68	Isthmia 1954	583/4	yes	73
6	Thasos 1977	518–527	yes	57
14	Corinth 1971b	527–565	no	36
5	Porto Rafti	518–527	no	31
20	Megara 1884	533–538	no	18
70	Priolithos Kalavryton	583/4	yes	15
52	Zogeria 1992.II	491–518	yes	14
3	Eleusis 1992.II	565–578	yes	12
69	Kleitoria	583/4	yes	10
50	Nemea 1979	576/7	yes	5
2	Eleusis 1992.I	491–518	no	3
51	Thebes 1995.IV	576/7	yes	3
43	Spata	569/70	yes	2

comparatively smaller number of minimi with other denominations. The most recent hoard with minimi is Pellene 1936, with the latest coin struck in 584/5. However, the most recent minimi-only hoard is Megara 1884, in which the latest coins were struck between 533 and 538. Therefore, the minimi-only hoard seems to have been a relatively short-lived phenomenon in Greece, which could be dated between c. 500 and c. 540. This was apparently a period of relative stability of the exchange rate between the solidus and the follis and of a considerable increase in weight for the follis, from 9.10g in 498 to 24.95g in 538 (the heaviest follis throughout the sixth and early seventh century).[9] In addition to minimi, hoards with latest coins struck during this period also include ancient Greek coins, especially coins of Sikyon and of the Macedonian king Philip II, all of which show no signs of being in regular circulation for 800 years or more after leaving the mint.[10] They must have been picked up in Corinth and re-introduced into circulation as minimi on the basis of their weight (Dengate 1981: 157). Minimi remained in circulation long after ceasing to be struck in any significant numbers, as shown by the Corinth 1971c hoard. In that hoard, minimi and earlier Greek and Roman coins represent over two thirds of the total value in copper coins (Dengate 1981: 162).[11]

Did currency in sixth-century Greece then circulate by weight and not by the stamped type? The evidence of hoards seems to contradict that idea. Had hoard owners been after heavy coins, then not only they would have avoided minimi – the most unsatisfactory medium for the storage of a capital sum – but they would have preferred folles to any other denomination. Moreover, they would have preferred the heaviest folles of all, those struck after 538 and before 550.[12] This may have indeed been the case for the owner of the small hoard found in Agios Nikolaos, in which the only follis was a heavy piece struck in 539/40. But in most other hoards, such folles were found only in relatively small numbers (Table 3.3). Similarly, the higher denominations struck before 538 are almost absent from hoards with the latest coins minted in the 580s, most probably because such coins had by then disappeared from circulation (Duncan 1993: 147).[13] A quick glance at the composition of any of those hoards shows that the selection of coins was not based on weight alone, but that the owner took into consideration several other criteria, such as denomination, mint, and year of minting (Shuvalov 1999: 105, in reference to the Thebes 1932 hoard). It has already been observed that while there were many more folles than half-folles in hoards with the latest coins struck between 510 and 540, and between 610 and 620, the number of half-folles is larger than that of folles in hoards with the latest coin struck between 565 and 585 (Morrisson et al. 2006: 50 fig. 4). It appears, therefore, that the owners of all those hoards were interested in the monetary (or face) value of the coins, most probably

Table 3.3 Sixth-century hoards with heavy folles struck between 538 and 550.

Date of latest coin	Hoard	Number of heaviest folles	Total number of folles
565–578	Thebes 1932	9	113
571/2	Thasos 1957	7	63
583/4	Eleusis 1893	7	117
584/5	Pellene 1936	7	107
565–578	Eleusis	5	12
575/6	Mantinea	4	7
577/8	Koutsi	4	13
582/3	Agia Kyriaki	3	22
583/4	Athens 1908	3	34
576/7	Nemea 1979	2	10
577/8	Megara	2	6
569/70	Laurion	1	9
569/70	Spata	1	7
575/6	Agios Nikolaos	1	1

because of the higher fiduciary nature of the larger copper denominations (Morrisson 1989: 251; Hahn 2000: 8). For example, the total weight of the Koutsi hoard is 278.605g, the equivalent of 20.43 folles if using the standard weight of the follis in 578 (13.64g), the date of the latest coins in the collection. The total amount of copper in that collection was worth 0.028 solidi in 578, when the solidus–follis ratio was 1:720. There are twenty-two coins in the Koutsi hoard, thirteen folles and nine half-folles. If taking the monetary (face) value into consideration, there are 17.5 folles in the Koutsi hoard, the value of which was equal to 0.024 solidi in 578, slightly less than that calculated on the basis of weight alone. Similarly, the total weight of the coins in the Thebes 1932 hoard is 2679.85g, the equivalent of 196.47 folles or 0.272 solidi at the same exchange rate as applied in the case of the Koutsi hoard. The total value of the 235 coins in the Thebes 1932 hoard is 173.2 folles, or 0.24 solidi. The difference between the face and the weight value is also negligible in the case of the Kenchreai 1963.II and Athens 1933a hoards.[14]

However, the monetary value of the copper coins varied considerably throughout the sixth century, as a consequence of the variations in reckoning the follis to the solidus (as money of account) introduced by several monetary reforms.[15] The value of a hefty collection of copper coins could suddenly drop to almost nothing. That much follows from the comparison between the total value of hoard collections calculated on the basis of the exchange rate between gold and copper in operation at the time of every one of the constituent coins, and that at the time of the latest coin (Table 3.4 and Fig. 3.2).[16] The difference is minimal or absent for very early (Petrochorion and Boeotia) or very late hoards (Solomos 1938, Nea Anchialos, Politika-Psachna, Chalkis, and Pellene 1982). In both cases, the earliest and the latest coins in each collection were struck at a distance of only a few years (only three or four for Chalkis and Nea Anchialos), too short indeed for the collection to be affected by variations in the value of the follis.[17] Assuming that they were buried shortly after the date of the latest coins, such hoards are therefore a direct indication of the amount of money their owners have put into saving. This, however, is not true for the majority of hoards in Greece with the latest coins struck between 540 and 600. At the time of their burial, the value of what may have been money set aside for savings had dropped considerably.[18] The owners of the Eleusis, Thebes 1932, Laurion, Spata, Thasos 1957, Mantinea, and Athens 1936 hoards thus appear to have lost more than 50 per cent of the accumulated value. Particularly vulnerable to depreciation were hoards with coins struck between 538 and 550, when the solidus was cheaper in relation to the follis than at any other time during the sixth and early seventh century. If, as some believe (MacDowall 1965: 266), the valuable old folles were still worth their face value for a while after 550, then by 580, the steep reduction in value of the new coins must have made it necessary to accumulate a much larger number of new coins in order to match the value of the old ones. Indeed, when examining the year-by-year accumulation in thirty-four hoards with the latest coins struck between 538 and 629, it is clear that in order to make up about the same amount of money, it was necessary to have a number of coins struck shortly before and after 570 much larger than of coins struck between 540 and 550. Similarly, a very large number of coins (mostly half-folles) struck between 565 and 578 appear in hoards buried after 580, but their value is equal to that of a smaller number of coins (mostly folles) struck between 610 and 615. Depreciation affected especially hoards with the latest coins struck in the late 570s or early 580s. Such hoards typically include heavier, high-value folles struck between 540 and 560, which are otherwise completely absent from hoards with the latest coin struck after 600. The evidence suggests therefore that between 565 and 585, a number of relatively large hoards were buried in Greece. Such hoards were collections

Table 3.4 The value in fractions of solidus of sixth- and early seventh-century hoards from Greece, calculated on the basis of the solidus–follis ratio at the time of each coin's minting and at the time of the latest coin.

	Hoard	Date of latest coin	Total value of coins at time of minting (in solidi)	Value in solidi at time of 'closing' (date of latest coin)
39	Thebes 1932	565–578	0.494	0.24
67	Eleusis 1893	583/4	0.442	0.307
71	Pellene 1936	584/5	0.3469	0.245
83	Solomos 1938	619/20	0.30	0.30
45	Thasos 1957	571/2	0.259	0.126
68	Isthmia 1954	583/4	0.1896	0.167
70	Priolithos Kalavryton	583/4	0.168	0.121
66	Athens 1908	583/4	0.1658	0.123
21	Petrochorion	537/8	0.142	0.142
22	Boeotia	538–562	0.123	0.123
61	Agia Kyriaki	582/3	0.0617	0.039
57	Athens 1971	579–582	0.0807	0.078
59	Athens 1936	581/2	0.055	0.028
26	Adam Zagliveriou	552–562	0.054	0.049
42	Laurion	569/70	0.054	0.023
34	Eleusis	565–578	0.0521	0.019
30	Athens 1933a	565–578	0.05	0.008
50	Nemea 1979	576/7	0.05	0.019
69	Kleitoria	583/4	0.0485	0.032
53	Koutsi	577/8	0.0427	0.024
43	Spata	569/70	0.038	0.017
56	Zogeria 1995	578–582	0.0384	0.056
89	Delos	624–629	0.0339	0.020
49	Mantinea	575/6	0.0324	0.011
84	Thasos 1979	615–624	0.0323	0.021
54	Megara	577/8	0.0314	0.017
82	Thasos	617/8 (?)	0.0239	0.019
80	Nea Anchialos	615/16	0.035	0.035
81	Politika-Psachna	615/16	0.0152	0.016
32	Corinth 1971c	565–578	0.0153	0.01
31	Athens 1933b	565–578	0.014	0.009
35	Kenchreai 1963.II	565–578	0.013	0.007
73	Chalkis	607/8	0.011	0.011
77	Pellene 1982	602–610	0.011	0.011
47	Agios Nikolaos	575/6	0.0067	0.003

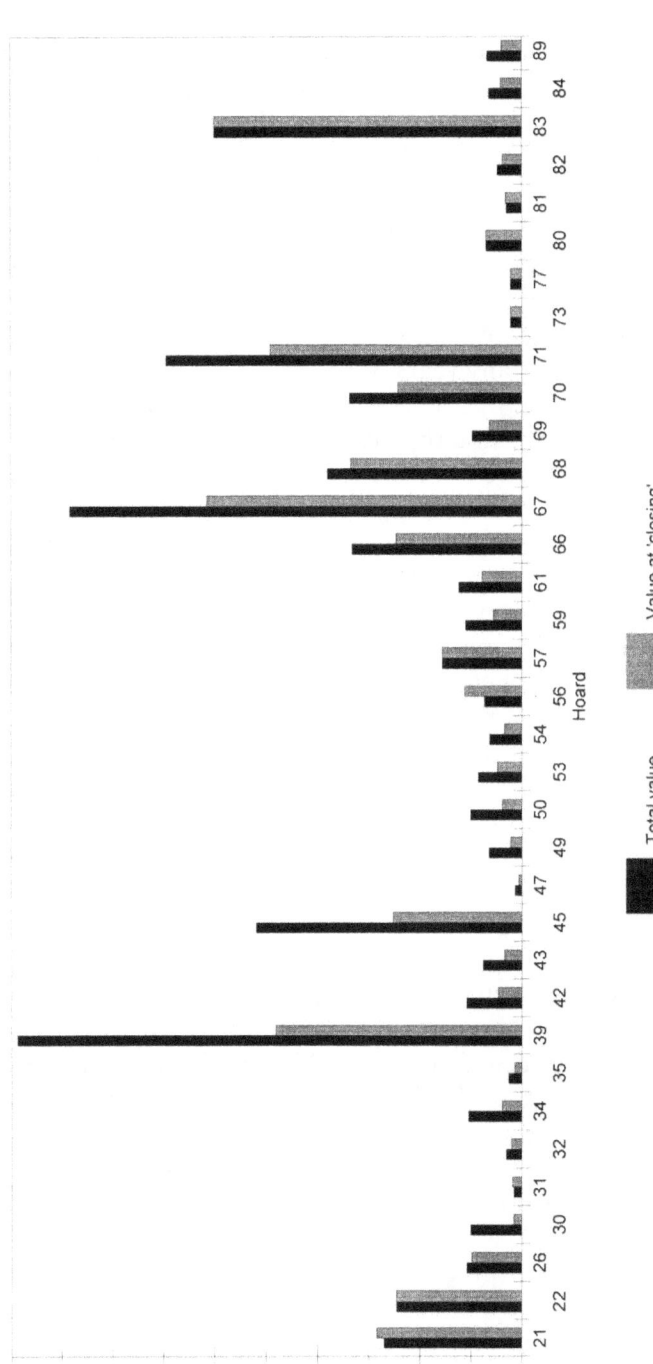

Figure 3.2 The value of thirty-five hoard collections from Greece, calculated on the basis of the exchange rate between gold and copper in operation at the time of every one of the constituent coins ('Total value'), and at the time of the latest coin ('Value at "closing"'), respectively. Numbers refer to the list in Table 3.4.

of coins of different dates and mints, some of which appear to have been selected for their weight and corresponding high value. 'Saving deposits' seems to be the best way to describe those hoards, especially because of the year-by-year, relatively long sequences of coins in their composition. It is not possible to decide whether the heavy, high-value coins were withdrawn from circulation shortly after being minted or some time after that. However, it is unlikely that such hoards were collections hastily put together at the time of their burial. The year-by-year sequence of coins strongly suggests that the accumulation in each one of them was a slow, gradual process, which may have taken many years. If so, then it is quite possible that the value of the withdrawn coins changed between the beginning of the accumulation process and the moment of burial. In other words, owners of hoards with latest coins struck between 565 and 585 had the greatest chance of being disappointed in their expectations and of seeing the value of their savings diminish over the years. This is in sharp contrast to the situation of hoards with the latest coins struck after 600, which were comparatively modest collections of very new coins. The owners of later hoards had little or no concern for the selection of coins struck before 585, but instead withdrew only new coins, the value of which, though much diminished in comparison to that of the early sixth-century follis, was nevertheless stable.

There is therefore a sharp break in coin accumulation in Greek hoards after the early 580s, and new coins appear briefly only after 600. Moreover, no hoards are known so far from Greece with the latest coins struck between 585 and 605. For two decades, hoarding seems to have completely ceased in Greece, after two other decades (565–585) in which it was very common. This is in sharp contrast to the situation in the northern Balkans, especially along the Lower Danube, where hoards have been found which include many coins struck between 585 and 605 (Curta 1996: 196 fig. 19 and 199 fig. 22). Why are there no coins in Greek hoards to have been struck for Emperor Maurice after 585? That this is no accident follows from the fact that such coins are also rare among single finds.[19] In Athens, much as in hoards, the number of coins drops abruptly in the 580s, and coins minted for Emperor Maurice after 585 are rare.[20] A similar phenomenon has been noted for Kenchreai.[21] The evidence thus suggests that the reason for the absence of any hoards with the latest coins struck between 585 and 602 is that fewer coins were in circulation in Greece during that period and, as a consequence, none was withdrawn from circulation. That coins from that period are also absent from later hoards substantiates the idea of a sudden gap in circulation. Furthermore, no fewer than four hoards of gold are known (Zogeria, Apidea, Eleusis 1885, and Patras 1986) in which the latest coins were struck at some point between 582 and 602.

There is no reason to believe that the gap in the circulation of copper was caused by the Slavic and Avar invasions, which clearly did not interrupt occupation of any of the major urban sites in Greece. On the contrary, some believe the absence of hoards of copper for the period between 585 and 605 to be a 'sign that conditions in Greece improved, while military events focused on the northern regions of the Balkans' (Nystazopoulou-Pelekidou 1986: 350). Hoards with the latest coins struck in the 590s have indeed been found so far only in the region of the Lower Danube, and have therefore been associated with Emperor Maurice's campaigns against the Sclavenes and the Avars, which started in 593 (Popović 1978: 623 and 629, 1980: 246; Curta 1996: 108; for Maurice's campaigns against the Sclavenes and the Avars, see Curta 2001b: 99–107). But if the presence of hoards in the north in the 590s may be associated with the military, could the same possibly be true for Greece between 565 and 585 or between 605 and 625? As we have seen, there is little evidence for the permanent presence of the military in southern Greece throughout the sixth century, with the exception of the large garrison stationed at Isthmia. Most hoards with the latest coins struck between 565 and 585 have been found in southern or central Greece, not far from Isthmia (Fig. 3.1). Moreover, a quick glance at their composition substantiates the idea of 'military deposits'. While coins struck under Emperor Justin I are mostly from Constantinople, more than half of all coins struck for Emperor Justin II were minted in Thessalonica (as opposed to only 2 per cent from Antioch), and the number of Thessalonican issues is even larger under Tiberius II (Morrisson et al.: 59 and 61 figs 10c and 10d; 63 fig. 11). In fact, more coins struck in Thessalonica throughout the sixth century have been found in Greece than in any other region of the Balkans. In Greece, the number of such coins is even larger than that of coins minted in Constantinople. The vast majority of those coins are half-folles struck for Emperor Justin II, which have been found in very large numbers not only in hoards, but also in urban sites, such as Athens and Corinth (Metcalf 2000: 175–6).[22] Some have explained the presence of such coins in those cities by means of trade (Duncan 1993: 149), others as a consequence of the movement of Roman troops, without any interference from trade networks (Morrisson et al. 2006: 63). The latter explanation seems more likely, especially when taking into consideration the distribution of all finds of sixth-century Thessalonican coins. It has long been noted that the peculiar denominations struck under Justinian in Thessalonica (pieces of 16 and 8 nummia), while quite common in hoards from Macedonia, are conspicuously absent from hoards found in central or southern Greece (Morrisson et al. 2006: 69 fig. 16; Metcalf 1962b: 147).[23] Out of 137 legible coins of Justinian from the Athenian Agora, only one has been identified as a 16-nummia piece struck in Thessalonica (Duncan 1993: 149).[24] By contrast, such coins are quite common in Thessalonica and on sites in the city's hinterland (Eleutheriadou et al. 1994: 495 for Thessaloniki; Galani-Krikou and Tsourti 2000: 351 for Rendina; Marki and Akrivopoulou 2003: 293 for Paliokastro; Makropoulou 2002: 370, for Polypetros; Moutsopoulos 1992a: 17 for Setina; for finds of 16-nummia pieces in the villages on the Aegean coast, see Georganteli 2005: 312). On the basis of die analysis, Michael Metcalf has estimated that the whole production of peculiar Thessalonican denominations under Justinian was between 15 and 45 million coins (Metcalf 1976: 27). That so few of them were found in central and southern Greece cannot be the result of accident. Similarly, the fact that the market in Athens and Corinth was flooded with Thessalonican coins struck after 562 – when the peculiar denominations were replaced with half-folles and 10-nummia pieces – suggests that trade was not responsible for the vagaries of the distribution of the copper coins of Thessalonica.[25] If that distribution could indeed be explained in terms of the movements of troops, then those could have very well been the 'young elite soldiers of the army' and 'those who serve in the great praetorium', who at the time of the 586 attack on Thessalonica were in the 'land of the Hellenes' under the command of the city prefect (*Miracles of St. Demetrios* 1 13.128). The soldiers would have been paid in gold, at least for their *donativa*, which they would have then taken to the imperial *campsor* attached to their unit in order to get their small change in copper coins.[26] The *campsor* must have carried large amounts of such coins with him (which he may have obtained directly from the mint), in order to meet the demands of the soldiers. It is unlikely that the *campsor* had anything but large denominations (folles and half-folles) available. The soldiers would then have brought those denominations to the market for procuring goods necessary for their daily subsistence.

While this scenario provides a reasonable explanation for the presence of large numbers of Thessalonican coins in Greece, it does not solve the problem of the hoards. It is not altogether impossible that some of them belonged to soldiers, but if so, were they never retrieved because their owners died in battle, perhaps against the Slavs or the Avars? There are good reasons to favour a negative answer to that question, if only for some hoards. While the specific circumstances of a hoard's burial and non-retrieval will remain unknown, collecting together a 'treasure' of coins in cash was a response more to general tendencies on the money market and in circulation than to times of war or social turmoil. Because of the accelerated depreciation of the follis, a poor man's savings were worth much less at the time of the burial than when the collection of coins had started.[27] Moreover, none of those collections of small change was worth more than half of a solidus, often much less. One could indeed wonder how profitable it may have been to attempt retrieving a hoard from hiding, the value of which had so dramatically decreased in the meantime because of the ongoing coin depreciation and accompanying inflation.

On the other hand, the idea that hoards represent first and foremost a reaction to a military crisis, such as that created by the invasion of the Slavs, is ultimately based on the assumption that hoards found within the same region, presumably that most hardly hit by the raid, have the latest coins struck at the same time. For example, the burial of all hoards with the latest coins struck in 583/4 (Athens 1908, Eleusis 1893, Isthmia, Kleitoria, and Priolithos Kalavryton) has been explained in terms of the Slavic invasion of the early 580s (Morrisson et al.: 226, 247, 250, 254, and 272).[28] They have all been found on both sides of the Hexamilion, within a relatively short distance of each other. Can they therefore have been buried at the time of a barbarian invasion, which is known from the written sources to have ended in 584? In order to draw such a conclusion, one needs to assume that their owners took the decision to withdraw from circulation the most recent coins from their collections (those struck in Emperor Maurice's second regnal year, 583/4) right before burying them, in hiding places from which they were then never retrieved. With one exception, all those coins were half-folles struck in Thessalonica, but no study of wear has so far been done on any of them. It is, however, very unlikely that they have been deposited in hoard collections immediately after leaving the mint.[29] They cannot therefore be regarded as evidence for the hoards being buried in 584. In reality, the hoards with latest coins struck in 583/4 may well have been buried at different moments in time after that, and because of different circumstances. This means that a much better case for burial at the time of the Slavic raids of the 580s may be made for hoards with latest coins struck earlier, in the late 570s, especially when found in an archaeological context indicating destruction (e.g., Athens 1933a, Athens 1933b, or Kenchreai 1963.I).[30] If the Slavic raids provoked panic in the countryside, then the hoards that may be associated with that are Koutsi and Megara, not Kleitoria and Pellene 1936.[31]

A much stronger correlation exists between Slavic or Avar invasions and hoards of gold. It is important to note that out of seventeen such assemblages known so far from Greece for the entire period between 500 and 670, only three have the latest coins struck before 565. The largest of such hoards are known from the islands in the Aegean Sea (Kratigos, Polichnitos, Rhodes, Samos 1983). In the case of the Kratigos and Samos 1983 hoards, the presence of dress accessories (necklaces, bracelets, and earrings) betrays the civilian status of their owners, who may have been refugees from Asia Minor fleeing the Persian armies (Morrisson et al. 2006: 72). Similar circumstances may have been responsible for the burial of the Thessaloniki hoard, in which the latest coins are four solidi and one tremissis struck for Emperor Tiberius II (578–582). As the preservation of the coins appears to be excellent, the collection, which was worth more than ninety solidi, may have been buried shortly after the date of the latest coins, perhaps at the time of the siege of 586.[32] Nothing indicates, however, that the burial of much smaller hoards of gold (Apidea, Patras 1986, Zogeria, or Eleusis 1885) may equally be attributed to the invasion of the Slavs (Table 3.5). The Patras 1986 hoard was found in a pot (for which no analogues are known either in Greece or elsewhere in the sixth- or early seventh-century Balkans) with no traces of use, which suggests that it was placed in hiding under circumstances very different from those involving the panic induced by an approaching barbarian invasion (Moutzali 2002: 183 and 187 fig. 2). Moreover, the hoards of gold with latest coins struck between 582 and 602 are typically collections of between four and thirteen solidi, all of which were minted in Constantinople.[33] Particularly interesting in this respect is the identity between the Apidea and the Eleusis 1884 hoards, each with six coins minted for Justin II, one for Tiberius II, and the latest one for Maurice. Collections of solidi such as those have been interpreted as *donativa*, imperial gifts of money distributed to the soldiers on special occasions (Curta 1996: 85–6).[34] This may also be true for hoards of a few solidi minted in Constantinople, with the last coins struck after 605 and before 630

Table 3.5 Sixth- to seventh-century hoards of gold from Greece.

Hoard	Date of the latest coin	Value in solidi
Samos 1983	622–627	286½
Athens 1876	c. 668	199⅓
Thessaloniki	578–582	93⅔
Arkessini	669–680	54⅓
Kratigos	616–625	32
Zogeria 1979	565–578	30
Patras 1987	609/10	20⅔
Polichnitos	616–625	17
Zogeria	582–600	13
Sane	613–616	11
Vasaras	602–610	10 (?)
Apidea	582–600	8
Eleusis 1885	584–602	8
Pinios	565–578	6
Solomos 1956	616–625	6
Paiania	607–609	5
Patras	582–600	4
Nestani	542–565	at least 3
'Peloponnese'	565–578	at least 3
Malaisina	607–609	at least 3
Amphipolis	542–562	3⅓

(Malaisina, Paiania, Vasaras, and Solomos 1956), given that the distribution of *donativa* is known to have survived as late as 641. All those hoards therefore indicate the presence of the Roman army, not of the Slavic marauders.

If, therefore, hoards of copper with large numbers of coins struck in Thessalonica after 562 may also be associated with the presence of the army, the only institution capable of injecting into the market such a large quantity of coins, then it is perhaps not an accident that the value of the Solomos 1938 hoard, calculated on the basis of the exchange rate in operation at the time of its latest coin, is the equivalent of a tremissis, or a third of a solidus, a coin which is otherwise not attested in Greece after 578, either in hoards or in single finds. In other words, some at least of the amounts accumulated in hoards of copper may have been the change their owners – possibly soldiers stationed in Greece – received in addition to a fixed amount payable in solidi, perhaps because other denominations of the gold coin were not available any more.[35]

Hoards of both gold and copper thus provide evidence more

of economic and social practices than of barbarian invasions. The owner of some collections of gold, especially those of high value, such as Samos 1983 or Thessaloniki, may indeed have buried their considerable wealth in order to prevent it from coming into the hands of barbarians, either Persians or Slavs. Similarly, hoards of copper such as Athens 1933a or Kenchreai 1963.II may have been buried in a hurry in the face of impending attack by the barbarians. But the vast majority of hoards of both gold and copper do not fit into this picture of generalised panic and devastating invasions. Instead, a great number of hoards of gold which may represent *donativa* signal the presence of the army during the 580s, the years of the troubles. Although indirectly attesting to a situation of military crisis in Greece, which made the presence of the army necessary, such hoards are nonetheless indications not of defeat, but of otherwise regular distributions of gifts of money to the troops. Soldiers or officers may have placed their savings under ground *custodiae causa*, not *ob metum barbarorum*.

On the other hand, contemporary, much more modest savings of copper coins may have been buried and never retrieved not because of the Slavic invasions, but because the accelerated depreciation and inflation had meanwhile rendered them virtually worthless, and, therefore, there was no point in recovering them any more. When taking into consideration their composition, hoards of copper from Greece may be divided into three groups. First, a number of hoards with the latest coins struck before 565, often from urban contexts (especially in Corinth), seem to have been collections of relatively small value. The presence in many of them of minimi, often in large numbers, suggests that those were small savings based primarily on the lowest denominations available on the market. That at least some of those hoards should indeed be regarded as saving deposits follows from the use of ceramic containers hidden in the ruins of formerly public buildings – the southern portico of the Roman Bath in Corinth or the Roman Odeon in Patras (Morrisson et al. 2006: 236 and 264). The circumstances leading their owners to commit to hiding such small savings are not at all clear and will probably remain forever unknown. However, by their very nature, large collections of minimi such as Chersonissos or Zacha are an indication of a flourishing monetary economy throughout the first half of the sixth century, and of the ability to accumulate some value in tiny pieces of metal which apparently circulated on the basis of their weight, and not of their face value. The capillaries of the urban economy of sixth-century Greece may have contained an even greater number of such trivial coins than the rate of survival would suggest, and this may well be the symptom of a great demand on the market for low denominations, in itself a sign of confidence in the fiduciary nature of the larger denominations of the copper currency. Indeed, those were years of heavy, high-value folles, which, because of their worth, were quickly withdrawn from circulation and hoarded. They are, however, rare in hoards from Greece, the owners of which seem to have had sufficient confidence in much smaller denominations, either the 16-nummia pieces struck in Thessalonica during Justinian's reign (Adam Zagliveriou) or minimi.

The situation began to change shortly after the end of that reign. While minimi continue to appear in hoards with latest coins struck after 565, sometimes in very large number (Olympia), they were only a much more modest addition to larger amounts of money in copper coins of higher denominations. There is a visibly larger number of hoards with the latest coins struck between 565 and 585, but none of them is worth more than half a solidus. The great number of hoards suggests that a large mass of coins was still in circulation in Greece. However, the small value of every one of those collections cannot be interpreted in the same way as hoards of minimi of the first half of the sixth century. Because of the continuous depreciation of the follis throughout the second half of that century, the value of each hoard must have deteriorated rapidly, with losses in some cases of as much as 50 per cent. The specific circumstances in which those hoards were buried varied considerably. Some of them were hidden in the urban ruins of now abandoned buildings (the Theatre in Thasos, or the stadium in Nemea), but others were found in rural contexts, in buildings of possibly secular function or in churches (Mantinea, Agia Kyriaki). Some were associated with layers of destruction, for which historians blamed the Slavic marauders of the early 580s.

An important feature of the hoards with latest coins struck during those years is the abundance of half-folles minted in Thessalonica, a phenomenon linked to a massive injection of coins from that mint into the markets in Greece, most probably because of the movements of troops from Thessalonica to central and southern Greece. That an equally impressive quantity of coins from Thessalonica appears in single finds from several urban sites in Greece strongly suggests that the presence of the army considerably altered the economic configuration of the region by creating new and increased demands within an environment seriously affected by inflation. Whether the additional stress put on the local economy by the presence of troops further aggravated the crisis remains unclear, but it appears that the population quickly lost confidence in the money in circulation. This may explain the low rate of retrieval, itself responsible for the large number of hoards known from Greece from this period. With the value of already small savings often cut by as much as half, there was really no incentive for any hoard owner to recover the hidden collection of coins.

That soldiers or officers of the army may have been among the owners of hoards from this period also follows from the analysis of hoards of gold, many of which include a relatively small number of solidi, which may have originated in payments of *donativa*. If the hoards of the 580s were indeed a military phenomenon, this would explain why the hoarding phenomenon stopped after 585. This could also explain the sudden reduction in the number of coins in circulation in Greece, which is visible in the rarity, if not lack, of coins struck for Emperor Maurice between 585 and 602. The troops responsible for the injection of Thessalonican half-folles into Greece in the 580s may have moved in the 590s to the north, on the Lower Danube front line as part of the military campaign Maurice then launched against the Sclavenes and the Avars. In Greece, an economy exhausted by the combined effects of inflation, barbarian raids, and overwhelming military demands was not given sufficient respite for recovery. Under Phokas and at the beginning of Heraklios' reign, the army re-appeared in Greece, as suggested by a new series of hoards of exclusively new copper coins and a few *donativum*-type hoards of gold. Most other, much larger collections of early seventh-century gold are known from hoards found on the Aegean islands, sometimes in association with dress accessories, a clear indication of the civilian status of their owners, who were probably refugees from Asia Minor. By the time the coins were struck, which are the latest in the Delos (624–629) and Athens 1972 (633/4) hoards, the majority of troops had already been moved in the opposite direction, from continental Greece to Asia Minor. Troops and coins were now restricted to the coastal areas around Thessalonica, Athens, and Corinth.

Notes

1. For an early critique of Sotiriou's views, otherwise inspired by Zakythinos, see Pallas 1955b: 102–5.
2. Aupert attributed to that destruction the traces of fire in the Bath of the

Theatre in Argos, as well as the layer of destruction in the Christian cemetery next to the modern-day gymnasium in that city.
3. For an attempt to 'reconstruct' on the basis of coin hoards a Slavic raid, which is not mentioned in any written source, see Popović 1981.
4. None of the three Greek hoards with latest coins struck for Emperor Anastasius (Corinth 1960, Eleusis 1992.I, and Zogeria 1992.II) has been found within any of the regions north of the Thermopylae Pass, which Comes Marcellinus mentioned as having been devastated by the 517 attack of the 'Getae'.
5. For the phrase 'currency habits', see Jones 1956: 30–1. Three hoards with the latest coins struck for Emperor Justinian (Corinth 1937, Megara 1979, and Patras 1938) have been found in ceramic containers (a small bottle-shaped jug and three pots), which is a clear indication of 'saving hoards'.
6. Five-nummia pieces struck under Anastasius or Justin I appear in the Athens 1933b hoard (six specimens). One five-nummia piece struck under Justinian is known from the Kenchreai 1963.I hoard. The largest number of five-nummia pieces found in Greek hoards (Athens 1971 with four specimens, Athens 1908 with seventeen specimens, and Eleusis 1893 with twenty-two specimens) were minted under Emperor Justin II. That such coins were in circulation in Greece at that time is confirmed by single finds of five-nummia pieces from contemporary sites, for which see Pallas 1965: 163, as well as Marki and Polychronaki 2000: 185–6.
7. For single finds of minimi indicating that they were indeed in circulation at the time of their hoarding, see Hohlfelder 1974: 74; Pallas 1976: 194; Galani-Krikou 1998b: 145–6; Kalantzi-Sbyraki 2004: 151; Callegher 2005: 229. There were over 350 minimi in the Athens 1933 hoard, which was found in a sixth-century mill outside the Late Roman walls. According to Metcalf 1962b: 140, this indicates that the miller's customers used that very small denomination to pay him.
8. According to Hahn 2000: 58, the striking of minimi ceased in the central mints during Justinian's reign. However, minimi were still struck in Carthage, Rome, and probably Antioch after 527 (Hahn 2000: 62 and 68–70).
9. Between 498 and 538, there were 360 folles to the solidus. After 538, the value of the follis in relation to the solidus increased even further, as the number of follis to the solidus dropped to 210. For the exchange rate between follis and solidus, see Hahn 1973a: 27–8, 1975: 15–16, 1981: 16–20; Duritat 1980. For somewhat different rates, see Morrisson 1989: 248 and Morrisson et al. 2006: 51. On the basis of variation in the weight standard of coins struck in Thessalonica, Hahn 2000: 65 has suggested that in Illyricum, the gold–copper ratio may have been different from that in the eastern provinces of the Empire.

10. The Corinth 1933, Corinth 1937, and Agios Nikolaos hoards each included one coin of Sikyon. Two such coins have been found in the Patras 1938 hoard, while the Corinth 1971b and Corinth 1971c hoards had three coins each.
11. The hoard also contains bronze scrap, which must have been collected for its bullion value.
12. The standard weight of the follis between 538 and 542 was 24.95g. The weight dropped to 21.83g between 542 and 550 (Banaji 2001: 224). No hoard in the Balkans is known to contain heavy folles struck between 538 and 542, except those discovered in Macedonia and Greece (Morrisson et al. 2006: 52).
13. The only pre-538 folles in hoards with the latest coins struck in the 580s are those from the Athens 1908 (one specimen) and Eleusis 1893 (two specimens) assemblages. MacDowall 1965: 266 believed that because of the steep reduction in weight of the new coins, reflecting a high order of inflation, the old, heavy coins must have been worth more than their face value.
14. In all those cases, the value is always small, the equivalent of a minute fraction of the solidus. Indeed, none of those hoards is worth a semissis, much less a single solidus (Duncan 1993: 148).
15. The changing gold–copper ratio indicates that the imperial policies established a compulsory rate of exchange, which may be associated with the government's attempts to finance wearisome wars, especially under Justinian (Hahn 1973b: 177).
16. Drawing such a comparison implies that coins entered hoards shortly after leaving the mint, which is unlikely to have happened. However, there is no way to establish for how long a coin may have been in circulation before being withdrawn for collection in a hoard. The comparison exercise has therefore only a heuristic value.
17. This is true even for early hoards, such as Petrochorion, with a gap of twenty-six years between the earliest and the latest coins. However, since all fifty-one coins in the collections were struck before 538 (when the exchange rate between gold and copper introduced by Emperor Anastasius' monetary reform in 498 was first modified), their value remained unaltered.
18. The only exceptions are Athens 1971 and Zogeria 1995, with the latest coins struck most probably between 578 and 580, at a time when the exchange rate between gold and copper was forcefully, albeit temporarily, brought back to its Justinianic level (1:216). As a consequence, the collection of coins in those hoards remained almost the same (Athens 1971) or was even slightly over-valued at the presumed time of burial (Zogeria 1995).
19. Only three folles (one struck in 586/7 and two others struck in 589/90) and a 10-nummia piece (struck in 586/7) are known from Andikira

(Boeotia), and only one follis (struck in of 590/1) from Kephalos in the Ambrakian Bay (Tsourti 2004: 126–7; Barla 1970: 96).

20. Excavations in the Athenian Agora produced twenty-five coins minted for Emperor Maurice, only eight of which could be dated with any degree of certainty after 585. Two of them were folles struck in Nicomedia and Antioch in 587/8 and 595/6, respectively (Thompson 1954: 69 and 104). Excavations in Corinth have produced so far 279 coins struck for Justin II and 70 coins struck for Phokas, but only 55 coins struck during the longer reign of Maurice. Out of nine coins minted for Maurice and discovered between 1896 and 1929, seven can be dated after 585 (Sanders 2002: 649; Edwards 1933: 129–30).
21. In Kenchreai, there are no finds of coins struck between 582 and 604 (Hohlfelder 1978: 71 and 74; Avramea 1997: 74).
22. Among finds from the Athenian Agora, the Thessalonican half-folles struck for Justin II outnumber all other issues from that reign combined (Metcalf 1962b: 142).
23. The only exception is Thebes 1932, with eight 16-nummia pieces. Such coins have also been found in the Thessaloniki 1966 (three specimens) and Thasos 1957 hoards (one specimen). A hoard said to have been from a dealer in Athens, which has eight 16-nummia pieces, is most probably from northern Greece (Weller and Metcalf 1969: 313; Morrisson et al. 2006: 228).
24. Four more pieces are known from Corinth.
25. On the other hand, half-folles struck in Thessalonica after 562 appear in some Greek hoards together with minimi (Nemea, Thebes 1995.IV, Argos 1983, Athens 1908, Isthmia, and Pellene 1936).
26. A funerary inscription was found in Hebdomon (Bakırköy) which was set up for an imperial *campsor* named John, who died on 21 August 554. He is said to have 'gone with the expedition', which may indicate that he died during a military campaign (Asdracha 1998: 494–6). On the other hand, a money-changer (*trapezites*) is mentioned in a fifth- to sixth-century funerary inscription from Corinth (Papanikola-Bakirtzis 2002: 71).
27. In times of inflation and coin depreciation, hoards have a tendency to reflect the mass of coins in circulation at the time when the monetary system was in balance (Bruun 1978: 114).
28. The same is true for hoards with latest coins struck in 582/3, such as Agia Kyriaki and Argos 1983 (Morrisson et al. 2006: 216 and 269).
29. Traces of wear are clearly visible on the photograph of the latest coin in the Priolithos Kalavryton hoard, a follis struck in Constantinople in 583/4 (Oikonomidou-Karamesini and Touratsoglou: 69 fig. 2.120).
30. However, an archaeological context of destruction does not always support the idea of associating a hoard with the Slavic invasion. According to Dengate 1981: 154, the Corinth 1971c hoard was hidden

above the pool of the Fountain of the Lamps, an area later destroyed by an earthquake, not by Slavs.
31. On the basis of traces of wear, Avramea 1997: 75 has already argued for c. 580 as a date of burial for the Koutsi hoard, with the latest coin struck in 577/8. See also Metcalf 2001: 146.
32. For the preservation of the coins, see Oikonomidou-Karamesini and Touratsoglou 1979: 289.
33. By contrast, large hoards of gold include coins struck in Thessalonica (Thessaloniki and Samos 1983; Morrisson et al. 2006: 391–2). Those were collections of coins of a nature very different from that of hoards of a smaller number of solidi struck in Constantinople.
34. Under Emperor Tiberius II, the accessional *donativum* was nine solidi and the quinquennial one five solidi (Hendy 1985: 188 and 646–7; Brandes 2002: 24–5).
35. Semisses struck for Maurice and Phokas appear, however, in the Patras 1987 hoard (Morrisson et al. 2006: 265). On the other hand, another way to explain collections of copper coins to the amount of a third of a solidus, such as Solomos 1938, is to point to the fact that taxes were paid to the lowest amount higher than the assessment value which could be paid in gold, with change in copper coins returned to the taxpayer to make up for the difference. Nothing is known, however, about the collection of taxes in Greece c. 620, the date of the latest coin in the Solomos 1938 hoard.

CHAPTER 4

Dark-Age Greece (c. 620 to c. 800)

The numismatic, sphragistic, and archaeological evidence strongly suggests that after 620, Greece entered a relatively long period of political instability and sharp demographic decline. For some fifty years between c. 620 and c. 670, Greece disappears from the radar of the written sources, which some have interepreted as the 'Dark Ages' separating Antiquity from the Middle Ages, an era of decline and ruin brought by Slavic invaders (Zakythinos 1966: 300, 302, and 316; Avramea 1997: 49). It has indeed been suggested that the significant number of hoards with latest coins struck in the early seventh century are an indication of the Slavic invasions of Greece at the beginning of Herakleios' reign (Metcalf 1962a and 2001: 129–30). Their composition, based almost exclusively on new coins, suggests, however, the presence of the Roman troops. The cluster of their latest coins between 610 and 620 strongly suggests that those small collections of copper were never retrieved because of the general withdrawal of Roman armies from the Balkans. With few exceptions,[1] there are no coins of Herakleios post-dating the withdrawal of troops on any site in Greece. Although in the early seventh century hoards of gold were still buried in Greece, after c. 630 gold finds are very rare in the southern Balkans. Only three hoards, two of gold and one of copper, are so far known for the entire period between c. 630 and c. 900.[2] With just one exception, all stray finds of seventh- and early eighth-century coins are of copper (Fig. 4.1).[3]

This picture of contraction is confirmed by the archaeological record. The occupation of most military sites or 'isles of refuge' that could be dated to the early seventh century does not seem to have continued beyond the reign of Herakleios (610–641). The latest coins found on the island of Kephalos in the Ambrakian Bay or at Glanorisi (Gantsa) near Limni (Evvoia) suggest that the occupation of both sites ceased before the end of that reign (Barla 1970: 97; Bowden 2003: 188; Sampson 1984–1985: 367; for 'isles of refuge', see Hood 1970). The early Byzantine fort identified on the island of

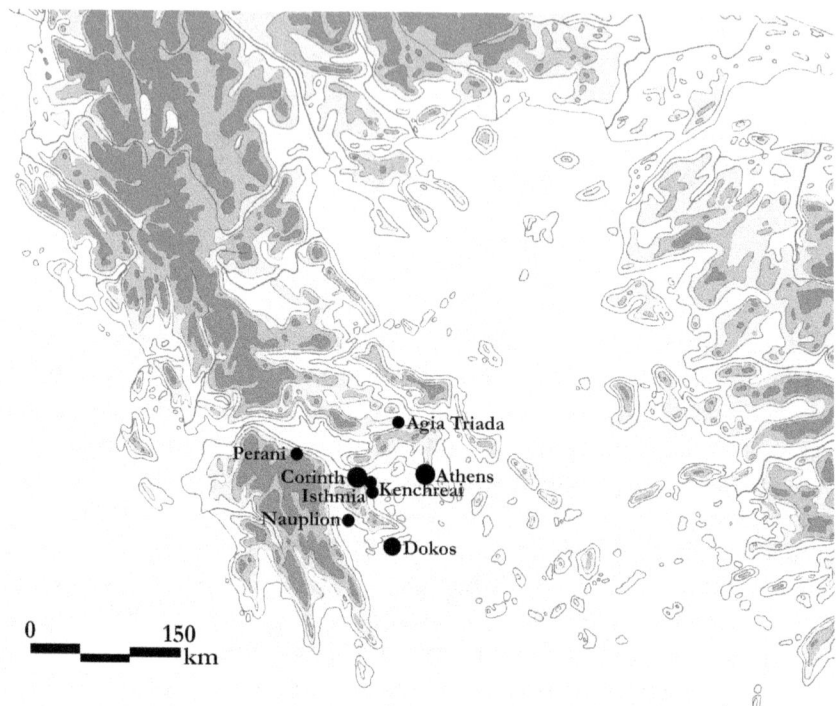

Figure 4.1 The distribution in Greece of single finds of coins struck after 630 and before 711. The smallest circles mark individual coins, larger circles 2 and over 100, respectively.

Dokos has two phases of occupation, one of which ends abruptly in the early seventh century. Judging from the existing evidence, the site remained unoccupied until the mid-seventh century (Kyrou 1995: 111).[4] The so-called 'squatter' occupation at the northern bay of the Hexamilion has produced cooking pots, including one with a handle and obliquely and vertically incised ornament, as well as a belt buckle. If the latter was indeed associated with the ceramic assemblage in question, this may be viewed as an indication of some occupation of the site during the first half of the seventh century (Gregory 1993b: pl. 25b).[5]

The only signs of building activity during the first two or three decades of that century have so far been recorded in Thessaloniki and Athens. Just before 620, the Church of Hagia Sophia in Thessaloniki was built on top of an earlier basilica. However, its impressive dome belongs to a second building phase, which is dated by an inscription to 690/1, while the interior decoration must be attributed to yet another phase, traditionally associated with the triumphal celebrations after Staurakios' campaign of 783 (Bouras 2006: 62).[6] In Athens, the Erechtheion seems to have been turned into a three-aisled basilica in the early seventh century, at the same time as the conversion into churches of the Temple of Hephaistos in the Agora and the Temple of Artemis Agrotera by the Ilissos (Kazanaki-Lappa 2000: 200).

Most cemeteries with the earliest burials dated to the sixth century do not appear to have continued after c. 620. The stone-lined grave accidentally found near a third-century burial chamber in Ladochori, near Igoumenitsa, produced a fragment of a dagger-like sword and a belt buckle with oval plate, both dated to the first few decades after 550 (Agallopoulou 1975).[7] The twenty-two graves excavated in Europos (prefecture of Kilkis) were extensively robbed, but a few surviving artefacts, especially a pair of gold earrings with open-work, star-shaped pendant, unmistakably point to a late sixth-century date (Savvopoulou 1992: 389 and pl. 114β).[8] No finds are known that could be securely dated to the seventh century. The same is true for the twenty-one stone-lined graves found in two separate, small cemeteries in Portochelion, near Kranidion (Argolis). The only chronologically sensitive artefact among the few grave goods from those graves is a belt buckle with shield-shaped end, with a good analogue among finds from Corinth (Rudolph 1979: 297–301 and 320 with fig. 14.57; Davidson 1952: pl. 114.2210).[9] A burial chamber found in Nea Anchialos between basilicas A and B produced a number of metal artefacts associated with scattered remains of several skeletons. The bracelet with pointed ends has a good analogue in a certainly contemporary assemblage in Keramidi, near neighbouring Karditsa in Thessaly, which has also produced a pair of earrings similar to one of the eleven earrings found in Nea Anchialos (Sotiriou 1956: 113–15 with pl. 41β; Liankouras 1965: 321 with pl. 381α). The associated buckles have good analogues in Crimea, which could be dated shortly before and after 600 (Veimarn and Aibabin 1993: 95 with 94 fig. 66.4). An African Red Slip bowl of Hayes' form 99A found in a pit by the cemetery excavated in 1983 in the Papathanassiou area of present-day Argos may be dated as late as c. 620, but the type was popular mainly during the sixth century (Oikonomou-Laniadou 2003: 32 and 35–6). Nothing else indicates that the cemetery remained in use after 600.

The only cemetery known so far to have begun in the sixth century and continued after 620 is Tigani, near Mezapos (Lakonia)

(Drandakis and Gkioles 1980 and 1983; Drandakis et al. 1981; Katsougiannopoulou 2001). Among the fifty-six graves excavated in the 1980s within a ruined basilica in the middle of an early Byzantine fort, some at least must be dated before the abandonment of the church.[10] The iron fibula with bent stem found in grave 8 is a dress accessory relatively common on sixth-century military sites in the Balkans (Drandakis and Gkioles 1980: 256; for iron fibulae with bent stem, see Uenze 1992: 149–50). The dates for most other graves in Tigani fall, however, within the seventh century.[11] Although no weapons have been found, Tigani is regarded as the graveyard of a relatively small garrison stationed throughout the seventh century on the western coast of the Mani Peninsula. However, this was clearly not an exclusively military cemetery. No proper sexing of the skeletons has so far been carried out, but such grave goods as the gold earrings in grave 25 or the bronze keys in graves 9 and 53 strongly suggest that there were also women among those buried inside the ruins of the sixth-century basilica (Drandakis and Gkioles 1980: 250, 254, 255, and 256, with pls 148ε and 149β; Drandakis et al. 1981: 249). While nothing indicates that the cemetery was in use after c. 700, it certainly continued after c. 630, possibly even after c. 650. No fewer than seven buckles of the Corinth type are known from burials within the Tigani basilica, four of which cluster within the southern aisle (Drandakis and Gkioles 1980: 253, 255, and pl. 149ε [graves 13 and 25]; Drandakis et al. 1981: 249, 251, and pl. 182γ [graves 32, 40, 42, and 45]).[12]

Exclusively seventh-century cemeteries similar to Tigani are typically smaller. Out of twelve graves excavated on two separate sites on Antikythera, only one produced a chronologically sensitive artefact, namely a seventh-century belt buckle with cross-shaped plate (Touchais et al. 2000: 849 and fig. 73; Pyrrou et al. 2006: 225–6 and 234 pl. 5.2).[13] Such buckles have also been found in a cemetery excavated to the west and northwest of the Church of St Dionysios the Areopagite in Athens. The latest of all thirty-five graves from that cemetery, which produced belt buckles of the Pergamon type, may not be dated after c. 650 (Travlos and Frantz 1965: 167 and pl. 43a).[14] A small cemetery with twenty-five stone-lined graves, some capped with tiles laid *a cappuccino*, was found accidentally in the early 1970s on Proussa Street in Edessa. Some of those early seventh-century graves contained two or even more skeletons and may have been used for members of the same family (Karamanoli-Siganidou 1973–1974: 709–10). Of the same date is a small group of inhumations found elsewhere in the city, one of which produced a buckle of the Boly-Želovce type (Gounaris 1984: 57 and 56 fig. 2ε; for Boly-Želovce-type buckles, see Ibler 1992: 140; Varsik 1992: 86–7; Prokopiou 1997: 339).

A date within the first half of the seventh century may also be assigned to a number of graves which were found either in small groups or isolated. Those are most unusual assemblages: although continuing in many ways the local burial traditions, they produced 'exotic' artefacts, which have hastily been interpreted as barbarian. Such is the case of a 'Slavic' bow fibula found in Nea Anchialos in a burial chamber to the north of the apse of basilica Δ (the cemeterial basilica), together with four skeletons with a west–east orientation (Fig. 4.2) (Sotiriou 1935: 60–4). Unfortunately, it is not known with which one of them the fibula was associated. Presumably, one of the skeletons was that of a female, and the fibula may have been attached to her funerary dress, much like the other artefact found in the burial chamber, a hinged belt buckle with circle-and-dot decoration. Such buckles are known from several sites in the eastern Mediterranean region and may be dated to the first half of the seventh century (Vida and Völling 2000: 28; Curta 2005b: 116–17). Two other contemporary female burials – one from Greece, the other from Albania – may serve as comparison for the Nea Anchialos assemblage. One of them was found in a small cemetery excavated in Edessa, and produced a pair of 'Slavic' bow fibulae, a belt buckle, and a knife (Petsas 1969: 307 with fig. 320).[15] The buckle is Syracuse-type, most typical of circum-Mediterranean assemblages of the first half of the seventh century.[16] The Edessa burial thus coincides in time with the burial with 'Slavic' bow fibula from Nea Anchialos. A slightly later but similar assemblage is a grave from the north Albanian cemetery at Kruje. The female burial produced two 'Slavic' bow fibulae and a Corinth-type buckle (Anamali and Spahiu 1963: 16, 34–5, 57–8, fig. 13 and pl. 12.2).[17]

What differentiates the Nea Anchialos, Edessa, and Kruje assemblages from other contemporary female burials in Greece (such as those in Tigani) is the association of fibula(e) and buckle, which is very rare in the southern Balkans. By contrast, this combination was relatively popular, c. 600, in Crimea, Hungary, and northeastern Poland (Mazuria). The three burials with 'Slavic' bow fibulae may thus be regarded as the southernmost examples of an essentially East European female fashion of the early seventh century. In all three cases 'Slavic' bow fibulae were associated with 'Byzantine' belt

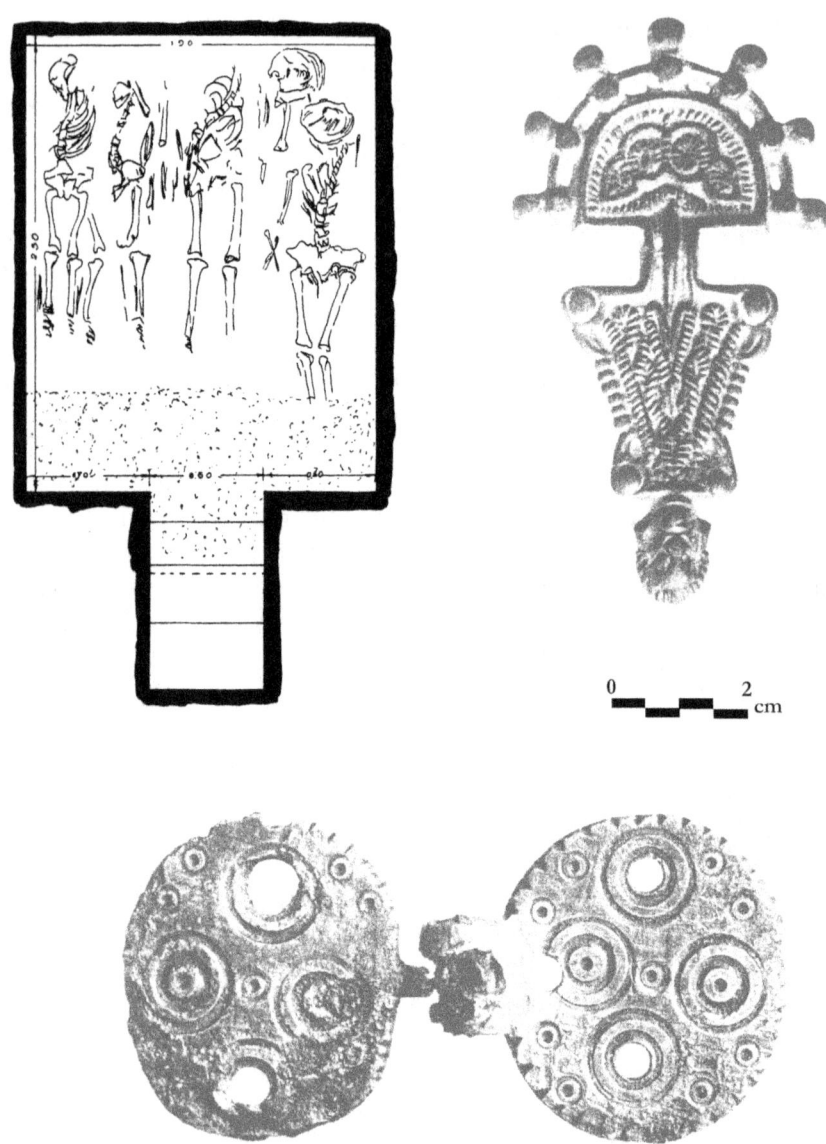

Figure 4.2 Nea Anchialos, burial chamber: plan and associated artefacts – a 'Slavic' bow fibula and a hinged buckle (after Sotiriou 1935: 61 fig. 11 and 63 figs 12–13)

buckles most typical of assemblages in the circum-Mediterranean area. Particularly interesting in this respect is the Nea Anchialos assemblage, because of its unusual association of a 'Slavic' bow fibula with a buckle, imitations of which have been found on sites in the northern Balkans, but never in the company of fibulae (Curta 2005b:

127). Similarly, Corinth- and Syracuse-type buckles never appear in association with fibulae and are more often found with male than with female burials (e.g., in Corinth, for which see Williams et al. 1974: 11 and pl. 2.8). The three burials at Nea Anchialos, Edessa, and Kruje seem therefore to combine, in unique ways, elements of 'Byzantine' and 'barbarian' burial traditions. In particular, the Nea Anchialos burial, which can otherwise be regarded as 'privileged' because of the use of a burial chamber, reflects preoccupation with marking the exceptional by means of a few artefacts that may be viewed as 'quoting' fashions known from other regions of early medieval Europe. The women buried in the chamber built next to basilica Δ in Nea Anchialos or in a simple grave pit at Edessa may well have been barbarian wives of men in Byzantine service. But the privileged status of the Nea Anchialos woman was rendered visible by access to a Christian burial site. Her burial may have thus have been meant to mirror the social position and privilege of her husband. Though imitations of specimens found elsewhere in Eastern Europe, most 'Slavic' bow fibulae found in Greece have more analogues among themselves than outside Greece. This has been interpreted as an indication that 'access and manipulation of such artefacts may have been strategies for creating a new sense of identity for local elites' (Curta 2005b: 133).

If Nea Anchialos and Edessa are known for female burials with 'Slavic' bow fibulae, the most famous seventh-century male burial in Greece is the stone-lined grave of the 'wandering soldier' found in 1938 in the colonnade of the South Stoa in Corinth (Fig. 4.3) (Davidson 1974). The grave was quickly interpreted as that of a Slavic mercenary or of an Avar or Bulgar warrior killed in battle against, or in the service of, Emperor Constans II (Davidson 1937: 233 with n. 1; Setton 1950: 520; Hrochová 1976: 130; Štefanovičová 1977: 126; Weithmann 1978: 104; Ivison 1996: 118; Avramea 1997: 97; Rashev 2000: 73). However the burial has never been properly studied in the context of the early medieval archaeology of Eastern Europe. As with the female graves in Nea Anchialos and Edessa, the burial assemblage in Corinth combines elements of different cultural origins in a most surprising way. The belt buckle found under the last vertebra has good analogues among small finds from earlier excavations in Corinth, as well as among stray finds from islands near the Argolid coast and from Olympia. However, its closest parallel was found in an Early Avar *female* burial assemblage in Nagyharsány (Hungary) together with a late sixth-century, silver, disc-shaped

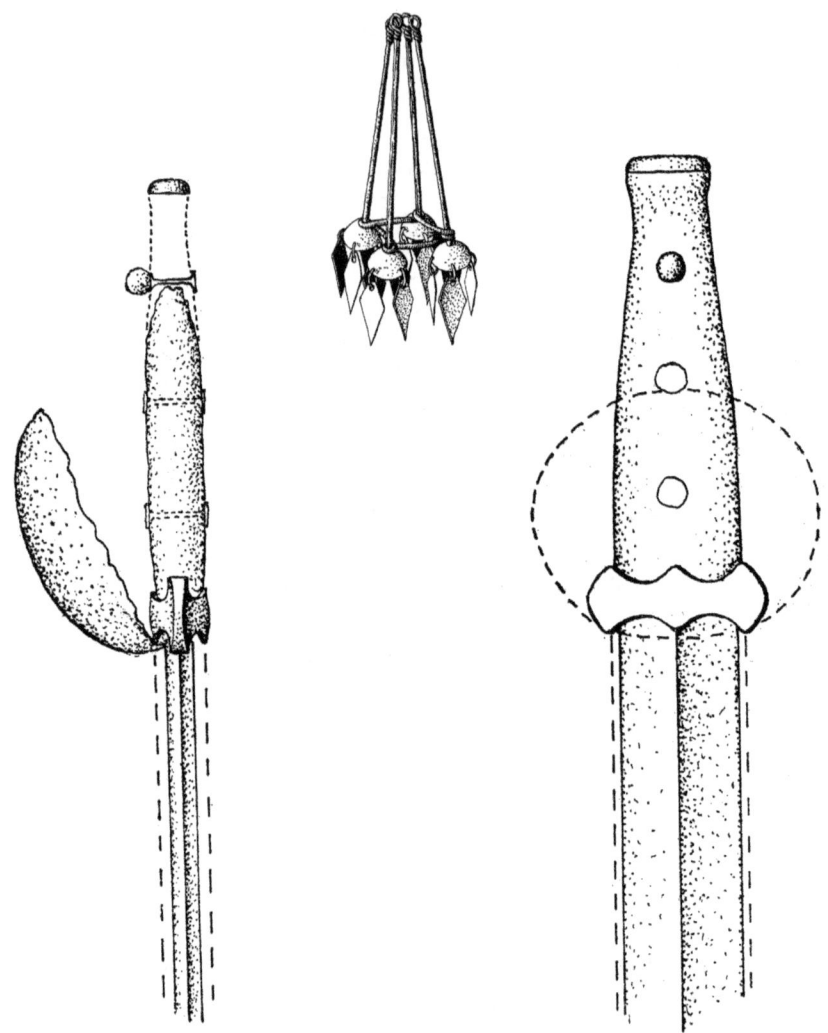

Figure 4.3 Corinth, the 'wandering soldier' grave: reconstructions of the bronze trinket and the sword with cross-bar and cup-like guard (after Davidson 1974: 516 fig. 1 and 520 fig. 5). Reproduced courtesy of the Trustees of the American School of Classical Studies at Athens.

brooch with an image of St George (Davidson-Weinberg 1974: pl. 110e; Davidson 1952: pl. 114.2209–10; Avramea 1997: 90 and pl. 4c8; Völling 1992: 495–6 and 494 fig. 1; for Nagyharsány, see Papp 1963: 131–2 and pl. 11.8; Garam 1993: 101–2 and fig. 1.3; for buckles of the Nagyharsány type, see Ibler 1992: 143). By contrast, analogues for the bronze trinket with lozenge-shaped pendants found in the right hand of the 'wandering soldier', an equally female piece of jewellery, are known only from seventh-century barrows in Latvia and Lithuania, as well as in the Smolensk region of Russia (Szymański 1968: 205–6; Sedov 1974: 58 and pl. 25.37–9; for settlement finds from Belarus, see Zverugo 2005: 103 and 121 fig. 68). Equally uncommon is a single amber bead discovered underneath the left hand, for no such artefacts are otherwise known from seventh- or eighth-century assemblages in the Balkans (Davidson 1974: 520 fig. 5 and pl. 111b). In Hungary, single amber beads appear towards the end of the Early Avar period (c. 570 to c. 630), often in association with amazing quantities of gold, in extraordinarily rich male burials (Tóth and Horváth 1992: 205–6; Kiss 2001: 105 and 269). Despite claims to the contrary, the handmade pot deposited by the right ankle of the 'wandering soldier' has nothing to do with the 'Slavic' pottery of the so-called Prague type. Instead, it is a specimen of a typically Early Avar pot with funnel-shaped neck, which has good analogues in Hungary, as well as in Siberia and central Asia (Vida and Völling 2000: 35; for the Corinth pot as 'Slavic', see Kilian 1980: 282; Hood 1988: 93). The exotic nature of the burial assemblage attributed to a 'wandering soldier' is further underlined by the associated double-edged sword with cross-bar, which is very similar to swords with cross-bars found in late Early Avar (mid-seventh-century) burials of warriors excavated in Hungary (Davidson 1974: 516 fig. 1, 518 fig. 3, 519 fig. 4, pl. 12a–c).[18] Such swords appear only in high-status male burials, as do single amber beads such as that from the 'wandering soldier' grave.

How, then, is the 'wandering soldier' grave to be interpreted? Most probably not in direct connection with the Early Avar assemblages in Hungary or the neighbouring regions, in which stone-lined graves with weapons are unknown.[19] The stone lining of the 'wandering soldier' grave has much more in common with contemporary burial assemblages in Greece than do its associated grave goods. The 'wandering soldier' grave stands out among Dark-Age burial assemblages in Greece as prominently as the presumably female burials with 'Slavic' bow fibulae from Nea Anchialos and Edessa. In all three cases, the extraordinary status of the deceased was emphasised either by exceptional grave goods or by privileged location. The message encoded in burial dress in those cases combined cultural elements of different origins in what amounted to nothing less than a statement about relative identity. That identity was most probably linked to the imagined position of the deceased within the social network.

The 'wandering soldier' grave is similar in this respect to another isolated, tile-lined grave which was found during the exploration of the Temple of Demeter to the northwest of the Asklepieion in Messini (Anagnostakis and Poulou-Papadimitriou 1997: 242–51).[20] As in Corinth, there was a handmade pot in the grave pit, which belongs to the same type of vessel with funnel-shaped neck so typical of early seventh-century burial assemblages from Hungary. Moreover, the grave produced a belt buckle with strap director of the Emling type, analogues for which are known only from the northern Adriatic coast and from Bavaria (Uenze 1966: 157–8). The 'wandering soldier' in Corinth may well have been a barbarian warrior, perhaps one of those Avars who had defected to the Romans in 602; one of the Turks in the Persian army who were sent in 591 to the Romans, having on their foreheads the symbol of the cross tattooed in black; or, finally, an officer of the Kök Turk troops that Yabghu Xa'kan left with Emperor Herakleios in 627 after the siege of Tiflis (Theophylact Simokatta, *History* 8.6; Theophanes Confessor, *Chronographia* 389 and 446–8). Nonetheless, those who buried the 'wandering soldier' in Corinth certainly did not want to make too strong a statement about his barbarian otherness. Interred in a stone-lined grave, like many others in Greece and the surrounding Mediterranean regions at that time, wearing a belt buckle and a bronze trinket more often associated with female burials, the 'wandering soldier' looks very different from his contemporaries in the Middle Danube region or in the steppe lands north of the Black Sea. Because of the associated weapon, the 'wandering soldier' grave may be compared with burial assemblages within the square tower near the western gate of the Acrocorinth and in the South Stoa in Corinth, which produced spear and arrow heads, but also more modest grave goods. That those poorer warriors were buried at about the same time as the 'wandering soldier' follows from the analysis of the spear heads and of the few artefacts, such as bronze chains (Davidson 1937: 230 and 232 with 231 fig. 2B; Ivison 1996: 116–17 and 115 fig. 5.6K, P, and R).[21] None of those graves was found within one and the same cemetery, and none was associated with any church building (*pace* Avramea 1997: 98).[22]

A great number of coins of Emperor Constans II (641–668) are known from both Corinth and Athens (Thompson 1954: 70–1; Edwards 1933: 132–3; Penna 1996: 199).[23] In Athens alone, the number of coins of Constans is four times larger than that of coins struck during the much longer reign of his father, Herakleios. Out of 817 coins of Constans II found in the Athenian Agora, 108 were struck in Constantinople in just one year (657). The reason for this unusually large number of coins may be the visit of Emperor Constans, who spent the winter of 662/3 in the city on his way to Italy (Hendy 1985: 662; *Liber Pontificalis*: 186; Paul the Deacon, *History of the Lombards* 5.6).[24] Indeed, more than 600 pieces found in Athens were minted before that date. Moreover, they seem to cluster along the axis of the Panathenaic Way, which may indicate the existence of a 'military or paramilitary encampment' on or near the Areopagus (Metcalf 1965: 213 and 2001: 125).[25] The rebuilding of the tetraconch in the Library of Hadrian was also dated to the second half of the seventh century and may have been associated with Emperor Constans II's visit of 662/3 (Frantz 1988: 73). In addition, the old colonnade of the Stoa of Attalos, which had already lost its original architectural integrity, was subdivided into rooms. In room 6, hundreds of terracotta roof tiles recovered from the fallen debris of the house destroyed sometime in the 630s were piled in neat rows for possible re-use. These alterations have been coin-dated to the reign of Constans II (Shear 1973: 397).[26]

Nothing similar is known from Corinth, although a number of isolated graves with Corinth-type buckles may be dated to the second half of the seventh century.[27] However, recent excavations at Isthmia revealed a group of rooms in the northwestern corner of the Bath, all with walls built in rough masonry. One of them had a cooking hearth, another had an apsidal structure at the south end. The associated quern stones bespeak the rural character of the occupation (Gregory 1993a). The ceramic material found in those rooms has been quickly dubbed 'Slavic ware', but a detailed analysis of both forms and decoration suggests a date in the mid- to late seventh century (Gregory 1993a: 151 and 1993b: 41; Vida and Völling 2000: 19). Indeed, single-handled pots with similar decoration have been found on the south side of the northeastern gate at Isthmia in association with a coin struck for Emperor Constans II in 655/6 (Gregory 1993b: 41, 85, and 123).

The evidence thus suggests that in Athens and, to a lesser extent, in Korinthia, small change was suddenly put into circulation on the eve of Constans II's Italian campaign (Metcalf 2001: 124).[28] Since a similar increase in number of coins struck for Constans has been noted in Sicily (Kislinger 1996: 29–30), it is possible that the sudden infusion of copper coins was associated with the military preparations preceding the mobilisation of the fleet for the war in Italy.

This hypothesis is further substantiated by the presence among the Athenian coins of a relatively large number of half-folles, all minted in a single year (659/60). Such coins are extremely rare in the rest of the Balkans. It would be hard to explain this surge as anything but the arrival in Athens of a group of people carrying coins available at that time in Constantinople. A number of coins from Sicily suggest that they were not bringing only coins produced in Constantinople.

Coins from Italy continued to reach Greece during the reign of Constantine IV. Five folles struck in Sicily for that Emperor between 668 and 674, as well as another for Tiberius III between 698 and 705, have been found during excavations in the southern part of the Agora of Corinth. Excavations in the Athenian Agora produced a Sicilian follis of Justinian II (Avramea 1997: 73; Thompson 1954: 71). That coins struck in Sicily were found in Greece could hardly be explained without reference to a fleet. If the surge in number of coins minted for Emperor Constans II can be associated with his preparations for the naval expedition to Italy, the presence and importance of the navy in Hellas during the reign of Constantine IV are highlighted in a passage from Book II of the *Miracles of St. Demetrios*, in which a *strategos* of the fleet named Sisinnios is said to have been ordered to go to Thessalonica together with his troops in order to sort out things related to accusations of conspiracy (*Miracles of St. Demetrios* 2.5).[29]

Book II of the *Miracles of St. Demetrios*, particularly the fourth homily, is an extremely valuable source for the contemporary situation in northern Greece, and without it there would be very little to say. The unknown author of Book II describes a powerful polity under the rule of the 'king' of the Rynchines, Perbundos. Other groups of Slavs existed in the vicinity of Thessalonica. There were also Slavs in the Strymon valley by the time the king of the Rynchines was arrested and executed, which led the Rynchines and their allies, the Sagudates, to attack Thessalonica. A third tribe, the Drugubites, later joined the alliance. The ensuing siege of the city is to be dated to 25 July 677 because of a clear reference to 'July 25 of the fifth indiction'. The Slavs appear as better organised than in any of the preceding sieges, with an army of special units of archers and warriors armed with slings, spears, shields, and swords. In a long story most probably derived from an oral account, the author of Book II mentions a Sclavene craftsman building a siege machine. There were also Slavic tribes living at a considerable distance from, and not taking part in the Slavic alliance against, Thessalonica. The

Belegezites, who lived near Thebes and Demetrias, even supplied the besieged city with grain (*Miracles of St. Demetrios* 2.3.219, 2.3.222, 2.4.231, 2.4.242, 2.4.255, 2.4.262, 2.4.271–6; for supplies of grain from the Belegezites, see the *Miracles of St. Demetrios* 2.4.254 and 2.4.268).[30] The author of Book II also refers to Slavic pirates raiding as close to Constantinople as the island of Proconnesos. The Emperor (whose name is not given) eventually decided to send an army to Thrace and to the 'land on the opposite side', against the Strymonian Slavs. Since the siege can be dated to 677, and we are specifically told that prior to the siege the Emperor was preparing for war against the Arabs, this expedition against the 'Sklaviniai' of southern Macedonia must have been ordered by Constantine IV. The successful campaign took place in 678, shortly after the failure of the Arab blockade of Constantinople (*Miracles of St. Demetrios* 2.4.277, 2.4.278, 2.4.232; for the date of Constantine IV's expedition, see Lemerle 1981: 131–3; Korres 1999: 163). As a consequence, it was possible for Archbishop John of Thessalonica to participate in the Sixth Ecumenical Council in Constantinople (680/1) together with the bishops of Athens, Argos, Lakedaimon, and Corinth (Riedinger 1979: 8 and 14; Petit 1900–1901: 214).[31]

Modern accounts of the history of Dark-Age Greece have been considerably influenced by one particular text: *On the Themes*, a work associated with Emperor Constantine VII Porphyrogennetos.[32] There is not much material relevant to the seventh or eighth centuries, but chapter 6 was long viewed, together with the *Chronicle of Monemvasia*, as a crucial piece of evidence for the Slavic presence in Greece. According to Porphyrogennetos, during the reign of Constantine V (741–775), the entire country 'was slavonicized and turned barbarian', as an indirect consequence of the plague of 746 that wiped out the native population and made room for the newcomers (Constantine Porphyrogennetos, *On the Themes* 6; see Maricq 1952: 338–40; for a different, but unconvincing interpretation of this passage, see Amantos 1939–1943: 217; Tsaras 1971).[33] Scholars have paid less attention to another chapter, in which Emperor Constantine VII refers to measures taken by Justinian II in 688 or 689. Following his defeat by the Bulgars in a mountain pass near Philippopolis (present-day Plovdiv), Emperor Justinian II settled groups of 'Scythians' around the gorges of the river Strymon, thus laying the foundations of the Strymon *kleisoura*, later to become the theme of the same name (Constantine Porphyrogennetos, *On the Themes* 3; see Melovski and Proeva 1987: 23–4).[34] Many historians believed the 'Scythians' to be either Slavs or Bulgars (for Scythians as Slavs, see Lemerle 1945: 125; Ferluga 1976: 45; for Scythians as Bulgars, see Pliakov 1989: 105; see also Ditten 1993: 172–3). To be sure, a scholium in a ninth-century manuscript with excerpts from Strabo's *Geographia* does indeed refer to 'Scythian Slavs' (Müller 1861: 574).[35] However, as Peter Charanis long since demonstrated, Constantine Porphyrogennetos often used 'Scythians' in reference to steppe nomads, such as Khazars or Magyars (Constantine Porphyrogennetos, *On the Themes* 1 and *On the Administration of the Empire* 13.24–8, 53.126 and 129; Charanis 1961: 143–4 with n. 14). Judging from the existing evidence, the creation of a Bulgar polity shortly before 700 drastically altered the balance of power in the northern Balkans, while driving the local Slavs into the orbit of the new state. Garrisoned outposts in the valley of the Lower Strymon were thus designed to protect the Via Egnatia, the major road across the Balkans from Constantinople to Thessalonica.

The late seventh century also witnessed the first major administrative re-arrangements in the southern Balkans. Shortly after the creation of the theme of Thrace in the 680s, a second theme must have already been in place when, in 695, Leontius, a former general of the Anatolian theme (Anatolikon), was appointed *strategos* of Hellas (Theophanes Confessor, *Chronographia* 368; Ostrogorski 1952: 65; Stratos 1975: 70).[36] During the second half of the seventh and the early eighth century, most Aegean islands were in Byzantine hands. In 653, Pope Martin I was kept prisoner on the island of Naxos on his way to Constantinople, after being arrested by the exarch of Ravenna (Jaffé 1885: 232–3). In 710, summoned to Constantinople to discuss controversial decisions of the Quinisext Council, Pope Constantine I met the *strategos* of the Karabisianoi theme on the island of Keos (*Liber Pontificalis*: 223; Frazee 1993: 215; Hendy 1985: 660; Avramea 1997: 100).

The evidence of seals shows that the theme of Hellas was an administrative unit, and not just an army, even though a great number of seals bespeak the significant role of the navy in the seventh- and especially eighth-century history of Greece (Mordtmann 1877; Veis 1914; Curta 2004b).[37] Hellas as an administrative unit is mentioned on the earliest dated seals known so far, those of *kommerkiarioi* (Mordtmann 1877: 291; Laurent 1962: 128–9).[38] The imperial *kommerkia* of Hellas are attested on seals dated between 730 and 740 (Fig. 4.4), a time when such seals are also attested for the theme of Thrace and for the maritime gateway of Thessalonica (Zacos

Figure 4.4 Anonymous seal of the imperial kommerkia *of Hellas, 736/7. The portraits are of Emperor Leo III (717–741) and his son Constantine. The inscription reads: 'The imperial* kommerkia *of Hellas' (after Mordtmann 1877: pl. 10).*

and Veglery 1972: 331–2; Likhachev 1924: 197; see also Brandes 2002: 365–8). This dovetails nicely with what is otherwise known about an intensified military presence in the Balkans during most of the eighth century. Indeed, the state control of both commercial exchange and tax collection which became the hallmark of Leo III's reform of 730/1, responsible for the appearance of the anonymous seals of imperial *kommerkia*, survived longer in those provinces, such as Thrace, that were vital to the provisioning of the armies engaged in war against Bulgaria (Dunn 1993: 14–15).This is definitely not the case of Greece (Hellas), from which both *kommerkiarioi* and the imperial *kommerkia* disappeared by the mid-eighth century (for the last seal of *kommerkiarios*, see Bon 1951: 205; Curta 2004b: 164).

The imperial *kommerkia* of Hellas operated in an economic environment which, though considerably diminished since the early seventh century, was not completely devoid of coins. On the contrary, *kommerkiarioi* in Hellas witnessed, but most probably did not contribute to, extraordinary injections of copper coinage into local markets, similar to those of the second half of the sixth century. There is an unusually large quantity of copper in Athens, which was minted for Emperor Philippikos (711–713), with a coin-per-regnal-year ratio second only to that of Constans II (Thompson 1940; Charanis 1955b: 165). Since among the thirty-one legible coins, only six obverse dies were represented, it has been suggested that those die-linked specimens formed a body of coin specifically transported from Constantinople and injected into the circulating medium at Athens (Metcalf 1967: 278). Responsible for this phenomenon must have been the military (Hendy 1985: 659). It has also been noted that all coins were struck during the second year of Philippikos' reign (712/13), the year in which a *kommerkiarios* first appeared in Thessalonica. All those coins are 10-nummia pieces struck over half-folles of Justinian II. Margaret Thompson initially proposed that they had been struck in a local mint, possibly in Athens, despite the fact that they all bear the mint mark of Constantinople. However, if struck in Constantinople, such coins are conspicuously absent from the finds of the Saraçhane excavation.[39] Moreover, coins struck for Emperor Philippikos do not appear in Sicily, despite the creation of that theme precisely at this moment in time (Kislinger 1996: 151–2).[40] The fact that coins of Philippikos are equally absent from Corinth strongly suggests that the headquarters of the theme of Hellas were in Athens. Peter Charanis believed that the surge of coins of Philippikos must be explained in reference to the mission of the *spatharios* Helias, who, shortly after the execution of Justinian II, was sent to the western provinces of the Empire to parade Justinian's head. According to Charanis, Philippikos struck new coins in order to replace those of the 'fallen tyrant'. Helias must have been responsible for the distribution of those coins to the inhabitants of Athens (Charanis 1955b: 168). However, all coins found in Athens are struck on older flans, in many cases badly so, which can hardly be evidence for the replacement of the 'fallen tyrant's'coinage. Copper struck for Philippikos has meanwhile been found in the northeastern Balkans, but nowhere else in the Peninsula (Poenaru-Bordea and Donoiu 1981–1982: 238; Peikov 2005: 158–9).[41]

The distribution of finds of late seventh and eighth-century coins in both Greece and the northeastern Balkans strongly suggests a connection between petty currency and coastal regions easily accessible by sea (Fig. 4.5). If the 10-nummia pieces minted for Philippikos and found in the Agora of Athens were indeed struck in Constantinople, then their presence in Greece should also be attributed to the navy. The distribution of seventh-century coins (Fig. 4.1) is still reminiscent of the distribution of hoards of sixth- and early seventh-century coins (Fig. 3.1), for finds cluster around the Isthmus of Corinth. However, the distribution of eighth-century coins brings out the significance of the eastern coast of Peloponnesos and the neighbouring Cyclades

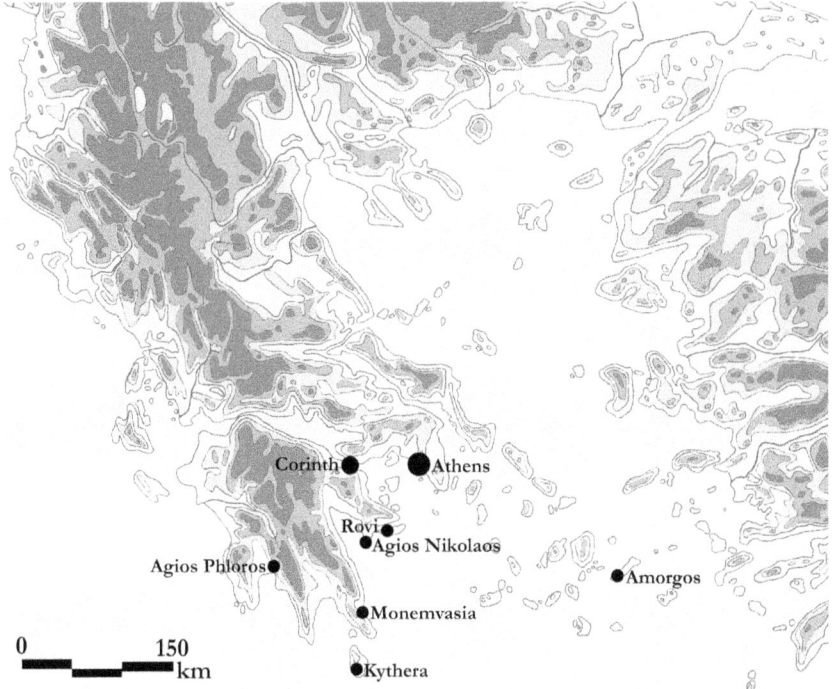

Figure 4.5 The distribution in Greece of single coins struck between 711 and 811. The smallest circles mark individual coins, larger cicrcles up to 20 and over 90, respectively.

(for coins in Cyclades during the eighth and ninth century, see Penna 2001). This is in fact the time of a dramatic re-organisation of the administration of the Aegean islands, which coincides in time with, or follows the creation of, the Kibyrrhaiotai in 732 (Malamut 1988: 305).[42] Moreover, half-folles and 10-nummia pieces found in Greece indicate the existence of local markets of low-price commodities, such as food in small quantities, serving a population that had direct access to both low-value coinage and sea-lanes (Curta 2005a: 124). Such small change implies the presence of oarsmen and sailors of either commercial or, more probably, war ships, who could rely on constant supplies of fresh food at certain points along the coast.

This interpretation is substantiated by the evidence of seals (Table 4.1). The number of seals of military officials, mainly of the navy, associated with Hellas is almost as large as that of seals of generals (*strategoi*) and officers of the land troops stationed in Thrace. The earliest mention of any military official in the Balkans refers to a

Table 4.1 Seventh- to early ninth-century seals of officers and officials associated with the Byzantine themes of Greece.

Office	Hellas	Thessalonike	Kephallenia	Peloponnesos	Total
Political					
archon	2				2
eparch		5			5
protonotarios	2	1			3
Military					
chartularios				1	1
droungarios	2				2
komes tes kortes	1				1
strategos	45	1	10	3	59
turmarch	2			2	4
Economic					
abydikos		5			5
anagrapheus				1	1
balnitoros		1			1
dioiketes	4	1		1	6
epoptes	1			1	2
kommerkiaros	9	14	1		24
kourator	1				1
Juridical					
krites		1			1

general of Hellas named George, whose seal has been dated to the late seventh or early eighth century (Konstantopoulos 1902: 160). No fewer than three other *strategoi* of Hellas are mentioned on seals dated to the eighth century (Konstantopoulos 1906: 161; Veis 1914: 198; Zacos and Veglery 1972: 1406). Two of them bore the title of *patrikios*, which suggests that they may have been of a rank equal to that of contemporary *kommerkiarioi*. It is important to note that the seal of one *strategos* of Hellas was found on the island of Rovi, an indication of the naval character of that theme (Avramea 1996: 14–15).[43] Another seal found on the island of Chenitsa, in the Argolid Bay, mentions a *strategos* of the Helladikoi, most probably the name of the soldiers in the theme of Hellas (Avramea 1997: 99; for the Helladikoi, see Charanis 1953). The number of seals of *strategoi* of Hellas increases visibly after the middle of the eighth century. One of them, Euphemianos, is mentioned on no fewer than thirteen seals, all from the same *boulloterion*, besides twenty-four other seals with the same name but a different titulature. All those seals must have belonged to an archive and point to Euphemianos' important position in the military and administrative organisation of the Empire (Zacos and Veglery 1972: 1066–8). The first *strategoi* of Kephallenia appear in the eighth century, those of Peloponnesos shortly before and after 800 (Zacos and Veglery 1972: 628–9, 1144, 1416, and 1782; Curta 2004b: 184 no. 70 and 187–8). The most important official in the administration of Thessalonica at that time was the eparch, mentioned on no fewer than seven different seals of the late eighth and early ninth century.[44] Most officers of a rank lower than a *strategos* appear to have been in the navy. Two *droungarioi* (navy commanders) of Hellas and Athens, respectively, appear in the eighth and early ninth century (Zacos and Veglery 1972: 1379 and 1733). Turmarchs (navy colonels) appear in Hellas in the late eighth century and at the same time in Peloponnesos, but nowhere else in the Balkans (Panchenko 1908: 133).[45] It was a turmarch named Agallianos who led the rebellion of the Helladikoi against Emperor Leo III in 726 (Theophanes Confessor, *Chronographia* 405; Oikonomides 1994a: 111).

During the eighth century, a number of seals attest the existence of *dioiketai* (Curta 2004b: 184 no. 67 and 185 no. 85). An interesting case is the late eighth- or early ninth-century seal of John of Thessalonica, who was *dioiketas* and *kommerkiarios* at the same time (Konstantopoulos 1906: 62). During the late eighth or early ninth century, several other officials appear to have had fiscal attributions. Two *epoptai* (officials whose task was to verify the tax assessment) are attested for Hellas and Peloponnesos (Konstantopoulos 1906: 73; Curta 2004b: 188 no. 145). There is also an *anagrapheus* of Peloponnesos, who was in charge of the cadastre, but could have also operated as land surveyor (Bon 1951: 191). Apparently, there were imperial estates in Hellas during the eighth century, as indicated by the seal of a *kourator* of Athens (Zacos and Veglery 1972: 1703).[46] Several *abydikoi* (officials in charge of the control of navigation) are attested for Thessalonica during the eighth and early ninth century (Zacos and Veglery 1972: 865, 1166–7, 1239, and 1385; Curta 2004b: 189 no. 176; Koltsida-Makri 2000: 250–1). Like *dioiketai*, *abydikoi* could also be *kommerkiarioi* or notaries at the same time.

Churchmen are the third most important group of officials mentioned on seventh- to early ninth-century seals concerning the Greek lands. The oldest are those of Paul, archbishop of Thessalonica, and Marinos, bishop of Athens (Curta 2004b: 180 no. 9; Zacos and

Veglery 1972: 631).⁴⁷ The bishops of Corinth appear on eighth-century seals, and they may have been metropolitans of Hellas, at least until the middle of the century, the earliest date at which Athens and Larissa are believed to have received metropolitan status (Zacos and Veglery 1972: 817–18 and 1390; Yannopoulos 1993b: 395). A bishop of Athens named John appears on no fewer than three seals and may have been the same bishop as the one whose death is mentioned in a graffito on a column of the Parthenon (Konstantopoulos 1902: 190; Curta 2004b: 167).⁴⁸ An archbishop of Nikopolis named John is also mentioned on an eighth-century seal (Curta 2004b: 182 no. 45).⁴⁹ During that century, there was also a bishop of Kerkyra named John (Curta 2004b: 194 no. 74). Slightly later seals mention bishops of Aigina, Monemvasia, and Troizen (Koltsida-Makri 1996: 252; Curta 2004b: 185 no. 101 and 188 no. 155; Zacos and Veglery 1972: 1123 and 1226). The attribution to a local bishop of the eighth-century seal of Basil, bishop of Orobe, which was found on the island of Rovi, is disputed (Penna 1995: 169; Avramea 1996: 16).⁵⁰ However, given that seals of churchmen rarely travel outside their dioceses, it is quite possible that Basil was the bishop of Rovi under Emperor Constantine V (Cheynet and Morrisson 1990: 109).

Much more difficult to interpret is the late seventh- or early eighth-century seal of a certain Peter, *archon* of Hellas (Curta 2004b: 183 no. 46; Papadimitriou 2004: 214–16). *Archontes* seem to have been local officials with various degrees of autonomy, but the seal of one Theodore, *archon* of Vagenetia (the coastal region opposite the island of Kerkyra), suggests that the title may have also been accorded to local chieftains (Bănescu 1938: 116–17; see also Frashëri 1998: 55; for Peter as a precursor to the *strategos* of Hellas, see Brandes 2002: 211 with n. 217). This may also be the case for Peter. Besides him, we know of another *archon* of Hellas named Dargaskavos, a name presenting a Slavic phonetism that predates the metathesis of the liquids, a phenomenon which linguists commonly date to c. 800 (Curta 2004b: 184 no. 63; Seibt 1999: 29 and 2003; for the chronology of the metathesis of the liquids, see Birnbaum 1975: 228 and 232). Nicholas Oikonomides has proposed that both Peter and Dargaskavos be viewed as *archontes* of the Slavs living in the immediate vicinity of, or even within the theme of, Hellas, perhaps in the valley of the river Spercheios (Oikonomides 1994a). Whether or not any group called itself 'Slavs' at that time, several other seals of *archontes*, which refer to tribes, and not territories, substantiate Oikonomides' interpretation. The Evidites had two *archontes*, Voidargos and John, mentioned on seals dated to the eighth and early ninth century (Seibt 1999: 29–30 and 2003: 463–4). Tichomiros appears on another seal as *archon* of the Belegezites, a Slavic tribe otherwise known from literary sources as living in the region of Thebes and Demetrias (Seibt 1999: 28; Ivanova 1995a: 154 and 202). A recently discovered seal of one Peter, *archon* of the Drugubites, points to the same literary source: the Drugubites appear in the *Miracles of St. Demetrios*, first as part of an alliance of Slavic tribes bent on conquering Thessalonica in 677, then as subjects of Emperor Constantine IV (668–685), who ordered them to feed the refugees coming from the Avar qaganate under the command of Kuver and Mauros (Kyriaki-Wassiliou 2004: 249; see the *Miracles of St. Demetrius* 2.1, 2.4.255, and 2.5.289).[51] Mauros' own seal describes him as *archon* of the Sermesianoi and the Bulgars, with the former being the name given to the refugee group because their ancestors had initially been settled by the Avars in the region of Sirmium. The seal also mentions Mauros' title of *patrikios*, but according to the *Miracles of St. Demetrios*, the Emperor had bestowed upon him the lofty title of *hypatos*, whereby Mauros became equal in rank to his contemporary Peter, the *archon* of Hellas (Nystazopoulou-Pelekidou 1991: 16–7; see the *Miracles of St. Demetrios* 2.5.292; for the Sermesianoi, see Pillon 2002).

Very little is known about the central and southern regions of Greece during the eighth century. According to Theophanes, in 725, 'the inhabitants of Hellas and the Cyclades' rose against Leo III and proclaimed a new emperor, Cosmas. The rebels sent a large fleet to Constantinople under the command of the turmarch of the theme, Agallianos (Theophanes Confessor, *Chronographia* 405). A few sources maintain that Dark-Age Athens was an important centre of learning. In a letter of 748 to St Boniface, Pope Zacharias calls Theodore of Tarsus, the archbishop of Canterbury (668–690), 'Greco-Latinus ante philosophus et Athenis eruditus'. However, Bede only knew that Theodore had a thorough command of Greek (Gundlach 1892: 357; Bede, *Ecclesiastical History of the English People* 4.1).[52] A tenth- or eleventh-century entry in the *Synaxarion of Constantinople* mentions a trip that St Stephen of Sougdaia (Surozh) allegedly made in the mid-eighth century to Athens, where he conversed and discussed at length with 'traditional philosophers and orators'. This bit of information does not appear in the saint's *Life*, preserved only in a fifteenth-century Russian version (Vasil'evskii 1915: 73 and 77–8). Finally, the unknown author of the eleventh-century *Gesta episcoporum Cameracensium* claimed that St Ghislenus, an Athenian by birth, had studied philosophy in his home town (Pertz 1844: 409; such claims have been uncritically reproduced by Herrin 1973: 77–8 and 121 with nn. 52 and 53; and Browning 1984: 299–300). There is no reason to treat those pieces of information as anything more than literary tropes. Nonetheless, and assuming that the headquarters of the theme of Hellas was indeed in Athens, the idea of sea travel to and from that city in the eighth century is not only possible, but also confirmed by other, independent sources. According to Theophanes, the plague of 745/6 'traveled like a spreading fire' from Sicily and Calabria to Monemvasia, Hellas, 'and the adjoining islands', before reaching Constantinople (Theophanes Confessor, *Chronographia* 422). The route along which the plague spread was that of the main line of communication between the westernmost provinces of the Empire and the capital. Whether or not Greece and the Aegean islands suffered any losses from the epidemics, by 755 the population growth must have been robust enough for Emperor Constantine V to bring to Constantinople several families from the islands, Hellas, and 'the southern parts' in an attempt to repopulate a city devastated by the plague (Theophanes Confessor, *Chronographia* 429; Kislinger 1992: 105–6; for the demographic significance of the 755 population transfers, see Yannopoulos 1993b: 391). In 766, he also 'collected artisans from different places', and brought to the capital five hundred clay-workers from Hellas and the islands (Theophanes Confessor, *Chronographia* 440). It is important to note that the few passages in Theophanes' *Chronographia* concerning Hellas show travel from, and not so much to, Greece. The situation appears to have been the reverse of that in the late seventh and early eighth century. Perhaps this also explains the remarkable decline of monetary circulation. In Athens, low denominations of the same value as the coins minted for Philippikos appear during the reign of Leo III, but the reign of Constantine V coincides in time with one of the lowest points in the monetary history of Dark-Age Greece.

Much has been made of the mention of Monemvasia, at the southernmost tip of Peloponnesos, in the account of the pilgrimage trip of Bishop Willibald of Eichstätt to the Holy Land (Guth 1982: 13–28; McCormick 2001: 131–2). The author of the story was a nun, Hugeburc of Heidenheim, who wrote down what she had been told by Willibald himself 'in dictation from his own mouth' (*Vita Willibaldi*, 86; English translation from Noble and Head

1995: 143–4). According to her, Willibald set out on his pilgrimage in 722. One year later, he sailed from Syracuse and 'reached the city of Monemvasia, in the land of Slavinia' (*Vita Willibaldi*, 93).[53] The sojourn in Monemvasia does not seem to have been long, but the fact that Hugeburc reports that the place was 'in the land of Slavinia' has been interpreted as an indication of a Slavic presence in the hinterland (Huxley 1988: 9; McCormick 2001: 131 and 508). The Latin word *Slawinia* is a calque of the Greek term *Sklavinia*, which refers to a more or less independent but loosely organised barbarian polity beyond the borders of the Empire. From the point of view of the Byzantine authorities in Constantinople, what mattered was not the precise description of the ethnic identities associated with any *Sklavinia*, but the fact that such polities were independent and potentially hostile. It is therefore important not to read too much into Hugeburc's mention of Monemvasia in the 'land of Slavinia'. What she probably meant was not that the city was surrounded by Slavs, but that the power of the Byzantine Emperor or of his local deputy ended at the very walls of the city: beyond that, it was barbarian land (Ronin 1995: 440; for *Sklavinia* in Byzantine and Carolingian sources, see Antoljak 1964: 11–12; Bertels 1987: 160–1). In any case, the 'land of Slavinia' was most probably not the name which those living in the environs of Monemvasia employed to refer to their country. Instead, the phrase betrays the administrative nature of Hugeburc or Willibald's source of information about what was beyond Monemvasia. As a consequence, the phrase is little more than a stereotype, albeit of administrative, not bookish origin.[54]

In contrast, the apocryphal *Life of St. Pancratius*, the first bishop of Taormina, may have employed eyewitness accounts. Recent studies have demonstrated that its author, Evagrius, was writing shortly after the introduction of the thematic organisation into Sicily (709/10), possibly before 695 (Stallman 1986: 156 and 247; for an earlier date of the first redaction, see Brandes 2005: 200–1 with n. 134). Evagrius placed the life of Pancratius, a disciple of St Peter who lived in the first century AD, in the context of his own lifetime. Pancratius' mission of conversion is thus set against the background of the first Arab attacks on Sicily, in the late seventh or early eighth century. One of Pancratius' converts was a local *hegemon* named Bonifatius. Portrayed as the *strategos* of the Sicilian theme residing in Taormina, Bonifatius was the supreme commander of the local troops, which he led in campaigns against 'tyrants' in Sicily or against barbarians abroad. At one time, he is described as organising a seaborne expedition into the regions of Dyrrachium and Athens. Upon returning to Sicily, he is confronted by St Pancratius, who claims that his prisoners look like Christians. Bonifatius assures him that they were Avars, who were about to be distributed among the soldiers in order to be baptised and taught Greek and Latin, the languages in use at that time in Taormina (Stallman 1986: 271).[55] Through the intermediary of a translator, the prisoners then declare that they used to worship fire, water, and their own swords (Stallman 1986: 271).[56] It is hard to establish the possible source of this story, but there can be no doubt about its authenticity.[57] In the eyes of eighth-century Sicilian Greeks, there were Avars in the environs of Athens, an indication perhaps that at that time the theme of Hellas still consisted of a narrow strip of land along the coast and that the authority of the *strategos* did not extend too far into the interior of central Greece or into Peloponnesos. This conclusion is confirmed by the analysis of the archaeological evidence.

In continental Greece, assemblages that can be safely dated to the eighth century are rare. The last chronological phase of the Tigani cemetery coincides in time with the beginnings of another cemetery, which was accidentally found in 1966 to the southwest of Ioannina (Vokotopoulou 1967). Only a few artefacts are known from the twenty-one graves excavated there, none of which has been properly published. The bronze bracelets and finger-rings point to a date within the second half of the seventh century, but it remains unclear whether or not the cemetery continued into the eighth century.[58] Recent excavations in the Panagia Field of Corinth revealed the seventh- to eighth-century occupation of the city. The house built on top of a sixth-century bath produced fragments of cooking pots in a very micaceous fabric similar to pottery found in Constantinople and dated between the late seventh and the early ninth century, one-handled jugs with flat bases, and an early Abbasid coin (Sanders 2003a: 35–44 with figs 10.1, 2 and 4; 12.1, 2004: 185–6; Warner Slane and Sanders 2005: 246 with n. 12 and 273–80). In addition, the Panagia Field excavations produced evidence of glazed pottery, especially fragments of Glazed White Ware chafing dishes produced in Constantinople between the late seventh and the late eighth century (Vroom 2005: 63). Fragments of Glazed White Ware have also been found at Pseira (Crete), as well as in Athens, but only sporadically elsewhere (Poulou-Papadimitriou 2001: 238–9 and 252 figs 7–8; Hayes and Petridis 2003: 531 figs 7–8 and 10–11; only one such fragment was found during the Berbati-Limnes survey of northern Argolis, for which see Hahn 1996: 424 and 432). Only two churches are known in Greece that could be securely dated to the late seventh or eighth century. The Church of St Peter in Alika near Vathia (Lakonia), not far from Tigani, was built with architectural fragments from ancient monuments and produced a coin struck for Emperor Tiberius III (698–705) (Kordosi 1981b: 419; Avramea 1997: 102; Kislinger 2001: 92). At Exampela, on the island of Siphnos, only an inscription survives from a Church of St Thomas, which is said to have been built in 787 (Bouras 2006: 59).[59]

At Aphiona, on the northwestern coast of Kerkyra, there was a small late seventh- and early eighth-century settlement site, of which only four houses have been excavated, one with two rooms. With one exception, all the buildings produced evidence of two occupation phases, the later of which is associated with a great quantity of broken tiles and fragments of limestone slabs from the superstructure. Most finds from the Aphiona settlement are of unglazed small jugs very similar to those found in the cemetery associated with the Church of St Dionysios the Areopagite in Athens, as well as of fragments of blue and green glassware.[60] Much as in Isthmia, fragments of millstones made of volcanic tufa have been found, which show trade connections with Italy, for the tufa in question is not native to Kerkyra. It is unclear whether the existence of two churches, one on the isthmus leading to the fortified peninsula, the other on the ridge of the hill, coincided in time with the settlement site (Bulle 1934: 213–17; Bowden 2003: 203–4).

A date after 700 can be firmly established for at least some of the about fifty stone-lined graves in the cemetery associated with the settlement site in Aphiona (Bulle 1934: 219–20, 223, 227, 222 fig. 26.24 [buckle of the Corinth type], 222 fig. 26.18 [pendant of the Komani class], and 222 fig. 26.7 [beads]). To be sure, the fragment of a belt buckle of the Corinth type found in grave 2 suggests that the beginnings of the cemetery may well be placed within the seventh century, possibly before 650. But the isolated finds of pendants of the Komani type and the melon-seed-shaped beads from grave 10 clearly point to a date after 700 (for pendants of the Komani type, see Garam 1980: 174–5; for melon-seed-shaped beads, see Vida and Völling 2000: 88). Much as in Tigani, the skeletal evidence shows that both females and children (including infants) were buried within one and the same cemetery. Some of the graves had more than one skeleton, in some cases as many as five, all male. An eighth-century date may also be advanced for the graves accidentally found in 1972 in neighbouring Palaiokastritsa (Agallopoulou 1973).[61]

Unique among the Dark-Age sites in Greece is the cemetery excavated in 1959 in Olympia, which produced thirty-two cremations, of which twenty-eight were in urns (Gialouris 1961–1962; Vryonis 1992; Vida and Völling 2000). As in Aphiona, there are some indications that the cemetery began at some point during the second half of the seventh century. For example, the flint steel found in burial 11 has a good analogue in a burial assemblage from one of the two annexes of the Kenchreai basilica, in which it was associated with two coins struck for Emperor Constans II (Vida and Völling 2000: pl. 10.11; Pallas 1981: 299 fig. 5c). A date within the seventh century may also be advanced for the urn in grave 1, with its vertically incised decoration, very similar to pottery found in Argos and Isthmia (Aupert 1980: figs 15 and 16; Gregory 1993b: 41, 85, and 123 with pls 25d and 45c).[62] On the other hand, early eighth-century melon-seed-shaped beads were found in graves 3 and 22. It remains unclear how far the chronology of the Olympia cemetery may reach into the eighth century, but nothing indicates a date after 800. Another contemporary, yet very different burial site was recently discovered in Agia Trias near Skliva (Ilia) during excavations of a Mycenaean-age cemetery (Vikatou 2002). Most interesting among the grave goods found together with the five stone- and brick-lined graves is a pair of earrings, each with four attached loops and granulated, triangular ornaments. Very similar earrings have been found in Abdera, Tigani (graves 10 and 54), as well as in a stone-lined grave at the eastern end of the northern aisle of the Kraneion basilica in Corinth (Vikatou 2002: 243 and 269 fig. 20; n.a. 1976: 132 fig. 1, pl. 97, fig. 99β; Bakirtzis 1983: 17 fig. 4 [where the burial is wrongly dated to the 'Late Byzantine' period]; Drandakis and Gkioles 1980: 254 with pl. 148δ; Drandakis et al. 1981: 249; Pallas 1972: 213 and 238 with pl. 222α). None of those analogues can be dated with precision, but grave 10 in Tigani was found in the middle of the nave of the ruined basilica, and its north–south orientation is in sharp contrast to all other neighbouring graves, which have a predominantly west–east orientation. This strongly suggests for grave 10 a date far different from that of the other graves in Tigani, but no conclusive evidence exists to place that date between 700 and 800.[63] A late date for the Agia Trias inhumations is, however, supported by other finds, such as the barrel-shaped bronze beads in grave 3, with good analogues in Abdera and in eighth- and ninth-century cemeteries excavated in southern and northeastern Bulgaria (Bakirtzis 1994: 160; Văzharova 1976: 137 with 139 fig. 86.2; Stoianova-Serafimova 1979: 789 with 798 fig. 7/2; for the chronology of cemeteries in southern Bulgaria, see Angelova and Koleva 2001). It is therefore possible that Agia Trias and Olympia coexisted throughout the second half of the seventh and the first half of the eighth century. As in Olympia, it is impossible to establish how far into the eighth century one can stretch the chronology of the Agia Trias cemetery.[64]

No eighth-century finds are so far known form mainland Greece that could match the Aphiona and Palaiokastritsa burial assemblages. There seems to have been a strong correlation between the presence of land troops stationed more or less permanently together with their families and burial assemblages that could safely be dated to the eighth century. This is certainly the case of the two cemeteries on Kerkyra, which are otherwise part of a group of burial sites stretching further up the coast into northern Albania and inland into Macedonia, and known, for lack of a better name, as the 'Komani culture' (the literature on the 'Komani culture' is considerable; see, more recently, Bowden 2003; Nallbani 2004a and 2004b). These sites have much in common with contemporary cemeteries excavated in Sicily or Sardinia, which have also been attributed to Byzantine garrisons stationed at key points in the defence system of those two islands (Orsi 1942: 113–15 and 124–7; Spanu 1998: 127 and 150; Riemer 2000: 156). Finally, Bulgarian archaeologists have recently established solid links between the 'Komani culture' and a number of cemeteries around Gotse Delchev, Smolian, and Zlatograd, just north of the present-day Greek–Bulgarian border, which they attributed to Byzantine garrisons stationed on the northern frontier of Thrace, perhaps to control the access to the Via Egnatia from across the Rhodopes (Angelova and Marvakov 2001; Angelova and Koleva 2001). To be sure, finds similar to those of Albania, Sardinia, and southern Bulgaria are known from several sites in Greece, such as Tigani, where a seventh-century cemetery cut through the floor of a sixth-century basilica. The relation between cemetery and church reminds one of the situation on such contemporary sites as Sv. Erazmo and Radolishte in Macedonia, Shurdhah in Albania, or Tharros in Sardinia, where seventh-century stone-lined graves cut through the floors of abandoned sixth-century churches (Maneva 1998: 846–7; Spahiu 1976: 155–6; Spanu 1998: 85; for Tigani, see also Avramea 1998: 55).

However, with the exception of Olympia and Agia Trias, no

assemblages have been so far found in continental Greece that could be clearly dated between 700 and 800. That burial activity ended by 700 on such sites as Tigani and, perhaps, Ioannina may indicate that the garrisons stationed there were withdrawn or had meanwhile become irrelevant. This may have something to do with the dramatic military changes already taking place during the second half of the seventh century. If the surge in numbers of coins minted for Emperor Constans II and found in Athens can be associated with his preparations for the sea expedition to Italy, the role of the navy in Hellas under Constantine IV is underscored by the episode of Sisinnios narrated in the *Miracles of St. Demetrios*. The creation of the theme of Hellas shortly before 700 and, in the course of the eighth century, of that of Kephallenia (Oikonomides 1976: 119; Wasilewski 1980: 36)[65] effectively made land troops stationed at key points in the interior unnecessary, as both administrative units existed almost exclusively in relation to the navy. It is perhaps no accident that the introduction of those themes coincides with that of the 'Slavic' client polities on the northern border of the theme of Hellas, which operated as a 'buffer zone' against Avar and Bulgar attacks from the north. The *archontes* of Hellas are mentioned throughout the eighth century, but by 750 their seals begin referring to individual tribal groups, such as Drugubites, Belegezites, or Evidites.

No such clients existed on the western frontier of the theme of Hellas. Can the cremation cemetery in Olympia therefore be in any way associated with the Slavs? Tivadar Vida's thorough analysis of both grave goods and their analogues has shown how comparisons consistently point to the Middle Danube region of the Avar qaganate. Iron torcs, for example, are unknown in the Balkans, but are particularly frequent on burial sites in Hungary and Slovakia during the Middle and Late Avar periods (Vida and Völling 2000: 61–76). The specific decoration of many urns found in Olympia has good analogues in Middle and Late Avar assemblages, but it is also attested on contemporary sites in the western Balkans, such as Kašić in Croatia or Mušići in Bosnia (Belošević 1968; Čremošnik 1975). But in the southern Balkans, the Olympia cemetery is unique, for no other cremation burials have so far been found anywhere in Greece, Albania, Macedonia, or southern Bulgaria. The Olympia cemetery began at some point during the second half of the seventh century. The community which used the cemetery must therefore have coexisted with the garrison in Tigani and with some of those who buried their dead in Corinth at some point before 700. Despite occasional links that could be established between grave goods found in all these burial assemblages, Olympia represents an archaeological phenomenon fundamentally different from anything that was in existence at that time in Greece. In other words, everything points to an intrusive group, and not to the 'cohabitation of Byzantine peasants and Slavs' (Sanders 1995: 455; Avramea 1997: 86). Whether or not one can call 'Slavs' those who buried their dead in Olympia is a matter of how the archaeological evidence is interpreted. In any case, that evidence has nothing to do with what has so far been found in those regions of northern Greece in which the author of Book II of the *Miracles of St. Demetrios* placed the Slavic tribes of the Drugubites, Belegezites, Berzites, and Rynchines. Instead, most analogues point to the Middle Danube region of the Avar qaganate and to its southern periphery. Despite claims to the contrary, the Olympia urns have nothing to do with the so-called Prague-type pottery, while the handmade pot found in the 'wandering soldier' grave in Corinth has much more to do with the pottery from Early and Middle Avar assemblages in Hungary than with 'Slavic ware'.

The creation of the theme of Hellas in the late seventh century did not result in a gradual extension of the imperial authority inland from the outposts on the coast, because at least initially Hellas was little more than a naval base. The *Sklaviniai* remained outside the area of direct Byzantine control, though still in the orbit of the newly created themes. This may explain why the perspective on developments in Greece remained Constantinopolitan and why sources based on information originating in the capital, such as the *Life of St. Willibald* and Theophanes' *Chronographia*, spoke exclusively of *Sklaviniai* and Slavs. By contrast, the author of Book II of the *Miracles of St. Demetrios*, a resident of Thessalonica, knew many tribes by name – Drugubites, Sagudates, Belegezites, Berzites, Rynchines. To him, there was an important difference between 'Slavs-as-friends' and 'Slavs-as-foes'. Some of the tribes he mentioned besieged Thessalonica. He described them as savage, brutish, and heathen. Others, like the Belegezites, were friendly and, at times, potential and important allies, who were able to supply the besieged city with food. That the *Life of St. Pancratius* distinguished between Avars and Slavs, although the former apparently spoke Slavic, is a further indication of ethnic groups being classified not in terms of language and culture, but in terms of their military and political potential. The situation in southern Greece is less clear, but nothing indicates a Byzantine *reconquista* of the western and northwestern region of Peloponnesos during the first half of the eighth century (Yannopoulos 1993b: 398). While the archaeological evidence, especially that from Olympia, points to an 'Avar', not 'Slavic' cultural component, the first tribal names (Ezerites and Milingoi) documenting a greater familiarity with the locals do not appear in written sources before the creation of the theme of Peloponnesos. In 783, an army led by the logothete of the Swift Course, Staurakios, moved from Constantinople to Thessalonica and Hellas 'against the Sklavinian tribes', and forced them to pay tribute to the Empire. According to Theophanes, Staurakios' army then moved into Peloponnesos and 'brought back many captives and much booty to the Roman Empire' (Theophanes Confessor, *Chronographia* 456–7).[66] It is important to note that although Staurakios is said to have moved against the Slavs, the exact ethnicity of his Peloponnesian prisoners is not mentioned. In any case, at least three important Peloponnesian centres were under imperial control in the 780s, as indicated by the participation of the bishops of Troizen, Monemvasia, and Patras in the Council of Nicaea, which restored the cult of the icons in 787 (Darrouzès 1975: 38). Some have even argued that the theme of Peloponnesos was created shortly after Staurakios' expedition (Živković 1999).

On the other hand, Staurakios' campaign had no impact on the Slavic clients of northern Greece. By the end of the eighth century, when the Studite brothers Theodore and Joseph (future archbishop of Thessalonike) were exiled to Thessalonike as punishment for having opposed the adulterous marriage of Constantine VI, their military escort did not travel overland along the Via Egnatia, from Constantinople to Thessalonica, but by sea, via Lemnos (Theodore the Studite, *ep.* 3, dated to 25 March 797; see also Tsorbarzoglou 2001: 131).[67] The trip took place in February and March, the worst months for navigation in the northern Aegean. The military party escorting the Studite brothers may have had very serious reasons to avoid the overland route, which they apparently judged to be much more dangerous than braving the strong winds of the Aegean Sea during a winter trip. Whether or not the danger on the Via Egnatia, which the escort tried to avoid, was in any way linked to the local 'Sklavinian tribes', subdued only a few years before by Staurakios, the situation in Boeotia was no better. In 799, prompted by conspirators from the theme of Hellas, Akamiros, the *archon* of the Belegezites, attempted to release the sons of Constantine V from their exile in Athens and to proclaim one of them as emperor (Theophanes Confessor, *Chronographia* 473–4; Oikonomides 1994a: 117; Vryonis

2003: 79; for the title of *archon*, see also Ferluga 1982 and Ditten 1983: 110–11).[68] The rebels were defeated and blinded, and nothing else is known about the Slavic *archon* (Theophanes Confessor, *Chronographia* 473–4; Vasmer 1941: 16; Yannopoulos 1993b: 350; Ditten 1993: 240; Oikonomides 1994a: 117). He must have been a successor of that Tichomiros mentioned on an eighth-century seal, but his alliance with the Helladikoi cannot be an accident. The *archontes* of the Belegezites had already been drawn into the political developments of the theme of Hellas. Akamiros was no barbarian chieftain, but a client ruler with knowledge of, and influence in, local Byzantine politics.

Notes

1. Besides the latest coin in the Athens 1972 hoard, only two coins minted for Emperor Herakleios after 630 are known from Greece, one from Athens (struck in Ravenna in 631/2), the other from Corinth (struck in Constantinople in 633/4) (Thompson 1954: 70; Edwards 1933: 131). According to Kissas 1988: 210, no fewer than twenty-six coins from the last years of Herakleios' reign have been found in a storage room excavated near a three-aisled basilica in Zoodochos Pigi near Kolchida (prefecture of Kilkis). Leaving aside the possibility of that being in fact a hoard, no details on the coins have been published for proper identification.
2. Athens 1972 and Athens 1876. According to Metcalf 2001: 124, the Athens 1876 hoard is in fact three separate hoards. Another hoard of gold with the latest coins struck for Emperor Leo III is from an unknown location in Attica, for which see Vryonis 1963. The only hoard of gold from that period from the Aegean islands is Arkessini.
3. The exception is a solidus struck for Justinian II between 705 and 710 and accidentally found in Athens (Penna 1996: 202 with n. 23).
4. During the second building phase of the fort, which is coin-dated to the reigns of Constans II and Constantine IV, a church was erected inside the walls, which was dedicated to St John the Theologian.
5. Most analogues of the Isthmia buckle are known from burial assemblages in Hungary dated to the first half of the seventh century (Garam 2001: 101).
6. An inscription on the mosaic in the apse mentions Empress Irene and her son, Constantine VI (780–797) (Spieser 1973: 159), and much of the sculptured decoration has also been dated to the eighth century (Mentzos 2001). The Church of Panagia Drosogiane in Naxos is dated by its wall paintings to the early seventh century, but such a foundation date has not been confirmed archaeologically.

7. For similar buckles found in burial assemblages in Crimea dated to the second half of the sixth century, see Veimarn and Aibabin 1993: 125–6 with 125 fig. 92.5, 30, and 31.
8. Similar earrings have been found in Magnisi (Sicily) together with a coin struck for Emperor Tiberius II (578–582) (Baldini Lippolis 1999: 74 and 92). The Europos cemetery also includes two burial chambers, the dating of which remains uncertain.
9. Good analogues for the Portochelion buckle are known from assemblages in Caričin Grad (Serbia) and Suuk Su (Crimea) securely dated to the sixth century (Mano-Zisi 1958: 312–13 with 326 fig. 36; Repnikov 1906: 22–3). One of the two cemeteries excavated in Portochelion produced the remains of an infant placed inside an amphora, a burial practice attested elsewhere on the Adriatic coast, in Italy, as well as in Crimea (Bowden et al. 2002: 207–8; Pioro 1990: 126 and fig. 35.1).
10. Some may be even earlier than the basilica, e.g., graves 2 and 6 (Laskaris 2000: 58–9). This is certainly true for grave 21, which was cut by the southern wall of the nave and must therefore ante-date the building of the church.
11. No fewer than six buckles of the Corinth type have been found in Tigani, some of which could be dated after c. 650 (Drandakis and Gkioles 1980: 253, 255, and pl. 149ε; Drandakis et al. 1981: 249, 251, and pl. 182γ). However, *pace* Sanders 1995: 456, nothing indicates that any of those buckles could be dated after 700.
12. Unlike all other buckles, the specimen in grave 25 is made of iron, not bronze. As such, it has good analogues in Corinth and in Apulia (Davidson 1952: pl. 114.2195–6; Riemer 2000: 155 and 422). Buckles of the Corinth type have also been found in Athens, the islands of Korakonissi, Daskaleio, Platea, Delos, and Crete (Avramea 1997: 89–90 and pl. 4a2, 4c2, and 4b6; Poulou-Papadimitriou 2005: 698–9). For the chronology of the Corinth-type buckles, see Nallbani 2005. No evidence exists to support the idea that such buckles were 'Orthodox "Byzantine" artifacts of the eighth century' (Sanders 1995: 456).
13. Similar buckles are known from several islands near the Argolid coast and from Crete (Avramea 1997: 89–90 and pl. 3.4ea, 4b1–3, and 4c5–6; Poulou-Papadimitriou 2005: 696 and 702 fig. 8). One such buckle was found in Samos in association with three coins struck for Emperor Herakleios, the last of them in 613/14 (Martini and Steckner 1993: 127–8). For the chronology of buckles with cross-shaped plate, see Schulze-Dörrlamm 2002: 197.
14. In grave 23, a buckle of the Pergamon type was associated with two other buckles of the Bologna and Boly-Želovce type, respectively. Another specimen was found in the Athenian Agora, for which see Setton 1950: 522 and fig. For the chronology of Pergamon-type buckles, see Neeft 1988: 4–6; Riemer 1995: 783.

15. No anthropological sexing of the skeleton has been carried out, which encouraged speculations about this being a male burial (Pallas 1981: 306). For the Edessa pair of fibulae and their analogues, see now Curta 2006a.
16. Similar buckles are known from a burial in Athens, as well as isolated finds on islands near the Argolid coast (Travlos and Frantz 1965: 167 and pl. 43a; Avramea 1997: 89–90 and pl. 4a1 and 4c1). For the chronology of Syracuse-type buckles, see Schulze-Dörrlamm 2002: 179; Garam 2001: 95; for a somewhat earlier dating, see Maurici 2000: 515.
17. The closest analogues for the Kruje fibulae were found together with a type of earring which is otherwise dated with coins struck for Emperor Constantine IV. This is not contradicted by what is otherwise known about Corinth-type buckles (Aibabin 1982: 172; Varsik 1992: 83).
18. Most authors have regarded the Corinth sword as 'Byzantine' despite the fact that the closest analogue for its cup-like guard is that of a long dagger from the seventh- to eighth-century Kudyrge cemetery in the Altai region of Central Asia (Bálint 1989: 254). For Avar-age analogues, see Nagy 1959: 62 and 94 pl. 27.1 (Aradac); Kiss 1996: 230 and 232 (Kölked); Müller 1996: 411 (Gyenesdiás); Szabó 1965: 42, 47–8, and 69 pl. 8.1–3 (Tarnaméra); Simon 1991.
19. Several Middle and Late Avar-age horseman burials are covered with stone slabs similar to those of contemporary burials in central Asia (Simon 1993). However, no parallel exists in Hungary and the neighbouring regions for stone-lined graves, the preferred form of inhumation in sixth-century cemeteries of Balkan cities and forts and in the Mediterranean area during the seventh century. Seventh-century graves lined and covered with roughly shaped stone slabs occur in Istrian and Sardinian cemeteries (Torcellan 1986: 42; Evans 1989: 301–2 and 307; Spanu 1998: 85 and 126).
20. Another cemetery with some fifty inhumations has been found over the Temenos of Asklepios (Themelis 2002: 34–8).
21. For those graves as warrior burials, see Charanis 1949: 257. For early seventh-century chains similar to that from Corinth, see Garam 2002. For Early Avar-age analogues for the spear heads, see Kiss 1977: 94 and 96 with pl. 37.30.6 and Török 1980–1981: pl. 13.1.
22. The two burials found within the church on the Acrocorinth (one of which may be that of a woman) produced no weapons, only belt buckles of the Boly-Želovce type (Ivison 1996: 117 and 116 fig. 5.7D, E).
23. In Athens, 817; in Corinth, 127. For stray finds from Greece, see Kyrou 1995: 112 fig. 5; Gregory 1993a: 151–3; Avramea 1997: 74; Galani-Krikou 1998b: 151. Metcalf 2001: 125 offers a tabulation of Athenian finds of coins struck for Constans II by *DOC* classes. His list has only 705 specimens, 146 of which belong to *DOC* classes 6 to 8, dated between 655 and 657/8.

24. Paul the Deacon's account of Constans II's campaign is based on the biography of Pope Vitalian in the *Liber Pontificalis*. As a consequence, he too claimed that the Emperor marched overland from Constantinople. However, given that communication by land between Constantinople and Thessalonica was re-established only under Constantine IV, it is unlikely that Constans crossed through southern Thrace and Macedonia to reach Athens (Stratos 1975: 171; Yannopoulos 1993b: 343; Hunger 1990: 49).
25. The large number of solidi struck for Emperor Constans II found in the Athens 1876 hoard(s), all of which belong to class VI, minted between 661 and 663 has also been attributed to the Emperor's visit to Athens in 662/3 (Metcalf 2001: 124).
26. It remains uncertain whether or not the chapel built on top of the spring house of the Asklepieion in Corinth may also be attributed to the same circumstances (Hattersley-Smith 1988: 413).
27. For example, the two graves, one with a female skeleton, found near Temple G in the southwestern corner of the Roman Forum (Williams et al. 1974: 11 with pl. 2.8). The associated belt buckle of the Corinth class has analogues in one of the two burials within the square tower by the western gate of the Acrocorinth, in the southern Stoa, and in the Hemicycle (Setton 1950: 522; Davidson 1952: 235, 272 and pl. 114.2192, 2195; Ivison 1996: 112 and 116 fig. 5.7C).
28. The *strategos* of the Karabisianoi is first mentioned in the 670s, but a Byzantine fleet was surely in existence before Constans II's campaign to Italy, as indicated by the events of 653/4 (Theophanes Confessor, *Chronographia* 345–6; Antoniadis-Bibicou 1966). According to Treadgold 1995: 72–5, the *strategia* of Karabisianoi was in fact created precisely at this moment in time, the goal of the Emperor's visit to Athens in 662/3 being to ready the Karabisianoi for his expedition to Italy.
29. Sisinnios was a *strategos* of the Karabisianoi.
30. The Drugubites also supplied food to immigrants from the Avar qaganate (*Miracles of St. Demetrios* 2.5.289). For the execution of Perbundos, see Leszka 2005. For the Slavic army besieging Thessalonica, see Zachopoulos 1992.
31. The presence of the five bishops in Constantinople is commonly interpreted as evidence that Corinth, Argos, Athens, and Lakedaimon were, like Thessalonica, under direct Byzantine control.
32. *On the Themes* has traditionally been dated after Emperor Constantine's death, but recent studies suggest that its final redaction, if not composition, may well be associated with the reign of Constantine's father, Leo VI (Lounghis 1973: 304–5; Pratsch 1994: 130–1).
33. The passage in *On the Themes* is a key argument for advocates of a late Slavic settlement in Greece (Zakythinos 1945: 94; Karagiannopoulos 1971: 460; Stratos 1975: 180).

34. The gorges of the river Strymon around which Justinian settled his 'Scythians' have been located between Roupel and Melenikon, two villages north of Sidirokastron and south of Melnik, near the modern Bulgarian–Greek border (Karagiannopoulos 1989: 689–90; Stavridou-Zafraka 1995b: 313–15; for a different location in the straits of Kavala, see Oikonomides 1996c: 10 with n. 5). For the Strymon *kleisoura*, see Rajković 1958. Emperor Constantine may have projected into the past an institution of his own lifetime, but his use of *kleisoura* to describe Justinian's establishment of 'Scythians' in the Strymon valley may not be an anachronism. The first frontier districts organised into 'passes', each under a *kleisourarch*, appeared in Cilicia under Emperor Herakleios. Some believe that, in addition to 'Scythians', Justinian II also settled 12,000 Mardaites in Peloponnesos, Kephallenia, and Epirus (Amantos 1932: 135–6; Ferluga 1984: 57). However, the Mardaites in question were moved from Lebanon to Asia Minor, not to the Balkans. The earliest mention of the Mardaites in relation to Peloponnesus cannot be dated before 800, at the earliest.
35. It has been suggested that the author of the scholium was one of Photios' disciples (Diller 1954: 31, 48, and 50; Lemerle 1971: 218 and 233).
36. For the creation of the theme of Thrace, see Lilie 1977: 27. Ostrogorski 1952: 65 placed Hellas in Peloponnesos, while Charanis 1970: 4 argued that the theme consisted of eastern-central Greece (including Attica), with a northern extension into Thessaly. See also Zakythinos 1965: 55; Koder and Hild 1976: 57; Yannopoulos 1993b: 393; Kalaitzakis 1996: 622–3; Avramea 1997: 37. The signature of the bishop of Corinth who attended as papal legate the Sixth Ecumenical Council in Constantinople (681) suggests that he represented the 'province' of Hellas (*Hellenon chora*), an early indication of the thematic organisation in Greece (Avramea 1997: 38, 172 and 185; Ohme 1989: 199–201). For a later date, between 693 and 695, see Živković 1999: 143.
37. Judging from the existing evidence, the initial character of the theme of Hellas may not have been very different from that of Sardinia and Sicily, which emerged as themes a few years later. Sardinia was a military unit collecting the remnants of the Exarchate of Africa, while Sicily comprised those parts of the Exarchate of Italy which were most exposed to raids from Arab-held Africa. Similarly, the creation of the theme of Hellas may have been a response to the first Arab attacks on Cyprus, Rhodes, Kos, and Crete (Moniaros 1998: 137)
38. *Kommerkiarioi* were high-ranking financial officers in charge of the collection of tax from various provinces, but actually residing in Constantinople (Brandes 2002: 503–4).
39. Only one half-follis of Philippikos has been found in the Saraçhane excavations (Harrison and Hayes 1986: 317–18). On the other hands, coins

of later emperors, which were found in the Athenian Agora, appear to have been struck in Constantinople over coins of Philippikos, the presence of which in the capital of the Empire is thus indirectly confirmed.

40. Nonetheless, coins were struck in Sicily for Philippikos, as demonstrated by a coin from Monemvasia (Penna 1996: 201).
41. Some of the coins of Philippikos found in Athens come from a new building phase within a house to the east of the Library of Patainos (Metcalf 2001: 126).
42. In 732, the thema of Aigaion Pelagos was split into the three smaller themes of Kibyrrhaiotai, Samos, and Aigaion Pelagos. A *strategos* of Kibyrrhaiotai is already attested for 732 by Theophanes Confessor, *Chronographia* 410.
43. The late eighth- or early ninth-century seal of another *strategos* of Hellas named Sisinnios was found in Palatitsia (prefecture of Imathia), in Central Macedonia (Kyriakidis 1941; Moschopoulos 2004: 138, who believes that to be Sissinios Triphylles, known as *strategos* of Thrace in 799).
44. Konstantopoulos 1906: 64; Zacos and Veglery 1972: 647, 985, 1300, 1395–6, and 1426; Curta 2004b: 184 no. 68. See also Konstantakopoulou 1985: 159–62. The city eparch may have been the official whose good will the usurper Artavasdus, besieged in Constantinople, was trying to win with bribes, a portion of which survived in the form of a hoard of silver coins struck for that usurper and found in 1891 in Thessaloniki. See Szemiothowa 1961; Metcalf 1963: 283.
45. Some turmarchs seem to have been important individuals, such as a certain Theophylact who bore the same title of *protospatharios* as two contemporary *strategoi* of Peloponnesos. The seal of a turmarch of Hellas named Leo was found in Constantinople, and it is quite possible that he was an officer of the navy stationed in Hellas (Likhachev 1991: 52–3; for turmarchs, see also Lounghis 2001: 415–16).
46. Another *kourator* named Leo appears on a late seventh- or eighth-century seal from the collection of the Byzantine Museum in Athens (Zikos 1977: 83–4). No place or provincial name is mentioned on the seal, but if this was a local official, then his seal may further substantiate the idea of imperial estates in Hellas.
47. This Paul is most probably the Monothelite archbishop deposed by Pope Martin I in 649 (Petit 1900–1901: 213). Many more archbishops of Thessalonica are mentioned on late eighth- and early ninth-century seals (Zacos and Veglery 1972: 962 and 978; Curta 2004b: 184 no. 82 and 189 no. 173).
48. John's predecessor was Theocharistos, whose death in 702 is mentioned in another graffito.
49. If this is indeed Nikopolis in Epirus, then the archbishop must certainly have resided outside that region.

50. According to Anagnostakis 1997: 319 and n. 94, Orobe is the name of a town in Anatolia.
51. According to Ivanova 1995a: 191, the Drugubites lived to the west of Thessalonica, around Veroia.
52. There is no basis for the claim that Theodore, who allegedly taught in Athens, was brought to Italy by Constans II in 651 or 652 (Savvidis 1987–1989: 101).
53. That Willbald travelled directly from Sicily to Monemvasia is a clear indication that in the early eighth century, in order to reach Constantinople from the western provinces, one needed to circumnavigate Peloponnesos (Kalligas 1990: 42; McCormick 2001: 502–8).
54. There is no reason to assume that the evidence of the *Life of St. Willibald* could be dimissed on the basis of its author being 'ignorant' (Zakythinos 1945: 20).
55. The first to notice the importance of this source for the question of the Avar presence in Greece were Kollautz and Miyakawa 1970: 282.
56. The Avar episode appears in two eleventh-century manuscripts, one from Vienna, the other from Moscow. According to both, the Avar prisoners were captured in the provinces (*eparchiai*) of Dyrrachium and Athens (Vasil'ev 1898: 416; Capaldo 1983: 13; Olajos 1994: 107–8; Papadimitriou 2004: 173–4; Curta 2004a: 530–2). For Avars speaking Slavic, see Curta 2004b: 143–4.
57. Nor is it possible to link this episode to the memories of Greek refugees from Peloponnesos, whom Evagrius allegedly met in Sicily (Stallman 1986: 273; Falkenhausen 1995: 361).
58. Most analogues point to assemblages of the so-called 'Komani culture' excavated in Macedonia, although good parallels may also be found among finds from Hungary dated to the Middle Avar period (630/650–700) (Malenko 1985: 291–3 and pl. 21.1–5; Kovrig 1963: 24, 55, and 56 with pls 16.1–2, 41.9 and 42–3).
59. The dating of most other churches in Greece said to be Dark-Age foundations must be regarded with suspicion, given that it is based exclusively on stylistic analysis and on analogues with well-dated monuments outside Greece. Such is the case of St John Riganas in Marton (near Aitolikon); the basilica at Mastron near Katochi (Aitoloakarnania); St Demetrios *Katsouri* in Plesioi near Arta; the church in Ano Epidavros (Argolis); St Cosmas and St Panteleimon on Kythera; St Nicholas on the islet of Prasoudi at the entrance into the Bay of Igoumenitsa; the three-aisled cemetery basilica outside the walls of Abdera; and the small basilica to the west of Polianthon near Komotini (prefecture of Rodopi) (Bouras 2006: 62 and 64; Vokotopoulos 1992: 181; Lampropoulou et al. 2001: 206–10; Avramea 1997: 101; Vasilikou 2004; Bakirtzis 1989: 45 and 48).
60. The earliest instance of deposition of one-handled jugs in graves,

signalling a new rite of funeral offering, is in the cemetery inside and around the basilica discovered in Stamata (Attika), but the practice is also attested in Sicily (Gkini-Tsophopoulou and Chalkia 2003: 755–7; Vroom 2003: 139 and 141; Puglisi and Sardella 1998: 779).

61. The strap end from grave 1 has good analogues in late eighth-century cemeteries in Slovakia and Austria. Buckles similar to that from grave 3 are known from Corinth (Davidson 1952: pl. 114.2217–18).

62. The urn in grave 19, which is equally decorated with vertical incisions, produced a melon-seed-shaped bead of a late seventh-century date (Vida and Völling 2000: pl. 13.2).

63. A seventh-century stone mould for the casting of similar earrings is known from Ruvo di Puglia in southern Italy (Baldini Lippolis 1999: 236 fig. 78). On the other hand, somewhat similar earrings have been found in tenth-century burial assemblages in Hungary (Schlunk 1940: 44 and 46; Fodor 1996: 323–4 with 323 fig. 1).

64. In the absence of any securely dated artefacts, both the beginning and the end of other, possibly Dark-Age cemeteries in Greece will remain unknown. This is particularly true for the cemeteries excavated in Meropi and Paliopyrgos (Epirus) near the Greek–Albanian border (Andreou 1980, 1983, and 1987). According to Ilias Andreou, at least some of the graves in both cemeteries must be dated between the seventh and the tenth century, but not a single artefact has been published to allow the verification of that conclusion. For two undoubtedly early medieval cemeteries of northern Thessaly, see Deriziotis and Kougioumtzoglu 2004.

65. Several seals of eighth-century *strategoi* of Kephallenia are known that ante-date the earliest mention of the theme in written sources.

66. The campaign is also mentioned by Michael the Syrian and the thirteenth-century chronicle of Gregory Barhebraeus, who adds that Staurakios left a garrison in the 'country of Peloponnesos'. According to Barhebraeus, those conquered by Staurakios were 'Arabs' (perhaps 'Avars'), not Slavs (Gregory Abū'l-Faraj Bar Hebraeus, *Chronography* 120; Olajos 1998; Oikonomides 1999–2000).

67. The letter narrating the events is the last document to mention an eparch of Thessalonike and the first one to mention the Hagia Sophia church in that same city (Cheynet and Flusin 1990: 198, 201 with n. 29, and 211 with n. 60).

68. Slavic *archontes* were apparently among the 'western commanders' whom Emperor Leo III ordered in 718 to assist in the suppression of the usurpation of Gregory-Tiberius in Sicily (Theophanes Confessor, Chronographia 398; Živković 2002b).

CHAPTER 5

Revival and expansion (c. 800 to c. 900)

'Nikephoros was holding the scepter of the Romans, and these Slavs who were in the province of Peloponnesus decided to revolt.' They first attacked their Greek neighbours, whose settlements they plundered, and then laid siege to the city of Patras, 'having with them African Saracens also'. Shortage of both food and water persuaded the inhabitants of Patras to consider the option of surrender. However, before doing so, they decided to try one more thing. Since the leaders of the city (*archontes*) had already informed the military governor (*strategos*), who at that time was in Corinth, about the attack of the Slavs, the Patraeans sent a scout 'to the eastern side of the mountains' in order to see if the military governor was indeed coming to their rescue. If he were to see the troops of the military governor approaching, the scout was to return to the city and dip his standard, but if not, he was to hold the standard straight, 'so they might for the future not expect the military governor to come'. The scout did not see anyone coming and was about to return to Patras with the standard erect when, through the intercession of St Andrew, God made his horse slip and the rider fell off, in the process dipping the standard. Emboldened by what they took to be good news, the Patraeans attempted a sortie against the Slavs. At this point, they saw St Andrew, 'mounted upon a horse and charging upon the barbarians', whom he routed and scattered and drove away from the city. Those Slavs who witnessed this terrible attack were so shocked and terrified that they immediately sought refuge in the very church dedicated to the saint, which apparently stood just outside the city walls. The military governor finally made his appearance three days later, and upon learning what had happened, immediately reported everything in detail to the Emperor.

> The emperor, learning these things, gave orders to this effect: 'Since the rout and total victory were achieved by the apostle, it is our duty to render to him the whole expeditionary force of the foe and the booty and the spoils.' And he ordained that the foemen themselves,

with all their families and relations and all who belonged to them, and all their property as well, should be set apart for the temple of the apostle in the metropolis of Patras, where the first-called and disciple of Christ had performed this exploit in the contest; and he issued a bull concerning these matters in that same metropolis.[1]

Thus described Emperor Constantine Porphyrogennetos in the mid-tenth century the way in which 'the Slavs were put in servitude and subjection to the church of Patras', an event that took place more than one hundred years earlier, in the reign of Nikephoros I (802–811). It has long been recognised that this account is in fact based on the oral, local tradition devoted to St Andrew.[2] St Andrew on horseback charging the Slavs is an image strikingly similar to that of the angel assisting Judas Maccabeus and his warriors against Lysis (II Maccabees 11:8; Turlej 1999: 398). Some have noticed similarities between the account in the *On the Administration of the Empire* and the information culled from the *Chronicle of Monemvasia*, as well as from a synodal letter of 1084 written by Patriarch Nicholas III the Grammarian for Emperor Alexios I Komnenos. The story, therefore, whether true or not, is not a figment of Emperor Constantine's imagination. Nor did he learn about it directly from some oral source. Instead, he must have had access to a written version of the story, which was also available to the author of the *Chronicle of Monemvasia* and to Patriarch Nicholas III (Kresten 1977; Belke 1996; Turlej 1998: 467). That written source was no other than the bull of Nikephoros I. However, a detailed, comparative study of Emperor Constantine's account and of other sources pertaining to the revolt of the Slavs around Patras leads to the conclusion that in fact Emperor Nikephoros I issued not one, but two consecutive bulls for Patras (Belke 1996: 8–9). The first one was issued in late 805 or early 806, and appears to have dealt with the rebuilding of the city or the city's walls; the elevation of the see of Patras to metropolitan rank; and the subordination of three bishoprics (Lakedaimon, Korone, and Methone) to the metropolitan of Patras (Kislinger 2001: 47–8). Rather than an attempt to convert the local barbarians to Christianity, the decision to raise the bishop of Patras to the rank of metropolitan may have been a response to the demographic growth in the area, itself caused by the transfer of population from other parts of the Empire. According to the *Chronicle of Monemvasia*, Lakedaimon, one of the suffragan sees of Patras, was repopulated with mixed people – 'Kaperoi, Thrakesians, Armenians, and others from different places and cities' (Kislinger 2001: 203). Paul Lemerle has advanced the idea of 'Kapheroi' being the Greek form of the Arab word *kafir*, 'apostate', which referred derogatorily to Arabs converted to Christianity, in other words, Muslims from the eastern provinces of the Empire who had accepted baptism (Lemerle 1963a: 20 with n. 28; Huxley 1977: 107 calls them 'akritic Moslems'). Thrakesians and Armenians were inhabitants of the Anatolian themes of Thrakesion and Armeniakon, respectively. If this interpretation is correct, then Emperor Nikephoros' first bull of 805 or 806 may have been an indirect recognition of the dramatic changes taking place in the demographic configuration of the theme of Peloponnesos, only a couple of decades after its implementation, as a consequence of the transfer of population from the central and eastern provinces of the Empire. Perhaps as a result of those changes, especially the presence of settlers who may have been drafted from military families and encroached onto their lands, the Slavs revolted in 807 or 808. They attacked the 'Greek' settlements and then put Patras under siege.[3] The revolt was quelled, and following that, Emperor Nikephoros issued a second bull – the one mentioned by Emperor Constantine in his account – which spelled out the details of the subordination of the defeated Slavs to the Church of Patras, as well as their obligations. They were supposed now to maintain 'like hostages the military governors and the imperial agents and all the envoys sent from foreign nations' and to collect 'the necessary funds' for covering the lodging and the meals of such high-ranking visitors 'by apportionment and subscription among their unit' (Constantine Porpyhrogennetos, *On the Administration of the Empire* 49; see Litavrin 1985: 1350–1, who believes that the Slavs had military obligations before their revolt; see also Anagnostakis and Lampropoulou 2001: 36–44, who argue that the relatively lenient obligations imposed on the Slavs derived from their decision to seek sanctuary in the Church of St Andrew).[4]

It is tempting to relate the arrival of the new settlers from the central and eastern provinces of the Empire to the sudden appearance of Impressed White Wares (also known as Glaze White Ware II) on several sites in Peloponnesos, at Argos, Corinth, as well as Sparta (Lakedaimon). Such wares were produced in the environs of Constantinople and distributed all across the Aegean, in continental Greece, as well as on the islands, with a cluster of finds around the Argolid Bay (Armstrong 2001: 58 and fig. 6.1; Megaw and Jones 1983: 242–3).[5] Some have associated the appearance of Impressed White Wares in Lakedaimon with the city's new (or re)foundation in the early ninth century, and have gone as far as to regard the use of table wares produced in Constantinople as a 'physical manifestation of the cultural aspect of the rehellenization of southern Greece' (Armstrong 2001: 64). Leaving aside the dubious assumption that Constantinopolitan table wares were used only by speakers of Greek, the chronology of the Impressed White Wares currently lacks the precision necessary for drawing such conclusions. There is nothing in the way of assigning a later date to the Impressed White Wares of Sparta, perhaps during the late ninth or even the tenth century.[6] So far, there are no archaeological correlates of the demographic and ethnic changes taking place in southern Greece during the first half of the century.[7] The excavation of a Byzantine monastery at Pseira, in Crete, has produced fragments of plain glazed wares (chafing dishes) dated to the late eighth and early ninth century (Poulou-Papadimitriou 2001: 239 and 253 fig. 9).[8] No such wares are so far known from any site in the Peloponnesos. At Corinth, there are no White Wares for the entire ninth century, as imports of such table wares from Constantinople resumed only after the mid-tenth century (Sanders 2003a: 37).[9]

It has recently been affirmed that a trade route from the Adriatic and Italy opened around 830 through the Gulf of Corinth and that from this moment onwards it became a regular point of passage for travellers heading north to Constantinople. In support of such a contention, the 'unmistakable refurbishing of older structures in Corinth' is cited, which is dated to 'the tenth and possibly ninth centuries' (McCormick 2001: 535–6). As far as the ninth century is concerned, the evidence in question is simply missing. No buildings of any significance have so far been found in Corinth which could be dated to the ninth century. It is not known where were the headquarters of the *strategos* of Peloponnesos, where the cathedral of the local metropolitan (Sanders 2002: 64–50). On the other hand, the numismatic evidence of single finds of copper coins from Corinth shows a surge during the reign of Emperor Theophilos (829–842), for which no fewer than 161 coins are known, in sharp contrast to only 6 from the previous reign of Michael II (820–829) and only 23 from the subsequent reign of Michael III (842–867) (Penna 1996: 273; Metcalf 2001: 114 [with only 157 coins struck for Theophilos]; Sanders 2002: 649 [with only 2 coins struck for Michael II and 18 for Michael III] and 2003b: 390). In addition, a hoard of six solidi is known from Corinth, with the latest coin struck between 830 and 840.[10] Folles minted for Theophilos are also known from Sparta and Naupaktos (Penna 1996: 245; Konstantinos 1981).[11] Since the north Italian fairs, especially those of Piacenza, grew dramatically during the ninth century, the monetary surge has been interpreted as evidence of the development of trade routes from Italy across the Isthmus (Metcalf 1979: 19–20 and 2001: 115). Others have gone as far as to suggest that the area of the Roman Forum in Corinth, in which no structures were built in the ninth century, but which produced large numbers of ninth-century coins, operated as the site of a fair (Sanders 2000: 165 and 2002: 650). If so, it is remarkable that besides coins, no other evidence of trade was found in the area, not even pottery presumably of Italian origin.[12] Instead, ceramic finds from Corinth strongly suggest that commercial contacts between the city and the Aegean and Adriatic seas were drastically curtailed by Arab fleets from Crete, Africa, and Sicily.

Crete was occupied in the 820s by a group of exiled Spanish Arabs, who had settled in Egypt under the leadership of Abū Hafs (Christides 1984: 85–6; Malamut 1988: 72–7). During the following decades, the emirate became a launching pad for a number of devastating raids on the Aegean islands (Savvidis 1993: 376 and 2000: 323). Cretan Arabs often competed for raiding territories with Muslim pirates from Africa. During the 820s, African pirates attacked the region of the Ambrakian Bay, as well as Aigina and Lesbos (for the Ambrakian Bay, see Constantine Akropolites, *Life of St. Barbaros* 3; Da Costa-Louillet 1961: 211; Chrysos 1997: 185; for Aigina, see the *Life of St. Athanasia of Aigina* 1; *Life of St. Theodora of Thessalonike* 3 and 6; see also Setton 1954: 313; Koder 1998: 76 [with a later dating to 840]; Pennas 2004: 16). According to Emperor Constantine Porphyrogennetos, African pirates had already visited the region of Patras in the early 800s, when they allied themselves to the local, Slavic rebels (*On the Administration of the Empire* 49).[13] In Peloponnesos, Emperor Nikephoros I's success against those rebels was short-lived. The Slavs revolted again 'in the days of the emperor Theophilos and his son Michael, and became independent and enslaved and pillaged and burned and stole' (*On the Administration of the Empire* 50). At some point after 842, during the first years of Michael III's reign, the *strategos* of Peloponnesos, *protospatharios* Theoktistos Bryennios, launched a major expedition against the rebels with a large army combining the troops of Thrace, Macedonia, 'and the rest of the western provinces'. Theoktistos managed to defeat and subdue the Slavs 'and other insubordinates of the province of Peloponnesos', except two groups, the Ezeritai and the Milingoi in the south.[14] A second expedition forced them to move from the plain of Sparta onto the slopes of the neighbouring Taigetos and Parnon Mountains.[15] Theoktistos imposed on both groups the payment of tribute, 60 solidi for the Milingoi and 300 solidi for the Ezeritai (*On the Administration of the Empire* 50; Ditten 1993: 250–2).[16]

Theoktistos' expeditions must have been the occasion for a significant concentration of troops in Corinth shortly before and after the death of Emperor Theophilos in 842. It may therefore be possible to explain the monetary surge in Corinth by means of the presence for a few years of thematic troops from Thrace, Macedonia, and other parts of the Empire, in much the same way as seventh- and eighth-century monetary surges in Athens have been explained (see Chapter 4). Moreover, out of twenty-three coins struck for Michael III and found in Corinth, sixteen are from a western mint, which suggests that some of the troops Theoktistos may have employed for his second expedition were indeed from the 'western provinces', namely from Byzantine Italy (Penna 1996: 273). The idea that the army and not trade was responsible for the sudden injection of copper into the local market in Corinth is further supported by the fact that so far no coins of Michael III are known from any site in Peloponnesos except Corinth, while coins of Theophilos have been found in Sparta (the region of intense fighting with the Milingoi and the Ezeritai), but nowhere else in Peloponnesos.

In Athens, the number of coins struck for the Emperors Michael II, Theophilos, and Michael III is comparatively small,[17] which suggests that in contrast to Peloponnesos, early ninth-century Hellas was a more peaceful province, which did not require the presence of large numbers of troops. All the meagre information we have about Athens during the early ninth century confirms this conclusion. In the early ninth century, the metropolis of Athens received its first suffragan sees, one of which was Skyros (Hunger 1990: 51). In 807, Theophano, an Athenian and a relative of Empress Irene (herself a member or a relative of the Athenian family Sarantapechoi), married Staurakios (Browning 1984: 301). A graffito on a column of the Parthenon refers to a *strategos* of Hellas names Leo Kotzes, who died in Athens in 848 and was probably buried on the Acropolis (Kazanaki-Lappa 2000: 204). A number of stone-lined graves, some with lids of marble slabs, have been found in a cemetery excavated around the ruined basilica at Olympos near Laurion. The associated artefacts – a buckle with rectangular plate and animal decoration, segmented glass beads and bronze earrings – point to a date between the late eighth and the first half of the tenth century, but the pottery found in those graves consists of one-handled jars with trefoiled mouths, as well as simple pitchers, all wheel-made and not unlike those found in the seventh-century cemetery around the Church of St Dionysios the Areopagite in Athens (Kotzias 1952: 122–4). Outside Attica, most analogues for the belt buckle with rectangular plate from Olympos are known from sites in northern and northwestern Greece (Kourenta-Raptaki et al. 1994: 117 and 116 fig. 20 with pl. 48 [Thebes]; Pennas 1973–1974: 843 and 844 fig. 1 [Philippi]; Papanikola-Bakirtzis 2002: 393 no. 482 [Servia near Kozani]; Mastrokostas 1971: 186–7 with 188 fig. 4–5 [Drymos near Vonitsa]; Symeonoglou 1985: pl. 103δ [Ithaka]; for another buckle from Attika, see Lazaridis 1960: 69 and pl. 57γ; for this type of belt buckles, see Pletn'ov 2005).

In Thebes, the series of medieval coin finds begins with six folles and a solidus struck for Emperor Theophilos (Galani-Krikou 1998b: 153). The seal of the first known bishop of Thebes has also been dated to the first half of the ninth century (Dunn 1995: 757). An early ninth-century inscription found to the north, in Thessaly, mentions another local bishop named Nikon and his see of Kaisareia (Velenis 1995). A renewed or new occupation of several sites in western Macedonia is attested by field surveys in the prefecture of Grevena, which produced ninth- and tenth-century pottery (Rosser 2005: 281).[18] Judging from the existing evidence, the roads going across Boeotia and Thessaly from north to south were relatively safe. In 833, Gregory of Dekapolis travelled overland from Thessalonike to Corinth, where he boarded a ship to take him to Reggio and then to Rome (Ignatios the Deacon, *Life of St. Gregory of Dekapolis* 23; for the date, see Tsorbazoglou 2001: 127).[19] He had much more trouble moving across the Via Egnatia between Chrysoupolis and Thessalonike. According to his biography written by Ignatios the Deacon around 855, at the crossing of a river, most probably the Strymon, Gregory encountered Sclavene bandits on small boats, who used to prey on commercial ships and occasional travellers (Ignatios the Deacon, *Life of St. Gregory of Dekapolis* 21).[20] A few years later, a *protokankellarios* and deputy *strategos* of Thessalonike travelled in the opposite direction (from Thessalonike to Constantinople) in the company of a monk named Anastasios. They went through 'difficult and terrible places', and had to embark at Maroneia in order to continue their trip by sea, despite the threat of Arab pirates (Ignatios the Deacon, *Life of St. Gregory of Dekapolis* 52; see Belke 2002: 58). Insecurity in the area was increased by Bulgar raids into Thrace in

812 or 813. It is most probably at this time that a newly founded fort at Didymoteichon was sacked. The conquerors carried as a trophy to Pliska, in northeastern Bulgaria, an inscription on a fragment of marble column mentioning the name of the fort (Giannopoulos 1975: 11–12; Asdracha and Bakirtzis 1980: 264).[21] At the beginning of the reign of Presian (836–852), another Bulgar army crossed the Rhodope Mountains into the region along the Aegean coast, as attested by a stone inscription found in Philippi. The purpose of the expedition is not clear, but the Bulgars encountered the Smoliani, a tribe on the lower course of the Nestos river, near the present-day Greek–Bulgarian border (Beshevliev 1963: 164–5; Petkov 2008: 12–13).[22] At some point during his longer sojourn in Thessalonike between 835 and 841, Gregory of Dekapolis left the city together with a young disciple and went to a *Sklavinia* in the hinterland. He returned quickly after foreseeing a great deal of bloodshed and unrest, which would be caused, for unknown reasons, by the leader (exarch) of the *Sklavinia* (Ignatios the Deacon, *Life of St. Gregory of Dekapolis* 49; Tsorbazoglou 2001: 128). Francis Dvornik believed that the *Sklavinia* in question was the territory of the Drugubites, who lived in the environs of Veroia (Dvornik 1926: 36). If so, the exarch who caused all the trouble may have been an *archon* like Peter, whose ninth-century seal mentions the rank of imperial *spatharios*, an indication that he owed his position of power to the Emperor (Kyriaki-Wassiliou 2004: 24; see also Tsorbazoglou 2001: 129, who argues against the location of the Sklavinia as proposed by Tsaras 1985). He may thus have had a position very similar to that of Methodius, the future bishop of Moravia, who is known to have been the *archon* of a *Sklavinia* prior to entering, in 850, the monastery on Mount Olympos in Bithynia (*Life of Methodius* 3; Nasledova 1956: 87).[23] Whether or not the *Sklavinia* which Gregory of Dekapolis was about to visit was indeed that of the Drugubites, an *archon* of Thessalonike mentioned on a ninth- or tenth-century seal as having the rank of imperial *strator* may well have been the ruler of a *Sklavinia* in the hinterland of the city, for throughout the ninth and tenth century, the region of Thessalonike was ruled by a *strategos*, not an *archon* (Koltsida-Makri 2000: 245 and 253).

The military threat from Bulgaria led to the rapid multiplication of themes in northern Greece: Macedonia shortly before 802, Strymon shortly before 809, and Thessalonike at some point between 796 and 811 (for Thessalonike, see Koltsida-Makri 2000: 245; for Macedonia, see Stavridou-Zafraka 1998; for Strymon, see

Karagiannopoulos 1989: 23–4; Stavridou-Zafraka 1995b). Most numerous after seals of the *kommerkiarioi* of Thessalonike are those of the military governors (*strategoi*) of the theme.[24] The archbishops of Thessalonike occupied a prominent position in the hierarchy of the church.[25] Joseph the Studite, the brother of Theodore who was exiled to Thessalonike in the 790s, twice served as archbishop (807–809 and 812–815; Petit 1900–1901: 216). Leo the Mathematician was also metropolitan of Thessalonike between 840 and 843.[26] Like him, the archbishop in office at the time when Gregory of Dekapolis visited the city must have been an iconoclast. Perhaps in an attempt to emphasise the misery brought about by iconoclasm, Ignatios the Deacon describes the city as infested by snakes, with corpses lying by the roadside and corrupt clerics stealing from the food reserved for the poor (Ignatios the Deacon, *Life of St. Gregory of Dekapolis* 38, 40, and 47; Mango 1985: 639).[27] Initially, at least, Gregory seems to have experienced some hard times, often lacking the basic means of subsistence. He lived in a cell by the Church of St Menas, which Ignatios located near the tomb of St David, outside the city walls (Ignatios the Deacon, *Life of St. Gregory of Dekapolis* 36 and 55; Makris 1997: 119; for the life of Gregory of Dekapolis in Thessalonike, see also Yannopoulos 1993a: 71–2). When he arrived in Thessalonike in 833, Gregory was received by the head of a community of hermits, named Mark (Ignatios the Deacon, *Life of St. Gregory of Dekapolis* 22). It remains unclear whether the said hermits lived inside or outside the walls. However, no fewer than five monasteries existed inside the city throughout the ninth century (Varinlioğlu 2005: 197).[28] No monumental buildings still standing are known for this period in Thessalonike. The chapel of St Euthymios attached to the basilica of St Demetrios is believed to have been erected shortly before or, more probably, after 900 (Velenis 2003: 14; for a much later date [1083], see Glavinas 2001).[29] A small funerary chapel was excavated at 90 Kassandrou Street; it was built on top of the ruins of a late antique house, and its dating to the ninth century was established only on the basis of the frescoes on its walls (Makropoulou and Tzitzimpase 1993: 361–4). The same is true for the church excavated between 1933 and 1936 at the corner of Egnatia and Dikasterion streets by Dimitrios Evangelidis, which has been dated to the first half of the ninth century on the basis of remains of frescoes (believed to be typical for the iconoclastic period) and interpreted as the *katholikon* of the Monastery of John the Baptist (Leontia), which was, however, founded only in the tenth century (Evangelidis 1937; Theocharidis 1978; Giros 1992: 431–2). There were several monasteries in the hinterland of the city, one of which was founded by St Euthymios the Younger (823/4–898), a monk from Mount Olympus in Bithynia. He spent some time at Mount Athos (859–864), before founding the Monastery of St Andrew in Peristera in 871 (Basil of Thessalonike, *Life of St. Euthymios the Younger* 7 and 22).[30] He came to Thessalonike in 864 to attend the funeral of his spiritual father, Abbot Theodore, and remained for four years in the city, where he was ordained deacon by Archbishop Theodore, the same prelate who appointed Theopista, St Theodora's daughter, as abbess of the convent of St Stephen in Thessalonike (Basil of Thessalonike, *Life of St. Euthymios the Younger* 24; *Life of St. Theodora of Thessalonike* 37; see Paschalidis 1991: 261–2; Tsorbazoglou 2001: 134 with n. 1). After returning to Athos for a while, he joined a number of monks seeking refuge from the Arab depredations first in Siderokausia on the Chalkidike, then in Euthymios' new foundation at Peristera, near modern Vrastama in the prefecture of Chalkidiki (Basil of Thessalonike, *Life of St. Euthymios the Younger* 25–7). According to Basil, the author of the *vita* of Euthymios, the saint relied on the support of the local community for building his monastery, from donations of money for the rebuilding of the *katholikon* to farm animals, fields, and vineyards (Basil of Thessalonike, *Life of St. Euthymios the Younger* 29).

A disciple of St Euthymios named John Kolobos ('the Dwarf') established another monastery at Hierissos (Monastery of Kolobos). Meanwhile, on Mount Athos the number of hermits was apparently sufficiently large to require the intervention of the Emperor. A bull of Basil I, issued in June 883, drew distinction between Athonites living outside the monastery and those 'who have pitched their frugal tents there', an indication that hermits and cenobitic communities coexisted at that time on the mountain. The bull gave the Athonites freedom from the 'vexations' of imperial officials and prohibited private individuals, peasants, and shepherds from entering the area of the mountain (Morris 1996: 41–2).

The measures taken during the last years of Michael III's reign for the fortification of Thessalonike and its environs, perhaps in response to Arab raids in the northern Aegean, as well as the conversion of Prince Boris of Bulgaria to Christianity and the subsequent peace with the Empire, opened a period of relative stability and prosperity for the northern parts of Greece.[31] In 869, the papal envoys to Constantinople travelled by land across the western Balkans and arrived in Thessalonike, where they were greeted by the imperial *protospatharios* Eustathios, who escorted them all the way to Selymbria, along the Via Egnatia (Belke 2002: 58).[32] At some point between 880 and 912, Harun ibn Yahya made the trip without any escort in the opposite direction, from Constantinople to Thessalonica.[33] A flourishing trade across the frontier with Bulgaria may be responsible for the simultaneous appearance of *kommerkiarioi* in many of the cities along or close to the main rivers linking southern Bulgaria with northern Greece, the Vardar, the Strymon, and the Nestos (Oikonomides 1991: 247). In Thessalonike, the number of seals of *kommerkiarioi* is larger than that of any other seals, and most of them must be dated to the late ninth and early tenth century (Koltsida-Makri 2000: 251).[34] Two *kommerkiarioi* of Thessalonike named Kosmas and Staurakios, both imperial *spatharioi*, are known from ninth- and tenth-century seals. They may well be the two 'greedy' merchants who in 893, with the tacit approval of Emperor Leo VI, moved to Thessalonike the Constantinopolitan trade with the Bulgarians, no doubt in order to tax it to their own advantage, a measure which sparked a four-year war between Symeon of Bulgaria and Emperor Leo VI (Oikonomides 1991: 247, who noted that Kosmas and Staurakios were from Hellas; Magdalino 1990, who attributes the measure to Emperor Leo's devotion to St Demetrius, the patron saint of Thessalonike).[35] It is important to note that no mention exists of hostilities or military operations in northern Greece. Symeon neither took advantage of the sack of Thessalonike by the fleet of Leo of Tripoli, nor tried to push the frontier with Byzantium closer to that great city of Macedonia.[36]

The recovery and burgeoning prosperity of the region during the last three decades of the ninth century is well illustrated in the archaeological record. A church was built in the late ninth century in the ruins of an early Byzantine basilica in Kolchis in the prefecture of Kilkis (Kissas 1988: 211). At Chrysoupolis (Kaledes near Amphipolis, prefecture of Serrai), fragments of Glazed White Wares II indicate commercial contacts with Constantinople beginning shortly before or after 900 (Dunn 1999: 406; for the identification of Chrysoupolis with Kaledes, see Dunn 1990: 327–9). There is clear evidence of a ninth-century re-occupation of Philippi.[37] The baptistery discovered to the east of the modern museum was turned into a three-aisled basilica, while a portion of an ancient, ruined house excavated only 22m from the Via Egnatia was turned into a dwelling with a kitchen, a lavatory, and storehouses (Kourkoutidou-Nikolaidou 1989: 467 and 1995: 174–5; Gounaris and Velenis 1989:

456–7 and 1990: 480–1). The French excavations of the eastern wing of the so-called 'House of the Beasts' (*Maison des Fauves*) in the southwestern part of the city revealed the existence of a house of circular form, whose contour was identified by means of twenty-one post holes (Provost and Foschia 2002: 114–15). Farther to the east, a large cemetery beginning in the ninth century was excavated outside the western walls of the abandoned city of Abdera (Bakirtzis 1989: 45). The graves in Abdera may be dated to the ninth century on the basis of the associated bronze beads, the best analogues of which have been found in grave 89 in Kiulevcha (northeastern Bulgaria) in association with a Carolingian disc-brooch (Bakirtzis 1994: 160 fig.; Văzharova 1976: 137 with 139 fig. 86.2). Later in the ninth or even the tenth century, an octagonal baptistery was built on the neighbouring Polystylon hill (n.a. 1994: 14).[38] At the entrance of the Lake Vistonis, a fish- and oyster-farm existed in the ninth and tenth century in Poroi, where excavations revealed the production of large quantities of shells, as well as of pottery used for the transportation of both fish and oysters (n.a. 1994: 18). On the southern shore of the lake, the excavation of a ruined church in Porto Lago produced three processional crosses made of iron and dated to the ninth century (Kourkoutidou-Nikolaou 1972).[39] Finally, two graves dug into a prehistoric barrow were excavated in 1999 at Spilaion (prefecture of Evros), across the Greek–Turkish border from Edirne (Touchais et al. 2000: 954; Triantaphyllos 1997: 628–9; 632 figs 13–14 [earrings and glass beads] and 15–16 [seal]). One of them produced two earrings with croissant-shaped pendants and glass beads, the other a seal belonging to the imperial *protospatharios* and Grand Logothete Marianos, Emperor Basil I's brother. While the seal can be precisely dated to 868/9, it also reveals the high status of the man, who was perhaps buried together with a letter or document bearing the seal of Marianos.[40]

The general atmosphere of stability does not seem to have been at all affected by sporadic raids by Arab pirates, such as the attacks of 840 and 860 on Lesbos or those of 879 on the islands in the northern Aegean by Arabs from the emirate of Crete (Niketas Magistros, *Life of Theoktiste of Lesbos* 18; Theophanes Continuatus, in Bekker 1838: 299–300; see also Koder 1998: 76).[41] The impact of Arab raiding on the Cyclades, as well as on the neighbouring islands of Evvoia and Samos, was much more serious. Under Emperor Basil I, the emir of Tarsos with a fleet of thirty ships attacked the Byzantine fortress of Euripos on Evvoia, dangerously close to Athens. The *strategos* of Hellas gathered men from the entire theme and successfully defended the city (Theophanes Continuatus, in Bekker 1838: 298–9; Setton 1954: 312). At that time, all the inhabitants of Aigina are said to have abandoned the island because of Arab depredations (*Life of St. Luke the Younger* 2).⁴² In 893, the Arabs destroyed three monasteries on Samos, while ruling over Patmos and exacting tribute from the inhabitants of Naxos (John Kaminiates, *The Capture of Thessaloniki* 70; Setton 1954: 313).⁴³ By 910, the island of Paros had fairly recently been abandoned because of the Arab raids (Niketas Magistros, *Life of Theoktiste of Lesbos* 4 and 9). Skyros and the Sporades do not appear to have suffered as much from Muslim attacks. A new episcopal church was erected in 895 inside the Byzantine fort on Skyros, as attested by an inscription mentioning the senior metropolitan of Athens and the local bishop. This is an example of the domed cross-in-square church, a building with two longitudinal walls with narrow openings supporting the dome, and the eastern arm of the cross forming the sanctuary together with the adjacent corner bays (Vokotopoulos 2000: 155; Bouras 2006: 70).⁴⁴ Some twenty-five ninth- to tenth-century churches of this type are known from Greece, but the most famous example of that type of architecture is the Church of the Virgin in Skripou (Orchomenos), in Boeotia (Fig. 5.1; Lazaridis 1973; Stikas 1975; Pallas 1990).⁴⁵ The founder is mentioned in no fewer than four inscriptions placed in different parts of the building. His name was Leo, and he was an imperial *protospatharios* and a member of the imperial household with a function connected to the Emperor's private fortune, perhaps a steward of the imperial domain (*kourator*). Given that the inscription on the northern façade gives the year of foundation as AM 6382 (873/4), the Emperor in question must have been Basil I, although Leo's long career must have begun under one of Basil's predecessors (Oikonomides 1994b: 482–3; Papalexandrou 1998: 130). At the end of that career, he apparently decided to relocate with his family to Boeotia, in order to claim his landholdings in the area of Orchomenos (Sotiriou 1931: 153–7; Megaw 1966: 23–4; Oikonomides 1994b). He wanted to make his grand intentions apparent, which explains the relatively large size of the church, the abundant sculptural decoration, the repetition of the name Leo in four separate inscriptions, and, last but not least, the commissioning of a scholar in Constantinople for a splendid epigram composed in archaic iambic trimeters for the inscription on the western wall (Oikonomides 1994b: 483–4; see Bouras 2006: 77, who complains about the meagre lighting of the

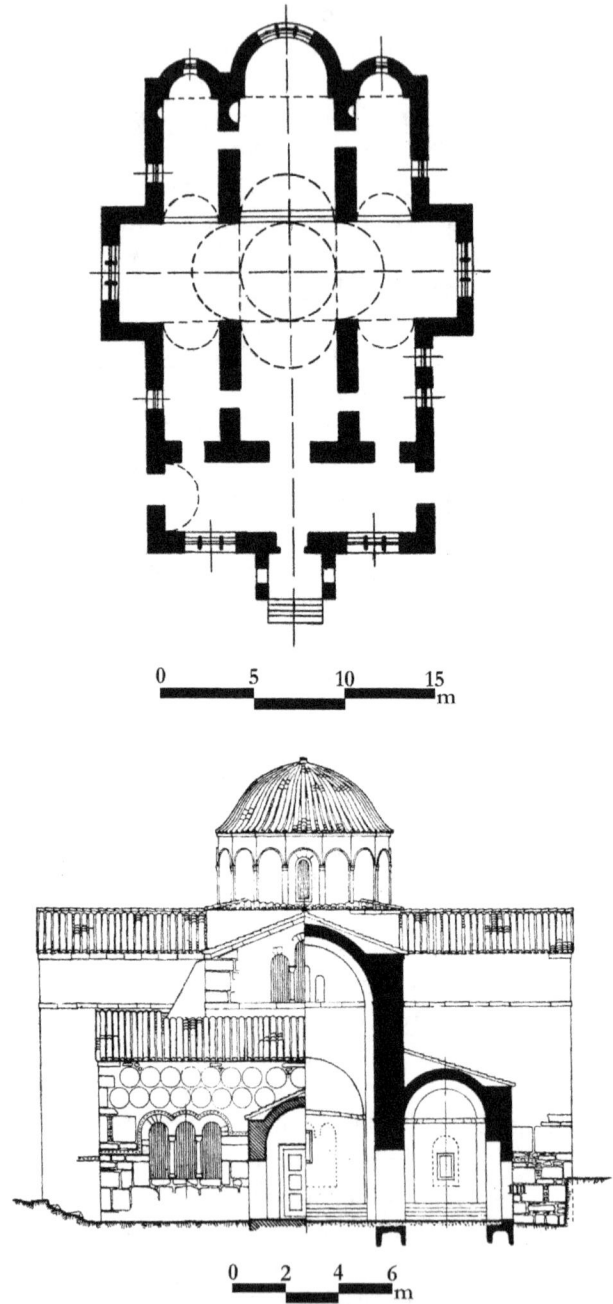

Figure 5.1 The Church of the Dormition of the Holy Virgin, Skripou (Orchomenos), Boeotia (873/4): plan and western end with cross-section (drawing by Hubert Megaw; after Sotiriou 1931: 122 fig. 3 and 124 fig. 5).

interior of the church and the supposedly clumsy carving of decorative reliefs as signs of the low level of technology available in Greece). The epigram explains that Leo was the owner of the fertile and well-watered land around the church, no doubt in the vicinity of the imperial estates (for which Leo may have served as *kourator*) in the region of Lake Kopais. Furthermore, the inscription on the southern façade mentions Patriarch Ignatios (847–858 and 867–877), most probably in an attempt to emphasise the political and religious affiliations of the founder, while at the same time pointing to his aspirations to a lifestyle typical of Constantinople. The walls of the church incorporate abundant ancient material taken from the ancient site at Orchomenos, but Skripou is also the earliest example of the use of large blocks of stone for the façade, a feature most typical of the architecture of tenth-century churches in Greece (Hadji-Minaglou 1994: 163–4).[46] The style of the architectural sculpture employed for the decoration of the church is an outstanding example of Constantinopolitan standards, but those responsible for its execution must have been the local carvers who had just finished working on the much smaller and slightly older Church of St Gregory the Theologian in Thebes, which, according to the dedicatory inscription, was built in 872 (Sotiriou 1924: 1–2, 2 figs 3–4).[47] The same craftsmen are believed to have been at work elsewhere in Boeotia and Evvoia (Megaw 1966: 18–19; Bouras 2006: 74). Skripou may therefore serve as evidence for the existence of a local workshop of stone carvers whose skills were apparently in high demand in the area in the 870s, a fact which in itself is a sign of relative prosperity.[48]

Domed, cross-in-square churches were also built in ninth-century Athens. The Church of the Prophet Elias at the Staropazaro near the Roman Agora in Athens, a monument otherwise known only from nineteenth-century drawings and engravings, has been rightly compared to the Church of the Virgin in Skripou (Bouras 2006: 80). Other churches in Athens, however, had a very different plan. Built on the northern slope of the Acropolis, the Church of St John Mangoutis, from which there survives only the dedicatory inscription with the year AM 6379 (870/1), was not a domed cross-in-square church, but a small, three-aisled, timber-roofed basilica (Kazanaki-Lappa 2000: 206; for the dedicatory inscription, see Konstantopoulos 1931: 253 with fig. 6).[49] The domed cross-in-square plan also appears in western Greece, for example in the Church of St Demetrios *Katsouri* in Plesioi near Arta, or in that of Episkopi in the prefecture of Evritania, now submerged by the waters of Lake

Kremasta (for St Demetrios *Katsouri*, see Vokotopoulos 1975: 56–69 and 181–3; Papadopoulou 2007: 25–8; for the church of Episkopi, see Orlandos 1961; Vokotopoulos 1975: 6–74 and 183).[50] If the use of the domed cross-in-square plan is to be associated in any way with the final establishment of Byzantine authority in any given region, it is tempting to attribute the appearance of churches of this type in western Greece to the creation, at some point between 880 and 899, of the theme of Nikopolis. Although a few ninth-century seals mention the archbishops of Nikopolis, it appears that that city was at the time abandoned and that the headquarters of the theme were in Naupaktos (Chrysos 1997: 187–8). No church, either of the timber-roofed or of the domed plan, is so far known from that city. In fact, none appears to have been built in southern Greece throughout the ninth century.[51] The absence of ninth-century buildings in Peloponnesos is at first glance surprising, given that the *Chronicle of Monemvasia* specifically links the ecclesiastical re-arrangements in Peloponnesos, especially the creation of a metropolis of Patras with three suffragan sees, to the conversion to Christianity of the local Slavs (Kislinger 2001: 202–3). Since at the council summoned by Photius in Constantinople in 879, Greece was represented by many metropolitans and bishops, the assumption is that revived sees, such as Naupaktos, or new ones, such as New Patras, had a primarily missionary function (Herrin 1973: 123). To be sure, local metropolitans came to play an important role in church politics. For example, the envoy of Patriarch Photios to Pope John VIII was Theodore, the metropolitan of Patras (Ganktzis et al. 1993: 473).[52] However, no metropolitan is known to have engaged in missionary activity. Among their suffragans, only St Peter of Argos is known for such an activity. He was born in Constantinople in 851 or 852 and went to Corinth when his brother Paul was appointed archbishop of that see by Patriarch Nicholas Mystikos, most probably during the latter's second term (912–925). Peter was then appointed bishop of Argos. His *vita*, which was perhaps written at some point after 927 by his successor, Bishop Constantine, mentions the destruction of property perpetrated by 'barbarians' in the eparchy of Argos. 'Barbarians', either the same or others, are said to have been persuaded by Peter's virtues to renounce the pagan faith of their ancestors and adopt Christianity. However, a prophecy just before Peter's death announced a three-year occupation of Peloponnesos by 'barbarians'. Those destroying houses in the region of Argos or subsequently converting to Christianity cannot therefore have been the local Slavs

(*Life of St. Peter of Argos* 13, 14, and 19; Vasiliev 1947: 176; Da Costa-Louillet 1961: 317 and 321–2).[53] Moreover, all new bishoprics in Peloponnesos were in the east or on the coast, away from the troubled areas of the interior (Dunn 1977: 78). There is therefore no link between the growth of church organisation in southern Greece and the supposed mission to convert the local Slavs.

Although no church has so far been found in Peloponnesos which could securely be dated to the ninth century, this was at the same time a period of great development of monasticism in southern Greece, particularly in the region of Patras. A monk attached to the Cathedral of St Andrew in that city received Basil (the future Emperor) with surprising honour when he came to Patras in c. 850 in the service of an imperial official named Theophilos. He later prophesised that Basil would become Emperor (Theophanes Continuatus, in Bekker 1838: 226). In 821 or 822, a monk named Niketas arrived at Karyoupoulis, where he subsequently wrote the *Life of St. Philaretos* (Etzeoglou 1988: 8–9). Before becoming bishop of Methone, Athanasios entered an unnamed monastery in Patras, of which he was also abbot, c. 850 (Vasiliev 1947: 188; Da Costa-Louillet 1961: 314). Just outside Patras, on Mount Klokova, ninth-century potsherds and architectural remains of rooms and a water tank have been associated with a monastic site (Katsaros 2001). Some scholars attribute this burst of monastic activity to iconodule refugees from other parts of the Empire (Lampropoulou et al. 1996: 99 and 2004: 90–1). There is, however, no record of any monk moving to Peloponnesos because of iconoclastic persecution. St Theodosius the Younger, an Athenian, established himself at some point after 920 in the hills of the province of Argos, where he lived as a hermit until his death (Lampropoulou 1994: 34; Lampropoulou et al. 1996: 82).[54] In 880, St Elias the Younger moved from Calabria to Sparta, where he found shelter in a church, perhaps in ruins, dedicated to the Unmercenary Saints Cosmas and Damian.[55] Together with his disciple Daniel he then went to Epirus, where he was arrested after being mistaken for an Arab spy. In 887, after being released, but before returning to Calabria, the two Italians went to Kerkyra, where St Elias predicted the election of a certain Demetrios from Reggio as local bishop, following 'the famous Pachomios' (*Life of St. Elias the Younger*, in Taibbi 1962: 42 and 44). When in 888 Calabria was attacked by Muslims, Elias and Daniel fled to Patras (*Life of St. Elias the Younger*, in Taibbi 1962: 56; Yannopoulos 1994: 198). St Elias Spelaiotes moved to the same city in c. 894. He lived for eight years in an abandoned tower on the outskirts of the city (Yannopoulos 1994: 198–9; Lampropoulou 1994: 32–3; see also Kourelis 2003: 148–9).[56]

The Arab marauders reached Peloponnesos as well. An Arab fleet from Crete under the renegade Photios attacked the western coast in 879, just one year before St Elias the Younger's first trip to Greece (Setton 1954: 312; Savvidis 1990: 52, 1991: 335, 1993: 374, and 2000: 333). A patrician named Niketas Ooryphas, then just a *droungarios*, was sent against the Arabs. From Constantinople, he sailed to Kenchreai, where he learned that the Muslims had ravaged Methone, Pylos, Patras, and the region around Corinth. He ordered his ships to be hauled in the middle of the night over the Isthmus of Corinth, from the Saronic to the Corinthian Gulf, and thus fell unexpectedly on the Muslim ships, which he destroyed (Theophanes Continuatus, in Bekker 1838: 300–2; Savvidis 1991: 335).[57] In 880, a fleet of 60 warships from Africa invaded Byzantine Italy, causing St Elias the Younger to leave for Sparta. They plundered and took captives as far as Kephallenia and Zante. The imperial admiral Basil Nasar was sent against them with a large fleet of triremes, biremes, and smaller vessels. He quickly reached Methone, but because of the desertion of some of his men, he was delayed by measures taken to restore discipline. Together with the *strategos* of Peloponnesos, John Kretikos, he attacked the Muslims, defeated them, and dedicated the captured ships to the church in Methone (Theophanes Continuatus, in Bekker 1838: 302–3; see also Setton 1954: 312; Savvidis 1990: 52 and 2000: 323).[58] When the Cretan emir Abdallah Umar II ibn Shuayub attempted to raid Peloponnesos, he was defeated by the local *strategos* Constantine Tessarakontapechys, without any help from the imperial navy (Savvidis 1990: 52 and 1993: 376). The attack must have taken place at the beginning of the reign of Leo VI, whose name is otherwise mentioned in an inscription from Corinth in relation to the building of a tower meant to signal by fire the attack of the 'bands of barbarians', most probably Arabs (Feissel and Philippidis-Braat 1985: 299–300; Rife 2008: 282–6 and 291–8, who identifies the optical telegraph in the inscription with the ruins of a watching tower on the Acrocorinth).

Since the Arab raids continued after 900, troops must have been stationed by then at key points around and across Peloponnesos. If its redating is correct, the inscription found during excavations in 1978 in the Tigani basilica which mentions a *komes* or officer of the fleet must be associated with the increased presence of the navy in southern Greece during the reign of Leo VI (Feissel and Philippidis-Braat 1985: 308; Avramea 1998: 56). This may also explain the presence in Corinth of a ninth-century seal of an *archon* of Dalmatia, given that the only possible connection between the two regions was by sea (Davidson 1952: 319; McCormick 2001: 534). On the other hand, in the war against the Arabs in Italy, including the siege and subsequent conquest of Taranto in 881, the Byzantines employed land troops from Peloponnesos, most probably recruited from among the local Slavs (Ditten 1993: 261–2). Ever since the expedition of Theoktistos Bryennios, a considerable number of troops must have been stationed in central and especially southern Greece, a region which therefore appears as highly militarised throughout the second half of the ninth century. However, with the exception of a spear and three arrow heads from Tiryns, in the hinterland of Argos, there is no archaeological support for the idea of such a heavy military presence (Kilian 1980: 283 and 286, 285 fig. 3.2–4, 8).[59] On the other hand, an unusually large number of copper coins struck for Leo VI have been found on many sites in central and southern Greece.[60] The largest number is that of Corinth (972 coins), more than three times the number of coins from the previous reign of Basil I (278 specimens; Sanders 2002: 649).[61] This is by far the largest number of coins for any emperor ruling between 600 and 900, and it is tempting to associate this massive injection of copper into the local market in Corinth with the presence of the military, much as in the case of the previous surge during the reign of Theophilos.

Nonetheless, the reign of Leo VI (886–912) also coincides with a significant expansion of the imperial domain in Peloponnesos. Shortly after the beginning of his reign, Leo sent a *protospatharios* named Zenobius to Naupaktos in order to take over the inheritance left for him by a very rich widow from Patras, Danielis (Theophanes Continuatus, in Bekker 1838: 321).[62] She had visited the Emperor in Constantinople, perhaps on the occasion of his coronation, and at her death, she left all her possessions to Leo. Zenobius was amazed at the quantity of money, gold, silver, and copper, in those possessions, as well as at the number of flocks and slaves. Danielis left eighty estates, for she owned 'a part of the Peloponnesos that was not small', over which she ruled almost like an empress (Theophanes Continuatus, in Bekker 1838: 319; Litavrin 2004: 22). The estates were apparently worked by slave labour, but Danielis appears to have run one or two workshops where the wool from the backs of her numerous sheep and the flax from her fields were made up into cloth and carpets and other woven goods (Runciman 1940: 427; Kourelis 2003: 138–9). While re-organising Danielis' estates after her death, Emperor Leo VI may have closed the workshops when sending the redundant slave population, which he previously freed from bondage, to the theme of Longobardia (Calabria), in order to repopulate a province previously devastated by Arab raids (Runciman 1940: 427; Turlej 1999: 393). It is perhaps under such circumstances that others, seeing that the conditions of Danielis' slaves had improved so dramatically, may have complained to the Emperor about the abuses of the metropolitan of Patras. At some point between 888 and 890, Leo issued a privilege 'containing a detailed account of what these same persons who are ascribed to the metropolitan are liable to provide, and forbidding him to exploit them or in any other way to hurt them unjustly at his whim' (Constantine Porphyrogennetos, *On the Administration of the Empire* 49; for the date, see Turlej 1999: 394).[63]

Leo's measures of freeing Danielis' slaves and legislating against the abuses of the metropolitan of Patras strongly suggest that during her lifetime Danielis had been able to amass relatively quickly a considerable wealth at the expense of less fortunate inhabitants of the region of Patras. She may even have had the support of the local metropolitan, who, in any case, seems to have taken advantage of the situation thus created to increase arbitrarily the obligations of his own subjects. Was Danielis a lady with power in local politics, the ninth-century equivalent of Akamiros, the *archon* of the Belegezites (see Chapter 4)? Some scholars believe so, and even regard her as an 'archontissa of a Peloponnesian Sklavinia in the process of peaceful and diplomatic absorption into the empire' (Ševčenko 1992: 192, reproducing the opinion of Hendy 1985: 207; see also Harvey 1989: 32; Jacoby 1991–1992: 458; for a critique of such claims, see Koutava-Delivoria 2001: 104).[64] To be sure, what we know about her amounts to more than Akamiros' intervention in the local politics of the theme of Hellas.[65] The mid-tenth century author of her story certainly implied that, if not the chief lady of the entire region of Patras, she definitely had grand plans and was just as well if not better connected in Constantinople than the *protospatharios* Leo, who at about the same time erected the Church of the Virgin in Skripou. According to the unknown continuator of Theophanes' *Chronographia*, Danielis first met Emperor Leo's father, Basil, in c. 850, when he came to Patras in the service of an imperial official named Theophilos or Theophilitzes.[66] Startled by the honour accorded to Basil by a local monk attached to the Church of St

Andrew, Danielis learned from him that Basil was destined to become Emperor soon. When Theophilos returned to Constantinople, Basil was forced by an illness to stay behind. Danielis took the opportunity to shower him with gifts of money and clothes, and even made him her son's spiritual brother, a gesture which led to the appointment of that son as *protospatharios* as soon as Basil became Emperor.[67] Danielis herself was loaded with honours and invited to come to Constantinople. She accepted the invitation and crossed the Gulf of Corinth by boat, and then travelled from Naupaktos by land. Because of her age, she is said to have moved in a litter carried by teams of slaves. In Constantinople she stayed in the Magnaura palace, where only visiting foreign princes or magnates could receive accommodation. As gifts for the Emperor she brought from Patras 300 young slaves, 100 of whom were eunuchs, 100 serving women, 100 linen garments dyed in kermes red (*sindonia*), 100 linen-and-wool cloths, 100 wool-free flax cloths, 100 other cloths of the finest woven thread, and many gold and silver vessels.[68] In addition, Danielis gave large estates in Peloponnesos to the Emperor, whom she regarded as her own son (and was accordingly treated as 'mother of the emperor'[69]). Around 880, Basil built a new church in the imperial palace. Danielis requested the dimensions of the building and ordered the manufacture of an enormous carpet with peacock-like patterns and precious stones sewn into it. She continued to send gifts to Constantinople every year after that until Basil's death in 886.

The story of Danielis is part of a tradition developed in the mid-tenth century in order to illustrate the prophecies about Basil's ascent to the imperial throne and to underscore 'Basil's moral integrity when, after his accession, he showed his gratitude to his earlier benefactors' (Rapp 1997: 305). As such, the story was modelled after old narrative patterns, resembling in minute details that of a widow named Kandaki in Pseudo-Kallisthenes' *Alexander Romance*, as well as the story of the queen of Sheba (I Kings 10:1–3; Anagnostakis 1989: 381–9). As a consequence, doubts have been raised about the authenticity of this story, especially since it was written down some seventy years after the events. However, if the account of Danielis' befriending Emperor Basil I was exaggerated, there is no reason to doubt that Basil's son Leo truly became the widow's heir. Emperor Constantine VII Porphyrogennetos' reference to his father's bull for Patras shows that there truly was an imperial concern with northwestern Peloponnesos under Leo VI, no doubt in connection with the disposition of Danielis' will in favour of the

Emperor. It is hard to imagine Danielis travelling all the way from Naupaktos to Constantinople in a litter, but there is no immediate reason to doubt that she could in fact have made that trip, given that the roads across Boeotia, Thessaly, Macedonia, and Thrace appear to have been relatively safe at the beginning of Basil I's reign (867–886).[70] The detailed description of the gifts Danielis brought to Constantinople suggests that the author of the account was familiar with high-quality cloths, although no indication of a textile industry exists for ninth-century Peloponnesos. Such evidence, however, is not missing for the tenth century, during which two industries related to fabrics are known to have flourished in Peloponnesos – parchment production and murex-shell purple-dye extraction (Constantine Porphyrogennetos, *On the Administration of the Empire* 52; Jacoby 1991–1992: 455–8; Kourelis 2003: 140–1). It is therefore possible that the unknown continuator of Theophanes' *Chronographia* projected into the past the realities of his own lifetime.[71] He may have exaggerated the number of slaves and estates which Danielis owned, but the intervention of Emperor Leo VI on the side of the subjects of the metropolitan of Patras – as reported some sixty years later by his son, Constantine VII Porphyrogennetos – shows that social inequality and bondage, even brutal exploitation were indeed harsh realities in the area in which Danielis is said to have had her estates. Moreover, the evidence of the inscriptions from Skripou indicates that estates in Boeotia – even if not as numerous as those of Danielis in Peloponnesos – were sufficiently large to provide revenue to pay for the expenses involved in building and decorating the Church of the Virgin. Neither Leo nor Danielis had any trade centres in the proximity of their estates, and one is left wondering how the putative abundance of produce could be turned into cash for the payment of the stone carvers in Skripou or the procurement of the gold, silver, and copper vessels which Danielis offered to the Emperor as gifts. Sixteen folles struck for Basil I which were found in Athens, seven in Thebes, four in Sparta, and 278 known from Corinth are simply not sufficient to support the idea of an active local trade which could make possible the acquisition of the financial means reported for both Leo and Danielis (for Athens, see Metcalf 1966; for Thebes, see Galani-Krikou 1998b: 155; for Corinth, see Sanders 2002: 649; for Sparta, see Penna 1996: 246).[72] There is no archaeological indication of long-distance trade on any of those sites, and no other sources hint at such commercial connections.[73]

It is perhaps no accident that in both cases, although in different ways, private fortunes were linked to the imperial domains. While the *protospatharios* Leo may have acquired his own estates during his service as steward of the imperial *kouratoreia*, Danielis bequeathed her whole property to the Emperor. Her reasons for doing so may have had less to do with her love for Basil I and his son than with her concern to protect her assets from members of her own family, local authorities, or the local church. It is possible that at the origin of Danielis' wealth was a grant of land for an imperial, possibly military official residing in Patras (Kourelis 2003: 136). If so, this could explain Danielis' willingness to transfer that wealth to the Emperor. However, other explanations may be considered as well. While her own son John had died before her, Danielis still had at least one heir, namely her grandson. Nothing is known about relatives of her deceased husband, but her eagerness to turn Basil I into her son's spiritual brother and the chronicler's insistence upon her regarding the Emperor as her own son suggest that Danielis lacked the support of her own family. On the other hand, she does not seem to have had any particularly strong roots in Patras. Seventy years after the elevation of the local bishop to metropolitan rank, Danielis appears to have been more concerned with decorating a basilica erected in distant Constantinople than with the endowment of the Church of St Andrew in Patras. If one is to believe that, following her visit to the imperial court, Danielis continued to send gifts to Constantinople every year throughout the reign of Basil I, then one is forced to conclude that Danielis was concerned more with maintaining excellent relations with the court then with using her extraordinary wealth to influence the local political scene in Peloponnesos. And if she truly did send that many gifts through so many years to the Emperor, then the production of her own estates and workshops was geared not towards markets that may have existed in the region, but towards obtaining political favours in Constantinople. Her strategy, however, could not work for too long. Danielis had no imitators. In the early tenth century, Patraeans who lived in Constantinople, like Arethas of Kaisareia, tried to influence the political developments in Peloponnesos, in which were involved members of the local nobility who manifested little concern with obtaining the favour of the Emperor in Constantinople.

Notes

1. Constantine Porphyrogennetos, *On the Administration of the Empire* 49.

2. Emperor Constantine himself cited the 'unwritten tradition' as his source (*On the Administration of the Empire* 49).
3. Emperor Constantine called the neighbours of the Slavs *Graikoi*, a term not used in any other part of his work. Ševčenko 1992: 192 believes the word to have been employed by Emperor Constantine's Slavic informant, an idea rightly rejected by Živković 2002a: 124 with n. 280. According to Koder 2003: 306, Emperor Constantine chose the word because in the mid-tenth century 'Hellenes' still had a strongly non-ethnic, religious meaning ('Hellenes'-as-pagans). In reality, 'Greeks' (*Graikoi*) may have been chosen to distinguish between non-Slavic natives and the mixed, perhaps Greek-speaking population brought from the eastern provinces of the Empire.
4. According to the *Chronicle of Monemvasia*, the general of the army sent to crush the rebellion of the Slavs was an Armenian, a member of the Skleros family (Kislinger 2001: 202).
5. The Impressed White Wares in Sparta were found during the 1905–1909 excavations of the ancient theatre, the ruined cavea of which produced evidence of an early medieval occupation.
6. Similarly, Glazed White Wares II have been found at Chrysoupolis, in northern Greece, but the occupation on most sites to the east of Thessalonike along the Via Egnatia cannot be dated before c. 900 (Dunn 1999: 406).
7. There is no basis for the idea that in the ninth century, the landscape of northwestern Peloponnesos witnessed a boom of habitation with a distinctive form of settlement (Kourelis 2003: 124).
8. Late eighth- or early ninth-century imitations of LR 5/6 amphorae (so-called 'silt bag-shaped jars') have been found in Herakleio (Poulou-Papadimitriou 2001: 244 and 259 fig. 20).
9. However, the local production of glazed pottery in Corinth, principally chafing dishes, began at some point in the ninth century (Sanders 2003b: 390).
10. Two other solidi of that same series are known from Patras and Tegea, with a third specimen found in Thessaloniki. Only one silver coin struck for Theophilos is known from Kythera (Metcalf 1979: 32; Penna 1996: 230, 257, and 263).
11. Such coins are rare in central and northern Greece. Only four folles struck for Theophilos are known from Athens, others have been found in Thebes, Amphissa, and Rendina (Thompson 1954: 72; Dunn 1995: 765; Galani-Krikou 2000: 351). Only three folles are known from Thessalonike (Drosogianni 1963: 248; Metcalf 1979: 31).
12. Some Italian influence can indeed be seen in the pottery produced locally in Corinth, but only from the thirteenth century onwards (Sanders 2000: 165 and 2002: 650). The fragment of a Chinese Marbled Ware bowl found in the Castle of Methone and dated to the late eighth or

early ninth century may indeed point to commercial contacts with distant markets, but there is no way to establish the exact point in time after its production at which the bowl reached the western coast of the Peloponnesos. The earliest Chinese pottery finds in Greece cannot be dated earlier than the thirteenth century (Kontogiannis 2002).

13. The attack of the African Saracens on Patras may not have coincided with the revolt of the local Slavs. In fact, in 808 or 809, the *strategos* of Kephallenia is known to have been, together with his fleet, in the northern Adriatic region around Venice, and the western coasts of Peloponnesos may thus have been left exposed (*Royal Frankish Annals*, s.a. 809; Kislinger 2001: 48).
14. The Milingoi and the Ezeritai are specifically linked to the region of Lakedaimon (Sparta). The mention of 'other insubordinates' suggests that the revolt of the Slavs may have been used as an opportunity for rebellion by other, non-Slavic groups of population, perhaps the Kapheroi, Thracians, and Armenians mentioned in the *Chronicle of Monemvasia*.
15. The Milingoi are believed to have relocated to the western side of the Taigetos (Birnbaum 1986: 16; Ilieva 1989–1990: 17–18).
16. According to Huxley 1988: 14, the Slavs initially held the plain of Sparta and were later pushed by the Byzantine conquest into the hills, where they became pastoralists.
17. Two of Michael II, four of Theophilus, and only one of Michael III (Thompson 1954: 72).
18. A ninth-century date is secured for ceramic fragments with olive-green or brown glaze.
19. Seventy years later (in 903), St Elias the Younger travelled safely in the opposite direction, from Naupaktos to Thessalonike. See *Life of St. Elias the Younger*, in Taibbi 1962: 110.
20. Gregory had embarked in Ainos and reached the seaport of Chrysoupolis. From there he took the road to Thessalonica. For the date of the *Life*'s composition, see Makris 1997: 28–9.
21. It is not known when the fort was restored, but a bishop of Didymoteichon named Nikephoros appears among the participants in the synod of 869/70, which took place in Constantinople (Darrouzès 1981: 285 with n. 595).
22. The inscription is fragmentary, but from the anti-Byzantine tone of the last sentences in the surviving text some have derived an anti-Byzantine goal of the expedition itself. It is, however, possible that the Bulgars were acting on behalf of Emperor Theophilos, to whom Presian would also offer military assistance against the Arabs. That much follows from the interpretation of another mutilated inscription from Vasilika (Chalkidiki), for which see Beshevliev 1985: 147. See also Ditten 1984; Curta 2006b: 165–6. For the Smoliani as living in the environs of Philippi, see Cheshmedzhiev 1997: 91.

23. Most historians believe that the Slavs over whom Methodius ruled in the name of the Emperor were those in the hinterland of Thessalonike, but others believe that his office must have been in some theme of Asia Minor, perhaps Opsikion (Tachiaos 1993–1994: 41–72).
24. Also numerous are the seals of *protonotarioi*, some of whom were at the same time *kommerkiarioi*, like a certain Constantine whose seal has been dated to the first half of the ninth century. By contrast, only two ninth-century turmarchs are known for Thessalonike (Koltsida-Makri 2000: 245, 248, and 254; 246 fig. 1 and 254).
25. In a letter of 25 September 860, Pope Nicholas I wrote to the archbishop of Thessalonike to confirm his responsibilities for supervising the provinces under his jurisdiction, namely Achaia, Thessaly, Old and New Epirus, Crete, Mediterranean and Ripuarian Dacia, Moesia, Dardania, and Praevalitana (Jaffé 1885: 343). Even though the jurisdiction of the archbishop of Thessalonike as described in the papal letter had much more to do with the sixth- than with the ninth-century situation, that letter is still a testimony of the prestige which the archbishop enjoyed within the church. On the other hand, this appears to have been the last letter any pope wrote to the archbishop in his capacity of vicar of the Church of Rome (Frazee 1993: 224).
26. He was followed by Antony, the first iconophile archbishop of Thessalonica, who died shortly after his appointment (*Life of St. Theodora of Thessalonike* 17; Petit 1900–1901: 217; Paschalidis 1994: 209–11).
27. A similar explanation may apply to the decision St Theodora's father took to leave the city, in order to escape the iconoclasts, and to live as a hermit in an 'area below Thoropa' (*Life of St. Theodora of Thessalonike* 7).
28. The convent of St Luke was 'on the road leading to the Kassandreotic Gate' on the east side of the city, close to the Via Egnatia (*Life of St. Theodora of Thessalonike* 9). A small monastery was excavated in the Upper City at 6 Thisseos Street (Karydas 1998: 152, 154, and 157 fig. 4).
29. For a piece of ninth-century funerary sculpture in Thessalonike, see, however, Pazaras 1988: 29–30 and pl. 17α.
30. For the *vita* of St Euthymios, which was written by Basil, archbishop of Thessalonike in the early tenth century, see Papachryssanthou 1974; Ioannidou-Gregoriou 1990. For St Euthymios as an example of the strong connection between the beginnings of Mount Athos and the monastic communities in Bithynia, see Morris 1996: 39. The first mention of the monks on Mount Athos refers to events taking place in Constantinople in 843 (Papachryssanthou 1975: 17–18).
31. The restoration of the fortress of Vardar in 861/2 is attested by an inscription mentioning the imperial *protospatharios* Marinos (perhaps

the *strategos* of Thessalonike) and the imperial *strator* Gagik (Kakikes) (Marki 1982: 144–5; 145 fig. 18; Kiourtzian 1991). For the relations between Boris and Byzantium, see Angelov 1995.

32. From Constantinople, the envoys returned in 870 on the same route, along the Via Egnatia, all the way to Dyrrachium. The Byzantine envoys to Rome may have travelled in 868 along the same route. For those trips, see McCormick 2001: 144–5, 939, and 941–2.
33. Ibn Yahya was a civilian captured by the Byzantines at Askalon, who may have been a slave in Constantinople prior to his trip to Rome. His account survives in Ibn Rusta's *Book of Precious Records*. (Wiet 1955: 143; Marquart 1903: 206–10; McCormick 2001: 557 and 957).
34. Involved in the flourishing trade with Bulgaria must also have been a *vardarios* of Thessalonike named Pardas, mentioned on a late eighth- or ninth-century seal (Koltsida-Makri 2000: 263).
35. Symeon's protestations have to do not with the new location for the Bulgarian trade – Thessalonike was closer to the Bulgarian border than Constantinople – but with the abolition of what may have been most-favoured-nation status for the Bulgarian merchants (Curta 2006b: 178–9).
36. This is further confirmed by the description of the situation in the region of Thessalonike on the eve of the Arab sack of the city in 904. According to John Kaminiates, 'ever since the sacrament of baptism had brought the Scythian people [Bulgarians] into the Christian fold and had made them share in the milk of true piety, the tumult of war died down, the murderous blade abandoned its work of butchery and the predictions of that mightiest voice of prophesy, Isaiah, were in our own times clearly fulfilled: for our swords were transformed into pruning hooks and our spears into ploughshares and war was in no place and peace governed all the neighboring territory and there was no material resource of which we did not enjoy a superfluity' (John Kaminiates, *The Capture of Thessaloniki* 9; Nasledova 1956: 66).
37. There is no basis for the idea that Philippi was still inhabited in the early ninth century or that it was occupied by Bulgar troops in 812 (Karagiannopoulos 1984).
38. The location of the cathedral of the local bishop named Demetrios who participated in the synod of 879 is not known (Darrouzès 1981: 285 with n. 614).
39. This may have been the church of the local bishop who participated in the synod of 879 (Darrouzès 1981: 285 with n. 595).
40. Upon his death, Leo V's envoy to Lesbos was buried in Constantinople with a letter from St Symeon of Lesbos 'as a resplendent mantle and a magnificent shroud' (*Lives of Sts. David, Symeon, and George of Lesbos* 16).
41. The situation on Lesbos, especially in the region of Mitylene, seems to

have been compounded by the famine of 842, which prompted Empress Theodora to suspend tax payments until 844, while organising shipments of food from neighbouring Smyrna (*Lives of Sts. David, Symeon, and George of Lesbos* 13; Koder 1998: 210).

42. For the trope of the abandoned island in ninth- and tenth-century Byzantine hagiography concerning the Aegean, see Caraher 2008: 272–3 and 276–7.
43. The Arab raids may have prompted the creation of a new theme of Samos shortly before 899 (Koder 1998: 78). The ninth-century fortifications on the island have, however, been dated to the reign of Theophilos (Malamut 1988: 140).
44. Unlike other churches of the same type, the Episkope in Skyros is half-buried in the steeply sloping ground.
45. The church was once the *katholikon* of a monastery, which was built on top of an early Byzantine building with mosaic pavement, perhaps a basilica. For the six building phases of the church, see Vogiatzis 1998.
46. Skripou is also the first monument in Greece to have used bricks laid obliquely in rows to form dentil bands for the decoration of the façade (Bouras 2006: 76).
47. The church was built by an imperial candidate, a title ranked lower than that of the *protospatharios* Leo.
48. Much has been made of the allegedly 'indiscriminate use of ancient members' for the building of the church in Skripou (Bouras 2006: 77). However, at a closer look, it appears that many of the spolia employed are in fact funerary stelae. Their use may have been a deliberate attempt to invoke the same antiquity to which the epigram on the western wall pointed (Papalexandrou 1998: 319–24).
49. The founder was a *droungarios*. The church was demolished in the nineteenth century (Browning 1984: 301). For ninth-century churches on the island of Aigina, in the Saronic Gulf southwest of Athens, see the *Life of St. Athanasia of Aigina* 11; *Life of St. Theodora of Thessalonike* 3.
50. The Church of St Basil of the Bridge (*tes Gephyras*) just outside Arta is of free-cross type and has been dated to the second half of the ninth century (Vokotopoulos 1975: 185 and 2000: 157).
51. The dating to the ninth century of the churches of St Prokopius near Tigani (Lakonia), St Andrew in Gortyna (Arkadia), and the Holy Saviour in Alagonia (prefecture of Messini) must be regarded with suspicion, as it is based on stylistic analogues (Avramea 1998: 51; Moutsopoulos 1997: 63–4 and 69; Dimitrokallis 1990: 121–31).
52. A metropolitan of Patras participated in the synod of 879 (Kresten 1977: 29). Two other metropolitans of Patras are known from seals dated to the first half of the ninth century.
53. In a funeral oration which St Peter of Argos wrote for the Unmercenary

Saints Cosmas and Damian, he asked them not to 'permit henceforth that the eyes of Scythians and Agarenes may look at us haughtily'. Vasiliev 1947: 189 convincingly identified both the 'Scythians' of the encomium and the 'barbarians' of the *Life of St. Peter of Argos* with King Symeon's Bulgarians who raided Greece between 918 and 924 (see Chapter 6).

54. St Theodosius the Younger was ordained priest by St Peter of Argos c. 920 (Yannopoulos 1997: 365).
55. Lampropoulou 1994: 31 believes that to be the *katholikon* of the Monastery of the Holy Unmercenaries in Vassaras. No evidence exists, however, that that church existed in the ninth century.
56. The family of St Athanasios, bishop of Methone, was from Catania and moved to Patras in the late 820s (Da Costa-Louillet 1961: 314; Ganktzis et al. 1993: 474–5).
57. Photios was slain, and some of the Muslim captives were subjected to torture, especially those who refused Christian baptism.
58. Most probably to recover his losses due to desertion, Nasar is said to have recruited Mardaites from Peloponnesos for his final and decisive attack on the Arabs (Theophanes Continuatus, in Bekker 1838: 320; Bon 1951: 75–6; Ditten 1993: 149 and 155–6; Kislinger 2001: 54).
59. All the weapons were found during excavations within the Bronze-Age fortification, one of them in the medieval cemetery on the acropolis. A ninth-century date is suggested by the single find of a *miliaresion* struck for Theophilos.
60. More sites in Peloponnesos than in any other part of Greece have produced folles struck for Leo VI: Kenchreai, Archaia Kleones, Argos, Sparta, Tegea, Kalamata, and Patras (Penna 1996: 240, 242, 246, 257, 261, and 263). According to Galani-Krikou 1998b: 158, ten folles have also been discovered in Thebes. Four coins of Leo VI are known from a private collection in Thessalonike, while three more folles have been found near the medieval fort at Vrya, near Nea Silata in Chalkidiki (Drosogianni 1963: 249; Pazaras and Tsanana 1991: 297). Only one solidus struck for Leo is so far known from Greece, the specimen from Velestino, for which see Intzesiloglou 1987: 271.
61. In Athens, the numbers of coins struck for Basil I and Leo VI are much smaller, at 17 and 81, respectively (Thompson 1954: 72). On the island of Samos, the largest number of ninth-century coins is that of specimens struck for Leo VI (Malamut 1988: 141 and 238). For a small hoard of folles struck for Leo VI from Veroia, see Pariente 1994: 758.
62. Zenobius may have arrived in Naupaktos in or shortly before 888 (Turlej 1999: 394). There is no reason to doubt the authenticity of this account, for Zenobius is specifically said to have received a copy of Danielis' will from the hands of her grandson (Litavrin 2004: 22).
63. Some assume that those complaining about the abuses of the

metropolitan were the Slavs made subject to him by the bull of Nikephoros I (Litavrin 1985: 1352).

64. The only reason for regarding Danielis as of Slavic origin is that she is said to have been named Danelis (or Danielis) after her husband, a detail which some have hastily associated with the Slavic (Russian) practice of married women changing their patronymic to their husband's first name. Assuming that this could apply to Danielis, there is, however, no evidence that such a practice existed in the ninth century among the Slavs. Moreover, the practice is well attested in eastern Macedonia during the first half of the fourteenth century within a clearly Greek-speaking population (Kravari 2005: 306).

65. What follows is a summary of the story of Danielis as narrated by Theophanes Continuatus, in Bekker 1838: 226–8 and 317–21.

66. Anagnostakis 1989: 378 believes that Theophilos/Theophilitzes may have arrived in Patras in the context of Theoktistos Bryennios' campaigns against the Slavs.

67. Besides money and clothes, Danielis gave Basil thirty slaves (Theophanes Continuatus, in Bekker 1838: 228).

68. For *sindonia* as linen, not silk cloths, see Mark 14:51–2 and 15:46, Matthew 27:59, and Luke 23:53; Bon 1951: 128. *Contra*: Laiou and Morrisson 2007: 67, who claim that from the ninth century onwards, Peloponnesos was referred to as Morea (the land of mulberries) because of the local silk industry. In fact, the earliest reference to Peloponnesos as Morea is the *Life of St. Meletios the Younger* written in the twelfth century by Nicholas, bishop of Methone (Bon 1951: 137). For the eunuchs offered as gifts by Danielis as possibly of Slavic origin, see Anagnostakis and Papamastorakis 2004: 74–5. For eunuchs as luxury slaves, see Patlagean 1993: 598.

69. The phrase appears to allude to the equivalent title of 'father of the emperor' first accorded by Basil's son Leo VI to his father-in-law Stylianos Zaoutzes (Rapp 1997: 307 with n. 97).

70. This is even true for the early 880s, when the carpet for the new church built by Basil I in Constantinople is said to been shipped by land from Patras. Had the carpet travelled by sea, the story of Danielis would have been less credible, because in the 880s Arab fleets from Africa and Crete are known to have controlled, if only briefly, the sailing lanes across the Ionian and the Aegean Seas.

71. Such an interpretation is further supported by the claim of the unknown continuator of Theophanes' *Chronographia* that the name of the precious textiles offered by Danielis as gifts had been corrupted from *sidonia* into *sendais* (Theophanes Continuatus, in Bekker 1838: 318). As David Jacoby has demonstrated, *sendais* (*sendes*) was a silk textile (sendal), the name of which is first attested in a tenth-century Byzantine military treatise (Jacoby 1991–1992: 459).

72. Two other folles struck for Basil I are known from Kythera and Volos, respectively (Penna 1996: 257; Oikonomidou-Karamesini 1966: 15). For a small hoard of folles struck for Basil I, found in Aigina, see Pennas 2004: 14–15 and 15 fig. 14.
73. According to Runciman 1940: 429, Danielis produced carpets for the market in Constantinople. But the giant carpet for the new basilica in Constantinople was a gift, not a commodity. In addition, transporting such bulky goods as carpets from Patras for sale on the market in Constantinople involved major logistical problems.

CHAPTER 6

The beginning of prosperity (c. 900 to c. 1050)

The series of victories against the Arabs obtained in the late ninth century by the Byzantine fleet in the Aegean and Ionian seas was abruptly interrupted after 900 by a number of bold, even spectacular attacks on major cities in Greece. Following an attack on Lemnos in 901, a Syrian fleet commanded by the emir of Tarsos, Damianos, sacked in 902 the city of Demetrias in the Pagasic Bay in Thessaly (Theophanes Continuatus, in Bekker 1838: 365; John Kaminiates, *The Capture of Thessaloniki* 14).[1] Shortly after that, the *protospatharios* Petronas, who had been commissioned by Emperor Leo VI to take temporary charge of the defence of Thessalonike, arrived in that city from Constantinople with alarming news of an impending Arab attack by a large fleet under the command of Leo of Tripoli (Abū Hārith).[2]

> He said that fugitives from the hands of those barbarians had arrived and had given the emperor prior information concerning their strategy, to the effect that they were now concentrating all their energies for a projected attack on the city, since they had been assured by many of those whom they had previously defeated that it was practically unwalled on the seaward side and would be an easy target for a seaborne attack. Once these dreadful tidings had been received, confused and panic-stricken rumours were rife throughout the city.[3]

John Kaminiates does not give any details as to the nature of the rumours, but historians have speculated that Leo of Tripoli, who had initially planned to attack Constantinople, may have been invited to do so by a conspiracy against Emperor Leo VI organised by Andronikos Dukas and Eustathios Argyros in cooperation with Patriarch Nicholas Mystikos (Jenkins 1948; Farag 1989: 138). If so, the swift replacement of Eustathios Argyros with admiral Himerios may have given the signal that the Arab fleet had nothing to gain from remaining in the Straits, and consequently, Leo passed by Lampsakos, Abydos, Tenedos, then northward to Imbros, Samothrake, before throwing anchor at Thasos, where Egyptian

The beginning of prosperity

ships from a different raiding party joined his fleet.[4] Meanwhile, the citizens of Thessalonike have begun plundering the cemeteries to the east and west of the city for tombstones from graves in which 'in olden times the pagans who dwelt there buried their dead'. Their goal was to build an underwater fence, which was meant to deny Leo's fleet access into the harbour (John Kaminiates, *The Capture of Thessaloniki* 17). The work was half-finished when Petronas was replaced with the *strategos* Leo Chitzilakis, who abandoned the initial plan and instead began to repair and to raise the height of the existing system of fortifications. Leo's short-lived accomplishments were in fact celebrated by an inscription on a large stone forming the lintel of a gate, which was found in 1879 during the demolition of the sea wall of Thessaloniki (Spieser 1973: 162).[5] Because of accidentally injuring himself, Leo too was replaced with another *strategos* named Niketas who arrived from Constantinople and who tried to recruit a force of archers from the neighbouring Sclavenes, 'both those who paid us tribute and those who were under the jurisdiction of the *strategos* of Strymon' (John Kaminiates, *The Capture of Thessaloniki* 20).[6] However, because of the incompetence of the commanders 'who had been put in charge' of the Sclavenes, only a few responded to the call to arms (John Kaminiates, *The Capture of Thessaloniki* 20).[7] Despite being placed 'at those points from which it was easiest to shoot accurately', when the Arabs broke into the city, the leaders of the Sclavene archers escaped through the gate near the Acropolis, by pushing the wings of the gate ajar, leaving 'one of their number on the spot to shut the gate behind them', and telling the terrified crowd at the gate that they were going to collect allies from the Strymon area, pretending that they had orders from the *strategos* of Thessalonike (John Kaminiates, *The Capture of Thessaloniki* 41).[8] Niketas does not seem to have contemplated the idea of a general evacuation of the city, both because of the churches in Thessalonike with all their valuables, and because of the concern that 'we would not know how to assuage the emperor's displeasure' (John Kaminiates, *The Capture of Thessaloniki* 21).

On 29 July 904, Leo's fleet of fifty-four ships, 'manned by a motley crowd of cut-throats and desperadoes, Ishmaelites who dwell in Syria, and Ethiopians, whose country borders on Egypt', appeared in the city's harbour (John Kaminiates, *The Capture of Thessaloniki* 18).[9] After two days of desperate resistance, the enemy broke into the city and a great massacre ensued. The population of Thessalonike appears to have been swollen with refugees 'from the islands already captured before' by the Arabs (John Kaminiates, *The Capture of Thessaloniki* 12). The booty collected from Thessalonike and the number of enslaved people were so large that Leo had to take with him a number of ships, which were in the city's harbour at the time of the attack, and which were normally used for the transportation of grain (John Kaminiates, *The Capture of Thessaloniki* 61).[10] The devastation of the city must have been serious, judging from the impression of sheer misery which Thessalonike left on St Elias the Younger, who visited the city less than a week after the withdrawal of Leo's fleet (*Life of St. Elias the Younger*, in Taibbi 1962: 110; Yannopoulos 1994: 215–16). However, both the city and the surrounding countryside recovered rapidly and would witness an accelerated economic growth throughout the second half of the tenth and the first half of the eleventh century (see Chapter 7).

Leo of Tripoli returned to the region of the northern Aegean in 911, when, together with Damianos of Tarsus, he intercepted and defeated near Chios the imperial armada under the command of admiral Himerios, which was headed to Crete for a full-scale invasion of the island (Theophanes Continuatus, in Bekker 1838: 376–7; Malamut 1988: 112).[11] In 921, Leo also thouroughly plundered Lemnos (Theophanes Continuatus, in Bekker 1838: 405; Malamut 1988: 84). While Leo kept himself busy in the northern Aegean, the emirs in al-Khandaq (Iraklion) controlled the Sea of Crete and the southern approaches to Peloponnesos. According to the *Life of St. Peter of Argos*, in the early tenth century Cretan marauders devastated the islands, as well as the villages and the cities on the coast, massacring those who resisted and enslaving those who yielded. Peter convinced them to return the captives for ransom, which they did constantly year after year, an indication that raids may have aimed not just at plundering the target region, but also at extorting ransom money (*Life of St. Peter of Argos* 14).[12] The *Life of St. Luke the Younger* shows that, fearing the Arabs of Crete, pilgrims from Rome going to Jerusalem travelled first to the northern shore of the Gulf of Corinth, then crossed central Greece to reach Athens, before embarking again (*Life of St. Luke the Younger* 9 and 21; Oikonomides 1992: 254). That local ships also avoided sailing around Cape Malea is further demonstrated by the problems St Theodore faced when attempting to cross over from Monemvasia to the deserted island of Kythera (*Life of St. Theodore of Kythera*, in Oikonomides 1967: 286; Malamut 1988: 112, who dates the events to c. 920).[13] Even Monemvasia was sacked in c. 950 by a fleet coming from Crete

(Savvidis 1990: 53). St Theodore eventually reached Kythera after boarding a warship of the Byzantine navy, which had just obtained a victory over the Arabs of Crete (*Life of St. Theodore of Kythera*, in Oikonomides 1967: 286–7; Niavis 1992: 264; Caraher 2008: 270). That island was eventually conquered forty years later by an expedition led by the new domestic of the East, Nikephoros Phokas, who put al-Khandaq under siege, and eventually stormed the city walls in the spring of 961. The massacre of the local population would have been complete, had not Nikephoros been able 'to restrain with difficulty the murderous impulses of the army' (Leo the Deacon, *History* 2.7). The description of the booty collected from al-Khandaq by the Byzantine forces mirrors that of the riches collected from Thessalonike by Leo of Tripoli's men:

> So they went through the houses and were rewarded with abundant and valuable booty. For it is said that the city of the Cretans contained great and inexhaustible wealth, since it had been very prosperous for a long time, had enjoyed good and kindly fortune, and had not suffered any of the abominations, such as disasters, that the vicissitudes of time usually bring about. By making use especially of the expeditions of pirates and corsairs, it had plundered the shores of both lands, and had stored away untold wealth as a result of such pursuits. When everything inside had been brought out, Nikephoros ordered his men to raze the circuit wall to the ground.[14]

The conquest of Crete effectively put an end to Muslim raiding and placed the Aegean Sea under Byzantine control, although sporadic attacks from Zirid Africa continued well into the first half of the eleventh century.[15] Crete became a theme, and so did Chios in the late tenth or early eleventh century (Malamut 1988: 310 and 316).[16] In the late tenth century, Byzantine coins began to reappear on several Aegean islands, on Thasos, Chios, and on Crete (Tsougarakis 1982). While most islands in the northern Aegean and the Saronic Gulf experienced depopulation and abandonment in the tenth century, the signs of economic recovery – increased monetary circulation, population growth, monumental architecture – appear on a number of islands in the Cyclades during the last quarter of that century. Even the painters of the frescoes in the rather modest cave church of the Kaloritissa in Naxos, which are dated to the tenth century, seem to have drawn inspiration from the style of the portraits in such prominent churches as Hagia Sophia in Constantinople or the Church of the Assumption in Nicaea, a strong indication of artistic and most probably economic ties with the capital of the

Empire and its hinterland (Skawran 2001: 77).[17] By 1000, pilgrims from Greece travelled to the Holy Land via the Aegean islands. Among them was a goldsmith from Athens who scratched his name on the wall of a cave at Gastria on Tinos (Malamut 1988: 213, 467, and 547). Several officials in the administration of the islands were in fact members of prominent families in mainland Greece. For example, Leo Kyparissiotes, the *strategos* of Chios in the early eleventh century, was a native of Kyparissia in Peloponnesos, while another *strategos* of Chios, Theodore Verivoes, was a member of an important family from Evvoia (Malamut 1988: 500).

According to John Kaminiates, on the eve of the Arab attack on Thessalonike, relations across the Bulgarian–Byzantine frontier just north of that city were peaceful, both parties being on 'friendly terms with each other' and refraining from 'any violent measures that lead to confrontation and armed conflict'. This had 'been their policy for some not inconsiderable time past' (John Kaminiates, *The Capture of Thessaloniki* 6).[18] Even allowing for the bias inherent in the rosy picture Kaminiates drew in his nostalgic description of his home town, his account is confirmed by all existing sources. No operations are known to have taken place in northern Greece during the four-year war which Symeon waged against Byzantium as a result of the transfer in 893 of the Bulgarian trade market from Constantinople to Thessalonike (see Chapter 5). By 904, the frontier ran only 22km to the north of Thessalonike, as attested by an inscription on a frontier landmark found in Nea Philadelphia (Beshevliev 1963: 216; Oikonomides 1995a). But in 916, Bulgarian armies devastated the territory of the theme of Thessalonike in retaliation for Empress Zoe's annulment of her son's engagement to Symeon's daughter and for her rejection of his imperial title. Following his victory over the Byzantine army at Anchialos (20 August 917) and his campaign against Prince Peter of Serbia, Symeon raided Greece in 918. In 921, he appears to have raided northern Greece again, this time reaching as far south as the Isthmus and ravaging northern Peloponnesos (Orgels 1964: 277). That much follows from one of the prophecies of St Luke the Younger ('Hellas will be smitten and the Peloponnese will see war'), as well as from a scholium of Arethas of Kaisareia on a manuscript of Dion Chrysostom, which mentions the Bulgarian occupation of the Kadmeia of Thebes (*Life of St. Luke the Younger* 24; Veis 1928: 337–8).[19] In central Greece, when 'the ruler of the Scythians (we know that in the vernacular they are called Bulgarians)' began 'enslaving and ravaging, depriving some of life and others of freedom, forcing them to pay tribute', the inhabitants either barricaded themselves in cities, or otherwise moved to Evvoia and Peloponnesos (*Life of St. Luke the Younger* 32). The villagers near Mount Ioannitza, on which St Luke lived as a hermit, fled to various islands in the Gulf of Corinth, but a group of Bulgarians pursued them on a stolen ship. Only a few villagers, together with St Luke, escaped the massacre by plunging into the sea (*Life of St. Luke the Younger* 33).[20] After the invasion, Luke moved to Corinth; he returned to Mount Ioannitza only in 927, when, at Symeon's death, his son Peter 'said farewell to blood and war and welcomed peace' with the Empire (*Life of St. Luke the Younger* 40).

Symeon's raids into Greece seem to have contributed to further problems in Peloponnesos. According to Constantine Porphyrogennetos, who wrote a few decades after the events,

> In the reign of the lord Romanos the emperor, the *protospatharios* John Proteuon, military governor in this same province, reported to the same lord Romanos concerning both Milingoi and Ezeritai that they had rebelled and neither obeyed the military governor nor regarded the imperial mandate, but were practically independent and self-governing, and neither accepted a head man at the hand of the military governor, nor heeded orders for military service under him, nor would pay other dues to the treasury.[21]

It appears that the Milingoi and the Ezeritai refused to accept as their *archontes* the men appointed by the *strategos* of Peloponnesos. Their dissatisfaction seems to have been fuelled by the sudden demands for troops for the mobilisation of the army of Peloponnesos in preparation for a campaign in Italy, following the defeat the Byzantine army suffered at Ascoli at the hands of the Lombard rebels (Constantine Porphyrogennetos, *On the Administration of the Empire* 51; see also Zakythinos 1945: 53; Orgels 1964: 277). While the report reached Constantinople, probably in the early 922, a new *strategos* of Peloponnesos was appointed in the person of Krinites Arotras, who had special orders to quell the rebellion of the Milingoi and Ezeritai, which was perhaps viewed as particularly dangerous in the circumstances created by the Bulgarian raids. Between March and November 922, Krinites waged war against the rebels, 'burning down their crops and plundering their land', and eventually forced them to submit to imperial authority and pay much higher tribute than before, probably in compensation for their reluctance to provide troops for the campaign in Italy. By the end of 922 or in early

923, Krinites was then appointed *strategos* of Hellas. His replacement in Peloponnesos, Bardas Platopydes, appears to have been the creature of Emperor Romanos I, who had staunch supporters in the theme. Bardas' term as *strategos* was marked by 'disorder and strife', for he intervened in the local conflict between the supporters of Romanos I and an aristocratic faction favourable to Constantine VII Porphyrogennetos and managed to expel from Peloponnesos a local *protospatharios* named Leo Agelastos, who was perhaps the leader of the 'legitimist' faction (Constantine Porphyrogennetos, *On the Administration of the Empire* 50).[22] Whether or not related to the conflict between the two political factions, a conspiracy was discovered, which is mostly known from Arethas of Kaisareia's *Apology*. Arethas, by then a resident of Constantinople, had visited his native province in order to participate in the reconsecration of churches, perhaps in connection with the devastation brought by the Bulgarian attacks. However, he later wrote the *Apology* in order to defend himself against accusations that he had tried to convince a certain notable of Patras named Symbatios to declare himself emperor. Symbatios had declined the offer and promptly denounced the plot, while sending to Constantinople, under imperial guard, two noblemen from Tegea, the *protospatharioi* Nicholas and Thomas (Shangin 1947: 249, 252, and 259).[23] Taking advantage of the 'disorder and strife' created in Peloponnesos, 'straight away the Slavesians made an attack upon this same province' (Constantine Porphyrogennetos, *On the Administration of the Empire* 50). The Slavesians were Byzantine troops recruited from among Slavs in Asia Minor and stationed in Peloponnesos and, perhaps, Hellas, as reinforcements for the local thematic army or as replacements for those soldiers of Peloponnesos who had preferred to redeem their military obligations during the mobilisation of troops for the Italian campaign.[24] It is interesting to note that, 'fearing lest they [the Slavesians] might join forces with the Slavs [the Milingoi and the Ezeritai] and bring about the total destruction of this same province', Emperor Romanos I agreed to reduce the tribute of the Peloponnesian Slavs to the level in existence before the campaign of Krinites Arotras. Some believe that the attack of the Slavesians resulted in a three-year occupation of Peloponnesos. This appears to be based on a wrong identification of the Slavesians with the barbarians who, following the death of Peter of Argos, 'for three years did possess Peloponnesos; they massacred people and thoroughly devastated the whole country, completely destroying the traces of former wealth and good order' (*Life of St. Peter of Argos* 19;

see also Vasiliev 1947: 172; Orgels 1964: 271–3). In fact, the description in the *Life of St. Peter of Argos*, albeit lacking in precision, better fits the situation between 921 and 923, in which the turmoil created by different factors may have appeared as ultimately having one single cause, namely the Bulgarian raid under Symeon. Twenty years later, 'the nation of the Turks (Magyars) overran Hellas' (*Life of St. Luke the Younger 50*; Kalaitzakis 1995–1997). A *strategos* of Thessalonike named Katakalon, who tried to stop them, was killed in battle. In Boeotia, St Luke and the villagers of Kalamion fled to the island of Ampelon in the Gulf of Corinth, a completely dry and waterless island (*Life of St. Luke the Younger 50*).[25] The Magyars withdrew only when the imperial *parakoimomenos* Theophanes met them and offered a five-year peace (Oikonomides 1973: 3).

But Peloponnesos was not the only region of Greece to witness such turbulence. An inscription on a marble slab placed in the wall at Christoupolis (Kavala) attributes the reconstruction of the ramparts in 926 to Basil Kladon, the *strategos* of Strymon, who may have resided in the city (Reinach 1882: 269).[26] The repair may have been needed because of damage caused by one of the earthquakes that rocked the region in the early tenth century.[27] If so, it was certainly a timely measure to protect the city against possible attacks from 'certain Slavs' in the region of Thessalonike, who in 927 'were rebels against the emperor Romanos and were depopulating his land'. The Slavs attacked the embassy to Constantinople led by Liudprand of Cremona's father, but the envoys resisted, killed the attackers, and even managed to capture two of their leaders, whom they then presented to the Emperor (Liudprand of Cremona, *Retribution* 3.24; Jenkins 1955: 208). The Slavs in the theme of Strymon are mentioned too by John Kaminiates as providing (an insufficient number of) archers for the defence of Thessalonike against the Arabs (*The Capture of Thessaloniki* 20). There were also Slavs in the Chalkidike. Several inhabitants of Hierissos who appear in tenth- and eleventh-century documents from the archives on Mount Athos had Slavic names or nicknames, which suggests that Slavic was spoken in the town at that time, perhaps as the main language. Several villages in the fertile coastal plain at the foot of the Pangaion Mountain – Radolibos, Obelos, and Dobrobikea – were Slavic and remained so well into the fourteenth century (Kravari 1998: 395–6). At some point during the reign of Emperor Romanos II (959–963), an imperial chrysobull for the Monastery of Kolobos, which was then renewed at least once in the eleventh century, granted to the monastic community in Hierissos forty dependent peasants (*paroikoi*) free from all public taxes as a compensation for the lands which had been taken from the monastery by 'Bulgarian Slavs' said to have settled in Hierissos (Dölger 1952: 7, 12, and 17; Soulis 1953: 67–9; Papachryssanthou 1992: 28–9).[28] The distinction between Slavs and Bulgarian Slavs seems to have been important, as the latter were newcomers whose arrival may have been facilitated by Symeon's campaigns of 918 and 921. A testimonial dated June 982 regarding an agreement between the inhabitants of Hierissos and John the Iberian, the founder of the Monastery of Iviron on Mount Athos, bears the signature of numerous persons with typically Slavic names: Basil Stroimir, Vlasios Vladko, Nicholas Detko, Antony Rokovina. In addition, one of the signatures is in Glagolitic letters (Soulis 1953: 71).

Examples of familiarity with the Slavic language(s) and possibly bilingualism are also known from southern Greece. Tenth-century scholia to Strabo's *Geography* written by scholiasts who were either from, or otherwise knew very well, the region of Patras never describe the local Slavs (called Sclaveni) as enemies. Moreover, they candidly list Slavic equivalents for those ancient place names which appear in Strabo's text, but were obviously not in use in the tenth century.[29] The Milingoi (but not the Ezeritai) appear again in connection with events taking place in Sparta in the 970s, which are mentioned in the *Life of St. Nikon* written between 70 and 180 years later.[30] A certain Antiochos, the *doux* of the Milingoi, came to a dependency of the monastery established by St Nikon and ordered it to be turned into an inn. He then built his court there, surrounding the place with a wall and bringing 'lewd and wild women in his tent' (*Life of St. Nikon* 59).[31] Later, 'a mixed group, both young and those whose impulses could not be controlled', recruited from among the Milingoi arrived at the monastery with spears (*Life of St. Nikon* 62).[32] The unknown author of the *Life* calls the Milingoi 'ethnics' ('whom the locals are accustomed to call Milengoi instead of Myrmidons'), a term which has been interpreted as indicating that the Slavs were pagans. However, as soon as the Milingoi saw St Nikon in their dreams setting loose upon them two ferocious dogs, 'they immediately become passionate in repentance and strongly smitten in their hearts', admitting their sin and asking their relatives to go to the monastery in order to obtain the saint's pardon (*Life of St. Nikon* 62). This strongly suggests that in the eyes of the unknown author of the *Life of St. Nikon*, the Milingoi were in fact Christian.[33]

Unlike the two Italians from Aquileia who settled in Sparta 'for the sake of trade', they never appear as 'foreigners, not natives', and in fact may have been perceived as just uncouth and rude neighbours. Two mid-eleventh-century donors who paid for the altar table of the church in Milia near Platsa (Messinia) may indeed have been speakers of Slavic.[34]

During the second half of the tenth century, Bulgarian raids resumed as part of the new Byzantine–Bulgarian war initiated by Emperor Nikephoros II Phokas. Following one such raid, against which not enough troops could apparently be gathered in time in Thessalonike, a young slave was taken captive to the fortress of Kolyndros, near Veroia. Only at the intervention of St Phantinos the Younger was he able to escape and to find his way to Kitros, where he took a boat back to Thessalonike (*Life of St. Phantinos the Younger* 49 and 61; see also Yannopoulos 1995: 489 and 492–3, who dates the event between 989 and 991). The Bulgarian raids led to the abandonment of the Gomaton monastery near Hierissos, which was later incorporated into the estates of the Great Lavra on Mount Athos (Stephenson 2003: 16; for the Gomaton monastery, see Papachryssanthou 1992: 132–4). During his brief sojourn in Larissa in 965, St Phantinos had predicted the conquest of the city by the Bulgarians (*Life of St. Phantinos the Younger* 36; Tsorbazoglou 2001: 135). Some twenty years later, after a long siege which drove the population of the city to starvation, Larissa was indeed taken by Samuel, who promptly removed a substantial number of inhabitants, as well as the relics of the local saint Achilleios (Kekaumenos, *Strategikon* 169–70).[35] Northern Greece was one of the main theatres of operation during the long war opposing Samuel to Emperor Basil II. Samuel may have been responsible for the building of such forts in the area as Longas in the prefecture of Kastoria, Setina near Achlada in the prefecture of Florina, and Moglena near Chrysi in the prefecture of Pella (for Longas, see Moutsopoulos 1992a: 2 and 1995a: 137–8; for Setina, see Moutsopoulos 1992a: 13, 15, and 18, as well as Moutsopoulos 1995b; for Moglena, see Evgenidou 1987: 16–18; Pariente 1993: 847). However, farther to the south and southeast forts were either built or restored by Emperor Basil II. This is clearly the case of a fort said to have been restored in 1015 by Constantine Diogenes, *katepano* of Thessalonike, in an inscription found in Mylovos (Aiginion, prefecture of Pieria) (Marki 1993 and 1997b; see also Stavridou-Zafraka 1995a). Both Rendina (prefecture of Thessaloniki) and Platamon (prefecture of Kavala) may have also been restored under Basil II (for Rendina, see Moutsopoulos 2001; for Platamon, see Loverdou-Tsigarida 1993 and 1997: 61; Marki and Loverdou-Tsigarida 1994: 533; Katsambalos and Loverdou-Tsigarida et al. 1995; Touchais et al. 2000: 890).[36]

In the 990s, Basil managed to take back some of the forts in northern Greece which had previously been in Samuel's hands, the most important of which was Veroia.[37] When leaving for the eastern front, the Emperor left behind Gregory of Taron as *doux* of Thessalonike.[38] In 997, Samuel raided the region of Thessalonike and captured Gregory's son. When Gregory tried to rescue him, he was ambushed and killed. As a consequence of Samuel's extraordinary military success, a number of important political figures appear to have defected to his side. First among them was a leading man of Thessalonike, the *magistros* Paul Bobos, who may well have been the man mentioned in a judicial judgement of November 996 issued by Nicholas, the judge (*krites*) of Thessalonike, Strymon, and Drougoubiteia, as having his property seized by the imperial fisc (Holmes 2005: 108). Another defector was John Malakenos, the *strategos* of Hellas, a man 'in the first rank not only' in Sparta, 'but in all Hellas and the land of Pelops' (*Life of St. Nikon* 43).[39] He was arrested at the order of the Emperor on an accusation of defection and insurrection, but St Nikon conveniently predicted for him safety, imperial favour, and even higher dignities (*Life of St. Nikon* 43).[40]

Samuel was able to take back Veroia, as well as other places in northern Thessaly, before raiding deep into mainland Greece. By the time a new domestic of the West, Nikephoros Ouranos, arrived at Thessalonike with a large number of troops, Samuel had reached as far south as Corinth. The *strategos* and judge of Peloponnesos, Basil Apokaukos, who 'was guarding the Isthmus there against the Bulgarian attack', feared the worst, but was eventually reassured by St Nikon that the destruction of the Bulgarians was imminent (*Life of St. Nikon* 43).[41] Historians have assumed that Nikon's prophecy referred to the victory obtained against Samuel by Nikephoros Ouranos, the *doux* of the West, in 997 at the river Spercheios (Pirivatrić 1997: 103–4; Holmes 2005: 409).[42] It may nonetheless be a more general reference to the fall of Samuel and his defeat at Basil II's hands, which are explicitly mentioned in chapter 43 of the *Life of St. Nikon*.

Basil returned to northern Greece in 1001, when he took Vodena (modern Edessa). In 1014, when the Byzantine field army was engaged under the Emperor's command in the mountain pass at Kleidion, a

Bulgarian counter-offensive force was sent to raid the hinterland of Thessalonike. Nikephoros Botaneiates, the local *doux*, was able to repel the attack, but when attempting to secure the road between western Macedonia and Thessalonike, in order for the field army to return safely for the winter, he was ambushed and killed by the Bulgarians (Holmes 2005: 412–13). One year later, Basil managed to recapture Vodena and to take Moglena. The former had reverted to the Bulgarians and, as a punishment for their betrayal, the Emperor ordered the deportation of its inhabitants. To conquer Moglena, the Byzantine troops led by Nikephoros Xiphias and Constantine Diogenes, the new *doux* of Thessalonike, had to sap the walls, after which they razed them to the ground, as Basil placed a garrison in the nearby fortress at Enotia (John Skylitzes, *History*, in Thurn 1973: 352). The Emperor was in Thessalonike in early 1015, but two years later he was busy besieging Kastoria and routing the Bulgarians near Vodena. He returned to Kastoria in 1018, after the surrender of the Bulgarian aristocrats, and moved through Thessaly to Athens, where he offered thanksgivings for his victory in the Church of the Virgin, the former Parthenon (Curta 2006b: 245–7; Kazanaki-Lappa 2000: 206). This was the first time since Constans II in the seventh century that an emperor had visited Athens. However, Basil II's victory did not put an end to military invasions from the north. Thessalonike was briefly under siege in 1040 by the Bulgarian rebels under Alusian (John Skylitzes, *History*, in Thurn 1973: 413, who claims that Alusian's army was 40,000 strong; see also Prinzing 1997: 8; Holmes 2005: 219). Peter Delian, the leader of the rebels, had previously captured many forts in northern Greece and secured the support of the inhabitants of the theme of Nikopolis, already in rebellion against a corrupt tax collector.[43] The Bulgarian troops pushed south into Boeotia, where they defeated the army of John Alekasseos, the *strategos* of Thebes and Hellas (John Skylitzes, *History*, in Thurn 1973: 411; Savvidis 1987: 36–7; Krsmanović 2008: 204). They eventually occupied Demetrias, where Delian appointed as governor 'an old soldier with experience in battle' named Litovoi (Lytovoes), who began repairing the crumbling walls of the city (Kekaumenos, *Strategikon* 75).[44] Betrayed by his new subjects, who sent word to the *doux* of Thessalonike to send reinforcements, Litovoi was eventually overthrown, captured, and handed over to the Byzantine authorities (Stephenson 2000: 130–1).

The prolonged military conflict with Bulgaria (969–1018) led to dramatic changes in the administrative organisation of northern

Greece. Much like the key frontier themes in the east, Thessalonike was put under the command of a *doux*, who was provided with units of heavy cavalry from the regiments of the field army (*tagmata*). However, the *doux* neither replaced nor eliminated the office of *strategos* of the theme, whose existence is attested by several late tenth- and early eleventh-century seals. The reason for this overlap of jurisdictions may be that the previously large theme of Thessalonike was now broken into four smaller themes: Veroia, Drougoubiteia, and Edessa, in addition of course to Thessalonike (Stavridou-Zafraka 2000: 134; Krsmanović 2008: 141).[45] A similar development took place in neighbouring Strymon. In the late tenth century, the theme was split into 'Strymon and Chrysava', to the south, and 'New Strymon', to the north (Dunn 1990: 319). In northern Greece, the multiplication and fragmentation of themes continued well after the conquest of Bulgaria, as eleventh-century *strategoi* were appointed over such key strongholds as Kastoria, with authority over their immediate hinterland, but not much more (Krsmanović 2008: 185–8).[46] Moreover, during the first half of the eleventh century, smaller themes, such as Boleron, Strymon, Drougoubiteia, and Thessalonike, were temporarily brought together in various combinations for financial, fiscal, or juridical purposes (Stavridou-Zafraka 2000: 135–7). By contrast, no comparable fragmentation is known for the themes in central and southern Greece. At a quick glance, the reason for the multiplication of themes in the north appears to have been military. However, since the early eleventh-century themes in the newly conquered territories in the central, northern, and eastern Balkans were much larger, an explanation is needed for the concomitant fragmentation and shrinking. One possible solution is offered by the examination of the distribution of finds of tenth- and eleventh-century coins (Table 6.1; Figs 6.1 and 6.2). With the exception of two hoards of gold and one of silver, most published specimens are of copper.[47] The majority of coins struck in the tenth and during the first half of the eleventh century have been found in central and southern Greece, particularly around the Isthmus, a distribution strikingly similar to that of seventh-century coin finds (Fig. 4.1). The contrast between northern and southern Greece is even sharper in the case of hoards of tenth-century coins, the majority of which are from the south. The considerably larger number of late tenth- and eleventh-century coins – the so-called 'anonymous folles' – found in Corinth have been interpreted as an indication of expanding markets (Metcalf 1974: 22). But if the coins found in Corinth indicate the

Table 6.1 Tenth- and early eleventh-century coins from continental Greece.

	Site	Denomination	Date	Number of specimens
1	Corinth	follis	913–959	2,327
2	Paleochora-Maroneia (Rhodopi)	follis	913–959	unknown
3	Philippi (Kavala)	follis	913–959	1
4	Thebes	follis	913–959	3
5	Athens	follis	913–919	6
6	Corinth	follis	913–919	45
7	Rendina (Chalkidiki)	follis	913–919	unknown
8	Athens	follis	920–944	59
9	Corinth (St. John)	follis	920–944	3 (hoard)
10	Corinth 1934.I	follis	920–944	110 (hoard)
11	Corinth 1965	follis	920–944	8 (hoard)
12	Corinth 1934.II	follis	920–944	21 (hoard)
13	Drama	follis	920–944	1
14	Kenchreai (Korinthia)	follis	920–944	4
15	Kephalos (Ambrakian Bay)	follis	920–944	1
16	Malthi (Messinia)	follis	920–944	139 (hoard)
17	Paleochora-Maroneia (Rhodopi)	follis	920–944	unknown
18	Platanos (Arkadia)	follis	920–944	1
19	Rendina (Chalkidiki)	follis	920–944	unknown
20	Sparta	follis	920–944	6
21	Stimanga (Korinthia)	follis	920–944	66 (hoard)
22	Thessaloniki	follis	920–944	1
23	Unknown location (Thessaly)	follis	920–944	1
24	Patras	follis	931–944	1
25	Thebes	follis	931–944	3 (hoard)
26	Argos	follis	945–950	1
27	Corinth 1934.II	follis	945–950	1 (hoard)
28	Drama	follis	945–950	1
29	Ilis (Ilia)	follis	945–950	1
30	Kenchreai (Korinthia)	follis	945–950	1
31	Limnai (Argolis)	follis	945–950	1
32	Patras	follis	945–950	1
33	Sparta	follis	945–950	14
34	Tegea (Arkadia)	follis	945–950	1
35	Trikala	follis	945–950	1
36	Athens	follis	945–959	192
37	Chrysi (Pella)	*nomisma*	945–959	16 (hoard)
38	Argos	follis	950–959	9 (hoard)
39	Killinis (Ilia)	follis	950–959	1
40	Sparta	follis	950–959	1

Table 6.1 (continued)

	Site	Denomination	Date	Number of specimens
41	Athens	follis	963–969	46
42	Chrysi (Pella)	*nomisma*	963–969	3 (hoard)
43	Corinth	follis	963–969	220
44	Platanos (Arkadia)	follis	963–969	1
45	Rendina (Chalkidiki)	follis	963–969	unknown
46	Sparta	follis	963–969	1
47	Tegea (Arkadia)	follis	963–969	1
48	Corinth	follis	970–1030	168 (hoard)
49	Corinth	follis	970–1030	96 (hoard)
50	Corinth	follis	970–1030	54 (hoard)
51	Corinth	follis	970–1030	over 4,000
52	Agios Sostis (Arkadia)	follis	970–976	1
53	Argos	follis	970–976	1
54	Athens	follis	970–976	104
55	Kephalos (Ambrakian Bay)	follis	970–976	2
56	Krestena (Ilia)	follis	970–976	1
57	Ligourion (Argolis)	follis	970–976	1
58	Limnai (Argolis)	follis	970–976	1
59	Patras	follis	970–976	4
60	Polystylon (Xanthi)	follis	970–976	2
61	Phlious (Korinthia)	follis	970–976	1
62	Sparta	follis	970–976	1
63	Thessaloniki	follis	970–976	2
64	Thebes	follis	976–1025	1
65	Thessaloniki	*histamenon*	976–1025	11 (hoard)
66	Archaia Kleones (Korinthia)	follis	976–1030/5	4
67	Athens	follis	976–1030/5	519
68	Epidauros (Argolis)	follis	976–1030/5	7
69	Ilis (Ilia)	follis	976–1030/5	2
70	Leonidion (Arkadia)	follis	976–1030/5	1
71	Olympia (Ilia)	follis	976–1030/5	2
72	Paleochora-Maroneia (Rhodopi)	follis	976–1030/5	unknown
73	Patras	follis	976–1030/5	2
74	Peleta (Arkadia)	follis	976–1030/5	1
75	Polystylon (Xanthi)	follis	976–1030/5	3
76	Psophis (Achaia)	follis	976–1030/5	1
77	Sparta	follis	976–1030/5	34
78	Tegea (Arkadia)	follis	976–1030/5	8
79	Thebes 1995	follis	976–1030/5	7 (hoard)
80	Thebes	follis	976–1030/5	1 (hoard)
81	Thebes	follis	976–1030/5	2
82	Thessaloniki	follis	976–1030/5	4

Table 6.1 (continued)

	Site	Denomination	Date	Number of specimens
83	Troizin (Attiki)	follis	976–1030/5	4
84	Valtetsi	follis	976–1030/5	1
85	Vrya (Chalkidiki)	follis	976–1030/5	5
86	Kenchreai (Korinthia)	*miliaresion*	989–1025	5 (hoard)
87	Thebes	follis	1023–1028	1 (hoard)
88	Thessaloniki	follis	1023–1028	2
89	Athens	follis	1028–1034	218
90	Thessaloniki	*histamenon*	1028–1034	2
91	Athens	follis	1030/5–1042	154
92	Paleochora-Maroneia (Rhodopi)	follis	1030/5–1042	unknown
93	Thebes	follis	1030/5–1042	1 (hoard)
94	Unknown location (Thessaly)	follis	1023–1028	1
95	Athens	follis	1042–1050	104
96	Corinth	follis	1042–1050	unknown (hoard)
97	Paleochora-Maroneia (Rhodopi)	follis	1042–1050	unknown
98	Skotoussa (Larisa)	follis	1042–1050	1
99	Thebes	follis	1042–1050	1
100	Thessaloniki	*histamenon*	1042–1050	1 (hoard)

expansion of monetary exchanges and of trade, the archaeological evidence for the latter is conspicuously absent. Conversely, from Thessalonike, a city for which there is plenty of written evidence of trade markets (see Chapter 7), the number of anonymous folles so far known is very small (Metcalf 1974: 22). Even allowing for the poor state of publication of coin finds from Thessalonike, finds of copper are rare in the hinterland of the city, especially when compared with the ubiquity of such finds in rural Peloponnesos. Moreover, the absence of gold and silver from a city (Corinth) with a supposedly rapidly expanding market is troubling, for the written sources clearly indicate that at least gold was locally available.[48] Other sources suggest that in order to be exchanged for luxury commodities, the gold available locally needed to be taken to Constantinople, presumably because such goods could not be found on the local market.[49] On the other hand, if the market was indeed expanding with the participation of foreign goods and merchants, it is surprising that, with the exception of fifteen badly worn coins struck for the emirs of Crete

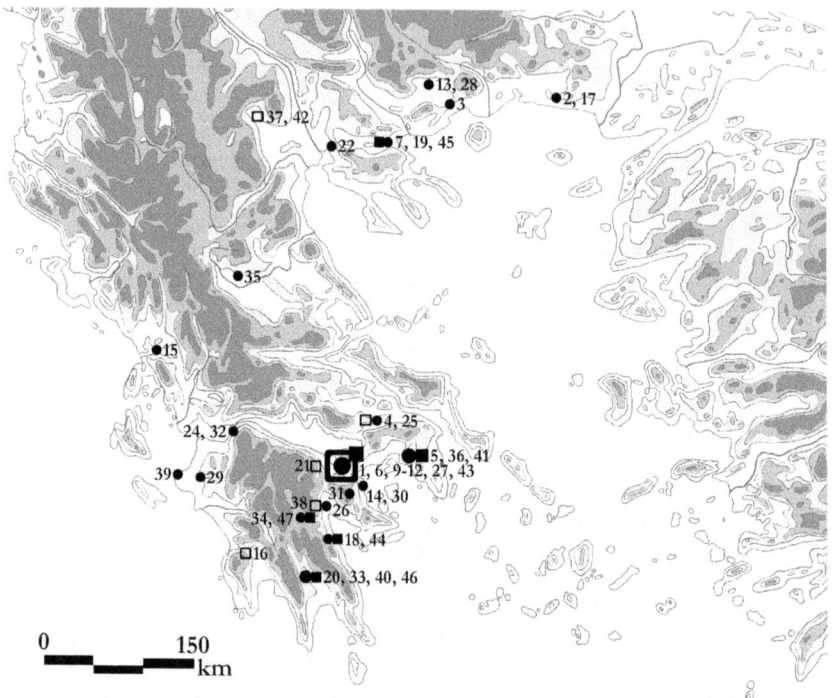

Figure 6.1 The distribution in Greece of hoard (marked by hollow squares), single, and stray (marked by circles) finds of coins struck between 913 and 959 (marked by circles) and between 963 and 969 (marked by solid squares). The smallest symbols mark finds up to 20, larger symbols up to 50, 100, and over 300 specimens. Numbers refer to the list in Table 6.1.

between 864 and 895, no non-Byzantine coins are known for this period from Corinth (Metcalf 1979: 48, who notes that the Cretan coins must have reached Corinth after the conquest of Crete in 961). The distribution of late tenth- and early eleventh-century coins may therefore not have economic reasons. Much as in the previous centuries, the army was responsible for the injection of coins into local markets. It has long been noted that the folles struck for Emperor Constantine VII Porphyrogennetos during the regency of his mother Zoe (913–919) are relatively rare in Greece (Table 6.1). By contrast, such coins are quite common in the Lower Danube region and in Dobrudja, where they signal the re-appearance of the imperial fleet during the military confrontation with Symeon of Bulgaria (Metcalf 1981: 235). A similar interpretation may be advanced for the late tenth- and early eleventh-century coins. Most anonymous folles

The beginning of prosperity 183

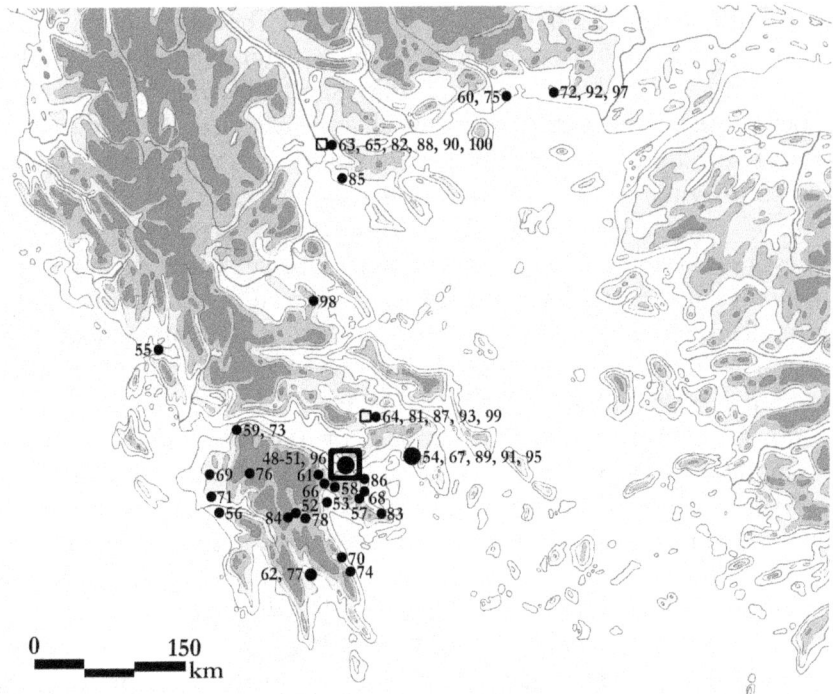

Figure 6.2 The distribution in Greece of hoard (marked by squares), single, and stray (marked by circles) finds of coins struck between 970 and 1050. The smallest symbols mark finds up to 20, larger symbols up to 50, 100, and over 300 specimens. Numbers refer to the list in Table 6.1.

from Corinth are varieties of class A, dated between 970 and 1030/5 (Metcalf 1970, who advanced the idea that some of those coins were struck in a local mint).[50] Over 4,000 such coins are so far known for this relatively short period, almost six times as many specimens as in Athens. They have been linked to the presence of the army, but they are rather rare in northern Greece, where much of the fighting took place (Metcalf 1979: 52). Can the coins be linked to soldiers from the thematic army of Hellas and Peloponnesos, returning home with the cash they had earned during the campaign? From the scarce information available about contemporary soldiers in the thematic army, it appears that instead of being paid, such soldiers often campaigned at their own expense.[51] Moreover, no indication exists that thematic troops were employed in the war against Samuel, although a *strategos* of Hellas was accused of favouring the Bulgarians, presumably after getting in touch with them in some way. There were two seals of a tenth-century *strategos* of Hellas named Theodore among those found in the vault of the Hagia Sophia Church in Thessalonike. However, the seals show only that somebody in Thessalonike, most probably a man of the church, received letters or messages from the military governor of Hellas, not that thematic troops from the south were present in Macedonia under the command of their *strategos* (Kissas 1990: 191–2).[52] Unlike the military, the presence in Thessalonike of civilians from southern Greece is well documented. In a story added at a later time to the collection of 'spiritually beneficial tales' written in the 960s or 970s by Paul, bishop of Monemvasia, men from that town are said to have gone to Thessalonike 'attending to their personal affairs' (Wortley 1996: 113).[53]

There is therefore little evidence for returning soldiers of the thematic armies introducing a large number of coins into the local market in Corinth. The presence of the military in that city is equally elusive, as no information exists of large units stationed in Corinth. Nonetheless, it is quite clear that the coins cannot be linked to any economic boom supposedly triggered by the explosion of long-distance trade. Throughout the first half of the tenth century, no ceramic imports reached Corinth either from the west or from the east. White Ware imports from Constantinople began to appear only after c. 950 in such shapes and forms as chafing dishes, dishes on low and tall pedestals, large bowls, and cups, all of which were apparently linked to feasting.[54] Locally manufactured imitations appeared as well, which indicates that feasting and not commerce must have been responsible for the adoption by local elites of such 'open' vessels as chafing dishes, bowls, or dishes with pedestals.[55] White Ware has also been found in Sparta, while Polychrome Ware, which appears in Corinth in the mid-eleventh century, has now been documented in northern Greece as well, at Thessaloniki, Vrya, and Synaxis (Armstrong 1993: 331; Waywell and Wilkes 1995: 454; Kanonidis 2003: 71–2; Pazaras and Tsanana 1991: 294; Tsanana 2003: 246; Bakirtzis 1994: 175).[56] A cup with yellow-brown glaze belonging to the earliest Polychrome Ware was among the finds from a cistern in the Agora of Athens, which also produced fragments of coarse unglazed ware.[57] Although important for documenting the relations between Constantinople and the main urban centres in the Byzantine provinces in Greece, neither White nor Polychrome Ware can therefore be cited as evidence of an increasing volume of trade on any market in any one of those centres. This is also true for another category represented in assemblages in northern Greece, so-called

Gouged Ware (or Fine Orange-Red Burnished Ware), which is dated from the mid-tenth to the late eleventh-century, and may have been imported from the Black Sea region (Vroom 2005: 68–9). Fine Orange-Red Burnished Ware pitchers were found in graves of the cemetery excavated in Polystylon, near Abdera, and fragments of Gouged Ware dated to the late tenth or eleventh century are known both from Thebes and from several rural sites in Boeotia (Bakirtzis 1983: 17 fig. 3; Vroom 2001: 183–4 and 2003: 145). It is important to remember that all those imported wares represent only a small percentage of the ceramic assemblages in which they were found, and which are dominated by locally produced wares. No remains of Polychrome Ware are known from Thebes, and salvage excavations elsewhere in the city produced only brown-glazed pottery (Koilakou 1992: 79).[58] Several sites in Boeotia are known for finds of so-called Otranto 1 amphorae, but it remains unclear whether such tenth- or early eleventh-century transportation jars were imported from South Apulia or produced locally, somewhere in Boeotia or in Corinth (Vroom 2003: 155–6 and 2005: 102–3).

At least some of the coins found in Corinth, as well as specimens scattered across Peloponnesos, may be associated with the campaign against the Milingoi and the Ezeritai in the early 920. Two out of four tenth-century hoards from Corinth contain only coins struck for Emperor Romanos I between 920 and 944. Given the state of preservation of the coins, the hoards with coins struck for Romanos I were probably concealed not long after the introduction of the new numismatic type represented in their composition (Penna 1996: 230 and 274). Similarly, since all hoards made up of anonymous folles of class A2 have been found in Corinth, it is possible to link them to the presence of troops in Corinth shortly before AD 1000. In fact, from the *Life of St. Nikon*, it appears that a judge (*praitor*) named Basil Apokaukos 'was guarding the isthmus there against the Bulgarian attack', quite possibly that of 997 (*Life of St. Nikon* 40). While it remains unclear whether the soldiers under his command were from the thematic army or not, Apokaukos was certainly not guarding the Isthmus alone.[59]

How large was the thematic army of Peloponnesos? During the early tenth century, the troops of Peloponnesos seem to have chosen to redeem their military obligations, instead of serving on campaigns outside the province. At the time of the general mobilisation for the 921 campaign in Italy, 'these same Peloponnesians opted against military service, but to give instead a thousand horses, with saddles and bridles, and one hundred pounds in ready money, and these they supplied with great readiness' (Constantine Porphyrogennetos, *On the Administration of the Empire* 51). Judging from the way in which the demand for horses was distributed among the most important lay and ecclesiastical authorities in Peloponnesos, in the early 920s the provincial troops cannot have been more 1,500 to1,600 men strong (Constantine Porphyrogennetos, *On the Administration of the Empire* 52; Oikonomides 1996c: 114). Exempt from this obligation were only the men who served in the local fleet of four warships, which policed the coasts and the seas around Peloponnesos; the purple-fishers, who must have worked for the imperial workshops in Constantinople; and the parchment-makers, who, like the purple-fishers, must have been furnishers of the imperial court (Oikonomides 1996c: 117). The largest contribution was that of the metropolitans of Patras and Corinth, each of four horses. Monasteries had to provide two horses each, but those without means paid only 'one horse between two' (*On the Administration of the Empire* 52). The list of lay aristocrats providing horses includes only holders of titles known as 'imperial' or 'of the retinue': *protospatharios*, spatharocandidate, *spatharios*, and *strator*.[60] Conspicuously absent from the list are dignitaries with so-called 'senatorial' titles, such as *dishypatos, hypatos, vestitor*, or *apo eparchon*. The *protospatharioi* represented the upper echelon of the local aristocracy, with one of them occupying the position of *strategos* of Peloponnesos. Occasionally, *protospatharioi* in Greece appear as founders of churches, as in the case of Christopher, *katepano* of Longobardia, who in 1028 built the Church of Panagia Chalkeon in Thessalonike, or the high-ranking official who in 1049 founded the Church of the Holy Theodores in Athens (Spieser 1973: 163–4; Mouriki 1980–1981: 80; Tsitouridou 1985: 9–11; Bouras 2000: 229). Krinites, the *strategos* of Hellas in the late 940s and of Peloponnesos in the following years, donated money for the building of the Church of St Barbara in Steiris, in order to apologise for his lack of deference towards St Luke (*Life of St. Luke the Younger* 59).[61] The *protoasekretis* John Lampardopoulos, chief secretary of Emperor Nikephoros II Phokas in 963, built the *katholikon* of the Monastery of the Philosopher in Dimitsana, Arkadia (Bouras 2006: 79; for the *katholikon* of the Monastery of the Philosopher near Dimitsana, see Konti 1985: 105–6). However, in all known cases those were office-holders from outside Greece, not members of native aristocratic families. Their reasons for building churches in Greece remain obscure, but from the available evidence it appears that none of them had local roots. In fact, no local aristocrats are known to have been founders of churches, although some may have joined already existing monasteries.[62] A funerary inscription from the Monastery of St Luke in Steiris mentions a certain Theodosius of good ancestry, who had been *anthypatos, patrikios, katepano*, and *vestes* before taking monastic vows. He may well be Theodosios Leobachos, the abbot of the monastery known from the rule of a religious confraternity created in Thebes in 1048 and devoted to an icon of the Holy Virgin kept in a convent in Naupaktos (Oikonomides 1992: 248; for the confraternity of Thebes, see Nesbitt and Wiita 1975). The Leobachoi were a prominent Theban family of landowners, one of the earliest known members of which had been an imperial *kourator* under Emperor Basil II (Nesbitt and Wiita 1975: 374).

In most other cases where the identity of the founder is known, churches were built not by local aristocrats, but by local churchmen. The oldest dedicatory inscription of tenth-century Greece is that found in Pallandion (Arkadia), which mentions that the Church of St Christopher was consecrated on 15 May 903 by Nicholas, bishop of Lakedaimon (Feissel and Philippidis-Braat 1985: 300; see also Avramea 1981: 33–4; Konti 1985: 115). Since no other name appears in the inscription, it is possible that the bishop was the founder as well. A century or so later, Bishop Eustathios of Vessaina restored a ruined, possibly early Byzantine basilica and thus built the Church of the Assumption in Aetolophos, prefecture of Larissa (Avramea and Feissel 1987: 368–9).[63] On the island of Crete, St Nikon is known to have built many churches and 'created priests and deacons and church-guardians and other officials' (*Life of St. Nikon*, 21).[64] Later, as he moved from Argos and Nauplion to Sparta and Mani, he crossed the 'Dorian land', where he built two churches (*Life of St. Nikon*, 31; Bon 1951: 72 with n. 2, who suggests that the 'Dorian land' was the territory later known as Tsakonia, which was located to the northeast of Sparta). On the site of one of Nikon's miracles (the bringing up of water to thirsty travellers), a house of prayer was built and dedicated to him by a local, who 'was a member of the order of monks' (*Life of St. Nikon*, 42). In Mani, the oldest dedicatory inscription is that from the Church of St Panteleimon in Ano Boularioi, which bears the date 991/2. The inscription mentions a priest-monk (*hieromonachos*) as the founder. In Sparta, a monk named Nikodemos established in 1027 a monastery at one end of a bridge over the Eurotas River, just outside the walls of the city (Feissel and Phlippidis-Braat 1985: 301–3).[65]

The distribution of tenth- and early eleventh-century churches in Greece (Table 6.2 and Fig. 6.3) shows a particularly big cluster in Peloponnesos, while large areas in central and northern Greece are devoid of any monuments.[66] Most tenth-century churches in Peloponnesos and central Greece are three-aisled basilicas, some of which appear to have been built on top of Late Roman ruins.[67] With the exception of two churches built in Kastoria with barrel vaults, all three-aisled basilicas from Greece are timber-roofed (Bouras 2006: 70).[68] By contrast, most tenth-century, single-naved churches with simple, timber roofs appear in northern Greece, often inside fortified settlements, such as Setina, Longas, or Platamon (for Setina and Longas, see Moutsopoulos 1992a: 6 and 13; for Platamon, see Marki and Loverdou-Tsigarida 1994: 533, Loverdou-Tsigarida 1993 and 1997: 61).[69] The largest and finest monuments of this period are domed cross-in-square churches, the earliest of which are massive buildings with very thick walls built in so-called megalithic masonry (stones in volume larger than 0.6 cubic metres), with no bricks and no traces of mortar, as in the case of the Church of the Assumption in Tegea or in that of the Church of the Holy Virgin *Panaxiotissa* in Gavrolimni (Bouras 2006: 70; for megalithic masonry, see Hadji-Minaglou 1994; for Tegea, see Orlandos 1973: 141–63; for Gavrolimni, see Vokotopoulos 1975: 80–6 and Konstantios 1981: 266–9).[70] Unlike other architectural types, the domed cross-in-square was employed not only for episcopal churches (such as Episkopi near Kissamos, on the island of Crete, for which see Malamut 1988: 198) but also for monastery churches (*katholika*, such as Koronisia, for which see Vokotopoulos 1975: 51–6). In addition, most rural churches built in southern Peloponnesos in the late tenth and early eleventh century are in fact of the same type. Most remarkable is a cluster of such churches in Deep Mani (Fig. 6.3, insert), within a short distance of each other. Some of them have walls covered in frescoes. Those of St Panteleimon in Ano Boularioi are related stylistically to the frescoes in the Church of St Peter in Palaiochora (second layer) and the Church of St George at Keria (first layer), which points to the existence of itinerant painters who worked within the restricted region of Deep Mani (Panayotidi 1999: 178 and 181–2; Kalopissi-Verti 2003: 339; see also Skawran 2001: 79; for the Church of St Panteleimon in Ano Boularioi, see Drandakis 1969–1970). This conclusion is confirmed by the examination of the sculptured decoration. Beginning with the mid-eleventh century, a stone carver named Niketas worked in a number of churches in

Table 6.2 Churches built in Greece between c. 900 and c. 1050.

	Site	Dedication	Date	Founder
1	Pallandion (Arkadia)	St Christopher	903	Bishop Nicholas of Lakedaimon
2	Dyo Ekklisies near Stamna (Aitoloakarnania)		Early 10th c.	
3	Kaisariani (Attiki), funerary chapel	Holy Archangels (Taxiarchs)	Early 10th c.	
4	Kastoria	Transfiguration of the Saviour	Early 10th c.	
5	Kastoria	Holy Archangels (Taxiarchs)	Early 10th c.	
6	Mavrika, near Agrinion (Aitoloakarnania)	Holy Trinity	Early 10th c.	
7	Patros-Riganokampo	St Irene	Early 10th c.	
8	Setina, near Achlada (Florina)		Early 10th c.	
9	Kastoria	Holy Virgin (Panagia) *Koumbdelidiki*	Mid-10th c.	
10	Mentzaina (Achaia)	Holy Virgin (Panagia)	Mid-10th c.	
11	Dimitsana (Arkadia), *katholikon*	Monastery of the Philosopher	963	John Lampardopoulos, *protoasekretis*
12	Aigion	St Nicholas	Second half of 10th c.	
13	Koropion (Attiki)	Transfiguration	Second half of 10th c.	
14	Tegea (Arkadia)	Assumption	Second half of 10th c.	
15	Zourtsa	Assumption	Second half of 10th c.	
16	Ano Boularioi (Lakonia)	St Panteleimon	991/2	Priest-monk
17	Kaki Vigla (Salamina)	Agia Sotira	Late 10th c.	
18	Koronisia (Arta), *katholikon*	Holy Virgin (Panagia) *Korakonisias*	Late 10th c.	
19	Episkopi (Evritania)	Assumption	10th c.	

Table 6.2 (continued)

	Site	Dedication	Date	Founder
20	Gavrolimni (Aitoloakarnania)	Holy Virgin (Panagia) *Panaxiotissa*	10th c.	
21	Kechrianika (Lakonia)	St Cyprian	10th c.	
22	Kernitsa (Achaia)	Assumption	10th c.	
23	Kissamos-Episkopi (Crete), episcopal church	St George	10th c.	
24	Longas (Kastoria)		10th c.	
25	Methoni	St Basil	10th c.	
26	Ochia (Lakonia)	Holy Virgin (Panagia)	10th c.	
27	Paliochora (Lakonia)	St Peter	10th c.	
28	Philerimos (Rhodes)		10th c.	
29	Platsa (Messinia)	St Nicholas	10th c.	
30	Polyportou near Eratini (Phokis)		10th c.	
31	Poroi (Xanthi)		10th c.	
32	Skala	St George	10th c.	
33	Synaxis near Maroneia (Rhodope), *katholikon*		10th c.	
34	Tairia near Monemvasia	Assumption	10th c.	
35	Vasiliko (Salamina)	St Gregory	10th c.	
36	Vathyrema (Larisa)	Holy Virgin (Panagia)	10th c.	
37	Ano Gardenitsa (Lakonia)	Holy Saviour (Agios Soter)	10th–11th c.	
38	Attali (Evvoia)	St Nicholas	10th–11th c.	
39	Beran Episkopi near Kastelli Milopotamou (Crete)		10th–11th c.	
40	Charouda (Lakonia)	St Michael (Agios Strategos)	10th–11th c.	
41	Chrysi (Pella)		10th–11th c.	
42	Erimos (Lakonia)	St Barbara	10th–11th c.	
43	Iraklion	Holy Virgin *Phorou*	10th–11th c.	

Table 6.2 (continued)

	Site	Dedication	Date	Founder
44	Platamon (Kavala)		10th–11th c.	
45	Potamoula (Aitoloakarnania)	Holy Virgin *Trimitou*	10th–11th c.	
46	Pyrgos Dirou (Lakonia)	St John	10th–11th c.	
47	Tsoukalario (Thasos)		10th–11th c.	
48	Thessaloniki	Holy Virgin *ton Chalkeon*	1028	Christopher, *katepano* of Longobardia
49	Aetolophos (Larisa)	Assumption	Early 11th c.	Bishop Eustathios of Vessaina
50	Asprokklisia (Trikala)	Holy Virgin (Panagia)	Early 11th c.	
51	Athens	Holy Apostles	Early 11th c.	
52	Athens	Holy Archangels (Taxiarchs)	Early 11th c.	
53	Athens	Holy Virgin (Panagia) *Lykodemou*	Early 11th c.	
54	Athens	St Catherine	Early 11th c.	
55	Distomo (Voiotia), *katholikon*	St Luke of Steiris	Early 11th c.	
56	Distomo (Voiotia)	Mother of God	Early 11th c.	
57	Kako Vouno near Kitta (Lakonia)	Asomatoi	Early 11th c.	
58	Kastoria	St Stephen	Early 11th c.	
59	Kastoria	Holy Unmercenaries	Early 11th c.	
60	Keria (Lakonia)	St John	Early 11th c.	
61	Kerkyra	Sts Jason and Sosipatros	Early 11th c.	
62	Thermon (Aitoloakarnania)	Holy Wisdom (Agia Sophia)	Early 11th c.	
63	Myriokephala (Rethimni), *katholikon*	Mother of God *Antiphonetria*	Early 11th c.	
64	Neochorion (Arkadia), *katholikon*	St Nicholas	Early 11th c.	
65	Olynthos (Chalkidiki)		Early 11th c.	

Table 6.2 (continued)

	Site	Dedication	Date	Founder
66	Orchomenos (Voiotia)	Holy Saviour (Agios Soter)	Early 11th c.	
67	Troizin (Attiki), episcopal church		Early 11th c.	
68	Athens	Holy Theodores (Agioi Theodoroi)	1049	
69	Koutipharis (Messinia)	Prophet Elias	Mid-11th c.	
70	Ligourion (Argolis), *katholikon*	St John the Theologian	Mid-11th c.	

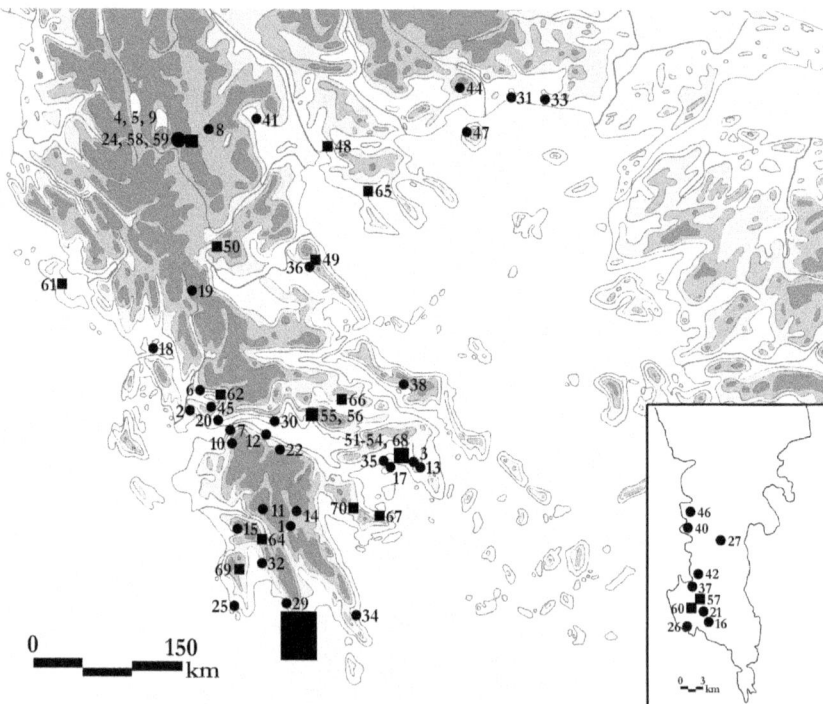

Figure 6.3 The distribution in Greece of churches dated to the tenth or tenth-to-eleventh century (marked by circles) and early eleventh century (marked by squares), respectively. The smallest symbols mark one church, the medium-sized two churches, and the largest four churches. Insert: the distribution of churches in Mani. Numbers refer to the list in Table 6.2.

southwestern Peloponnesos. His contribution is often acknowledged in inscriptions on altar tables which mention his name, in one case followed by the phrase 'from the country of Mani' (Feissel and Philippidis-Braat 1985: 304–5).[71] Why were so many churches built in a relatively short period of time in Mani? And by whom?

In the absence of any contextual information deriving from the written sources or from the archaeological excavation of any tenth- or eleventh-century site in Mani, either around or away from the many contemporary churches in the region, it is very difficult to explain the reasons behind this building boom. Some have attributed it to the missionary activity of St Nikon and observed that church building on such a scale did not resume in the region before the second half of the eleventh century (Megaw 1932–1933: 153; Kalopissi-Verti 2003: 339). However, no mention exists in the *Life of St. Nikon* of churches being built in Mani while or after the saint visited the region. In Sparta, Nikon may have taken the initiative in building the church of the monastery he eventually dedicated to the Saviour, the Mother of God, and St Kyriake. He may even have assumed symbolically the pose of a founder when, during a procession from the cathedral to the marketplace where he intended to build the new church, he 'put three stones on his shoulders and carried them', to everybody's amazement (*Life of St. Nikon* 35).[72] Nonetheless, he did not pay for the building. Instead, all the people of Sparta, 'both leaders and private citizens', are said to have participated in the building, some giving money, others promising to give, contributing what was needed, or offering to work. When lime was short, a man from Sthlavochorion procured a sufficient quantity. When wine for the workers was short, one of the poorest men in town brought wine of the worst quality for the workers, which required a miracle-making effort from Nikon in order to become drinkable (*Testament of Nikon the Metanoeite for the Church and Monastery of the Savior, the Mother of God and St. Kyriake in Lakedaimon*, in Thomas and Hero 2000: 318; *Life of St. Nikon* 35 and 36). As for Nikon, when unable to pay his workers, he agreed to put a chain about himself and be dragged like a slave through the whole city by the neck. Apparently impressed by this display of abnegation, the most prominent men in Sparta agreed to pay his debt to the workers (*Life of St. Nikon* 38).[73] No information exists about the most prominent men of Mani in the tenth or early eleventh century, and the only founder known from Nikon's lifetime is the priest-monk mentioned in the inscription from Ano Boularioi. However, half a century later, two men named Staninas and Pothos donated the money for the altar table in the Church of St Nicholas in Milia, which was carved by Nikitas the marble-carver (Feissel and Philippidis-Braat 1985: 304–5). No title accompanies the names of the two men in the inscription, but it may not be too far-fetched to assume that they were members of the local elite. In any case, for that many churches to be erected within a relatively short time and in a short distance of each other, somebody had to pay for both materials and labour in the same way the most prominent men of Sparta ultimately did for St Nikon's building projects. Nikon was able to erect just one monastery church in Sparta, a provincial city of some prominence. By contrast, it is not at all clear who may have had the financial means in the distant and relatively isolated Mani to support the building of no fewer than five domed cross-in-square churches (Ochia, Ano Gardenitsa, Erimos, Kako Vouno near Kitta, and Keria) within less than 5km of each other, a distance almost equal to that separating St Nikon's monastery in Sparta from one of its dependencies in Parorion (*Testament of Nikon the Metanoeite for the Church and Monastery of the Savior, the Mother of God and St. Kyriake in Lakedaimon*, in Thomas and Hero 2000: 319). Even if all those churches were modest in size, building in stone of the size and quantity involved for each one of them meant high costs for the workers needed, as well as for the level of skill required, and a correspondingly high level of prosperity. During much of the tenth and eleventh century, the only source of marble was the ruins of ancient monuments, but the costs of quarrying and moving stone, even from a relatively short distance, must have been considerable. Large projects such as each church may have represented also involved extraordinary methods of recruitment, for except cutters, masons, and painters, most of the labour force was probably unskilled. In the mid-tenth century, Emperor Constantine Porphyrogennetos knew of Mani that it was a 'waterless and inaccessible' region, which, however, could bear 'the olive, whence their comfort is' (*On the Administration of the Empire* 50; see also Anagnostakis 1996: 125).[74] If, as in Sparta, the production of olive oil was ultimately the source of prosperity for the region, then that prosperity correlates well with such indicators of economic growth as the building of churches.[75] The local oil may thus have been the source of the considerable funds necessary for the erection of the tenth- and early eleventh-century churches of Mani. In other words, and even if contextual information is lacking, the churches themselves are an indication of the relative prosperity of the region before, during, and shortly after St Nikon's lifetime. It is remarkable that the various afflictions lamented by the author of the *Life of St. Nikon* and other sources pertaining to tenth-century Peloponnesos, the most serious of which were the epidemic of plague signalled in Sparta and the Bulgarian raids, had no measurably adverse effect on the building boom. Moreover, the churches built during the tenth century in Mentzaina, Aigion, Kernitsa, Tegea, and Zourtsa, or in Ligourion in the mid-eleventh century, show that Mani was not the only prosperous region of Peloponnesos (for Mentzaina, Aigion, and Zourtsa, see Moutzali 1984, Lampropoulou and Moutzali 1997: 336, and Bouras 1971; for Kernitsa, see Lampropoulou and Moutzali 1993: 381; for Tegea, see Vokotopoulos 2000: 157; for Ligourion, see Mamaloukos 1984).

The construction of churches, which in Peloponnesos proceeded vigorously only after c. 900, continued unabated after c. 1000, especially in central and northern Greece, where new and more sophisticated architectural types and techniques of decoration were introduced. Of the two churches in the Monastery of St Luke the Younger near Distomo, in Boeotia, the *katholikon* is older than the Church of the Virgin and is crowned with a wide dome (8.98m in diameter and 5.22m high) resting on a shallow, polygonal drum (Chatzidakis 1997: 18; for the chronological relation between the *katholikon* and the Church of the Virgin, see Stikas 1972: 311; Pallas 1985; Connor 1992: 294; Mylonas 1990a and 1992: 118–19 and 120; Schminck 2003: 350).[76] This is one of the first examples of the domed cross-in-octagon type in Greece. In Athens, the first of the elaborate churches built in the first half of the eleventh century is the Holy Apostles in the Agora, whose octagonal dome with double-light windows and arched cornices is another illustration of the same architectural sophistication (Bouras 2000: 229).[77] Of a similar date and type is the Church of Panagia Lykodemou in Athens. The elaborate ornamentation of its façade consists of a combination of stone and brick, with the latter in a pattern imitating Kufic (Arabic) characters. The decoration of the façade with so-called cloisonné masonry (dressed stones laid in regular courses and horizontally and vertically framed by bricks) is typical of domed cross-in-square churches built in the early eleventh century, such as the Church of Sts Jason and Sosipatros in Kerkyra, the Church of the Virgin in the Monastery of St Luke the Younger, or the Church of St Catherine in Athens (Megaw 1931–1932: 104 with n. 2 and 107; Chatzidakis 1997: 13; Vokotopoulos 2000: 159).[78] Similarly, the decoration of the façade of the Church of the Holy Theodores in Athens and of the southern façade of the Church of Our Lady of the Coppersmiths (*Panagia ton Chalkeon*) in Thessaloniki consists of relief ceramic plaques and glazed tiles, respectively, both bearing decorative designs and pseudo-Kufic lettering (Bouras 2000: 229; Tsitouridou 1985: 22–4). While the Church of the Holy Theodores is known to have been built by an imperial official, the ornamental concept of the *katholikon* of the Monastery of St Luke the Younger was inspired by the decoration of the Hagia Sophia in Constantinople: in both cases, the portrait of Christ Pantokrator is placed in the narthex, in the lunette above the 'imperial pillars', together with the inscription 'I am the light of the world' (John 8:12). In fact, the exceptional quality of the building and its mosaics, which may be dated to the 1030s, bespeak a Constantinopolitan founder or patron, either Eudokia, the daughter of Emperor Constantine VIII, or the future Constantine IX, who before becoming Emperor in 1042 served as supreme judge (*dikastes*) of Hellas (Stikas 1972: 311; Schminck 2003: 350–1 and 379–80; Mylonas 1992: 120; for the date of the mosaics, see Mouriki 1980–1981: 86).[79] An equally Constantinopolitan origin has been proposed for the artist(s) who painted the frescoes in the Church of Our Lady of the Coppersmiths (*Panagia ton Chalkeon*) in Thessaloniki, as well as those of the second layer in the church of Episkopi (Evritania) now in the Byzantine Museum in Athens (Papadopoulos 1966; Mouriki 1980–1981: 80 and 87).[80] The Constantinopolitan associations of those monuments prompted imitation on a smaller scale by less well-to-do patrons, perhaps local potentates, as in the case of the Church of St Nicholas in Olynthos (Chalkidiki), which is very similar to the Church of Our Lady of the Coppersmiths (*Panagia ton Chalkeon*) in size, morphology, and decoration (Vokotopoulos 1995).

The Monastery of St Luke the Younger near Distomo is not the only one in Greece to display Constantinopolitan associations. The Monastery of St John the Baptist in Thessalonike, also known as Leontia, was founded shortly before 946 by members of the imperial family and richly endowed with estates and dependent workers (*paroikoi*) (Theocharidis 1978: 6–7). A chrysobull of Emperor Constantine IX (1042–1055) for Nea Mone on the island of Chios gave them a house (*xenodocheion*) in Constantinople to be used by the monks when visiting the capital (Morris 1995: 49). Imperial patronage is even more prominent in the late tenth and early eleventh century for a number of monasteries on Mount Athos. Among the earliest cenobitic communities on Mount Athos was the Monastery of St Nikephoros of Xeropotamou, which was most probably established during the reign of Romanos I (920–944). It became rich through an important donation of land, most probably from that same Emperor, which was then confirmed by Constantine VII and Romanos II in 956 (Binon 1942: 205; Papachryssanthou 1975: 65–8). Athanasios, the founder of the Great Lavra, arrived at Athos in 958 from Mount Kyminas in Asia Minor, but shortly before or after the conquest of al-Khandaq by Nikephoros Phokas, he joined the future emperor on the island of Crete. He returned to Mount Athos with sufficient funds from the future Emperor to build a new monastery in a place near the southern tip of the peninsula, at Melana, where Athanasios had withdrawn to live as a hermit before his departure for Crete (*Life of St. Athanasios the Athonite* 12 and 21–3; Lemerle 1963b: 75–6; Lemerle et al. 1970: 33–6; Papachryssanthou 1975: 75–7). By 963, as a *katholikon*, cells for five monks, and a refectory had already been built, Athanasios drew up rules for his community, which introduced a more advanced form of monastic settlement combining the virtues of cenobitic and eremitic life (Mylonas 1984 and 1987; for Athanasios' rule, see Thomas and Hero 2000: 221–8). In 964, Emperor Nikephoros II Phokas granted to the newly established Lavra three relics, including a fragment of the Holy Cross and the head of St Basil of Kaisareia (Lemerle et al. 1970: 103–5).[81] The chrysobull confirmed two other imperial rulings in favour of the Lavra, one of which established an annual payment of 244 gold coins from the imperial treasury for the maintenance of eighty monks. In addition, the Lavra was to receive in-kind payments every year, and the Monastery of St Andrew at Peristera, which had been founded in 871 by St Euthymios the Younger (see Chapter 5), together with all its properties. By virtue of its founder ascending the imperial throne, the Lavra became an imperial monastery. After the assassination of Nikephoros II Phokas, the new Emperor, John Tzimiskes, doubled the cash annuity for the Lavra. In addition, at some point between 970 and 972 he issued a comprehensive *typikon* concerning the organisation of the monastic communities on Mount Athos (Thomas and Hero 2000: 235–42; Papachryssanthou 1975: 95–102). When in 978 Emperor Basil II confirmed the previous privileges granted by Nikephoros II Phokas and John Tzimiskes, the end result was an increase of financial assistance for the Great Lavra to a level where over six times as many monks could be supported as initially stipulated by Athanasios (Lemerle et al. 1970: 111–14).

The Monastery of St Clement was granted in 979–80 as a base for a group of Georgian noblemen – John the Iberian, his son Euthymios, and John Tornik, their relative – who established Iviron with the support of the Iberian prince David of Upper Tao. The rules drawn up by Euthymios, who served as the second abbot, applied the same concept of cenobitic life as employed by Athanasios for the Lavra: a community for the majority of the monks, with a small number of hermitages for more experienced monks who desired to live separately (Nastase 1985: 253–6).[82] Vatopedi was founded at some point between 970–972 (the date of John Tzimiskes' *typikon*, which does not mention the monastery) and 985 (the date of the first mention of the monastery in a document of Iviron). The founders were three noblemen from Adrianople in Thrace, Nicholas, Athanasios, and Antony. Much like Iviron, Vatopedi was not a new foundation, for the founders are said to have restored an old, abandoned monastery which had been sacked by Arabs in the ninth century (Oikonomides 1999: 15; Pazaras 2001b: 10).[83] Not much is known about the attitude of Emperor Basil II towards Vatopedi, but the unity of the sculptured decoration of the *katholikon*, and the precision with which it was executed, betray the work of a team of stone cutters working to a specific design. The range and quality of the Vatopedi sculptures are seen only in a few monuments in major centres of the tenth and eleventh century, especially in Constantinople. If Vatopedi started as a relatively obscure foundation, by the middle of the eleventh century it was ranked second only to the Great Lavra (Pazaras 2001b: 10 and 102).

By the middle of the eleventh century, there may have been as many as 3,000 monks on Mount Athos, with 300 in Iviron and 700 in the Great Lavra (Morris 1995: 224 and 2000: 158). A little more than a century from the foundation of the Great Lavra in 963, half of the monasteries now in existence on the peninsula were founded (Burridge 1996: 173). In the *typikon* issued for the Athonites by Emperor Constantine IX in 1045, the Great Lavra, Iviron, and Vatopedi appear along with several other houses, such as Xeropotamou, Docheiariou, and Esphigmenou, which are still in existence (Thomas and Hero 2001: 291). John Tzimiskes' *typikon* of 970 or 972 was signed by no fewer than 47 abbots, heads of recognisable monastic communities. Even if many of those communities consisted of little more than two or three hermits, most probably disciples of the 'abbot', the *typikon* still proves that in 970 or 972 there were already several cenobitic communities on Mount Athos. By 1000, the dominant form of monasticism in the peninsula was that of cenobitic houses. The last hermits on Mount Athos, those of Chalou at the southern tip of the peninsula, had formed their own monastery in 991 (Morris 1995: 45).

Notes

1. Tarsos was an important frontier city and it had a formidable naval force. The emir Damianos appears to have been independent from the Tulunid regime in Syria and in fact acted in support of the Abbasid caliph al-Mutawakil (892–902). Together with Leo of Tripoli, Damianos attacked Egypt in 904, the first step towards its subjugation by al-Mutadid in 905 (Odetallah 1995: 98).
2. In Arabic sources, Leo is more often referred to as Ghulām Zurāfā ('the page of Zurāfā'), because he had been an attendant in the house of the chamberlain at the Abbasid court in Baghdad, who was nominated governor of Tripoli in 863 by the caliph al-Musta'īn (Odetallah 1995: 98; Farag 1989: 135).
3. John Kaminiates, *The Capture of Thessaloniki* 16–17; see also Frendo 1997: 207. The authenticity of John Kaminiates' account of the sack of Thessalonike has been disputed by Kazhdan 1978, but convincingly defended by Christides 1981, Frendo 1997: 208–23, and Frendo and Fotiou 2000: xxxvii–xl.
4. From Thasos, Leo took 'seven stone-throwing engines heavily protected on all sides', which he later used against Thessalonike (John Kaminiates, *The Capture of Thessaloniki* 29). According to Odetellah 1995: 99, the Egyptian ships joined Leo's fleet near Cyprus, before moving against Constantinople.
5. The inscription mentions the restoration of the wall by the imperial *protospatharios* and *strategos* of Thessalonike, Leo Chitzilakis, during the reign of Leo VI and at the time of Archbishop John of Thessalonike.
6. In a previous paragraph, Kaminiates explained that the inhabitants of some of the villages in the plain between Thessalonike and Veroia were Drugubites and Sagudates 'who pay their taxes to the city' (*The Capture of Thessaloniki* 6). For the status of the tenth-century Drugubites and Sagudates, see Nasledova 1956: 85.
7. Kaminiates accuses those commanders of spending more time on intriguing against their associates, 'madly intent on taking bribes and well-versed in the art of preferring this type of acquisition to all other', an indication that they needed to be bought up for military service.
8. It is worth noting that the Sclavenes within the neighbouring theme of Strymon are viewed as allies, not subjects.
9. Some Arabic sources place the sack of Thessalonike in March 903, others in July 904. The latter must be the correct date, for it is corroborated by Byzantine sources (Kazhdan 1978: 302; Farag 1989: 135;

Frendo 1997: 206). The 'Ethiopians' were Sudanese warriors on the Egyptian ships (Christides 1981: 8).

10. One such ship, headed probably to Thessalonike, was intercepted at the southern tip of the island of Peristera in the archipelago of the Sporades. The crew was massacred, and their ship was probably taken as well (*The Capture of Thessaloniki* 67). When, on 26 August 904 the fleet eventually reached Crete, the total number of prisoners counted was 22,000, 'out of all of whom, with the exception of those of us who were being detained pending the exchange of prisoners [with the Byzantines], there was not a single boy who had grown his first beard, nor, in all those thousands, was there even one woman of mature years' (*The Capture of Thessaloniki* 73).
11. A second attempt to take Crete in 949 ended in complete failure (Theophanes Continuatus, in Bekker 1838: 438; Leo the Deacon, *History* 1.2).
12. Those events must be placed before 920, when Peter attended a church council in Constantinople which had been summoned by Patriarch Nicholas Mystikos (Vasiliev 1947: 166).
13. According to Caraher 2008: 269–70 and 272, the *Life of St. Theodore of Kythera* was written in Monemvasia, not long after Bishop Paul committed to writing his own 'spiritually beneficial tales' in the 960s or 970s. There is little chronological precision in the *Life*, but St Theodore is known to have died in 922, only eleven months after taking up residence as a hermit in the ruins of an abandoned church on the island.
14. Leo the Deacon, *History* 2.8. Four years later (965), when Cyprus was conquered as well, the Byzantine conquest of the eastern Mediterranean was complete.
15. In 993, Arab pirates perhaps from Africa intercepted on Lemnos a ship carrying a Serbian embassy to Constantinople (Ostrogorsky 1949). In 1032, the *strategos* of Nauplion, Nikephoros Karantenos, defeated in the Adriatic an African fleet which had raided Kerkyra (John Skylitzes, *History*, in Thurn 1973: 385–6; Savvidis 1990: 53, 1991: 291, and 1994: 362; Prinzing 1997: 8). Kerkyra was also raided at some point during the middle third of the tenth century by Narentan pirates from Croatia, the 'Scythians' mentioned in the *Life of St. Arsenios* as being chased, attacked, and eventually killed by the inhabitants of the island in retaliation for the capture of their beloved bishop (Da Costa-Louillet 1961: 328 and 367–9).
16. The earliest *strategos* of Crete known by name is Michael, attested on a seal dated to c. 1000.
17. In the features of the Apostles on the apse wall, one can recognise the style of the frescoes in the Rotunda of Thessaloniki, but there are also stylistic connections with the frescoes in Çavuşin and New Tokalı Kilise (Cappadocia).

18. According to Kaminiates, ever since Prince Boris' conversion to Christianity in 865, 'war was in no place, and peace governed all the neighboring territory' (*The Capture of Thessaloniki* 9).
19. For the identification of Symeon's second campaign into Greece as the devastation of Peloponnesos predicted by St Luke, see Bazaiou-Barabas 1989: 384. For the link between Symeon's expedition and the scholium of Arethas of Kaisareia, see Vasiliev 1947: 187. The *Life of St. Luke the Younger* was written not long after the saint's death in 953 (Neville 1998: 22).
20. Throughout the 920s, several Bulgarian raids appear to have threatened central Greece, for a few years after the events of 921, because of 'hostile attacks', the master of a harbour on the southern shore of the Gulf of Corinth forbade boats from crossing over into Hellas. When St Luke attempted to cross over in a boat, he was arrested and severely beaten (*Life of St. Luke the Younger* 38).
21. Constantine Porphyrogennetos, *On the Administration of the Empire* 50. For the chronology of events, see Jenkins 1955: 205; Orgels 1964: 277–8.
22. Leo Agelastos would later resurface in a high-ranking position under Constantine VII Porphyrogennetos (Jenkins 1955: 207).
23. The conspiracy also involved the metropolitan of Patras and a certain poet named Chrysochoos.
24. The Slavesians are also mentioned in *On ceremonies*, in Reiske 1830: 651, as troops recruited for the 911 expedition to Crete. They were among the troops under Nikephoros Phokas, who, in 961, stormed and eventually took al-Khandaq (Theophanes Continuatus, in Bekker 1838: 480–1; Ditten 1993: 265–7). Ferjančić 1955: 40 believed the Slavesians to be a group of Slavs under Bulgarian control, while Orgels 1964: 274 saw them as Slavic rebels from the Byzantine themes of Thrace or Macedonia. Needless to say, there is no evidence of the Slavesians being either under the control of the Bulgarians or in some way associated with the Byzantine themes in the eastern Balkans.
25. There were relics of an unknown saint on the island, whom Luke invoked for the cure of his genital affliction (*Life of St. Luke the Younger* 51).
26. Christoupolis is mentioned on several tenth-century seals of *archontes* and *kommerkiarioi* (Stavridou-Zafraka 2000: 131 with n. 8).
27. Veroia was considerably damaged by an earthquake in c. 900 (John Kaminiates, *The Capture of Thessaloniki* 14).
28. 'Bulgarian Slavs' living in a village named Livadia also appear in the Georgian *Life of St. Gregory of Athonite*, who was abbot of Iviron between 1045 and 1056 (Grigoriou-Ioannidou 2000).
29. The scholium at *Geographia* 3.155a explains that the Slavs drink beer instead of wine. Another scholium mentions that Rhion near Patras

was called at the time in Slavic Velviskon. Three other scholia mention place names of Slavic origin, Verzitia, Lousitza, and Varasava (Diller 1954: 35, 37–9, and 49).

30. The date of the *Life* can be established on the basis of what its author has to say about him, namely that he had become abbot of the Monastery of St Nikon in Lakedaimon 'at the time of the concurrent eleventh indiction, the 6650th year' (*Life of St. Nikon* 68). The year 6650 of the Byzantine era is AD 1142, but that does not fit with the eleventh indiction, so emendations have been proposed which give the year 6656 (AD 1148) or the year 6550 (AD 1042). Most commentators prefer the latter, for there are indications in the text that the author of the *Life of St. Nikon* may well have known Nikon personally (Sullivan 1987: 6–7; Rosenqvist 1996: 102; *contra*: Waywell and Wilkes 1994: 426).

31. The dependency was located in a village characteristically called Sthlavochorion, which is mentioned in the much earlier *Testament of Nikon the Metanoiete for the Church and Monastery of the Savior, the Mother of God, and St. Kyriake in Lakedaimon* (Thomas and Hero 2000: 319). It is important to note that the story of Antiochos, the *doux* of the 'ethnics', is part of a long list of miracles performed by St Nikon at some point after his death. The events therefore may be dated to the first half of the eleventh century.

32. The story of the Milingoi and their attack on the monastery's stock is also a post-mortem miracle of St Nikon. The episode must therefore have taken place between Nikon's death (1005) and the earliest date advanced for the composition of the *Life* (1042). During his lifetime, Nikon does not appear to have had any interaction with the Milingoi or any other 'ethnics'.

33. One of the two manuscripts of the *Life of St. Nikon* contains a version of the text closer to the now lost original, according to which the Milingoi mentioned in chapter 62 agreed to 'bring candles and incense to this holy monastery every year' (Rosenqvist 1996: 100). For the Milingoi as Christian, see also Avramea 1998: 57. To be sure, the Milingoi had a different social organisation, for they are said to have fellow tribesmen, in addition to a 'barbaric and untamed nature'.

34. One of the two names is Staninas. The name of the other donor is Pothos, but his father's name is Syrakos (Feissel and Philippidis-Braat 1985: 304–5). Avramea 1998: 57 regards Staninas and Pothos as 'Hellenized Slavs'. Similarly, Oikonomides 2004 regarded the *Testament* of St Nikon as a source for the 'Byzantinization of Peloponnesos, specifically of its Slavic-speaking inhabitants'.

35. Samuel's attack on Larissa is commonly dated to 976. However, such a military campaign makes much more sense in the context of the events of the late 980s and 990s (Stavrakos 1999: 3; Holmes 2005: 402). Tăpkova-Zaimova 1966 has associated Samuel's attack on Larissa

with the local revolt mentioned in an anonymous, tenth-century letter (Darrouzès 1960: 357). The author of the letter describes as current events the defeat inflicted upon the rebels by the *strategos* of Hellas, who was just about to storm their stronghold at Ezeros. The relics which Samuel removed must have been taken from the Church of St Achilleios in which St Phantinos the Younger is said to have preached in 965 (*Life of St. Phantinos the Younger* 36; Yannopoulos 1995: 478).

36. The fort at Rendina may have been occupied since the first half of the tenth century, as indicated by coin finds (Galani-Krikou and Tsourti 2000: 351).
37. This, or the subsequent Bulgarian reconquest, may be the event responsible for the destruction of a building with two wine presses and a kiln which was excavated in Veroia in the early 1990s (Pariente 1994: 758).
38. For the office of *doux* of Thessalonike and its late tenth- and early eleventh-century titulars, see Tzanis 1996; Krsmanović 2008: 52–5, 134–5.
39. On his seal found in Constantinople, Malakenos appears as *strategos* of Peloponnesos, but two other seals have a person by that name holding the office of *strategos* of Longobardia and Macedonia, respectively (Stavrakos 1999: 5–6). Going over to Samuel's side seems to have been on the mind of a sufficiently large number of people for Kekaumenos' paternal grandfather, who was also *strategos* of Hellas, to fake a defection in order to allow the inhabitants of Larissa to harvest. Kekaumenos' maternal grandfather, Demetrios Polemarchios, actually fought with Samuel against Basil II (Kekaumenos, *Strategikon* 76 and 169).
40. While describing the circumstances in which Malakenos was slandered 'by some malicious men' to the Emperor, the author of the *Life of St. Nikon* in the same breath adds that the Emperor in question was no other than Basil II, through whom 'the late Samuel, the leader of the Bulgarian nation who was invincible in power and unsurpassed in strength, was destroyed' and 'the numberless Bulgarian phalanx was struck down and humbled'. Since the slanderers accused Malakenos of defection and insurrection, it is quite possible that at stake was the support Samuel may have received from the *strategos* of Hellas.
41. The seal of Basil Apokaukos was found in the American excavations of Corinth (Davidson 1952: 2764). For judges of Peloponnesos during the tenth and early eleventh century, see Limousin 1999: 301–2.
42. Both Samuel and his son, Gabriel Radomir, were wounded before escaping by hiding among the corpses of the slain, while 12,000 of their men are said to have been captured. Samuel and his son managed to flee to 'the hills of Aitolia and from there travel across the Pindos Mountain ridges, finding refuge in Bulgaria' (John Skylitzes, *History*, in Thurn 1973: 340–2; Krsmanović 2008: 53).
43. Shortly after Emperor Basil II's death in 1025, a revolt broke out in

Naupaktos against the *strategos* of Nikopolis, Georgios (nicknamed 'Morogeorgios'), who was also the local tax collector. Georgios was killed in the process, while his estates were plundered. The revolt was caused apparently by Georgios' arbitrary exactions on the inhabitants of the theme, but it is possible that his own reason for doing that was the decision of the government to collect taxes not just for 1025, but also for the two previous years, which happened to be years of bad harvest and famine. The local metropolitan may also have participated in the revolt (Prinzing 1997: 17).

44. This may have been the first time the walls of Demetrias were repaired after the Arab attack of 902.
45. Veroia, which was located to the southwest of Thessalonike, included the coast of Pieria, while Drougoubiteia extended northwest from the city. The *strategos* of Drougoubiteia appears in the 990s in the documents from the archives on Mount Athos, while the judges (*kritai*) of the theme are known from eleventh-century seals.
46. A *strategos* of Kastoria named John Dukitzes is mentioned on a seal dated to the mid-eleventh century (Iordanov 2006: 145).
47. The two hoards of gold have been found in Thessaloniki (Marki 2000: 247–8; Burkhalter and Philippa-Touchais 2003: 958) and Chrysi (Oikonomidou 1991). For the hoard of silver from Kenchreai, see Penna 1996: 230. For single finds from Paleochora in Maroneia, see Doukata 1991 and Doukata-Demertzi 1992: 701. For Philippi, see Gounaris and Velenis 1993: 535. For coins from Polystylon, see Bakirtzis 1982: 22 and 25. For single finds from Rendina, see Galani-Krikou and Tsourti 2000: 351. For hoard and single finds from Thebes, see Galani-Krikou 1997: 118, 1998a: 276, and 1998b: 158–9. For stray finds from Thessaly, see Oikonomidou-Karamesini 1966. For hoard, single, and stray finds from Peloponnesos, including Corinth, see Penna 1996: 230–64.
48. The bishop of Corinth presented a gift of gold to St Luke. That that was a gift of money follows from the fact that after initially refusing it, Luke was eventually convinced to accept one coin of the total amount offered (*Life of St. Luke the Younger* 42).
49. At some point after the death of St Nikon, a tax collector arrived in Sparta at a time when the new abbot of the Monastery of St Nikon was in Constantinople, in order to obtain an imperial chrysobull for the protection of the monastery against 'evil designs'. Confronted by St Nikon in a 'waking vision', the tax collector made a donation of seventy-two gold coins, which the monks used to buy 'holy pyxes and other fine vessels' from Constantinople (*Life of St. Nikon* 58).
50. For the classification of anonymous folles, see Thompson 1954: 109–15.
51. That much is known about a soldier named Michael Argyromytes, who was healed with oil from the lamp in the *katholikon* of the Monastery of St Nikon (*Life of St. Nikon* 65).

52. The seals were found along with another of a *strategos* of Thessalonike named Leo, as well as the seal of an archbishop of Thessalonike named Niketas.
53. The men were relatives of Martha, the abbess of the Convent of the Mother of God in Monemvasia.
54. Chafing dishes were placed on the table as a sort of portable brazier and cooking pot at the same time. The food in the upper bowl was kept warm by charcoal placed in the lower stand. Like dishes with tall pedestals, chafing dishes were therefore more appropriate for banquets, where food was shown before being consumed (Vroom 2003: 231). White Ware is a generic term for both utilitarian pottery in a coarse, gritty, grey-white fabric, and finer pottery delicately painted, so-called Polychrome Ware (Armstrong et al. 1997).
55. Imitations may be distinguished from genuine imports on the basis of glaze colour: while genuine imports are commonly green-glazed, their imitations were dipped into a solution of yellow glaze (Sanders 2003a: 40).
56. For Polychrome Ware, see Sanders 2001: 91–2 and 2003a: 41. The earliest variety is decorated with geometrical and figural ornaments in blue-green, manganese, and yellow-brown.
57. The deposit also contained a fragment of a chafing dish in brown-glazed ware with upside-down handles, a feature most typical of the second half of the tenth century (Frantz 1938: 430 and 433–4).
58. Similarly, only one fragment of early tenth-century plain glazed ware was found during the Boeotia field survey (Vroom 2003: 147).
59. If those were thematic troops, then their number must have been relatively small, which could explain Basil Apokaukos' fear of the Bulgarians. According to Limousin 1999: 298–9, after c. 925, the thematic troops of Peloponnesos were not operational any more and may have been disbanded, with the exception of a small police force of *taxiotai*.
60. These titles were of military origin and at least initially applied to servants of the emperor (Oikonomides 1996c: 116).
61. The chapel of St Barbara was the first church built on the site of the present-day Monastery of St Luke in Steiris (Stikas 1972: 311; Pallas 1985: 94; Connor 1992: 294; Mylonas 1992: 118).
62. According to Epstein 1980: 200 and 202, the churches of St Stephen, the Taxiarchs, Koubdeliki, and Holy Unmercernaries in Kastoria were all built by local potentates during the Bulgarian rule on small plots of land outside the town's walls. This may well be true, although no direct evidence exists to prove the point in the form of inscriptions.
63. That the church in Aetolophos may indeed be a refoundation also follows from its architecture: it is a large, three-aisled, timber-roofed basilica with a short narthex (Nikonanos 1979: 16–27).

64. Like the bishop of Vessaina, Nikon too restored an old, abandoned church, which he rededicated to St Photeine.
65. The inscription was carved on a column of the bridge and mentioned the protection for the monastery granted by the Emperor and his deputies in the theme of Peloponnesos, the *strategos* and the judge (*krites*), specifically against the bishop of Lakedaimona and his clergy (Neville 1998: 76).
66. Mentioned in the sources are several urban churches which have neither survived nor been identified by archaeological means. For example, in Corinth, St Nikon is said to have preached in the marketplace, 'above the arch which is there, where the divine church of our Lord and Savior Jesus Christ is situated' (*Life of St. Nikon* 28). In Sparta, he spoke to the people in front of the 'central church', presumably the cathedral in which the liturgy was celebrated by the local bishop Theopemptos (*Life of St. Nikon* 35). When Peter of Argos died, the funerary service was performed in the Church of the Mother of God in Argos (*Life of St. Peter of Argos* 22). When in Thessalonike, St Phantinos visited the Church of St Anysia (*Life of St. Phantinos the Younger* 46). The precise location of all those churches remains unknown. The only churches in Corinth which could be dated to the tenth century are the three-aisled basilica near the Kenchrean Gate and the single-naved building underneath the twelfth-century church on the Bema (Shelley 1943: 184 and 189; Scranton 1957: 45).
67. This is particularly the case of the church in Mentzaina which was built during the second or third quarter of the tenth century over the ruins of a late Roman building, perhaps the bath of a large *villa rustica* (Moutzali 1984: 31 and 33). Several other churches of the basilical type are known from tenth-century Peloponnesos. For Patras-Riganokampo, see Pariente 1991: 871 and Moutzali 1994: 147–9. The excavation of the church produced a coin dated between 931 and 944 (Lampropoulou 2004: 102; Moutzali 2004: 135–6 and 145 fig. 7). For Aigion, see Lampropoulou and Moutzali 1997: 336. For Zourtsa, see Bouras 1971. The same type appears in Thessaly (Vathyrema and Aetolophos), southern Epirus (Potamoula), and Macedonia (Chrysi and Kastoria) (Nikonanos 1979: 16–34; Vokotopoulos 1975: 29–35 and 189–91; Pariente 1993: 847; Moutsopoulos 1992b: 113–44). The latest examples of three-aisled basilicas are the churches of St Stephen and the Holy Unmercenaries in Kastoria, as well as the chapel of St Gregory near Vasiliko on the island of Salamina, all of which are dated to the first half or the middle of the eleventh century (Moutsopoulos 1992b: 203–26; Pallas 1987: 227; Aslanidis and Pinatsis 1994: 180–2). For a different dating of the Church of St Stephen in Kastoria, based on the frescoes, see Siomkos 2005: 45–132.
68. The two exceptions from Kastoria are the Church of the Holy Archangels and the Church of the Holy Unmercenaries.

69. A small, aisleless church was built in the tenth or eleventh century on top of a fourth- or fifth-century burial structure in Tsoukalario, on the island of Thasos (Dadaki 1997). The single-naved type is also sporadically attested in southern Epirus (Dyo Ekklisies; Vokotopoulos 1975: 41–4), Thessaly (Asprokklisia; Nikonanos 1979: 86–90), and Peloponnesos (Tairia; Kalligas et al. 2002: 486).
70. The domed cross-in-square church is the only tenth- and early eleventh-century type known from the Aegean islands (Georgopoulou 1972; Kollias 2004).
71. The Greek name of the country was actually 'Maina', which is believed to be the region of the interior, away from the coast (Drandakis 1972; Avramea 1998: 56–7; Bouras 2005: 2).
72. The three stones may in turn be a symbol of the triple dedication of the church. For the identification of the *katholikon* of the Monastery of St Nikon with the church found in the Roman Stoa at Sparta, see Waywell and Wilkes 1994: 426–8; Kourinou-Pikoula 1998.
73. Because they knew he had no money, the stoneworkers wanted to cut corners and install a column which was shorter than the others.
74. Emperor Constantine mistakenly placed Mani 'on the tip of Malea, that is, beyond Ezeron towards the coast' (Avramea 1998: 52–5).
75. That the production of olive oil was a lucrative business in Sparta is demonstrated by the fact, among others, that the Monastery of St Nikon had a workshop where 'the fruits of the olive trees were customarily crushed and with tools and stone weights oil squeezed out' (*Life of St. Nikon* 67). That Nikon's later success in Sparta and elsewhere could be attributed to olive oil is symbolically depicted in an episode of the *vita* which is set on the deserted island of Salamina, where the ship taking Nikon from Damala to Athens stopped for a while. 'Now the others returned to the ships rather quickly; but he alone delayed his return, since he foresaw what was going to happen. Scarcely then did he return from the island soaked with olive oil, when the sailors greatly reproached him for his slowness. And they wondered on account of the great amount of olive oil on so uninhabited an island, but especially at his bath in it. The situation remained unexplained because of an unspoken plan, the saint being willing to reveal this to none of the men' (*Life of St. Nikon* 23; see also Anagnostakis 1996: 127).
76. Chatzidakis 1969 and 1972b attributed the building of the *katholikon* to an abbot named Philotheos, whose portrait appears three times in the frescoes, of which the one in the northeastern chapel shows him offering the church to St Luke.
77. For the Church of the Taxiarchs near the Roman Agora, which was demolished in 1850, see Bouras 2001: 69–70.
78. Another typical feature of early eleventh-century churches is the replacement of arcade windows with double or triple windows.

79. Chatzidakis 1997: 47 notes that the hierarchs depicted in the *prothesis* and the *diakonikon* represent the provinces of the Empire, with St Dionysios the Areopagite and St Hierotheos for Hellas (Athens), St Achilleios for Thessaly (Larissa), and Sts Jason and Sosipatros for Kerkyra.
80. Closely related to the frescoes in Thessaloniki are those of the first layer in the apse and dome of the *katholikon* of the Monastery of Myriokephala built in Crete by St John Xenos.
81. Athanasios travelled to Constantinople both before and perhaps after the granting of Nikephoros II's chrysobull. St Phantinos saw him in Thessalonike in 966, perhaps on the point of embarking for Constantinople (*Life of St. Phantinos the Younger* 39).
82. A little later, Leo, the brother of Duke Pandulf II of Benevento (981–1014), arrived at Athos with six disciples. Initially accommodated at Iviron, he was soon able to build his own monastery, which was separate from the monastery of the Amalfitans first mentioned in the early eleventh century.
83. A number of older sculptures re-used for the present-day *katholikon* as well as recent excavations inside the *katholikon* seem to confirm that the church was built on top of an older, possibly early Byzantine basilica.

CHAPTER 7

Early medieval Greece and the Middle Byzantine economy

On a hot summer day in the 990s, St Nikon was on his way back to Sparta from Corinth in the company of a group of men who enjoyed 'the sweet grace' of his words. They were all travelling by foot and as they passed by Amyklion and were approaching Sparta, Nikon's companions witnessed one of his most astounding miracles.

> It was then summertime and the season of the high noon and violent heat and unbearable warmth. Those sharing the journey with the holy man, as has been said, were besieged terribly by thirst. For there was not on all that road either a spring-fed stream or river's flow or a snow-fed torrent or any other natural source of water at all. These men were stricken to the ground in the middle of the road; their breathing was cut short by the continuous heat and the choking resulting from this and they were violently pressed to give up their lives. Seeing that they were about to be in grave danger and taking pity on their weakness, the saint gave himself up to prayer as was his custom. Then, with his cross-bearing staff he struck the ground on which he stood and prayed. O your wonders, my Christ! Water immediately was given from the hollows of the earth – the sweetest and the most radiant and the most fit to drink. Those who were overcome by thirst and almost dead, having taken their fill of this, were revived and regained their strength.[1]

After living for seven years in Steiris, and feeling that his end was near, on a day of 953 St Luke decided to bid farewell to all his friends, neighbours, and acquaintances. Three months later, he was severely ill in his cell, and everybody expected him to die.

> When those who dwelt in the villages round about learned this, even though there was a terrible storm and indescribable snow was falling, so that the roads were nearly impassable and the people housebound, nevertheless, nothing could prevent them from traveling to see him. All of them gathered together and remained by him until the ninth hour, paying no attention to food or to returning home.[2]

Those two episodes, which took place at a distance of less than fifty years within the tenth century, illustrate very well the contrasts of the Mediterranean climate of Greece, with very hot summers in the arid lowlands of the interior of Peloponnesos and abundant winter snowfall at the foot of Mount Parnassos in Boeotia. No comparable data exists for the earlier period, but it is likely that the climate conditions remained the same between c. 500 and c. 1050. Throughout the early Middle Ages, much as during the Roman period as well as the subsequent Late Byzantine and post-Byzantine period, a mild Mediterranean climate existed only in the coastal areas within the isotherm of an average temperature of 3 degrees centigrade in January, which is the limit of oleiculture (Laiou and Morrisson 2007: 8). Climate conditions remained, therefore, relatively constant and most if not all changes in vegetation and landscape which took place during the early Middle Ages can be attributed almost exclusively to human activity. For Peloponnesos, the environmental survey of the Argolid Exploration Project has shown that, at least in the southern Argolid, the gap in settlement activity between the seventh and the ninth century coincides with a regeneration of pine and *maquis*, which is evident in the pollen spectra of coastal lagoons. When settlements re-appeared after c. 800 in the headwaters of the Ermioni and Pikrodavni streams, the land was cleared rapidly and intensively, which led to serious erosion, showing in the alluvial deposits of the Upper Flamboura valley (Andel et al. 1986: 122). In central and northern Greece, a steady decline in arboreal pollen-values and an advance of plants associated with agriculture and woodland clearance began by 900 at Pertoulion (prefecture of Trikala; Athanasiadis 1975: 112 and 123) and by 1000 at Litochorion (prefecture of Pieria; Dunn 1992: 244–5).[3] In a sequence from Lake Volvi (Chalkidiki), there is a peak in arboreal pollen-values during the early Middle Ages, possibly before the ninth century. Similarly, at Gravouna (prefecture of Kavala), at the foot of Mount Lekane, the trajectory of arboreal pollen-values for oak suggests a gradual cumulative decline beginning with the ninth or tenth century (Dunn 1992: 245–6).[4]

The importance of land clearing taking place during the early Middle Ages is also highlighted by place names of Slavic origin which refer to deforestation, such as Terpitsa or Strevina, both derived from *trěbiti*, 'to clear the woods' (Vasmer 1941: 60 and 76; Malingoudis 1985: 69 and 1987: 47).[5] In Arkadia, some 140 place names are known which derive from the Slavic word for 'yoke' (e.g., Zogovisti), which point to extensive agriculture practised in the area, no doubt in the aftermath of land clearance. The kind of agriculture practised is betrayed, on the other hand, by the frequency of place names derived from the Slavic word for 'harrow' (e.g., Vrana). Given that the particular phonetism of all those place names shows no metathesis of the liquids, a linguistic phenomenon which cannot be dated before c. 800, this may be a further indication of the approximate date at which the extensive cultivation of the lands began (Malingoudis 1985: 70 and 1987: 52; for the chronology of the metathesis of the liquids, see Birnbaum 1975: 228 and 232).

During the second half of the sixth century, the form of agriculture practised in Greece must have been a complex mixture of crop cultivation and animal husbandry. The tilling tools (two mattocks and four pickaxes) found in the hoard of agricultural implements discovered in 1877 in Olympia were mostly suitable for work in viticulture, arboriculture, and horticulture (Völling 1995: pls 95.a–d and 96.3–4). Two spades (only one of which survived) point to similar activities (Völling 1995: pl. 96.2). These were tools used on small fields to be worked by a single or very few individuals. Nothing indicates the cultivation of crops on large estates. Instead, everything points to a combination of garden, orchard, and most probably vineyard. Most harvesting implements from the Olympia hoard were also used for 'the pruning of fruit trees, shrubs, and vines, as well as for the harvesting of fruits' (Völling 2002: 200).[6] The production of wine is attested by the small-sized wine press found in one of the rooms of the house excavated in 1878 between the northeastern corner of the palaestra and the gate of the Gymnasium (Chapter 1; Fig. 1.4). The conclusion drawn from the analysis of the Olympia hoard is confirmed by the tools recovered from the excavation of the episcopal palace in Louloudies (prefecture of Pieria): billknives and mattocks (Papanikola-Bakirtzis 2002: 124–5). Unlike Olympia, however, the site in Louloudies produced evidence of oleiculture, in the form of olive oil presses (see Chapter 1). Such presses are also known from Athens and the hinterland of Patras, while local oleiculture may have prompted the production of Late Roman 2 amphorae in the vicinity of Portochelion (see Chapter 1; Sodini 1984: 359; Callegher 2005: 228). By contrast, there are no signs of olive oil production in Pyrgouthi (Argolis), and the palaeobotanical study of samples from a farmstead on that site showed that its inhabitants ate barley, wheat, rye, millet, and oats, which they most probably produced locally. That some regions of Peloponnesos produced grain follows also from the fact that in 533, Belisarius was able to procure large quantities of bread for his army from the hinterland of Methone (Prokopios of Kaisareia, *Wars* 3.13.20). As in Olympia, the farmstead in Pyrgouthi included a wine press, and as in Louloudies, there were numerous animals around, for faunal assemblages include bones of sheep, goats, pigs, and cattle.[7]

There is no comparable evidence for the 'Dark Ages' (seventh and eighth centuries). The existence of estates is attested by a boundary marker from Rhodes, which is dated to that period (Papanikola-Bakirtzis 2002: 123). Similarly, the seal of a *kourator* of Athens shows that imperial estates existed in or near that city during the eighth century (Zacos and Veglery 1972: 1703). Nothing indicates, however, that any of those estates were under cultivation. The quern stones found in Isthmia and Aphiona (see Chapter 4) point to the consumption of cereal-based foods, but cannot prove the cultivation of crops. It is in fact doubtful that the grain was produced locally. The sites in Tigani and Aphiona were located on narrow peninsulas by the sea, with little if any land available for agriculture. If the fields were in the interior, then no agricultural tools have so far been found which could support the idea of self-sufficient communities. Neither the location nor the economic profile is known for the community, which buried its dead in the cremation cemetery in Olympia. Nothing indicates that the kind of agriculture practised on that site in the late sixth century was still in existence during the seventh or the early eighth century. Pollen-analysis studies on various sites in Greece have confirmed that during the 'Dark Ages' the absence of any agricultural activity made possible the large-scale regeneration of wood- and scrublands. One economic strategy taking advantage of this phenomenon was bee-keeping, the archaeological remains for which are particularly prominent for the 'Dark Ages' in the form of ceramic beehives found at Corinth and Isthmia, on Aigina and Crete, as well as in Boeotia (Vroom 2005: 50–1; Papanikola-Bakirtzis 2002: 135).[8] Given that bee-keeping requires large numbers of flowers in relatively open areas, such as meadows or grazing fields, finds of beehives may be treated as indirect evidence for a shift from crop cultivation to pastoral farming.

Given the poor state of the archaeology of medieval settlements in Greece, there is currently no archaeological evidence for the revival of agricultural activity in the ninth century, which is, however, known from the written sources. The local community in Peristera provided farm animals, fields, and vineyards for the Monastery of St Andrew established by St Euthymios the Younger (Basil of Thessalonike,

Life of St. Euthymios the Younger 29). If the story of Danielis may be taken at face value, her estates worked by slaves produced flax, while the many sheep which she had provided the wool for the cloth, carpets, and other textiles which she generously donated as gifts to Emperor Basil I. The existence of cultivated fields is at least implied by the epigram in the inscription on the western wall of the Church of the Virgin in Skripou. In addition, the founder of that church may have served as *kourator* for imperial estates in the region of Lake Kopais (see Chapter 5). The evidence for cultivation of crops and fields becomes somewhat richer after 900. The grim aftermath of an Arab raid into Peloponnesos in the 920s is described in terms of crop fields and stores pillaged, with people eating grass and plants (*Life of St. Peter of Argos* 13; Morris 1995: 114). A refugee from Aigina, St Luke's grandfather moved in the early tenth century to a 'certain village called Kastorion', where he soon found himself in conflict over land with his neighbours. He went to Constantinople to request imperial assistance in the matter and was granted 'imperial letters and put in contact with the person who tends to imperial injunctions'. The imperial official divided the village and its lands and, while bringing peace in the conflict, arranged for both parties to live in security (*Life of St. Luke the Younger* 2; Neville 1998: 28; for Kastorion as present-day Thisvi in the Bay of Domvraina, see Dunn 2006). Small peasant properties also existed on the island of Crete after the Byzantine conquest of 961, often squeezed between larger estates worked by tenants (Malamut 1988: 426).[9]

In sharp contrast to such small properties, the estates of the Athonite monasteries appear enormous. According to the *typikon* of John Tzimiskes, which was based on a thorough investigation of the situation at Athos by a committee set up at the special order of the emperor, by 970 there were already individual monks at Athos 'who possessed fields and sold them, then purchased others in turn, and sold them again for the sake of profit and shameful gain' (Thomas and Hero 2000: 238). In the late tenth and early eleventh century, Athonite monasteries expanded beyond the Holy Mountain into the fertile agricultural areas to the northeast and northwest (Fig. 7.1). The Great Lavra possessed land as far away from Mount Athos as Chrysoupolis, while Iviron owned property on Kassandra and the Chalkidike. When acquiring the Monastery of Kolobos in Hierissos, the Iviron also gained property in the valley of the Strymon near Ezoba, thus becoming the most prominent land-owning monastery on Mount Athos, with an estimated property of 80,000 *modioi*

Figure 7.1 The distribution of estates of the Athonite monasteries of the Great Lavra (marked by circles) and Iviron (marked by squares) during the late tenth and the first half of the eleventh century (data after Morris 1995).

(about 8,000 hectares; Morris 1995: 228–9).[10] Although by 1029, the monastery had lost much of its property, which was confiscated by the emperor as punishment for the treason of Abbot George, all estates were eventually returned before 1070 (Harvey 1996: 91).

Much of the monastic property was gained through donation, but a considerable quantity was also acquired through outright purchase. The monks were usually able to outbid their lay neighbours in competition for klasmatic lands (i.e., abandoned lands which had been granted tax relief for thirty years, then withdrawn from the fiscal unit before becoming state property). This is most obvious in the case of the mammoth sale of klasmatic land which was undertaken in 941 by a tax assessor (*epoptes*) of Thessalonike named Thomas (Lemerle et al. 1970: 91–5; Harvey 1989: 57; Morris 2000: 160–1).[11] The Monastery of St Andrew at Peristera purchased two properties in the Peninsula of Kassandra totalling 1,800 *modioi* (c. 180 hectares), of which 1,200 are said to have been already under cultivation. The monks of St Andrew paid 36 *nomismata* for the land, while a local peasant named Nicholas was able to buy only 100 *modioi* (c. 10 hectares) for his 2 *nomismata* (Lemerle et al. 1970: 95–7). Unlike him, a group of thirteen peasants put their money together to buy 950 *modioi* of klasmatic land in the region of Hierissos for 19 *nomismata*. However, a few years later, when the land was re-assessed and the price doubled, the peasants found themselves short of cash. The Monastery of Xeropotamou quickly produced 38 *nomismata*, outbid the peasants, and thus acquired the land (Harvey 1989: 57; Morris 2000: 161).

While estates are well documented in the rich archives of Mount Athos, there is comparatively little information about what was cultivated on the land accumulated by the Athonite monasteries. John Kaminiates describes the hinterland of Thessalonike as 'decked out with vineyards, copses and gardens' (*The Capture of Thessaloniki* 6). One of the posthumous miracles attributed to St Luke the Younger mentions a peasant in a village near Steiris in Boeotia who was digging a silo inside his house for the storage of grain, barley, or legumes (*Life of St. Luke the Younger* 80; the silo was called *gouba* in the vernacular). By 1037, the theme of Hellas supplied Constantinople with large quantities of grain (John Skylitzes, *History*, in Thurn 1973: 411). Barley bread was the daily diet of St Luke the Younger on Mount Ioannitza, as well as of the inhabitants of Euripos (Chalkis) on Evvoia (*Life of St. Luke the Younger* 20; *Life of St. Nikon* 27). In addition to barley bread, St Luke also ate vegetables from his own garden, which is said to have had all sorts of plants, including cumin (*Life of St. Luke the Younger* 30).[12] The production of wine in a small wine vat is described in a miracle of St George, the ninth-century bishop of Mytilene on Lesbos:

> But George, the servant of God, asked his brother for a prayer and ordered two men to tread in the vat while he himself stood by and sang psalms of David. O Thy wondrous miracles, Christ, Who grants the desire of those who hope in Thee! For one could then see such streams of juice pouring and flowing from the vat that not only did they fill the storage jars one-hundredfold, but there was also enough in abundance for every container that each member of the clergy and the poor happened to bring.[13]

Tenth- and early eleventh-century wine presses have been found during archaeological excavations in Veroia and Vrya near Nea Silata, in Chalkidiki (Pariente 1994: 758; Pazaras and Tsanana 1991: 294). By 1000, Mount Athos was self-sufficient in wine. Monks sold large quantities of wine to 'laymen from the Zygos river in towards the Mountain' (*Typikon of Emperor John Tzimiskes*, in Thomas and Hero 2000: 238). The Great Lavra on Mount Athos owned many vineyards at Mylopotamos, Metrophanous, Bouleuteria, Pisson, Katadaimon, and in the village of Zitetza (Morris 1995: 224). One large vineyard at Thessalonikea on the small peninsula of Platys was apparently valuable enough for the second abbot of Iviron, Euthymios, to pay 200 gold coins for it, although the initial price had been only 34 *nomismata*. Oleiculture is well attested in Peloponnesos for Sparta (see Chapter 6), but olive oil was also produced in northern Greece. At the beginning of the eleventh century, the abbot of the Monastery of St Nicholas *tou Chrysokamerou* on Mount Athos donated an orchard with 300 olive trees to his cousin, Xenophon, the founder of the monastery which was to bear his name (Morris 1995: 227).

No archaeological finds of agricultural implements are known from early medieval Greece which could be compared to those of the sixth-century hoard from Olympia or the tools discovered during excavations in Louloudies.[14] References to tools are also absent from written sources. It is therefore very difficult to reconstruct the production process in agriculture. Many scholars assume that the characteristic plough remained the ardshare known since Roman times, because shallow tillage was more suitable to the dryer regions of Greece. Since ploughing with the ardshare is rarely if ever more than 12cm deep, tillage with ardshares implied the use of harrows as well. If place names of Slavic origin in Greece are of any use in this context, especially in the absence of other sources, then it is perhaps not an accident that many of them derive from names for such tools as harrow and mattock (Malingoudis 1985: 69). The first water mills of early medieval Greece appear in the Lavra archives. In the early eleventh century, the small monastery *ton Roudabon* on Mount Athos purchased land for six *nomismata* near a stream in the village of Radochosta in order to build mills. One of them is said to have been restored, which implies that an old mill had been in existence there before the monks purchased the land (Harvey 1989: 131).[15] In most rural communities, however, peasants preferred to grind their own flour by hand using hand-mills not unlike that of St Luke which was stolen by sailors visiting his hut while he was away (*Life of St. Luke the Younger* 49). Nor is there any evidence of restoring the fertility of the soil through manuring. Most producers needed sufficient and permanent grazing fields for their animals, since nothing indicates that they were concerned with root crops to stall-feed their animals regularly. Michael Choirosphaktes attacked the dependency of the Monastery of St Nikon because the animals of the monastery were harming his fields, which bordered the territory of the dependency (*Life of St. Nikon* 60).[16] This suggests that the tenants working for the dependency did not have enough pasture land of their own. Conversely, on Mount Athos, emperors had to intervene repeatedly in favour of the monks to prevent the encroachment onto the Holy Mountain of herds of animals belonging to the inhabitants of neighbouring communities, especially of Hierissos. The dependency of the Monastery of St Nikon in Sparta had enough animals to attract attacks from the Milingoi, who wanted to steal them (*Life of St. Nikon* 62). Stock breeding on a relatively large scale is also implied by St Nikon's request for the 'leading men' of Sparta to 'tear down the slaughter houses in the vicinity of the church of St Epiphanios' (*Testament of Nikon the Metanoiete for the Church and Monastery of the Savior, the Mother of God and St. Kyriake*, in Thomas and Hero 2000: 317). The local *doux* had a 'man from a foreign land' hired as trainer for his many horses (*Life of St. Nikon* 71). That certain areas of Peloponnesos may have specialised in horse breeding follows from the fact that 1,000 horses were demanded from the theme as part of the commutation of military service for Emperor Romanos I's 921 campaign to Italy (see Chapter 6).

Whether independent freeholders or tenants, the vast majority of the peasants in tenth- and early eleventh-century Greece lived in villages, such as Enorion near Argos, 'a place which is the home of farmers and rustics' (*Life of St. Nikon* 29).[17] In the early tenth century, there was 'a mixture of villages' in the plain between Veroia and Thessalonike, while other villages surrounded Mount Ioannitza, as well as Steiris (John Kaminiates, *The Capture of Thessaloniki* 6; *Life of St. Luke the Younger* 19, 28, 33, and 64). A document from Lavra dated to 952 mentions a number of isolated farms, but most peasants in tenth-century Macedonia lived in typically small villages, with no more than 100 peasant houses, separated by small gardens, vineyards, or fields. Village territories ranged between 15 and 20 square kilometres, a fifth of which was under cultivation (Lefort 2005: 295). As described in documents from the Athonite archives, peasant houses consisted of rooms grouped around a courtyard, with a superstructure of timber and adobe (Lefort 1979: 256).[18] Villages had leaders called *meizoteroi* in a Lavra document of 974, an Iviron document of 996, and another document of Lavra of 1008. Such leaders managed the communal property, and acted on behalf of their villages for sales and purchases of land. Large monastic estates were worked by tenants (*paroikoi*), who were controlled by *oikonomoi* (managers) residing in granges called *metochia*, which often had a church and buildings flanking an inner courtyard (Lefort

1979: 258). Tenants were often brought from somewhere else, as in the case of the property which the monastery of Iviron owned at Dobrobikea (see Fig. 7.1). At some point during the tenth century, for reasons that remain unknown, that village was abandoned by its inhabitants. After thirty years, the village property reverted to the fisc and became klasmatic land, which was purchased shortly before 1031 by the monks at Iviron. The monastery brought tenants from the outside, who took over the fields abandoned by the inhabitants of Dobrobikea and may also have restored the houses abandoned in their village (Lefort 1979: 260).[19]

Some villages were probably abandoned because of the devastation brought by the military campaigns of the late tenth century. A document of Iviron dated to 996 mentions peasants moving onto the monastery's estates because their villages had been destroyed by the Bulgarians (Lefort 1979: 256). Others moved behind the walls of the many fortifications built in the region. In 1044, all inhabitants of the fortified town (*kastron*) of Ardameri in Chalkidiki are said to have been peasant landowners with property just outside the town's walls (Harvey 1989: 201).[20] Some of the villages fortified in the early tenth century, like Hermeleia in eastern Chalkidiki, became towns. Mentioned as village (*kome*) in the early tenth century, Hermeleia was a *kastron* in 1047. Ezoba, Chrysoupolis, Vrya, Kassandreia, and Hierissos were also tenth- and early eleventh-century *kastra* along the Via Egnatia, the valley of the Strymon River, and the road from Thessalonike to Athos (Lefort 1979: 253–4).[21] Unlike in towns or *kastra*, there were very few craftsmen in villages. A list of tenants in the region of Hierissos, which is dated to 974, contains only two names of trades – mason and blacksmith – but no craftsmen existed among the twenty-four peasants known to have been residents of Dobrobikea in the early eleventh century. Even in Ardameri, the only inhabitant mentioned in 1044 as having a non-agricultural occupation was a certain Kalotas Amaxa, a wagon-maker (Lefort 2002: 308–9; Harvey 1989: 201).

In 968, when leaving Crete for Epidauros, St Nikon brought with him from Crete a bag of sea-salt (*Life of St. Nikon* 22). While the existence of salt pans on the island is beyond any doubt, it remains unclear whether salt production was part of the rural economy or, perhaps, associated with specialised craftsmen residing in such urban centres as the newly conquered al-Khandaq (Iraklion).[22] Specialisation may have been more advanced in fishing. To be sure, in the early tenth century, the Koronia and Volvi lakes in northern

Chalkidiki kept 'the tables of the neighboring villages' as well as of Thessalonike supplied with fish (John Kaminiates, *The Capture of Thessaloniki* 5).[23] However, the fish- and oyster-farm in existence during the ninth and tenth century in Poroi, at the entrance into Lake Vistonis, must have produced for the market in Constantinople (n.a. 1994: 18).[24] Similarly, the purple-fishers (*konchyleutai*) in the theme of Peloponnesos, who in 921 were exempted from any obligation to provide horses for Emperor Romanos I's expedition to Italy, must have worked for the imperial workshops in Constantinople (Constantine Porphyrogennetos, *On the Administration of the Empire* 52; Oikonomides 1996c: 117). Purple-shells were collected by hand or by means of baited baskets, and the extraction from the molluscs of the dye-producing glands must have taken place in the vicinity of the coast on which the shells were gathered. The dyestuff was then probably sent to Constantinople (Jacoby 1991–1992: 455–6). It is quite possible that the dye for some of the precious purple fabrics which the Byzantine authorities confiscated in 968 from Liudprand of Cremona came from Peloponnesos (Liudprand of Cremona, *Embassy* 53–4). No silk industry existed in Peloponnesos before the middle of the eleventh century. The many textiles and carpets which Danielis offered in the late ninth century to Emperor Basil I may have well been made in local workshops, most probably in Patras. However, no evidence exists so far of any textile industry in Peloponnesos before the late tenth century. When St Nikon convinced the 'chief men' of Sparta to expel the local Jews from the city, a certain John Aratos opposed him and brought a Jew back 'on the pretext of some task, by which garments are accustomed to be finished' (*Life of St. Nikon* 35). John Aratos' worker may have been employed in the 'shearing of the surface of woolen cloth, which obliterated any visible weave and rendered the fabric much finer and smoother' (Jacoby 1991–1992: 455).

In the sixth and early seventh century, almost the entire artisanal production was city-based. A wide variety of trades are known from sixth-century funerary inscriptions from Corinth, from millers, fishermen, and fullers to furriers, sandal-makers, grave-diggers, innkeepers, and dealers in second-hand clothes (Feissel and Philippidis-Braat 1985: 359–60, 362–3, and 365). Sixth-century glass-making is documented archaeologically for Philippi, Argos, and Corinth, while pottery production is known from contemporary Delphi (Koukouli-Chryssanthaki and Karadedos 1999: 80–1; Oikonomou-Laniadou 2003: 6–7; Hattersley-Smith 1988: 403; Petridis 2003). In Athens, where a glass-maker is attested by at least one funerary inscription, lamps were produced on a relatively large scale in the sixth century, although no evidence exists of organisation in large workshops (Papanikola-Bakirtzis 2002: 119; Karivieri 1998: 424). It is not clear where exactly in the theme of Hellas had resided the 500 tile-makers whom Emperor Constantine V moved to Constantinople in order to repair the aqueduct of Valens, but at least some of them may have been involved in the pottery production of such centres as Athens and Corinth (Theophanes Confessor, *Chronographia* 440). In the tenth century, glazed wares in red and grey fabric, as well as so-called Otranto amphorae, were produced in Corinth, although neither kilns nor wasters have so far been found to confirm the local production of such wares in Greece (Vroom 2005: 73 and 103).[25] The parchment-makers (*chartopoioi*) in Peloponnesos, who received exemption from the procurement of horses during the 921 expedition to Italy and who most probably produced for the market in Constantinople, may also have resided in Corinth. The same may be true about the blacksmiths involved in the production of 3,000 spears and 200,000 arrows which the theme of Peloponnesos provided for the 949 expedition to Crete (Bon 1951: 131 with n. 6).[26] On his way to the Holy Land, a goldsmith from Athens signed his name on the wall of a cave at Gastria on Tinos (Malamut 1988: 547). Craftsmen seem also to have been active on the island of Thasos, from which in 904 Leo of Tripoli took seven stone-throwing engines for the siege of Thessalonike. Glass bracelets have been found in Rendina, Philippi, and Corinth, but a larger numbers are known from Thessaloniki, which raises the possibility of a glass-working workshop operating in that city (Antonaras 2006: 424 with n. 16, 426 fig. 2, 427 fig. 3, 428 fig. 4, 429 figs 7–8, 431 fig. 12). Tenth- to eleventh-century pottery workshops have been excavated outside the eastern wall of Thessalonike, near the Kassandra Gate and the White Tower. The site was known as Kaminia ('kilns') in the early tenth century and the pottery workshops may have been privately owned (Bakirtzis 2007: 108).

In the sixth as well as in the tenth century, Thessalonike was an important centre of regional and trans-Mediterranean trade. Among the most generous donors to the Church of St Demetrios in the sixth century were rich merchants, possibly owners of ships and shipyards. Throughout the eighth and ninth centuries, the city maintained its status of maritime gateway of commerce, for imperial officials named *kommerkiarioi* were permanently on site to tax commercial transactions. Eighth- and ninth-century seals mention several *abydikoi* of Thessalonike who were involved in the control of the navigation, which suggests that the trade in question must have been at least partially seaborne. By contrast, in the early tenth century, because of the Via Egnatia and the travellers who wanted to stop in the city to supply themselves with everything they needed, 'a motley crowd of foreigners and townspeople thronged the streets' of Thessalonike engaging in commercial transactions. The lucrative trade was at the origin of a great many private fortunes based on gold, silver, and precious stones, 'while silk garments were as common an item of manufacture as were woolens elsewhere' (John Kaminiates, *The Capture of Thessaloniki* 9). Of all the goods mentioned, silk is the most certain sign of long-distance trade, but John Kaminiates claimed that it was the commerce with Bulgaria that was responsible for the prosperity of Thessalonike before the Arab sack of the city in 904. According to him, 'mighty rivers, rising from the land of the Scythians . . . lavish much abundance on the city through . . . being navigable upstream by seagoing vessels, as a result of which a cunningly contrived assortment of profits from commodities flows down those waters' (*The Capture of Thessaloniki* 6). The abundance in Thessalonike and its hinterland of the seals of ninth- and tenth-century *kommerkiarioi* and of other imperial officials involved in the taxation of the local trade (some with such specific names as *vardarios*, derived from Vardar, one of the 'mighty rivers' mentioned by John Kaminiates) strongly suggests that Kaminiates' is an accurate description of the situation shortly before and after AD 900. That foreigners engaged in trade in Thessalonike at that time further shows the ambit of the commercial network of which the city was a key component. Given the move, in 893, of the central market for the trade with Bulgaria from Constantinople to Thessalonike, it is quite possible that some of those foreigners were Bulgarians. However, the city was visited several times in the course of the ninth and tenth centuries by embassies from Italy or the lands under Frankish rule, and it is not impossible that either the envoys or others following in their footsteps engaged in commercial transactions in Thessalonike. It has been suggested that following the Byzantine conquest of the Balkans and the Hungarian conversion to Christianity in c. 1000, Thessalonike became the southern outlet of the trade from Central Europe via Belgrade (Ferluga 1993: 485–6). Throughout the early Middle Ages, therefore, the most important commercial centre of Greece was in the north, not in the south.

Despite the fact that money does not figure prominently in the main hagiographic texts referring to the regions of central and southern Greece during the tenth century, the evidence of coin finds from Corinth and Athens is far more impressive than that of Thessalonike (see Chapter 6).[27] Is it therefore possible to envisage such an economic growth in Peloponnesos during the ninth century as to treat Corinth, where the largest number of coins in early medieval Greece have so far been found, as the hub of the East Mediterranean trade? Michael McCormick has put forward the idea of a tremendous transformation taking place in trans-Mediterranean trade in the 830s, which had Corinth at its centre (McCormick 2001: 535–6).[28] However, neither the archaeological nor the written sources support that idea. There is nothing in the archaeological record of ninth- and tenth-century Corinth to indicate a considerable economic growth, much less the transformation of the city into a port-of-trade for international commerce. Moreover, the multiple surges in finds of tenth- and early eleventh-century coins may in fact have been associated with the periodical appearance of troops in the theme of Peloponnesos (see Chapters 5 and 6). There can be no doubt that the money brought by the soldiers temporarily stationed in Corinth was used to purchase goods from the local markets, but the trade in question was neither as developed as previously thought, nor based on commodities that would have transformed the city into a centre of regional or international trade. To judge from the archaeological evidence, there was little difference between the seventh- and eighth-century troops stationed in Corinth, on one hand, and those visiting the city in the ninth, tenth, or early eleventh century, on the other hand. In both cases, the large amount of money available almost exclusively in low and very low denominations served for the purchase of relatively cheap goods, perhaps food and other means of daily subsistence. The association between low-denomination coinage and local markets in which fresh food, such as vegetables and fruit, were sold is confirmed by the written sources. A poor woman living in the dependencies of the Monastery of St Nikon earned her living by selling bread, and fruit was sold in the local market in Sparta for money (*Life of St. Nikon* 71 and 75). Monks had purses with money in their monastery cells, but the amounts accumulated by such means must have been modest (*Life of St. Nikon* 75).[29] The first indications that commodities were available in local markets which attracted merchants from afar cannot be dated before c. 1000. According to the *Life of St. Nikon*, two Italians ('Latins') from Aquileia settled in Sparta 'for the sake of trade' (*Life of St. Nikon* 74). It is unfortunately not clear what the goods were in which the two Italians were trading, but the story is part of a posthumous miracle of St Nikon and must therefore be dated after 1005. The episode may well be a mirror of the economic conditions in Sparta in the mid-eleventh century (or even later), when the *Life of St. Nikon* was apparently written. It is not before the twelfth century that the Venetians began to export large quantities of olive oil from Corinth and Sparta (Harvey 1989: 147; Laiou and Morrisson 2007: 146).

Did early medieval Greece, then, have a subsistence economy with only marginal commercial activity, as Elisabeth Malamut once characterised the economy of the islands in the Aegean Sea during that same period (Malamut 1988: 436)? The current understanding of the development of the Byzantine economy between the sixth and the eleventh century is that a short period of wealth and prosperity during the first half of the sixth century was followed by a longer period of 'decay', crisis, and transformation between the mid-sixth and the early eighth century. The restructuring, recovery, and controlled expansion of the Byzantine economy between the eighth and the tenth century were characterised by strong state influence. As the economic situation began to improve during the late tenth century, the role of the state was tempered, and with increased production in the countryside, intensification of activity in secondary production, and growth of trade, the state eventually abandoned its control over the economy (Laiou and Morrisson 2007: 23–4, 38, 89, and 164). The analysis of the evidence available for Greece partially confirms this scenario, from which, however, it also departs in significant ways. Both archaeological and numismatic data show that there was indeed a period of remarkable prosperity in Greece during the first half of the sixth century, the last period of growth for many of the numerous urban centres in the region. It is not altogether clear what was the origin of that prosperity, but from the few indications in the written sources, it appears that the Greek lands produced sufficient grain to feed the troops of an Empire waging war on many fronts at the same time. This was not any more an economy of large estates with rural villas, but one of isolated, single-family farmsteads, making more intensive use of their cultivated land. Whether the occupants of those small farmsteads were independent freeholders or tenants, the state was able to siphon off outside Greece the substantial surplus which the rural economy of Greece was capable of producing. While in the fourth century the most important commercial activities had been those inside the Aegean region, by 500 the region had opened up to long-distance trade with the Near East, the southern parts of Asia Minor, and Africa. The number of African imports, especially fine wares, increased considerably during this period, especially in southern Greece. This change in commercial relations can be explained not by means of an economic re-bounce, but rather as an indication of state intervention, specifically in relation to the distribution of the *annona* (Abadie-Reynal 1989a: 151–2, 155–6, and 159). The barbarian invasions of the second half of the sixth century might not have had as important an impact as they did without state pressure on the local economy to continue working under the same conditions as in the previous period, in order to provide support for the military units temporarily stationed in the region or on campaign in the northern regions of the Balkans.

Unlike those regions, Greece did not benefit much from Justinian's programme of fortification. This may have encouraged the early abandonment of some urban sites (e.g., Demetrias) and the concentration of the population in other, supposedly better defended cities. It is interesting to note that in those cases of abandonment which have been better studied (e.g., Delphi), the last phase of occupation coincides with the development of some industrial function in the form of either glass or pottery production. It remains unclear for whom the workshops in Delphi were producing in the 590s, but most similar sites were abandoned only gradually and without any signs of violence. However, the abandonment of urban sites disrupted the capillaries of the local economy, for in certain parts of Greece there were no more markets for the agricultural products of the countryside. The rural areas were also deserted at a pace and with consequences which are not yet fully understood, mainly because of lack of excavations in rural areas. The withdrawal of the local elites in the aftermath of the abandonment of various regions by the central administration or by the military contributed to a rapid decline of cities such as Nikopolis, Amphipolis, or Delphi. By contrast, the continuous presence of the central administration in cities such as Thessalonica, Corinth, or Athens may have been responsible for the continuity of occupation, if not of economic function as well. The general withdrawal of troops from the Balkans in c. 620 gave the final blow to a regional economy much weakened by state intervention and military catastrophe. The collapse is well illustrated by, among other things, the relatively rapid regeneration of wood- and scrubland in many parts of Greece, in itself an indication of the absence of any agricultural activity, as well as of sporadic human occupation, if any at all.

There was, however, no 'decay' or crisis in those territories which remained under the control of the Empire between c. 620 and c. 820. Instead, the mechanisms at work seem to have been designed, again, to serve the army. Although next to nothing is known about agricultural or secondary production in any part of Greece during the 'Dark Ages', the presence of seals of *kommerkiarioi* suggests that something was exchanged on the local markets in sufficient quantities to be taxed by the state. Moreover, the presence of late seventh- and eighth-century coins in Corinth and Athens has been interpreted as a sign of the occasional presence of large numbers of troops, for whose needs the local population may have catered. The scarce evidence available points therefore to considerable shrinking and relative impoverishment, but also, and perhaps more importantly, to an economy beyond the level of subsistence, since it could be controlled by the state and geared towards meeting the demand of the military. On a much smaller scale because of both territorial losses and demographic decline, the situation in the 'Dark Ages' may therefore not have been very different from that of the late sixth and early seventh century.

The transformation came in the late eighth and early ninth century. Through state intervention, groups of population on the fringes of Byzantine territory were transferred to, and gradually incorporated into, the themes of Hellas and Peloponnesos. With the exception of episodic revolts, the incorporation of the Slavic clients on the northern frontier of Hellas took place peacefully. In the case of Peloponnesos, the process involved violence and military campaigning, with at least two groups, the Milingoi and the Ezeritai, successfully resisting assimilation. Unlike in northern Greece, large numbers of people from different parts of the Empire were settled in Peloponnesos. Kapheroi, Thrakesians, and Armenians were soon followed by Mardaites, Tzakonians, and Jews, creating a mosaic of ethnic and regional identities which will be discussed in Chapter 10. Some of those groups served as auxiliaries either for the thematic troops or for the navy. The reason for their settlement was therefore military, not economic. This is not the case, however, for the many refugees from the islands in the Aegean Sea, which during the ninth and early tenth century were the target of raids by Arabs from Crete or Africa. State intervention, as well as historical circumstances, thus contributed to a substantial increase in population, which is ultimately the sign of the ninth- and tenth-century phase of recovery. Growth was, however, slow. Land clearing and the increase of the area under cultivation became prominent only after 900, while the expansion of secondary production and the growth of trade cannot be dated before 1000.

By the early eighth century, Hellas was little more than a military outpost for the imperial navy. Two centuries later, its grain fed the population of Constantinople. Seventh-century Thessalonica relied on supplies of grain from the outside for its survival. In the early tenth century, although grain was still coming onto the local market from outside, possibly from Hellas, Thessalonike was a major centre of regional and inter-regional trade. The first half of the tenth century is a period of intense political and military conflict in Peloponnesos. After 950, however, the region witnessed an explosion of church building (see Chapter 6). This may be interpreted as the sign of the relative prosperity of those who, instead of serving in the imperial army in Italy, preferred to redeem their military obligations and were capable of paying in full a large amount of money to the imperial treasury, in addition to providing horses for the imperial army. Boeotia underwent significant economic revival from the late tenth century onwards, which is indirectly demonstrated by five or six new bishoprics established there in the eleventh century (Dunn 1995).

Among the first to witness the revival of the rural economy in Boeotia may have been the imperial *protospatharios* Leo, the founder of the Church of the Virgin at Skripou. However, among the first to bring about that revival were refugees from the islands such as St Luke's grandfather. In northern Greece, the monasteries on Mount Athos were the spear head of recovery in the tenth century and accelerated growth in the eleventh century. Nonetheless, neither economic recovery nor controlled expansion could automatically lead to an expansion of the local markets or to the integration of ninth- and tenth-century Greece into the network of international commerce. The only exception is Thessalonike, which was already a gateway for Bulgarian trade in the early tenth century. It was only the accelerated growth of the eleventh century that turned both Thessalonike and Corinth into major centres of international (as opposed to just Bulgarian) trade. From the seventh to the tenth century, the most important intervention of the state in the regional economy of Greece was through the army. Local markets continued to operate throughout the 'Dark Ages' in order to offer relatively cheap goods, such as fresh food or other means of subsistence, to soldiers and sailors in the navy. The ninth- and tenth-century recovery may have been indirectly brought about by military concerns, especially in those areas, such as Peloponnesos, to which entire groups of population were transferred from other parts of the Empire. Besides the army, only the monasteries could trigger changes in the rural economy of the magnitude associated with the accelerated growth of the eleventh century. Economic prosperity returned to the Greek lands after five centuries or so through a combination of factors, only one of which was the intervention of the state. In early medieval Greece, the driving force behind economic growth was the agricultural production of fields owned by freeholders or of large estates in monastic or private property.

Notes

1. *Life of St. Nikon* 42; Constantelos 1985: 310. The miracle took place after the visit St Nikon paid to Basil Apokaukos in Corinth. Given that the *praitor* was afraid of 'the attack of the Bulgarian nation', the year may have well been 997, when Samuel's raiding campaign is known to have reached Corinth. For the water miracles of St Nikon imitating Moses, see Imellou 1999: 42–3.
2. *Life of St. Luke the Younger* 64. Violent winter storms were also on the mind of the members of the confraternity of Thebes, who were in charge with the organisation of the monthly processions with the icon of the Holy Virgin in the convent of Naupaktos (Nesbitt and Wiita 1975: 369). For a description of a rainy, but very cold winter in Thessalonike, see the *Life of St. Theodora of Thessalonike* 31–3.
3. During the Dark Ages (seventh to ninth century), the vegetation in Litochorion contained a higher proportion of tree species than in any previous or subsequent period.
4. After the conquest of Crete by the Byzantine troops in 961, monks such as John Xenos had to clear the land before building their monasteries (Malamut 1988: 478).
5. The forty-four instances of the place name Lazos identified in southwestern Peloponnesos point to a similar phenomenon.
6. Crop farming and the use of hand tools are also betrayed by such vessels as the marble bowls found in Thessaloniki, which were used in drying, kneading, and pounding various foodstuffs – pulses, grains, vegetables, nuts, or spices (Tzitzibassi 2000).
7. Animal husbandry in Louloudies is at least suggested by finds of bells for cattle (Papanikola-Bakirtzis 2002: 124–5, 132–3).
8. Most ceramic beehives found in Greece have been dated between the mid-sixth and the mid-eighth century. Beehives were among the pottery

forms produced in the late sixth-century pottery workshop in Delphi (Petridis 2003: 445 and fig. 5).
9. The *strategos* of Nikopolis in 1025, Georgios, owned large estates near Naupaktos, which were plundered in the course of the revolt against him (Prinzing 1997: 17).
10. By the end of the eleventh century, the Lavra had 47,052 *modioi* (c. 4,700 hectares) of land in the theme of Boleron-Strymon-Thessalonike.
11. No fewer than 14,000 *modioi* (c. 1,400 hectares) were sold in 941. Possession of klasmatic lands was advantageous because the price was no more than twenty-four times the tax to be paid for the land before abandonment. Moreover, after purchase the tax was reduced to a twelfth of the original tax during the period of bringing the land back to cultivation.
12. Luke's sister Kale is said to have taken care of his garden.
13. *Lives of Sts. David, Symeon, and George of Lesbos* 32.
14. The purpose of the pickaxe found in a seventh-century grave within the square tower at the western gate of the Acrocorinth together with weapons and a bronze chain may not have been agricultural (Davidson 1937: 230 and 232, 231 fig. 2J).
15. According to the *Lives of Sts. David, Symeon, and George of Lesbos* 13, there was a mill in or near Mitylene in the early ninth century.
16. The animals in question appear to have been sheep, for Choirosphaktes' men set fire to the sheepfolds.
17. Nikon is said to have gone 'through all the other villages (*komopoleis*)' in Arkadia (*Life of St. Nikon* 31).
18. In the late tenth century, a house in Hierissos which belonged to a monastery was taken apart and the materials were easily recovered (Lefort 2005: 292 with nn. 14–15).
19. The new hamlets created for tenants were no more than 2 square kilometres in area (Lefort 2005: 294).
20. Ardameri appears as a bishopric in the early tenth century under the name Herkoulon (Darrouzès 1981: 278; Lefort 1979: 253).
21. Besides fortification, the difference between village and *kastron* was that the latter served as residence for state officials, garrison officers, bishops, and clergy.
22. In the seventh century, a salt pan in Thessalonike was the property of the Emperor, who donated it to the Church of St Demetrios (Vasiliev 1943, who nonetheless believed the donation to have been a salt shop or storehouse, not pan).
23. Fishing hooks have been found on the site of the ninth- to eleventh-century monastery excavated in Synaxis near Maroneia (Papanikola-Bakirtzis 2002: 156).
24. Moreover, the containers employed for the shipping of fish and oysters were apparently produced on site, as evidenced among other things

by finds of dies for amphora stamps. One such die was found at Porto Lago, and another is known from Synaxis (Papanikola-Bakirtzis 2002: 83).
25. A kiln was found during the excavation in the early 1990s of a tenth-century building in Veroia, but nothing is known about the kinds of pottery which were produced there (Pariente 1994: 758).
26. An equal quantity of weapons was delivered by the *archon* of Chalkis in Evvoia for the theme of Hellas, and by the *strategos* of Nikopolis, whose headquarters were in Naupaktos.
27. For monetary transactions as rarely mentioned in hagiographic texts, see Neville 1998: 43.
28. Contrast that with the opinion of Choumanidis 2001: 46, according to which the regional economy of Peloponnesos was not fully integrated within the Empire before the reign of Basil I (867–886).
29. Moreover, St Nikon himself instructed his monks to keep the revenue from the monastery's dependencies in Sthlavochorion and Parorion 'stored up and collected in the Church of the Savior, not only the yield of the vineyards and small farms and olive trees, but also the yield of fruit-bearing and non-fruit bearing trees' (*Testament of Nikon the Metanoiete for the Church and Monastery of the Savior, the Mother of God and St. Kyriake*, in Thomas and Hero 2000: 319). The ideal of autarky thus worked against the participation of the monks in profit-making transactions in the market.

CHAPTER 8

Social structures and Byzantine administration in early medieval Greece

The secular elites of sixth-century Greece formed an evanescent social group. By 500, most of them lived in urban villas lavishly decorated with mosaic floors or marble revetment, as in Argos, Delphi, or Athens (see Chapter 2). They laid their dead in frescoed burial chambers, often inside basilicas for the building or decoration of which they served as patrons (see Chapter 1). While urban villas completely disappeared before 600, the use of burial chambers attached or adjacent to existing basilicas continued well into the seventh century. However, those burying their dead in Nea Anchialos shortly after 600 neither had the same social status nor employed the same elements of material culture for the representation of their power as their sixth-century predecessors. Although the privileged status of the woman buried in a chamber built next to basilica Δ in Nea Anchialos was rendered visible by access to a Christian burial site, the message encoded in her burial dress combined cultural elements of different origins in an attempt to create a new way of expressing social power (see Chapter 4). Similarly, the 'wandering soldier' from Corinth was buried in a stone-lined grave – a type of grave most common in the circum-Mediterranean region – but with grave goods hinting at barbarian fashions from the Middle Danube region or the steppe lands north of the Black Sea. The archaeological evidence thus suggests that the withdrawal of the old, city-based aristocracy both from political life and, quite possibly, from Greece altogether was followed by a dramatic transformation of the cultural construction of social power. By the time Emperor Herakleios withdrew the army from the Balkans, leaving only a modicum of Byzantine administration in a few coastal cities, the representation of aristocratic identity had already adopted elements of barbarian inspiration, if not origin. At the same time, military offices became the dominant political positions, which turned the army into the only pathway to local power. The large number of military officials, mainly of the navy, associated with the theme of Hellas which are mentioned on seventh- and eighth-century seals strongly suggests that in Dark-Age Greece, as well as elsewhere in the Empire, 'military hierarchies became the dominant public positions' (Wickham 2005: 236).

There is no evidence of continuity between the sixth-century aristocracy and the military men of the late seventh and eighth century. The militarisation of aristocratic identity and values went hand in hand with a competition for imperial titles. Many of the ninth- to tenth-century *strategoi* of Peloponnesos, Kephallenia, Nikopolis, Thessalonike, and Strymon bore such lofty titles as imperial *protospatharios* or spatharocandidate, which suggest that those men were at the top of the hierarchy in their respective provinces because they were linked to the hierarchy at the court in Constantinople. However, there is no indication that they also belonged to local aristocratic families.[1] The imperial *protospatharios* Kontoleon, the *strategos* of Kephallenia in 1010 and that of Hellas in 1024, was a member of the Armenian family Tornik (Malamut 1988: 486).[2] Several other *strategoi* of Samos were of Armenian origin, beginning with Romanos Lekapenos, the future Emperor (Malamut 1988: 501–2).[3] By 900, imperial *protospatharioi* were founders of churches, such as that in Skripou, a form of power representation which reminds one of the sixth-century parameters of aristocratic identity in Greece. Moreover, and if the story of Danielis is to be treated as authentic, the very purpose of wealth accumulated in the province was to obtain a place in the hierarchy of the imperial court in Constantinople. The son of Danielis was appointed *protospatharios* as soon as Basil assumed the imperial power, while she became the 'Mother of the Emperor'. To judge from the archaeological evidence, the simple possession of a letter from an important *protospatharios* was sufficient for the representation of status in death, as in the case of the man buried in a grave excavated in Spilaion (see Chapter 5). *Protospatharioi* were the cream of the local aristocracy in tenth-century Peloponnesos, members of which bore imperial but not senatorial titles, as no dignitaries existed in the province who were not 'of the imperial retinue' (Oikonomides 1996c: 116 and 118–19).[4] However, after 900, there is a marked change in the relations between the local and the imperial hierarchies. As those on whom emperors had bestowed lofty imperial titles were able to use their position in the imperial hierarchy to acquire land and increase their wealth, they became more interested in local power networks, which did not always have the interest of the imperial government at heart. It has long been noted that, judging from the hagiographic sources of the tenth century (primarily the *Life of St. Luke the Younger* and the *Life of St. Nikon*), the presence of the imperial power in Greece is seen not so much through steady local government as in a traffic of officials and regular subjects between Constantinople and the provinces.[5] By 700, local authority lay with those who were linked to the court hierarchy in Constantinople. Three hundred years later, those in power in Greece were the ones who could influence others, whose good reputation carried weight, who could use violence with impunity, and who could command bands of men to establish 'order'. Such people were not necessarily at the top of the social hierarchy. Moreover, the power of some of them may have originated outside the normal pathway taken by most members of the local aristocracy associated with the imperial administration. Antiochos, the *doux* of the Milingoi near Sparta, had control over a band of men whom he could order to turn a dependency of the Monastery of St Nikon into an inn, while building nearby his own court (*aulaia*), which he surrounded with a wall and used as a place of pleasure (*Life of St. Nikon* 59). In doing so, Antiochos may have imitated the behaviour of members of the provincial aristocracy, such as Krinites, the *strategos* of Hellas, who invited St Luke the Younger to a luxurious banquet in his own 'court'. But in terms of his aspirations, the *doux* of the Milingoi was only a pale imitation of the late eighth-century *archon* of the Belegezites, Akamiros, who attempted to release the sons of Constantine V from their exile in Athens and to proclaim one of them as emperor. Others were less eager to demonstrate their control of both people and space, but more successful in climbing to positions of power. Tichomiros, the eighth-century *archon* of the Belegezites, was an imperial *spatharios*, much like his contemporaries, who were eparchs of Thessalonike or *strategoi* of Thrace and Kephallenia (for Tichomiros' seal, see Seibt 1999: 28; for contemporary seals of eparchs of Thessalonike with the title of imperial *spatharios*, see Zacos and Veglery 1972: 647; Curta 2004b: 184; for *strategoi* of Thrace and Kephallenia with that same title, see Mushmov 1934: 342; Zacos and Veglery 1972: 628–9 and 998). There is therefore no reason to treat him as in any way different from other members of the local aristocracy. Similarly, the early tenth-century *archontes* of the Sclavenes in the hinterland of Thessalonike and in the theme of Strymon appear to have been so well integrated into the fabric of the provincial society that they became (in)famous for not responding to the calls of the imperial authorities in the absence of bribes, and for successfully 'intriguing against their associates' (John

Kaminiates, *The Capture of Thessaloniki* 20). Those *archontes* may not have had political aspirations as high as those of Akamiros, but they were certainly in a position to play hardball with the imperial administration, and could extricate themselves from the mess in Thessalonike after the city's conquest by Leo of Tripoli by (falsely) claiming that they were acting on the orders of the *strategos* (*The Capture of Thessaloniki* 41). Their corruption highlights the mechanisms for social promotion that had previously secured the success of more respectable members of the local aristocracy.

There is plenty of evidence – both written and sphragistic – for the presence of government officials in the provinces, but no source portrays them as active participants in the regulation of society. Public power in early medieval Greece was with the local elites, 'the small-town big-wigs' (Neville 1998: 48 and 276). By 900, many of them belonged to families which had gained prominence at the local level. One of the names inscribed on the walls of the *katholikon* of the Monastery of St George in the ancient Temple of Hephaistos in the Athenian Agora is Rendakios (d. 967), a family name which also appears on the seals of a tenth-century imperial *protospatharios* in Peloponnesos (Marki 1982: 101–3).[6] Two members of the same family appear in the Cadaster of Thebes, which is dated to the second half of the eleventh century (Marki 1982: 103–5; Harvey 1989: 74; Neville 1998: 270; for a list of individuals named Rendakios, see also Malingoudis 1994).[7] Even if they could not compare with the large aristocratic families of the Empire, the Rendakioi were brokers of local power. Individuals like them must have been among the 'chief men' (*hoi te prouchontes*) who, together with 'the rest of the people', approached St Nikon in Amyklion (probably Nikli near Tegea) to implore him to come with them to Sparta and put an end to the plague (*Life of St. Nikon* 33; see also Christou and Nikolaou 1990: 211–12). The 'most prominent men' of Sparta were among those who backed Nikon's building plans and agreed to pay his debt to the workers employed for his church (*Life of St. Nikon* 37).[8] Some appear to have been literate, as St Nikon is said to have asked for a written agreement with the 'leading men' of Sparta that, in exchange for his putting a stop on the plague, they would expel the Jews from the city and tear down the slaughter houses in the vicinity of the church of St Epiphanios (*Testament of Nikon the Metanoiete for the Church and Monastery of the Savior, the Mother of God and St. Kyriake*, in Thomas and Hero 2000: 317). Others, like John Aratos, vehemently opposed the saint; he is called 'nobleman' only sarcastically (*Life of*

St. Nikon 35; see also Savvidis 1995: 129, according to whom the events must have taken place at some point between 975 and 986/7). In fact, and despite the use of family names, there does not seem to be any nobility of blood in tenth- and early eleventh-century Greece. Michael Choirosphaktes was 'illustrious and renowned', second to none in Lakonia in honour, reputation, 'and various properties and powers', in the force of his words, generosity (*megalopsyia*), and worldly wisdom. However, next to nothing is known about his family or genealogy.[9] He certainly exercised a great deal of local power, for he gathered 'no small band of men' with whom he attacked one of the two dependencies of the Monastery of St Nikon, seized the oldest monk there, and managed to beat and humiliate him in front of his retainers, before setting fire to the fences and sheepfolds of the monastery's tenants (*Life of St. Nikon* 60).

What did aristocrats do to show their status, besides acting arrogantly or violently? The hallmark of aristocratic life is of course feasting. Krinites, the *strategos* of Hellas, invited St Luke the Younger to a luxurious lunch, at which he met his guests 'not seated in polite fashion upon a couch' but 'reclined on a mattress', and with his belt not at his loins 'but rather much lower, in no way different from the heathens' (*Life of St. Luke the Younger* 59). Krinites made a very bad impression on St Luke, who even left the party to withdraw to a monastery near Thebes, where the *strategos* later came to apologise. While Krinites' sagging clothing may have attracted St Luke's criticism for being indecent, the idea that the appropriate position at a banquet was seated, not reclined, has a much deeper meaning. It has long been noted that by the ninth century, customs in the Empire had begun to change, at least for the well-to-do classes: guests at feasts, instead of reclining around the dining table, were now sitting upright on high-backed benches around larger tables. However, the tradition of reclining on the sigma-shaped couch seems to have persisted longer during certain festive banquets at the imperial court than in the average household (Constantine Porphyrogennetos, *On Ceremonies* 1–2; Vroom 2003: 315 and 327). Since the reclining position was the rule at court, Krinites was simply imitating the behaviour of the higher echelons of the elite hierarchy. No details are given as to what was offered at the lunch, but according to St Luke Krinites' intention was to entertain guests who 'craved luxury' (*Life of St. Luke the Younger* 59).[10]

Tenth-century aristocrats also kept themselves busy competing in games. In Sparta, they played *tzykanion* (a tenth-century version of polo) in the central market area, together with the local *strategos*, who was 'fond of sports and delighted greatly in games' (*Life of St. Nikon* 39; for *tzykanion*, see Christou and Nikolaou 1990: 214–15). They all made such a racket that St Nikon had to get out of the church and scold them for interrupting the service. Like John Aratos, the *strategos* did not hesitate to show his anger and ordered Nikon to leave Sparta, only to ask for his return as soon as he had an attack requiring a saintly intervention. Others did not need to be punished in such a way in order to make a display of piety. A number of distinguished citizens of Thebes established a lay confraternity in 1048 which was dedicated to the promotion of an icon of the Holy Virgin kept in a convent in Naupaktos. Every month, the icon was taken out in procession to another church in the confraternity. Many participants were members of the aristocratic families owning land in the environs of Thebes. Gregory Kalandos, for example, had a wealthy relative named Theodore who later appeared in the Cadaster of Thebes as owning land in the village of Tache. A female member of the confraternity, Maria Kamateros, was married to a member of one of the most prominent families in eleventh-century Hellas (Nesbitt and Wiita 1975).

When not feasting or playing games, most members of the local aristocracy appear to have spent their time squabbling over local politics. The *archontes* of Kerkyra were in conflict with the local *strategos*, who brought charges against them before Emperor Constantine VII Porphyrogennetos. When summoned to Constantinople, the *archontes* took with them Bishop Arsenios as a witness, although he was already old and the trip had to be taken in the middle of winter, the worst sailing season of the year (Da Costa-Louillet 1961: 329).[11] Even more serious was the conflict between the *strategos* of Peloponnesos, Bardas Platopydes, and the provincial supporters of Constantine VII Porphyrogennetos against the usurper Romanos Lekapenos (see Chapter 6). The 'disorder and strife' created by the appointment in 923 of Bardas ended with the expulsion from Peloponnesos of a *protospatharios* named Leo Agelastos, who may have well been the leader of the 'legitimists', since he resurfaced after 945 in a high-ranking position under Emperor Constantine VII (Jenkins 1955: 207). The tensions in the theme of Peloponnesos were very serious indeed, and may have verged on usurpation. According to Arethas of Kaisareia, an aristocrat from Patras named Symbatios was asked to declare himself emperor. Arethas' purpose in writing the *Apology*, our main source for those events, was to defend himself against accusations of having pushed Symbatios to assume the imperial power. In reality, there were many more people in high positions involved in that affair. One of them was the metropolitan of Patras. The masterminds behind the plot were apparently two *protospatharioi* from Tegea, Nicholas and Thomas. After Symbatios denounced the conspiracy, they were promptly arrested and sent to Constantinople under imperial guard (Shangin 1947: 249, 252, and 259). A *strategos* of Hellas named Pothos Argyros was also accused in 944 of participation in a conspiracy against Emperor Constantine VII and was called to Constantinople. Not knowing what to do, he consulted his friend, St Luke the Younger, who reassured him that it was safe to go (*Life of St. Luke the Younger* 58). In Constantinople, the tensions created by the politically polarised aristocracy of the themes of Hellas and Peloponnesos may have encouraged the use of ethnic stereotypes in order to blacken the reputation of political rivals. A high-ranking official and man of letters, Niketas Magistros, rose to political prominence as a supporter of Romanos I.[12] He married his daughter Sophia to the Emperor's son Christopher (who died in 931), but fell from grace in 927, was tonsured a monk, and exiled on the shore of the Hellespont. In the context of the regime change of 945, Niketas may have tried to obtain an imperial pardon, but he died soon after 946 or 947. Constantine Porphyrogennetos does not seem to have held him in favour. The Emperor even reproduced some of the ethnic insults targeted at Niketas at court. A native of Sparta, Niketas apparently pretended to be of noble origin (Niketas Magistros, *epp.* 2, 4, and 5). However, to his enemies, Niketas was just a 'shrewd face, Slavic through and through' (Constantine Porphyrogennetos, *On the Themes* 2.6; see also Maricq 1952: 339–40; Anagnostakis 1996: 126; Pratsch 2005: 503–5; Kaldellis 2007: 94). For the educated snobs at the imperial court in Constantinople, Peloponnesos appeared in the mid-tenth century as a thoroughly Slavicised country (see Chapter 10). Conversely, some members of the local aristocracy felt that their interests were served better by foreign rulers than by Constantinople. In the long war which Basil II waged against Bulgaria, both Paul Bobos, one of the leading men of Thessalonike, and John Malakenos, the *strategos* of Hellas whose disgrace is mentioned in the *Life of St. Luke the Younger*, sided with the Bulgarian Emperor Samuel. Though probably not a native of Hellas, Malakenos appears to have commanded some respect among the local aristocrats, for he was 'in the first rank not only in the city of the Laconians, but in all Hellas and the land of Pelops' (*Life of St. Nikon* 43). The accusations against him were at least as serious as those levelled at the two conspirators from Tegea who wanted Symbatios of Patras as emperor. The latter were escorted to Constantinople by an imperial guard. Basil II sent 'two satraps leading legions of soldiers' to arrest Malakenos. The *strategos*, rightly fearing for his life, was only comforted by St Nikon's prophecy. The aristocrats of Vodena (Edessa) were not as lucky. After the city was reconquered by Basil in 1015, the Emperor ordered the deportation of all inhabitants, including, one may presume, the 'leading men' of the city.[13]

Elites resided in cities where they apparently had access to schools and baths. St Luke the Younger went to a school in Corinth, but left in disappointment at his classmates' behaviour (*Life of St. Luke the Younger* 34). He later sent a monk to Corinth to look for Theophylaktos the Wise, a 'teacher of pagan wisdom' whom St Luke knew to be 'a person renowned at that time for virtue' (*Life of St. Luke the Younger* 47). Shortly after being cured by St Luke, the son of one of 'those who held first place' in Thebes went to the bath (*Life of St. Luke the Younger* 45).[14] However, next to nothing is known about urban housing in early medieval Greece, especially aristocratic houses or palaces. Nor are there any excavations of rural courts, such as that built by Antiochos, the *doux* of the Milingoi, near the dependency of the Monastery of St Nikon in Sparta. In the 'spiritually beneficial tales' of Bishop Paul of Monemvasia, an *archon* of Peloponnesos is said to have had a private chapel in his house, but it is not clear where exactly that house was (Wortley 1996: 92). A glimpse into the daily life of an aristocratic house is offered by luxury objects of personal use made of ivory, such as the late tenth- or early eleventh-century comb found during excavations in Chalkis (Evvoia), which may have belonged to an aristocratic woman (Georgopoulou-Meladini 1973: 508 and pl. 330 α and β; Georgopoulou-Meladini and Papadakis 1974: 39–42).[15] Much as in the sixth and early seventh century, women may have been viewed as mirrors of the social status of their husbands. Upon the death of both her parents, a young girl from the 'country of the Hellads' was adopted by 'one of the ruling class' from Larissa, who married her to his son. However, his relatives criticised the son (and not the father) for having married a poor woman of lowly birth (Wortley 1996: 104). Tenth-century female burials also illustrate the vicarious representation of the status of aristocratic males through their womenfolk (Fig. 8.1). The richest burials of the tenth century are the female

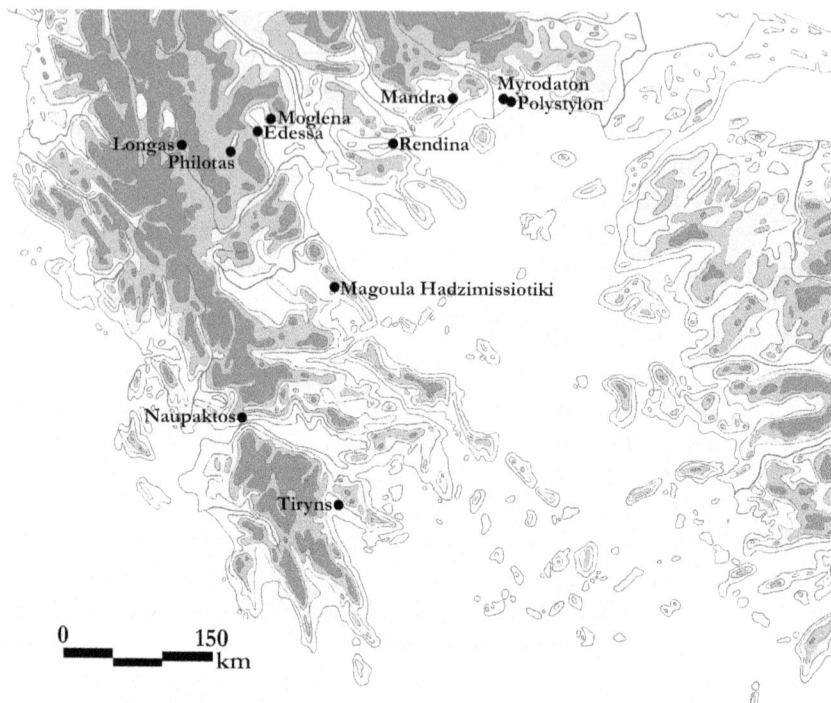

Figure 8.1 The distribution in Greece of tenth- and early eleventh-century cemeteries and isolated graves.

graves in a small cemetery accidentally found in Naupaktos on Apokaukou Street. One of them produced a crescent-shaped, golden earring decorated on front and back with enamel, as well as two finger-rings, one of which was of gold (Petritaki 1987: 175).[16] Two finger-rings, one of gold, and two gold earrings with crescent-shaped, narrow ends have also been found in another grave. They are the first gold artefacts to be found in burial assemblages in Greece dated after c. 600. They must have belonged to women of high status, perhaps wives or sisters of the *strategoi* of Nikopolis residing in Naupaktos. Such a high position in the local hierarchy follows from the analysis of some of the analogues known for the dress accessories with which the females of Naupaktos were buried. Two earrings similar to that with enamel decoration have been found together with silver coins struck in 959 for Emperors Constantine VII Porphyrogenitus and Romanos II in a hoard from Kastana, near Preslav (Bulgaria). The hoard also includes diadem plates representing scenes from the life of Alexander the Great, which have been rightly associated with the

Macedonian dynasty in power in Constantinople. The diadem was certainly meant for a member of the Bulgarian royal family and may have been, much like the earrings and the other components of the hoard, a gift from the Byzantine imperial family (Totev 1993: 52–8). High social status may also have been marked by the rich decoration of the tomb, as in the case of the marble slab with a round and soft relief from Rendina, which is very similar to closure panels in the Church of St Sophia in Kiev, dated to the 1040s or 1050s (Pazaras 1988: 126). If the tomb was located in a church built inside the fort at Rendina, then there is a good chance that the person buried there was either a patron or a member of a family of patrons of the church.

A number of isolated female graves from early medieval Greece may also be regarded as 'privileged', if not aristocratic as well. Unlike the rich burials in Naupaktos, the tenth-century grave excavated in Myrodaton (prefecture of Xanthi) contained only a necklace with 121 glass beads, bronze earrings, and finger-rings. However, the grave was dug into an Iron-Age barrow (Kranioti 1984: 281; for the dating, see also Štefanovičová 1997: 358). A ninth-century grave similarly dug into a prehistoric burial mound in Spilaion (prefecture of Evros) produced the seal of a high-ranking official of the court in Constantinople, which suggests a comparatively high social status for the deceased (Triantaphyllos 1997). In northern Greece, burial in pits dug into pre-existing barrows may therefore have been a practice restricted to only a few selected individuals. A single, isolated stone-lined grave of a woman was found in 1934 in Thessaly, on an island (Magoula Hadzimissiotiki) in the middle of the now completely drained Lake Karla, to the west of Mount Pelion and to the north of Volos. The burial assemblage included two earrings, one of which was of silver with four barrel-shaped attachments, a bronze bracelet, and three finger-rings, in addition to fragments of an iron belt buckle (Grundmann 1937: 56 and 67). The earring is a specimen of Sokol's class 14, with many analogues in rather modest burial assemblages excavated in Macedonia and Kosovo (Sokol 2006: 236–42; for analogues, see Jovanović 1976: pl. 1; Kepeska 1992: 249 and fig. 5). Again, the privileged status of the Magoula Hadzimissiotiki woman follows not so much from the associated dress accessories as from the peculiar, isolated location of the burial on an island in the middle of a lake. This may also be true for the isolated grave found inside the Mycenaean fortification at Tiryns (Kilian 1980: 286, 285 pl. 49.3, and 284 fig. 3.7). The burial assemblage produced only a twisted iron bracelet, but the peculiar location of the grave points to an inhumation of special status. Privileged burials were, however, not restricted to females. A number of graves surrounded the apse of a single-naved church in Longas. All of them were infant burials, and their special status in the eyes of the Christians who used the church follows from the fact that all graves were dug inside a rectangular precinct attached to the apse (Moutsopoulos 1992a: 6). This is a most unusual arrangement, given that in contemporary fort graveyards, grave pits appear on all sides around the church, as in Moglena or Polystylon (Evgenidou 1987: 17–18 [eighteen graves]; Bakirtzis 1983: 17 [thirty-six graves]).

Some of the graves in Moglena produced pectoral crosses. There were also crosses among the grave goods from the still unpublished cemetery from Edessa.[17] Very similar crosses have been found in Corinth (Davidson 1952: pl. 110. 2073–4 and 2077–9). An isolated grave found in the ruins of the Kraneion basilica in Corinth produced a bronze, tang-less buckle (Ivison 1996: 116 fig. 5.7G [grave GR.28.08]). Such buckles are believed to have been used for book covers, because of the association with rivets for book bindings in a small hoard from Troianov most (Serbia; Garašanin and Vašić 1987: 94 and 103 figs 15–16) and with writing instruments on the fortified site at Ruino (Bulgaria; Atanasov 1991: pl. 2.11, 14).[18] If this interpretation is correct, then the grave in the ruins of the Kraneion basilica may well be that of a churchman, perhaps a reader. Fingerrings, as well as interwoven bracelets and bracelets with flattened, round ends, were found in some of the 177 graves of a large cemetery excavated in Philotas (prefecture of Florina), the largest early medieval cemetery so far excavated in Greece (Ziota and Moskanis 1997: 51–2 and 55 pls 11–14).[19] A comparatively small cemetery with forty-seven graves (forty-five of which are stone-lined) was excavated around a funerary chapel in Mandra, 4km north from Philippi. As in Philotas, the Mandra graves produced bronze bracelets with flattened, round ends and bronze finger-rings (Pennas 1977: 291).

Large cemeteries like that of Philotas may have been village or town graveyards for the common people, which the members of the local aristocracy may have avoided, taking care to be buried within a church or at least a symbolic site adjacent to it. Nevertheless, society in the villages or towns in question may have been considerably stratified. The documents in the archives on Mount Athos show that villages in the Chalkidike and the neighbouring regions had leaders in charge of the communal property and who represented their communities in commercial transactions involving land. In 982, the

Monastery of Iviron agreed to a twenty-nine-year lease of land for the inhabitants of Hierissos, who, in addition to allowing the monks to occupy some land of theirs in the vicinity of Longos, agreed to pay 100 *nomismata*. That the inhabitants of Hierissos were able to raise such a large sum of money is an indication that at least some of them were relatively wealthy (Harvey 1989: 231).[20] Some of the independent freeholders in the theme of Thessalonike were *stratiotai*, peasants occupying their own land who were liable for providing either a soldier for the thematic army or a cash payment instead (Harvey 1990: 253). In the mid-tenth century, thematic soldiers or sailors represented an important part of the population of medium landowners in the Aegean islands, people who did not have to do any cultivation themselves, and often appear, as in Chalkidiki, as village leaders (Malamut 1988: 473). *Stratiotai* from different parts of the Empire, whom the author of the *Chronicle of Monemvasia* knew as 'Kapheroi, Thrakesians, Armenians, and others from different places and cities', were settled in Peloponnesos under Emperor Nikephoros I (Kislinger 2001: 203). By 900, they were probably not much richer than others in the Empire, but the *stratiotai* of Peloponnesos were clearly men of some means, since they were all able to redeem their military obligations at the time of the 921 expedition to Italy organised by Emperor Romanos I. In the early eleventh century, a Spartan soldier of Corinthian origin named Michael Argyromytes was capable of campaigning at his own expense. He must therefore have been the owner of some important estates around Sparta. In fact, the imperial novel of 947 clearly stipulated that each sailor of the themes of the Aegean Sea, Samos, and Kibyrrhaiotai had to own an estate worth at least four pounds of gold (Malamut 1988: 473). Large numbers of *stratiotai* – Armenians, Romans, 'and other rabble' (Leo the Deacon, *History* 2.8)[21] – were settled on Crete following the conquest of the island in 961. Their descendants, the independent peasants of the village of Pege, donated a small property from their land for the Monastery of John Xenos at Myriokephala (Malamut 1988: 426).

Very little is known about the daily life of such people, with only a few glimpses offered by saints' lives. St Luke the Younger's parents owned land in the village of Kastorion, which had been separated from the lands of the others by a boundary established by an imperial official. They also had livestock and apparently an abundance of clothes for young Luke to distribute to the poor (*Life of St. Luke the Younger* 4 and 6). Their diet consisted of cheese, eggs, and fruit, which Luke refused to eat. On one occasion, Luke's parents cooked fish with meat together in a single pot, which they placed in the middle of the table for the entire family to eat from it. Luke 'took the fish when his father offered it', an indication that younger members of the family could not dip into the common pot without approval from the head of the family (*Life of St. Luke the Younger* 3). Nothing is said about the particular position of the family members around the table, but the simplicity of this fish-with-meat meal is in sharp contrast with the luxury with which St Luke would later be treated at the table of the *strategos* of Hellas. A few farmers in the theme of Thessalonike may have known how to read and write, like that inhabitant of Hierissos who signed in Glagolitic letters the 982 agreement with John the Iberian, the founder of the Monastery of Iviron. However, most of them were illiterate. On a document from the Great Lavra for the villagers of Radochosta, which is dated to 1008, out of fourteen signatures, twelve are by the hand of the scribe.

By 1050, there were very few if any *stratiotai* left in Greece, and the number of independent freeholders had dropped dramatically. The transformation is not fully understood in all its details, especially for the region of southern Greece, but it must have started at least one hundred years earlier. It has been estimated that the lay and ecclesiastical aristocracy of Peloponnesos, which probably numbered between 500 and 1,000 people, was supported by a population of at least 15,000 *paroikoi* (Oikonomides 1996c: 123). While it is clear that many *paroikoi* of the later period were descendants of families of *stratiotai*, the dependency of others appears to have been the result of punishment for rebellion. The Slavs who revolted and attacked Patras in the early ninth century were given to the Church of St Andrew in that city, together 'with all their families and relations and all who belonged to them, and all their property as well' (Constantine Pophyrogennetos, *On the Administration of the Empire* 49). Throughout the ninth century they were the object of abuse by the metropolitan of Patras, to such a degree that Emperor Leo VI had to intervene – perhaps in the context of disposing of the property which Danielis had left to the emperor – in order to curb their exploitation and their unjust treatment at the metropolitan's whim. Elsewhere, *paroikoi* were newly arrived settlers who, unlike *stratiotai*, had no state-guaranteed privileges or protection. In 1049, a chrysobull of Emperor Constantine IX gave to the Monastery of Nea Mone on Chios 'the Jews who lived on this island', fifteen families totalling about seventy-five persons. They were to pay their head-tax to the monastery, instead of the state, which effectively turned them into the *paroikoi* of Nea Mone (Malamut 1988: 166; Oikonomides 1995b: 218 and 220).

In northern Greece, the process of encroachment of the powerful onto the land of village communities is better understood because of the evidence surviving in the archives of Mount Athos (Lefort 2005: 290). Because of imperial cash donations and privileges, the powerful Athonite monasteries could easily outbid the independent freeholders in purchasing large amounts of klasmatic land, and they could also force some of them to renounce their own lands. Sometimes, the collective action of the peasants was effective in preventing the encroachment of the monasteries on village property. For example, in 980, the monastery of Iviron decided to sort out once and for all the disputes it had with the inhabitants of Siderokausia over lands near Belikradou and Arsenikea in the Chalikidike. Complaints had been made that the monks allowed their animals to trample the crops of the peasants, and even occupied lands which did not in fact belong to them. Moreover, they had brought *paroikoi* from elsewhere to work the disputed lands and had installed mills on somebody else's property. The inhabitants of Siderokausia acting collectively brought their case to Nicholas, the judge (*krites*) of Thessalonike and Strymon, who eventually ruled in their favour (Morris 2000: 163). In most other cases, because the Athonite monasteries could take their claims way beyond the local thematic courts and right up to the imperial judges in Constantinople, they were often able to win against independent freeholders. However, there were also peasants who willingly submitted themselves to the authority of the Monastery of Iviron, as their villages had been destroyed by Bulgarian raids (Lefort 1979: 256). The descendants of those who had owned land a generation or two before now worked as tenants for ecclesiastical landlords. In other cases, such as Dobrobikea (see Chapter 7), the *paroikoi* living in a certain village were not the descendants of the villagers who had previously abandoned their houses in that village. Similarly, the *paroikoi* who laboured on the fields of the dependency of the Monastery of St Nikon do not seem to have had any local connections. They lacked any protection when attacked by the men of Michael Choirosphaktes.[22] Similarly, a family of *paroikoi* belonging to that same dependency could be attacked in the middle of the night with impunity. The attackers were kidnapping the daughter of the family, whom they were planning to sell into slavery, when St Nikon intervened to save her and punish the perpetrators of the crime (*Life of St. Nikon* 70).

The distinction between free and not free in early medieval Greece appears to have been closely associated with the use of violence. When St Nikon requested of the leading men of Sparta that, in exchange for his working to take the plague out of the city, they would expel all the Jews, the only opposition came from a man named John Aratos. He 'asserted that the removal of the Jews outside the city was not just or reasonable', and even brought back, apparently for his own interest, a Jew who knew how to finish garments. Nikon's reaction was immediate: 'He seized a club which was lying near-by and inflicting many blows on the Jew drove him out of the city and seemed more fearful to his enemies than Herakles with his club, as they say' (*Life of St. Nikon* 35). There is no other episode in the *Life of St. Nikon* to depict the saint as acting as violently as in that of the Jew of John Aratos. Why did he beat the Jew? After all, his true enemy was John Aratos, who in fact did not hesitate to attack Nikon violently, to abuse, to shove, and to frighten him with threats. To John Aratos, Nikon 'answered in only a gentle voice' (*Life of St. Nikon* 35). The Jew, who only obeyed the command of John Aratos, and never spoke to Nikon directly, bore the brunt of Nikon's wrath. The conclusion can only be that the Jew in question was not a free man, but most probably a dependant of John Aratos, perhaps his *paroikos*, of a status not unlike that of his coreligionists on the island of Chios in the mid-eleventh century. If there were many more Jews like that among Aratos' *paroikoi*, his verbal and, possibly, physical violence against St Nikon may be explained as a protest against Nikon's measure to expel the Jews, which obviously harmed Aratos' economic interests. In the story of a posthumous miracle of St Nikon mentioned above, Michael Choirosphaktes dared to beat Zosimos, the oldest monk of the dependency of the saint's monastery, because of regarding him as inferior in status (*Life of St. Nikon* 60). Like the Jew of John Aratos, Zosimos neither resisted nor in any way communicated his opinion about Choirosphaktes' actions. But because the latter's men had attacked the dependency on account of its tenants trespassing onto his lands, Zosimos was regarded as the ultimate culprit and consequently stripped of his cloak, mantle, and status as manager of the dependency. In other words, Choirosphaktes reduced Zosimos to the status of a slave, worthy only of being beaten with rods and cut with blows. A similar conclusion may be drawn from the analysis of two episodes from the *Life of St. Luke the Younger*. Mistaken for a runaway slave by soldiers laying ambushes to collect runaway slaves, St Luke the Younger was beaten and imprisoned before being released when recognised by others as not being of lower class, and when 'his identity and status were attested' (*Life of St. Luke the Younger* 8; Neville 1998: 26). St Luke was physically assaulted a second time later in his life by the master of a harbour on the southern shore of the Gulf of Corinth. Because of 'hostile attacks' by Bulgarians, the harbour master forbade any boats to cross over to Hellas. When St Luke was caught trying to cross over, he was apprehended and severely beaten (*Life of St. Luke the Younger* 38). That tenth-century slaves in Greece were to expect beating whenever they disobeyed their masters or ran away is quite clear from the first episode. It is only when his identity and status were properly attested that Luke was freed from the temporary position of slavery in which he was placed by his captors' ignorance. Less clear is the second episode, primarily because of the lack of information as to the social status of the harbour master. If, as is quite possible, he had received his orders from the military authorities of Peloponnesos, then he may have not only mistaken St Luke for a person of lower status, as the soldiers of the first episode did, but also applied the disciplinary measures necessary to reinforce the orders. In both cases, beating was as much a punishment as a symbolic way to reduce a free man's status to that of a slave. The existence of slaves in early medieval Greece is otherwise amply documented in the sources, leaving the impression that it was quite normal to purchase, sell, or own slaves (Patlagean 1993: 597). Danielis is said to have owned so many that, following her death, Emperor Leo VI freed 3,000 of her slaves in order to settle them in the theme of Longobardia.[23] Slaves appear also in saints' lives. A man, 'a slave by fate but free by faith', who suffered from dropsy came to the nunnery of St Athanasia of Aigina to ask for the intercession of the saint (*Life of St. Athanasia of Aigina* 16). In a posthumous miracle, St Phantinos intervened to free a young slave from Bulgarian captivity and return him to his master in Thessalonike (*Life of St. Phantinos* 61). Some slaves may have been prisoners of war, such as the 'Scythian' (Bulgarian) child whom an *archon* of Peloponnesos bought in the early tenth century in order to give him to the priest serving in his domestic chapel to be brought up and taught the sacred letters (Wortley 1996: 92).

There were many poor people in late tenth- and early eleventh-century Greece, especially in cities such as Larissa or Sparta (Wortley 1996: 104; *Life of St. Nikon* 36). In Thessalonike, beggars, otherwise not mentioned in Ignatios the Deacon's *Life of St. Gregory of Dekapolis*, appear shortly after 950 in the *Life of St. Phantinos* (*Life of St. Phantinos* 47; Yannopoulos 1995: 489). Elsewhere, they appear whenever famine strikes ill-prepared communities. Just outside Mytilene, two poor men approached St George of Lesbos returning from the mill and begged him for a little flour (*Lives of Sts. David, Symeon, and George of Lesbos* 13).[24] Instead of begging, a poor woman living in the dependencies of the Monastery of St Nikon earned her living by selling bread (*Life of St. Nikon* 71 and 75). The impoverished peasants in the environs of Sparta turned to brigandage, which appears to have been a matter sufficiently serious to require St Nikon's intervention (*Life of St. Nikon* 57).[25] However, there is no evidence of social dissent in early medieval Greece which could be compared with the urban violence in Thessalonica shortly after 600, when

> people were drunk in the public squares on the blood of their neighbors, and they attacked each other in their homes and pitilessly murdered those within, so that they who lived in the upper stories were flung down to the earth – women and children, the old and the young, who because of their weakness could not escape by flight – and citizens, like rough barbarians, plundered friends and relations and burned down their buildings.[26]

The cause of violence in Thessalonica was most probably political, not primarily social, and the same may be true for the bloodshed and unrest in the *Sklavinia* near the city, which St Gregory of Dekapolis was about to visit at some point between 835 and 841 (Ignatios the Deacon, *Life of St. Gregory of Dekapolis* 49; see Chapter 5). Nothing similar is known from those regions of Greece for which there is evidence of an accelerated social differentiation during the tenth or early eleventh century. In early medieval Greece, the transition from a 'peasant-mode society' to a 'feudal-mode society' took place relatively peacefully during the second half of the tenth century, with little if any evidence, of peasant revolts or violent resistance. Of all phases of that transition so far identified for early medieval Europe, it is the 'steady reduction of areas of continuing peasant autonomy inside the overall dominance of the feudal model' that is most visible in Greece between the ninth and the first half of the eleventh century (Wickham 2005: 588).

Notes

1. At the end of his term as judge (*praitor*) of Peloponnesos, Basil Apokaukos 'was about to return home' when visiting Sparta to pay homage at the tomb of St Nikon and to obtain some holy ointment in a

vessel, in order to take it with him *at home* 'for sanctification and relief from misfortunes and remedy for diseases' (*Life of St. Nikon* 50).
2. Kontoleon also served as *katepano* of Bari, but before him many other *strategoi* of Kephallenia were also imperial officers in Italy. For example, a certain Eupraxias Mousoulikes was a *strategos* of both Kephallenia and Sicily in 880. One of his successors, Symbatikios, was a *strategos* of Macedonia, Thrace, Kephallenia, and Longobardia in 892.
3. John Kourkouas (before 1008) and George Theodorakanos (1025–1028) were also of Armenian origin.
4. *Protospatharios*, spatharocandidate, *spatharios*, and *strator* were titles 'of the imperial retinue'. *Dishypatos, hypatos, vestitor, silentiarios*, and *apo eparchon* were 'senatorial' titles.
5. When they came to Hellas, imperial officials had no protection against local thieves. This is best illustrated by the envoy Emperor Romanos I sent to Egypt in 937/8 with a large amount of gold to be distributed as gifts. The gold was stolen in the dead of night and only St Luke was capable of recovering it and identifying the culprit (*Life of St. Luke the Younger* 44).
6. The name also appears on another seal of the same person, but with the title of imperial spatharocandidate.
7. Some of those mentioned in the Cadaster of Thebes are said to have been *protospatharioi* and *spatharioi*, but such titles had been greatly debased by the mid-eleventh century. The individuals in question wielded only locally significant power.
8. The 'chosen men of the city' (*tous logadas tes poleos*) were among those whom Nikon called to his deathbed (*Life of St. Nikon* 45).
9. A member of the Choirosphaktes family named Nikitas was *strategos* of Hellas in the late tenth or early eleventh century (Nesbitt and Oikonomides 1994: no. 8.51). References to noble descent are rare in the sources and, when they appear, they are difficult to distinguish from mere rhetorical devices. St Theodora of Thessalonike was married at a young age to 'a man from a prominent family' of Aigina, while St Athanasia was from a 'well-born' family from that same island (*Life of St. Theodora of Thessalonike* 5; *Life of St. Athanasia of Aigina* 1).
10. This was apparently an opportunity to show off, and it is likely that there were chafing dishes on Krinites' table
11. The *strategos* in question may have been that of Kerkyra, not Kephallenia, for the former became a separate theme in the course of the tenth century (Roux 1996: 73; Prinzing 1997: 6).
12. For the biography of Niketas Magistros, see Westerink 1973: 23–38. He was related to the Rendakios family (Theophanes Continuatus, in Bekker 1838: 399; Anagnostakis 1996: 132).
13. The inhabitants of Larissa learned the lesson and in 1040, when the city

was taken by the rebels of Peter Delian, they secretly established contact with the *doux* of Thessalonike before overthrowing the Bulgarian governor by themselves, and handing him to the Byzantine authorities.
14. Baths also existed in ninth-century Mytilene (Lesbos) and Thessalonike, and they were visited by women as well (*Lives of Sts. David, Symeon and George of Lesbos* 3; *Life of St. Theodora of Thessalonike* 19). In Thebes, some women were regarded as 'distinguished citizens' (*Life of St. Luke the Younger* 61).
15. The comb has a relief decoration representing two opposing lions on one side and two peacocks flanking a fountain on the other side.
16. Very similar earrings are known from the Kanellopoulos and Stathatos collections and may also have been found in Greece (Brouskari 1985: 146; Coche de la Ferté 1957: 18–24 and pls 2 and 2bis). The dating is based on a specimen now in the collection of the Museum of Late Antique and Byzantine Art in Berlin, the central medallion of which has a portrait of Emperor John Tzimiskes (969–976) (Schlunk 1940).
17. In addition to pectoral crosses, the grave goods from Edessa include a lyre-shaped belt buckle and bronze finger-rings (Papanikola-Bakirtzis 2002: 395, 444, 447, and 500–1).
18. Similar buckles have been found in Constantinople, but also on tenth-century sites in Macedonia, Romania, and Albania (Harrison and Hayes 1986: 266; Lilčić 1996: 80–1; Teodor 1984: 108 and 115 fig. 61.13; Hidri 1991: pl. 11.6, 7).
19. The cemetery began in the tenth century, but appears to have continued through the eleventh and early twelfth century.
20. In the early eleventh century, on Skyros, a *koubouklisios* named John and his wife Glykeria donated to the Great Lavra a house which had been inherited from John's family and which they had turned into a little monastery, with a grazing field of unknown area in the vicinity (Malamut 1988: 426).
21. According to Theophanes Continuatus, in Bekker 1838: 474, 476, and 481, the settlers came from the themes of Thrace and Macedonia.
22. The fences and sheepfolds of the tenants were destroyed, but their houses appear to have been spared.
23. According to Runciman 1940: 429, it is remarkable that Danielis used slave labour, which must have been rare in the ninth-century Empire.
24. The association between famine and the distribution of flour is also an important motif in the *Life of St. Peter of Argos* 13.
25. To judge by this miracle, the brigands had a village with huts and a church dedicated to the Archangel Michael, as well as tilled fields.
26. *Miracles of St. Demetrios* 1.112–13; English translation from Hoddinott 1963: 148–9.

CHAPTER 9

Christianity in early medieval Greece

Judging by the extant and distribution of the network of bishoprics, sixth-century Greece must have been a thoroughly Christianised province of the Empire. By 550 there were fifty-seven episcopal sees in Greece, with the large concentration in the province of Achaia (Zeiller 1926: 225).[1] Bishops had a wide variety of ecclesiastical and civilian powers and the large number of churches in existence or built during the sixth century illustrates the ubiquity and considerable influence of the church in the life of the inhabitants of the provinces of Achaia, Epirus Vetus, Thessaly, Macedonia Prima, and Rhodope during the last century of Roman power (see Chapter 1). The highest-ranking man of the church in sixth century Greece was the archbishop of Thessalonica, but his influence over the Achaian, Thessalian, Macedonian, and Epirote bishops had diminished considerably by 550, primarily because of the Monophysite archbishop Dorotheos and the opposition he faced from the bishops of the Dacian and Macedonian dioceses. The bishops of Epirus Vetus and Thessaly turned to Rome, soon followed by their colleagues in other sees in Greece. However, such developments had no immediate consequences, primarily because of the accelerated regionalisation of the church organisation after c. 600 and the subsequent abandonment of the provinces in the southern Balkans by the Roman army and administration, whose presence was maintained only on a few key coastal points. During the subsequent centuries, several other archbishops of Thessalonica espoused non-Orthodox beliefs. Pope Martin I declared Archbishop Paul deposed in 649 for his Monotheletic views, and Leo the Mathematician, a moderate iconoclast, was archbishop of Thessalonike between 839/40 and 843 (Petit 1900–1901: 213 and 217).

By that time, Thessalonike had long ceased to be the most important see in Greece. At the Sixth Ecumenical Council in Constantinople (680/1), the archbishop of Thessalonica still signed as vicar of the pope. The papal legate at that time was the bishop of

Corinth, who represented the 'province' of Hellas (*Hellenon chora*), which some historians have interpreted as an early indication of the existence of a theme with that name (Avramea 1997: 38, 172, and 185; Ohme 1989: 199–201; see Riedinger 1979: 14). The bishops of Athens, Argos, and Lakedaimon were also present, but no other bishop from the former provinces of Achaia, Thessaly, Macedonia, or Epirus Vetus.[2] By contrast, at the Quinisext Council (*in Trullo*) of 692/3, the bishops of Thessalonica, Edessa, Amphipolis, and Philippi were all present, but not those of Athens, Corinth, Argos, or Lakedaimon (Yannopoulos 1993b: 395). A century later, in 787, eleven sees from Crete and fifteen from the other islands and from continental Greece were represented at the Council of Nicaea, which restored the cult of the icons (Laurent 1943: 69–70; Darrrouzès 1975: 37–8; Yannopoulos 1993b: 395 and 398–9; Browning 1984: 301; Avramea 1997: 188). The absence of Corinth, Athens, Traianoupolis, and Thessalonike is remarkable, but so is the absence of the see of Lakedaimon at the same time as the first appearance of such new Peloponnesian bishops as those of Troizen and that of Monemvasia. During the eighth century, Corinth had an archbishop, like Thessalonike (for the first seals of archbishops of Corinth, see Zacos and Veglery 1972: 817–18 and 1390; for the first seals of archbishops of Thessalonica, see Zacos and Veglery 1972: 978; Curta 2004b: 184). The sees of both Athens and Patras were elevated to metropolitan status in the early ninth century, most probably under Patriarch Tarasios (784–806), who presided over the Council of Nicaea.[3] By 900, the metropolitan of Athens had ten suffragan bishops within his jurisdiction, both on several islands and in continental Greece (Darrouzès 1981: 283; Kazanaki-Lappa 2000: 206). An equal number of suffragan sees were under the jurisdiction of the metropolitans of Larissa and Rhodes, respectively (Darrouzès 1981: 284–5).[4] Thebes may have also reached metropolitan status by that time, but unlike Athens, nothing is known about its suffragan sees before the twelfth century.[5] Kerkyra was a metropolitan see in the mid-eleventh century, but by 1000 several islands in the Aegean and Ionian Seas had already become sees of newly established bishoprics (Ikaria, Astypaleia, Nisyros).[6] The greatest number of bishoprics was that of northern Greece. However, the situation in the early tenth century is not clear, mostly because of problems of manuscript transmission associated with the lists of bishoprics subject to the patriarch of Constantinople, known as *notitiae episcopatuum*. All manuscripts containing *notitia* 7, which was compiled at the beginning of the tenth century under Patriarch Nicholas Mystikos, list among the suffragan sees of Thessalonike a bishopric of Drougoubiteia. This may have well been the area to the northwest of Thessalonike, which was inhabited by the Drugubites and was later organised as a theme of the same name.[7] By contrast, only a few manuscripts have a bishop of the 'Turks' or 'Vardariotes' as a suffragan of the archbishop of Thessalonike. The bishopric may have well been established only during the second half or towards the end of the tenth century, for the 'Turks' in question were Magyars settled in the Vardar valley, whom Emperor Basil II recruited for his campaigns against Samuel (*Life of St. Athanasios the Athonite* 58; Lemerle 1963b: 81; for the bishopric of the 'Turks' [Vardariotes], see Laurent 1940; Konidares 1952). *Notitia* 7 lists eight suffragan sees each for the metropolitans of Traianoupolis (now Traianoupoli, prefecture of Evros) and Naupaktos, respectively, but only six for Philippi, the smallest metropolis in northern Greece.[8]

During the reign of Nikephoros I, Patras was elevated to the rank of metropolis with three suffragan sees – Lakedaimon, Korone, and Methone. According to *notitia* 7, in the early tenth century, Corinth had seven suffragan sees: Damala, Argos, Monemvasia, Kephallenia, Zakynthos, Zemaina, and Maina. To the list of the suffragan sees of Patras, *notitia* 7 added Bolaina. This list is then repeated in *notitia* 9, which was first completed in 946, then revised between 970 and 976 (Darrouzès 1981: 282, 284, 302, and 303; see also Bon 1951: 106–8 and 208–9). To some, the distribution of bishoprics in *notitiae* 7 and 9 outlines the territory under direct Byzantine control in eastern Peloponnesos. According to such views, the outliers (Bolaina, Patras, and Methone) must have been created for the specific purpose of converting the local Slavs in the regions newly (re)conquered by the Byzantines (Yannopoulos 1993b: 390–3 and 399).[9] This, however, is to take the evidence of the *notitiae episcopatuum* too far. First, it appears that neither *notitia* 7 nor *notitia* 9 (nor, for that matter, any subsequent list of bishoprics) may be treated as comprehensive. The existence of a tenth-century bishopric of Kernitza (now Kernitsa, near Aigion), otherwise not attested in any list before c. 1100, is documented by the seal of Bishop Paul.[10] Second, there is no evidence of any mission to the Slavs in Peloponnesos during the ninth, tenth, or eleventh century. To Emperor Constantine Porphyrogenitus, the only people in need of conversion in the region were the 'inhabitants of the city of Maina', who are specifically said to have been 'not of the race of the aforesaid Slavs, but of the ancient Romans' (Constantine

Porphyrogennetos, *On the Administration of the Empire* 50).[11] Later in the century, St Nikon's missionary activity on the island of Crete is described in terms of efforts to bring back to Christianity those inhabitants of the island who 'by time and fellowship with the Saracens, alas! were led astray to their customs and foul and unhallowed rites' (*Life of St. Nikon* 20). Initially, Nikon adopted an aggressive style of preaching, focused on his favourite theme of repentance.[12] The reaction was immediate: they 'cried out against this strange and foreign preaching' and 'violently opposed the just man, wishing to destroy him'. In the face of such opposition, Nikon changed his strategy. Taking some aside 'whom he knew to be different from the others in their knowledge and acceptance of good', he eventually managed to bring the Cretans to the point where, 'believing he was an apostle sent from God', they 'made known his deeds throughout the island' (*Life of St. Nikon* 20). Nothing of the sort is known about Nikon's activity in Peloponnesos. While he preached repentance to the inhabitants of Euripos (Chalkis) on Evvoia, he neither encountered opposition, nor had to go to the lengths required by his dealings with the Cretans (*Life of St. Nikon* 26).[13] In Peloponnesos, Nikon does not appear to have been concerned with the conversion of anyone, either Greek or Slav.

Moreover, the distribution of bishoprics known from *notitiae episcopatuum* is in sharp contrast to the distribution of churches dated with some degree of certainty to the tenth or eleventh century (Fig. 6.3; for the distribution of bishoprics, see the maps in Yannopoulos 1993b: 390 and Turlej 2001: 164). The largest cluster of tenth- to early eleventh-century churches in Peloponnesos is that from Deep Mani, which many historians believe to have been within the diocese of Maina (see Chapter 6). If the number of churches is in any way related to the process of Christianisation, then those converted before 900 in Deep Mani, according to Constantine Porphyrogennetos, were natives, not Slavs. By contrast, there are remarkably few churches in eastern Peloponnesos, the area with the largest concentration of early medieval bishoprics. The churches built in central and southwestern Peloponnesos may have been within the episcopal jurisdiction of one of four outliers – Bolaina, Methone, Korone, or Lakedaimon. The Church of St Christopher in Pallandion was certainly consecrated by the bishop of Lakedaimon, Nicholas, in 903 (see Table 6.2). Nothing is known about diocesan boundaries in the early tenth century, but it is remarkable that in charge of the consecration of that church was the bishop of Lakedaimon, even though Pallandion is closer to

Argos than to Sparta. The bishop of Lakedaimon, a suffragan of the metropolitan of Patras, may have had special reasons for committing to stone the memory of the consecration of a church in the northern parts of his diocese bordering the area of jurisdiction of the bishop of Argos, who was a suffragan of the metropolitan of Corinth. The consecration of the church in Pallandion took place at a moment when the relations between Patras and Corinth may have deteriorated because of disputes over the areas of their respective metropolitan jurisdictions.

It has recently been suggested that the main text of the *Chronicle of Monemvasia* may have been written in 900 or 901 to support the claims which the metropolitan of Patras had to the suffragan see of Lakedaimon against the metropolitan of Corinth, perhaps in anticipation of the diocesan re-organisation reflected in episcopal *notitia* 7, issued under Patriarch Nicholas Mystikos at some point between 901 and 907 (Kislinger 2001: 106; Madgearu 2005: 75–6).[14] It has long been noted that the author of the *Chronicle* had no knowledge of any bishop of Bolaina being a suffragan of the metropolitan of Patras, an indication that he must have written his work before the drafting of *notitia* 7 (Koder 1976: 79). If, as seems likely, that author wrote in Constantinople, his intention must have been to provide a basis for the metropolitan of Patras to claim the see of Lakedaimon. Since the bishop of that see had long been a suffragan of Corinth, the only way to justify his subordination to Patras was to claim that the old Lakedaimon in existence during the 'thirty-second year of the reign of Justinian the Great' was destroyed by the barbarian invasions, which prompted its inhabitants to abandon the city and to move to Sicily. Lakedaimon was then refounded by Emperor Nikephoros I, who repopulated the city with 'Kapheroi, Thrakesians, Armenians, and others from different places and cities' (Kislinger 2001: 201 and 203).[15] To give further weight to the argument, the author of the *Chronicle of Monemvasia* – no doubt a learned churchman with access to a number of sixth-, seventh-, and ninth-century sources – introduced the Avars into the narrative, in order to explain that, after subjugating 'all of Thessaly and Greece, Old Epirus, Attica, and Euboea', they also conquered Peloponnesos, destroying and driving out the native 'Hellenic nations', and finally settling in the region, which they hold for 218 years (Kislinger 2001: 201; for the sources of the *Chronicle of Monemvasia*, see Kislinger 2001: 25–9; Madgearu 2005: 28–31). At the origin of this picture of devastation seems to be a passage in Evagrius' *Ecclesiastical History*, according to which the Avars plundered and conquered cities and forts in Greece (see Chapter 1). However, those whom the *strategos* Skleros defeated under Emperor Nikephoros I, after 218 years of barbarian rule, were Slavs, not Avars (Evagrius, *Ecclesiastical History* 6.10; see Curta 2004a). While ordering the conversion of the defeated Slavs to Christianity, the Emperor recalled the old inhabitants from the lands to which their ancestors had initially fled. The inhabitants of Patras, who had gone to Calabria, returned together with their bishop, in time for his elevation to the rank of metropolitan.

There is of course no reason to take this story at face value, despite the controversy surrounding the authenticity of the *Chronicle of Monemvasia* ever since the early nineteenth century, when Jakob Philipp Fallmerayer used the source to claim that the modern Greeks were descendants not of the ancient Greeks, but of Slavs and Albanians (see Chapter 10). However, less attention has been paid to the reasons for such an elaborate story, complete with chronological details and geographical references. The *Chronicle of Monemvasia* is not a chronicle properly speaking, but a compilation of sources concerning Avars and Slavs and referring to the foundation of the metropolitan see of Patras, and of the city and bishopric of Lakedaimon. Monemvasia is therefore not at the centre of the narrative. It has been argued that the text was written in order to be used in negotiations with the metropolitan of Corinth over the status of the metropolitan of Patras (Setton 1950: 517, who, following Kyriakidis 1947: 28, 51, and 92, believed the *Chronicle* to be a forgery of ecclesiastical origin, perpetrated by or on behalf of the metropolitan of Patras).[16] If so, it is perhaps important to note that in the *Chronicle of Monemvasia*, Patras and Lakedaimon were not the only cities abandoned at the time of the barbarian invasions. The inhabitants of Argos left their city and fled to 'the island called Orobe', while those of Corinth moved to Aigina (Kislinger 2001: 201). In other words, to the author of the *Chronicle of Monemvasia*, the havoc brought by the barbarian invasions completely destroyed the network of bishoprics in existence before that, so much so that Corinth – itself a victim of the devastation – could not operate any more as the only metropolitan in the region. In fact, while Corinth remained within the eastern part of Peloponnesos, which 'because of its ruggedness and inaccessibility remained free from the Slavs' (Kislinger 2001: 201) and continued to be ruled by a *strategos* appointed by the emperor, the remainder of the region had to be reconquered. Although Corinth had been the only metropolis in that region before the barbarian invasions, the subsequent devastation, depopulation, and reconquest of (western and central) Peloponnesos required the creation of a new metropolis, Patras. The author of the *Chronicle of Monemvasia* most probably wanted to forestall accusations of infringement of canon law, which clearly prohibited the coexistence of two metropolitans within one and the same province (Kresten 1977: 24–5 with n. 44; Turlej 2001: 91 and 94–5; Kislinger 2001: 102). Such accusations were to be expected from the patriarchal synod, and, as already mentioned, the *Chronicle* may have well been written in Constantinople by a learned man of the church. Although there is no indication that any accusations based on canon law were ever targeted at the metropolitan of Patras, there is some evidence of rivalry between suffragans of Patras and Corinth. The author of the *Chronicle of Monemvasia*, in his efforts to emphasise the relative importance of the metropolis of Patras, associated the refounding of Patras under Emperor Nikephoros I with his desire 'to rebuild the churches that the barbarians had destroyed, and to Christianise the barbarians themselves' (Kislinger 2001: 202–3; Turlej 2001: 110). To judge by the evidence of the *Chronicle*, the conversion of the Slavs to Christianity was a direct consequence of the creation of the bishopric of Lakedaimon and its subordination, together with Methone and Korone, to the metropolis of Patras. In the early tenth century, not everybody agreed with that version of events. According to the author of the *Life of St. Peter of Argos*, when he became bishop of that city – a suffragan of the metropolitan of Corinth – all those who had lost their homes to barbarian incursions found hospitable shelter in Argos. Peter's virtues, and not any missionary activity from other episcopal centres in Peloponnesos, were the key factor which eventually won over the minds of the barbarians, who renounced their pagan faith and adopted Christianity (*Life of St. Peter of Argos* 12–13; Vasiliev 1947: 172). The barbarians of the *Chronicle of Monemvasia* are most probably not the same as those in the *Life of St. Peter of Argos*, in either chronological or ethnic terms. Nonetheless, those contrasting stories underline the importance each bishopric (or metropolis), in its efforts to advance its own political interests, attached to the conversion of barbarians to Christianity, for which there is otherwise no corroborating evidence. When in 903 he decided to consecrate a church in Pallandion, on the border between his diocese and that of Argos, Bishop Nicholas of Lakedaimon may thus have symbolically claimed that territory for his own area of jurisdiction.

The two churches which St Nikon built shortly after each other in 969 or 970 in the 'Dorian land' near Sparta were within the area of jurisdiction of Bishop Nicholas' successor, Theopemptos. Nikon spoke to the local people of Sparta gathered in front of the episcopal church, and he also asked Bishop Theopemptos to organise a procession to the marketplace with the holy clergy and the people in order to mobilise them for the building of his own church (*Life of St. Nikon* 31 and 35).[17] Far from submitting to the authority of the local bishop, St Nikon was apparently capable of recruiting him for his own cause. Relations with holy men turning into monks may not have always been that smooth. In early 1027, a monk named Nikodemos built a bridge over the river Eurotas and, in addition, a monastery church at the end of the bridge, just outside Lakedaimon. He placed the church under the protection of the emperor and of his deputies, the *strategos* and the judge (*krites*), and specifically asked that 'the bishop of this same city, with his clergy, not be allowed to exercise any authority in this church, not even to set foot in it' (Zakythinos 1957: 99–100; Feissel and Philippidis-Braat 1985: 301–3; Thomas and Hero 2000: 324; for the *Testament* of Nikodemos as inspired by St Nikon's, see Gerolymatou 2004: 42). Nikodemos was perhaps a former member of the local aristocracy, with sufficient wealth and spirit of independence to bypass the bishop's area of jurisdiction. Elsewhere in Peloponnesos, bishops may have been more successful in controlling their flocks. A generation before Nikodemos, when a Peloponnesian priest named Pardos desired to become a monk, he first approached Bishop Paul of Monemvasia. His request was fulfilled, but he immediately had to return to his home town, named Eniklion, at the request of his father, who may have disagreed with his son's decision (Wortley 1996: 68; the location of Eniklion is not known).

Some of the tenth- and eleventh-century bishops and members of the higher clergy had considerable wealth. John Kaminiates' father was 'exarch of the whole of Hellas', an ecclesiastical position believed to be equal to that of bishop (John Kaminiates, *The Capture of Thessaloniki* 55). He gathered a considerable amount of wealth in the form of gold- and silverware, which he used to redeem his and his sons' lives from Leo of Tripoli in 904. More than sixty years later, when returning from Constantinople, Liudprand of Cremona noted that bishops in 'Greece' were 'rich in gold coins', but 'poor in servants and tools'. According to him, the bishop of Leukas paid to the emperor no less than one hundred gold coins, which probably was the amount needed to redeem the military obligations of his diocese (Liudprand of Cremona, *Embassy* 63).[18] Similarly, at the time of Emperor Romanos I's expedition to Italy (921), the metropolitans of Corinth and Patras provided eight horses together as a contribution to the general payment for which the Peloponnesians opted rather than military service (Constantine Porphyrogennetos, *On the Administration of the Empire* 52). Six years later, on his way to Constantinople, the metropolitan of Corinth stopped on Mount Ioannitza to pay a visit to St Luke the Younger and to offer him a gift of gold. When Luke refused, he did not hesitate to rebuke him: 'If you have no need at all for this gift, offer it to those who do need it. Now you seem to think the commandment to do good to others is empty and irrational, and you reject that nobility of mind that combines the love of God with the love of man' (*Life of St. Luke the Younger* 42; Luke's visitor is specifically called 'archbishop'). Luke accepted the criticism, in addition to only one coin of the amount offered. He may have done so because he needed the metropolitan's instructions in a matter of the utmost concern to him: how could a solitary like Luke 'participate in the divine and awesome mysteries', with no congregation and no priest around? The metropolitan took the opportunity to instruct Luke on proper liturgical practice:

> Now to begin with, a priest should be present, but if he is unavoidably absent, place a vessel containing what has already been sanctified upon the holy table, if it is a chapel, but if it is a cell, upon a very clean bench. Then, spreading out a covering, place on it the holy portions, and, lighting the incense, sing the psalms of the *typika* or the Trisagion along with the Creed. After three genuflections, fold your hands and take with your mouth the esteemed body of Christ our God, saying the Amen. In place of eucharistic wine, you may drink a cup of ordinary wine, but this cup should not be shared afterwards with another person. Next, put the remaining portions with the covering in the vessel, taking care lest a pearl fall out and be trampled.[19]

St Luke's circumstances were of course unusual, since he was expected to play the parts of both the faithful and, to some extent, the priest. The metropolitan's advice is therefore tailored to a special size. Nonetheless, it still reveals, as if in sharp relief, the 'zero degree' of standard liturgical practice. Perhaps the most important conclusion one can draw from this tenth-century description of the performance of the eucharistic rite is that it could all take place within the small cell of a solitary. This is consistent with what is otherwise known about liturgy in Middle Byzantine churches. Judging from the size of the churches built in tenth- and early eleventh-century Greece (see Chapter 6), many of which are considerably smaller than sixth-century basilicas, the performance of liturgical services must have appeared as quasi-'private', with little movement within a narrow space inside the church, especially in front of the sanctuary, and a greater emphasis on the symbolism of gestures and body posture.[20]

Since he was not a priest, Luke could not celebrate the Divine Liturgy. The Holy Communion he was advised to take consisted of eucharistic bread previously sanctified elsewhere by an ordained priest.[21] He must also have obtained from a church the incense which he was to burn when taking communion. Unlike eucharistic bread or incense, it may have been much more difficult to obtain eucharistic wine, for the metropolitan advises Luke to use ordinary wine instead. Although that wine had not been consecrated, like the eucharistic bread, the cup from which Luke was supposed to drink it was automatically assigned a symbolic value, for he was not to share it with another person after receiving communion. The exact meaning of the metropolitan's instructions is not easy to decipher, but it appears that in the absence of both priest and chalice, Luke was to receive the Holy Gifts separately – first the Body, and then the Cup. Instead of the Communion hymn, Luke was supposed to sing either psalms from the various offices in existence at that time or 'the Trisagion along with the Creed'. Both the Thrice Holy Prayer and the 'symbol of faith' were key components of the liturgy, which preceded the sanctification of the Species. In other words, before receiving communion, Luke was to replicate in a much abbreviated form the sequence of events in a standard liturgical service. Bending his knees three times, he was then to take the Communion cloth with both hands folded, and the Body of Christ with his mouth. In all three respects (genuflection, holding the covering with both hands, and taking the Body of Christ), the metropolitan's instructions are most probably an accurate description of the way in which he himself gave Communion to the faithful in tenth-century Corinth. Those instructions, however, turned St Luke's cell into a sacred space. His cup was not a mere cup anymore, and his bench became an altar table.

The sanctification of space could be further enhanced by religious processions. Liturgical parades had been a common feature of Christian practice since Late Antiquity. In tenth-century Greece, processions celebrated the foundation of new churches. St Nikon asked the bishop of Lakedaimon to get involved in a procession with the 'holy clergy and all the people' from the cathedral to the marketplace, 'where the cross was standing' (*Life of St. Nikon* 35;

Testament of Nikon the Metanoeite for the Church and Monastery of the Savior, the Mother of God and St. Kyriake in Lakedaimon, in Thomas and Hero 2000: 317). During the procession, Nikon put three stones on his shoulders – most probably a symbol of the triple dedication of his future church – and carried them to the marketplace. He delivered powerful speeches for the participants both before and after the procession. Besides offering an opportunity for Nikon to mobilise the community for his pet project, the procession may have offered a good opportunity for the 'leading men' of Sparta to display both piety and political power. Some 'generously furnished money', while others, like the *strategos* of Peloponnesos, donated an entire village, Perissos (*Testament of Nikon the Metanoeite for the Church and Monastery of the Savior, the Mother of God and St. Kyriake in Lakedaimon*, in Thomas and Hero 2000: 320).

The late tenth and early eleventh century also witnessed an increase in pilgrimage. Around AD 1000, as we have seen, on his way to the Holy Land, a goldsmith from Athens stopped on the island of Tinos, and signed his name on the wall of a cave at Gastria (Malamut 1988: 213, 467, and 547). Pilgrims also travelled to see living holy men in action, to draw inspiration from their ascetic practices, and occasionally to witness their formidable powers. In a place of Peloponnesos 'which the local inhabitants are accustomed to call Moros', St Nikon withdrew to a cave and asked the local priests and monks to be given the monastic habit, as he 'was worn out by disease and suffering ill in his body' (*Life of St. Nikon* 32). Shortly after that, however, 'a multitude of people gathered desiring to obtain his blessing (*eulogia*)'. As they were all very thirsty and 'in that place there was no water nor any flow of a spring', Nikon immediately showed his miraculous powers 'before the eyes of all' by striking the earth with his cross-bearing staff to bring water to the surface. Later Nikon repeated the water miracle in front of a group of people who were travelling with him from Corinth to Sparta. Not only were they 'astounded at the wonder of the miracle', but on the site of the spring produced by Nikon's miracle-working staff a house of prayer dedicated to him was built 'by one of the local inhabitants' (*Life of St. Nikon* 42). Its purpose was to produce 'defense against thirst for all wayfarers'. The monastery came into being in the holy place around the spring and may in time have become an attractive destination for local pilgrims.

The purpose of travelling to such places was to obtain *eulogia*, a word which meant both 'benediction' (such as the blessing which Nikon gave to the crowd gathered in Moros) and the material conduits for the transfer of the divine or saintly powers. The great emphasis placed in the tenth and eleventh centuries on a tactile form of piety can be seen in the description in the *Life of St. Nikon* of some of the saints' personal belongings on display around his tomb. Nikon's flask, 'which was expensively fashioned of Sardian stone', was used by all pilgrims to drink the water 'through which the holy chest is cleansed from within by a sponge' (*Life of St. Nikon* 17). When touched, the chain with which Nikon was dragged through Lakedaimon in order to convince the prominent men of the city to pay his debt to the workers is said to have been capable of 'setting people free from disease and weakness' (*Life of St. Nikon* 37).[22] *Eulogia* could also be a simple medallion with a holy image, which was produced on the pilgrimage site by means of special moulds, such as the eighth-century specimen found in the basilica of St Demetrios in Thessalonike (Mentzos 1996). More than souvenirs, such *eulogiai* were to be taken home by the pilgrims as tokens of the blessings they enjoyed while visiting the site.

'Portable' too was the precious and life-giving substance which exuded from the remains or the tombs of saints. At the end of his term as judge of Peloponnesos, Basil Apokaukos travelled to Sparta to pay homage at the tomb of St Nikon, but also to obtain some holy ointment (myrrh) in a vessel, in order to bring it home with him 'for sanctification and relief from misfortunes and remedy for diseases' (*Life of St. Nikon* 50).[23] The appearance of myrrh in the cult of St Nikon was by no means unique. Following the victory over iconoclasm in 843, myrrh began to flow from the remains of a great number of saints (Bakirtzis 2002: 179). In tenth-century Thessalonike, fragrant healing ointment miraculously exuded not just from the sarcophagus containing the remains of St Theodora, but also from her icon (*Life of St. Theodora of Thessalonike* 54 and 61). In 1040, Emperor Michael IV, in the hope of achieving cure for his advanced illness (apparently a form of acute epilepsy), came to the shrine of St Demetrios in Thessalonike (John Skylitzes, *History*, in Thurn 1973: 405). What he was seeking was most probably the myrrh gushing forth from the saint's tomb. This was the same myrrh which, according to John Skylitzes, the citizens of Thessalonike rubbed on their bodies before going into battle against the Bulgarian rebels under Alusian, who besieged the city in 1040 (John Skylitzes, *History*, in Thurn 1973: 413; see also Macrides 1990: 194).[24]

The therapeutic aspect was an essential part of the cult of saints in early medieval Greece. All fifteen posthumous miracles reported at the end of the *Life of St. Luke the Younger* are about the healing of a wide variety of afflictions, from demonic possession to cancer and blindness. St Luke's favourite remedy for any kind of disease was olive oil from the lamp hanging above his tomb (*Life of St. Luke the Younger* 71–3, 75, 80, 81, and 84; for olive oil in the *Life of St. Peter of Argos*, see Anagnostakis 1996: 127).[25] Olive oil from the lamp is also a prominent feature in the miracles and the cult of St Theodora of Thessalonike (*Life of St. Theodora of Thessalonike* 47 and 56).[26] The author of Theodora's *vita*, a learned cleric, even played on the homophony between the Greek words for olive oil (*elaion*) and mercy (*eleos*; *Life of St. Theodora of Thessalonike* 49). Cure might often come about through a dream, especially when the suppliant was allowed to sleep near the tomb of the saint. A boy and a man, both possessed by demons, were visited and healed by St Theodora while they were asleep (*Life of St. Theodora of Thessalonike* 50–1; for incubation, see also the *Life of St. Luke the Younger* 76). The origin and social background of the suppliants varied considerably. St Demetrios' tomb was visited by emperors, that of St Nikon by local judges. Monks 'from various mountains' and the wife of a *strategos* of Hellas appealed to St Theodora of Thessalonike (*Life of St. Theodora of Thessalonike* 56 and 59). People from as far as Thermopylae and Evvoia came to St Luke the Younger's tomb, and that of St Nikon in Sparta was visited by people from 'the environs of Corinth' as well as 'the coastal area of Kalamata' (*Life of St. Luke the Younger* 81–2; *Life of St. Nikon* 52 and 56). Women are prominent among suppliants at St Luke's tomb, both old and young, some appealing for themselves, others for their children (*Life of St. Luke the Younger* 69–72).

Early medieval holy men had powerful rivals. When in Argos, St Nikon visited the house 'of that John, who was surnamed Blabenterios'. He and his daughter were suffering because of the 'wiles and spells of a sorcerer'. Nikon's remedy was to find the very spot where the sorcerer had buried his spell – images or objects fashioned in the likeness of his victims – 'near the roots of a tree which stood in the courtyard of those people' (*Life of St. Nikon* 30). Those who could not afford to hire holy men against black magic had to make do with finger-ring amulets, such as those found in Corinth and carrying the image of the Medusa, as well as inscriptions, both being prophylactic means to ward off the evil eye (Papanikola-Bakirtzis 2002: 486).[27] Apotropaic devices were also needed because of the many demons believed to populate the landscape. A series of late ninth- and tenth-century buckles with rectangular plates decorated with images of lions or such fantastic animals as griffins are believed to be just such amulets, as the images in question were expected to drive back the evil forces potentially threatening to attack the persons wearing such dress accessories (Pletn'ov 2005: 81).[28] Awe-inspiring images of animals operated as shields against demons, which were also imagined to take an animal form when entering or exiting the human body. Demons were believed to live underground, which rendered any wells or crevasses particularly dangerous. When a girl from Euripos, whom her mother had sent to fetch water, lowered the bucket into a well, a demon from the abyss entered her body in the form of a crow. When her desperate mother appealed to St Nikon for assistance, he started first to pray for the victim. He tied her up, and praying some more together with the people gathered to watch the exorcism, he approached the well. He then reproved the demon, who immediately 'left the girl in the form of a crow before the eyes of all and crept back into the well'. After this episode, the inhabitants of Euripos decided to fill in the well 'up to the level of the ground' in order to prevent any other incidents (*Life of St. Nikon* 27).[29] Later in his life, Nikon had to confront demons again, this time in the form of wasps. When deciding to build his church on the site of a cross planted in the marketplace, he apparently did not know what the excavation could reveal:

> For the foundation was just being dug and had advanced to considerable depth when a very large stone was encountered which couldn't be moved . . . The stone was pushed by a boundless and numberless multitude and remained absolutely unmoved. But when the saint tried and only touched it with his hand, it seemed lighter than a feather and was most easily removed from the foundations. At the removal of the rock demons, who haunted the place to the great detriment of the inhabitants, and on account of whom, I believe, it was ordained that the church be built there, leapt forth in the form of wasps from the foundation and struck violently and wounded those toiling in the task.[30]

Nikon intervened, reproached the demons, and drove them from that place to the 'bottomless depths'. According to another version of the story, the wasp-demons returned at the time of the feast of St Kyriake, to whom the church was dedicated. Nikon had asked a senior priest to celebrate the liturgy on that special occasion. The wasps made their appearance during the liturgical service, but dropped dead in front of Nikon and the senior priest. At the Gospel reading, however, they revived and fled 'to the bank of the river' (*Testament of Nikon the Metanoeite for the Church and Monastery of the Savior, the Mother of God and St. Kyriake in Lakedaimon*, in Thomas and Hero 2000: 318).

Nikon's ability to combat demons, hot weather, and disease is the unmistakable mark of a holy man (for Nikon's biography, see the *Life of St. Nikon*; see also Galanopoulos 1933; Lampsidis 1982; Sullivan 1987). Born at some point between 930 and 935 in a wealthy family of the theme of Armeniakon, he spent twelve years in a monastery, before moving to Crete 'just when the island had been snatched from the hands of the Agarenes and preserved for the Roman Empire in the time of Nikephoros, emperor of blessed memory'. He remained seven years on the island, working for the conversion of its inhabitants. He then moved to continental Greece in 968, and visited Athens, Thebes, Corinth, Argos, Naupaktos, and many other places in Peloponnesos, before settling in Sparta, c. 970. He died shortly before or after the year 1000.[31] His *vita*, written in the mid-eleventh century, at the earliest, by someone who became an abbot of the Monastery of St Nikon, describes him in strong colours: an unflinching, yet compassionate man with an incredible energy and an obsessive concern with repentance. Those are features captured in the earliest known portrait of the saint, a mosaic in the northern arm of the cross-shaped *katholikon* of the Monastery of St Luke the Younger (Fig. 9.1). Nikon had a strong physical frame and remarkable endurance: he crisscrossed Peloponnesos on foot several times, often travelling at a rapid pace on hot summer days, apparently without suffering from heat and thirst like everybody else. He had a loud voice, which could cover the racket produced by the game of *tzykanion*, in which the local *strategos* and his playmates engaged not far from the church of the Monastery of St Nikon. He was also an impulsive man, eager to reproach not just demons, but also brigands, even when on the point of paying with his life for such brashness (*Life of St. Nikon* 57). Nikon did not avoid society and, despite his ascetic habits, he gladly took the leading role in the community, a manager and an arbiter at the same time. His was not the typical life of a solitary, for he constantly acted on behalf of his community in dealing either with the divine or with the more earthly authorities (*Life of St. Nikon* 1: 'For he mingled with society without defiling the beauty of his soul').

By contrast, St Luke the Younger was more committed to the ideals of eremitical life (for the biography of St Luke, see the *Life of*

Figure 9.1 St Nikon Metanoiete, *mosaic on the northern side of the nave in the* katholikon *of the Monastery of St Luke the Younger near Distomo (after Diez and Demus 1931: fig. 25).*

St. Luke the Younger; see also Papadopoulos 1935a). Born in 896 in the village of Kastorion (now Thisvi) in Boeotia, he was the son of relatively wealthy parents descended from refugees from Aigina. Luke became a monk in 910, but unlike Nikon, he lived only for a short while in a monastery in Athens, after running away from home.[32] He then began a solitary life on Mount Ioannitza. In 927, he moved to Peloponnesos, where he remained in the service of a stylite in Zemena for ten years. He returned to Mount Ioannitza, but moved in 940 to the neighbouring village of Kalamion. Three years later, he fled together with the villagers to the island of Ampelon in the Gulf of Corinth, where he remained until 946. He finally moved to Steiris, where he died in 953, at the age of 57. He was buried inside his cell, which was later turned into an oratory, around which grew the monastery dedicated to St Luke the Younger. Luke was in constant search of an ascetic life. His repeated wish to withdraw marks his unhappy encounters with society. He was attacked and badly beaten twice – by the soldiers who mistook him for a runaway slave and again by the harbour master who caught him trying to cross the Gulf of Corinth on a boat. When the Bulgarians attacked the island on which Luke and a number of villagers had fled, he escaped only by plunging into the sea. Though spending twenty years of his life on Mount Ioannitza, Luke also travelled to Thebes, either to pay visits to his friend Antonios, the abbot of a monastery outside the city, or in response to the invitation of the local *strategos*, Krinites. While Nikon's physical endurance figures prominently in his *vita*, Luke appears as much more dedicated to spiritual exercise. To be sure, he, like Nikon, 'was frozen by cold and scorched by burning heat and, in addition, unceasingly consumed by an infestation of lice'. However, he much preferred 'the unsocial life of the wilderness' to the company of men or women (*Life of St. Luke the Younger* 20). He talked to deer and vipers. When praying, he is said to have 'levitated about one cubit above the ground as if being raised up towards God' (*Life of St. Luke the Younger* 7).

The third holy man of tenth-century Greece is John Xenos (for the biography of John Xenos, see his *Autobiography* in Petit 1924; Tomadakis 1983–1986). He was born to wealthy parents in 970 at Siba (probably Sivas to the east of the Bay of Mesara) in southern Crete. He pursued a solitary life for several years, wandering around the island, before building a church for Sts Eutychios and Eutychianos in the vicinity of Rethymno. He then decided to build a monastery dedicated to the Mother of God *Antiphonetria* in Myriokephala, southwest from Rethymno. He also built churches in many other places in the hinterland of Rethymno. In every one of them he left those of his disciples who were ordained monks. When returning to Myriokephala, he bought arable land from the local peasants and established a dependency in order to secure the means of subsistence for the twelve monks in that monastery. Unlike Nikon and Luke, John Xenos travelled to Constantinople in order to obtain privileges for his foundations. He indeed obtained a chrysobull from Emperor Romanos III (1028–1034), who awarded John's foundation in Myriokephala an annuity, as well as monastic clothes. Patriarch Alexios Studites (1025–1043) also gave John a foundation charter for Myriokephala, which recognised the independence of the monastery through exemption from interference by both lay and ecclesiastical officials (for the *Testament* of John Xenos for his monastery at Myriokephala, see Thomas and Hero 2000: 146). Like Luke, John Xenos spent much of his lifetime as a solitary. Like Nikon, he built many churches and a monastery. Unlike both Nikon and Luke, he managed, however, to attract the imperial and patriarchal support for his small house.

All three saints have in common a preoccupation with establishing communities of ascetics, many of whom were their dedicated disciples. Both Nikon and Luke lived in monasteries before becoming solitaries. In that respect, they were different from other early medieval saints of Greece, such as St Athanasios of Methone, St Peter of Argos, or St George of Lesbos, who, despite starting their careers as monks, were later remembered for their deeds as bishops. Having practised asceticism from a very young age, none of those men had any family ties. Luke constantly chagrined his widowed mother by running away from home, while Nikon had long rejected his very wealthy father when he moved to Crete. By contrast, St Theodore of Kythera started as a married man and died as a hermit, in complete isolation (for the biography of Theodore, see the *Life of St. Theodore of Kythera* in Oikonomides 1967; Caraher 2008). A native of Korone, Theodore grew up in Nauplion. He was already married when he was ordained deacon by the local bishop. Longing for the life of an ascetic, Theodore travelled to Rome, perhaps as a pilgrim, but later returned to Peloponnesos to live in Monemvasia, as far as possible from his family. To isolate himself even more, he eventually took up residence as a hermit on the deserted island of Kythera, where he died shortly after that. His body was found by hunters coming from Monemvasia, who decided to bury it in the ruins of the Church of Sts Sergios and Bacchus, which later became the *katholikon* of the monastery dedicated to St Theodore. Theodore's story is remarkably similar to that of St Theoktiste (for the biography of Theoktiste, see Niketas Magistros, *Life of Theoktiste of Lesbos*). She was a native of Lesbos, who had entered a local convent at an early age. She was eighteen when taken captive by a party of Arab marauders, but managed to escape her captors on the deserted island of Paros. She lived there as a hermit for thirty-five years, before being discovered by a hunter from Evvoia. Theoktiste died shortly after the hunter's second visit to the island, but not before taking the Holy Communion he had brought for her. Like Nikon, Theoktiste had taken monastic vows at a very young age. Although, like Theodore, she is remembered for having been a hermit on a deserted island, she never enjoyed the same level of popularity as the two most important female saints of early medieval Greece, St Athanasia of Aigina and St Theodora of Thessalonike. Like Theodore, Athanasia and Theodora had both been married before taking monastic vows. Both natives of Aigina, they were born to wealthy families, members of which were later killed in battle with Arab raiders. Forced into marriage by their own families, both saints decided to withdraw from the world and take monastic vows after the deaths of their husbands. Both became abbesses in their respective monasteries. However, unlike Theodora, Athanasia built several churches on her native island, before joining a monastery in Constantinople. She returned to Aigina shortly before her death at some point during the first half of the ninth century. Theodora was twenty-five when she entered the convent of St Stephen in Thessalonike and remained a nun in that convent for the rest of her life, without travelling anywhere. Nonetheless, soon after her death in 892, her cult was sufficiently developed for her portrait to appear in the mid-eleventh century frescoes of the Church of Hagia Sophia in Thessalonike. Athanasia of Aigina and Theodora of Thessalonike thus stand in sharp contrast to Theoktiste of Lesbos. While the latter was a true hermit, the biographies of the former two female saints of early medieval Greece are associated with the virtues of an emphatically cenobitic life.

After the middle of the tenth century, such virtues were also embraced by the monastic community on Mount Athos. Unlike other monastic communities in the Empire, the hermits on the Mount Athos had developed at a very early stage a loose organisation. Its purpose was not just to represent the Athonite community in dealings with the civilian and ecclesiastical authorities, but also to be the administrator of the many klasmatic lands which the hermits had under their control. In 908 their 'chief hermit' (*protos hesychastes*) complained to the emperor about the encroachment of the flocks of the monasteries beyond Athos onto the mountain itself (Papachryssanthou 1975: 114; Morris 1995: 44).[33] During the second half of the tenth century, the Athonites acquired a legal persona represented by the *protos* and the assembly of elders, which initially met three times a year at the Lavra of Karyes, at Christmas, Easter, and the feast of the Assumption (Papachryssanthou 1975: 116).[34] The *protos* was assisted by a council of abbots, which by the mid-eleventh century was reduced to just three, the abbots of the Great Lavra, Vatopedi, and Iviron (Papachryssanthou 1975: 117; Morris 1996: 44).[35]

In the early tenth century, most Athonites lived either as isolated hermits or within lavras with minimal rules for communal life. St Athanasios is credited with the introduction of strictly cenobitic communities on Mount Athos, following his move there in 959. However, Athanasios was initially an advocate of eremitical monasticism.[36] After joining an Athonite hermit on Zygos, then near Karyes, he moved to the southernmost tip of the peninsula, to a place called Melana, where he began to live as a solitary (*Life of St. Athanasios the Athonite* 14, 19, and 21; Lemerle 1963b: 72–4). When he later drafted the rule for his Great Lavra, Athanasios permitted five of his monks, to whom he referred as 'kelliots' ('cell-monks') or 'hesychasts', to pursue a solitary life, each one together with his own disciple. Nonetheless, when setting up his lavra with funds from Nikephoros Phokas, instead of building separate cells for hermits Athanasios decided to dispose them in a rectangle around a *katholikon*. He defended his choice in unambiguous terms:

> For before God and the angels I bear witness that those who persevere in genuine obedience and who remain firm in the love of God and in true affection for one another do not take second place to those carrying on the struggle special to solitude. But they shall be found to be superior and deemed worthy of eternal crowns by the good and impartial judge.[37]

The monks were to eat and pray together, private acts of charity were not permitted, and hospitality was to be offered not by individuals, but by the community as a whole. In spite of its name, Athanasios' Lavra was therefore much closer to the Studite ideals of cenobitic life. In fact, the Lavra was the first community organised on the basis of the Studite principles not just on Mount Athos but in the whole of Greece (Ware 1996: 16).

That Athanasios' foundation of the Great Lavra was inspired by the *Testament* of Theodore the Studite is clear from a quick glance at his rule or *typikon* (Thomas and Hero 2000: 250–65; for the *Testament of Theodore the Studite for the Monastery of John Stoudios in Constantinople*, see Thomas and Hero 2000: 75–80; see Ware 1996: 6). No fewer than fourteen sections of the former (out of a total of twenty-four) were incorporated, often word for word, in Athanasios' *typikon*. There are also direct quotations from Theodore the Studite: 'You shall not possess anything of this world nor store up anything for yourself as your own, not even one piece of silver', or 'You shall always be vigilant that all things in the community be held in common and be indivisible and that nothing be owned on the part of any individual, not even a needle' (*Typikon of Athanasios the Athonite for the Lavra Monastery*, in Thomas and Hero 2000: 258–9; the quotations are from the *Testament of Theodore the Studite for the Monastery of John Stoudios in Constantinople*, for which see Thomas and Hero 2000: 77–8). Even the prohibition to own female animals is taken from the *Testament* of Theodore of Stoudios, along with the rule against the possession of slaves and servants. Like Theodore of Stoudios, Athanasios forbade female animals because he did not want his monks to engage in stock breeding, which could easily lead to profit-making activity, itself an incentive to hire servants or to use slave labour. In other words, his concern was with maintaining the ideal of apostolic poverty and a simplicity of lifestyle in the monastery (*Typikon of Athanasios the Athonite for the Lavra Monastery*, in Thomas and Hero 2000: 259: 'You shall not possess a slave either for your use or for the monastery entrusted to you or for the fields since man was created in the image of God. This institution has been allowed only to those in worldly life just as marriage. For necessary duties you shall not have an animal from among those of the female race since you have completely renounced the female sex').[38] To Athanasios, monks were 'called to sorrow, not to delights', a reminiscence of the old idea of monastic life as a form of inner martyrdom (Thomas and Hero 2000: 257).[39] He also endorsed the established Studite practice of 'disclosure of thoughts', whereby the monks laid 'before the superior their thoughts and hidden deeds' and conformed to whatever their superior decided on that basis (*Rule of Athanasios the Athonite for the Lavra Monastery*, in Thomas and Hero 2000: 228).[40]

The new, cenobitic ideals also found an architectural form of expression. The Great Lavra was from the beginning designed to have a courtyard plan with a free-standing church in the middle, surrounded on all sides by inward-facing cells and dependencies, which backed on to the enclosure walls guarded by a tower.[41] The refectory, built at some point between 963 and 976, consisted of a cross-shaped building with marble tables brought probably from Constantinople (Mylonas 1987: 154). The first *katholikon* of the Great Lavra was a cross-in-square church, to which Anastasios later added two choirs (*chorostasiai*) in order to accommodate the needs of a more elaborate liturgy using a larger number of chanters. Such an architectural innovation seems to have been applied first (in 965) to the three-aisled, timber-roofed basilica at Karyes (Monastery of the Protaton), where the assembly of the elders gathered three times a year. The resulting quasi-triconch plan was then introduced to the *katholikon* of the Great Lavra and subsequently became the hallmark of the church architecture on Mount Athos (Mylonas 1984: 98–9, 1979: 144–6 and 150).

Notes

1. There were twenty-one bishops in Achaia, nine in Epirus Vetus, eleven in Thessaly, fourteen in Macedonia Prima, and two in Crete. In the early tenth century, there were eighty-four episcopal sees in Greece.
2. The bishop of Athens who attended the Sixth Ecumenical Council may well have been that Andrew whose death in 693 is mentioned in a graffito on a Parthenon column (Laurent 1943: 63).
3. Patras is mentioned as archbishopric under Emperor Nikephoros I in the *Chronicle of Monemvasia* (Kislinger 2001: 202). The first archbishop of Athens mentioned in the inscriptions on the columns of the Parthenon is Germanos, who died in 841; the first metropolitan is Philip, who died in 981.
4. The metropolitan of Larissa was present at the council of 879, together with five of his suffragan bishops.
5. In a letter to the *strategos* of Hellas, Patriarch Nicholas Mystikos explicitly refers to an 'archbishop of Thebes' (Nicholas Mystikos, *ep*. 34). A metropolitan of Thebes named Germanos is mentioned on two tenth-century seals (Dunn 1995: 758). At least three bishoprics – Opous, Zaratova, and Kastorion (St Luke's home town, present-day Thisvi) – may have been the suffragan sees of Thebes during the tenth century.
6. Those and other island bishoprics were under the jurisdiction of the metropolitan of Rhodes (Darrouzès 1981: 304; Malamut 1988: 146–7).
7. The Drugubites within the flock of the bishop of Drougoubiteia lived in villages located in the plain between Thessalonike and Veroia. According to John Kaminiates, they were paying taxes to the city of Thessalonike (*The Capture of Thessaloniki* 6). Similarly, the bishopric of Smolaina, which is first mentioned in *notitia* 7 as a suffragan of the metropolitan of Philippi, was organised on the lower course of the Nestos River, near the present-day Greek–Bulgarian border (Darrouzès 1981: 285). That

was most probably where the Smoliani lived, who are mentioned in the inscription of Philippi (Beshevliev 1963: 164–5; Cheshmedzhiev 1997: 91).

8. Peritheorion, which appears in *notitia* 7 as a suffragan see of Traianoupolis, is listed under the metropolis of Philippi in *notitia* 9, compiled during the reign of John Tzimiskes (Darrouzès 1981: 112–13, 285, and 304). Of all eight suffragan sees of Naupaktos, three were in Akarnania (Bounditza, Aetos, Acheloos) and two in Epirus (Rogoi and Ioannina). The metropolitans of Traianoupolis, Naupaktos, and Philippi participated in the council of 879 together with some of their suffragan bishops (Darrouzès 1981: 284 with n. 575 and 285 with n. 595).

9. Neither Bolaina nor Zemaina can be located with certainty. However, the former was almost certainly in western Peloponnesos, within the borders of the present-day prefecture of Ilia (Bon 1951: 107). If the Zemaina in the list is the same as Zemena, where the stylite lived whom St Luke served for ten years, then the town must have been between Corinth and Patras (*Life of St. Luke the Younger* 35; Turlej 2001: 113 with n. 124).

10. Kernitza does not appear as a suffragan bishopric of Patras before the turn of the twelfth century (Darrouzès 1981: 362; Turlej 2001: 118–19). Similarly, although the see is not listed in *notitia* 9, a bishop of Hierissos, who was a suffragan of the archbishop of Thessalonike, appears in a document from the Monastery of Iviron, which is dated to 982 (Darrouzès 1981: 299; Živojinović 1973).

11. The conversion of those people is dated to the reign of Emperor Basil I (867–886). No indication exists that the barbarians, whom St Peter of Argos inspired to renounce paganism and to embrace Christianity, were Slavs (*Life of St. Peter of Argos* 14).

12. The repetitive nature of Nikon's message of repentance (*metanoia*) may indicate not just an emphasis on the need for a change of mind and heart in his audience, either generally or in respect of specific sins. Nikon may have also felt the need for an inner compensation for personal traumas and experiences. In other words, he may have preached repentance in order to compensate for his own profound sense of guilt as the son of a wealthy family, who 'saw and learned of the great suffering and hardship of those living' on his father's estates as dependent peasants. They were 'always devoting themselves to working the earth', so much so that, when he saw them, Nikon supposedly exclaimed: 'What purposelessness, oh the deceit of life; truly in vain does each man vex himself' (*Life of St. Nikon* 3; Constantelos 1985: 305).

13. If anything, the fact that initially his speeches about repentance attracted only the children of Evvoia, who believed 'this unusual preaching to be a game', may indicate that their parents were

indifferent. The episode may also be a narrative strategy employed by the author of the *vita* to introduce the miracle of the child who, through the intervention of the saint, escaped unscathed after falling from the wall of the city.

14. The date 900/1 follows from a note at the beginning of the version of the *Chronicle* in a manuscript from the Monastery of Kutlumus (Athos 3293), dated to the fifteenth or sixteenth century: 'From the days of the Avars until now, 95 years'. Since, according to the *Chronicle of Monemvasia*, the 'days of the Avars' ended with the victory of the *strategos* Skleros in 805 or 806, the 'now' of the composition must be 900 or 901. Several changes and additions were made to the main text written in the early tenth century which reflect much later events in that century (Madgearu 2005: 65–8).

15. Nikephoros appears to have re-established not just the city, but also the bishopric of Lakedaimon. When the Justinianic city was abandoned because of the invasion of the barbarians, its bishop, together with that part of his flock which did not go to Sicily, moved to an 'inaccessible place by the seashore', where they all built another city named Monemvasia.

16. According to Turlej 1998: 455 with n. 23, the *Chronicle* is an 'exposé', an elaborate report on the circumstances leading to the establishment of the metropolis of Patras.

17. Theopemptos 'had his origins in Athens'. For his seal, see Nesbitt and Oikonomides 1994: no. 29.3.

18. The bishop in question must in fact have been an archbishop (Malamut 1988: 345). Not all bishops in Greece were poor in servants. The metropolitan of Corinth who visited Luke had an entourage, some of whose members were asked to present the gift to the saint.

19. *Life of St. Luke the Younger* 42.

20. Some of the smallest early medieval churches so far found in Greece could clearly meet the demands for basic service. The tenth- or early eleventh-century church excavated in the Platamon fort produced a liturgical marble vessel with carved decoration which is believed to be either a baptismal font or a *phiale* for holy water (Loverdou-Tsigaridi 1997: 61 and 63–4).

21. Similarly, St Theoktiste of Lesbos, a solitary, when meeting a hunter coming onto her deserted island, asked him to place 'in a clean vessel a portion of the most pure gifts, the body of our Lord Jesus Christ' and to bring it to her the next time he would come again. Following her request, when he was 'ready to go hunting' with his companions on Paros, he put 'in a small box a portion of the divine flesh of the Lord' and gave it to St Theoktiste. The eucharistic bread must have been consecrated by a priest in Evvoia (Niketas Magistros, *Life of Theoktiste of Lesbos* 18–19). For a seventh- to eighth-century seal from Aigina, with

which the eucharistic bread was stamped, see Papanikola-Bakirtzis 2002: 196.
22. The chain was on display above Nikon's tomb, next to the saint's cowl.
23. No 'vessels' (ampullae) for the collection of myrrh survive from early medieval Greece which could be compared to the sixth-century ampullae from Nea Anchialos or Rhodes (Papanikola-Bakirtzis 2002: 173–4).
24. However, the earliest evidence for pilgrims coming to Thessalonike to obtain myrrh from the tomb of St Demetrius cannot be dated before 1100 (Bakirtzis 1990).
25. A healing miracle involving olive oil from the lamp is also reported for St Nikon (*Life of St. Nikon*, 65). However, this may simply indicate the influence of the *Life of St. Luke the Younger*, a text from which the author of the *Life of St. Nikon* drew for a number of elements in his own work (Rosenqvist 1996: 95–6).
26. In St Theodora's case, olive oil is instrumental in the conversion of an iconoclastic heretic (*Life of St. Theodora of Thessalonike* 57).
27. No *phylacteria* are known from early medieval Greece, except that attached to a golden necklace found in a seventh-century hoard in Kratigos near Mytilene (Lesbos), for which see Papanikola-Bakirtzis 2002: 530; see also Bartelink 1973.
28. Buckles decorated with griffins have been found in Thebes and Ithaka (Kourenta-Raptaki et al. 1994: 116 fig. 20 and pl. 48; Symeonoglou 1985: pl. 103δ). Specimens with images of lions are known from Philippi and Corinth (Pennas 1973–1974: pl. 634δ; Davidson 1952: pl. 115.2215). Two buckles from Corinth, one from Crete (Werner 1955: pl. 7B2), and another from Laurion (Davidson 1952: pl. 115.2213–14; Lazaridis 1960: pl. 57γ) are decorated with images of some kind of carnivores, perhaps lions, attacking deer. Two buckles, one from Tigani on Samos (Vinski 1974: pl. 3.2), the other from Crete (Werner 1955: pl. 7B1), are decorated with a composition consisting of a human mask (or bust) flanked by two opposing horse heads. A similar buckle has recently been found in Messini (personal information from Nikos Tsivikis). An image of a wolf (or dog) appears on a buckle from Drymos, which has an eagle on the inner side (Mastrokastas 1971: 188 figs 4–5). A similar buckle from Chersonesos in Crimea has four doves on the back, which suggests that while the image on the outside may have been of a fantastic or otherwise frightening animal, that on the inside was a strong symbol of Christian protection (Vinski 1974: 62 and pl. 1.10).
29. When exorcised, other demons looked like human excrement. See the *Life of St. Theodora of Thessalonike* 51.
30. *Life of St. Nikon* 36.
31. The early date is advanced by Dennis F. Sullivan, the later one by Odysseus Lampsidis (Sullivan 1987; Lampsidis 1982). In fact, all

that the *vita* has to say about the date of Nikon's death is that it took place a 'sufficient time' after the recalling in 997 of John Malakenos to Constantinople, under accusations of siding with Samuel of Bulgaria (*Life of St. Nikon* 44).

32. St Luke is regarded as the first in a list of prominent monks in the early medieval history of Greece. That list also includes St Nikon, St Christodoulos of Patmos, and St Meletios the Younger (Papadopoulos 1935a: 193).
33. Conflicts between Athonites and their neighbours led to a demarcation of the border of Athos, which is first mentioned in 943 in relation to the conflict between the Athonites and the inhabitants of the town of Hierissos (now Ierisos, in Chalkidiki) (Papachryssanthou 1975: 56–9; Morris 1996: 43). Along with the archbishop of Thessalonike, also involved in this demarcation was Katakalon, the *strategos* of Thessalonike who would soon after that be killed by Magyar marauders.
34. The *typikon* of Emperor John Tzimiskes reduced the annual assemblies to just one, to be summoned on the feast of the Virgin (15 August), but in the early eleventh century, the practice of holding three assemblies per year was re-established.
35. The *protos* represented Athos in any dealings with the civilian or ecclesiastical authorities, with the Emperor, the patriarch, or the local authorities in Thessalonike. When Nikephoros Phokas wished to search out his spiritual father Athanasios, the judge (*krites*) of Thessalonike charged with finding him approached the *protos* of Athos for assistance (*Life of St. Athanasios the Athonite* 16; Lemerle 1963b: 73; Papachryssanthou 1975: 73, 115, and 124).
36. There is nonetheless no evidence of his sudden 'conversion' to cenobitic life, especially not under the influence of the Rule of St Benedict, as claimed by Leroy 1953 and 1963. As Papachryssanthou 1975: 78–9 long since pointed out, the revolutionary character of the introduction of the strictly cenobitic community of the Great Lavra follows less from Athanasios' alleged 'conversion' than from the fact that when the founder became an emperor, his foundation automatically turned into an imperial foundation. It is Nikephoros Phokas' lavish donation to the Lavra which created a large *koinobion*, for which there was no precedent or parallel on Mount Athos.
37. *Typikon of Athanasios the Athonite for the Lavra Monastery*, in Thomas and Hero 2000: 262. The *typikon* indicates that the kelliots were to live not far from the Lavra and were expected to be obedient to its abbot like any other brethren.
38. The entire paragraph has been lifted, word for word, from the *Testament of Theodore the Studite for the Monastery of John Stoudios in Constantinople* (Thomas and Hero 2000: 77). See also Leroy 1963: 114.

39. *Typikon of Athanasios the Athonite for the Lavra Monastery*, in Thomas and Hero 2000: 262.
40. Athanasios is said to have 'received the thoughts' of his fellow monks not only during Matins in the chapel, but also throughout the day (Ware 1996: 11). The *typikon* of Emperor John Tzimiskes (known as the *Tragos*) refers to the 'disclosure of thoughts' when stipulating that 'no one is allowed to ridicule or publicly expose the thoughts and confessions of anyone' (*Typikon of Emperor John Tzimiskes*, in Thomas and Hero 2000: 237). This shows that the 'disclosure of thoughts' was a widespread practice in the monastic community of Mount Athos.
41. Very few monasteries in existence in Greece during the tenth century have been studied architecturally and archaeologically. There is therefore no way so far to tell whether or not the Great Lavra was a novelty in early medieval Greece. However, judging from the results of Charalambos Bakirtzis' excavations in Synaxis near Maroneia, it appears that the idea of a free-standing *katholikon* and a regular arrangement of both cells and dependencies around it did not exist anywhere in Greece before the foundation of the Great Lavra. In Synaxis, a monastery was established in the ninth and tenth centuries within the ruins of an early Byzantine basilica. The plan of the pre-existing church dictated the specific arrangement of the monastic buildings, given that many of them re-used the still standing walls of the sixth-century basilica. There were five apartments on the southern side, one of which had a fireplace and may have served as the porter's lodge. The refectory was in the southern wing of the transept of the early Byzantine basilica. Opposite the entrance into the refectory was the *katholikon*, an aisle-less church with tiled roof, whose floor was paved with re-used marble slabs from the ruins of the sixth-century basilica. On the latter's northern side, there were five more apartments (Bakirtzis 1996: 48–9).

CHAPTER 10

Conclusion: *the people of early medieval Greece*

It has been a major argument of this book that, following the general abandonment of the Balkan provinces under Emperor Herakleios, the army, either land (thematic) troops or the navy, played a fundamental role in the early medieval history of Greece. The military created the political and administrative infrastructure which secured the survival of Roman (Byzantine) power in coastal areas and on several islands. Land troops may have been responsible for the repopulation of large parts of Peloponnesos in the early ninth century, while the first social hierarchies in 'Dark-Age' Greece were essentially military. Around 1000, high-ranking officials such as Krinites, the *strategos* of Hellas, or Christopher, the *katepano* of Longobardia, were prominent patrons of churches. The presence of the navy also created the need for local markets on which monetary exchanges continued, albeit on a much reduced scale. As late as the early eleventh century, the military continued to be a key factor in the injection of coins into the local economy, both in urban centres and in the countryside.

Within the general framework defined by the ubiquity of the army in early medieval Greece, three features are especially striking. The first is the remarkable absence of any attempts at usurping the imperial power, which are otherwise well documented for the themes of Anatolikon, Opsikion, and Armeniakon. In Greece, all such attempts were nipped in the bud, most famously at the beginning of Romanos I and Constantine VII Porphyrogennetos' joint rule (920–944). Charges of treason and defection to the enemy were levelled at several key officers, including at least one military governor of Hellas, during the long war between Basil II and Samuel of Bulgaria. None of them, however, tried to use the opportunity to challenge the imperial authority directly, which may explain why, in the end, none was found guilty and none was punished. Three emperors – Constans II, Justinian II, and Basil II – are known to have visited the Greek lands, and the Byzantine grip on those lands was sufficiently strong to secure the cooperation, if not also the loyalty, of the local aristocrats.

A particularly good illustration of that loyalty is the story of the Bulgarian governor of Larissa, Litovoi, who, after taking care of the city's fortifications in 1040, was nonetheless overthrown, captured, and handed to the *strategos* of Thessalonike by the inhabitants of the city. Similarly, Symbatios of Patras sent to Constantinople under imperial guard the masterminds of the conspiracy of the early 920s, before any intervention by the imperial authorities. Kekaumenos would later advise anyone forced by unusual circumstances to betray the Emperor to follow the example of his paternal grandfather, the *strategos* of Hellas, and keep the emperor informed at all times about the reasons for such actions (*Strategikon* 169 and 171).

On the other hand, the written sources contain several examples of members of the military and administrative hierarchies in the Greek lands sporting so-called 'imperial titles' associated with the court. *Protospatharioi*, for example, were the cream of the local aristocracy during the tenth century, members of which occupied the position of *strategos* and were patrons of the first churches built in early medieval Greece. Danielis invested a good portion of her legendary wealth to obtain the title of *protospatharios* for her son and that of 'Mother of the Emperor' for herself. As the value of such lofty titles diminished, many of those who had gained access to imperial favour and resources came to control substantial amounts of land. Not an 'aristocracy of office' any more, such people became an economically dominant and socially powerful group of landowners who had a say in local politics on the basis of their good reputation, but who could also use 'legitimate' violence perpetrated by bands of men under their command in order to establish 'order'. No title was attached to the name of any of the prominent men of Sparta who backed St Nikon's initiatives. Nonetheless, small-town big-wigs like them (Neville 1998: 48 and 276) were brokers of local power.

The presence of the army in Greece had more to do with neighbouring areas of military conflict – with the Arabs in the ninth and tenth century or with the Bulgarians shortly before and after the year 1000 – than with territorial expansion. The traditional view of early medieval Greece as a region gradually (re)taken from the barbarians, after c. 750, by Byzantine troops initially stationed in coastal forts is in part the product of the particular way in which the sources, especially the *Chronicle of Monemvasia*, have been manipulated by scholars. Most soldiers in the thematic troops were expected to serve in expeditions overseas, such as that organised in 921 by Romanos I against the Lombard rebels in Italy. When the revolt of the Milingoi and Ezeritai broke out in Peloponnesos, the army sent against the rebels under the command of the *strategos* of Peloponnesos consisted of troops recruited from outside the province, namely from Thrace, Macedonia, 'and the rest of the western provinces' (Constantine Porphyrogennetos, On the Administration of the Empire 50). From the point of view of Emperor Constantine VII, the Milingoi and the Ezeritai were not intruders to be eliminated by military action, but locals with special status, from whom tribute needed to be extracted, if necessary by force. When troops recruited elsewhere, such as the Slavesians, revolted, the proper course of action was to reduce the tribute paid by the Milingoi and the Ezeritai, in order to prevent an alliance between foreign and local rebels.

To distinguish precisely between those identities, Emperor Constantine Porphyrogennetos employed two different names, Slavesians (*Sklavesianoi*) and Slavs (*Sthlavoi*). The latter were clearly a local population, for they too had revolted in the past, had attacked the dwellings of their neighbours, the Greeks (*Graikoi*), and had put Patras under siege (*On the Administration of the Empire* 49). Those rebels, against whom the *strategos* of Peloponnesos was expected to come from Corinth, are then called by a third name, Sclavenes (*Sklavenoi*). It is against the Sclavenes that the inhabitants of Patras organised their sortie, and it is for them that the Emperor Nikephoros I later issued a bull which reduced them to the status of subjects of the metropolis of Patras. The Sclavenes, but not the Slavs (*Sklavoi*), are twice called barbarian, most probably because of their behaviour, and not because they were thought to be from outside the Empire, since they are specifically said to have been 'in the province of Peloponnesos'. There was a single Sclavene *ethnos* (*ethnos ton Sklavenon*, On the Administration of the Empire 49), but many Slavonic nations (*ethne Sklavinika*, On the Administration of the Empire 29; see also *para ton Sklavikon ethnon* at the beginning of chapter 30). That Emperor Constantine's terminology is not erratic is proved by the fact that the Sclavenes appear only in chapter 49 of the treatise *On the Administration of the Empire* regarding Peloponnesos, while the Slavs are also mentioned in the chapters on the Rus' and their tributaries (chapters 9 and 37), as well as in the chapter on Dalmatia (chapter 29). To Emperor Constantine, 'Slavs' was an umbrella term, not an individual ethnic group. By contrast, 'Sclavene' was meant to denote a social and political configuration which was specific to Peloponnesos. In that respect, Emperor Constantine's usage is not different from the narrative strategies of other early medieval authors who wrote about the early Slavs (e.g., Fredegar, for which see Curta 1997: 152–3). That the Sclavenes of Peloponnesos were Slavs may not be surprising at all. But it is important to note that they were so to the same degree as the Croats, the Serbs (including the 'unbaptised' ones), the Zachlumites, the Terbouniotes, the Oultines, the Dervlenines, and the Lenzenines (*On the Administration of the Empire* 29, 31, and 37). Similarly, 'Milingoi' and 'Ezeritai' were names for two groups of Slavs who, like the Sclavenes before them, refused to submit to the power of the emperor, and were practically independent and self-governing under Emperor Romanos I (*On the Administration of the Empire* 50). By contrast, all those who in Peloponnesos had been subdued and forced to accept Byzantine rule are simply called 'Slavs'.

When did all those 'Slavs' come to Peloponnesos? According to Constantine Porphyrogennetos, the land was Slavicised (*esthlavothe*) and barbarised after the plague of 745/6 (*On the Themes* 6; Stathakopoulos 2004: 382–5). Some of the emperor's older contemporaries pushed the antiquity of the Peloponnesian Slavs even farther back into history. The learned cleric who compiled the *Chronicle of Monemvasia* in the early tenth century scoured the historical sources for evidence of an earlier devastation which could be linked to the disappearance of the bishopric of Lakedaimon and, with that, of the claims which the metropolitan of Corinth had to that see in the tenth century. The beginning of barbarian rule was thus set at a much earlier time:

> Having thus conquered and settled the Peloponnesos, the Avars have held it for two hundred and eighteen years, from the year 6096 [AD 587] from the creation of the world, which was the sixth year of the reign of Maurice, to the year 6313 [AD 805], which was the fourth year of the reign of Nikephoros the Old who had Staurakios as son. They were subject neither to the emperor of the Romans, nor to anyone else.[1]

Neither the *Chronicle of Monemvasia* nor Constantine Porphyrogennetos can in fact be trusted as a reliable source for what happened in Greece between the seventh and the ninth century. The evidence examined in Chapter 4 shows that, while the author of Book II of the *Miracles of St. Demetrios* knew a number of 'Slavic' groups by name, no source indicates the presence of any such groups in southern Greece before c. 700. In fact, Constantine Porphyrogennetos is the first source to shed light on the Slavs of Peloponnesos. And his interest was neither ethnographic nor historic. In the early tenth century, factions supporting either Romanos I or Constantine Porphyrogennetos were almost at war with each other in Hellas and Peloponnesos. The political atmosphere in Constantinople was poisoned with the rumours from the provinces about the expulsion of faction leaders or aborted attempts at usurping the imperial power. At court, Greece was viewed as a backward country. As John Geometres put it in one of his epigrams, 'having seen Greece (*Hellas*), not the land of barbarians, you have become barbarised in your speech as well as your manners' (Cramer 1963: 285; English translation in Oikonomides 1992: 253). Political enemies from Hellas were therefore compared to barbarians. The claims to noble lineage of Niketas Magistros, who was born of a Spartan father and an Athenian mother, were ridiculed. An epigram about him which circulated in court circles encapsulates the notion of linguistic barbarity which the educated elites in Constantinople may have had about Greece: it employs a Slavic word ('gorazd', in the sense of 'shrewd') with a Greek ending (*garasdoeides*) to refer to Niketas' facial traits, which are further said to have been 'Slavic through and through' (Constantine Porphyrogennetos, *On the Themes* 6; Pratsch 2005: 504). The ethnic insult is supposed to deride Niketas' claims to noble lineage and perhaps his education (Ševčenko 1992: 193–4, who adds Niketas' affiliation with the 'Lekapenos clan'). His barbarity is apparently opposed to the 'civilised' manners and language in use at the imperial court. Was Niketas, then, a Slav? In order to draw such a conclusion, one would have to ignore completely the context of the epigram and the emphasis placed on the contrast between barbarians and civilisation, and not between Slavs and Greeks (or Romans). Similarly, to take at face value the idea that the Slavs arrived in Greece after the plague of 745/6 is to turn a blind eye to the fact that the author of Book II of the treatise *On the Themes* attributes the event to the reign of 'that Constantine, who bore the name of dung', a ruler whose reputation had been long and thoroughly blackened before *On the Themes* was composed.[2] It is important also to note that by claiming that the entire country was Slavicised and barbarised, the author of Book II wanted to point out that no one had been left of noble origin and that, as a consequence, Niketas' claims were without any basis, for being born of a Spartan father and an Athenian mother, he could not but have been barbarian. There is therefore no reason to take as historical evidence the nasty gossip about a disgraced supporter of Romanos I. Whether or not the plague of 745/6 had any role in facilitating a Slavic settlement in Greece, the evidence of the anonymous comment in *On the Themes* cannot be taken at face value, for its author's goal was to score political points, not to relate historical facts.

The evidence discussed in Chapter 4 strongly suggests an early presence of people in northern Greece whom the author of Book II of the *Miracles of St. Demetrios* knew both by their respective tribal names (Drugubites, Sagudates, Belegezites, or Rynchines) and by the more general term of 'Sclavenes' (*Sklavenoi*). On the other hand, no evidence exists of a Sclavene (or 'Slavic') presence in southern Greece before 700. Moreover, the archaeological evidence pertaining to 'barbarians' in Dark-Age Greece may be understood only in the context of analogues with assemblages discovered outside Greece. Such analogues do not point either to the territories across the Lower Danube where early Byzantine authors placed the Slavs, or to the regions in northern Greece which were inhabited in the late seventh century by those called 'Sclavenes' in the *Miracles of St. Demetrios*. Instead, the ceramic material and the metal artefacts found in cremation burials in Olympia have many and very clear analogues in the Middle Danube region of the Avar qaganate or in the steppe lands north of the Black Sea. It may well be that the author of the *Chronicle of Monemvasia* muddled Avars and Slavs with the purpose of tracing a history of the 'barbarian occupation' of Peloponnesos as far back in time as possible. But the same cannot be true for the *Life of St. Pancratius*, according to which there were Avars in the region of Athens in the late seventh or early eighth century. It is important to note that 'Avars' and 'Slavs' are labels employed by outsiders, not the names those people, whoever they were, may have employed for themselves. When calling the hinterland of Monemvasia 'the land of Slavinia', Hugeburc of Heidenheim (or Willibald of Eichstätt, whose biography she wrote) may have had in mind the 'land of the barbarians', not necessarily the land of the Slavs in an ethnic sense. Be that as it may, the earliest information about the 'Slavs' in the Peloponnesos long post-dates the establishment of the theme by that name, even though the creation of a metropolitan of Patras and the settlement of groups of population from other parts of the Empire may well have been connected with the first major conflict between the Byzantine authorities and the local Slavic tribes.

The author of the *Chronicle of Monemvasia*, Arethas of Kaisareia, and Constantine Porphyrogennetos knew about a single 'Sclavene nation' (*Sthlavinos/Sklauinos/Sklavenos ethnos*) in existence in

Peloponnesos at the time of Emperor Nikephoros I's two bulls for the metropolis of Patras (Kislinger 2001: 201; Westerink 1972: 241; *On the Administration of the Empire* 49; see Chapter 5). It is no doubt from the text of one of those bulls that the reference to the 'Sclavene nation' was taken by all three sources, which suggests an official, perhaps administrative origin for such an ethnic terminology. The author of the *Chronicle of Monemvasia* linked the 'Sclavene nation' to the Avars of the sixth-century sources which were available to him in Constantinople. By contrast, Constantine Porphyrogennetos moved forward in time in order to associate the 'Sclavene nation' with the 'Slavs' of more recent times. 'In the days of the emperor Theophilus and his son Michael', therefore, there was no 'Sclavene nation' any more, just 'Slavs of the province of Peloponnesos' who revolted against Byzantine rule. Furthermore, some of the 'insubordinates of the province of Peloponnesos' were now known by their own names, Milingoi and Ezeritai. The source of information for the two groups is specifically said to have been a golden bull of Emperor Romanos I (920–944), which reduced the tribute imposed on the Milingoi and the Ezeritai in the aftermath of a particularly destructive campaign against them led by the *strategos* of Peloponnesos, Krinitas Arotras (*On the Administration of the Empire* 50). Since the two groups first appear in the context of the expedition of Theoktistos Bryennios, which took place during the first years of Michael III's reign (842–867), it is possible that the bull of Romanos contained a short history of the conflict with the Milingoi and the Ezeritai, which Emperor Constantine used as the main source for the narrative in chapter 50 of *On the Administration of the Empire*. The impression one gets from that chapter is that the conflict with the Byzantine authorities had set the Milingoi and the Ezeritai apart from the other 'Slavs' of Peloponnesos, who, following the expedition of Theoktistos Bryennios, had submitted to imperial rule. Moreover, Emperor Constantine knew that the Milingoi and the Ezeritai had been pushed 'towards Lacedaemonia and Helos' and forced to settle on either side of 'a great and very high mountain called Pentadaktylos'. In other words, to Emperor Constantine, the Milingoi and the Ezeritai were not native to southern Peloponnesos, but arrived there as refugees from the region farther to the north, in which Theoktistos Bryennios waged his war against the 'Slavs and other insubordinates'. This opens the possibility of the Milingoi and the Ezeritai being not remnants of migrants from the Slavic homeland in East Central Europe with a fully fledged identity (so Birnbaum

Conclusion: the people of early medieval Greece

1986), but new ethnic groups which emerged at some point during the second half of the ninth century in reaction to Byzantine military campaigns. The distinction between the 'Sclavene nation', on one hand, and the Slavic Milingoi and Ezeritai, on the other hand, may be attributed to Emperor Constantine's use of two different sources, the bulls of Nikephoros I and Romanos I, respectively. While the former was concerned with subordinating the 'Sclavene nation' to the metropolis of Patras, the latter had to recognise the independence of the Milingoi and the Ezeritai, who, despite paying tribute to the local *strategos* (60 *nomismata* for the Milingoi, 300 *nomismata* for the Ezeritai), were 'practically independent and self-governing, and neither accepted a head man at the hand of the military governor, nor heeded orders for military service under him' (Constantine Porphyrogennetos, *On the Administration of the Empire* 50). The different positions in which those groups found themselves in relation to the imperial authority required a different terminology. The idea that they were all Slavs is Emperor Constantine's, the result of his efforts to bring his sources to a common denominator.[3] In reality, the Milingoi were neither subdued to the metropolis of Patras (or any of its suffragan sees), nor forced to pay a tribute as large as that of the Ezeritai. By the mid-eleventh century, the best way to describe their status was to call them 'ethnics' (*Life of St. Nikon* 59 and 62). They now had a *doux* of their own, who could order a dependency of the Monastery of St Nikon (most probably that in Sthlavochorion, now Amykles; see Oikonomides 2004: 30) to be turned into an inn, next to which he then built his court, surrounding it with a wall (*Life of St. Nikon* 59). To the author of the *Life of St. Nikon*, who served as abbot of the monastery dedicated to the saint and thus knew about them from experience, the Milingoi had a tribal society and a 'barbaric and untamed nature' (*Life of St. Nikon* 62). Nonetheless, they were capable of repentance and knew that in order to obtain forgiveness for their sins, they had to bring candles and incense to the monastery, which strongly suggests that they were Christian (see Chapter 6).

Did the Milingoi speak Slavic? Emperor Constantine Porpyhrogennetos repeatedly mentions the 'Slavic language' (*Sklavenisti*) from which he translates the names of several tribes in Dalmatia, as well as the names of the Dnieper rapids (*On the Administration of the Empire* 9).[4] However, he offers no translation for the names of the Milingoi and the Ezeritai and apparently knew of no place in Greece whose name was of Slavic origin. That such names did exist and that

Slavic was in use in tenth-century Peloponnesos is demonstrated by scholia to Strabo's *Geography*, which provide current names for ancient toponyms. Thus, Rhium and Chalkis near Patras were called at that time in Slavic Velviskon and Varasava, respectively (Diller 1954: 38–9). Nothing indicates, however, that such place names of Slavic origin were used only by speakers of Slavic. A great number of the many place names of Slavic origin known from twentieth-century Peloponnesos are formed directly from Slavic loans in modern Greek (Vasmer 1941; Malingoudis 1981).[5] They may have been introduced not by speakers of Slavic, but by speakers of Greek. Similarly, there were several individuals in early medieval Greece with surnames of Slavic origin which appear in written sources of the tenth (Rendakios Helladikos) or eleventh century (Constantine Rendakios from Athens; Lagos Rendakios; Rendakios, son of Geros; Michael Garasdes; John of Melgota; Lichozismos; and Vaklikas).[6] Even though the names are of Slavic origin, the individuals thus named were speakers of Greek, not Slavic. Although there is no way to know what the language was which the *doux* of the Milingoi used to order the building of his court, no evidence exists that interpreters were necessary in order to communicate with the Milingoi. In order for the Milingoi and the Ezeritai to 'send to the lord Romanus, the emperor, requesting and praying that the increments to their tribute should be forgiven them', some of them must have been fluent in that language which was understood at the imperial court.[7] Moreover, in order for the Milingoi and the Ezeritai to understand that their tribute had been reduced accordingly, some of them must have been able to read the Greek text of the bull issued by Emperor Romanos I in their favour. When the Milingoi who attacked the dependency of the Monastery of St Nikon in order to steal the animals, the saint's intervention made them aware of their mistake and, as a consequence, they asked 'their relatives' to go to the monastery and obtain the saint's pardon (*Life of St. Nikon* 62). It is hard to imagine how such dealings would have been possible without knowledge of Greek. It has long been noted that the number of Slavic loans in Greek, which appear to be from Common Slavic and may thus be dated before the eighth century, is smaller than that of loans with much later linguistic features (Pătruţ 1970: 27–8 and 1972; for the minimal influence of Common Slavic on Greek, see also Moutsos 1987; for Slavic loans in modern Greek, see Bornträger 1989). Several place names in Greece are compounds in which one part is Greek and the other Slavic. For example, in Gavrolimni, the former part derives from the Slavic word for 'beech' and the latter is the Greek word for 'lake'. Such compounds are a clear indication of frequent codeswitching between languages and of bilingualism. Moreover, they signal second language acquisition in a bilingual environment. That second language must have been Greek, and not Slavic, since the tendency to form compound words is greater in Greek than in any Slavic language (Malingoudis 1983: 105).

Bilingualism must have also been a prominent feature in the life of the Drugubites and Sagudates from the 'mixture of villages' between Veroia and Thessalonike (John Kaminiates, *The Capture of Thessaloniki* 6). Both groups had participated in the siege of Thessalonica in the aftermath of the execution of Perbundos, the 'king' of the Rynchines (*Miracles of St. Demetrios* 2.4.255). In 677, the Drugubites had their own 'kings' who led the attack, but a few years later, when they were ordered by Emperor Constantine IV to feed the refugees from the Avar qaganate under Kuver and Mauros, no mention is made of any 'kings' or chieftains (*Miracles of St. Demetrios* 2.5.289). More than a century later, during the first half of the ninth century, the Drugubites had their own *archon*, Peter, whose seal shows that he had the title of imperial *spatharios*, which must have been granted by the emperor (Kyriaki-Wassiliou 2004: 249). During the tenth century, much like the Milingoi of Peloponnesos, the Drugubites were Christian, for a bishopric of Drougoubiteia is listed among the suffragan sees of Thessalonike in *notitia* 7, compiled in the early 900s under Patriarch Nicholas Mystikos and Emperor Leo VI (see Chapter 9). A theme of Drougoubiteia was also organised shortly before 1000, and its military governor is mentioned several times in documents from the archives of Mount Athos (see Chapter 6). Unlike the Milingoi, the Drugubites apparently submitted at an early date to the imperial authority, although they must have preserved a great deal of autonomy under their own *archontes*. Their special status secured the survival of the name and, perhaps, of a certain sense of tribal identity. Although the ethnic name was eventually transferred to that of an administrative unit, no indication exists that by the time the theme of Drougoubiteia came into being its inhabitants felt, or were regarded by others as, in any way different from those of the neighbouring themes of Veroia and Thessalonike. Did they speak Slavic? As with the Milingoi, the absence of any information about interpreters or linguistic barriers in communication strongly suggests widespread bilingualism. The hinterland of Thessalonike is, after all, the region in which was spoken the Slavic dialect from which Constantine and Methodius are believed to have fashioned the Old Church Slavonic into which they translated the religious texts for their mission to Moravia. As Emperor Michael III allegedly told Constantine before sending him on that mission, 'all Thessalonians speak pure Slavic' (*Life of Methodius* 5). The implication is that they did so in addition to Greek – in other words, that they were bilingual. Even though he wrote his name (possibly Gregory or George) in Glagolitic, the person who signed a testimonial dated to June 982 regarding an agreement between the inhabitants of Hierissos in Chalkidiki and John the Iberian, the founder of the Monastery of Iviron, must have been able to understand the terms of the agreement in Greek. Similarly, all the other witnesses whose surnames are of Slavic origin, but whose names were written in Greek letters, were without any doubt speakers of Greek.

The Drugubites are the only seventh-century group of Sclavenes mentioned in Book II of the *Miracles of St. Demetrios* to have developed a sense of regional identity out of a client polity later incorporated into the Empire. The Sagudates are mentioned together with the Drugubites in John Kaminiates' *Capture of Thessaloniki*, but there was never a theme or a bishopric of Sagudatia. The Belegezites, who lived near Thebes and Demetrias, supplied grain to those besieged in Thessalonica by the coalition of Rynchines, Sagudates, and Drugubites (*Miracles of St. Demetrios* 2.4.254 and 2.4.268). More than a century later, an *archon* of the Belegezites named Akamiros unsuccessfully tried to free the sons of Constantine V from their exile in Athens and to proclaim one of them emperor (Theophanes Confessor, *Chronographia* 473–4). One of his eighth-century successors, Tichomiros, was imperial *spatharios*, which suggests that by then the *archon* of the Belegezites was an imperial client. That after c. 800 no mention is made of the Bel(ege)zites may indicate that their polity had by then been absorbed within the theme of Hellas. If the Baiunetes mentioned in the *Miracles of St. Demetrios* have anything to do with Vagenetia, the coastal region near Kerkyra, then it is important to note the existence of an *archon* of Vagenetia at the same time and with the same title of imperial *spatharios* as Tichomiros, the *archon* of the Belegezites (*Miracles of St. Demetrios* 2.179; Bănescu 1938: 116–17; see also Soustal 2004: 22). Another *archon*, named Hilarion, is known from his seal dated to the late ninth or early tenth century (Schlumberger 1895: 226). He was probably a contemporary of the bishop of Vagenetia who participated in the church synod of 879 (Chrysos 1997: 184). However, both the episcopal see and any administrative structure of Vagenetia disappear from the radar of the written sources after c. 950.[8] While the Berzetes and the Rynchines of the *Miracles of St. Demetrios* are not known from any subsequent sources, the Evidites are known only from two eighth- and early ninth-century seals of their *archontes*, one of whom had a Slavic name, Voidargos (*Miracles of St. Demetrios* 2.179 and 2.231–3; Seibt 1999: 29–30 and 2003: 463–4).

Though not mentioned in the *Miracles of St. Demetrios*, the Smoliani appear in the inscription of Philippi (Beshevliev 1963: 164–5). Whether the Bulgar army to which the inscription refers encountered the Smoliani in the region of Philippi or elsewhere, a bishopric of Smolaina is mentioned for the first time as a suffragan of Philippi in the early tenth century (Darrouzès 1981: 285; for the later theme of the Smolenoi, see Cheshmedzhiev 1997: 92–3). Much like the Drugubites, the Smoliani left their name to a Byzantine ecclesiastical and administrative structure, but nothing indicates the survival of their tribal identity. By contrast, the Sclavene archers in the theme of Strymon, whom Niketas, the *strategos* of Thessalonike, summoned to the defence of his city against Leo of Tripoli, were led by their own *archontes*, which suggests that they enjoyed some degree of autonomy inside the theme (John Kaminiates, *The Capture of Thessaloniki* 20). Their commanders were not independent leaders, for they had been appointed, probably by the emperor or by the local *strategos*. John Kaminiates accuses them of corruption, and if those *archontes* were Sclavenes themselves, they certainly had no problems speaking Greek. That much follows from the fact that, just when Leo of Tripoli's men burst into Thessalonike, the *archontes* escaped through one of the city's gates and told the terrified crowd they left behind that they had orders from the *strategos* to collect reinforcements from the Strymon area (John Kaminiates, *The Capture of Thessaloniki* 41).

As well as revealing the organisational and administrative structures in existence during the early Middle Ages, the evidence discussed above shows how misconstrued is the so-called 'Slavic problem' in the historiography of medieval Greece. It is clear that 'Sclavene' and 'Slav' were labels used by outsiders in order to simplify a much more complicated ethnic and political configuration. No group called itself by such names at any point in time. The Slavs are an invention of the Byzantine authors, for no evidence exists that any Milingoi and Drugubites, for example, ever thought of themselves as part of any ethnic or political entity larger than the very groups to which they belonged. Nor do they seem to have felt at any time that their respective groups were somehow related to each other linguistically or politically. Even though they probably spoke mutually intelligible dialects, no sense of solidarity united the 'Slavs' beyond temporary military alliances such as that of 677 for the attack on Thessalonica. Because 'Slavs' could be used metonymically to refer to barbarians, all things Slavic came to represent the opposite of 'civilisation' or cultural sophistication. Whatever ethnographic interest may have existed in relation to the 'Slavs', it quickly gave way to ethnic stereotypes. To say that behind his pretentious poses as an educated man, Niketas Magistros was nothing more than a bumpkin, one only needed to refer to his 'Slavic face' using a composite word with a Slavic root, such as only rustics having an incomplete or poor knowledge of Greek could have uttered. In Constantinople, the political advantages which bilingualism may have offered to the inhabitants of early medieval Greece could turn into symbols of inadaptability and rusticity.[9]

In reality, no facial features distinguished the Milingoi or the Drugubites from their non-Slavic neighbours, while the bilingualism derided by the *littéraires* of Constantinople was more a factor of specific political conditions than of an incomplete assimilation. Although an important component of provincial life, the 'Slavs' were by no means the only one. 'Kapheroi, Thrakesians, Armenians, and others from different places and cities' settled in Peloponnesos in the early ninth century (Kislinger 2001: 203; see also Ditten 1993: 341–3), while Armenians 'and other rabble' came to Crete in the aftermath of the island's conquest in 961 (Leo the Deacon, *History* 2.8). The Kapheroi may well have been converted Arabs from the eastern frontier of the Empire, but not all references to 'Amalekites' need to be interpreted in an ethnic sense, as a reference to Arabs. For example, one of the miracles attributed to St Theodora of Thessalonike involved a man named Elias, 'who was of Amalekite extraction' and who is said to have been devoted 'by ancestral tradition' to the iconoclast heresy (*Life of St. Theodora of Thessalonike* 57). Much like Emperor Leo V, who is mentioned elsewhere in the text (*Life of St. Theodora of Thessalonike* 11), Elias is called Amalekite not because of being of Arab descent, but because of endorsing the Islamic rejection of icons.

According to the *Chronicle of Monemvasia*, the Lakonian shepherds and farmers dislodged by the barbarian invasions moved into the rugged area around Monemvasia known as Tzakonia (Kislinger

2001: 201).[10] However, Emperor Constantine Porphyrogennetos describes the Tzekones as impoverished soldiers, who participated in campaigns with state support and were normally employed in the garrisons of forts – a combination of soldiers and policemen (*On Ceremonies*, in Reiske 1830: 696; Ahrweiler 1963: 248).[11] Tzakonia would appear to have been a mountain region in close proximity to trouble-making neighbours, such as the Ezeritai. This was the region in which Tzekones were settled in the course of the ninth and tenth century, probably as garrisons along the roads linking Corinth to Monemvasia or on the coast. A similar role may have been played by the 'Turks' or 'Vardariotes' – Magyar prisoners of war settled in the valley of the Vardar River, who converted to Christianity, and were later recruited into Emperor Basil II's army on campaign against Samuel of Bulgaria (*Life of St. Athanasios the Athonite* 58; Laurent 1940; Oikonomides 1973). A conspicuously military character may be recognised in the case of the Mardaites. The continuator of Theophanes Confessor and Emperor Constantine Pophyrogennetos both mention their presence in Kephallenia and Peloponnesos (Theophanes Continuatus, in Bekker 1838: 303 and 311; Constantine Porphyrogennetos, *On Ceremonies*, in Reiske 1830: 655, 656, and 665; see also Bon 1951: 75–6; Ahrweiler 1966: 399; Malamut 1988: 164; Ditten 1993: 155–6). They seem to have been moved to the Greek lands from Pamphylia to serve as reinforcements for the local naval forces, because of their excellent reputation as sailors. In 880, they were indeed recruited for the fleet of the admiral Basil Nasar operating on the western coast of Peloponnesos against African warships, which had just raided Kephallenia and Zante (Theophanes Continuatus, in Bekker 1838: 320; Bon 1951: 75–6; Ditten 1993: 149 and 155–6; Kislinger 2001: 54).

Others moved willingly to Peloponnesos, such as the two 'Latins' from Aquileia who settled in Sparta 'for the sake of trade' during the first half of the eleventh century, after the death of St Nikon (*Life of St. Nikon* 74). Two centuries earlier, there were communities of Athinganoi ('untouchables') on the island of Aigina. They may have arrived there from Asia Minor. Their heretical practices of Judaic inspiration did not prevent St Athanasia from extending charity to them during a famine (*Life of St. Athanasia of Aigina* 2). Her attitude contrasts sharply with that of St Nikon towards the Jews of Sparta (Niavis 1994: 311–12). Nikon wanted nothing less than to drive 'outside of their city the Jewish race which lived among them' (*Life of St. Nikon* 33). He appears to have singled out the Jews, their 'abominable customs and the pollution of their worship', as the main cause of the pestilence against which his assistance was requested by the 'chief men and the rest of the people of Lakedaimon'. In his *Testament*, St Nikon mentions as particularly outrageous the fact that there were slaughter houses in the immediate vicinity of the Church of St Epiphanios (*Testament of Nikon the Metanoeite for the Church and Monastery of the Savior, the Mother of God and St. Kyriake in Lakedaimon*, in Thomas and Hero 2000: 317). Since he asked the inhabitants of Lakedaimon, as a pre-condition for his taking action against the plague, to 'slaughter on Saturday and observe the feast on Sunday', the implication must be that those working in if not also owning the slaughter houses whose demolition he ordered were Jews (Constantelos 1985: 308). Judging from Nikon's violent reaction against them, the Jews of Sparta were very well integrated into local society, so much so that the author of the *Life of St. Nikon* puts into Nikon's mouth a quotation from Jeremiah 37:14 ('Your ways have done these things to you') in which he accused the inhabitants of Lakedaimon of cohabitation with the Jews. Such an accusation provoked anger among some of the leading men in town. One of them, John Aratos, may have employed Jews for finishing garments. That, in fact, is why he brought back a Jewish worker in direct opposition to St. Nikon (*Life of St. Nikon* 35; Savvidis 1995). Nikon's outburst of violence against the Jew suggests that the latter was not free, but perhaps in some way dependent upon John Aratos, probably his *paroikos* (see Chapter 8). His status may not have been very different from that of the fifteen Jewish families on the island of Chios who, according to an imperial chrysobull of 1049, were dependants (*paroikoi*) of the local monastery of Nea Mone (Oikonomides 1995b).

It has recently been argued that in Byzantium, 'ethnic origins were irrelevant' and that to the inhabitants of the Empire ethnicity 'was only a curiosity about first- or second-generation Romans or an antiquarian construction' (Kaldellis 2007: 95). The evidence presented so far directly shows such conclusions to be wrong, at least for early medieval Greece. There is perhaps no better illustration of how real ethnic boundaries could be than a few cases of mistaken identity. St Luke the Younger was mistaken for a runaway slave because of his poor clothing. Similarly, St Elias the Younger was arrested in Butrint under suspicion of being an Arab spy (*Life of St. Elias the Younger*, in Taibbi 1962: 40 and 42). In his case, the element of confusion may have been the saint's turban. Difference – whether social or religious – mattered, and ethnic difference was important in both out- and in-group relations. That Arabs, Bulgarians, and Magyars, long after their conversion to Christianity, were still recognisable to outsiders as Kapheroi, Scythians, and Turks, respectively, cannot be explained either as curiosity or as antiquarian construction. The categories of 'Arab' and 'Kapheroi' may not have overlapped completely and their definition in Constantinople (where the *Chronicle of Monemvasia* was most probably written) may have been different from that in Greece. Moreover, exactly how Kapheroi and Turks thought of themselves will remain unknown. Yet the existence in early medieval Greece of a sharp distinction between 'us' and 'them', which is a key component of ethnic identity, cannot be denied. The 'natives' were regarded as fundamentally different from all other peoples, especially the invaders. Arethas of Kaisareia, a native of Patras, blamed the 'Sclavene nation' for the destruction and exile of the 'native, Hellenic nations' (*eggene hellenika ethne*) of Peloponnesos, which seems to be a classicising reference to the Hellenic tribes of the Dorians and Epoioi (Westerink 1972: 241; Kislinger 2001: 39; Koder 2003: 306, who believes the 'Hellenic nations' to refer to pagans; Kaldellis 2007: 117–18, who wrongly views the 'Hellenic nations' as 'mere Romans who lived in Hellas').[12] To the author of the *Life of St. Nikon*, two Italians from Aquileia who had settled in Lakedaimon were 'foreigners, not natives', and the Milingoi were 'ethnics' (*Life of St. Nikon* 62 and 74; for the usage of Lakedaimon and Lakedaimonia to refer to Sparta, see Vasilikopoulou-Ioannidou 1979). He was writing as a 'native', for he had been (or perhaps still was) the abbot of the Monastery of St Nikon in Sparta.

Neither Arethas nor the author of the *Life of St. Nikon* had any specific name for the 'natives'. Niketas Magistros claimed to be a Lakonian and a 'son of Sparta', but apparently lacked an identity beyond the regional level (*epp*. 2, 4, and 5; Koutrakou 1993).[13] Similarly, when citing from Homer and Herodotus in reference to Thessaly, his goal was to appeal to the sense of regional pride of his letter's addressee – the archbishop of Thessalonike, who was a native of Larissa (*ep*. 23). Constantine Porphyrogennetos describes those living in the hinterland of Patras, who were not Slavs, as *Graikoi* (*On the Administration of the Empire* 49). His reason for doing so may have been that in the mid-tenth century 'Hellenes' still had a strongly non-ethnic meaning ('Hellenes'-as-pagans), while *Helladikoi* referred strictly to the troops of the theme of Hellas, not Peloponnesos (Koder 2003: 306; Kaldellis 2007: 117 and 184–5). According to the Emperor Constantine, those living in Peloponnesos during his lifetime used the term 'Hellenes' to refer not to themselves, but to the inhabitants of the city of Maina, 'because in the very ancient times they were idolaters and worshippers of images after the fashion of the ancient Hellenes' (*On the Administration of the Empire* 50). There was, however, an ethnic difference between *Graikoi* and the inhabitants of Maina. The latter are said to be 'not of the race (*genea*) of the aforesaid Slavs, but of the ancient Romans (*Rhomaioi*)'. That Emperor Constantine has in mind Latin Romans, and not just the population of Greece in Antiquity, follows from the explanation he gives elsewhere for the fact that in ancient times the whole of Italy was in the possession of the Romans: 'I mean, when Rome was the imperial capital' (*On the Administration of the Empire* 27).[14] Whether or not the tenth-century inhabitants of Mani were truly of Roman descent is irrelevant at this point. What matters is that they *appeared* to be so to the Emperor in Constantinople, and as a consequence they needed to be distinguished from the *Graikoi* on the outskirts of Patras. The latter may have referred to people who, unlike the 'Hellenes' of Mani, had a much more recent history in Peloponnesos. A Latin name with pejorative connotations, *Graikoi* had been used in the sixth century to insult soldiers in the Roman army which had invaded the Vandal and the Ostrogothic kingdoms (Prokopios of Kaisareia, *Wars* 4.27.38, 5.18.40, 5.29.11, 7.9.12, 7.21.4, 7.12.12–14, 8.23.25). Among speakers of Greek, the term was employed derogatorily in reference to soldiers recruited in Greece (Prokopios of Kaisareia, *Secret History* 24.7; Kaldellis 2007: 115).[15] But by the early tenth century, its meaning had changed. In his *Taktika*, Emperor Leo VI describes how his father, Basil I, persuaded the Slavs to abandon their ancient customs, to accept baptism, and to enrol as soldiers in the Roman army, while at the same time being able to turn them into *Graikoi* (*graikosas*; *Taktika* 18.101; Tăpkova-Zaimova 1964: 120; Dagron 1987: 220–1). What Leo VI means is perhaps something more than just to say that the Slavs learned how to speak Greek, for he avoids using the verb *hellenizein*, which when applied to language had no pagan connotations (Kaldellis 2007: 116, who believes that Emperor Leo 'viewed all Greek things, including his language, from a Roman point of view'). In other words, by learning Greek, the Slavs had gone only half way through the process of becoming subjects of the Emperor, i.e., true Romans. The *Graikoi* were only half-civilised inhabitants of the Empire. As Theophanes Confessor put it, in order for the process to be complete, one needed both the 'language of the *Graikoi*' and the 'customs of the Romans' (Theophanes Confessor, *Chronographia* 455).[16] Emperor Constantine Porphyrogennetos even advanced the idea that 'Hellenic' had initially been not the name of a people, but the name of a language later associated with the *Graikoi* (*On the Themes* 2.5). The implication is that *Graikoi* were people who spoke 'Hellenic', but were neither Hellenes (pagans), nor Romans.[17] The *Graikoi* near Patras, whose houses were attacked by the 'Sclavene nation', may therefore have been speakers of Greek from other parts of the Empire, who had been settled in Peloponnesos during the reign of Nikephoros I.[18]

The *Graikoi*, however, had no special homeland. Since Greek language acquisition was the precondition for civilisation, the *Graikoi* could theoretically be found anywhere in the Empire, and not only in Greece. Both Prokopius of Kaisareia and Emperor Constantine Porphyrogenitus used the term 'Peloponnesians' to refer to the inhabitants of Peloponnesos, in general (Prokopios of Kaisareia, *Secret History* 26.31–4; Constantine Porphyrogennetos, *On the Administration of the Empire* 51). Similarly, most references to Macedonians in Byzantine texts are in a geographical or administrative and not ethnic sense. The Byzantine Macedonian may well have been of some other ethnicity; as long as he was from 'the land of the Macedonians', he could be regarded as Macedonian, as in the case of Basil I, who is otherwise said to have been of Armenian origin (Tarnanidis 2000: 44 and 47). Was there a 'land of the Hellenes'? Although the phrase was occasionally used to refer to Greece, it was either poetic licence or as a periphrasis for the theme of Hellas, and not as an indication of a particular ethnicity. When the city of Thessalonica was attacked by Sclavenes and other barbarians in 586, no troops were available to come to its rescue, for 'the young elite soldiers of the army' and 'those who serve in the great praetorium' were at that time on campaign in the 'land of the Hellenes' (*Miracles of St. Demetrios* 1 13.128). Archbishop John, the author of Book I of the *Miracles of St. Demetrios*, obviously had no pagans in mind, and no sixth-century province could be referred to periphrastically as the 'land of the Hellenes'. He must therefore have been referring to the central and southern regions of what is now Greece, in contrast to Macedonia and the hinterland of Thessalonica (Charanis 1955a: 170–1). The same may be true about the phrase '(from) the province of the Hellenes' (*Hellenon chora*) added after the signature of the archbishop of Corinth in the minutes of the last two sessions of the Sixth Ecumenical Council in Constantinople, which took place in 681 (Riedinger 1979: 14). Given that the theme of Hellas is first mentioned in the context of events taking place a few years later, in 695, some have suggested that the 'province of the Hellenes' was just a periphrasis for the newly (or about to be) created administrative province (Avramea 1997: 38, 172, and 185; see also Ohme 1989). If so, it is important to note that after its first mention such periphrastic ways to refer to the name of the theme, as well as any references to Hellenes in an administrative sense, disappeared from the sources. Those rising in rebellion against Leo III and proclaiming one of themselves emperor in 725 were the 'inhabitants of Hellas and the Cyclades' (Theophanes Confessor, *Chronographia* 405). When needing to repopulate the city of Constantinople, after the devastation wrought by the plague of 745/6, Emperor Constantine V brought to the capital several families from the islands, Hellas, and the 'southern parts' (Theophanes Confessor, *Chronographia*, 429).[19] To refer to the inhabitants of Hellas, Theophanes Confessor never used 'Hellenes', but preferred the term *Helladikoi* (Theophanes Confessor, *Chronographia*, 405 and 474).[20] *Helladikos* was also used as a surname, and it seems that in all known cases the name indicated one's place of origin (the theme of Hellas), not ethnicity (Greek) (Anagnostakis 1996: 131–2).

Nonetheless, it has sometimes been suggested that *Helladikoi* was what 'native Greeks' were called in the early Middle Ages by authors concerned with an increasingly theological meaning of the term 'Hellenes'. It is further assumed that despite being called by terms of administrative origin, such as Macedonians or Peloponnesians, the 'native Greeks' could be distinguished from other inhabitants of the Empire. Byzantine Greeks were, in the words of Demetrios Constantelos, 'conscious of their continuity with the ancient Greeks' (Constantelos 1985: 309). That argument, however, is demonstrably wrong and has by now been seriously challenged. A recent examination of Hellenism in Byzantium concluded that no clear notion exists that the Greek nation survived into Byzantine times, and that the ethnic identity of those who who lived in Greece during the Middle Ages is best described as Roman (Kaldellis 2007). Over a century ago, John Bagnall Bury reached the same conclusion: 'The people of the three themes, Hellas, Peloponnesus, and Nicopolis, were all Rômaioi; but were not linked together by any narrower name, which could serve to mark them out as a sort of national unity, distinct from other Greek-speaking subjects of the empire' (Bury 1892: 81). Although no direct evidence exists that the people of early medieval

Greece called themselves Romans, the lack of any special names besides those of administrative origin (Macedonian, Peloponnesian, or *Helladikoi*) strongly suggests that ethnicity was a measure of the cultural distance between inhabitants of the Empire and barbarians. In other words, ethnic traits mattered for the classification of those who were not yet (or not at all) subjects of the emperor. No such traits were necessary for those who were already subjects of the emperor; they did not need a special, collective name, because they were not a separate category, but the norm against which categories were defined. John Kaminiates was proud of being from Thessalonike and St Luke the Younger was regarded as a luminary of Hellas. In both cases, however, the audience of their respective stories was 'Roman'. Clearly, there was no need to stress the obvious.

Notes

1. Kislinger 2001: 201; English translation from Charanis 1950: 148.
2. Book II of the treatise *On the Themes* is believed to have been composed by an anonymous author around 1000, some fifty years after Constantine Porphyrogennetos' death (Pertusi 1952: 47–9; Westerink 1973: 23; Ševčenko 1992: 185 with n. 47).
3. The 'Sclavene nation' is called 'Slavs' only in the title of chapter 49.
4. Most translations are of course incorrect. For example, 'Paganoi' does not mean 'unbaptised' in the Slavonic language (*ton Sklabon glossan*; *On the Administration of the Empire* 29 and 36); 'Croats' does not mean 'those who occupy much territory' (*On the Administration of the Empire* 31); 'Terbunia' is not 'strong place', and 'Kanali' is not 'wagon-load' in Slavonic (*On the Administration of the Empire* 34).
5. There are also cases of place names of Slavic origin which are not *in situ* creations. For example, Kalavryta, a name derived from the Slavic hydronym *kolovrăt'*, referred initially not to the present-day town, but to the nearby river (Malingoudis 1983: 106).
6. Even the name of the Leobachoi, a prominent Theban family of landowners, is of Slavic origin (Malingoudis 1994: 19–20 with n. 22).
7. Conversely, when in 768/9 Emperor Constantine V sent emissaries to the Slavic chieftains to offer them silken vestments in exchange for freeing the Christian captives whom they had long since taken from Imbros, Tenedos, and Samothrake (Nikephoros, *Short History* 86), the language of communication may have been Slavic.
8. The place name Vagenetia resurfaced in the early thirteenth century and even appears in Ottoman sources of the sixteenth century (Soustal 2004: 22).
9. Another way to use language to make fun of someone's 'rustic' origins

was to use one instead of two lambdas for the surnames of people like John Eladas, a *magistros* who under Leo VI collected the money from those in the provinces in the west who had opted against military service (Constantine Porphyrogennetos, *On the Administration of the Empire* 51). John may have been a supporter of Romanos I against Constantine Porphyrogennetos, and the suppression of one lambda may have been a way to present him as 'rustic' and uncouth by reference to olive oil (*eladion*). See Anagnostakis 1996: 122, 125, and 133 with n. 2.

10. Taking the *Chronicle of Monemvasia* and a letter of the fifteenth-century metropolitan of Kiev at face value, some have wrongly assumed that Tzakonia was a corrupt form of Lakonia (Koukoules 1926; Chatzidakis 1927; Symeonidis 1972: 57–70 and 87–103).

11. During the Late Byzantine period, the 'tzakonike' service consisted of sentinel duty at the gates, night-watch and process serving, the watch over the *kastron*, and the enforcement of the orders of civilian magistrates (Kislinger 2001: 54 with n. 440).

12. On this particular point, Arethas of Kaisareia may have reworked a passage, or simply drawn inspiration, from Prokopios of Kaisareia, according to whom the 'Huns' invading Achaia in 539 or 540 bypassed Thermopylae and 'destroyed all the Hellenes except the Peloponnesians' (*Wars* 2.4.11).

13. While Niketas did not stake any claim to Greek ethnicity when writing that his father was Spartan and his mother Athenian (*ep.* 2; Vryonis 1978: 252 with n. 2), he nonetheless cannot be regarded as 'a Roman who happened to have been born in Sparta' (Kaldellis 2007: 94). In reality, Niketas never claimed to be Roman.

14. In addition, whenever he (wrongly) translates place or tribal names from the 'language of the Romans' Emperor Constantine has Latin in mind (*On the Administration of the Empire* 27, 29, and 32).

15. That the term was derogatory is further substantiated by Prokopios' comment: 'as if it were wholly impossible for any man from Hellas to be a decent man' (*Secret History* 24.7). The derogatory meaning also follows from the word's usage in ninth-century inscriptions from Bulgaria, such as those carved for the Bulgar rulers Kormesis and Malamir and found in Madara and Shumen, respectively (Beshevliev 1963: 98–9 and 156).

16. Leo VI has a different order of things in his description of the civilising policies of Basil I towards the Slavs: first 'ancient' customs, then language (*graikosas*), baptism, and finally recruitment into the Emperor's army (presumably, as a symbol of loyalty).

17. In addition, the Greek spoken by *Graikoi* may not have been the same as that in use within the polite society of Constantinople, and certainly not the same as the literary Greek of the early medieval sources. The

author of the *Life of St. Luke the Younger* drew that distinction when describing the destruction perpetrated in central Greece by 'Scythians', about whom 'we know that in the *vernacular* (they) are called Bulgarians' (*Life of St. Luke the Younger* 32; emphasis added).
18. As Peter Charanis put it, 'some of them were pure Greeks (the Calabrians), others were not so pure, but doubtless hellenized' (Charanis 1949: 85). Leaving aside the pervasive fallacy of ethnic purity, it is significant that, much like Emperor Constantine Porphyrogennetos, Charanis believed that in order to become Greek, one needed first (or at least) to be Hellenised (i.e., to speak Greek). Kislinger 2001: 54 believes that the *Graikoi* were the population of Peloponnesos not yet organised as a theme.
19. Similarly, when in 766 he 'collected artisans from different places', the 500 clay-workers whom the Emperor brought to Constantinople were not Hellene, but 'from Hellas and the islands' (Theophanes Confessor, *Chronographia* 440; Charanis 1955a: 172).
20. The word was not Theophanes' invention. To John Malalas, who was writing in the mid-sixth century, Empress Eudokia was both *Helladike*, because she was from Greece, and Hellene, for she was a pagan (John Malalas, *Chronographia* 353 and 355; Charanis 1953: 618).

Bibliography

Primary sources

Agathias of Myrina, *Histories*. Ed. R. Keydell, Berlin: De Gruyter, 1967.
Basil of Thessalonike, *Life of St. Euthymios the Younger*. Ed. L. Petit, in *Revue de l'Orient Chrétien*, 8, 1903, pp. 155–205 and 503–36.
Bede, *Ecclesiastical History of the English People*. Eds B. Colgrave and R. A. B. Mynors, Oxford: Clarendon Press, 1969.
Collection avellana. Ed. O. Guenther, Vienna: Tempsky, 1895.
Comes Marcellinus, *Chronicle*. Ed. T. Mommsen and trans. B. Croke, Sydney: Australian Association for Byzantine Studies, 1995.
Constantine Akropolites, *Life of St. Barbaros*, in A. Papadopoulos-Kerameus, *Analekta hierosolymitikes stachiologias*, vol. 1. Ed. V. Kirshbaum. St Petersburg, 1891, pp. 405–20.
Constantine Porphyrogennetos, *On the Administration of the Empire*. Ed. G. Moravcsik and trans. R. J. H. Jenkins, Washington, DC: Dumbarton Oaks Center for Byzantine Studies, 1967.
—, *On Ceremonies*. Ed. A. Vogt, Paris: Les Belles Lettres, 1935–1940.
—, *On the Themes*. Ed. A. Pertusi, Vatican: Biblioteca Apostolica Vaticana, 1952.
Evagrios, *Ecclesiastical History*. Eds J. Bidez and L. Parmentier. London: Methuen, 1898.
George of Pisidia, *Bellum Avaricum*, in *Poems*. Ed. A. Pertusi. Ettal: Buch-Kunstverlag, 1959.
Gregory Abū'l-Faraj Bar Hebraeus, *Chronography*. Ed. E. A. W. Budge. London: Oxford University Press, 1932.
Gregory the Great, *Registrum epistolarum*. Eds P. Ewald and L. M. Hartmann, MGH *Epistolae* 1.2, Berlin: Weidmann, 1887 and 1899.
Ignatios the Deacon, *Life of St. Gregory of Dekapolis*. Ed. G. Makris, Stuttgart/Leipzig: B. G. Teubner, 1997.
Isidore of Seville, *Chronicon*. Ed. T. Mommsen, MGH *Auctores antiquissimi* 11, Chronica Minora 2, Berlin: Weidmann, 1894, pp. 267–303.
John of Biclar, *Chronicle*. Ed. T. Mommsen, MGH *Auctores antiquissimi* 11. Chronica Minora 2, Berlin: Weidmann, 1894, pp. 211–39.
John of Ephesus, *Ecclesiastical History*. Ed. E. I. Brooks, Paris: Typographeo Reipublicae, 1935; trans. E. I. Brooks, Paris: Typographeo Reipublicae, 1936.
John Kaminiates, *The Capture of Thessaloniki*. Ed. G. Böhlig and trans. D. Frendo and A. Fotiou, Perth: Australian Association for Byzantine Studies, 2000.
John Malalas, *Chronographia*. Ed. L. Dindorf, Bonn: E. Weber, 1831; trans.

E. Jeffreys, M. Jeffreys, and R. Scott, Melbourne: Australian Association for Byzantine Studies, 1986.
Kekaumenos, *Strategikon*. Ed. M. D. Spadaro, Alessandria: Edizioni dell'Orso, 1998.
Leo VI, *Taktika*. Ed. G. T. Dennis. Washington, DC: Dumbarton Oaks Center for Byzantine Studies, 2010.
Leo the Deacon, *History*. Ed. M. Ia. Siuziumov, Moscow: Nauka, 1988; trans. A.-M. Talbot and D. F. Sullivan, Washington, DC: Dumbarton Oaks Research Library and Collection, 2005.
Liber Pontificalis. Ed. T. Mommsen, Berlin: Weidmann, 1898.
Life of Methodius. Ed. O. Kronsteiner, Salzburg: Institut für Slawistik der Universität Salzburg, 1989.
Life of St. Athanasia of Aigina. Ed. L. Carras, in A. Moffatt (ed.), *Maistor: Classical, Byzantine, and Renaissance Studies for Robert Browning*, Canberra: Australian Association for Byzantine Studies, 1984, pp. 212–24; trans. L. Sherry, in A.-M. Talbot (ed.), *Holy Women of Byzantium*, Washington, DC: Dumbarton Oaks Research Library and Collection, 1996, pp. 137–58.
Life of St. Athanasios the Athonite. Ed. L. Petit, in *Analecta Bollandiana*, 25, 1906, pp. 12–87.
Life of St. Luke the Younger. Ed. D. Z. Sophianos, Athens: Ekdosis Akritas, 1989; trans. C. L. Connor and W. R. Connor, Brookline: Hellenic College Press, 1994.
Life of St. Nikon. Ed. and trans. D. F. Sullivan, Brookline: Hellenic College Press, 1987.
Life of St. Peter of Argos. Ed. K. T. Kyriakopoulos, Athens: Hieras Metropoleos Argolidos.
Life of St. Phantinos the Younger. Ed. E. Follieri, Brussels: Société des Bollandistes, 1993.
Life of St. Theodora of Thessalonike. Ed. S. A. Paschalidis, Thessaloniki: Hiera Metropolis Thessalonikes, 1991; trans. A.-M. Talbot, in A.-M. Talbot (ed.), *Holy Women of Byzantium*, Washington, DC: Dumbarton Oaks Research Library and Collection, 1996, pp. 159–237.
Liudprand of Cremona, *Retribution*. Ed. P. Chiesa, Turnhout: Brepols, 2001; trans. P. Squatriti, Washington, DC: Catholic University of America Press, 2007.
—, *Embassy*. Ed. P. Chiesa, Turnhout: Brepols, 2001; trans. P. Squatriti. Washington, DC: Catholic University of America Press, 2007.
Lives of Sts. David, Symeon, and George of Lesbos. Ed. J. van den Gheyn, in *Analecta Bollandiana*, 18, 1899, pp. 209–59; trans. D. Abrahamse and D. Domingo-Forasté, in A.-M. Talbot (ed.), *Byzantine Defenders of Images: Eight Saints' Lives in English Translation*, Washington, DC: Dumbarton Oaks Research Library and Collection, 1998, pp. 149–241.
Menander the Guardsman, *History*. Ed. R. C. Blockley, Liverpool: F. Cairns, 1985.
Michael the Syrian, *Chronicle*. Ed. J. B. Chabot. Paris: Typographeo Reipublicae, 1963.
Miracles of St. Demetrios. Ed. Paul Lemerle, Paris: Centre National de la Recherche Scientifique, 1979.
Nicholas Mystikos, *Epistulae*. Ed. R. J. H. Jenkins and L. G. Westerink, Washington, DC: Dumbarton Oaks Center for Byzantine Studies, 1973.
Nikephoros, *Short History*. Ed. C. Mango, Washington, DC: Dumbarton Oaks, Research Library and Collection, 1990.

Niketas Magistros, *Epistulae*. Ed. L. G. Westerink, Paris: Editions du Centre National de la Recherche Scientifique, 1973.
—, *Life of Theoktiste of Lesbos*. In *Acta Sanctorum Novembris*, vol. 4, Brussels: Société des Bollandistes, 1925, pp. 224–33 ; trans. A. Hero, in A.-M. Talbot (ed.), *Holy Women of Byzantium*, Washington, DC: Dumbarton Oaks Research Library and Collection, 1996, pp. 95–116.
Paul the Deacon, *History of the Lombards*. Eds L. K. Bethmann and G. Waitz, Hanover: Hahnsche Buchhandlung, 1878.
Prokopios of Kaisareia, *Buildings*. Ed. J. Haury and trans. H. B. Dewing, Cambridge, MA: Harvard University Press, 1940.
—, *Secret History*. Ed. J. Haury and trans. H. B. Dewing, Cambridge, MA: Harvard University Press, 1935.
—, *Wars*. Ed. J. Haury and trans. H. B. Dewing, 5 vols, Cambridge, MA: Harvard University Press, 1914–1928.
Royal Frankish Annals. Ed. F. Kurze. Hanover: Hahn, 1895.
Theodore the Studite, *Epistulae*. Ed. Georgios Fatouros, Berlin: De Gruyter, 1992.
Theophanes Confessor, *Chronographia*. Ed. C. de Boor, 2 vols, Leipzig: B. G. Teubner, 1883 and 1885; trans. C. Mango and R. Scott, Oxford/New York: Clarendon Press/Oxford University Press, 1997.
Theophylact Simokatta, *History*. Eds C. de Boor and P. Wirth, Stuttgart, 1972; trans. M. and M. Whitby, Oxford: Clarendon Press, 1986.
Vita Willibaldi episcopi Eischstetensis. Ed. O. Holder-Egger. MGH *Scriptores* 15, Hanover: Weidmann, pp. 80–117.

SECONDARY SOURCES

Abadie-Reynal, C. (1989a), 'Céramique et commerce dans le bassin égéen du IVe au VIIe siècle', in G. Dagron (ed.), *Hommes et richesses dans l'Empire byzantin*, Paris: P. Lethielleux, pp. 143–62.
— (1989b), 'Les amphores protobyzantines d'Argos (IVe–VIe siècles)', in V. Déroche and J. M. Spieser (eds), *Recherches sur la céramique byzantine*, Athens/Paris: Ecole Française d'Athènes/De Boccard, pp. 47–56.
Adelson, H. L. and G. Kustas (1964), 'A sixth century hoard of minimi from the Western Peloponnese', *American Numismatic Society. Museum Notes*, 11, pp. 159–205.
Agallopoulou, P. (1973), 'Palaiokastritsa', *Archaiologikon Deltion*, 28: 2, pp. 423–4.
— (1975), 'Ladochori Hegoumenitsas', *Archaiologikon Deltion*, 30: 2, p. 239.
Ahrweiler, H. (1963), 'Les termes Tsakones-Tsakonia et leur évolution sémantique', *Revue des Etudes Byzantines*, 21, pp. 243–9.
— (1966), *Byzance et la mer: La marine de guerre, la politique et les institutions maritimes de Byzance aux VIIe–XVe siècles*, Paris: Presses Universitaires de France.
Aibabin, A. I. (1982), 'Pogrebeniia konca VII–pervoi poloviny VIII v. v Krymu', in A. K. Ambroz and I. Erdélyi (eds), *Drevnosti epokhi velikogo pereseleniia narodov V–VIII vekov. Sovetsko-vengerskii sbornik*, Moscow: Nauka, pp. 165–92.
Amantos, K. (1932), 'Mardaitai', *Hellenika*, 5, pp. 130–6.

— (1939–1943), 'Hoi Slaboi eis ten Hellada', *Byzantinisch-neugriechische Jahrbücher*, 17, pp. 210–21.
Anagnostakis, I. (1989), 'To episodios tes Danielidas. Plerophories katemerinou biou e mythoplastika stoicheia?', in C. Maltezou (ed.), *He kathemerine zoe sto Byzantio. Tomes kai synecheis sten hellenistike kai romaike paradose. 15–17 septembriou 1988*, Athens: Kentro Byzantinon Ereunon, pp. 375–90.
— (1996), 'Elladika paramythia kai elladike paramythia sto Byzantio tou 10ou aiona', in *Elia kai ladi. D' triemero ergasias. Kalamata, 7–9 Maiou 1993*, Athens: Politistiko technologiko idryma ETVA, pp. 121–50.
— (1997), 'He cheiropoiete keramike anamesa sten Istoria kai ten Archaiologia', *Byzantiaka*, 17, pp. 285–330.
— (2000), 'Hoi peloponnesiakoi skoteinoi chronoi: to slabiko problema. Metamorphoseis tes Peloponnesou e tes ereunas', in E. Grammatikopoulou (ed.), *Hoi metamorphoseis tes Peloponnesou (4os–15os ai.)*, Athens: Ethniko Idryma Ereunon, pp. 19–34.
Anagnostakis, I. and A. Lampropoulou (2001), 'Mia periptose epharmoges tou byzantinou thesmou tou asylou sten Peloponneso. He prosphyge ton Slabon sto nao tou Agiou Andrea Patron', *Symmeikta*, 14, pp. 29–47.
Anagnostakis, I. and T. Papamastorakis (2004), 'Ho monachos tou Agiou Andrea sten Patra kai he apeikonise tou sto kheirographo tou Skylitze', in V. Konti (ed.), *Ho monakhismos sten Peloponneso 40s–15os ai.*, Athens: Institouto Byzantinon Ereunon, pp. 63–85.
Anagnostakis, I. and N. Poulou-Papadimitriou (1997), 'He protobyzantine Messene (5os–7os aionas) kai problemata tes kheiropoietes keramikes sten Peloponneso', *Symmeikta* 11, pp. 229–322.
Anagnostakis, I., V. Konti, A. Lampropoulou, and A. Panopoulou (2002), 'Choros kai enoteta tes dytikes Peloponnesou', in P. G. Themelis and V. Konti (eds), *Protobyzantine Messene kai Olympia. Aktikos kai agrotikos choros ste Dytike Peloponneso. Praktika tou Diethnous symposiou, Athena, 29–30 maiou 1998*, Athens: Hetaireia Messeniakon Archaiologikon Spoudon/Institouto Byzantinon Ereunon, pp. 65–81.
Anamali, S. and H. Spahiu (1963), 'Varrëza e herëshme mesjëtare e Krujës', *Buletin i Universitetit shtetëror të Tiranës*, 17: 2, pp. 3–85.
Andel, T. H. v., C. N. Runnels, and K. O. Pope (1986), 'Five thousand years of land use and abuse in the Southern Argolid, Greece', *Hesperia*, 55, pp. 103–28.
Andreou, E. (1980), 'Meropi kai Paliopyrgos Pogoniou', *Archaiologikon Deltion*, 35, pp. 303–7.
— (1983), 'Meropi', *Archaiologikon Deltion*, 38, pp. 229–30.
— (1987), 'Paliopyrgos Pogoniou', *Archaiologikon Deltion*, 42, pp. 307–8.
Angelov, P. (1995), 'Kniaz Boris I prez pogleda na vizantiicite', *Minalo* 2: 1, pp. 23–31.
Angelova, S. and R. Koleva (2001), 'Zur Chronologie frühmittelalterlicher Nekropolen in Südbulgarien', in M. Wendel (ed.), *Karasura, I. Untersuchungen zur Geschichte und Kultur des alten Thrakien. 15 Jahre Ausgrabungen in Karasura. Internationales Symposium Čirpan/Bulgarien, 1996*, Weissbach: Beier & Beran, pp. 263–70.
Angelova, S. and T. Marvakov (2001), 'Über zwei Nekropolen aus Südwestbulgarien', in L. Galuška, P. Kouřil, and Z. Měřínský (eds), *Velká Morava mezi východem a západem. Sborník příspěvku z mezinárodní vedecké konference. Uherské*

Hradište, Stare Město 28.9.–1.10.1999, Brno: Archeologický ústav Akadémie věd České Respubliky, pp. 13–27.

Antoljak, S. (1964), 'Unsere "Sklavinien"', in *Actes du XIIe Congrès International d'Etudes Byzantines. Ochride, 10–16 septembre 1961*, Belgrade: Comité Yougoslave des Etudes Byzantines, pp. 9–13.

Antonaras, A. (2006), 'Gyalina mesobyzantina brachiolia. Symbole se themata diadoses, paragoges, typologias kai chreses', *Deltion tes christianikes archaiologikes hetaireias*, 27, pp. 423–34.

Antoniadis-Bibicou, H. (1965), 'Villages désertés en Grèce. Un bilan provisoire', in *Villages désertés et histoire économique, XIe–XVIIIe siècle*, Paris: SEVPEN, pp. 343–417.

— (1966), 'A propos de la première mention d'un "stratège des Caravisiens"', *Byzantinoslavica*, 27, pp. 70–91.

Armstrong, P. (1993), 'Byzantine Thebes: excavations on the Kadmeia, 1980', *Annual of the British School at Athens*, 88, pp. 295–335.

— (2001), 'From Constantinople to Lakedaimon: impressed white wares', in J. Herrin, M. Mullett, and C. Otten-Froux (eds), *Mosaic. Festschrift for A. H. S. Megaw*, Athens: British School at Athens, pp. 57–67.

Armstrong, P., H. Hatcher, and M. Tite (1997), 'Changes in Byzantine glazing technology from the ninth to thirteenth centuries', in G. D. d'Archimbaud (ed.), *La céramique médiévale en Méditerranée. Actes du VIe Congrès de l'AIECM2, Aix-en-Provence (13–18 novembre 1995)*, Aix-en-Provence: Narration, pp. 225–9.

Arthur, P. (1998), 'Eastern Mediterranean amphorae between 500 and 700: a view from Italy', in L. Sagu (ed.), *Ceramica in Italia: VI–VII secolo. Atti del Convegno in onore di John W. Hayes, Roma, 11–13 maggio 1995*, Florence: Insegna del Giglio, pp. 157–84.

Asdracha, C. (1994–1995), 'Inscriptions chrétiennes et protobyzantines de la Thrace orientale et de l'île d'Imbros (IIIe–VIIe siècles)', *Archaiologikon Deltion*, 49–50, pp. 279–356.

— (1998), 'Inscriptions chrétiennes et protobyzantines de la Thrace orientale et de l'île d'Imbros (IIIe–VIIe siècles). Présentation et commentaire historique', *Archaiologikon Deltion*, 53, pp. 455–521.

Asdracha, C. and C. Bakirtzis (1980), 'Inscriptions byzantines de Thrace (VIIIe–XVe siècles). Edition et commentaire historique', *Archaiologikon Deltion*, 35, pp. 241–82.

Aslanidis, K. and C. Pinatsi (1994), 'Naodomia tes meses byzantines periodou ste Salamina', *Archaiologikon Deltion*, 49–50, pp. 165–94.

Atanasov, G. (1991), 'Khristianski pametnici ot rannosrednovekovnata krepost do selo Ruino, Dulovsko', *Dobrudzha*, 8, pp. 28–50.

Athanasiadis, N. (1975), 'Zur postglazialen Vegetationsentwicklung von Litochoro Katerinis und Pertouli Trikalon (Griechenland)', *Flora*, 164, pp. 99–132.

Athanassopoulou-Penna, V. (1979), '"Thesauros" nomismaton 6-ou m. Ch. aiona apo ten perioche ton Thebon', *Archaiologike ephemeris: ekdidomene tes archaiologikes hetaireias*, 118, pp. 200–13.

Augustinos, G. (1989), 'Culture and authenticity in a small state: historiography and national development in Greece', *East European Quarterly*, 23, pp. 17–31.

Aupert, P. (1980), 'Objets de la vie quotidienne à Argos en 585 ap. J.-C', in *Etudes argiennes*, Athens: Ecole Française d'Athènes, pp. 395–457.

— (1989), 'Les Slaves à Argos', *Bulletin de Correspondance Hellénique*, 113: 1, pp. 417–19.

Avramea, A. (1981), 'La géographie du culte de Saint Christophe en Grèce à l'époque méso-byzantine et l'évêché de Lacédémone au début du Xe siècle', in H. Ahrweiler (ed.), *Geographica Byzantina*, Paris: Centre de Recherches d'Histoire et Civilisation Byzantines, pp. 33–6.

— (1983), 'Nomismatikoi "thesauroi" kai memonomena nomismata apo ten Peloponneso', *Symmeikta*, 5, pp. 49–90.

— (1996), 'Anekdota molybdoboulla apo ta nesia tou Argolikou kolpou', *Symmeikta*, 10, pp. 11–25.

— (1997), *Le Peloponnèse du IVe au VIIIe siècle. Changements et persistances*, Paris: Publications de la Sorbonne.

— (1998), 'Le Magne byzantin: problèmes d'histoire et de topographie', in M. Balard, J. Beaucamp, J.-C. Cheynet, C. Jolivet-Lévy, M. Kaplan, B. Martin-Hisard, P. Pagès, C. Piganiol, and J.-P. Sodini (eds), *Eupsychia. Mélanges offerts à Hélène Ahrweiler*, Paris: Publications de la Sorbonne, pp. 49–52.

— (2005), 'Les villages de la Thessalie, de Grèce centrale et du Péloponnèse (Ve–XIVe siècle)', in J. Lefort, C. Morrisson, and J.-P. Sodini (eds), *Les villages dans l'Empire byzantin, IVe–XVe siècles*, Paris: Lethielleux, pp. 213–23.

Avramea, A. and D. Feissel (1987), 'Inventaires en vue d'un recueil des inscriptions historiques de Byzance. IV. Inscriptions de Thessalie (à l'exception des Météores)', *Travaux et mémoires du Centre de Recherches d'Histoire et Civilisation Byzantines*, 10, pp. 357–98.

Bakirtzis, C. (1982), 'Anaskaphe Polystylou Abderon', *Praktika tes en Athenais Archaiologikes Hetaireias*, 137, pp. 18–26.

— (1983), 'Anaskaphe Polystylou Abderon', *Praktika tes en Athenais Archaiologikes Hetaireias*, 138, pp. 13–19.

— (1985), 'Anaskaphe ste Synaxe Maroneias', *Praktika tes en Athenais Archaiologikes Hetaireias*, 140, pp. 80–92.

— (1987), 'Anaskaphe Synaxis Maroneias', *Praktika tes en Athenais Archaiologikes Hetaireias*, 142, pp. 186–97.

— (1989), 'Western Thrace in the early Christian and Byzantine periods: results of archaeological research and the prospects, 1973–1987', *Byzantinische Forschungen*, 14, pp. 41–58.

— (1990), 'Byzantine ampullae from Thessaloniki', in R. Ousterhout (ed.), *The Blessings of Pilgrimage*, Urbana: University of Illinois Press, pp. 140–9.

— (1994), 'Byzantine Thrace (AD 330–1453)', in V. Papoulia, M. Meraklis, C. Symeonidis, T. Korres, K. Hatzopoulos, and P. Hidiroglu (eds), *Thrace*, Athens: General Secretariat of the Region of East Macedonia-Thrace, pp. 151–210.

— (1996), 'Byzantine monasteries in eastern Macedonia and Thrace (Synaxis, Mt. Papikion, St. John Prodromos Monastery)', in A. Bryer and M. Cunningham (eds), *Mount Athos and Byzantine Monasticism. Papers from the Twenty-Eighth Spring Symposium of Byzantine Studies, Birmingham, March 1994*, Aldershot/Brookfield: Variorum, pp. 47–54.

— (2002), 'Pilgrimage to Thessalonike: the tomb of St. Demetrius', *Dumbarton Oaks Papers*, 56, pp. 175–92.

— (2007), 'Imports, exports, and autarky in Byzantine Thessalonike from the seventh to the tenth century', in J. Henning (ed.), *Post-Roman Towns, Trade, and Settlement in Europe and Byzantium*, Berlin/New York: De Gruyter, pp. 89–118.

Baldini Lippolis, I. (1999), *L'oreficeria nell'impero di Costantinopoli tra IV e VII secolo*, Bari: EdiPuglia.

Bálint, C. (1989), *Die Archäologie der Steppe. Steppenvölker zwischen Volga und Donau vom 6. bis zum 10. Jahrhundert*, Vienna/Cologne: Böhlau.

Banaji, J. (2001), *Agrarian Change in Late Antiquity: Gold, Labour, and Aristocratic Dominance*, Oxford/New York: Oxford University Press.

Bănescu, N. (1938), 'O colecție de sigilii bizantine inedite', *Memoriile secției de științe istorice*, 3: 20, pp. 115–26.

Barišić, F. (1953), *Čuda Dimitrija Solunskog kao istoriski izvori*, Belgrade: Srpska Akademija Nauka.

Barla, C. N. (1965), 'Anaskaphai Kephalou Ambrakikou', *Praktika tes en Athenais Archaiologikes Hetaireias*, 120, pp. 78–84.

— (1966), 'Anaskaphai Kephalou Ambrakikou', *Praktika tes en Athenais Archaiologikes Hetaireias*, 121, pp. 95–102.

— (1967), 'Anaskaphai Kephalou Ambrakikou', *Praktika tes en Athenais Archaiologikes Hetaireias*, 122, pp. 28–32.

— (1970), 'Anaskaphai Kephalou Ambrakikou', *Praktika tes en Athenais Archaiologikes Hetaireias*, 125, pp. 90–7.

Bartelink, G. J. M. (1973), 'Phylakterion-phylacterium', in *Mélanges Christine Mohrmann. Recueil nouveau offert par ses anciens élèves*, Utrecht/Anvers: Spectrum, pp. 25–60.

Bazaiou-Barabas, T. (1989), 'Semeioma gia ten epidrome tou tzarou Symeon kata tes kyrios Helladas (arches 10ou aiona)', *Symmeikta*, 8, pp. 383–7.

Bekker, I. (1838), *Theophanes Continuatus, Ioannes Cameniata, Symeon Magister, Georgius Monachus*, Bonn: E. Weber.

Belke, K. (1996), 'Einige Überlegungen zum Sigillion Kaiser Nikephoros' I. für Patrai', *Jahrbuch der österreichischen Byzantinistik*, 46, pp. 81–96.

— (2002), 'Roads and travel in Macedonia and Thrace in the middle and late Byzantine period', in R. Macrides (ed.), *Travel in the Byzantine World. Papers from the Thirty-Fourth Spring Symposium of Byzantine Studies, Birmingham, April 2000*, Aldershot/Burlington: Ashgate, pp. 73–90.

Belošević, J. (1968), 'Ranosrednjovjekovna nekropola u selu Kašić kraj Zadra', *Diadora*, 4, pp. 221–46.

Bendall, S. (1977), 'Byzantine hoards', *Coin Hoards*, 3, p. 82.

— (1993), 'A hoard of 16 nummia coins of Thessalonica', *Numismatic Chronicle*, 101: 5, p. 152.

Bertels, K. (1987), 'Carantania. Beobachtungen zur politisch-geographischen Terminologie und zur Geschichte des Landes und seiner Bevölkerung im frühen Mittelalter', *Carinthia*, 177, pp. 87–190.

Beshevliev, V. (1963), *Die protobulgarischen Inschriften*, Berlin: Akademie Verlag.

— (1985), 'Zur Deutung der protobulgarische Inschrift von Vassilika, Chalkidike', *Jahrbuch der österreichischen Byzantinistik*, 35, pp. 143–8.

Biers, J. C. (1985), *The Great Bath on the Lechaion Road*, Princeton: American School of Classical Studies.

Binon, S. (1942), *Les origines légendaires et l'histoire de Xéropotamou et de Saint-Paul*, Louvain: Bureaux du Muséon.

Bintliff, J. L. (2007), 'The contribution of region survey to the late antiquity debate: Greece in its Mediterranean context', in A. G. Poulter (ed.), *The Transition to Late Antiquity on the Danube and Beyond*, Oxford: Oxford University Press, pp. 649–78.

Birnbaum, H. (1975), *Common Slavic. Progress and Problems in its Reconstruction*, Columbus, OH: Slavica.

— (1986), 'Noch einmal zu den slavischen Milingen auf der Peloponnes', in R. Olesch and H. Rothe (eds), *Festschrift für Herbert Bräuer zum 65. Geburtstag am 14. April 1986*, Cologne: Böhlau, pp. 15–26.

Blanchet, A. (1900), *Les trésors de monnaies romaines et les invasions germaniques en Gaule*, Paris: E. Leroux.

— (1936), 'Les rapports entre les dépots monétaires et les événements militaires, politiques et économiques', *Revue Numismatique*, 39, pp. 1–70, 205–69.

Bon, A. (1950), 'Le problème slave dans le Péloponèse à la lumière de l'archéologie', *Byzantion*, 20, pp. 13–20.

— (1951), *Le Peloponnèse byzantin jusqu'en 1204*, Paris: Presses Universitaires de France.

Bonifay, M. (2005), 'Observations sur la diffusion des céramiques africaines en Méditerranée orientale durant l'Antiquité tardive', in F. Baratte, V. Déroche, C. Jolivet-Lévy, and B. Pitarakis (eds), *Mélanges Jean-Pierre Sodini*, Paris: Association des Amis du Centre d'Histoire et Civilisation de Byzance, pp. 565–81.

Bornträger, E. W. (1989), 'Die slavischen Lehnwörter im Neugriechischen', *Zeitschrift für Balkanologie*, 25, pp. 8–25.

Boura, L. (1980), *Ho glyptos diakosmos tou Naou tes Panagias sto Monasteri tou Hosiou Louka*, Athens: Vivliotheke tes en Athenais Archaiologikes Hetaireias.

Bouras, C. (1971), 'Zourtsa, une basilique byzantine au Péloponnèse', *Cahiers Archéologiques*, 21, pp. 137–49.

— (1974), 'Houses and settlements in Byzantine Greece', in P. Oliver and O. V. Doumanes (eds), *Oikismoi sten Hellada*, Athens: Ekdose 'Architektonikon Thematon', pp. 30–52.

— (2000), 'Middle Byzantine Athens: planning and architecture', in C. Bouras, M. B. Sakellariou, K. S. Staikos, and E. Touloupa (eds), *Athens from the Classical Period to the Present Day (5th century B.C.-A.D. 2000)*, New Castle, DE: Oak Knoll Press, pp. 222–45.

— (2001), 'The Middle Byzantine Athenian Church of the Taxiarchs near the Roman Agora', in J. Herrin, M. Mullett, and C. Otten-Froux (eds), *Mosaic. Festschrift for A. H. S. Megaw*, London: British School of Athens, pp. 69–74.

— (2005), 'Unfinished architectural members in Middle Byzantine Greek churches', in J. J. Emerick and D. M. Deliyannis (eds), *Archaeology in Architecture: Studies in Honor of Cecil L. Striker*, Mainz: Philipp von Zabern, pp. 1–9.

— (2006), *Byzantine and Post-Byzantine Architecture in Greece*, Athens: Melissa.

Bowden, H. and D. Gill (1997), 'Late Roman Methana', in C. Mee and H. Forbes (eds), *A Rough and Rocky Place. The Landscape and Settlement History of the Methana Peninsula, Greece. Results of the Methana Survey Project Sponsored by the British School at Athens and the University of Liverpool*, Liverpool: Liverpool University Press, pp. 84–91.

Bowden, W. (2001), 'A new urban élite? Church builders and church building in late-antique Epirus', in L. Lavan (ed.), *Recent Research in Late-Antique Urbanism*, Portsmouth: Journal of Roman Archaeology, pp. 57–68.

— (2003), *Epirus Vetus. The Archaeology of a Late Antique Province*, London: Duckworth.

Bowden, W., R. Hodges, and K. Lako (2002), 'Roman and late-antique Butrint: excavations and survey 2000–2001', *Journal of Roman Archaeology*, 15, pp. 199–230.

Brandes, W. (2002), *Finanzverwaltung in Krisenzeiten: Untersuchungen zur byzantinischen Administration im 6.-9. Jahrhundert*, Frankfurt: Löwenklau.

— (2005), 'Das Gold der Menia. Ein Beispiel transkulturellen Wissentransfers', *Millennium*, 2, pp. 175–226.

Brooner, O. (1935), 'Excavations at Corinth, 1934', *American Journal of Archaeology*, 39, pp. 53–75.

Brouskari, M. S. (1985), *The Paul and Alexandra Canellopoulos Museum. A Guide*, Athens: M. Brouskari.

Browning, R. (1984), 'Athens in the "Dark Age"', in B. Smith (ed.), *Culture and History. Essays Presented to Jack Lindsay*, Sydney: Hale and Iremonger, pp. 297–303.

Brubaker, L. (2004), 'Elites and patronage in early Byzantium: the evidence from Hagios Demetrios in Thessalonike', in J. Haldon and L. I. Conrad (eds), *The Byzantine and Early Islamic Near East VI. Elites Old and New in the Byzantine and Early Islamic Near East*, Princeton: Darwin Press, pp. 63–90.

Bruun, P. (1978), 'Site finds and hoarding behaviour', in R. A. G. Carson and C. M. Kraay (eds), *Scripta nummaria Romana. Essays presented to Humphrey Sutherland*, London: Spink and Son, pp. 109–23.

Bulle, H. (1934), 'Ausgrabungen bei Aphiona auf Korfu', *Mitteilungen des Deutschen Archäologischen Instituts. Athenische Abteilung*, 39, pp. 147–240.

Burkhalter, F. and A. Philippa-Touchais (2003), 'Fouilles et découvertes archéologiques en Grece en 2001 et 2002', *Bulletin de Correspondance Hellénique*, 127, pp. 683–1108.

Burridge, P. (1996), 'The architectural development of the Athonite monastery', in A. Bryer and M. Cunningham (eds), *Mount Athos and Byzantine Monasticism: Papers from the Twenty-Eighth Spring Symposium of Byzantine Studies, Birmingham, March 1994*, Aldershot/Brookfield: Variorum, pp. 171–88.

Bury, J. B. (1892), 'The Helladikoi', *English Historical Review*, 7, pp. 80–1.

Caillet, J.-P. (1987), 'Les dédicaces privées de pavements de mosaïque à la fin de l'Antiquité. Occident européen et monde grec: données socioéconomiques', in X. Barral i Altet (ed.), *Artistes, artisans et production artistique au Moyen Age. Colloque international. Centre National de la Recherche Scientifique, Université de Rennes – Haute Bretagne, 1–6 mai 1983*, Paris: Picard, pp. 15–38.

Callegher, B. (2005), 'La circulation monetaire à Patras et dans les sites ruraux environnants (VIe–VIIe siècle)', in J. Lefort, C. Morrisson, and J.-P. Sodini (eds), *Les villages dans l'Empire byzantin, IVe–XVe siècles*, Paris: Lethielleux, pp. 225–35.

Cambi, N. (1978), 'Starokrščanska crkvena arhitektura na području Salonitanske metropolije', *Arheološki vestnik*, 29, pp. 606–26.

Capaldo, M. (1983), 'Un insediamento slavo presso Siracusa nel primo millennio d. C.', *Europa Orientalis*, 2, pp. 5–17.

Caraher, W. R. (2008), 'Constructing memories: hagiography, church architecture, and the religious landscape of Middle Byzantine Greece: the case of St. Theodore of Kythera', in W. R. Caraher, L. J. Hall, and R. S. Moore (eds), *Archaeology and History in Roman, Medieval, and Post-Medieval Greece. Studies on Method and Meaning in Honor of Timothy E. Gregory*, Aldershot/Burlington: Ashgate, pp. 267–80.

Chaneva-Dechevska, N. (1999), *Rannokhristianskata arkhitektura v Bălgariia IV–VI v.*, Sofia: Universitetsko izdatelstvo 'Sv. Kliment Okhridski'.

Charanis, P. (1946), 'Nicephorus I, the savior of Greece from the Slavs (810 AD)', *Byzantina-Metabyzantina*, 1, pp. 75–92.

— (1949), 'On the question of the Slavonic settlements in Greece during the Middle Ages', *Byzantinoslavica*, 10, pp. 254–8.

— (1950), 'The chronicle of Monemvasia and the question of the Slavonic settlements in Greece', *Dumbarton Oaks Papers*, 5, pp. 141–66.

— (1952), 'On the capture of Corinth by the Onogurs and its recapture by the Byzantines', *Speculum*, 27, pp. 343–50.

— (1953), 'The term Helladikoi in Byzantine texts of the sixth, seventh and eighth centuries', *Epeteris Hetaireias Byzantinon Spoudon*, 23, pp. 615–20.

— (1955a), 'Hellas in the Greek sources of the sixth, seventh, and eighth centuries', in K. Weitzmann (ed.), *Late Classical and Mediaeval Studies in Honor of Albert Mathias Friend, Jr.*, Princeton: Princeton University Press, pp. 161–76.

— (1955b), 'The significance of coins as evidence for the history of Athens and Corinth in the seventh and eighth centuries', *História*, 4: 2–3, pp. 163–72.

— (1959), 'Ethnic changes in the Byzantine Empire in the seventh century', *Dumbarton Oaks Papers*, 13, pp. 25–44.

— (1961), 'The transfer of population as a policy in the Byzantine Empire', *Comparative Studies in Society and History*, 8: 2, pp. 140–54.

— (1970), 'Observations on the history of Greece during the Early Middle Ages', *Balkan Studies*, 11, pp. 1–34.

— (1971), 'Graecia in Isidore of Seville', *Byzantinische Zeitschrift*, 46, pp. 22–5.

Chatzidakis, G. N. (1927), 'Tsakones', *Byzantinische Zeitschrift*, 27, pp. 321–4.

Chatzidakis, M. (1969), 'A propos de la date et du fondateur de Saint-Luc', *Cahiers Archéologiques*, 19, pp. 127–50.

— (1972a), 'Peri mones Hosiou Louka neotera', *Hellenika*, 25, pp. 298–313.

— (1972b), 'Précisions sur le fondateur de Saint-Luc', *Cahiers Archéologiques*, 22, pp. 87–8.

Chatzidakis, N. (1997), *Hosios Loukas*, Athens: Melissa.

Cheshmedzhiev, D. (1997), 'On the question of the localization of the Slav tribe Smoljani', *Bulgarian Historical Review*, 25: 1, pp. 89–93.

Chevalier, P. (1988), 'Les baptistères paléochrétiens de la province romaine de Dalmatie', *Diadora*, 10, pp. 111–63.

— (2005), 'Les autels paléochrétiens des provinces d'Epirus Vetus, Epirus Nova et de Praevalis', *Hortus Artium Medievalium*, 11, pp. 65–80.

Cheynet, J.-C. and B. Flusin (1990), 'Du monastère Ta Kathara à Thessalonique: Théodore Stoudite sur la route d'exil', *Revue des Etudes Byzantines*, 49, pp. 249–85.

Cheynet, J.-C. and C. Morrisson (1990), 'Lieux de trouvaille et circulation des sceaux', *Studies in Byzantine Sigillography*, 2, pp. 105–36.

Choumanidis, L. T. (2001), 'Peri tes oikonomias tes Peloponnesou epi Basileiou A' (867–886)', in S. P. Spentzas (ed.), *Byzantio, ho kosmous tou kai he Europe.*

Praktika A' epistemonikes synanteses tes "Diethnou epistemonikes hetaireias plethonikon kai byzantinon meleton". Mystras, 26–28 maiou 2000, Athens: Diethnes Epistemonike Hetaireia Plethonikon kai Byzantion Meleton, pp. 31–47.

Christides, V. (1981), 'Once again Caminiates' "Capture of Thessaloniki"', Byzantinische Zeitschrift, 74, pp. 7–10.

— (1984), The Conquest of Crete by the Arabs (ca. 824), a Turning Point in the Struggle Between Byzantium and Islam, Athens: Akademia Athenon.

Christou, E. and K. Nikolaou (1990), 'Stoicheia gia ten koinonia kai ton kathemerino bio sten perioche tes Lakonikes (10–12os ai.) apo hagiologika keimena', Byzantinai Meletai. Diethnes Epistemonike Hepeteris Byzantines kai Metabyzantines Ereunes, 2, pp. 206–30.

Chrysanthopoulos, E. (1957), 'Ta biblia Thaumaton tou agiou Demetriou, to chronikon tes Monemvasias kai ai slabikai epidromai eis ten Ellada', Theologia, 28, pp. 115–57.

Chrysos, E. (1997), 'The Middle Byzantine period (sixth century–1204)', in M. V. Sakellariou (ed.), Epirus. 4000 Years of Greek History and Civilization, Athens: Ekdotike Athenon, pp. 182–95.

Coche de la Ferté, E. (1957), La collection Hélène Stathatos: les objets byzantins et post-byzantins, Limoges: A. Bontemps.

Connor, C. L. (1992), 'Hosios Loukas as a victory church', Greek, Roman and Byzantine Studies, 33, pp. 293–308.

Constantelos, D. J. (1985), 'Lives of saints, ethical teachings and social realities in tenth-century Byzantine Peloponnesos', Greek Orthodox Theological Review, 30, pp. 297–310.

Cormack, R. (1968), 'Ninth-century monumental painting and mosaic in Thessaloniki', PhD dissertation, London: London University.

Cramer, J. A. (1963), Anecdota graeca e codd. manuscriptis Bibliothecarum Oxoniensium, Amsterdam: A. M. Hakkert.

Čremošnik, I. (1975), 'Die Untersuchungen in Mušići und Žabljak. Über den ersten Fund der ältesten slawischen Siedlung in Bosnien', Wissenschaftliche Mitteilungen des bosnisch-herzegowinischen Landesmuseums, 5, pp. 91–176.

Crow, J. (2001), 'Fortifications and urbanism in late antiquity: Thessaloniki and other eastern cities', in L. Lavan (ed.), Recent Research in Late-Antique Urbanism, Portsmouth: Journal of Roman Archaeology, pp. 57–68.

Curta, F. (1996), 'Invasion or inflation? Sixth- to seventh-century Byzantine coin hoards in Eastern and Southeastern Europe', Annali dell'Istituto Italiano di Numismatica, 43, pp. 65–224.

— (1997), 'Slavs in Fredegar and Paul the Deacon: medieval "gens" or "scourge of God"?', Early Medieval Europe, 6: 2, pp. 141–67.

— (2001a), 'Peasants as "makeshift soldiers for the occasion": sixth-century settlement patterns in the Balkans', in T. S. Burns and J. W. Eadie (eds), Urban Centers and Rural Contexts in Late Antiquity, East Lansing: Michigan State University Press, pp. 199–217.

— (2001b), The Making of the Slavs. History and Archaeology of the Lower Danube Region, c. 500–700, Cambridge/New York: Cambridge University Press.

— (2004a), 'Barbarians in Dark-Age Greece: Slavs or Avars?', in T. Stepanov and V. Vachkova (eds), Civitas divino-humana. V chest na profesor Georgi Bakalov, Sofia: Centăr za izsledvaniia na bălgarite Tangra TanNakRa IK, pp. 513–50.

— (2004b), 'L'administration byzantine dans les Balkans pendant la "grande brèche": le témoignage des sceaux', *Bizantinistica. Rivista di studi bizantini e slavi*, 6, pp. 155–90.

— (2005a), 'Byzantium in Dark-Age Greece (the numismatic evidence in its Balkan context)', *Byzantine and Modern Greek Studies*, 29, pp. 113–46.

— (2005b), 'Female dress and 'Slavic' bow fibulae in Greece', *Hesperia*, 74: 1, pp. 101–46.

— (2006a), 'Slavic bow fibulae? Werner's class I D revisited', *Acta Archaeologica Academiae Scientiarum Hungaricae*, 57, pp. 423–74.

— (2006b), *Southeastern Europe in the Middle Ages, 500–1250*, Cambridge/New York: Cambridge University Press.

Da Costa-Louillet, G. (1961), 'Saints de Grèce aux VIIIe, IXe et Xe siècles', *Byzantion*, 31, pp. 309–69.

Dadaki, S. (1997), 'Anaskaphe taphikou ktismatos sto Tsoukalario Thasou', *To Archaiologiko ergo ste Makedonia kai Thrake*, 11, pp. 609–16.

Dagron, G. (1987), '"Ceux d'en face". Les peuples étrangers dans les traités militaires byzantins', *Travaux et mémoires du Centre de Recherches d'Histoire et Civilisation Byzantines*, 10, pp. 207–32.

Daly, L. W. (1942), 'Echinos and Justinian's fortifications in Greece', *American Journal of Archaeology*, 46, pp. 500–8.

Darrouzès, J. (1960), *Epistoliers byzantins du Xe siècle*, Paris: Institut Français d'Etudes Byzantines.

— (1975), 'Listes épiscopales du concile de Nicée (787)', *Revue des Etudes Byzantines*, 33, pp. 5–76.

— (1981), *Notitiae episcopatuum ecclesiae Constantinopolitanae. Texte critique, introduction et notes*, Paris: Institut Français d'Etudes Byzantines.

Davidson, G. R. (1937), 'The Avar invasion of Corinth', *Hesperia*, 6, pp. 227–39.

— (1952), *The Minor Objects*, Princeton: American School of Classical Studies in Athens.

— (1974), 'A wandering soldier's grave in Corinth', *Hesperia*, 43, pp. 512–21.

Dawkins, R. M. and J. P. Droop (1910–1911), 'Byzantine pottery from Sparta', *Annual of the British School at Athens*, 17, pp. 23–8.

Dengate, J. A. (1981), 'Coin hoards from the Gymnasium area at Corinth', *Hesperia*, 50, pp. 147–88.

Deriziotis, L. and S. Kougioumtzoglu (2004), 'Anakalyptontas ten agnoston christianiken Perraibiken Tripolin', in I. Kakouris, S. Choulia, and T. Albani (eds), *Thorakion. Aphieroma ste mneme tou Paulou Lazaride*, Athens: Ypourgeio Politismou, Genike Dieuthynse Archaioteton kai Politistikes Klironomias, Dieuthynse Metavyzantinon Archaioteton, pp. 63–74.

Diehl, C. (1889), *L'Eglise et les mosaïques du couvent de Saint-Luc en Phocide*, Paris: E. Thorin.

Diez, E. and O. Demus (1931), *Byzantine Mosaics in Greece. Hosios Lucas and Daphni*, Cambridge, MA: Harvard University Press.

Diller, A. (1954), 'The scholia on Strabo', *Traditio*, 10, pp. 29–50.

Dimitriadis, G. M. (2001), 'Nicopolis, la capitale paléochrétienne d'Epire', *Mésogeios*, 12, pp. 13–36.

Dimitrokallis, G. (1990), *Agnostoi vyzantinoi naoi Hieras Metropoleos Messenias*, Athens: G. Dimitrokallis.

Ditten, H. (1983), 'Prominente Slawen und Bulgaren im byzantinischen Diensten (Ende des 7. bis Anfang des 10. Jahrhunderts)', in H. Köpstein and F. Winkelmann (eds), *Studien zum 8. und 9. Jh. im Byzanz*, Berlin: Akademie Verlag, pp. 95–119.
— (1984), 'Herrschte 837 u.Z. Krieg oder Frieden zwischen Byzanz und Bulgarien?', *Etudes Balkaniques*, 20: 4, pp. 62–79.
— (1991), 'Soziale Spannungen in dem von Slawen bedrohten Thessalonike des ausgehenden 6. und des 7. Jh. n. Chr. Zu den Wechselwirkungen zwischen äußerer Bedrohung und inneren Verwicklungen', in F. Winckelmann (ed.), *Volk und Herrschaft im frühen Byzanz. Methodische und quellenkritische Probleme*, Berlin: Akademie Verlag, pp. 18–32.
— (1993), *Ethnische Verschiebungen zwischen der Balkanhalbinsel und Kleinasien vom Ende des 6. bis zur zweiten Hälfte des 9. Jahrhunderts*, Berlin: Akademie Verlag.
Dölger, F. (1952), *Ein Fall slavischer Einsiedlung im Hinterland von Thessalonike im 10. Jahrhundert*, Munich: Verlag der Bayerischen Akademie der Wissenschaften.
Doukata, S. (1991), 'Euremata palaiokhristianikes kai byzantines periodou sten Paleokhora Maroneias', *To Arkhaiologiko ergo ste Makedonia kai Thrake*, 5, pp. 497–513.
Doukata-Demertzi, S. (1992), 'Anaskaphe Paleochoras Maroneias 1992', *To Archaiologiko ergo ste Makedonia kai Thrake*, 6, pp. 695–709.
Drandakis, N. V. (1969), 'Byzantina kai metabyzantina mnemeia Lakonikes', *Archaiologike ephemeris: ekdidomene tes archaiologikes hetaireias*, 108, pp. 1–11.
— (1969–1970), 'Agios Panteleemon Mpoularion', *Epeteris Hetaireias Byzantinon Spoudon*, 37, pp. 437–58.
— (1972), 'Niketas marmaras', *Dodone. Istoria kai arkhaiologia*, 1, pp. 21–44.
Drandakis, N. V. and N. Gkioles (1980), 'Anaskaphe sto Tegani tes Manes', *Praktika tes en Athenais Archaiologikes Hetaireias*, 135, pp. 247–58.
— (1983), 'Anaskaphe sto Tegani tes Manes', *Praktika tes en Athenais Archaiologikes Hetaireias*, 138, pp. 264–70.
Drandakis, N. V., N. Gkioles, and C. Konstantinidi (1981), 'Anaskaphe sto Tigani Manis', *Praktika tes en Athenais Archaiologikes Hetaireias*, 136, pp. 241–53.
Drosogianni, P. A. (1963), 'Thessalonike', *Archaiologikon Deltion*, 18: 2, pp. 235–54.
Duncan, G. L. (1993), *Coin Circulation in the Danubian and Balkan Provinces of the Roman Empire AD 294–578*, London: Royal Numismatic Society.
Dunn, A. W. (1990), 'The Byzantine topography of southern Macedonia: a contribution', in T. Petrides (ed.), *Mneme D. Lazaride. Polis kai chora sten archaia Makedonia kai chora sten Thrake. Praktika archaiologikou synedriou, Kavala, 9–11 maiou 1986*, Thessaloniki: To Hypourgeio, pp. 307–32.
— (1992), 'The exploitation and control of woodland and scrubland in the Byzantine world', *Byzantine and Modern Greek Studies*, 16, pp. 235–98.
— (1993), 'The *kommerkiairios*, the *apotheke*, the *Dromos*, the *vardarios*, and *The West*', *Byzantine and Modern Greek Studies*, 17, pp. 3–24.
— (1995), 'Historical and archaeological indicators of economic change in Middle Byzantine Boeotia and their problems', *Epeteris tes Hetaireias Boiotikon Meleton*, 2, pp. 755–74.
— (1999), 'From polis to kastron in southern Macedonia: Amphipolis, Khrysoupolis,

and the Strymon Delta', in A. Bazzana (ed.), *Archéologies des espaces agraires méditerranéens au Moyen Age. Actes du colloque de Murcie (Espagne) tenu du 8 au 12 mai 1992*, Madrid/Rome: Casa de Velázquez/Ecole Française de Rome, pp. 399–413.
— (2002), 'Was there a militarisation of the southern Balkans during Late Antiquity?', in P. Freeman (ed.), *Limes XVIII. Proceedings of the XVIIIth International Congress of Roman Frontier Studies*, Oxford: Archaeopress, pp. 705–12.
— (2006), 'The rise and fall of towns, loci of maritime traffic, and silk production: the problem of Thisvi-Kastorion', in E. Jeffreys (ed.), *Byzantine Style, Religion and Civilizatin. In Honour of Sir Steven Runciman*, Cambridge: Cambridge University Press, pp. 38–71.
Dunn, M. (1977), 'Evangelism or repentance? The re-Christianisation of the Peloponnese in the ninth and tenth centuries', *Studies in Church History*, 14, pp. 71–86.
Durliat, J. (1980), 'La valeur relative de l'or, de l'argent et du cuivre dans l'empire protobyzantin (IVe–VIIe siècle)', *Revue Numismatique*, 22: 6, pp. 138–54.
Dvornik, F. (1926), *La vie de Saint Grégoire Décapolite et les Slaves macédoniens au IXe siècle*, Paris: Champion.
Edwards, K. (1933), *Corinth. Results of Excavations Conducted by the American School of Classical Studies at Athens*, Cambridge: Cambridge University Press.
— (1937), 'Report on the coins found in the excavations at Corinth during the years 1930–1935', *Hesperia*, 6: 2, pp. 241–56.
Eiwanger, J. (1981), *Keramik und Kleinfunde aus der Damokratia-Basilika in Demetrias*, Bonn: Rudolf Habelt.
Eleutheriadou, K., I. Kanonidis, N. Karydas, D. Makropoulou, E. Marki, G. Papazotou, and E. Pelekanidou (1994), 'Nomos Thessalonikes. 9e Ephoreia Byzantinon Archaioteton', *Archaiologikon Deltion*, 49, pp. 487–530.
Epstein, A. W. (1980), 'Middle Byzantine churches of Kastoria: dates and implications', *Art Bulletin*, 62, pp. 190–206.
Etzeoglou, R. (1988), 'Karyoupolis, mia ereipomene byzantine pole. Schediasma istorikes geographias tes boerioanatolikes Manes', *Lakonikai spoudai*, 9, pp. 3–60.
Evangelidis, D. (1937), 'Eikonomachika mnemeia en Thessaloniki', *Archaiologike ephemeris: ekdidomene tes archaiologikes hetaireias*, 83, pp. 341–51.
Evans, H. M. A. (1989), *The Early Medieval Archaeology of Croatia A.D. 600–900*, Oxford: BAR.
Evgenidou, D. (1987), 'Servia and Moglena, two Byzantine cities of Macedonia', *Historikogeographika*, 2, pp. 15–22.
Falkenhausen, V. von (1995), 'Arethas in Italien?', *Byzantinoslavica*, 56, pp. 359–66.
Fallmerayer, J. P. (1830), *Geschichte der Halbinsel Morea während des Mittelalters. Ein historischer Versuch*, Stuttgart/Tübingen: J. G. Cotta.
— (1835), *Welchen Einfluß hatte die Besetzung Griechenlands durch die Slaven auf das Schicksal der Stadt Athen und der Landschaft Attica? Oder nähere Begründung der im ersten Bande der Geschichte von Morea während des Mittelalters aufgestellten Lehre über die Entstehung der heutigen Griechen*, Stuttgart/Tübingen: J. G. Cotta.

— (1845), *Fragmente aus dem Orient*, Stuttgart/Tübingen: J. C. Cotta.
Farag, W. A. (1989), 'Some remarks on Leo of Tripoli's attack on Thessaloniki in 904 A. D.' *Byzantinische Zeitschrift*, 82, pp. 133–9.
Feissel, D. (1983), *Recueil des inscriptions chrétiennes de Macédoine du IIIe au VIe siècle*, Athens/Paris: Ecole Française d'Athènes/De Boccard.
Feissel, D. and A. Philippidis-Braat (1985), 'Inventaires en vue d'un recueil des inscriptions historiques de Byzance, III. Inscriptions du Péloponnèse (à l'exception de Mistra)', *Travaux et mémoires du Centre de Recherches d'Histoire et Civilisation Byzantines*, 9, pp. 267–395.
Ferjančić, B. (1955), 'O upadu Zklavisiiana na Peloponez za vreme Romana Lekapena', *Zbornik radova Vizantološkog Instituta*, 3, pp. 37–48.
Ferluga, J. (1976), *Byzantium on the Balkans. Studies on the Byzantine Administration and the Southern Slavs from the VIIth to the XIIth Centuries*, Amsterdam: Adolf M. Hakkert.
— (1982), 'Archon. Ein Beitrag zur Untersuchung der südslawischen Herrschertitel im 9. u. 10. Jh. in lichte der byzantinischen Quellen', in N. Kamp and J. Wollasch (eds), *Tradition als historische Kraft*, Berlin/New York: De Gruyter, pp. 254–66.
— (1984), 'Untersuchungen zur byzantinischen Ansiedlungspolitik auf dem Balkan von der Mitte des 7. bis zur Mitte des 9. Jahrhunderts', *Zbornik radova Vizantološkog Instituta*, 23, pp. 49–61.
— (1993), 'Mercati e mercanti fra Mar Nero e Adriatico: il commercio nei Balcani dal VII al'XI secolo', in *Mercati e mercanti nell'alto medioevo: l'area euroasiatica e l'area mediterranea*, Spoleto: Presso la Sede del Centro, pp. 443–98.
Finlay, G. (1877), *A History of Greece from its Conquest by the Romans to the Present Time, B.C. 146 to A.D. 1864*, Oxford: Clarendon Press.
Finley, J. H. (1932), 'Corinth in the Middle Ages', *Speculum*, 7, pp. 477–99.
Fodor, I. (1996), *'Őseinket felhozád . . . ' A honfoglaló magyarság. Kiállítási katalógus*, Budapest: Magyar Nemzeti Múzeum.
Frantz, M. A. (1938), 'Middle Byzantine pottery in Athens', *Hesperia*, 7, pp. 429–67.
— (1988), *The Athenian Agora. XXIV: Late Antiquity: A.D. 267–700*, Princeton American School of Classical Studies in Athens.
Frashëri, K. (1998), 'Les Albanais et Byzance aux VIe–XIe siècle', in C. Gasparis (ed.), *Hoi Albanoi sto Mesaiona*, Athens: Institouto Byzantinon Ereunon, pp. 47–57.
Frazee, C. A. (1993), 'The Balkans between Rome and Constantinople in the early Middle Ages 600–900 AD', *Balkan Studies*, 2, pp. 213–28.
Frendo, D. and A. Fotiou (2000), *John Kaminiates, The Capture of Thessaloniki*, Perth: Australian Association for Byzantine Studies.
Frendo, J. D. C. (1997), 'The Miracles of St. Demetrius and the capture of Thessaloniki. An examination of the purpose, significance and authenticity of John Kaminiates' De Expugnatione Thessalonicae', *Byzantinoslavica*, 58, pp. 205–24.
Galani-Krikou, M. (1992), 'Nomismata', *Archaiologikon Deltion*, 47, pp. 69–71.
— (1997), 'Thebai: 10os–14os aionas. He nomismatike martyria apo ten Hagia Triada', *Symmeikta*, 11, pp. 113–50.
— (1998a), 'Nomismatikoi thesauroi ton meson chronon apo te Theba," *Deltion tes christianikes archaiologikes hetaireias*, 20, pp. 275–84.
— (1998b), 'Thebai 6os–15os aionas. He nomismatike apo to Politistiko Kentro', *Symmeikta*, 12, pp. 141–70.

— (2000), 'Theba: 6os–15os ai. m. Ch. He nomismatike martyria apo ten anaskaphe sto Politistiko Kentro', *Epeteris tes Hetaireias Boiotikon Meleton*, 3, p. 901.
Galani-Krikou, M. and I. Tsourti (2000), 'Makedonike Rentina. He nomismatike martyria (anaskaphes 1976–1996)', in P. Adam-Veleni (ed.), *To nomisma sto makedoniko choro. Praktika B' epistemonikes synanteses. Nomismatokopeia, kyklophoria, eikonographia, istoria. Archaioi, byzantinoi kai neoteroi chronoi*, Thessaloniki: University Studio Press, pp. 347–54.
Galani-Krikou, M., G. Nikolaou, M. Oikonomidou, I. Touratsoglou, and I. Tsourti (2002), *Syntagma byzantinon 'thesauron' tou Nomismatikou Mouseion (SBTh)*, Athens: Hypourgeio Politismo, Nomismatiko Mouseio.
Galanopoulos, M. E. (1933), *Bios, politeia, eikonographia, thaumata kai asmatike akolouthia tou hosiou kai theophorou patros hemon Nikonos tou 'Metanoeite'*, Athens: Ioannis & Aristotelis Papanikolaou.
Ganktzis, D., M. Leontsini, and A. Panopoulou (1993), 'Peloponnesos kai notia Italia: stathmoi epikoinonias ste mese byzantine periodo', in N. G. Moschonas (ed.), *He epikoinonia sto Byzantio. Praktika tou B' diethnous symposiou, 4–6 oktobriou 1990*, Athens: Kentro Vyzantinon Ereunon, pp. 469–86.
Garam, É. (1980), 'Spätawarenzeitliche durchbrochene Bronzescheiben', *Acta Archaeologica Academiae Scientiarum Hungaricae*, 32, pp. 161–80.
— (1993), 'Die awarenzeitlichen Scheibenfibeln', *Communicationes Archaeologicae Hungariae*, pp. 99–134.
— (2001), *Funde byzantinischer Herkunft in der Awarenzeit vom Ende des 6. bis zum Ende des 7. Jahrhunderts*, Budapest: Magyar Nemzéti Múzeum.
— (2002), 'Ketten und Schlüssel in frühawarenzeitlichen Frauengräber', *Communicationes Archaeologicae Hungariae*, pp. 153–76.
Garašanin, M. and M. Vašić (1987), 'Castrum Pontes. Izveshtaj o iskopavanjima u 1981. i 1982. godina', *Đerdapske sveske*, 4, pp. 71–116.
Georgakas, D. J. (1950), 'The mediaeval names Melingi and Ezeritae of Slavic groups in the Peloponnesus', *Byzantinische Zeitschrift*, 43, pp. 301–33.
Georganteli, E. S. (2005), 'L'espace rural dans la province de Rhodope: le témoignage de la numismatique', in J. Lefort, C. Morrisson, and J.-P. Sodini (eds), *Les villages dans l'Empire byzantin, IVe–XVe siècles*, Paris: Lethielleux, pp. 307–18.
Georgopoulou, M. (1972), 'Agios Nikolaos Attales Euboias', *Archaiologika analekta ex Athenon*, 5, pp. 57–63.
Georgopoulou-Meladini, M. (1973), 'Chalkis – Hodos Phabierou 10 (oikopedon N. Papageorgopoulou)', *Archaiologikon Deltion*, 28, pp. 314–15.
Georgopoulou-Meladini, M. and N. Papadakis (1974), 'Archaika kai mesaionika euremata en Chalkidi', *Archaiologika analekta ex Athenon*, 7, pp. 35–43.
Georgopoulou-Verra, M. (2002), 'He prote oikodomike phase tou kastrou tes Patras', in P. G. Themelis and V. Konti (eds), *Protobyzantine Messene kai Olympia. Aktikos kai agrotikos choros ste Dytike Peloponneso. Praktika tou Diethnous symposiou, Athena, 29–30 maiou 1998*, Athens: Hetaireia Messeniakon Archaiologikon Spoudon/Institouto Byzantinon Ereunon, pp. 161–73.
Gerolymatou, M. (2004), 'Peloponnesiakes mones kai exousia (10os–11os ai.)', in V. Konti (ed.), *Ho monachismos sten Peloponneso 40s–15os ai.*, Athens: Institouto Byzantinon Ereunon, pp. 37–53.
Gerolymou, K. G. (1999), 'Dyo nees epigraphes apo to Argos', *Horos*, 13, pp. 49–56.

Gerstel, S. E. J. (1998), 'Medieval Messenia', in J. L. Davis (ed.), *Sandy Pylos. An Archaeological History from Nestor to Navarino*, Austin: University of Texas Press, pp. 211–42.

Gialouri, A. (2004), 'Palaiokhristianike basilike kato apo to nao tou Agiou Ioanou tou Theologou sten Tithorea Phthiotidos', in I. Kakouris, S. Choulia, and T. Albani (eds), *Thorakion. Aphieroma ste mneme tou Paulou Lazaride*, Athens: Ypourgeio Politismou, Genike Dieuthynse Archaioteton kai Politistikes Klironomias, Dieuthynse Metavyzantinon Archaioteton, pp. 87–100.

Gialouris, N. (1961–1962), 'Perioche Olympias', *Archaiologikon Deltion*, 17: 2, pp. 105–7.

Giamalidis, C. A. (1913), 'Archaiai ekklesiai Epidaurou kai ton perix chorion', *Athena. Syngrama periodikon tes en Athenais Epistemonikes Hetaireias*, 25, pp. 405–29.

Giannopoulos, P. A. (1975), 'Didymoteichon. Geschichte einer byzantinischen Festung', PhD dissertation, Cologne: University of Cologne.

Ginkel, J. J. v. (1998), 'Making history: Michael the Syrian and his sixth-century sources', in R. Lavenant (ed.), *Symposium Syriacum VII. Uppsala University, Department of Asian and African Languages, 11–14 August 1996*, Rome: Pontificio Istituto Orientale, pp. 351–8.

Giros, C. (1992), 'Remarques sur l'architecture monastique en Macédoine orientale', *Bulletin de Correspondance Hellénique*, 116, pp. 409–43.

Gkini-Tsophopoulou, E. (1980), 'Palaiochristianike basilike ste these "Mygdaleza" Attikes', *Archaiologike ephemeris: ekdidomene tes archaiologikes hetaireias*, 119, pp. 85–96.

— (1990), 'Stamata', *Archaiologikon Deltion*, 45, pp. 90–2.

— (2001), 'The Mesogeia from early Christian times to the Ottoman conquest', in S. A. Idea and K. Tsouni (eds), *Mesogaia. History and Culture of Mesogeia in Attica*, Athens: Eleftherios Venezelos Athens International Airport, pp. 148–221.

Gkini-Tsophopoulou, E. and E. Chalkia (2003), 'Taphike palaiochristianike keramike apo ten Attike: hoi periptoseis tes Stamatas kai tes Anabysos', in C. Bakirtzis (ed.), *7o Diethnes Synedrio Mesaionikes Keramikes tes Mesogeiou. Thessalonike, 11–16 oktobriou 1999. Praktika*, Athens: Edition de la Caisse de Recettes Archéologiques, pp. 755–8.

Glavinas, A. (2001), 'Ho chronos anidrysis tou parekklesiou tou agiou Euthymiou ston hiero nao Agiou Demetriou Thessalonikes', *Byzantiaka*, 21, pp. 99–118.

Gounaris, G. (1984), 'Chalkines porpes apo to Oktagono ton Philippon kai ten Kentrike Makedonia', *Byzantiaka*, 4, pp. 49–59.

— (1989), 'L'archéologie chrétienne en Grèce de 1974 à 1985', in *Actes du XIe Congrès International d'Archéologie Chrétienne. Lyon, Vienne, Grenoble, Genève et Aoste (21–28 septembre 1986)*, Rome: Ecole Française de Rome, pp. 2687–711.

Gounaris, G. and G. M. Velenis (1989), 'Panepistemiake anaskaphe Philippon 1989', *To Archaiologiko ergo ste Makedonia kai Thrake*, 3, pp. 451–7.

— (1990), 'Panepistemiake anaskaphe Philippon 1990', *To Archaiologiko ergo ste Makedonia kai Thrake*, 4, pp. 477–86.

— (1993), 'Panepistemiake anaskaphe Philippon 1993', *To Archaiologiko ergo ste Makedonia kai Thrake*, 7, pp. 531–40.

Grabar, A. (1975), 'La sculpture byzantine en Grèce', *Corso di cultura sull'arte ravennate e bizantina*, 22, pp. 225–31.

Greatrex, G. (1994), 'The dates of Procopius' works', *Byzantine and Modern Greek Studies*, 18, pp. 101–14.
— (1995), 'Procopius and Agathias on the defences of the Thracian Chersonese', in C. Mango and G. Dagron (eds), *Constantinople and its Hinterland. Papers from the Twenty-Seventh Spring Symposium of Byzantine Studies, Oxford, April 1993*, Aldershot: Variorum, pp. 125–9.
Grégoire, H. (1952a), 'Le communiqué arabe sur la prise de Thessalonique (904)', *Byzantion*, 22, pp. 371–8.
— (1952b), 'L'étymologie slave du nom des Melingi et des Ezerites', *Nouvelle Clio*, 4, pp. 293–8.
Gregory, T. E. (1984), 'Cities and social evolution in Roman and Byzantine southeast Europe', in J. Bintliff (ed.), *European Social Evolution*, Bradford: University of Bradford, pp. 267–76.
— (1985), 'An early Byzantine complex at Akra Sophia near Corinth', *Hesperia*, 54, pp. 411–28.
— (1987), 'The early Byzantine fortifications of Nikopolis in comparative perspective', in E. Chrysos (ed.), *Nikopolis I. Proceedings of the First International Symposium on Nikopolis (23–29 September 1984)*, Preveza: Demos Prevezas, pp. 253–61.
— (1992), '*Kastro* and *diateichisma* as responses to early Byzantine frontier collapse', *Byzantion*, 62, pp. 235–53.
— (1993a), 'An early Byzantine (Dark-Age) settlement at Isthmia: preliminary report', in T. E. Gregory (ed.), *The Corinthia in the Roman Period Including the Papers Given at a Symposium Held at the Ohio State University on 7–9 March, 1991*, Ann Arbor: Journal of Roman Archaeology Supplementary Series, pp. 149–60.
— (1993b), *The Hexamilion and the Fortress (Isthmia V)*, Princeton: American School of Classical Studies at Athens.
— (2000), 'Procopius on Greece', *Antiquité tardive*, 8, pp. 105–14.
Gregory, T. E. and P. N. Kardulias (1990), 'Geophysical and surface surveys in the Byzantine fortres at Isthmia, 1985–1986', *Hesperia*, 59: 3, pp. 467–511.
Grigoriou-Ioannidou, M. (2000), 'Hoi "Bulgari qui Sclavi appellantur" ston Bio tou Agiou Georgiou tou Agioreitou (1009–1065)', *Byzantina*, 21, pp. 143–50.
Grundmann, K. (1937), 'Magula Hadzimissiotiki. Eine steinzeitliche Siedlung in Karla-See', *Mitteilungen des Deutschen Archäologischen Instituts. Athenische Abteilung*, 62, pp. 56–69.
Gundlach, W., ed. (1892), 'Epistolae aevi merowingici collectae', in W. Gundlach and E. Dümmler (eds), *Epistolae Merowingici et karolini aevi*, Berlin: Weidmann, pp. 434–68.
Guseinov, R. A. (1969), '"Khronika" Mikhaila Siriica i "Vseobshchaia istoriia" Bar Ebreia kak istochniki po istorii iugo-vostochnoi Evropy (IX–XII vv.)', in V. Tăpkova-Zaimova et al. (eds), *Actes du premier Congrès International des Études Balkaniques et Sud-Est Européennes*, Sofia: Editions de l'Académie Bulgare des Sciences, pp. 209–19.
Guth, K. (1982), 'Die Pilgerfahrt Willibalds ins Heilige Land (723–728/9). Analyse eines frühmittelalterlichen Reiseberichts', *Sammelblatt des Historischen Vereins Eichstätt*, 75, pp. 13–28.
Hadji-Minaglou, G. (1994), 'Le grand appareil dans les églises des IXe–XIIe siècles de la Grèce du sud', *Bulletin de Correspondance Hellénique*, 118: 1, pp. 161–97.

Hahn, M. (1996), 'The early Byzantine to modern periods', in B. Wells (ed.), *The Berbati-Limnes Archaeological Survey, 1988–1990*, Jonsered: Åströms Förlag, pp. 345–451.

Hahn, W. (1973a), *Moneta Imperii Byzantini*, Vienna: Verlag der Österreichischen Akademie der Wissenschaften.

— (1973b), 'Some remarks on the historical value of the sixth century Byzantine copper currency', *Journal of Numismatic Fine Arts*, 1: 10, pp. 177–8.

— (1975), *Moneta Imperii Byzantini. Von Justinus II. bis Phocas (565–610)*, Vienna: Verlag der Österreichischen Akademie der Wissenschaften.

— (1981), *Moneta Imperii Byzantini. Von Heraclius bis Leo III./Alleinregierung (610–720)*, Vienna: Verlag der Österreichischen Akademie der Wissenschaften.

— (2000), *Money of the Incipient Byzantine Empire (Anastasius I–Justinian I, 491–565)*, Vienna: Österreichische Forschungsgesellschaft für Numismatik.

Haldon, J. F. (1997), *Byzantium in the Seventh Century. The Transformation of a Culture*, 2nd edn, Cambridge: Cambridge University Press.

Harrison, R. and J. Hayes (1986), *Excavations at Saraçhane in Istanbul*, Princeton/Washington, DC: Princeton University Press/Dumbarton Oaks Research Library and Collection.

Harvey, A. (1989), *Economic Expansion in the Byzantine Empire 900–1200*, Cambridge: Cambridge University Press.

— (1990), 'Peasant categories in the 10th and 11th centuries', *Byzantine and Modern Greek Studies*, 14, pp. 250–6.

— (1996), 'The monastic economy and imperial patronage from the tenth to the twelfth century', in A. Bryer and M. Cunningham (eds), *Mount Athos and Byzantine Monasticism. Papers from the Twenty-Eighth Spring Symposium of Byzantine Studies, Birmingham, March 1994*, Aldershot/Brookfield: Variorum, pp. 91–7.

Hattersley-Smith, K. (1988), 'Byzantine Public Architecture, Between the Fourth and the Early Seventh Centuries A.D., with Special Reference to the Towns of Macedonia', PhD dissertation, Oxford: Oxford University.

Hayes, J. W. and P. Petridis (2003), 'Rapport régionaux: Grèce', in C. Bakirtzis (ed.), *7o Diethnes Synedrio Mesaionikes Keramikes tes Mesogeiou. Thessalonike, 11–16 oktobriou 1999. Praktika*, Athens: Edition de la Caisse de Recettes Archéologiques, pp. 529–36.

Heather, P. (1996), *The Goths*, Oxford: Blackwell.

Hellenkemper, H. (1987), 'Die byzantinische Stadtmauer von Nikopolis in Epeiros: ein kaiserlicher Bauauftrag des 5. oder 6. Jahrhundert?', in E. Chrysos (ed.), *Nikopolis I. Proceedings of the First International Symposium on Nikopolis (23–29 September 1984)*, Preveza: Demos Prevezas, pp. 243–51.

Hendy, M. F. (1985), *Studies in the Byzantine Monetary Economy c. 300–1450*, Cambridge: Cambridge University Press.

Henning, J. (1987), *Südosteuropa zwischen Antike und Mittelalter. Archäologische Beiträge zur Landwirtschaft des I. Jahrtausends u. Z.*, Berlin: Akademie Verlag.

Herrin, J. (1973), 'Aspects of the process of hellenization in the early Middle Ages', *Annual of the British School at Athens*, 68, pp. 113–26.

Hidri, S. (1991), 'Materiale arkeologijke nga bazilika e Arapajt', *Iliria*, 21: 1–2, pp. 203–18.

Hjohlman, J., A. Penttinen, and B. Wells (2005), *Pyrgouthi. A Rural Site in the*

Berbati Valley from the Early Iron Age to Late Antiquity. Excavations by the Swedish Institute at Athens, 1995 and 1997, Stockholm: Svenska Institutet i Athen.

Hoddinott, R. (1963), *Early Byzantine Churches in Macedonia and Southern Serbia: A Study of the Origins and the Initial Development of East Christian Art*, London: Macmillan.

Hohlfelder, R. H. (1970), 'A small deposit of bronze coins from Kenchreai', *Hesperia*, 39, pp. 68–72.

— (1973), 'A sixth century hoard from Kenchreai', *Hesperia*, 42, pp. 89–101.

— (1974), 'A conspectus of the early Byzantine coins in the Kenchreai Excavation Corpus', *Byzantine Studies*, 1: 1, pp. 73–7.

— (1975), 'Barbarian invasions into Central Greece in the sixth century of the Christian era: more evidence from Corinthia', *East European Quarterly*, 9: 3, pp. 251–8.

— (1976), 'Migratory peoples' incursions into Central Greece in the late sixth century: new evidence from Kenchreai', in M. Berza and E. Stănescu (eds), *Actes du XIVe Congrès International des Etudes Byzantines. Bucarest, 6–12 septembre 1971*, Bucharest: Editura Academiei Republicii Socialiste România, pp. 333–8.

— (1978), *Kenchreai, Eastern Port of Corinth. Results of Investigations by the University of Chicago and Indiana University for the American School of Classical Studies in Athens. III. The Coins*, Leiden: Brill.

Holmes, C. (2005), *Basil II and the Governance of Empire (976–1025)*, Oxford: Oxford University Press.

Honigmann, E. (1939), *Le Synekdèmos d'Hiéroklès et l'opuscule géographique de Georges de Chypre*, Brussels: Editions de l'Institut de Philologie et d'Histoire Orientales et Slaves.

Hood, S. (1970), 'Isles of refuge in the early Byzantine period', *Annual of the British School at Athens*, 65, pp. 37–44.

— (1988), 'Some exotic pottery from prehistoric Greece', *Slovenská Archeológia*, 36: 1, pp. 93–7.

Hrochová, V. (1976), 'Problèmes des agglomérations slaves au Peloponnèse', *Etudes Balkaniques*, 12: 1, pp. 128–30.

Hunger, H. (1990), 'Athen in Byzanz: Traum und Realität', *Jahrbuch der österreichischen Byzantinistik*, 40, pp. 43–61.

Huxley, G. L. (1977), 'The second Dark Age of the Peloponnese', *Lakonikai spoudai*, 3, pp. 84–110.

— (1988), *Monemvasia and the Slavs: A Lecture on Some Works of Historical Geography in the Gennadius Library of the American School of Classical Studies at Athens*, Athens: G. Huxley.

Ibler, U. (1992), 'Pannonische Gürtelschnallen des späten 6. und 7. Jahrhunderts', *Arheološki vestnik*, 43, pp. 135–48.

Iliadi, A. K. (2003), *Ta 'thaumata' tou Agiou Demetriou hos istorikes peges. Epidromes kai slabikes epoikiseis enteuthen tou Dounabeos*, Trikala: Vogiatzouglou Thrasyvoulos.

Ilieva, A. (1989–1990), 'The mountain in the geographical and cultural space of the Peloponnese during the Middle Ages (before the Tourkokratia)', *Historikogeographika*, 3, pp. 11–24.

Imellou, S. D. (1999), 'He "hydatos blysis" katopin thaumatos ston bio Nikonos tou "Metanoeite". Synapheis thaumatikes kai alles diegeseis', *Epeteris Hetaireias Byzantinon Spoudon*, 7, pp. 39–84.

Intzesiloglou, A. (1987), 'Velestino', *Archaiologikon Deltion*, 42, pp. 270–1.

Ioannidou-Gregoriou, M. (1990), 'Zetemeta stratologias sto Byzantio: he periktose tou Hosiou Euthymiou', *Byzantiaka*, 10, pp. 149–58.

Iordanov, I. (2006), *Byzantine Seals with Family Names*, Sofia: Bulgarian Academy of Sciences.

Irmscher, J. (1992), 'Der Peloponnes in der justinianischen Epoche', *Sileno*, 18, pp. 75–81.

Ivanov, S. A. (1995), 'Georgii Pisida', in S. A. Ivanov, G. G. Litavrin, and V. K. Ronin (eds), *Svod drevneishikh pis'mennykh izvestii o slavianakh*, Moscow: 'Vostochnaia literatura' RAN, pp. 65–74.

Ivanova, O. V. (1995a), 'Chudesa Sv. Dimitriia Solunskogo', in S. A. Ivanov, G. G. Litavrin, and V. K. Ronin (eds), *Svod drevneishikh pis'mennykh izvestii o slavianakh*, Moscow: 'Vostochnaia literatura' RAN, pp. 91–211.

— (1995b), 'Isidor Sevil'skii', in S. A. Ivanov, G. G. Litavrin, and V. K. Ronin (eds), *Svod drevneishikh pis'mennykh izvestii o slavianakh*, Moscow: 'Vostochnaia literatura' RAN, pp. 353–8.

Ivison, E. A. (1996), 'Burial and urbanism at late antique and early Byzantine Corinth (c. AD 400–700)', in N. Christie and S. T. Loseby (eds), *Towns in Transition. Urban Evolution in Late Antiquity and the Early Middle Ages*, Aldershot: Scolar Press, pp. 99–125.

Jacoby, D. (1991–1992), 'Silk in western Byzantium before the fourth crusade', *Byzantinische Zeitschrift*, 84–5, pp. 452–500.

Jaffé, P., ed. (1885), *Regesta pontificium Romanorum ab condita ecclesia ad annum post Christum natum MCXCVIII*, Leipzig: Veit.

Jenkins, R. H. J. (1948), 'The flight of Samonas', *Speculum*, 23, pp. 217–35.

— (1955), 'The date of the Slav revolt in Peloponnese under Romanus I', in K. Weitzmann (ed.), *Late Classical and Mediaeval Studies in Honor of Albert Mathias Friend, Jr.*, Princeton: Princeton University Press, pp. 204–11.

Jones, A. H. M. (1956), 'Numismatics and history', in R. A. G. Carson and C. H. V. Sutherland (eds), *Essays in Roman Coinage Presented to Harold Mattingly*, Oxford: Oxford University Press, pp. 25–36.

Jovanović, V. (1976), 'Über den frühmittelalterlichen Schmuck von Cečen auf Kosovo', *Balcanoslavica*, 5, pp. 123–45.

Kalaitzakis, P. (1995–1997), 'Oungroi Tourkoi ston helladiko khoro kata ton 10o aiona', *Vyzantinos Domos*, 8–9, pp. 211–16.

— (1996), 'Autokratoras e agios? To koinoniko kai politistiko hypobathro henos dilemmatos kai he periptose tou Hosiou Louka (896–7 Febr. 953 m. Ch.)', *Byzantinai Meletai. Diethnes Epistemonike Hepeteris Byzantines kai Metabyzantines Ereunes*, 7, pp. 518–28.

Kalantzi-Sbyraki, E. (2004), 'To nesi ton Spetson kata tous "skoteinous chronous"', in I. Kakouris, S. Choulia, and T. Albani (eds), *Thorakion. Aphieroma ste mneme tou Paulou Lazaride*, Athens: Ypourgeio Politismou, Genike Dieuthynse Archaioteton kai Politistikes Klironomias, Dieuthynse Metavyzantinon Archaioteton, pp. 149–58.

Kaldellis, A. (2004), *Procopius of Caesarea. Tyranny, History, and Philosophy at the End of Antiquity*, Philadelphia: University of Pennsylvania Press.

— (2007), *Hellenism in Byzantium. The Transformations of Greek Identity and the Reception of the Classical Tradition*, Cambridge/New York: Cambridge University Press.

Kalligas, A. G., H. A. Kalligas, and R. S. Stroud (2002), 'A church with a Roman inscription in Tairia, Monemvasia', *Annual of the British School at Athens*, 97, pp. 469–90.

Kalligas, H. (1990), *Byzantine Monemvasia. The Sources*, Monemvasia: Akroneon.

Kalopissi-Verti, S. (2003), 'Epigraphic evidence in Middle-Byzantine churches of the Mani (patronage and art production)', in M. Aspra-Vardavaki (ed.), *Lampedon. Aphieroma ste mneme tes Ntoulas Mourike*, Athens: Panepistemiakes Ekdoseis, pp. 339–54.

Kanonidis, I. (2003), 'Mesobyzantine ephyalomene keramike me leuko pelo apo anaskaphes oikopedon ste Thessalonike', in C. Bakirtzis (ed.), *7o Diethnes Synedrio Mesaionikes Keramikes tes Mesogeiou. Thessalonike, 11–16 oktobriou 1999. Praktika*, Athens: Edition de la Caisse de Recettes Archéologiques, pp. 71–6.

Kaplan, M. (1992), *Les hommes et la terre à Byzance du VIe au XIe siècle. Propriété et exploitation du sol*, Paris: Publications de la Sorbonne.

Karagiannopoulos, I. (1971), 'Zur Frage der Slavenansiedlungen auf dem Peloponnes', *Revue des Etudes Sud-Est-Européennes*, 9, pp. 443–60.

— (1984), 'Wurde Philippoi von Krum im J. 812 erobert?', *Godishnik na Sofiiskiia Universitet 'Kliment Ohridski'. Istoricheski Fakultet*, 76: 2, pp. 217–22.

— (1989), *Les Slaves en Macédoine. La prétendue interruption des communications entre Constantinople et Thessalonique du 7e au 9e siècle*, Athens: Comité National Grec des Etudes du Sud-Est Européen.

— (1990), 'To kiborio tes Ekklesias tes Korinthou', *Lakonikai spoudai*, 10, pp. 79–85.

— (1996), 'Zur Frage der Slavenansiedlung im griechischen Raum', in A. Hohlweg (ed.), *Byzanz und seine Nachbarn*, Munich: Südosteuropa-Gesellschaft, pp. 177–218.

Karagiorgou, O. (2001a), 'Demetrias and Thebes: the fortunes and misfortunes of two Thessalian port cities', in L. Lavan (ed.), *Recent Research in Late-Antique Urbanism*, Portsmouth: Journal of Roman Archaeology, pp. 182–215.

— (2001b), 'LR2: a container for the military annona on the Danubian border?', in S. Kingsley and M. Decker (eds), *Economy and Exchange in the East Mediterranean during Late Antiquity. Proceedings of a Conference at Somerville College, Oxford – 29th May, 1999*, Oxford: Oxbow Books, pp. 129–66.

Karamanoli-Siganidou, M. (1973–1974), 'Edessa', *Archaiologikon Deltion*, 29: 2, pp. 709–10.

Kardaras, G. (2005), 'The episode of Bousas (586/7) and the use of siege engines by the Avars', *Byzantinoslavica*, 63, pp. 53–65.

Kardulias, P. N. (1992), 'Estimating population at ancient military sites: the use of historical and contemporary analogy', *American Antiquity*, 57: 2, pp. 276–87.

— (1993), 'Anthropology and population estimates for the Byzantine fortress at Isthmia', in T. E. Gregory (ed.), *The Corinthia in the Roman Period Including the Papers Given at a Symposium Held at the Ohio State University on 7–9 March, 1991*, Ann Arbor: Journal of Roman Archaeology Supplementary Series, pp. 139–48.

— (2005), *From Classical to Byzantine: Social Evolution in Late Antiquity and the Fortress at Isthmia, Greece*, Oxford: Archaeopress.
Karivieri, A. (1998), 'The Athenian lamp industry and lamp trade from the fourth to the sixth century', in N. Cambi and E. Marin (eds), *Radovi XIII. Međunarodnog Kongresa za starokršćansku arheologiju. Split-Poreč (25.9.–1.10. 1994)*, Vatican/Split: Pontificio Istituto di Archeologia Cristiana/Arheološki Muzej, pp. 421–8.
— (2001), 'Anaskaphe sten Arethousa to 2001', *To Archaiologiko ergo ste Makedonia kai Thrake*, 15, pp. 181–6.
Karydas, N. (1998), 'Byzantine mone sten odo Theseos', *To Archaiologiko ergo ste Makedonia kai Thrake*, 12, pp. 151–64.
Katsambalos, K. and K. Loverdou-Tsigarida (1995), 'Magnetic prospection at sites of archaeological interest: the castle of Platamon', in I. Liritzis and G. Tsokas (eds), *Archaeometry in South Eastern Europe. Second Conference in Delphi, 19th–21st April 1991*, Rixensart: Conseil de l'Europe, pp. 471–8.
Katsaros, V. (2001), 'Agnosto ereipomeno byzantino monasteri sten Kake Skala tes Klokobas', in K. Mauropoulou-Tsioume and E. Kyriakoudes (eds), *Aphieroma ste mneme tou Sotere Kissa*, Thessaloniki: University Studio Press, pp. 135–60.
Katsougiannopoulou, C. (2001), 'Einige Überlegungen zum byzantinischen Friedhof in Tigani auf dem Peloponnes', in E. Pohl, U. Recker, and C. Theune (eds), *Archäologisches Zellwerk. Beiträge zur Kulturgeschichte in Europa und Asien. Festschrift für Helmut Roth zum 60. Geburtstag*, Rahden: Marie Leidorf, pp. 461–9.
Kavvadia-Spondyle, A. (2002), 'Protobyzantine Pylia', in P. G. Themelis and V. Konti (eds), *Protobyzantine Messene kai Olympia. Aktikos kai agrotikos khoros ste Dytike Peloponneso. Praktika tou Diethnous symposiou, Athena, 29–30 maiou 1998*, Athens: Hetaireia Messeniakon Arkhaiologikon Spoudon/Institouto Byzantinon Ereunon, pp. 219–28.
Kazanaki-Lappa, M. (2000), 'Athens from Late Antiquity to the Turkish conquest', in C. Bouras, M. B. Sakellariou, K. S. Staikos, and E. Touloupa (eds), *Athens from the Classical Period to the Present Day (5th century B.C.–A.D. 2000)*, New Castle, DE: Oak Knoll Press, pp. 196–219.
Kazhdan, A. P. (1978), 'Some questions addressed to the scholars who believe in the authenticity of Kaminiates' "Capture of Thessalonica"', *Byzantinische Zeitschrift*, 71: 2, pp. 301–14.
Kepeska, L. (1992), 'Slovenska nekropola kaj s. Dunje-Mariovo', *Macedoniae Acta Archaeologica*, 13, pp. 245–52.
Keramopoulos, A. D. (1926), 'Palaiai christianikai kai byzantiakai taphai en Thebais', *Archaiologikon Deltion*, 10, pp. 124–36.
Kilian, K. (1980), 'Zu einigen früh- und hochmittelalterlichen Funden aus der Burg von Tiryns', *Archäologisches Korrespondenzblatt*, 10, pp. 281–90.
Kiourtzian, G. (1991), 'Note prosopographique sur une inscription du rempart de Thessalonique (861/862)', *Revue des Etudes Byzantines*, 49, pp. 247–53.
— (1997), 'Le Psaume 131 et son usage funéraire dans la Grèce, les Balkans et la Cappadoce la haute époque byzantine', *Cahiers Archéologiques*, 45, pp. 31–9.
— (2000), *Recueil des inscriptions grecques chrétiennes des Cyclades, de la fin du IIIe au VIIe siècle après J.-C.*, Paris: De Boccard.
Kislinger, E. (1992), 'Lakedaimonia, Demenna kai to Khronikon tes Monembasias', *Byzantinai Meletai. Diethnes Epistemonike Hepeteris Byzantines kai Metabyzantines Ereunes*, 3, pp. 103–21.

— (1996), 'Byzantinische Kupfermünzen aus Sizilien (7.–9. Jh.) im historischen Kontext', *Jahrbuch der österreichischen Byzantinistik*, 45, pp. 25–36.
— (1998), 'Ein Angriff zu viel', *Byzantinische Zeitschrift*, 91, pp. 49–58.
— (2001), *Regionalgeschichte als Quellenproblem. Die Chronik von Monembasia und das sizilianische Demenna. Eine historisch-topographische Studie*, Vienna: Verlag der Österreichischen Akademie der Wissenschaften.
Kiss, A. (1977), *Avar Cemeteries in County Baranya*, Budapest: Akademiai kiadó.
— (1996), *Das awarenzeitlich-gepidische Gräberfeld von Kölked-Feketekapu A*, Innsbruck: Universitätsverlag Wagner.
— (2001), *Das awarenzeitliche Gräberfeld in Kölked-Feketekapu B*, Budapest: Magyar Nemzeti Múzeum/Magyar Tudományos Akadémia Régészeti Intézete.
Kissas, S. K. (1988), 'He anaskaphe sten Kolchida Kilkis', *To Archaiologiko ergo ste Makedonia kai Thrake*, 2, pp. 207–17.
— (1990), 'Molybdoboulla apo ta hyperoa tes Agias Sophias Thessalonikes', *Studies in Byzantine Sigillography*, 2, pp. 185–202.
Kitromilides, P. M. (1998), 'On the intellectual content of Greek nationalism: Paparrigopoulos, Byzantium and the Great Idea', in D. Ricks and P. Magdalino (eds), *Byzantium and the Modern Greek Identity*, Aldershot/Brookfield: Ashgate, pp. 25–33.
Koder, J. (1976), 'Arethas von Kaisareia und die sogenannte Chronik von Monemvasia', *Jahrbuch der österreichischen Byzantinistik*, 25, pp. 75–80.
— (1986), 'Anmerkungen zu den Miracula Sancti Demetrii', in N. A. Stratos (ed.), *Byzantion. Aphieroma ston Andrea N Strato*, Athens: no publisher, pp. 523–38.
— (1998), *Aigaion Pelagos: die nördliche Ägäis*, Vienna: Verlag der Österreichischen Akademie der Wissenschaften.
— (2003), 'Griechische Identitäten im Mittelalter. Aspekte einer Entwicklung', in A. Avramea, A. Laiou, and E. Chrysos (eds), *Byzantio kratos kai koinonia. Mneme Nikou Oikonomidou*, Athens: Institouto Byzantinon Ereunon, pp. 297–319.
Koder, J. and F. Hild (1976), *Tabula Imperii Byzantinii 1: Hellas und Thessalia*, Vienna: Verlag der Österreichische Akademie der Wissenschaften.
Koilakou, C. (1992), 'Theba', *Archaiologikon Deltion*, 47, pp. 72–84.
Kolias, T. G. (2003), 'Byzance dans les manuels d'histoire grecs', in M.-F. Auzépy (ed.), *Byzance en Europe*, Paris: Presses Universitaires de Vincennes, pp. 61–71.
Kollautz, A. (1983), 'Orient und Okzident am Ausgang des 6. Jh. Johannes, Abt von Biclarum, Bischof von Gerona, der Chronist des westgotischen Spaniens', *Byzantina*, 12, pp. 463–506.
Kollautz, A. and H. Miyakawa (1970), *Geschichte und Kultur eines völkerwanderungszeitlichen Nomadenvolkes: Die Jou-Jan der Mongolei und die Awaren im Mitteleuropa*, Klagenfurt/Bonn: Rudolf Habelt.
Kollias, I. E. (2004), 'Treis mesobyzantines ekklesies tes Astypalaias', in I. Kakouris, S. Choulia, and T. Albani (eds), *Thorakion. Aphieroma ste mneme tou Paulou Lazaride*, Athens: Ypourgeio Politismou, Genike Dieuthynse Archaioteton kai Politistikes Klironomias, Dieuthynse Metavyzantinon Archaioteton, pp. 137–48.
Koltsida-Makri, I. (1996), *Byzantina molybdoboulla sylloges Orphanide-Nikolaide Nomismatikou Mouseiou Athenon*, Athens: Khristianiki Archaiologiki Hetaireia.
— (2000), 'He byzantine Thessalonike mesa apo te sigillographike martyria (8os–10os ai.)', in P. Adam-Veleni (ed.), *To nomisma sto makedoniko khoro. Praktika B' epistemonikes synanteses. Nomismatokopeia, kyklophoria, eikonographia,*

istoria. Archaioi, byzantinoi kai neoteroi chronoi, Thessaloniki: University Studio Press, pp. 243–67.

Konidares, G. (1952), 'He prote mneia tes episkopes Vardarioton Tourkon hypo ton Tessalonikes', *Theologia*, 23, pp. 87–94.

Konstantakopoulou, A. (1985), 'L'éparque de Thessalonique: les origines d'une institution administrative (VIIIe–IXe siècles)', in T. P. Giochalas (ed.), *Hellenikes anakoinoseis sto E' Diethnes Synedrio Spoudon Notioanatolikes Europes. Beligradi: 11–17 Septembriou 1984. Communications grecques présentées au Ve Congrès International des Etudes du Sud-Est Européen. Belgrade: 11–17 septembre 1984*, Athens: Hellenike Epitrope Spoudon Notioanatolikis Europis, pp. 157–62.

Konstantinos, D. (1981), 'Naupaktos', *Archaiologikon Deltion*, 36, p. 293.

Konstantios, D. N. (1981), 'Neotera stoicheia se byzantinous naous tes Aitoloakarnanias', *Epeirotika Chronika*, 23, pp. 266–84.

— (1992), 'Epeiros. He archaiologike ereuna gia te byzantine kai metabyzantine periodo (problemata, synkomide, aitemata, prooptikes)', *Epeirotika Chronika*, 30, pp. 61–87.

Konstantopoulos, K. M. (1902), 'Byzantiaka molybdoboulla en to Ethniko Mouseio Athenon', *Journal International d'Archéologie Numismatique*, 5, pp. 189–228.

— (1906), 'Byzantiaka molybdoboulla en to Ethniko Mouseio Athenon', *Journal International d'Archéologie Numismatique*, 9.

— (1930), *Byzantiaka molybdoboulla sylloge Anastasiou K.P. Stamoule*, Athens: Typois Hetaireias P.D. Sakellarios.

— (1931), 'Epigraphe ek tou naou tou agiou Ioannou Mankoute', *Epeteris Hetaireias Byzantinon Spoudon*, 8, pp. 244–55.

Konti, V. (1985), 'Symbole sten historike geographia tes Arkadias (395–1209)', *Symmeikta*, 6, pp. 91–124.

— (1997), 'Biotechnike drasterioteta sten perioche ton Halieon Ermionidas (6os–7os ai.)', in T. A. Gritsopoulos and K. L. Kotsonis (eds), *Praktika tou E' diethnous synedriou Peloponnesiakon spoudon. Argos-Nauplion, 6–10 septembriou 1995*, Athens: Hetaireia Peloponnesiakon Spoudon, pp. 335–56.

Kontogiannis, N. D. (2002), 'A fragment of a Chinese marbled ware bowl from Methoni, Greece', *Bizantinistica. Rivista di studi bizantini e slavi*, 4, pp. 39–46.

Kordosi, M. S. (1981a), 'He slabike epoikese sten Peloponneso me base ta slabika toponymia', *Dodone. Istoria kai archaiologia*, 10, pp. 381–427.

— (1981b), *Symbole sten historia kai topographia tes perioches Korinthou stous mesous chronous*, Athens: Vivliopoleio D. N. Karavia.

Korres, T. (1998), 'Some remarks on the first major attempts of the Avaroslavs to capture Thessaloniki (597 and 614)', *Byzantina*, 19, pp. 171–85.

— (1999), 'Paratereseis schetikes me ten pempte poliorkia tes Thessalonikes apo tous Slabous (676–678). Palaiotere ereuna kai neoteres ermeneies', *Byzantiaka*, 19, pp. 137–65.

Kosso, C. K. (1993), 'Public policy and agricultural practice: an archaeological and literary study of late Roman Greece', PhD dissertation, Chicago: University of Illinois at Chicago.

Kotzias, N. C. (1952), 'Anaskaphai tes basilikes tou Laureotikou Olympou', *Praktika tes en Athenais Archaiologikes Hetaireias*, 107, pp. 92–128.

Kougeas, S. B. (1912), 'Epi tou kaloumenou chronikou "Peri tes ktiseos tes Monemvasias"', *Neos Hellenomnemon*, 9, pp. 473–80.

Koukoules, P. (1926), 'Tsakonia kai Tsakones', *Byzantinische Zeitschrift*, 26, pp. 317–27.
— (1936), 'Peri ten byzantinen oikian', *Epeteris Hetaireias Byzantinon Spoudon*, 12, pp. 76–138 and 583–4.
Koukouli-Chryssanthaki, C. and G. Karadedos (1999), 'Anaskaphikes ereunes sto theatro ton Philippon', *To Ackhaiologiko ergo ste Makedonia kai Thrake*, 13, pp. 69–86.
Koumousi-Vgenopoulou, A. (1996), 'Anaskaphikes "martyries" tou seismou tou 552 m. Ch. sten Patra', *Archaiologika analekta ex Athenon*, 29–31, pp. 51–6.
Kourelis, K. (2003), 'Monuments of rural archaeology: medieval settlements of northwestern Peloponnese', PhD dissertation, Philadelphia: University of Philadelphia.
Kourenta-Raptaki, A. (2004), 'Palaiochristianike Antikyra. Mia prote proseggise', in I. Kakouris, S. Choulia, and T. Albani (eds), *Thorakion. Aphieroma ste mneme tou Paulou Lazaride*, Athens: Ypourgeio Politismou, Genike Dieuthynse Archaioteton kai Politistikes Klironomias, Dieuthynse Metavyzantinon Archaioteton, pp. 109–22.
Kourenta-Raptaki, A., C. Koilakou, and M. Galani-Krikou (1994), 'Nomos Boiotias. 1e Ephoreia Byzantinon Archaioteton', *Archaiologikon Deltion*, 49, pp. 109–27.
Kourinou-Pikoula, E. (1998), 'O naos tou Hosiou Nikonos tou Metanoiete', *Lakonikai spoudai*, 14, pp. 89–104.
Kourkoutidou-Nikolaidou, E. (1972), 'Chalkoi stauroi ek tou Perithesorio', *Archaiologika analekta ex Athenon*, 5, pp. 375–81.
— (1989), 'He basilike tou Mouseiou Philippon', *To Archaiologiko ergo ste Makedonia kai Thrake*, 3, pp. 465–71.
— (1995), 'Philippoi. Apo ten palaiochristianike ste byzantine pole', in *Diethnes Symposio 'Byzantine Makedonia, 324–1430 m. Kh.', Thessalonike, 29–31 Oktobriou 1992*, Thessaloniki: Hetaireia Makedonikon Spoudon, pp. 171–82 and 378.
Kourkoutidou-Nikolaidou, E. and M. Michailidis (2002), *He basilike tes Agias Paraskeus sten Kozane. Paratereseis se hena mnemeio tou 2 misou tou 6ou ai.*, Thessaloniki: Hypourgeion Politismou Ephoreia Byzantinon Archaioteton Thessalonikes.
Koutava-Delivoria, V. (2001), 'Qui était Danielis?', *Byzantion*, 71: 1, pp. 98–109.
Koutrakou, N. A. (1947), *Byzantinai meletai VI. Hoi Slaboi en Peloponneso*, Thessalonike: Hetaireia Makedonikon Spoudon.
— (1993), 'He eikona tes Spartes. Ideologematika schemata kai pragmatikoteta stous mesous byzantinous chronous', *Byzantinai Meletai. Diethnes Epistemonike Hepeteris Byzantines kai Metabyzantines Ereunes*, 4, pp. 222–43.
Kovrig, I. (1963), *Das awarenzeitliche Gräberfeld von Alattyán*, Budapest: Akademiai kiadó.
Kranioti, L. (1984), 'Myrodato', *Archaiologikon Deltion*, 39, pp. 281–3.
Kravari, V. (1998), 'L'hellénisation des Slaves de Macédoine orientale au témoignage des anthroponymes', in M. Balard, J. Beaucamp, J.-C. Cheynet, C. Jolivet-Lévy, M. Kaplan, B. Martin-Hisard, P. Pagès, C. Piganiol, and J.-P. Sodini (eds), *Eupsychia. Mélanges offerts Hélène Ahrweiler*, Paris: Publications de la Sorbonne, pp. 387–95.

— (2005), 'Le prénom des paysans en Macédoine orientale (Xe–XIVe siècle)', in J. Lefort, C. Morrisson, and J.-P. Sodini (eds), *Les villages dans l'Empire byzantin, IVe–XVe siècles*, Paris: Lethielleux, pp. 301–6.
Kresten, O. (1977), 'Zur Echtheit des sigillion des Kaisers Nikephoros I. für Patras', *Römische Historische Mitteilungen*, 19, pp. 15–78.
Krivov, M. V. (1995), 'Siriiskii "Smeshannyi khronikon"', in S. A. Ivanov, G. G. Litavrin, and V. K. Ronin (eds), *Svod drevneishikh pis'mennykh izvestii o slavianakh*, Moscow: 'Vostochnaia literatura' RAN, pp. 517–18.
Kroll, J. H., G. C. Miles, and S. G. Miller (1973), 'An early Byzantine and a late Turkish hoard from the Athenian Agora', *Hesperia*, 42, pp. 301–9.
Krsmanović, B. (2008), *The Byzantine Province in Change (on the Threshold between the 10th and the 11th Century)*, Belgrade/Athens: Institute for Byzantine Studies/Institute for Byzantine Research.
Kyriakidis, S. P. (1941), 'Sissinios, strategos tes Hellados', in *Epitymbion Chrestou Tsounta*, Athens: no publisher, pp. 680–3.
— (1947), *Byzantinai meletai VI. Hoi Slaboi en Peloponneso*, Thessalonike: Hetaireia Makedonikon Spoudon.
Kyriaki-Wassiliou, A. (2004), 'Neue Siegel der 1. Hälfte des 9. Jh. aus Südostbulgarien. Mit einem Appendix zu den Drugubiten', in V. Iotov and I. Lazarenko (eds), *Numizmatichni i sfragistichni prinosi kăm istoriiata na zapadnoto Chernomorie. Mezhdunarodna konferenciia, Varna, 12–15 septemvri 2001 g.*, Varna: Zograf, pp. 246–52.
Kyriakopoulos, K. T. (1976), *Agiou Petrou episkopou Argous bios kai logoi*, Athens: Hieras Metropoleos Argolidos.
Kyrou, A. K. (1995), 'Periplaneseis hagion leipsanon kai mia agnoste kastropoliteia ston Argoliko', *Peloponnisiaka*, 21, pp. 97–118.
Laiou, A. E. and C. Morrisson (2007), *The Byzantine Economy*, Cambridge/New York: Cambridge University Press.
Lampropoulou, A. (1994), *Ho asketismos sten Peloponneso kata te mese Byzantine periodo*, Athens: Idryma Goulandri-Horn.
— (2004), 'Ho monachismos sten Achaia kata te mesobyzantine periodo: synthekes exaploses kai anaptyxes', in V. Konti (ed.), *Ho monachismos sten Peloponneso 40s–15os ai.*, Athens: Institouto Byzantinon Ereunon, pp. 87–112.
Lampropoulou, A. and A. G. Moutzali (1993), 'Nea stoichia gia ten episkope Kernitzas', in *Praktika tou IV Diethnous Synedriou Peloponnesiakon Spoudon (Korinthos, 9–16 Septembriou 1990)*, Athens: Hetaireia Peloponnesiakon Spoudon, pp. 373–86.
— (1997), 'Ho mesobyzantinos naos tou Agiou Nikolaou Aigialeias. Symbole sten istoria tes mones Taxiarkhon', *Symmeikta*, 11, pp. 323–50.
Lampropoulou, A., I. Anagnostakis, V. Konti, M. Leontsini, and A. Panopoulou (1996), 'Ho monachismos sten Peloponneso kata te mese byzantine periodo', in K. Nikolaou (ed.), *Taseis tou orthodoxou monachismou, 9os–20os aiones. Praktika tou Diethnous Symposiou pou diorganotheke sta plaisia tou Programmatos 'Hoi dromoi tou orthodoxou monachismou. Poreuthentes mathete'. Thessalonike, 28 Septembriou–2 Oktobriou 1994*, Athens: Institouto Byzantinon Ereunon, pp. 77–103.
Lampropoulou, A., I. Anagnostakis, V. Konti, and A. Panopoulou (2001), 'Symbole sten ermeneia ton archaiologikon tekmerion tes Peloponnesou kata tous

"skoteinous aiones"', in E. Kountoura-Galake (ed.), *Hoi skoteinoi aiones tou Byzantiou (7os–9os ai.)*, Athens: Ethniko Idryma Ereunon/Institouto Byzantinon Ereunon, pp. 189–229.

Lampsidis, O. (1982), *Ho ek Pontou hosios Nikon ho Metanoeite. Keimena, scholia*, Athens: Epitrope Pontiakon Meleton.

Laskaris, N. G. (2000), *Monuments funéraires paléochrétiens (et byzantins) de Grèce*, Athens: Editions Historiques Stéfanos D. Basilopoulos.

Lauer, R. (1993), 'Jakob Philipp Fallmerayer und die Slaven', in E. Thurnher (ed.), *Jakob Philipp Fallmerayer. Wissenschaftler, Politiker, Schriftsteller*, Innsbruck: Universitätsverlag Wagner, pp. 125–57.

— (1996), 'Gräkoslaven und Germanoslaven bei Jakob Philipp Fallmerayer', in R. Lauer and P. Schreiner (eds), *Die Kultur Griechenlands in Mittelalter und Neuzeit. Bericht über das Kolloquium der Südosteuropa-Kommission 28.–31. Oktober 1992*, Göttingen: Vandenhoeck & Ruprecht, pp. 31–8.

Laurent, J. (1895), 'Sur la date des églises St. Démétrius et Ste. Sophie à Thessalonique', *Byzantinische Zeitschrift*, 4, pp. 420–34.

Laurent, V. (1940), 'Ho Vardarioton etoi Tourkon (L'évêque des Vardariotes, c'est-à-dire des Turcs)', in S. Georgiev, V. Beshevliev, and I. Duichev (eds), *Sbornik v pamet na Prof. Petăr Nikov*, Sofia: Kultura, pp. 275–89.

— (1943), 'L'érection de la métropole d'Athènes et le statut ecclésiastique de l'Illyricum au VIIIe siècle', *Revue des Etudes Byzantines*, 1, pp. 58–72.

— (1962), *Les sceaux byzantins du Médaillier Vatican*, Vatican: Biblioteca Apostolica Vaticana.

Lazaridis, P. (1960), 'Anaskaphe Dagla para to Markopoulon Mesogeion', *Archaiologikon Deltion*, 16, pp. 69–72.

— (1965), 'Nea Anchialos', *Archaiologikon Deltion*, 20: 2, pp. 326–34.

— (1973), 'Mone Skripous', *Archaiologikon Deltion*, 28, pp. 290–3.

Lefort, J. (1979), 'En Macédoine orientale au Xe siècle: habitat rural, communes et domaines', in *Occident et Orient au Xe siècle. Actes du IXe Congrès de la Société des Historiens Médiévalistes de l'Enseignement Supérieur Public (Dijon, 2–4 juin 1978)*, Paris: Les Belles Lettres, pp. 251–79.

— (2002), 'The rural economy, seventh to twelfth centuries', in A. E. Laiou (ed.), *The Economic History of Byzantium from the Seventh through the Fifteenth Century*, Washington, DC: Dumbarton Oaks Research Library and Collection, pp. 231–310.

— (2005), 'Les villages de Macédoine orientale au Moyen Age (Xe–XIVe siècle)', in J. Lefort, C. Morrisson, and J.-P. Sodini (eds), *Les villages dans l'Empire byzantin, IVe–XVe siècles*, Paris: Lethielleux, pp. 289–99.

Lemerle, P. (1945), *Philippes et la Macédoine orientale à l'époque chrétienne et byzantine. Recherches d'histoire et d'archéologie*, Paris: De Boccard.

— (1951), 'Une province byzantine: le Péloponnèse', *Byzantion*, 21, pp. 341–53.

— (1963a), 'La chronique improprement dite de Monemvasie: le contexte historique et légendaire', *Revue des Etudes Byzantines*, 21, pp. 5–49.

— (1963b), 'La vie ancienne de saint Athanase l'Athonite composée au début du XIe siècle par Athanase de Lavra', in *Le millénaire du Mont Athos, 963–1963. Etudes et mélanges*, Chevetogne: Editions de Chevetogne, pp. 60–100.

— (1971), *Le premier humanisme byzantin: notes et remarques sur enseignement et culture à Byzance des origines au Xe siècle*, Paris: Presses Universitaires de France.

— (1981), *Les plus anciens recueils des Miracles de Saint Démétrius et la pénétration des Slaves dans les Balkans. II: Commentaire*, Paris: Editions du Centre National de la Recherche Scientifique.
Lemerle, P., A. Guillou, and N. Svoronos (1970), *Actes de Lavra*, Paris: P. Lethielleux.
Leroy, J. (1953), 'S. Athanase et la Règle de S. Benoît', *Revue d'Ascétique et de Mystique*, 29, pp. 108–22.
— (1963), 'La conversion de S. Athanase l'Athonite à l'idéal cénobitique et l'influence studite', in *Le millénaire du Mont Athos, 963–1963. Etudes et mélanges*, Chevetogne: Editions de Chevetogne, pp. 101–20.
— (1964), 'Les deux Vies de saint Athanase l'Athonite', *Analecta Bollandiana*, 82, pp. 409–29.
Leszka, M. J. (2005), 'Kilka uwag na temat śmierci Prebuda, kśięcia Rynchinów', *Slavia Antiqua*, 46, pp. 57–62.
Liakos, S. N. (1971), *Ti pragmati esan hoi sklabenoi (=Asseclae) epoikoi tou thematos Thessalonikos (Drougouvitai, Rynchinoi, Saroudatoi)*, Thessaloniki: no publisher.
— (1977), *Ti esan ethnophyletika hoi Abarosklabenoi: protomosaionikoi epoikoi tes Peloponnesou*, Thessaloniki: no publisher.
Liankouras, A. G. (1965), 'Keramidi', *Archaiologikon Deltion*, 20: 2, p. 321.
Liebeschuetz, J. H. W. G. (2000), 'The government of the late Roman city, with special reference to Thessaloniki', in J. Burke and R. Scott (eds), *Byzantine Macedonia: Identity, Image, and History. Papers from the Melbourne Conference, July 1995*, Melbourne: Australian Association for Byzantine Studies, pp. 116–27.
— (2001), *Decline and Fall of the Roman City*, Oxford: Oxford University Press.
Likhachev, N. P. (1924), 'Datirovannye vizantiiske pechati', *Izvestiia Rossiiskoi Akademii istorii material'noi kul'tury*, 3, pp. 153–224.
— (1991), *Molivdovuly grecheskogo Vostoka*, Moscow: Nauka.
Lilčić, V. (1996), 'Nauchno-istrazhuvachki proekt severo-zapadna Makedonija vo docnata antika i sredniot vek Polog, Kichevija, Poreche', *Makedonsko nasledstvo*, 2, pp. 53–84.
Lilie, R.-J. (1977), '"Thrakien" und "Thrakesion". Zur byzantinischen Provinzorganisation am Ende des 7. Jahrhunderts', *Jahrbuch der österreichischen Byzantinistik*, 26, pp. 7–47.
Limousin, E. (1999), 'L'administration byzantine du Péloponnèse (Xe–XIIe siècle)', in J. Renard (ed.), *Le Péloponnèse. Archéologie et histoire. Actes de la rencontre internationale de Lorient (12–15 mai 1998)*, Rennes: Presses Universitaires de Rennes, pp. 295–311.
Litavrin, G. G. (1985), 'Iz kommentariia k 49-oi glave truda Konstantina Bagrianorodnogo "Ob upravlenii imperiei"', *Byzantina*, 13: 2, pp. 1347–53.
— (2004), 'Peloponnesskaia magnatka Danilikha: legenda i deistvitel'nost", in N. A. Makarov, A. V. Chernecov, and N. V. Lopatin (eds), *Vostochnaia Evropa v srednevekov'e. K 80-letiiu Valentina Vasil'evicha Sedova*, Moscow: Nauka, pp. 20–6.
Lounghis, T. C. (1973), 'Sur la date du "De Thematibus"', *Revue des Etudes Byzantines*, 31, pp. 299–305.
— (2001), 'Some gaps in a social evolution theory as research directions', in E. Kountoura-Galake (ed.), *Hoi skoteinoi aiones tou Byzantiou (7os–9os ai.)*, Athens: Ethniko Idryma Ereunon/Institouto Byzantinon Ereunon, pp. 171–88.

Loverdou-Tsigarida, K. (1993), 'Nea anaskaphika euremata sto Kastro tou Platamona', *To Archaiologiko ergo ste Makedonia kai Thrake*, 7, pp. 235–9.
— (1997), 'Marmarino leitourgiko skeuos apo to kastro tou Platamona', *Mouseio Byzantinou Politismou*, 4, pp. 54–70.
Loverdou-Tsigarida, K., V. Messis, E. Mastora, V. Karagianni, and M. Kontogiannopulou (2001), 'To telos tes anaskaphes ereunas sten Krania N. Panteleemona Pierias', *To Arkhaiologiko ergo ste Makedonia kai Thrake*, 15, pp. 415–23.
MacDowall, D. (1965), 'The Byzantine coin hoard found at Isthmia', *Archaeology*, 18, pp. 264–7.
Mackay, P. A. (1963), 'Procopius' De Aedificiis and the topography of Thermopylae', *American Journal of Archaeology*, 67, pp. 241–55.
Macrides, R. J. (1990), 'Subversion and loyalty in the cult of St. Demetrios', *Byzantinoslavica*, 51: 2, pp. 189–97.
Madgearu, A. (2005), 'Studiu introductiv', in V. Cotiugă (ed.), *To peri tes ktiseos tes Monemvasias Chronikon. Cronica Monemvasiei*, Iaşi: Performantica, pp. 13–84.
Magdalino, P. (1990), 'St. Demetrios and Leo VI', *Byzantinoslavica*, 51: 2, pp. 198–201.
Makris, G. (1997), *Ignatios Diakonos und die Vita des Hl. Gregorios Dekapolites*, Stuttgart/Leipzig: B. G. Teubner.
Makropoulou, D. (2002), 'Topographika nomou Kilkis', *To Archaiologiko ergo ste Makedonia kai Thrake*, 16, pp. 361–74.
Makropoulou, D. and A. Tzitzimpase (1993), 'Sostike anaskaphike ereuna sten hodo Kassandrou 90', *To Archaiologiko ergo ste Makedonia kai Thrake*, 7, pp. 355–72.
Malamut, E. (1988), *Les îles de l'Empire byzantin (VIIIe–XIIe siècles)*, Paris: Université de Paris I-Panthéon-Sorbonne.
Malenko, V. (1985), 'Ranosrednovekovnata materijalna kultura vo Okhrid i Okhridsko', in M. Apostolski (ed.), *Okhrid i Okhridsko niz istorijata*, Skopje: Sobranie na opshtina Okhrid, pp. 269–315.
Malingoudis, P. (1981), *Studien zu den slawischen Ortsnamen Griechenlands 1. Slawische Flurnamen aus der messenischen Mani*, Wiesbaden: Franz Steiner.
— (1983), 'Toponymy and history. Observations concerning the Slavonic toponymy of the Peloponnese', *Cyrillomethodianum*, 7, pp. 99–111.
— (1985), 'Za materialnata kultura na rannoslavianskite plemena v Gărciia', *Istoricheski pregled*, 41: 9–10, pp. 64–71.
— (1987), 'Slaviano-grecheskii simbioz v Vizantii v svete toponimii', *Vizantiiskii Vremennik*, 48, pp. 44–52.
— (1988), *Slaboi ste mesaionike Hellada*, Thessaloniki: Ekdoseis Vanias.
— (1994), 'Zur sozialen und ethnischen Assimilierung der Slaven in Byzanz: der Fall der Rhendakioi', *Godishnik na Sofiiskiia Universitet – Centăr za slaviano-vizantiiski prouchvaniia 'Ivan Duichev'*, 87, pp. 13–20.
Mamaloukos, S. V. (1984), 'Enas agnostos byzantinos naos sten Argolida. Ho Agios Ioannes ho Theologos Paliou Ligouriou', *Deltion tes christianikes archaiologikes hetaireias*, 12, pp. 409–40.
Maneva, E. (1998), 'La survie des centres paléochrétiens de Macédoine au Haut Moyen Age', in N. Cambi and E. Marin (eds), *Radovi XIII. Međunarodnog*

Kongresa za starokrščansku arheologiju. Split-Poreč (25.9.–1.10. 1994), Vatican/ Split: Pontificio Istituto di Archeologia Cristiana/Arheološki Muzej, pp. 843–58.
Mango, C. (1985), 'On re-reading the Life of St. Gregory the Decapolite', *Byzantina*, 13: 1, pp. 633–46.
— (1995–1996), 'The conversion of the Parthenon into a church: the Tübingen theosophy', *Deltion tes christianikes archaiologikes hetaireias*, 18, pp. 201–3.
Mano-Zisi, Đ. (1958), 'Iskopavanja na Carichinom Gradu 1955 i 1956 godine', *Starinar*, 7–8, pp. 311–28.
Maricq, A. (1952), 'Notes sur les Slaves dans le Péloponnèse et en Bithynie et sur l'emploi de "Slave" comme appellatif', *Byzantion*, 22, pp. 337–56.
Marín, J. R. (1991–1992), 'La "cuestión eslava" en el Peloponeso bizantino (siglos VI–X)', *Bizantion Nea Hellás*, 11–12, pp. 205–44.
Marki, E. (1982), 'Sympleromatika archaiologika stoicheia gia to phrourio Bardariou Thessalonikes', *Makedonika. Syngrama periodikon tes Hetaireias Makedonikon Spoudon*, 22, pp. 133–53.
— (1993), 'Epigraphe tou Basileiou B' Boulgaroktonou apo tou Mylobo', in I. Karagiannopoulos (ed.), *13' Panellenio Historiko Synedrio (29–31 Maiou 1992). Praktika*, Thessaloniki: Ekdoseis Vanias, pp. 133–42.
— (1997a), 'Deux tombeaux monumentaux protobyzantins récemment découverts en Grèce du nord', *Cahiers Archéologiques*, 45, pp. 19–24.
— (1997b), 'Ho Agios Georgios tes Megales kai agnoste epigraphe tou Basileiou B' Boulgaroktonou', in K. Vavouskos (ed.), *Mneme Manole Andronikou*, Thessaloniki: Hetaireia Makedonikon Spoudon, pp. 141–52.
— (2000), 'Anaskaphon Thessalonikes eranismata', *To Archaiologiko ergo ste Makedonia kai Thrake*, 14, pp. 247–57.
— (2001a), 'Kamarotos taphos me toichographies apo ten Pylaia', in C. Mauropoulou-Tsioume and E. Kyriakoudes (eds), *Aphieroma ste mneme tou Sotere Kissa*, Thessaloniki: University Studio Press, pp. 273–81.
— (2001b), 'Taphiko sygkrotema kai naiskos apo te dytike nekropole tes Thessalonikes', *To Archaiologiko ergo ste Makedonia kai Thrake*, 15, pp. 321–30.
Marki, E. and S. Akrivopoulou (2003), 'Anaskaphe agrepaules sto Paliokastro Oraiokastrou', *To Archaiologiko ergo ste Makedonia kai Thrake*, 17, pp. 281–98.
Marki, E. and M. Cheimonopoulou (2003), 'Céramique de l'époque paléochrétienne tardive de la fouille de Louloudies en Piérie', in C. Bakirtzis (ed.), *7o Diethnes Synedrio Mesaionikes Keramikes tes Mesogeiou. Thessalonike, 11–16 oktobriou 1999. Praktika*, Athens: Edition de la Caisse de Recettes Archéologiques, pp. 703–12.
Marki, E. and K. Loverdou-Tsigarida (1994), 'Nomos Pierias. 9e Ephoreia Byzantinon Archaioteton', *Archaiologikon Deltion*, 49, pp. 531–4.
Marki, E. and M. Polychronaki (2000), 'Nomismatikes sygkentroseis kai thesauros apo to episkopiko sygkrotema ton Louloudion', in P. Adam-Veleni (ed.), *To nomisma sto makedoniko choro. Praktika B' epistemonikes synanteses. Nomismatokopeia, kyklophoria, eikonographia, istoria. Archaioi, byzantinoi kai neoteroi chronoi*, Thessaloniki: University Studio Press, pp. 183–94.
Marquart, J. (1903), *Osteuropäische und ostasiatische Streifzüge. Ethnologische und historisch-topographische Studien zur Geschichte des 9. und 10. Jahrhunderts (ca. 840–940)*, Leipzig: Dieterich'sche Verlagsbuchhandlung, T. Weicher.

Martini, W. and C. Steckner (1993), *Das Gymnasium von Samos. Das frühbyzantinische Klostergut*, Bonn: Habelt.

Mastrokostas, E. I. (1971), 'Palaiochristianikai basilikai Drymou Bonitses', *Archaiologika analekta ex Athenon*, 4, pp. 185–95.

Mattingly, H. (1931), 'A late Roman hoard from Corinth', *Numismatic Chronicle*, 11, pp. 229–33.

Maurici, F. (2000), 'Ancora sulle fibbie da cintura di eta bizantina in Sicilia', in R. M. C. Bonacasa (ed.), *Byzantino-Sicula IV. Atti del I Congresso internazionale di archeologia della Sicilia bizantina (Corleone, 28 luglio–2 agosto 1998)*, Palermo: Istituto Siciliano di Studi Bizantini e Neoellenici, pp. 513–57.

Mauropoulou-Tsioumi, C. (1992), *Byzantine Thessaloniki*, Thessaloniki: Rekos.

McCormick, M. (2001), *Origins of the European Economy. Communications and Commerce, A.D. 300–900*, Cambridge: Cambridge University Press.

Megaw, A. H. S. (1931–1932), 'The chronology of some Middle Byzantine churches', *Annual of the British School at Athens*, 32, pp. 90–130.

— (1932–1933), 'Byzantine architecture in Mani', *Annual of the British School at Athens*, 33, pp. 137–62.

— (1966), 'The Skripou screen', *Annual of the British School at Athens*, 61, pp. 1–32.

Megaw, A. H. S. and R. E. Jones (1983), 'Byzantine and allied pottery: a contribution by chemical analysis to problems of origin and distribution', *Annual of the British School at Athens*, 38, pp. 235–63.

Melovski, K. and N. Proeva (1987), 'Makedonija vo deloto *De Thematibus* na Konstantin VII Porfirogenit ', *Živa Antika*, 37: 1–2, pp. 19–37.

Mentzos, A. (1996), 'Lithini "sphragida" eulogias', *Mouseio Byzantinou Politismou*, 3, pp. 18–27.

— (2001), 'Ho glyptos diakosmos tes Agias Sophias ste Thessalonike', in C. Mauropoulou-Tsioume and E. Kyriakoudes (eds), *Aphieroma ste mneme tou Sotere Kissa*, Thessaloniki: University Studio Press, pp. 315–34.

Metcalf, D. M. (1962a), 'The Aegean coastlands under threat: some coins and coin hoards from the reign of Heraclius', *Annual of the British School at Athens*, 57, pp. 14–23.

— (1962b), 'The Slavonic threat to Greece circa 580: some evidence from Athens', *Hesperia*, 31, pp. 134–57.

— (1963), 'The coinage of Thessaloniki, 829–1204, and its place in Balkan monetary history', *Balkan Studies*, 4, pp. 277–88.

— (1965), 'Frankish petty currency from the Areopagus at Athens', *Hesperia*, 34, pp. 203–33.

— (1966), 'Ražba follů Basilia I. a organizace jejích mincoven', *Numismatický sborník*, 9, pp. 95–127.

— (1967), 'How extensive was the issue of folles during the years 775–820?', *Byzantion*, 37, pp. 270–310.

— (1970), 'Interpretation of the Byzantine Rex Regnantium folles of class "A", 970–1030', *Numismatic Chronicle*, 10, pp. 199–219.

— (1973), 'Corinth in the ninth century: the numismatic evidence', *Hesperia*, 42, pp. 180–251.

— (1974), 'Byzantine coins minted in Central Greece under Basil II', *Nomismatika Chronika*, 3, pp. 21–5.

— (1976), *The Copper Coinage of Thessalonica under Justin I*, Vienna: Verlag der Österreichischen Akademie der Wissenschaften.
— (1979), *Coinage of South-Eastern Europe, 820–1396*, London: Royal Numismatic Society.
— (1981), 'The copper coinage of Constantine VII with Zoe in the Balkans', *Buletinul Societății Numismatice Române*, 75–6: 129–30, pp. 253–5.
— (1988), 'The minting of gold coinage at Thessalonica in the fifth and sixth centuries and the gold currency of Illyricum and Dalmatia', in W. Hahn and W. E. Metcalf (eds), *Studies in Early Byzantine Gold Coinage*, New York: American Numismatic Society, 1988, pp. 65–109.
— (2000), 'Mint-activity in Byzantine Thessaloniki', in P. Adam-Veleni (ed.), *To nomisma sto makedoniko choro. Praktika B' epistemonikes synanteses. Nomismatokopeia, kyklophoria, eikonographia, istoria. Archaioi, byzantinoi kai neoteroi chronoi*, Thessaloniki: University Studio Press, pp. 171–82.
— (2001), 'Monetary recession in the Middle Byzantine period: the numismatic evidence', *Numismatic Chronicle*, 161, pp. 111–55.
Meyer, G. (1894), *Neugriechische Studien*, Vienna: F. Tempsky.
Miller, S. G. (1983), 'Excavations at Nemea, 1982', *Hesperia*, 52: 1, pp. 70–95.
Moniaros, X. (1995–1996), 'Slabikes epidromes sto Aigaio stis arches 7ou ai. He periptose tes Chiou', *Byzantina*, 18, pp. 285–302.
— (1998), 'Arabikes epidromes ste Chio ton 7o aiona', *Byzantiaka*, 18, pp. 131–50.
Mordtmann, A. D. (1877), 'Plombs byzantins de la Grèce et du Peloponnèse', *Revue Archéologique*, 33, pp. 289–98.
Morgan, C. H. (1942), *The Byzantine Pottery*, Princeton: American School of Classical Studies in Athens.
Morris, R. (1995), *Monks and Laymen in Byzantium, 843–1118*, Cambridge: Cambridge University Press.
— (1996), 'The origins of Athos', in A. Bryer and M. Cunningham (eds), *Mount Athos and Byzantine Monasticism. Papers from the Twenty-Eighth Spring Symposium of Byzantine Studies, Birmingham, March 1994*, Aldershot/Brookfield: Variorum, pp. 37–46.
— (2000), 'The Athonites and their neighbors in Macedonia in the tenth and eleventh centuries', in J. Burke and R. Scott (eds), *Byzantine Macedonia: Identity, Image, and History. Papers from the Melbourne Conference, July 1995*, Melbourne: Australian Association for Byzantine Studies, pp. 157–67.
Morrisson, C. (1989), 'Monnaie et prix Byzance du Ve au VIIe siècle', in G. Dagron (ed.), *Hommes et richesses dans l'Empire byzantin*, Paris: P. Lethielleux, pp. 239–64.
— (1996), 'Nummi byzantins et barbares du VIe siècles', in E. Kypraiou (ed.), *Charakter. Aphieroma ste Manto Oikonomidou*, Athens: Ekdose tou Tameiou Archaiologikon Poron kai Apallotrioseon, pp. 187–93.
— (1998), 'La circulation monétaire dans les Balkans à l'époque justinienne et post-justinienne', in N. Cambi and E. Marin (eds), *Radovi XIII. Međunarodnog Kongresa za starokršćansku arheologiju. Split-Poreč (25.9.–1.10. 1994)*, Vatican/Split: Pontificio Istituto di Archeologia Cristiana/Arheološki Muzej, pp. 919–30.
Morrisson, C., V. Popović, and V. Ivanišević (2006), *Les trésors monétaires byzantins des Balkans et d'Asie Mineure (491–713)*, Paris: Lethielleux.
Moschopoulos, G. D. (2004), *He Kampania (Roumlouki) sta byzantina chronia. Istoria, topographia, laographia*, Thessaloniki: University Studio Press.

Mouriki, D. (1980–1981), 'Stylistic trends in monumental painting of Greece during the eleventh and twelfth centuries', *Dumbarton Oaks Papers*, 34–6, pp. 77–124.
Moutsopoulos, N. K. (1987), 'Anaskaphe ston ochyro byzantino oikismo tes Rentinas', *Praktika tes en Athenais Archaiologikes Hetaireias*, 142, pp. 149–60.
— (1989), 'Protes paratereseis sten oikistike tou byzantiou ochyrou oikismou tes Rentinas (6os–14os aionas)', *To Archaiologiko ergo ste Makedonia kai Thrake*, 3, pp. 291–301.
— (1992a), 'Anaskaphes byzantinon kastron ste D. Makedonia', *To Archaiologiko ergo ste Makedonia kai Thrake*, 6, pp. 1–26.
— (1992b), *Ekklesies tes Kastorias, 9os–11os aionas*, Thessaloniki: Parateretes.
— (1995a), 'Anaskaphikes ergasies kai ereunes se byzantinous oikismous kai kastra tes Makedonias kai tes Thrakes (1992–1993): Melete byzantinon kai metabyzantinon ekklesion', *Byzantiaka*, 15, pp. 133–54.
— (1995b), 'Ho monochoros dromikos naos sto kastro tes Setinas', in *Diethnes Symposio 'Byzantine Makedonia, 324–1430 m. Ch.', Thessalonike 29–31 oktobriou 1992*, Thessaloniki: Hetaireia Makedonikon Spoudon, pp. 217–29.
— (1997), 'O Agios Andreas Gortynas', *Epistemonike Epeterida Polytechnikes Scholes Thessalonikes. Tmema Architektonon*, 14, pp. 59–93.
— (2001), *Rentina II. To Byzantino kastro tes Mygdonikes Rentinas*, Athens: Techniko Epimetelerio Helladas.
Moutsos, D. (1987), 'Early Graeco-Slavic contacts and the problem of mutual interference', *Zeitschrift für Balkanologie*, 23, pp. 36–66.
Moutzali, A. G. (1984), 'Neotera stoicheia apo te byzantine basilike tes Koimeses tes Theotokou ste Mentzaina Achaias', *Archaiologika analekta ex Athenon*, 17, pp. 21–42.
— (1991), 'He pole ton Patron kata ten protobyzantine periodo', in A. D. Rizakis (ed.), *Archaia Achaia kai Eleia. Anakoinoseis kata to proto diethnes symposio, Athena, 19–21 maiou 1989*, Athens: Kentron Hellenikis kai Romaikis Archaiotitos tou Ethnikou Idrymatos Ereunon, pp. 259–64.
— (1994), 'Topographika tes mesaionikas Patras', in V. Katsaros (ed.), *Antiphonon. Aphieroma ston kathegete N. V. Drandaki*, Thessaloniki: Ekdoseis P. Pournara, pp. 132–57, 624.
— (2002), 'He pole ton Patron kata ton 6o kai 7o aiona', in P. G. Themelis and V. Konti (eds), *Protobyzantine Messene kai Olympia. Aktikos kai agrotikos choros ste Dytike Peloponneso. Praktika tou Diethnous symposiou, Athena, 29–30 maiou 1998*, Athens: Hetaireia Messeniakon Archaiologikon Spoudon/Institouto Byzantinon Ereunon, pp. 174–88.
— (2004), 'Hagia Eirene Riganokampou Patron', in V. Konti (ed.), *Ho monachismos sten Peloponneso 40s–15os ai.*, Athens: Institouto Byzantinon Ereunon, pp. 131–45.
Müller, K., ed. (1861), *Geographici graeci minores*, Paris: Firmin-Didot.
Müller, R. (1996), 'Das Gräberfeld von Gyenesdiás', in F. Daim, K. Kaus, and P. Tomka (eds), *Reitervölker aus dem Osten. Hunnen + Awaren. Burgenländische Landesausstellung 1996. Schloß Halbturn, 26. April–31. Oktober 1996*, Eisenstadt: Amt der Burgenländischen Landesregierung, pp. 411–16.
Mushmov, N. A. (1934), 'Vizantiiski olovni pechati ot sbiraka na Narodniia Muzei', *Izvestiia na Bălgarskiia arkheologicheski institute*, 8, pp. 331–49.
Mylonas, P. M. (1979), 'Les étapes successives de construction du protaton au Mont Athos', *Cahiers Archéologiques*, 28, pp. 143–60.

— (1984), 'Le plan initial du Catholicon de la Grande Lavra, au Mont Athos, et la génèse du type du catholicon athonite', *Cahiers Archéologiques*, 32, pp. 89–112.
— (1987), 'La trapéza de la Grande Lavra au Mont Athos', *Cahiers Archéologiques*, 35, pp. 143–57.
— (1990a), 'Domike ereuna sto ekklesiastiko synkrotema tou Hosiou Louka Phokidos', *Archaiologia*, 36, pp. 6–30.
— (1990b), 'Gavits arméniens et Litae byzantines. Observations nouvelles sur le complexe de Saint-Luc en Phocide', *Cahiers Archéologiques*, 38, pp. 99–122.
— (1992), 'Nouvelles remarques sur le complexe de Saint-Luc en Phocide', *Cahiers Archéologiques*, 40, pp. 115–22.
n.a. [no author] (1976), 'Anaskaphe sta Abdera', *Praktika tes en Athenais Archaiologikes Hetaireias*, 131, pp. 131–7.
— (1994), *Byzantine Thrace. A New Field Opened for Archaeological Research*, Athens: Ministry of Culture.
Nagy, S. (1959), 'Nekropola kod Aradca iz ranog srednieg veka', *Rad Vojvodanskih Muzeja*, 8, pp. 45–102.
Nallbani, E. (2004a), 'Résurgence des traditions de l'Antiquité tardive dans les Balkans occidentaux: étude des sépultures du nord de l'Albanie', *Hortus Artium Medievalium*, 10, pp. 25–42.
— (2004b), 'Transformations et continuité dans l'ouest des Balkans: le cas de la civilisation de Komani (VIe–IXe siècles)', in P. Cabanes and J.-L. Lamboley (eds), *L'Illyrie méridionale et l'Epire dans l'Antiquité. IV. Actes du IVe colloque international de Grenoble, 10–12 octobre 2002*, Paris: De Boccard, pp. 481–90.
— (2005), 'Précisions sur un type de ceinture byzantine: la plaque-boucle du type Corinthe au Haut Moyen Age', in F. Baratte et al. (eds), *Mélanges Jean-Pierre Sodini*, Paris: Association des Amis du Centre d'Histoire et Civilisation de Byzance, pp. 655–72.
Nasledova, R. A. (1956), 'Makedonskie slaviane konca IX–nachala X v. po dannym Ioanna Kamenniaty', *Vizantiiskii Vremennik*, 11, pp. 82–97.
Nastase, D. (1985), 'Les débuts de la communauté oecuménique du Mont Athos', *Symmeikta*, 6, pp. 251–314.
Neeft, K. (1988), 'Byzantijnse gespen en riembeslag in Amsterdam', *Vereniging van Vrienden Allard Pierson Museum Amsterdam: Mededelingenblad*, 43, pp. 4–6.
Nesbitt, J. W. and N. Oikonomides (1994), *Catalogue of Byzantine Seals at Dumbarton Oaks and in the Fogg Museum of Art*, Washington, DC: Dumbarton Oaks Research Library and Collection.
Nesbitt, J. W. and J. Wiita (1975), 'A confraternity of the Comnenian era', *Byzantinische Zeitschrift*, 68, pp. 360–84.
Neville, L. A. (1998), 'Local provincial elites in eleventh-century Hellas and Peloponnese', PhD dissertation, Princeton: Princeton University.
Niavis, P. E. (1992), 'Hoi arabikes epitheseis ste Lakonike kata te mesobyzantine periodo', *Byzantinai Meletai. Diethnes Epistemonike Hepeteris Byzantines kai Metabyzantines Ereunes*, 3, pp. 261–75.
— (1994), 'Bioi peloponnesion agion tes Mesobyzantines periodou: istorikokoinonika dedomena', *Byzantinai Meletai. Diethnes Epistemonike Hepeteris Byzantines kai Metabyzantines Ereunes*, 5, pp. 307–22.
Niederle, L. (1906), 'Michal Syrský a dějiny balkánských Slovanů v VI. století', in

G. Friedrich and K. Krofta (eds), *Sborník prací historických k žé. narozeninám Jaroslava Golla*, Prague: Náklad Hist. Klubu, pp. 48–54.

— (1910), *Život starých Slovanů*, Prague: Bursík a Kohout.

Nikonanos, N. (1979), *Byzantinoi naoi tes Thessalias apo to 10o aiona hos ten kataktese tes perioches apo tous Tourkous to 1393*, Athens: Tameio Archaiologikon Poron kai Apallotrioseon.

Noble, T. F. X. and T. Head, eds (1995), *Soldiers of Christ: Saints and Saints' Lives from Late Antiquity and the Early Middle Ages*, University Park: Pennsylvania State University Press.

Nystazopoulou-Pelekidou, M. (1986), 'Les Slaves dans l'Empire byzantin', in *The 17th International Byzantine Congress. Major Papers. Dumbarton Oaks/ Georgetown University, Washington D.C., August 3–8, 1986*, New Rochelle, NY: Aristide D. Caratzas, pp. 345–67.

— (1991), 'Sceaux byzantins, improprement appelés protobulgares', *Byzantiaka*, 11, pp. 15–22.

— (1993), *Slabikes egkatastaseis ste mesaionike Hellada. Genike episkopese*, Athens: Idryma Goulandri-Chorn.

— (1999), 'He ethnike tautoteta tou mesaionikou ellenismou sten ellenike istoriographia tou 19ou ai.', in *Byzance et l'hellénisme: l'identité grecque au Moyen-Age. Actes du Congrès International tenu à Trieste du 1er au 3e octobre 1997*, Paris: Association Pierre Belon, pp. 87–101.

Ober, J. (1987), 'Pottery and miscellaneous artifacts from fortified sites in northern and western Attica', *Hesperia*, 56, pp. 197–227.

Odetallah, R. Kh. (1995), 'Leo Tripolites-Ghulām Zurāfa and the sack of Thessaloniki in 904', *Byzantinoslavica*, 56, pp. 97–102.

Ohme, H. (1989), 'Der Terminus "chora" als "Provinzbezeichnung" in synodalen Bischofslisten des 6.–8. Jahrhunderts', *Byzantinische Zeitschrift*, 82, pp. 191–201.

Oikonomides, N. (1967), 'Ho bios tou hagiou Theodorou Kytheron (10os ai.) (12 Maiou – BHG3, ar. 2430)', in P. K. Boumpoulides (ed.), *Praktika III Panioniou Synedriou, 23–29 Septembriou 1965*, Athens: no publisher, pp. 281–91.

— (1973), 'Vardariotes – W.l.nd.r – V.n.nd.r: Hongrois installés dans la vallée du Vardar en 934', *Südost-Forschungen*, 32, pp. 1–8.

— (1976), 'Constantin VII Porphyrogénète et les thèmes de Céphalonie et de Longobardie', in H. Arhweiler (ed.), *Documents et études sur les institutions de Byzance (VIIe–XVe s.). Collected Essays of Nicolas Oikonomides*, London: Variorum Reprints, pp. 118–23.

— (1991), 'Le kommerkion d'Abydos, Thessalonique et le commerce bulgare au IXe siècle', in V. Kravari, J. Lefort, and C. Morrisson (eds), *Hommes et richesses dans l'Empire byzantin*, Paris: P. Lethielleux, pp. 241–8.

— (1992), 'The first century of the monastery of Hosios Loukas', *Dumbarton Oaks Papers*, 46, pp. 245–55.

— (1994a), 'L'archonte slave de l'Hellade au VIIIe siècle', *Vizantiiskii Vremennik*, 55: 2, pp. 111–18.

— (1994b), 'Pour une nouvelle lecture des inscriptions de Skripou en Béotie', *Travaux et mémoires du Centre de Recherches d'Histoire et Civilisation Byzantines*, 12, pp. 479–94.

— (1995a), 'Horos Rhomaion kai Boulgaron', in *Diethnes Symposio 'Byzantine*

Makedonia, 324–1430 m. Kh.', Thessalonike, 29–31 Oktobriou 1992, Thessaloniki: Hetaireia Makedonikon Spoudon, pp. 239–43 and 385.

— (1995b), 'The Jews of Chios (1049): a group of excusati', *Mediterranean Historical Review*, 10: 1–2, pp. 218–25.

— (1996a), 'Byzantino Batopaidi: mia mone tes hypseles aristokratias', in *Hiera Megiste Mone Batopaidiou. Paradose, historia, techne*, Hagion Oros: no publisher, pp. 44–53.

— (1996b), 'The medieval Via Egnatia', in E. Zachariadou (ed.), *The Via Egnatia under Ottoman Rule (1380–1699)*, Rethymnon: Crete University Press, pp. 9–16.

— (1996c), 'The social structure of the Byzantine countryside in the first half of the Xth century', *Symmeikta*, 10, pp. 105–25.

— (1999), 'Mone Batopediou: Ta pronomia tou IA' aiona', in P. Gounarides (ed.), *Hiera Mone Batopediou: Istoria kai tekhne*, Athens: Institouto Byzantinon Ereunon, pp. 15–22.

— (1999–2000), 'A note on the campaign of Staurakios in the Peloponnese (783/4)', *Zbornik radova Vizantološkog Instituta*, 38, pp. 61–6.

— (2004), 'Opsime hierapostole ste Lakonia', in V. Konti (ed.), *Ho monachismos sten Peloponneso 40s–15os ai.*, Athens: Institouto Byzantinon Ereunon, pp. 29–35.

Oikonomidou, M. (1991), '"Thesauros" chryson nomismaton apo te Chryse Edesses (10os aionas)', in *Euphrosynon. Aphierona ston Manoel Chatzidake*, Athens: Tameio Arkhaiologikon Poron kai Apallotrioseon, pp. 435–8.

Oikonomidou-Karamesini, M. (1966), 'Nomismata ek tou mouseiou tou Bolou', *Thessalika*, 5, pp. 15–17.

— (1991), 'Proimos byzantinos "thesauros" chalkinon nomismaton apo ten Korinthia', in *Harmos. Timetikos tomos ston kathegete N. K. Moutsopoulo gia ta 25 chronia pneumatikes tou prosphoras sto panepistemio*, Thessaloniki: Aristotelio Panepistemio Thessalonikes, pp. 1289–94.

Oikonomidou-Karamesini, M. and P. A. Drosogianni (1989), 'A hoard of gold Byzantine coins from Samos', *Revue Numismatique*, 31, pp. 145–82.

Oikonomidou-Karamesini, M. and I. Touratsoglou (1979), 'The 1948 Thessaloniki hoard of 6th century Byzantine gold coins: a contribution to the study of the mint of Thessaloniki', *Numismatica e antichità classiche*, 8, pp. 289–312.

Oikonomou, A. (1988), 'Lampes paléochrétiennes d'Argos', *Bulletin de Correspondance Hellénique*, 112, pp. 481–501.

Oikonomou-Laniadou, A. (2003), *Argos paléochrétienne. Contribution à l'étude du Peloponnèse byzantin*, Oxford: Archaeopress.

Olajos, T. (1985), 'Contribution à la chronologie des premières installations des Slaves dans l'Empire byzantin', *Byzantion*, 55, pp. 506–15.

— (1994), 'Quelques remarques sur une peuplade slave en Hellade', *Vizantiiskii Vremennik*, 55: 2, pp. 106–10.

— (1998), 'Une source inobservée concernant l'histoire des Slaves du Péloponnèse', in G. Kukovecz and N. Abdi (eds), *La Méditerranée et l'Europe: Histoire et politique*, Szeged: Universitas Szegediensis de Attila József nominata, pp. 39–44.

— (2000), 'Megjegyzések a korai szlávok Bizánci inváziójának kronológiájához', in F. Piti and G. Szabados (eds), *'Magyaroknak eleiről': Ünnepi tanulmányok a hatvan esztendős Makk Ferenc tiszteletére*, Szeged: Szegedi Középkorász Műhely, pp. 393–400.

Orgels, P. (1964), 'En marge d'un texte hagiographique (Vie de Pierre d'Argos, 19): la dernière invasion slave dans le Peloponnèse', *Byzantion*, 34, pp. 271–85.

Orlandos, A. K. (1961), 'O en Eurytania Byzantinos naos tes Episkopes', *Archeion ton byzantinon mnemeion tes Hellados*, 9, pp. 6–19.

— (1973), 'Palaiochristianika kai byzantina mnemeia Tegeas-Nykliou', *Archeion ton byzantinon mnemeion tes Hellados*, 1, pp. 3–176.

Orsi, P. (1942), *Sicilia bizantina*, Rome: Arte Grafiche Aldo Chicca.

Ostrogorski, G. (1949), 'Un ambassade serbe auprès de l'empereur Basile II', *Byzantion*, 19, pp. 187–94.

— (1952), 'Postanak tema Khelada i Peloponez', *Zbornik radova Vizantološkog Instituta*, 1, pp. 64–77.

Paliouras, A. D. (2004), *Byzantine Aitoloakarnania. Symbole ste byzantine kai metabyzantine mnemeiake techne*, Agrinion: Iphitos.

Pallas, D. I. (1955a), 'Ai "barbarikai" porpai tes Korinthou', *Hellenika*, 14, pp. 340–96.

— (1955b), 'Ta archaiologika tekmeria tes kathodou ton barbaron eis ten Hellada', *Hellenika*, 14, pp. 87–105.

— (1957), 'Anaskaphe tes basilikes tou Lechaiou', *Praktika tes en Athenais Archaiologikes Hetaireias*, 112, pp. 95–104.

— (1960), 'Anaskaphe en Lechaio', *Praktika tes en Athenais Archaiologikes Hetaireias*, 115, pp. 144–70.

— (1961), 'Anaskaphe basilikes Lechaiou', *Praktika tes en Athenais Archaiologikes Hetaireias*, 116, pp. 137–66.

— (1962), 'Anaskaphai Lechaiou 1956-1960', *Archaiologikon Deltion*, 17, pp. 69–78.

— (1965), 'Anaskaphike ereunai en Lechaio', *Praktika tes en Athenais Archaiologikes Hetaireias*, 120, pp. 137–66.

— (1970), 'Über die Datierung eines Kapitells der Basilika von Lechaion (Korinth)', *Byzantinische Zeitschrift*, 63, pp. 69–70.

— (1972), 'Anaskaphe tes basilikes tou Kraneiou', *Praktika tes en Athenais Archaiologikes Hetaireias*, 127, pp. 205–50.

— (1976), 'Anaskaphike tes basilikes tou Kraneiou en Korintho', *Praktika tes en Athenais Archaiologikes Hetaireias*, 131, pp. 163–95.

— (1979), 'Corinthe et Nicopolis pendant le haut Moyen Age', *Felix Ravenna*, 18, pp. 93–142.

— (1981), 'Données nouvelles sur quelques boucles et fibules considerées comme avares et slaves et sur Corinthe entre le VIe et le IXe siècles', *Byzantinobulgarica*, 7, pp. 295–318.

— (1985), 'Zur Topographie und Chronologie von Hosios Loukas: eine kritische Übersicht', *Byzantinische Forschungen*, 78, pp. 94–107.

— (1987), 'Archaiologikes episemanseis ste Salamina', *Archaiologikon Deltion*, 42, pp. 169–230.

— (1988), 'Die Baptiserien und das Kirchengebäude im altchristlichen Griechenland', in M. Restle (ed.), *Festschrift für Klaus Wessel zum 70. Geburtstag in memoriam*, Munich: Maris, pp. 215–30.

— (1989), 'Le baptistère dans l'Illyricum oriental', in *Actes du XIe Congrès International d'Archéologie Chrétienne. Lyon, Vienne, Grenoble, Genève et Aoste (21-28 septembre 1986)*, Rome: Ecole Française de Rome, pp. 2485–90.

— (1990), 'He Panagia tes Skripous hos metaplase tes palaiochristianikes architektonikes se mesaionike byzantine', *Epeteris Hetaireias Stereoelladikon Meleton*, 6, pp. 1–80.
Panayotidi, M. (1999), 'Un aspect de l'art provincial. Témoignage des ateliers locaux dans la peinture monumentale', in E. S. Smirnova (ed.), *Drevnerusskoe iskusstvo. Vizantiia i drevniaia Rus'. K 100-letiiu Andreia Nikolaevicha Grabara (1896–1990)*, St. Petersburg: DB, pp. 178–92.
Panchenko, B. A. (1908), 'Kollekcii Russkago Arkheologicheskago Instituta v Konstantinopol'e. Katalog molivdovulov', *Izvestiia Russkogo arkheologicheskogo instituta v Konstantinople*, 13.
Panov, M. B. (2001), 'On the Slav colonization and the ethnic changes in Macedonia by the end of the 6th and the first half of the 7th century', *Balcanica Posnaniensia*, 11–12, pp. 23–33.
Papachryssanthou, D. (1974), 'La Vie de Saint Euthyme le Jeune et la métropole de Thessalonique la fin du IXe et au début du Xe siècle', *Revue des Etudes Byzantines*, 32, pp. 225–45.
— (1975), *Actes du Prôtaton*, Paris: P. Lethielleux.
— (1992), *Ho Athonikos monachismos. Arches kai organose*, Athens: Morphotiko Hydryma Ethnikes Trapezes.
Papadimitriou, P. G. (2004), 'Thesmiske skheseis kai stadia ensomatoses ton Slabikon plethousmon ste byzantine autokratoria kata to deutero miso tou 7ou aiona', *Byzantina*, 24, pp. 167–218.
Papadopoulos, C. (1935a), 'Ho hosios Loukas ho "neos" (896–953)', *Theologia*, 13, pp. 193–223.
— (1935b), *Symbolai eis ten historian tou monachikou biou en Helladi*, Athens: Phoinikos.
Papadopoulos, K. (1966), *Die Wandmalereien des 11. Jahrhunderts in der Kirche Panagia ton Chalkeon in Thessaloniki*, Graz/Cologne: Böhlau.
Papadopoulou, V. N. (2007), *Byzantine Arta and its Monuments*, Athens: Archaeological Receipts Fund.
Papalexandrou, A. (1998), 'The Church of the Virgin of Skripou: architecture, sculpture and inscriptions in ninth-century Byzantium', PhD dissertation, Princeton: Princeton University.
Papanikola-Bakirtzis, D., ed. (2002), *Kathemerine zoe sto Byzantio. Thessalonike, Leukos Pyrgos, Oktobrios 2001–Ianouarios 2002*, Athens: Ekdoseis Kapon.
Paparrigopoulos, K. (1843), *Peri tes epoikeseos Slabikon tinon phylon eis ten Peloponneson*, Athens: Em. Antouiadou.
— . (1858), *Historikai pragmateiai*, vol. 1, Athens: L. D. Vilaras.
Papoulia, V. (1995), 'To problema tes eirenikes dieisdyseos ton Slabon sten Hellada', in *Diethnes Symposio 'Byzantine Makedonia, 324–1430 m. Kh.', Thessalonike, 29–31 Oktobriou 1992*, Thessaloniki: Hetaireia Makedonikon Spoudon, pp. 255–65 and 386–7.
Papp, L. (1963), 'A nagyharsányi avarkori temető', *Janus Pannonius Múzeum Évkönyve*, 9, pp. 113–41.
Pariente, A. (1991), 'Chronique des fouilles et découvertes archéologiques en Grèce en 1990', *Bulletin de Correspondance Hellénique*, 115: 2, pp. 835–957.
— (1993), 'Chronique des fouilles et découvertes archéologiques en Grèce en 1992', *Bulletin de Correspondance Hellénique*, 117: 2, pp. 757–896.

— (1994), 'Chronique des fouilles et découvertes archéologiques en Grèce en 1993', *Bulletin de Correspondance Hellénique*, 118: 2, pp. 695–843.
Paschalidis, S. A. (1991), *Ho bios tes hosiomyroblytidos Theodoras tes en Thessalonike*, Thessaloniki: Hiera Metropolis Thessalonikes.
— (1994), 'Enas omologetes tes deuteres eikonomachias: ho archiepiskopos Thessalonikes Antonios (+844)', *Byzantina*, 17, pp. 189–216.
Patlagean, E. (1993), 'Byzance et les marchés du grand commerce, vers 830–vers 1030. Entre Pirenne et Polanyi', in *Mercati e mercanti nell'Alto Medioevo: L'area Euraseatica e l'area Mediterranea*, Spoleto: Presso la sede del Centro, pp. 587–632.
Pătruţ, I. (1970), 'Primele relaţii slavo-romano-greceşti şi durata limbii slave comune', *Romanoslavica*, 17, pp. 21–30.
— (1972), 'Pierwsze kontakty językowe słowiańsko-romańsko-greckie a okres trwania języka prasłowiańskiego', *Rocznik Sławistyczny*, 33: 1, pp. 7–19.
Pazaras, T. N. (1988), *Anaglyphes sarkophagoi kai epitaphies plakes tes meses kai hysteres byzantines periodou sten Hellada*, Athens: Ekdose tou Tameiou Archaiologikon Poron kai Apallotrioseon.
— (1995), 'Sculpture in Macedonia in the Middle Byzantine period', in J. Burke and R. Scott (eds), *Byzantine Macedonia. Identity, Image, and History: Papers from the Melbourne Conference, July 1995*, Melbourne: Australian Association for Byzantine Studies, Australian Catholic University, pp. 28–40.
— (1998), 'Anaskaphe ste these "Mpgiadoudi" Epanomes (1998)', *To Archaiologiko ergo ste Makedonia kai Thrake*, 12, pp. 241–52.
— (1999), 'Anaskaphe palaiochristianikes basilikes sto "Mpgiadoudi" Epanomes (1999)', *To Archaiologiko ergo ste Makedonia kai Thrake*, 13, pp. 141–51.
— (2001a), 'Anaskaphe palaiochristianikes basilikes sto Mbgiadoudi Epanomes 2000–2001', *To Archaiologiko ergo ste Makedonia kai Thrake*, 15, pp. 289–98.
— (2001b), *Ta byzantina glypta tou katholikou tes mones Batopediou*, Thessaloniki: University Studio Press.
Pazaras, T. and E. Tsanana (1991), 'Anaskaphikes ereunes ste Beria N. Syllaton (1991)', *To Archaiologiko ergo ste Makedonia kai Thrake*, 5, pp. 289–301.
Peikov, A. (2005), 'Moneti na imperator Filipik Bardan ot Severoiztochna Bălgariia', in V. Giuzelev (ed.), *Kulturnite tekstove na minaloto. Nositeli, simvoli i idei. Materiali ot iubileinata mezhdunarodnata nauchna konferenciia v chest na 60-godishninata na prof. d.i.n. Kazimir Popokonstantinov. Veliko Tărnovo, 29–31 oktomvri 2003*, Sofia: Universitetsko izdatelstvo 'Sv. Kliment Okhridski', pp. 158–9.
Pelekanidis, S. (1955), 'He exo ton teichon palaiochristianike basilike ton Philippon', *Archaiologike ephemeris: ekdidomene tes archaiologikes hetaireias*, 94, pp. 114–79.
Pelekides, S. (1923), 'Anaskaphe Edesses', *Archaiologikon Deltion*, 8, pp. 259–69.
Penna, V. (1995), 'The island of Orovi in the Argolid: bishopric and administrative center', *Studies in Byzantine Sigillography*, 5, pp. 163–73.
— (1996), 'He zoe stis byzantines poleis tes Peloponnesou: he nomismatike martyria (8os–12os ai. m. Ch.)', in A. P. Tzamalis (ed.), *Mneme Martin J. Price*, Athens: Hellenic Numismatic Society, pp. 195–288.
— (2001), 'Nomismatikes nyxeis gia te zoe stis Kyklades kata tous 8o kai 9o aiones', in E. Kountoura-Galake (ed.), *Hoi skoteinoi aiones tou Byzantiou (7os–9os ai.)*, Athens: Ethniko Idryma Ereunon/Institouto Byzantinon Ereunon, pp. 398–413.

Pennas, C. (1973–1974), 'Philippoi', *Archaiologikon Deltion*, 29: 2, pp. 843–6.
— (1977), 'Philippoi', *Archaiologikon Deltion*, 32, pp. 291–2.
— (2004), *He byzantine Aigina*, Athens: Tameio Archaiologikon Poron kai Apallotrioseon.
Peristeri, K. (1990), 'Prote anaskaphike ereuna sten Akropole Platanias', *To Archaiologiko ergo ste Makedonia kai Thrake*, 4, pp. 469–76.
Pertusi, A., ed. (1952), *De thematibus*, Vatican: Biblioteca Apostolica Vaticana.
Pertz, G. H., ed. (1844), *Chronica et annales aevi Salici*, Hanover: Hahn.
Petit, L. (1900–1901), 'Les évêques de Thessalonique', *Echos d'Orient*, 4, pp. 212–21.
— (1903), 'Vie et office de Saint Euthyme le Jeune', *Revue de l'Orient Chrétien*, 8, pp. 155–205 and 503–36.
— (1906), 'Vie de saint Athanase l'Athonite', *Analecta Bollandiana*, 25, pp. 12–87.
— (1924), 'Saint Jean Xénos ou l'Eremite d'après son autobiographie', *Analecta Bollandiana*, 42, pp. 5–20.
Petkov, K. (2008), *The Voices of Medieval Bulgaria, Seventh–Fifteenth Century. The Records of a Bygone Culture*, Leiden/Boston: Brill.
Petridis, P. (1997), 'Delphes dans l'antiquité tardive: première approche topographique et céramologique', *Bulletin de Correspondance Hellénique*, 121, pp. 681–95.
— (2003), 'Ateliers de potiers protobyzantins à Delphes', in C. Bakirtzis (ed.), *7o Diethnes Synedrio Mesaionikes Keramikes tes Mesogeiou. Thessalonike, 11–16 oktobriou 1999. Praktika*, Athens: Edition de la Caisse de Recettes Archéologiques, pp. 443–6.
— (2005), 'Un exemple d'architecture civile en Grèce: les maisons protobyzantines de Delphes (IVe–VIIe s.)', in F. Baratte, V. Déroche, C. Jolivet-Lévy, and B. Pitarakis (eds), *Mélanges Jean-Pierre Sodini*, Paris: Association des Amis du Centre d'Histoire et Civilisation de Byzance, pp. 193–204.
Petritaki, M. (1987), 'Naupaktos', *Archaiologikon Deltion*, 42, pp. 169–75.
Petsas, P. (1969), 'Archaiotetes kai mnemeia Kentrikes Makedonias', *Archaiologikon Deltion*, 24, pp. 302–11.
Philadelpheus, A. (1924), 'Byzantina angeia ek ton anaskaphon palaias Korinthou', *Deltion tes christianikes archaiologikes hetaireias*, 1, pp. 22–47.
Picard, O. (1979), 'Trésors et circulation monétaire à Thasos du IVe au VIIe siècle après J.-C.', in *Thasiaca*, Athens: Ecole Française d'Athènes, pp. 411–54.
Piérart, M. and G. Touchais (1996), *Argos. Une ville grecque de 6000 ans*, Paris: Centre National de la Recherche Scientifique.
Pietri, C. (1984), 'La géographie de l'Illyricum ecclésiastique et ses relations avec l'Eglise de Rome (Ve–VIe siècles)', in *Villes et peuplement dans l'Illyricum protobyzantin. Actes du colloque organisé par l'Ecole Française de Rome (Rome, 12–14 mai 1982)*, Rome: Ecole Française de Rome, pp. 21–59.
Pillon, M. (2002), 'L'exode des Sermésiens et les grandes migrations des Romains de Pannonie dans les Balkans durant le Haut Moyen Age', *Etudes Balkaniques*, 38: 3, pp. 103–41.
— (2005), 'Armée et défense de l'Illyricum byzantin de Justinien à Héraclius (527–641). De la réorganisation justinienne l'émergence des "armées de cité"', *Erytheia*, 26, pp. 7–85.
Pioro, I. S. (1990), *Krymskaia Gotiia (Ocherki etnicheskoi istorii naseleniia Kryma v pozdnerimskii period i rannee srednevekov'e)*, Kiev: Lybid'.

Pirivatrić, S. (1997), *Samuilova drzhava: obim i karakter*, Belgrade: Vizantoloshki Institut SANU.

Pletn'ov, V. (2005), 'Buckles with animal images from north-east Bulgaria (9th–10th c. A.D.)', *Archaeologia Bulgarica*, 9: 1, pp. 75–86.

Pliakov, Z. (1989), 'La région de la Moyenne Struma aux VIIe–IXe siècles', *Palaeobulgarica*, 13: 2, pp. 100–15.

Poenaru-Bordea, G. and I. Donoiu (1981–1982), 'Contribuţii la studiul pătrunderii monedelor bizantine în Dobrogea în secolele VII–X', *Buletinul Societăţii Numismatice Române*, 75–6: 129–30, pp. 237–51.

Pohl, W. (1988), *Die Awaren: ein Steppenvolk im Mitteleuropa, 567–822 n. Chr.*, Munich: Beck.

Popović, V. (1978), 'La descente des Koutigoures, des Slaves et des Avares vers la Mer Egée: le témoignage de l'archéologie', *Comptes Rendus de l'Académie des Inscriptions et Belles-Lettres*, 6, pp. 597–649.

— (1980), 'Aux origines de la slavisation des Balkans: la constitution des premières sklavinies macédoniennes vers la fin du VIe siècle', *Comptes Rendus de l'Académie des Inscriptions et Belles-Lettres*, 8, pp. 230–57.

— (1981), 'Une invasion slave sous Justin II inconnue des sources écrites', *Numizmatičar*, 4, pp. 111–26.

Poulou-Papadimitriou, N. (1986), 'Lampes paléochrétiennes de Samos', *Bulletin de Correspondance Hellénique*, 110, pp. 583–610.

— (2001), 'Byzantine keramike apo ton elleniko nesiotiko choro kai apo ten Peloponneso (7os–9os ai.): mia prote prosengise', in E. Kountoura-Galake (ed.), *Hoi skoteinoi aiones tou Byzantiou (7os–9os ai.)*, Athens: Ethniko Idryma Ereunon/Institouto Byzantinon Ereunon, pp. 231–96.

-- (2002), 'Byzantines porpes. He periptose tes Messenes kai tes Eleuthernas', in P. G. Themelis and V. Konti (eds), *Protobyzantine Messene kai Olympia. Aktikos kai agrotikos khoros ste Dytike Peloponneso. Praktika tou Diethnous symposiou, Athena, 29–30 maiou 1998*, Athens: Hetaireia Messeniakon Arkhaiologikon Spoudon/Institouto Byzantinon Ereunon, pp. 125–36.

— (2005), 'Les plaques-boucles byzantines de l'île de Crète (fin IVe–IXe siècle)', in F. Baratte, V. Déroche, C. Jolivet-Lévy, and B. Pitarakis (eds), *Mélanges Jean-Pierre Sodini*, Paris: Association des Amis du Centre d'Histoire et Civilisation de Byzance, pp. 687–704.

Pratsch, T. (1994), 'Untersuchungen zu "De Thematibus" Kaiser Konstantins VII. Porfirogennetos', in P. Speck (ed.), *Varia V*, Bonn: Rudolf Habelt, pp. 13–145.

— (2005), 'Zur Herkunft des Niketas Magistros (*um 870; +frühestens 946/947) aus Lakonien', *Byzantion*, 75, pp. 501–6.

Prinzing, G. (1997), 'Epirus und die ionischen Inseln im Hochmittelalter. Zur Geschichte der Region im Rahmen des Themas Nikopolis und der Inselthemen Kerkyra und Kephallenia im Zeitraum ca. 1000–1204', *Südost-Forschungen*, 56, pp. 1–25.

Prokopiou, E. (1997), 'Byzantines porpes apo ten Amathounta kai ten Palaia Sylloge tou Kypriakou Mouseiou', in D. Christou, D. Pileidou, M. Hieronymidou, G. Chatzisavvas, and E. Dousi (eds), *He Kypros kai to Aigaio sten archaioteta apo ten proistoriko periodo hos ton 7o aiona m. Ch., Leukosia 8–10 Dekembriou 1995*, Nicosia: Tmema Archaioteton, pp. 333–42.

Provost, S. and L. Foschia (2002), 'He "oikia ton agrion zoon" stous Philippos hoi nees anaskaphes (2001–2002)', *To Archaiologiko ergo ste Makedonia kai Thrake*, 16, pp. 107–18.

Puglisi, M. and A. Sardella (1998), 'Priverno: la ceramica acroma e dipinta di V–VI secolo', in L. Saguì (ed.), *Ceramica in Italia: VI–VII secolo. Atti del Convegno in onore di John W. Hayes, Roma, 11–13 maggio 1995*, Florence: Insegna del Giglio, pp. 777–85.

Pyrrou, N., A. Tsaravopoulos, and C. O. Bojică (2006), 'The Byzantine settlement of Antikythira (Greece) in the 5th–7th centuries', in S. A. Luca and V. Sîrbu (eds), *The Society of the Living, the Community of the Dead (from Neolithic to the Christian Era). Proceedings of the 7th International Colloquium of Funerary Archaeology*, Sibiu: Universitatea 'Lucian Blaga', pp. 224–38.

Rajković, M. (1958), 'Oblast Strimona i tema Strimon', *Zbornik radova Vizantološkog Instituta*, 5, pp. 1–7.

Rapp, C. (1997), 'Ritual brotherhood in Byzantium', *Traditio*, 52, pp. 285–326.

Rashev, R. (2000), *Prabălgarite prez V–VII vek*, Sofia: Faber.

Reinach, S. (1882), 'La reconstruction des murs de Cavalla au Xe siècle', *Bulletin de Correspondance Hellénique*, 6, pp. 267–75.

Reiske, J. J., ed. (1830), *Constantini Porphyrogeniti Imperatoris de cerimoniis aulae Byzantinae libri duo*, Bonn: E. Weber.

Repnikov, N. (1906), 'Nekotorye mogil'niki oblasti krymskikh gotov', *Izvestiia imperatorskoi arkheologicheskoi kommissii*, 19, pp. 1–80.

Riedinger, R. (1979), *Die Präsenz- und Subskriptionslisten des VI. oekumenischen Konzils (680/1) und der Papyrus Vind. G. 3*, Munich: C. H. Beck.

Riemer, E. (1995), 'Byzantinische Gürtelschnallen aus der Sammlung Diergardt im Römisch-Germanischen Museum Köln', *Kölner Jahrbuch für Vor- und Frühgeschichte*, 28, pp. 777–809.

— (2000), *Romanische Grabfunde des 5.–8. Jahrhunderts in Italien*, Rahden: Leidorf.

Rife, J. L. (2008), 'Leo's Peloponnesian fire-tower and the Byzantine watch-tower on Acrocorinth', in W. R. Caraher, L. J. Hall, and R. S. Moore (eds), *Archaeology and History in Roman, Medieval and Post-Medieval Greece. Studies on Method and Meaning in Honor of Timothy E. Gregory*, Aldershot/Burlington: Ashgate, pp. 281–306.

Ronin, V. K. (1995), 'Zhitie Villibal'da, episkopa Eikhshtettskogo', in S. A. Ivanov, G. G. Litavrin, and V. K. Ronin (eds), *Svod drevneishikh pis'mennykh izvestii o slavianakh*, Moscow: 'Vostochnaia literatura' RAN, pp. 439–40.

Rosenqvist, J. O. (1996), 'The text of the Life of St. Nikon "Metanoiete" reconsidered', in J. O. Rosenqvist (ed.), *Leimon. Studies Presented to Lennart Rydén on His Sixty-Fifth Birthday*, Uppsala: Almqvist & Wiksell International, pp. 93–111.

Rosser, J. (2001), 'Evidence for a Justinianic garrison behind Thermopylae at the Dhema Pass', in J. Herrin, M. Mullett, and C. Otten-Froux (eds), *Mosaic. Festschrift for A. H. S. Megaw*, London: British School at Athens, pp. 33–41.

— (2005), 'Dark Age settlements in Grevena, Greece (southwestern Macedonia)', in J. Lefort, C. Morrisson, and J.-P. Sodini (eds), *Les villages dans l'Empire byzantin, IVe–XVe siècles*, Paris: Lethielleux, pp. 279–87.

Roux, M. (1996), 'Pour une histoire de Corfou byzantine (Xe–XIIe s.)', *Peri istorias*, 1, pp. 71–86.

Rudolph, W. W. (1979), 'Excavations at Porto Cheli and vicinity. Preliminary report V: the early Byzantine remains', *Hesperia*, 48, pp. 294–320.

Runciman, S. (1940), 'The widow Danielis', in *Etudes dédiées à la mémoire d'André M. Andréadès*, Athens: Pyrsos, pp. 425–31.

Sampson, A. (1984–1985), 'Chersaia kai nesiotika kataphygia tes proimes byzantines periodou sten Euboia kai anatolike Boiotia', *Archeion euboikon meleton*, 26, pp. 363–72.

Sanders, G. D. R. (1995), 'Pottery from medieval levels in the orchestra and lower cavea', *Annual of the British School at Athens*, 90, pp. 451–7.

— (2000), 'New relative and absolute chronologies for 9th to 13th century glazed wares at Corinth: methodology and social conclusions', in K. Belke et al. (eds), *Byzanz als Raum: Zu Methoden und Inhalten der historischen Geographie des östlichen Mittelmeerraumes*, Vienna: Verlag der Österreichischen Akademie der Wissenschaften, pp. 153–73.

— (2001), 'Byzantine polychrome pottery', in J. Herrin, M. Mullet, and C. Otten-Froux (eds), *Mosaic. Festschrift for A. H. S. Megaw*, Athens: British School at Athens, pp. 89–104.

— (2002), 'Corinth', in A. E. Laiou (ed.), *The Economic History of Byzantium from the Seventh through the Fifteenth Century*, Washington, DC: Dumbarton Oaks Research Library and Collection, pp. 647–54.

— (2003a), 'An overview of the new chronology for 9th to 13th century pottery at Corinth', in C. Bakirtzis (ed.), *7o Diethnes Synedrio Mesaionikes Keramikes tes Mesogeiou. Thessalonike, 11–16 oktobriou 1999. Praktika*, Athens: Edition de la Caisse de Recettes Archéologiques, pp. 35–44.

— (2003b), 'Recent developments in the chronology of Byzantine Corinth', in C. K. William and N. Bookidis (eds), *Corinth XX. The Centenary, 1896–1996*, Princeton: American School of Classical Studies at Athens, pp. 647–54.

— (2004), 'Problems in interpreting rural and urban settlement in southern Greece, AD 365–700', in N. Christie (ed.), *Landscapes of Change: Rural Evolutions in Late Antiquity and the Early Middle Ages*, Aldershot: Ashgate, pp. 163–93.

Savvidis, A. G. K. (1987), 'He byzantine Theba, 996/7–1204 m. Ch.' *Historikogeographika*, 2, pp. 33–52.

— (1987–1989), 'Theodore of Tarsus, Greek archbishop of Canterbury in A.D. 668/9–690', *Epeteris Hetaireias Byzantinon Spoudon*, 47, 97–108.

— (1990), 'Morea and Islam, 8th–15th centuries', *Journal of Oriental and African Studies*, 2, pp. 47–75.

— (1991), 'On Pylos-Navarino-Zonklon in the Byzantine period (late 6th–early 13th centuries)', *Byzantina*, 16, pp. 335–8.

— (1993), 'Peloponnesos kai Mousoulmanoi: hoi Arabikes epidromes kai hoi plerophories ton Arabon syngrapheon (8os–13os aiones)', *Byzantinai Meletai. Diethnes Epistemonike Hepeteris Byzantines kai Metabyzantines Ereunes*, 4, pp. 370–84.

— (1994), 'Ta problemata schetika me to Byzantino Nauplio', *Byzantiaka*, 14, pp. 355–74.

— (1995), 'Ho Lakon Ioannes Aratos kai hoi Ioudaioi tes Spartes sta tele tou 10ou aiona', *Byzantinai Meletai. Diethnes Epistemonike Hepeteris Byzantines kai Metabyzantines Ereunes*, 6, pp. 123–40.

— (2000), 'Peloponnesus mediaevalis. A review essay a propos of a new collective manual on the medieval Morea', *Byzantion*, 70, pp. 309–30.
Savvopoulou, T. (1992), 'Europos', *Archaiologikon Deltion*, 47, pp. 389–91.
Schlumberger, G. (1895), *Mélanges d'archéologie byzantine*. Paris: Ernest Leroux.
Schlunk, H. (1940), 'Eine Gruppe datierbarer byzantinischer Ohrringe', *Berliner Museen. Berichte aus den Preussischen Kunstsammlungen*, 61, pp. 42–7.
Schminck, A. (2003), 'Hosios Loukas: eine kaiserliche Stiftung?', in V. N. Vlyssidou (ed.), *He autokratoria se krise? To Byzantio ton 11o aiona (1025–1081)*, Athens: Ethniko Idryma Ereunon. Institouto Byzantinon Ereunon, pp. 349–80.
Schultz, R. W. and S. H. Barnsley (1901), *Byzantine Architecture in Greece. Monastery of Saint Luke of Stiris in Phocis, and the Dependent Monastery of Saint Nicholas in the Fields, near Skripou, in Boeotia*, London: Macmillan.
Schulze-Dörrlamm, M. (2002), *Byzantinische Gürtelschnallen und Gürtelbeschläge im Römisch-Germanischen Zentralmuseums. Teil I: Die Schnallen ohne Beschläg, mit Laschenbeschläg und mit festem Beschläg des 6. bis 7. Jahrhunderts*, Mainz: Verlag des Römisch-Germanischen Zentralmuseums/Rudolf Habelt.
— (2003), 'Gleicharmige Bügelfibeln der Zeit um 600 aus dem byzantinischen Reich', *Archäologisches Korrespondenzblatt*, 33, pp. 437–44.
Scranton, R. (1957), *Mediaeval Architecture in the Central Area of Corinth*, Princeton: American School of Classical Studies at Athens.
Sedov, V. V. (1974), *Dlinnye kurgany krivichei*, Moscow: Nauka.
Seibt, W. (1999), 'Siegel als Quelle für Slawenarchonten in Griechenland', *Studies in Byzantine Sigillography*, 6, pp. 27–36.
— (2003), 'Weitere Beobachtungen zu Siegeln früher Slawenarchonten in Griechenland', in A. Avramea, A. E. Laiou, and E. Chrysos (eds), *Byzantio kratos kai koinonia. Mneme Nikou Oikonomidou*, Athens: Institouto Byzantinon Ereunon, pp. 459–66.
Setton, K. (1950), 'The Bulgars in the Balkans and the occupation of Corinth in the 7th century', *Speculum*, 25, pp. 502–43.
— (1952), 'The emperor Constans II and the capture of Corinth by the Onogur Bulgars', *Speculum*, 27, pp. 351–62.
— (1954), 'On the raids of the Moslems in the Aegean in the ninth and tenth centuries and their alleged occupation of Athens', *American Journal of Archaeology*, 58: 4, pp. 311–19.
Ševčenko, I. (1992), 'Re-reading Constantine Porphyrogenitus', in J. Shepard and S. Franklin (eds), *Byzantine Diplomacy. Papers from the Twenty-Fourth Spring Symposium of Byzantine Studies, Cambridge, March 1990*, Aldershot/Brookfield: Ashgate/Variorum, pp. 167–96.
Shangin, M. A. (1947), 'Pisma Arefy – novyi istochnik o politicheskikh sobytiiakh v Vizantii 931–934 gg.', *Vizantiiskii Vremennik*, 26: 1, pp. 235–60.
Shear, T. L. (1973), 'The Athenian Agora: excavations of 1972', *Hesperia*, 42, pp. 359–407.
Shelley, J. M. (1943), 'The Christian basilica near the Cenchrean Gate at Corinth', *Hesperia*, 12, pp. 166–89.
Shuvalov, P. V. (1999), 'Sluchainye fluktuacii ili prednamerennyi otbor? (Tri klada folisov poslednei chetverti VI v.)', *Stratum+*, 6, pp. 104–10.
Sidiropoulos, K. (2002), 'He nomismatike kyklophoria sten hysteromaike kai protobyzantine Messene. Typiko paradeigma e istorike exairese?', in P. G. Themelis

and V. Konti (eds), *Protobyzantine Messene kai Olympia. Aktikos kai agrotikos choros ste Dytike Peloponneso. Praktika tou Diethnous symposiou, Athena, 29–30 maiou 1998*, Athens: Hetaireia Messeniakon Archaiologikon Spoudon/ Institouto Byzantinon Ereunon, pp. 99–124.

Simon, L. (1991), 'Korai avar kardok', *Studia Comitatensia*, 22, pp. 263–346.

— (1993), 'Adatok a szablyák kialakulásáról', *A Herman Otto Múzeum Évkönyve*, 30–1, pp. 171–94.

Siomkos, N. (2005), *L'église Saint-Etienne à Kastoria. Etude des différentes phases du décor peint (Xe–XIVe siècles)*, Thessaloniki: Kentro Vyzantinon Ereunon.

Skawran, K. M. (1982), *The Development of Middle Byzantine Painting in Greece*, Pretoria: University of South Africa.

— (2001), 'Peripheral Byzantine frescoes in Greece: the problem of their connections', in J. Herrin, M. Mullett, and C. Otten-Froux (eds), *Mosaic. Festschrift for A. H. S. Megaw*, London: British School of Athens, pp. 75–83.

Skedros, J. C. (1999), *Saint Demetrios of Thessaloniki: Civic Patron and Divine Protector, 4th–7th Centuries CE*, Harrisburg: Trinity Press International.

Skopetea, E. (1997), *Fallmerayer: technasmata tou antipalou deous*, Athens: Themelio.

Snively, C. S. (1984), 'Cemetery churches of the early Byzantine period in Eastern Illyricum: location and martyrs', *Greek Orthodox Theological Review*, 29, pp. 117–24.

— (1998), 'Intramural burial in the cities of the late antique diocese of Macedonia', in N. Cambi and E. Marin (eds), *Radovi XIII. Međunarodnog Kongresa za starokršćansku arheologiju. Split-Poreč (25.9.–1.10. 1994)*, Vatican/Split: Pontificio Istituto di Archeologia Cristiana/Arheološki Muzej, pp. 491–8.

Sodini, J.-P. (1984), 'L'habitat urbain en Grèce à la veille des invasions', in *Villes et peuplement dans l'Illyricum protobyzantin. Actes du colloque organisé par l'Ecole Française de Rome (Rome, 12–14 mai 1982)*, Rome: Ecole Française de Rome, pp. 341–97.

— (1995), 'La ville de Thasos à l'époque protobyzantine: les lacunes de la topographie', in *Diethnes Symposio 'Byzantine Makedonia, 324–1430 m. Kh.', Thessalonike 29–31 Oktobriou 1992*, Thessaloniki: Hetaireia Makedonikon Spoudon, pp. 279–94.

— (2000), 'Productions et échanges dans le monde protobyzantin (IV–VIIe s.): le cas de la céramique', in K. Belke, F. Hild, J. Koder, and P. Soustal (eds), *Byzanz als Raum. Zu Methoden und Inhalten der historischen Geographie des östlichen Mittelmeerraumes*, Vienna: Verlag der Österreichischen Akademie der Wissenschaften, pp. 181–208.

Sokol, V. (2006), *Hrvatska srednjovjekovna arheološka baština od Jadrana do Save*, Zagreb: Golden Marketing/Tehnička Knjiga.

Sotiriou, G. A. (1924), 'Ho en Thebais byzantinos naos Gregoriou tou Theologou', *Archaiologike ephemeris: ekdidomene tes archaiologikes hetaireias*, pp. 1–26.

— (1929a), 'Ai christianikai Thebai tes Thessalias', *Archaiologike ephemeris: ekdidomene tes archaiologikes hetaireias*, 75, pp. 1–158.

— (1929b), 'Byzantinai basilikai Makedonias kai palaias Hellados', *Byzantinische Zeitschrift*, 30, pp. 568–76.

— (1935), 'Anaskaphai Neas Anchialou', *Praktika tes en Athenais Archaiologikes Hetaireias*, 93, pp. 52–72.

— (1937), 'He byzantine glyptike tes Ellados kata ton 7on kai 8on aiona', *Archaiologike ephemeris: ekdidomene tes archaiologikes hetaireias*, 83, pp. 171–84.

— (1939), 'Anaskaphai en Nea Anchialo', *Praktika tes en Athenais Archaiologikes Hetaireias*, 97, pp. 53–72.

— (1956), 'Anaskaphai en Nea Anchialo', *Praktika tes en Athenais Archaiologikes Hetaireias*, 111, pp. 110–18.

Sotiriou, M. G. (1931), 'Ho naos tes Skripous tes Boiotias', *Archaiologike ephemeris: ekdidomene tes archaiologikes hetaireias*, 77, pp. 119–57.

Soulis, G. C. (1953), 'On the Slavic settlement in Hierissos in the tenth century', *Byzantion*, 23, pp. 67–72.

Soustal, P. (1991), *Tabula Imperii Byzantini 6: Thrakien (Thrake, Rodope und Haimimontus)*, Vienna: Verlag der Österreichischen Akademie der Wissenschaften.

— (2004), 'The historical sources for Butrint in the Middle Ages', in R. Hodges, W. Bowden, and K. Lako (eds), *Byzantine Butrint: Excavations and Surveys, 1994–99*, Oxford: Oxbow, pp. 20–6.

Soustal, P. and J. Koder (1981), *Nikopolis und Kephallenia*, Vienna: Verlag der Österreichischen Akademie der Wissenschaften.

Spahiu, H. (1976), 'La ville haute-médiévale albanaise de Shurdhah (Sarda)', *Iliria*, 5, pp. 151–67.

Spanu, P. G. (1998), *La Sardegna bizantina tra VI e VII secolo*, Oristano: S'Alvure.

Speck, P. (1993), 'De miraculis Sancti Demetrii qui Thessalonicam profugus venit', in S. Kotzabassi and P. Speck (eds), *Varia IV: Beiträge*, Bonn: Rudolf Habelt, pp. 255–532.

Spieser, J.-M. (1973), 'Inventaires en vue d'un recueil des inscriptions historiques de Byzance. I. Les inscriptions de Thessalonique', *Travaux et Mémoires du Centre de Recherches d'Histoire et Civilisation Byzantines*, 5, pp. 145–80.

— (1984), 'La ville en Grèce du IIIe au VIIe siècle', in *Villes et peuplement dans l'Illyricum protobyzantin. Actes du colloque organisé par l'Ecole Française de Rome, Rome 12–14 mai 1982*, Rome: Ecole Française de Rome, pp. 315–40.

Stallman, C. J. (1986), 'The "Life" of S. Pancratius of Taormina', PhD dissertation, Oxford: Oxford University.

Stathakopoulos, D. C. (2004), *Famine and Pestilence in the Late Roman and Early Byzantine Empire. A Systematic Survey of Subsistence Crises and Epidemics*, Burlington: Ashgate.

Stavrakos, C. (1999), 'Die Vita des hl. Nikon Metanoeite als Quelle zur Prosopographie der Peloponnes im späten 10. Jahrhundert', *Südost-Forschungen*, 58, pp. 1–7.

Stavridou-Zafraka, A. (1995a), 'Bodena, mia byzantine pole-kastro tes Makedonias', in G. Kioutoutskas (ed.), *He Edessa kai he periokhe tes. Istoria kai politismos. Praktika A' Panelleniou Epistemonikou Symposiou (Edessa, 4 Dekembriou 1992)*, Edessa: Vagourde, pp. 165–78.

— (1995b), 'Ta themata tou Makedonikou chorou. To thema Strymonos', in *Diethnes Symposio 'Byzantine Makedonia, 324–1430 m. Kh., Thessalonike, 29–31 Oktobriou 1992*, Thessaloniki: Hetaireia Makedonikon Spoudon, pp. 307–19 and 89–90.

— (1998), 'Ta themata tou Makedonikou chorou. To thema Thessalonikes os tis arches 10ou ai.', *Byzantina*, 19, pp. 157–70.

— (2000), 'The development of the theme organisation in Macedonia', in J. Burke and R. Scott (eds), *Byzantine Macedonia: Identity, Image, and History. Papers from the Melbourne Conference, July 1995*, Melbourne: Australian Association for Byzantine Studies, pp. 128–38.

Štefanovičová, T. (1977), 'Beitrag zur Frage der slawischen Ansiedlung Griechenlands', *Etudes Balkaniques*, 13: 2, pp. 126–8.

— (1997), 'Slavic settlement of Greece in the light of archaeological sources', in V. V. Sedov (ed.), *Etnogenez i etnokul'turnye kontakty slavian*, Moscow: Institut Arkheologii RAN, pp. 352–61.

Stephenson, P. (2000), *Byzantium's Balkan Frontier. A Political Study of the Northern Balkans, 900–1204*, Cambridge: Cambridge University Press.

— (2003), *The Legend of Basil the Bulgar-Slayer*, Cambridge/New York: Cambridge University Press.

Stikas, E. (1964), 'Anaskaphe palaiochristianikes basilikes Γ Amphipoleos', *Praktika tes en Athenais Archaiologikes Hetaireias*, 119, pp. 41–3.

— (1966), 'Anaskaphe Amphipoleos', *Praktika tes en Athenais Archaiologikes Hetaireias*, 121, pp. 24–9.

— (1972), 'Nouvelles observations sur la date de construction du catholicon et de l'église de la Vierge du monastère de Saint Luc en Phocide (Travaux de restauration exécutés au monastère)', *Corso di cultura sull'arte ravennate e bizantina*, 19, pp. 311–30.

— (1975), 'L'église byzantine de Scripou (Orchoménos) en Béotie', *Corso di cultura sull'arte ravennate e bizantina*, 22, pp. 385–400.

Stoianova-Serafimova, D. (1979), 'Die neuentdeckte mittelalterliche Nekropole beim Dorf Tuchovište, Kreis Blagoevgrad', in B. Chropovsky (ed.), *Rapports du IIIe Congrès International d'Archéologie Slave. Bratislava, 7–14 septembre 1975*, Bratislava: VEDA, pp. 789–804.

Stratos, A. N. (1975), *Byzantium in the Seventh Century*, Amsterdam: Adolf M. Hakkert.

Struck, A. H. (1905), 'Die Eroberung Thessalonikes durch die Sarazenen im Jahre 904', *Byzantinische Zeitschrift*, 14, pp. 535–62.

Sullivan, D., ed. (1987), *The Life of Saint Nikon*, Brookline: Hellenic College Press.

Svoronos, I. N. (1904), 'Thesauroi byzantinon chryson nomismaton ek ton anaskaphon tou en Athenais Asklepieiou', *Journal International d'Archéologie Numismatique*, 7, pp. 143–60.

— (1909), 'Heurema Dipylou', *Journal International d'Archéologie Numismatique*, 12, pp. 6–9.

Symeonidis, C. P. (1972), *Hoi Tsakones kai he Tsakonia. Symbole sten hermeneia ton onomaton kai tou homonymou byzantinou thesmou ton kastrophylakon*, Thessaloniki: Kentron Vyzantinon Ereunon.

Symeonoglou, S. (1985), 'Anaskaphe Ithakes', *Praktika tes en Athenais Archaiologikes Hetaireias*, 140, pp. 201–15.

Sythiakaki, V. (2004), 'Korinthiazonta kionokrana me staurous eggegrammenous se kyklo. He symbole ton ergasterion tes Magnesias', in I. Kakouris, S. Choulia, and T. Albani (eds), *Thorakion. Aphieroma ste mneme tou Paulou Lazaride*, Athens: Ypourgeio Politismou, Genike Dieuthynse Archaioteton kai Politistikes Klironomias, Dieuthynse Metavyzantinon Archaioteton, pp. 179–96.

Szabó, J. G. (1965), 'Az Egri múzeum avarkori emlékanyaga I. Kora-avarkori sírleletek tarnamérárol', *Agria*, 3, pp. 29–71.

Szádeczky-Kardoss, S. (1986), 'Die Nachricht des Isidorus Hispalensis und des spanischen Fortsetzers seiner "Historia" über einen Slaweneinfall in Griechenland', in N. Nikolov, S. Szádeczky-Kardoss, and T. Olajos (eds), *Szlávok-Protobolgárok-Bizánc*, Szeged: József Attila University Press, pp. 51–61.

Szemiothowa, A. (1961), 'Les rares monnaies antiques du Musée National de Varsovie', *Wiadomości Archeologiczne*, 5, pp. 85–90.

Szymański, W. (1968), 'Niektóre aspekty kontaktów słowiańsko-baltyjskich w świetle wyników badań w Szeligach, pow. Płock', *Archeologia Polski*, 13, pp. 188–210.

Tachiaos, A. E. (1993–1994), 'Some controversial points relating to the life and activity of Cyril and Methodius', *Cyrillomethodianum*, 17–18, pp. 41–72.

Taibbi, G. R., ed. (1962), *Vita di Sant'Elia il Giovane*, Palermo: Istituto Siciliano di Studi Bizantini e Neoellenici.

Tanoulas, T. (1997), *Ta Propylaia tes Athenaïkes Akropoles kata ton Mesaiona*, Athens: Archaiologike Hetaireia.

Tăpkova-Zaimova, V. (1964), 'Sur quelques aspects de la colonisation slave en Macédoine et en Grèce', *Etudes Balkaniques*, 1, pp. 111–23.

— (1966), 'Autour de la pénétration du tzar bulgare Samuel dans les régions de la Grèce proprement dite', *Byzantinobulgarica*, 2, pp. 237–9.

Tarnanidis, I. (2000), 'The Macedonians of the Byzantine period', in J. Burke and R. Scott (eds), *Byzantine Macedonia. Identity Image and History. Papers from the Melbourne Conference, July 1995*, Melbourne: Australian Association for Byzantine Studies, pp. 29–49.

Tavlakis, I., D. Bitzikopoulos, and V. Maladakis (2003), 'Anaskaphe palaiochristianikon basilikon ste Barbara Chalkidikes', *To Archaiologiko ergo ste Makedonia kai Thrake*, 17, pp. 391–402.

Teodor, D. G. (1984), *Continuitatea populaţiei autohtone la est de Carpaţi. Aşezările din secolele VI–XI e.n. de la Dodeşti-Vaslui*, Iaşi: Junimea.

Thavoris, A. (1975), 'The Slavs and Slav toponyms and their endings in Greece', *Cyrillomethodianum*, 3, pp. 190–218.

Themelis, P. G. (2000), 'Anaskaphe Messenes', *Praktika tes en Athenais Archaiologikes Hetaireias*, 155, pp. 82–4.

— (2002), 'Hysteromaike kai protobyzantine Messene', in P. G. Themelis and V. Konti (eds), *Protobyzantine Messene kai Olympia. Aktikos kai agrotikos choros ste Dytike Peloponneso. Praktika tou Diethnous symposiou, Athena, 29–30 maiou 1998*, Athens: Hetaireia Messeniakon Archaiologikon Spoudon/Institouto Byzantinon Ereunon, pp. 20–58.

Theocharidis, G. I. (1978), 'Mia exaphanismena megale mone tes Thessalonikes, he mone tou Prodromou', *Makedonika. Syngrama periodikon tes Hetaireias Makedonikon Spoudon*, 18, pp. 1–23.

Thomas, J. P. and A. C. Hero, eds (2000), *Byzantine Monastic Foundation Documents*, Washington, DC: Dumbarton Oaks Research Library and Collection.

Thompson, M. (1940), 'Some unpublished bronze money of the early eighth century', *Hesperia*, 9: 3, pp. 358–80.

— (1954), *The Athenian Agora. Results of Excavations Conducted by the American School of Classical Studies at Athens*, Princeton: Princeton University Press.

Thurn, H., ed. (1973), *Ioannis Scylitzae Synopsis historiarum*, Berlin/New York: De Gruyter.

Thurnher, E. (1995), *Jahre der Vorbereitung. Jakob Fallmerayers Tätigkeiten nach der Rückkehr von der zweiten Orientreise 1842–1845*, Vienna: Verlag der Österreichischen Akademie der Wissenschaften.
Tomadakis, N. B. (1983–1986), 'Ho agios Ioannes ho Xenos kai Eremites en Krete (10os–11os ai.)', *Epeteris Hetaireias Byzantinon Spoudon*, 46, pp. 1–117.
Torcellan, M. (1986), *Le tre necropoli altomedioevali di Pinguente*, Florence: All'insegna di Giglio.
Török, G. (1980–1981), 'Avar kori temető Csengelén (Szeged-Csengele, Feketehalom)', *Móra Ferenc Múzeum Evkönyve*, 1, pp. 43–62.
Totev, T. (1993), *The Preslav Treasure*, Shumen: Antos.
Tóth, E. H. and A. Horváth (1992), *Kunbábony. Das Grab eines Awarenkhagans*, Kécskemét: Museumdirektion der Selbstverwaltung des Komitats Bács-Kiskun.
Touchais, G. (1982), 'Chronique des fouilles et découvertes archéologiques en Grèce en 1981', *Bulletin de Correspondance Hellénique*, 106, pp. 529–631.
Touchais, G., T. Boloti, B. Detournay, S. Huber, A. Philippa-Touchais, and Y. Varalis (1996), 'Chronique des fouilles et découvertes archéologiques en Grèce en 1995', *Bulletin de Correspondance Hellénique*, 120: 3, pp. 1109–349.
Touchais, G., B. Detournay, A. Philippa-Touchais, and Y. Varalis (1998), 'Chronique des fouilles et découvertes archéologiques en Grèce en 1996 et 1997', *Bulletin de Correspondance Hellénique*, 122: 2, pp. 705–988.
Touchais, G., S. Huber, and A. Philippa-Touchais (2000), 'Chronique des fouilles et découvertes archéologiques en Grèce en 1999', *Bulletin de Correspondance Hellénique*, 24: 2, pp. 753–1023.
Traquair, R. (1908), 'Laconia III. The churches of western Mani', *Annual of the British School at Athens*, 15, pp. 177–213.
Travlos, J. and A. Frantz (1965), 'The church of St. Dionysios the Areopagite and the palace of the archbishop of Athens in the 16th century', *Hesperia*, 34: 3, pp. 157–202.
Treadgold, W. (1995), *Byzantium and its Army, 284–1081*, Stanford: Stanford University Press.
Triantaphyllos, D. (1997), 'Enas diachronikos tymbos sto Spelaio Evrou', *To Archaiologiko ergo ste Makedonia kai Thrake*, 11, pp. 625–32.
Tsanana, A. (2003), 'The glazed pottery of Byzantine Vrya (Vrea)', in C. Bakirtzis (ed.), *7o Diethnes Synedrio Mesaionikes Keramikes tes Mesogeiou. Thessalonike, 11–16 oktobriou 1999. Praktika*, Athens: Edition de la Caisse de Recettes Archéologiques, pp. 245–50.
Tsaras, G. (1971), 'Le verbe εσλαβώθη chez Constantin Porphyrogénète', *Cyrillomethodianum*, 1, pp. 26–57.
— (1985), 'Kai amphimeiktous tinas komas', *Byzantina*, 13, pp. 179–200.
Tsitouridou, A. (1985), *The Church of the Panagia Chalkeon*, Thessaloniki: Institute for Balkan Studies.
Tsorbarzoglou, P. G. (2001), 'The "Megalopolis of Thessaloniki" and its world according to the hagiographical texts of the middle Byzantine period', in J. Burke and R. Scott (eds), *Byzantine Macedonia: Art, Architecture, Music, and Hagiography. Papers from the Melbourne Conference July 1995*, Melbourne: National Centre for Hellenic Studies and Research/La Trobe University, pp. 127–40.
Tsougarakis, D. (1982), 'Economic and everyday life in Byzantine Crete through

numismatic evidence', *Jahrbuch der österreichischen Byzantinistik*, 32, pp. 457–65.

Tsourti, I. (2004), 'Antikyra Boiotias. Nomismatike martyria', in I. Kakouris, S. Choulia, and T. Albani (eds), *Thorakion. Aphieroma ste mneme tou Paulou Lazaride*, Athens: Ypourgeio Politismou, Genike Dieuthynse Archaioteton kai Politistikes Klironomias, Dieuthynse Metavyzantinon Archaioteton, pp. 123–8.

Turlej, S. (1998), 'The so-called Chronicle of Monemvasia. A historical analysis', *Byzantion*, 68, pp. 446–68.

— (1999), 'The legendary motif in the tradition of Patras. St. Andrew and the dedication of the Slavs to the Patras Church', *Byzantinoslavica*, 60, pp. 374–99.

— (2001), *The Chronicle of Monemvasia. The Migration of the Slavs and Church Conflicts in the Byzantine Source from the Beginning of the 9th Century*, Cracow: Towarzystwo Wydawnicze 'Historia Iagellonica'.

Tzanis, G. (1996), 'Hoi dioketes tou thematos Thessalonikes kata te basileia tou autokratora Basileiou B' (976–1025)', *Byzantiaka*, 16, pp. 245–63.

Tzitzibassi, A. (2000), 'Marmarina aggeia kathemerines chrises', *Mouseio Byzantinou Politismou*, 7, pp. 18–31.

Uenze, S. (1966), 'Die Schnallen mit Riemenschlaufe aus dem 6. und 7. Jahrhundert', *Bayerische Vorgeschichtsblätter*, 31, pp. 142–81.

— (1992), *Die spätantiken Befestigungen von Sadovec. Ergebnisse der deutsch-bulgarisch-österreichischen Ausgrabungen 1934–1937*, Munich: C. H. Beck.

Ulbert, T. (1984), 'Die religiöse Architektur im östlichen Illyricum', in *Actes du Xe Congrès International d'Archéologie Chrétienne. Thessalonique, 28 septembre–4 octobre 1980*, Vatican/Thessaloniki: Pontificio Istituto di Archeologia Cristiana/ Hetaireia Makedonikon Spoudon, pp. 161–79.

Vakalopoulos, A. (1940), 'To kastro tou Platamona', *Makedonika. Syngrama periodikon tes Hetaireias Makedonikon Spoudon*, 1, pp. 58–76.

— (1968), 'Nouveaux renseignements sur l'histoire de la forteresse de Platamon', in K. N. Triantaphyllos (ed.), *Actes de la VIIIe réunion scientifique de l'Institut International des Châteaux Historiques*, Athens: Technikon Epimeleterion tes Hellados, pp. 27–32.

Varinlioğlu, G. (2005), 'Urban monasteries in Constantinople and Thessaloniki: distribution patterns in time and urban topography', in J. J. Emerick and D. M. Deliyannis (eds), *Archaeology in Architecture: Studies in Honor of Cecil L. Striker*, Mainz: Philipp von Zabern, pp. 187–98.

Varsík, V. (1992), 'Byzantinische Gürtelschnallen im mittleren und unteren Donauraum im 6. und 7. Jahrhundert', *Slovenská Archeológia*, 40: 1, pp. 77–103.

— (1993), 'Zu manchen Problemen der Verbreitung byzantinischer Schnallen im mittleren und unteren Donauraum', in J. Pavuj (ed.), *Actes du XIIe Congrès international des sciences préhistoriques et protohistoriques, Bratislava, 1–7 septembre 1991*, Bratislava: Institut Archéologique de l'Académie Slovaque des Sciences, pp. 207–12.

Vasil'ev, A. (1898), 'Slaviane v' Grecii', *Vizantiiskii Vremennik*, 5, pp. 404–38 and 626–70.

Vasil'evskii, V. G. (1915), *Trudy*, vol. 3, St. Petersburg: Tipografiia Imperatorskoi Akademii nauk.

Vasiliev, A. A. (1943), 'An edict of Emperor Justinian II', *Speculum*, 18, pp. 1–13.

— (1947), 'The "Life" of St. Peter of Argos and its historical significance', *Traditio*, 5, pp. 163–91.
Vasilikopoulou-Ioannidou, A. (1979), 'Lakonia, Lakones eis tous byzantinous syngrapheis', *Lakonikai spoudai*, 4, pp. 3–13.
Vasilikou, N. (2004), 'Ereipomenos naos ste nesida Prasoudi Egoumenitsas. Symbole sten topographia ton epeirotikon akton', in I. Kakouris, S. Choulia, and T. Albani (eds), *Thorakion. Aphieroma ste mneme tou Paulou Lazaride*, Athens: Ypourgeio Politismou, Genike Dieuthynse Archaioteton kai Politistikes Klironomias, Dieuthynse Metavyzantinon Archaioteton, pp. 101–8.
Vasmer, M. (1941), *Die Slaven in Griechenland*, Berlin: Verlag der Akademie der Wissenschaften.
Văzharova, Z. (1976), *Slaviani i prabălgari po danni na nekropolite ot VI–XI v. na teritoriiata na Bălgariia*, Sofia: Izdatelstvo za Bălgarskata Akademiia na Naukite.
Veimarn, E. V. and A. I. Aibabin (1993), *Skalistinskii mogil'nik*, Kiev: Naukova Dumka.
Veis, N. A. (1914), 'Zur Sigillographie der byzantinischen Themen Peloponnes und Hellas', *Vizantiiskii Vremennik*, 21, pp. 90–110 and 192–235.
— (1928), 'Ai epidromai ton Boulgaron hypo ton tzaron Symeon kai ta ta schetika scholia tou Aretha Kaisareias', *Hellenika*, 1, pp. 337–56.
Velenis, G. M. (1995), 'Kaisareia, pempte pole Makedonias', *Egnatia*, 5, pp. 53–75.
— (2003), *Mesobyzantine naodomia ste Thessalonike*, Athens: Akademia Athenon. Kentro Ereunas tes Byzantines kai Metabyzantines.
Veljanovska, F. (1987), 'Skeletot od episkopskata bazilika vo Stobi', *Macedoniae Acta Archaeologica*, 11, pp. 233–9.
Veloudis, G. (1970), 'Jakob Philipp Fallmerayer und die Entstehung des neugriechischen Historismus', *Südost-Forschungen*, 29, pp. 43–90.
Vickers, M. (1971), 'The stadium at Thessaloniki', *Byzantion*, 41, pp. 339–48.
— (1974), 'The late Roman walls of Thessalonica', in E. Birley, B. Dobson, and M. Jarrett (eds), *Roman Frontier Studies 1969. Eighth International Congress of Limesforschung*, Cardiff: University of Wales Press, pp. 249–55.
Vida, T. and T. Völling (2000), *Das slawische Brandgräberfeld von Olympia*, Rahden: Marie Leidorf.
Vikatou, O. (2002), 'To christianiko nekrotapheio sten Agia Triada Heleias. Symbole ste melete tes cheiropoietes keramikes', in P. G. Themelis and V. Konti (eds), *Protobyzantine Messene kai Olympia. Aktikos kai agrotikos choros ste Dytike Peloponneso. Praktika tou Diethnous symposiou, Athena, 29–30 maiou 1998*, Athens: Hetaireia Messeniakon Arkhaiologikon Spoudon/Institouto Byzantinon Ereunon, pp. 238–70.
Vinski, Z. (1967), 'Kasnoantički starosjedioci u Salintanskoj regiji prema arheološkoj ostavštini predslavenskog supstrata', *Vjesnik za arheologiju i historiju Dalmatinsku*, 69, pp. 5–98.
— (1974), 'O kasnim bizantskim kopčama i o pitanju njihova odnosa s avarskim ukrasnim tvorevinama', *Vjesnik Arheološkog Muzeja u Zagrebu*, 8, pp. 57–81.
Vogiatzidis, I. K. (1949), 'He thesis tes kyrios Hellados entos tou byzantinou kratous', *Epeteris Hetaireias Byzantinon Spoudon*, 19, pp. 252–8 and 405–6.
Vogiatzis, S. (1998), 'Parastereseis sten oikodomike istoria tes Panagias Skripous ste Boiotia', *Deltion tes christianikes archaiologikes hetaireias*, 20, pp. 116–28.
Vokotopoulos, P. L. (1975), *He ekklesiastike architektonike eis ten dytiken sterean*

Hellada kai ten Epeiron. Apo tou telous tou 7ou mechri tou telous tou 10ou aionos, Thessaloniki: Kentron Byzantinon Ereunon.
— (1992), *He ekklesiastike architektonike eis ten dytiken sterean Hellada kai ten Epeiron. Apo tou telous tou 7ou mechri tou telous tou 10ou aionos*, 2nd edn, Thessaloniki: Kentron Byzantinon Ereunon.
— (1995), 'Ho byzantinos naos tes Olynthou', in *Diethnes Symposio 'Byzantine Makedonia, 324–1430 m. Kh., Thessalonike, 29–31 Oktobriou 1992*, Thessaloniki: Hetaireia Makedonikon Spoudon, pp. 45–56 and 392.
— (2000), 'Church architecture in Greece during the Middle Byzantine period', in O. Z. Pevny (ed.), *Perceptions of Byzantium and its Neighbors (843–1261)*, New York: Metropolitan Museum of Art, pp. 154–67.
Vokotopoulou, I. P. (1967), 'Neochoropoulon Ioanninon', *Archaiologikon Deltion*, 22: 2, pp. 342–4.
Völling, T. (1992), 'Byzantinische Kleinfunde aus Olympia', in O. Brehm and S. Klie (eds), *ΜΟΥΣΙΚΟΣ ΑΝΗΡ. Festschrift für Max Wegner zum 90. Geburtstag*, Bonn: Habelt, pp. 491–8.
— (1995), 'Ein frühbyzantinischer Hortfund aus Olympia', *Mitteilungen des Deutschen Archäologischen Instituts. Athenische Abteilung*, 110, pp. 425–59.
— (1996), '"Neuer Most aus alten Löwenköpfen". Ein frühbyzantinisches Gemach der alten Grabung in Olympia', *Mitteilungen des Deutschen Archäologischen Instituts. Athenische Abteilung*, 111, pp. 391–410.
— (2001), 'The last Christian Greeks and the first pagan Slavs in Olympia', in E. Kountoura-Galake (ed.), *Hoi skoteinoi aiones tou Byzantiou (7os–9os ai.)*, Athens: Ethniko Idryma Ereunon/Institouto Byzantinon Ereunon, pp. 302–23.
— (2002), 'Early Byzantine agricultural implements from Olympia (5th/6th centuries AD)', in P. G. Themelis and V. Konti (eds), *Protobyzantine Messene kai Olympia. Aktikos kai agrotikos choros ste Dytike Peloponneso. Praktika tou Diethnous symposiou, Athena, 29–30 maiou 1998*, Athens: Hetaireia Messeniakon Arkhaiologikon Spoudon/Institouto Byzantinon Ereunon, pp. 195–207.
Voutsaki, S. (2003), 'Archaeology and the construction of the past in nineteenth-century Greece', in H. Hokwerda (ed.), *Constructions of Greek Past. Identity and Historical Consciousness from Antiquity to the Present*, Groningen: Egbert Forsten, pp. 231–55.
Vroom, J. (2001), 'Byzantine garbage and Ottoman waste: medieval and post-medieval pottery from some rubbish pits at Pelopidou Street, Thebes', in V. S. Aravantinos et al. (eds), *Thèbes: Fouilles de la Cadmée*, Pisa: Istituti Editoriali e Poligrafici Internazionali, pp. 181–233.
— (2003), *After Antiquity. Ceramics and Society in the Aegean from the 7th to the 20th Century A.C. A Case Study from Boeotia, Central Greece*, Leiden: Faculty of Archaeology, Leiden University.
— (2005), *Byzantine to Modern Pottery in the Aegean. An Introduction and Field Guide*, Utrecht: Parnassus Press.
Vryonis, S. (1963), 'An Attic hoard of Byzantine gold coins (688–741) from the Thomas Whittemore collection and the numismatic evidence for the urban history of Byzantium', *Zbornik radova Vizantološkog Instituta*, 8, pp. 291–300.
— (1978), 'Recent scholarship on continuity and discontinuity of culture: Classical Greeks, Byzantines, modern Greeks', in S. Vryonis, Jr (ed.), *Byzantina kai*

Metabyzantina. The 'Past' in Medieval and Modern Greek Culture, Malibu: Undena Publications, pp. 237–56.
— (1981a), 'The evolution of Slavic society and the Slavic invasions in Greece. The first major Slavic attack on Thessaloniki, A.D. 597', *Hesperia*, 50, pp. 378–90.
— (1981b), 'Review of Michael W. Weithmann, "Die slavische Bevölkerung auf der griechischen Halbinsel. Ein Beitrag zur historischen Ethnographie Südosteuropas" (München, 1978)', *Balkan Studies*, 22: 2, pp. 405–39.
— (1992), 'The Slavic pottery (jars) from Olympia, Greece', in S. Vryonis, Jr (ed.), *Byzantine Studies. Essays on the Slavic World and the Eleventh Century*, New Rochelle/New York: Aristide D. Caratzas, pp. 15–42.
— (2003), 'Byzantium, its Slavic elements and their culture (sixth to ninth centuries)', *Symmeikta*, 28, pp. 63–85.
Waage, F. O. (1935), 'Middle Byzantine pottery from the excavations at Corinth', *American Journal of Archaeology*, 39, p. 115.
Waldmüller, L. (1976), *Die ersten Begegnungen der Slawen mit dem Christentum und den christlichen Völkern vom VI. bis VIII. Jahrhundert*, Amsterdam: Adolf M. Hakkert.
Ware, K. (1996), 'St. Athanasios the Athonite: traditionalist or innovator?', in A. Bryer and M. Cunningham (eds), *Mount Athos and Byzantine Monasticism: Papers from the Twenty-Eighth Spring Symposium of Byzantine Studies, Birmingham, March 1994*, Aldershot/Brookfield: Variorum, pp. 4–16.
Warner Slane, K. and G. D. R. Sanders (2005), 'Corinth: late Roman horizons', *Hesperia*, 74, pp. 243–97.
Wasilewski, T. (1980), 'Le thème maritime de la Dalmatie byzantine dans les années 805–822 et sa reconstitution par l'empereur Michel III', *Acta Poloniae Historica*, 41, pp. 35–49.
Waywell, G. B. and J. J. Wilkes (1994), 'Excavations at Sparta: the Roman Stoa, 1988–1991. Part 2', *Annual of the British School at Athens*, 89, pp. 377–432.
— (1995), 'Excavations at the ancient Theatre of Sparta 1992–4: preliminary report', *Annual of the British School at Athens*, 90, pp. 435–60.
Weithmann, M. W. (1978), *Die slavische Bevölkerung auf der griechischen Halbinsel. Ein Beitrag zur historischen Ethnographie Südosteuropas*, Munich: Rudolf Trofenil.
— (1985), 'Anthropologisches Fundgut zur Einwanderung der Slaven in Griechenland. Eine Materialzusammenstellung', *Homo*, 36, pp. 103–9.
Weller, H. L. and D. M. Metcalf (1969), 'A hoard of Byzantine 16 nummi coins minted at Thessaloniki in the time of Justinian I', *Balkan Studies*, 10, pp. 311–14.
Werner, J. (1953), *Slawische Bronzefiguren aus Nordgriechenland*, Berlin: Akademie Verlag.
— (1955), 'Byzantinische Gürtelschnallen des 6. und 7. Jahrhunderts aus der Sammlung Diergardt', *Kölner Jahrbuch für Vor- und Frühgeschichte*, 1, pp. 36–48.
Westerink, L. G. (1972), 'Marginalia by Arethas in Moskow Greek Ms. 231', *Byzantion*, 42, pp. 241–2.
— (1973), *Niketas Magistros. Lettres d'un exilé (928–946)*, Paris: Editions du Centre National de la Recherche Scientifique.
Whitby, M. (1988), *The Emperor Maurice and His Historian: Theopylact Simocatta on Persian and Balkan Warfare*, Oxford: Clarendon Press.

Wickham, C. (2005), *Framing the Early Middle Ages. Europe and the Mediterranean, 400–800*, Oxford: Oxford University Press.
Wiet, G. (1955), *Ibn Rusteh: Les atours précieux*, Cairo : Publications de la Société de Géographie d'Égypte.
Williams, C. K., J. Macintosh, and J. E. Fisher (1974), 'Excavation at Corinth, 1973', *Hesperia*, 43: 1, pp. 1–76.
Wortley, J., ed. (1996), *The Spiritually Beneficial Tales of Paul, Bishop of Monembasia and of Other Authors*, Kalamazoo/Spencer: Cistercian Publications.
Wozniak, F. E. (1982), 'The Justinianic fortification of interior Illyricum', in R. L. Hohlfelder (ed.), *City, Town, and Countryside in the Early Byzantine Era*, New York: Columbia University Press, pp. 199–209.
— (1987), 'Nikopolis and the Roman defense of Epirus', in E. Chrysos (ed.), *Nikopolis I: Proceedings of the First International Symposium on Nikopolis (23–29 September 1984)*, Preveza: Demos Prevezas, pp. 263–7.
Xanalatos, D. A. (1937), 'Beiträge zur Wirtschafts- und Sozialgeschichte Makedoniens im Mittelalter, hauptsächlich auf Grund der Briefe des Erzbischofs Theophylaktos von Achrida', PhD dissertation. Munich, Ludwig Maximilian Universität.
Yannopoulos, P. A. (1980), 'La pénétration slave en Argolide', in *Etudes argiennes*, Athens: Ecole Française d'Athènes, pp. 323–71.
— (1990–1993), 'Les Slaves chez Ménandre', *Epeteris Hetaireias Byzantinon Spoudon*, 48, pp. 27–35.
— (1993a), 'Ho boreioelladikos choros kata ton Bio Gregoriou to Dekapolitou', *Parnassos*, pp. 45–55.
— (1993b), 'Métropoles du Péloponnèse mésobyzantin: un souvenir des invasions avaro-slaves', *Byzantion*, 63, pp. 388–400.
— (1994), 'La Grèce dans la Vie de s. Elie le Jeune et dans celle de S. Elie le Spéléote', *Byzantion*, 64, pp. 193–221.
— (1995), 'La Grèce dans la Vie de S. Fantin', *Byzantion*, 65: 2, pp. 475–94.
— (1997), 'Ho episkopikos katalogos tou Byzantinou Argos', in T. A. Gritsopoulos and K. L. Kotsonis (eds), *Praktika tou E' diethnous synedriou Peloponnesiakon spoudon. Argos-Nauplion, 6–10 septembriou 1995*, Athens: Hetaireia Peloponnesiakon Spoudon, pp. 361–8.
Zachopoulos, C. (1992), 'He polemike ischys ton "Sklabinon" sten "5e poliorkia" tes Thessalonikes kai hoi scheseis tous me to byzantino kratos sten idia periodo', in I. Karagiannopoulos (ed.), *12' Panellenio Historiko Synedrio (29–31 Maiou 1992). Praktika*, Thessaloniki: Ekdoseis Vanias, pp. 39–64.
Zacos, G. and A. Veglery (1972), *Byzantine Lead Seals*, Basle: J. J. Augustin.
Zaimov, I. (1967), *Zaselvane na bălgarskite slaviani na Balkanskiia poluostrov. Prouchvane na zhitelskite imena v bălgarskata toponimiia*, Sofia: Izdatelstvo za Bălgarska Akademiia na Naukite.
— (1968), 'Anciens noms bulgares dans la partie sud de la Péninsule balkanique', in V. Georgiev, I. Gălăbov, and I. Zaimov (eds), *Actes du Premier Congrès International des Etudes Balkaniques et Sud-Est Européennes*, Sofia: Editions de l'Académie Bulgare des Sciences, pp. 389–414.
Zakythinos, D. A. (1945), *Hoi Slaboi en Helladi. Symbolai eis ten historian tou mesaionikou Hellenismou*, Athens: Aetos.
— (1957), 'Kastron Lakedaimonos', *Hellenika*, 15, pp. 95–111.
— (1965), *He Byzantine Hellas, 392–1204*, Athens: Ekdoseis E. G. Vagionake.

— (1966), 'La grande brèche dans la tradition historique de l'hellénisme du septième au neuvième siècle', in *Charisterion eis Anastasion K. Orlandon*, Athens: Archaiologike Hetaireia.

Zastěrová, B. (1976), 'Zu einigen Fragen aus der Geschichte der slawischen Kolonisation auf dem Balkan', in H. Köpstein and F. Winkelmann (eds), *Studien zum 7. Jahrhundert in Byzanz. Probleme der Herausbildung des Feudalismus*, Berlin: Akademie Verlag, pp. 59–72.

Zavadskaia, I. A. (2002), 'Baptisterii Khersonesa (k istorii kreshchal'nogo obriada v rannevizantiiskogo period)', *Materialy po arkheologii, istorii i etnografii Tavrii*, 9, pp. 251–72.

Zeiller, J. (1926), 'Les premiers siècles chrétiens en Thrace, en Macédoine, en Grèce et Constantinople', *Byzantion*, 3, pp. 215–31.

Zeiss, H. (1940), 'Avarenfunde in Korinth?', in *Serta Hoffileriana. Commentationes gratulatorias Victori Hoffiler sexagenario obtulerunt collegae, amici, discipuli, A.D. XI kal. mar. MCMXXXVII*, Zagreb: Zaklada Tiskare Narodni Novina, pp. 95–9.

Zikos, N. (1977), 'Molybdoboulla tou Byzantinou Mouseiou Athenon', *Archaiologikon Deltion*, 32, pp. 80–90.

Ziota, C. (1998), 'Kitrine Limne 1998. Anaskaphe sto Xeropegado Koiladas', *To Archaiologiko ergo ste Makedonia kai Thrake*, 12, pp. 503–16.

Ziota, C. and K. Moskanis (1997), 'Apo ten archaiologike ereuna sten archaia Eordaia. He anaskaphe ston Philota Phlorinas', *To Archaiologiko ergo ste Makedonia kai Thrake*, 11, pp. 43–55.

Živkov, S. (2003), 'Christian adaptations in Athens in Late Antiquity (end of 5th–beginning of 7th century)', *Hortus Artium Medievalium*, 9, pp. 213–19.

Živković, T. (1997), 'Prilog hronologij avarsko-slovenskih odnosa 559–578. godine', *Istorijski časopis*, 42–3, pp. 227–36.

— (1999), 'The date of the creation of the theme of Peloponnese', *Symmeikta*, 13, pp. 141–55.

— (2002a), *Južni Sloveni pod vizantijskom vlaštju, 600–1025*, Belgrade: Istorijski Institut/Službeni Glasnik.

— (2002b), 'The strategos Paul and the archontes of the Westerners', *Symmeikta*, 15, pp. 161–76.

— (2008), *Forging Unity. The South Slavs Between East and West: 550–1150*, Belgrade: Institute of History.

Živojinović, M. (1973), 'Sur l'époque de la formation de l'évêché d'Hiérissos', *Zbornik radova Vizantološkog Instituta*, 14–15, pp. 155–8.

Zverugo, I. G. (2005), *Belaruskae Paville u zhaleznym veku i rannim siaredneviakoui*, Minsk: Instytut Gistoryi NAN Belarusi.

Index

Abadie-Reynal, Catherine, 64
Abdallah Umar II ibn Shuayub, 152
Abdera, 122, 145
Abū Hafs, 139
Abū Hārith *see* Leo of Tripoli
Achaia, 15, 18, 28, 33, 48, 59, 76, 249, 250
Achilles, Bishop of Larissa, 33
Adam Zagliveriou, 91
Adrianople, 1
Africa, 15, 21, 135, 139, 152, 169, 224, 225
Agallianos, turmarch, 115, 117
Agapetus, pope, 33
Agia Kyriaki, 27, 28, 91
Agia Paraskevi, 34
Agia Trias, 122–3
Agia Varvara, 34
Agios Nikolaos, 69, 79
agriculture, 35, 210–11
Aigina, 116, 139, 147, 212, 213, 254, 264, 267, 289
Aigion, 28, 195
Akamiros, 126–7, 154, 232, 233, 286
Akra Sophia, 38
al-Khandaq *see* Iraklion
Albania, 123, 124
Albanians, 1, 254
Alexander 'Snips', 13
Alexios I Komnenos, 136
Alexios Studites, patriarch, 266
Alkison, Bishop of Nikopolis, 32, 51
Alusian, 177, 260
American School of Classical Studies in Athens, 6
Amphipolis, 28, 50, 63, 65, 224, 250

amphorae, 24, 37, 39, 40, 53, 64–5, 185, 220
ampullae, 54
Amyklion, 209, 233
Anastasius, emperor, 32, 58, 77
Anchialos, 17
Andikira, 28, 53
Ano Gardenitsa, 194
Antikythera, island of, 100
Antiochos, *doux*, 174, 232, 237
Aphiona, 121, 123, 212
Apidea, 85, 88
Appiaria, 17
Arabs, 11, 109, 135, 137, 139, 141, 144, 146–7, 151, 152, 153, 154, 166, 167, 173, 198, 213, 221, 225, 252, 266, 267, 277, 288, 290, 291
archon, 9, 116–17, 127, 135, 142, 153, 154, 232–3, 235, 237, 245, 285, 286, 287; *see also* titles
Ardameri, 218
Arethas of Kaisareia, 7, 157, 170, 172, 235, 281, 291
Argos, 56–7, 58, 59, 63, 64, 68, 99, 109, 137, 150, 151, 153, 187, 219, 230, 250, 251, 253, 254, 255, 263
army
   Byzantine, 9, 10, 140, 178, 182–3, 185–6, 222, 225, 226, 230, 276
   Roman, 15, 18, 39, 40, 64, 85–6, 89, 91–2, 97
arrows, 24, 106, 153, 220
Arsenios, Bishop of Kerkyra, 235
Arta, 31

Askra, 63
Astypaleia, 250
Athanasios, Bishop of Methone, 151
Athens, 6, 9, 13, 48, 53–5, 58, 62, 63, 68, 80, 81, 84, 85, 87, 88, 90, 92, 98, 99, 106–7, 108, 109, 112, 115, 116, 117–18, 120, 124, 126, 140, 146, 149, 156, 168, 170, 177, 183, 184, 211, 212, 219, 222, 230, 232, 250, 263, 264, 281, 286
Athos, Mount, 5, 144, 173, 175, 196–9, 213–16, 217, 218, 226, 240, 243, 267–70, 285
Attica, 23, 28, 141, 253
Avars, 16–18, 20, 62, 68, 76, 85, 92, 105, 106, 117, 120, 124, 125, 126, 253–4, 279, 281, 282, 285

Baiunetes, 19, 286
Balkans, 9, 10, 17, 18, 20, 24, 31, 32, 39, 40, 48, 58, 63, 65, 68, 85, 100, 102, 105, 108, 111, 112, 115, 124, 230, 276
bandits, 141, 263
baptisteries, 34, 52, 55, 56, 57, 59, 145, 146
Bardas Platopydes, 172, 235
Barnsley, Sidney Howard, 6
Basil I, 144, 146, 147, 151, 153, 213, 219, 231, 292, 293
Basil II, 175–7, 187, 197, 236, 251, 276, 289
Basil Apokaukos, 176, 185, 260
Basil Nasar, 152, 289
basilica, 24, 26, 27, 28, 31–2, 34, 35, 50, 51, 52, 53, 54, 56, 57, 58, 61, 68, 99, 100, 145, 188, 230
   cemeterial, 27, 34, 56, 57
   see also church
baths, 38, 49, 53, 54, 55, 57, 58, 61, 62, 237
beads
   amber, 105
   bronze, 122, 145
   glass, 121, 122, 140, 146, 239
beehives, 53, 212
Belegezites, 9, 19, 68, 109, 117, 124, 125, 126, 232, 281, 286

Berbati, river, 38, 121
Berzetes, 19, 125, 287
Bgadoudi, 26, 27
bishops, 31, 32, 33, 34, 57, 59, 115–16, 141, 147, 150, 249–57, 266
Bolaina, 251, 253
Boleron, theme of, 178
bracelets, 88, 99, 120, 220, 239, 240
bridges, 187, 256
British School of Archaeology in Athens, 6
buckles, 8, 98, 99, 100, 101, 102, 103, 106, 140–1, 239, 240, 262
   Boly-Želovce class, 101
   Corinth class, 100, 101, 103, 107, 121
   Emling class, 106
   Nagyharsány class, 103–4
   Pergamon class, 100
   Sucidava class, 24
   Syracuse class, 103
Bulgaria, 23, 40, 111, 123, 123, 124, 142, 144, 170, 174, 221, 236, 238, 276, 289
Bulgarians, 170, 171, 175, 176, 177, 183, 185, 195, 218, 221, 243, 245, 265, 277, 291
Bulgars, 20, 109, 110, 117, 124, 141–2
burial, 58
   chamber, 26, 40, 49, 55, 57–8, 99, 101, 230
   children, 55, 121, 240
   female, 26, 100, 103, 106, 121, 237–9
   in church, 27
   male, 26, 103–5, 121
   mass, 55, 61–2
   warrior, 105, 106
Byzantine Museum in Athens, 7

canoes, 19
capitals, column, 28, 31, 50
cemetery, 49, 56, 57, 59, 99–101
   cremation, 11, 122
   inhumation, 24, 99–100, 120, 121, 122–3, 140, 146

chafing dishes, 120, 138, 158n, 184
Chaldkidike, 173, 213, 219, 240, 241, 243
Chalkis, 81, 237
chapel, 143, 237
　funerary, 143
Charanis, Peter, 2, 3, 18, 110, 112
Chenitsa, island of, 114
Chersonissos, 90
Chios, 168, 169, 244, 290
　theme of, 169
Christianity, 10, 11, 103, 174, 249–70, 284, 285, 289, 291
Christopher, *katepano*, 186, 276
Christoupolis *see* Kavala
Chronicle of Monemvasia, 2, 7, 109, 136, 150, 241, 253, 254–5, 277, 279, 281, 282, 288, 291
chrysobulls, 136, 137, 144, 196, 197, 242, 266, 278, 282, 290
Chrysoupolis, 141, 145, 158n, 213, 218
church, 6, 8, 9, 10, 11, 17, 51, 54, 99, 121, 123, 135, 137, 143, 145, 147, 152, 172, 175, 187–8, 193–4, 217, 239, 255, 256, 262, 265, 267, 276, 277
　Assumption in Aetolophos, 187
　Assumption in Tegea, 188
　cave, 169
　cross-in-octagon, 195
　cross-in-square, 147, 188, 194, 270
　Dormition of the Holy Virgin in Skripou, 147–9, 154, 213, 226, 231
　Hagia Sophia in Thessaloniki, 5, 98, 184, 267
　Holy Apostles in Athens, 195
　Holy Theodores in Athens, 186, 196
　Holy Virgin *Panaxiotissa* in Gavrolimni, 188
　Panagia *ton Chalkeon* in Thessaloniki, 186, 196
　Panagia Lykodemou in Athens, 195
　Prophet Elias at Starapazaro, 149

　St Andrew in Patras, 135, 151, 154–5, 157, 242
　St Barbara in Steiris, 186
　St Catherine in Athens, 195
　St Christopher in Pallandion, 187, 252–3, 254
　St Demetrios in Thessaloniki, 5, 28, 31, 48, 49, 62, 143, 220, 260
　St Demetrios *Katsouri* in Plesioi, 149
　St Dionysios the Areopagite in Athens, 100, 141
　St George at Keria, 188, 194
　St Gregory the Theologian in Thebes, 149
　St John Mangoutis, 149
　St Nicholas in Milia, 194
　St Nicholas in Olynthos, 196
　St Panteleimon in Ano Boularioi, 187, 188
　St Peter in Alika, 121
　St Peter in Palaiochora, 188
　Sts Jason and Sosipatros in Kerkyra, 195
　Sts Sergios and Bacchus in Kythera, 266
　single-naved, 188
　Virgin in Athens, 177
cisterns, 57, 151
cities, 10, 13, 14, 16–18, 40, 48–65
climate, 210
coins, 6, 8, 9, 10, 13, 22, 23, 35, 38, 39, 49, 50, 55, 57, 58, 61, 62, 65, 69–92, 97, 106–8, 111–12, 113, 121, 122, 124, 137–8, 140, 141, 156, 178, 181, 182–3, 185, 238, 256–7, 276
combs, 237
Comes Marcellinus, 15, 61
confraternities, religious, 187, 235
Constans II, 106–7, 111, 122, 124, 177, 276
Constantine I, pope, 110
Constantine IV, 108, 109, 117, 124, 285
Constantine V, 109, 116, 118, 126, 220, 232, 280, 286, 294
Constantine VI, 126

Constantine VII Porphyrogenitus, 2, 109–10, 136, 139, 155, 171, 172, 194, 197, 235, 236, 251, 276, 278–80, 281, 282–3, 289, 291, 293
Constantine VIII, 196
Constantine IX, 196, 198, 242
Constantine Diogenes, 177
Constantinople, 1, 3, 32, 33, 34, 39, 48, 50, 51, 61, 77, 85, 88, 107, 108, 109, 110, 112, 117, 118, 119, 126, 137, 144, 147, 150, 153, 154, 156, 166, 167, 170, 172, 173, 181, 186, 196, 213, 219, 220, 221, 226, 236, 239, 243, 253, 256, 257, 265, 267, 269, 277, 282
conversion, 10, 119, 136, 137, 144, 150–1, 221, 251, 254, 255, 263, 273n, 289, 291
Corfu *see* Kerkyra
Corinth, 6, 9, 13, 14, 17, 23, 31, 33, 34, 39, 48, 55–6, 57, 59, 60–1, 62, 63, 64, 68, 77, 79, 85, 86, 90, 92, 99, 103, 106, 107, 108, 109, 112, 116, 122, 124, 135, 137, 139, 140, 141, 150, 152, 153, 156, 176, 178, 181, 182, 184, 185, 186, 209, 212, 219, 220, 222, 223, 226, 230, 237, 240, 250, 251, 253, 254–5, 257, 259, 261, 263, 278, 289, 293
council, church
  II Nicaea, 126, 250
  Quinisext (*in Trullo*), 110, 250
  Sixth Ecumenical, 109, 249, 293
Crete, 33, 64, 139, 146, 152, 168, 169, 181, 187, 197, 212, 213, 218, 220, 225, 241, 250, 252, 263, 265–6, 288
  theme of, 169
crops, 37, 211, 215
cross
  pectoral, 240
  processional, 146
Cutrigurs, 15, 20

Damala, 251
Damianos, emir, 166, 168
Danielis, 153–7, 213, 219, 231, 242, 245, 277
Danube, 16
Delos, 92
Delphi, 52–3, 54, 58, 63, 64, 65, 219, 224, 230
Demetrias, 48, 52, 53, 63, 68, 109, 116, 166, 177, 224, 286
Demetrios, Bishop of Philippi, 33
Demus, Otto, 6
Dhema, mountain pass, 23, 24
Didymoteichon, 142
Diehl, Charles, 5
Dion, 27
Dobrobikea, 173, 218, 243
Dodona, 15, 22, 31
Dokos, island of, 98
Dometios, Bishop of Nikopolis, 51
Dorotheos, Archbishop of Thessalonica, 32, 249
Drougoubiteia
  bishopric, 251, 285
  theme of, 176, 178, 251, 285
Drugubites, 9, 19, 76, 108, 116, 124, 125, 142, 251, 270n, 281, 285–6, 287, 288
Drymos, 27, 141
Dvornik, Francis, 142
Dyrrachium, 120

earrings, 26, 88, 99, 100, 122, 140, 146, 238, 239
earthquakes, 10, 13, 20, 48, 59–61, 173
Echinos, 48, 59
Ecole Française d'Athènes, 5
Edessa, 7, 100, 101, 176, 177, 237, 240, 250
  theme of, 178
Egypt, 139
Eleusis, 81, 85, 87, 88
Enorion, 217
Enotia, 177
eparch of Thessalonica, 115, 232
Epidauros, 218
Epirus, 15, 18, 28, 31, 32, 39, 61, 69, 151, 249, 250, 253
Episkopi, 149, 196

Erimos, 194
Ermioni, 40, 210
ethnicity, 11, 125, 278–95
eulogia, 259–60
Euripos, 146, 215, 252, 262
Europos, 99
Eurotas, river, 187, 256
Eusebios, Archbishop of Thessalonica, 33
Eustathios, Bishop of Vessaina, 187, 191
Evagrius, 17, 253
Evidites, 9, 116, 124, 287
Evvoia, 146, 149, 170, 171, 253, 261, 267
Exampela, 121
exorcism, 262
Ezerites, 9, 126, 139–40, 171, 172, 185, 225, 278, 279, 282–3, 284, 289
Ezoba, 213, 218

Fallmerayer, Jakob Philipp, 1, 8, 254
family, 3, 19, 157
feasts, 234
fibulae, 8
 'Slavic' 101
 with bent stem, 23, 100
finger-rings, 120, 238, 239, 240, 261
Finlay, George, 6
forts, 7, 16–17, 21–4, 40, 97–8, 147, 175, 188, 253
Frantz, Alison, 6
frescoes, 8, 26, 40, 143, 169, 196

Gastria, 170, 220, 259
George of Pisidia, 19
German Institute in Athens, 5
Glagolitic, letters, 174, 242, 286
Glanorisi, 97
glassware, 121, 219
Gortyna, 64
graffiti, 23, 116, 140
Graikoi, 158n, 278, 291–3
Gravouna, 210
Gregory of Taron, 176
Gregory the Great, pope, 33–4

Hadrian, Bishop of Thebes, 33
Harun ibn Yahya, 145
Helladikoi, 2, 114, 115, 127, 291, 294, 295
Hellas, 13, 173, 256, 295
 theme of, 5, 9, 108, 110, 111, 112, 113–14, 115, 116, 117, 118, 124, 125, 126, 127, 131n, 140, 170, 172, 176, 177, 183, 184, 186, 196, 215, 220, 225, 226, 230, 234, 236, 242, 245, 250, 261, 276, 277, 280, 286, 291, 293, 294
Hellenes, 18, 32, 86, 291–2, 293–4, 296n
Herakleios, emperor, 18, 19, 20, 63, 68, 92, 97, 106, 230
Hermeleia, 218
Hermione, 32
Hexamilion, 15, 23, 41n, 48, 98
Hierissos, 173, 174, 175, 214, 217, 218, 241, 242, 286
Hierokles, 48
Himerios, admiral, 166, 168
hoards, 10, 35, 60, 68–92, 97, 137, 178, 185, 211, 238
Hormisdas, pope, 32
houses, 35, 36, 37, 49, 52, 53, 54, 56, 58, 60, 107, 120, 121, 145–6, 237
Hungary, 101, 105, 124, 221

iconoclasm, 143, 151, 260, 273n, 288
icons, 4, 187, 227n, 235, 250, 260, 288
Ignatios, patriarch, 149
Ignatios the Deacon, 141, 245
Ikaria, 250
Imbros, 166, 295n
inscriptions, 5, 14, 23, 26, 27, 32, 40, 49, 51, 52, 56, 57, 61, 98, 121, 141, 142, 147, 149, 152, 156, 167, 170, 175, 187, 193, 220, 261, 270n, 287, 296n
Ioannina, 120, 124
Ioannitza, Mount, 171, 215, 217, 257, 264–5
Iraklion, 168, 169, 197, 218
Irene, empress, 140
Isidore of Seville, 18, 19
Isthmia, 15, 23, 85, 87, 107, 212

Italy, 15, 21, 107, 108, 124, 138, 140, 152, 153, 171, 172, 175, 185, 217, 219, 220, 221, 222, 226, 241, 257, 277, 289, 291, 292
Ithaka, 141

Jews, 219, 225, 233, 242, 244, 289–90
John, Archbishop of Thessalonica, 16, 17, 18, 21, 62, 109, 293
John Alekasseos, 177
John Aratos, 219, 233, 235, 244, 290
John Geometres, 280
John Kaminiates, 166, 173, 256, 286, 287, 295
John Lampardopoulos, 186
John Malakenos, 236
John of Biclar, 16
John of Ephesus, 16, 17
John Proteuon, 171
John Tzimiskes, 197, 198
John Xenos, 265–6
Joseph, Archbishop of Thessalonike, 126, 143
Jovianus, Bishop of Palaiopolis, 32
judges, 176, 185, 196, 204n, 243, 246n, 256, 260, 261
Justin I, 24, 58, 59
Justin II, 22, 35, 38, 39, 56, 57, 62
Justinian I, 13, 22, 23, 24, 32, 33, 34, 35, 38, 48, 49, 53, 58, 59, 61, 77, 86, 253
Justinian II, 108, 109, 112, 276

Kako Vouno, 194
Kalamata, 261
Kalamion, 265
Kallion, 31
Kaminiates, John, 5
Kapheroi, 136–7, 225, 241, 253, 288, 291
Karabisianoi, 110
Karla, lake, 239
Karyoupolis, 151
Kassandreia, 48, 218
Kastoria, 177, 178, 188
  lake, 23
Kastorion *see* Thisvi
Kastro, 26

katepano, 175, 187, 276
katholikon, 143, 188, 195, 197, 198, 204n, 233, 266, 268, 269, 270
Kavala, 5, 173
Kenchreai, 80, 84, 88, 90, 122, 152
Keos, 110
Kephalari, 28
Kephallenia, 152, 251, 289
  theme of, 115, 124, 231, 232
Kephalos, island of, 28, 31, 34, 97
Keramidi, 99
Kerkyra, 15, 20, 33, 116, 121, 123, 151, 235, 250, 286
Kernitsa, 195, 251
Kibyrrhaiotai, 113, 241
Kilkis, 26
kilns, 24, 40, 53, 203n, 220, 229n
Kitros, 175
Kleidion, pass, 176
Kleitoria, 87, 88
Klokova, Mount, 151
Kolchis, 145
Kolyndros, 175
kommerkia, 110–11, 112, 114, 115, 143, 145, 220, 221, 224
kommerkiarioi see kommerkia
Komotini, 22
Kopais, lake, 149, 213
Koromilia, 28
Korone, 136, 251, 255, 266
Koronisia, 188
Kougeas, Sokrates, 7
kourator, 115, 147, 187, 212, 213
Koutsi, 80, 88
Kratigos, 88
Kremasta, lake, 150
Krinites Arotras, 171–2, 186, 232, 234, 265, 276, 282
Kyparissia, 170
Kythera, 168, 266

Ladochori, 99
Lakedaimon *see* Sparta
Lamia, 28
lamps, 39, 53, 54, 63, 64, 220
Larissa, 34, 116, 175, 237, 245, 250, 277, 291
Laurent, Joseph, 5

Laurion, 81
Lechaion, 28, 31, 56, 59
Lemerle, Paul, 5, 19, 136
Lemnos, 126, 166, 168
Leo III, 111, 115, 117, 294
Leo V, 288
Leo VI, 145, 152, 153, 166, 242, 245, 285, 292
Leo of Tripoli, 145, 166, 220, 233, 256, 287
Leo the Mathematician, 143, 249
Lesbos, 139, 146, 266
Leukas, 256
Life of St. Luke the Younger, 168, 232, 236, 244, 261
Life of St. Nikon, 7, 11, 174, 176, 185, 193, 232, 260, 263, 282, 291
Life of St. Pancratius, 119–20, 125, 281
Life of St. Peter of Argos, 168, 173, 255
Life of St. Phantinos, 245
Ligourion, 195
linguistics, 4, 5, 6, 8, 116, 211, 284–5
Litochorion, 210
Litovoi, 177, 277
liturgy, 257–8, 262–3
Liudprand of Cremona, 173, 219, 256
Longas, 23, 175, 188, 240
Longobardia, theme of, 154, 186, 245, 276
Louloudies, 24, 26, 27, 211, 216

McCormick, Michael, 222
Macedonia, 15, 23, 28, 33, 48, 69, 86, 109, 123, 124, 139, 140, 141, 145, 156, 184, 217, 239, 249, 250, 293
  theme of, 142, 177, 278, 293
Magnesia, 28
Magoula Hadzimissiotiki, 239
Magyars, 110, 173, 251, 289, 291
Maina *see* Mani
Malaisina, 89
Malingoudis, Phaedon, 8
Mandra, 240
Mani, 6, 8, 100, 187, 188, 193, 251, 252, 292
Mantinea, 81, 91

Mardaites, 131n, 163n, 225, 289
Maroneia, 8, 141
Martin I, pope, 110, 132n, 249
masonry, 188, 195
mattocks, 35, 211, 216
Maurice, emperor, 17, 51, 55, 84, 279
Megara, 78, 88
Megaw, Arthur H. S., 6
Melana, 197
Menander the Guardsman, 16
Mentzaina, 195
Messenia *see* Messini
Messini, 58, 63, 106
Metcalf, Michael, 68
Methone, 39, 136, 151, 152, 212, 251, 255
Meyer, Gustav, 5
Michael II, 137, 140
Michael III, 137, 139, 140, 144, 282, 286
Michael IV, 260
Michael Choirosphaktes, 216, 234, 243, 244
Michael the Syrian, 17
Milia, 175
mills, 54, 58, 216, 228n, 243, 246
Milingoi, 9, 126, 139–40, 171, 172, 174, 185, 217, 225, 232, 237, 277, 279, 282–3, 284, 285, 287, 288, 291
Miracles of St. Demetrios, 16, 17, 18, 19, 48, 50, 62, 69, 108, 117, 124, 125, 279, 281, 286, 287, 293
Moglena, 175, 176, 240
monastery, 7, 54, 137, 143–4, 147, 151, 160n, 174, 186, 187, 256, 259, 263, 264, 266
  Docheiariou, 198
  Esphigmenou, 198
  Gomaton, 175
  Great Lavra, 175, 197, 198, 213, 215, 217, 242, 268–9, 270
  Iviron, 174, 197–8, 213, 216, 217, 241, 242, 243, 286
  Mother of God *Antiphonetria* in Myriokephala, 241, 265–6
  Nea Mone in Chios, 196, 242, 290

of Kolobos in Hierissos, 144, 173, 213
of the Philosopher in Dimitsana, 186
Protaton (Karyes), 268, 270
St Andrew in Peristera, 144, 197, 212, 214
St George in Athens, 233
St John the Baptist (Leontia) in Thessalonike, 143, 196
St Luke in Steiris, 5, 6, 187, 195, 196, 265
St Nicholas *tou Chrysokamerou*, 216
St Nikephoros of Xeropotamou, 197
St Nikon in Sparta, 216, 217, 222, 232, 234, 237, 243, 246, 263, 283, 284, 291
St Stephen in Thessalonike, 144, 267
Vatopedi, 198
Xeropotamou, 198, 215
Monemvasia, 116, 118, 119, 126, 168, 250, 251, 254, 266, 281, 289
Monophysites, 33
Mordtmann, Andreas David, 5
mosaics, 27, 28, 31, 32, 38, 51, 52, 53, 57, 58, 196
Moutsopoulos, Nikolaos, 7
Mylovos, 175
Myrodaton, 239
myrrh, 260
Mytikas, 26
Mytilene, 246

Naupaktos, 137, 150, 153, 154, 156, 187, 235, 238, 251, 263
Nauplion, 187, 266
navy, Byzantine, 9, 107–8, 110–11, 112, 124, 152, 166, 168, 186, 225, 226, 230, 276, 289
Naxos, 110, 147, 169
Nea Anchialos, 28, 31, 64, 68, 81, 99, 101, 230
Nea Philadelphia, 170
Nemea, 39, 91
Neposi, 22
Nestos, 22, 142, 145
Nicholas III the Grammarian, patriarch, 136

Nicholas, Bishop of Lakedaimon, 187, 252, 254
Nicholas Mystikos, patriarch, 150, 166, 251, 253, 270n, 285
Nikephoros I, 135–7, 139, 241, 251, 253, 254–5, 278, 279, 282, 283, 293
Nikephoros II Phokas, 169, 175, 186, 197, 268–9
Nikephoros Botaneiates, 177
Nikephoros Ouranos, 176
Nikephoros Xiphias, 177
Niketas Magistros, 236, 280, 288, 291
Niketas Ooryphas, 152
Nikopolis, 15, 28, 31, 32, 33, 34, 51, 58, 116, 150, 224
  theme of, 150, 177, 231, 238, 294
Nisyros, 250
notitiae episcopatuum, 250–1

Ochia, 194
Oikonomides, Nicholas, 116
Olympia, 5, 11, 34, 35, 58, 63, 91, 103, 122–5, 126, 211, 212, 281
Olympos, 34, 140
Orchomenos *see* Skripou
Ostrogoths, 15, 20, 39, 69
oysters, 146, 219

paganism, 174, 292
Paiania, 89
palace, 24, 52, 53, 237
Palaiokastritsa, 122, 123
Palaiopolis, 28, 31, 32
paleobotany, 37, 211
Palestine, 32, 64
Paliambela, 27
Paliokastro, 38
Palioklisi, 28
Paparrigopoulos, Konstantinos, 1, 3, 4, 7
Parnassos, Mount, 210
Parnon, Mount, 140
paroikoi, 174, 196, 217, 242–3, 244, 290
Paros, 34, 147, 267
Patmos, 147

Patras, 27, 39, 57, 60, 85, 88, 90, 126, 135–7, 139, 150, 151, 152, 153–4, 155, 157, 174, 186, 211, 219, 235, 237, 242, 250, 251, 253, 254, 255, 257, 277, 278, 281, 282, 283, 284, 291, 292, 293
patrikios, 114, 117; see also titles
Paul, Archbishop of Thessalonica, 115, 249
Paul, Bishop of Monemvasia, 184, 237, 256
peasants, 13, 14, 214–15, 246, 265, 271n
Pellene, 69, 78, 81, 88
Peloponnesos, 9, 11, 13, 15, 112, 120, 126, 140, 150–1, 152, 153, 155, 156, 168, 170, 171, 173, 181, 188, 193, 195, 210, 211, 213, 216, 217, 219, 220, 222, 225, 226, 227, 233, 237, 241, 242, 251, 252, 253, 254–5, 256, 257, 263, 264, 266, 276, 278, 279, 281, 282, 284, 285, 288, 289, 291, 292, 293, 294
  theme of, 5, 9, 115, 126, 135, 137, 139, 176, 183, 185–6, 219, 231, 235, 236, 259, 260, 280
pendants, 121
Perbundos, 108, 285
Pertoulion, 210
Peter Delian, 177
Petit, Paul, 5
Petrochorion, 81
Philippi, 28, 31, 50, 58, 141, 142, 145, 219, 220, 250, 251, 287
Philippias, 31
Philippikos, emperor, 111–12
Philippopolis, 109
Philotas, 240
Phoinike, 31
Phokas, emperor, 92
Photike, 22, 31
pilgrimage, 31, 170, 259–60, 266
pirates, 109, 139, 141, 146, 168
place names, 3, 8, 174, 210–11, 216, 283–5
plague, 2, 10, 18, 48, 59, 61–2, 109, 118, 195, 244, 279, 280, 290, 294
Platamon, 7, 175, 188

Pliska, 142
plowshares, 37, 216
Polichnitos, 88
Politika-Psachna, 68, 81
Polystylon, 185, 240
Poroi, 146, 219
Porto Lago, 146
Portochelion, 38, 40, 64, 99, 211
pottery, 6, 7, 98, 107, 120, 121, 141, 146, 151
  African Red Slip, 38, 56, 63, 77, 99
  Central Greek Painted, 44n, 64, 66n
  Fine Orange-Red Burnished see pottery: Gouged
  glazed, 120, 137, 185, 220
  Glazed White I, 65, 120
  Glazed White Ware see Impressed White
  Gouged, 185
  handmade, 105, 106, 122, 125
  Impressed White, 137–8, 145, 184
  in the grave, 121
  Late Roman C, 38
  Phocaean Red Slip, 63
  Polychrome, 184
Presian, 142
press
  for olive oil, 24, 35, 39, 54, 211
  for wine, 35, 36, 203n, 211, 212, 215
Priolithos Kalavryton, 87
processions, 258–9
Prokopios of Kaisareia, 13–14, 20–1, 23, 39, 48, 59, 60, 61, 293
protospatharios, 9, 132n, 139, 145, 147, 153, 154, 155, 160n, 166, 171, 172, 186, 226, 231, 233, 235–6, 277; see also titles
Pseira, 120, 137
Pylos, 152
Pyrgouthi, 35, 39, 40, 64, 211, 212

querns, 35, 107, 121, 212, 216

Radolibos, 173
Reinach, Salomon, 5
relics, 175, 197, 203n
Rendakios, 233, 247n, 284

Rendina, 7, 22, 86, 175, 220, 239
Rethymno, 265
Rhodes, 88, 250
Rhodope
  mountains, 22, 123, 142
  province, 33, 249
Romanos I, 172, 185, 197, 219, 235, 236, 241, 257, 276, 277, 278, 280, 282, 283, 284
Romanos II, 173
Romanos III, 266
Rome, 33, 34, 141, 168, 249, 266
Rovi, island of, 114, 116
Rynchines, 76, 108, 125, 281, 285, 286, 287

Sagudates, 19, 76, 108, 281, 285, 286
saints, 260–1
  Achilleios, 175
  Andrew, 135–6
  Athanasia of Aigina, 245, 267, 289
  Athanasios of Methone, 266
  Athanasios the Athonite, 5, 197, 268
  Constantine (Cyril), 286
  Demetrios, 19, 51, 52, 261
  Elias Spelaiotes, 151–2
  Elias the Younger, 151, 152, 159n, 168, 290
  Euthymios the Younger, 5, 144, 197, 212
  George of Lesbos, 215, 246, 266
  Gregory of Dekapolis, 141–2, 143, 246
  Kyriake, 193, 262
  Luke the Younger, 170, 173, 186, 209, 213, 215, 226, 232, 234, 236, 237, 241, 244–5, 257, 261, 263–5, 266, 290, 295
  Methodius, 142, 286
  Nikon, 174, 176, 187, 193–5, 209, 217, 219, 223, 232, 235, 237, 244, 246, 252, 255, 258–9, 260, 261, 262, 263, 264, 265, 266, 267, 277, 289
  Peter of Argos, 150, 172, 266
  Phantinos the Younger, 175, 245
  Theodora of Thessalonike, 144, 260, 261, 267, 288

Theodore of Kythera, 168, 266, 267
Theodosius the Younger, 151
Theoktiste of Lesbos, 266–7, 272n
Samos, 63, 88, 90, 146, 147
  theme of, 241
Samothrake, 166, 295n
Samuel, emperor, 175, 176, 236, 251, 276, 289
Sanders, Guy, 61
Sarantapechoi, family, 140
Sardinia, 123
scales, weighing, 35
scholia, 110, 174, 284
schools, 52, 117–18, 237
Sclavenes, 15, 16, 17, 19, 20, 62, 69, 141, 167, 232, 278–9, 281–7, 291, 293; see also Slavs
Schultz, Robert Weir, 6
seals, lead, 5, 6, 9, 10, 110–11, 113–17, 127, 141, 142, 146, 161n, 178, 184, 221, 231, 239, 250, 251, 272n, 285
Serbia, 40
Servia, 141
Setina, 23, 86, 175, 188
shipwrecks, 40
Sicily, 107, 108, 112, 118, 119, 123, 253
sickles, 37
Siderokausia, 144, 243
Siphnos, 121
Sirmium, 17, 117
Sklaviniai, 109, 119, 125, 142, 154, 246, 281
Skripou, 147–9, 156
Skyros, 140, 147
slaves, 153–4, 155, 156, 168, 175, 193, 213, 243, 244–5, 269
Slavesians, 172, 278
Slavic, language, 125, 173–4, 175, 210–11, 283–6, 288
Slavs, 1, 8, 9, 10, 17, 18, 68, 76, 85, 87, 88, 89, 90, 91, 92, 97, 108, 109, 110, 116, 119, 124, 125, 126, 135, 137, 139, 150–1, 153, 173–4, 225, 242, 251, 252, 254, 278–88, 291, 292
Smoliani, 142, 270n, 287

soldiers *see* stratiotai
Solomos, 68, 81, 89
sorcerers, 261
Sotiriou, Giorgios A., 7, 68
Soulinari, 34
Sparta, 6, 32, 109, 136, 137, 140, 151, 152, 156, 174, 175, 176, 184, 187, 193, 195, 209, 216, 217, 222, 223, 232, 233, 234, 235, 236, 237, 241, 244, 245, 250, 251, 252, 253, 254, 255, 256, 258, 259, 260, 263, 277, 289, 290, 291
Spata, 81
spears, 24, 106, 108, 153, 174, 220
Spercheios, 116, 176
Spilaion, 146, 231, 239
Stamata, 26, 27, 34
Stathakopoulos, Dionysios, 61
Staurakios, 99, 126
Stephen, Bishop of Larissa, 33
Stobi, 26
strategoi, 5, 9, 108, 110, 113–14, 119, 132n, 135, 137, 139, 140, 141, 143, 147, 152, 166, 170, 171, 172, 173, 176, 178, 183, 184, 186, 231, 232, 233, 234, 235, 236, 237, 238, 242, 254, 256, 259, 261, 263, 265, 276, 277, 278, 287
stratiotai, 9, 241, 242
Struck, Adolf Hermann, 5
Strymon, 108, 109, 110, 141, 145, 167, 213, 218, 287
    theme of, 5, 109, 142, 167, 173, 176, 178, 231, 232, 243, 287
swords, 99, 108
Symeon of Bulgaria, 145, 170, 173, 174, 182
Synaxis, 8, 26, 31, 184, 219, 275n

Taigetos, Mount, 140
Taranto, 153
Tarasios, patriarch, 250
Tarsos, 146, 166
taxes, 40, 96n, 111, 115, 131n, 177, 221, 224, 242
Tegea, 172, 195, 236, 237
Thasos, 31, 49, 50, 63, 64, 65, 68, 81, 91, 166, 169, 220

Thebes, 7, 32, 48, 52, 59, 68, 79, 80, 81, 109, 116, 141, 156, 170, 185, 187, 234, 235, 237, 250, 263, 265, 286
Theodore, Archbishop of Thessalonike, 144
Theodore, Metropolitan of Patras, 150
Theodore of Stoudios, 126, 143, 268–9
Theodosios Leobachos, 187
Theoktistos Bryennios, 139–40, 153, 282
Theopemptos, Bishop of Lakedaimon, 256
Theophanes Confessor, 117, 118, 125, 154, 289, 292
Theophilos, emperor, 137, 139, 140, 153, 282
Theophylact Simocatta, 1, 17
Thermopylae, 13–15, 21, 23, 40, 261
Thessalonica *see* Thessaloniki
Thessalonike *see* Thessaloniki
    theme of, 142, 170, 176, 178, 231, 241, 242, 243, 277
Thessaloniki, 5, 6, 16, 17, 18, 19, 20, 21, 22, 23, 24, 26, 27, 28, 32, 34, 48, 49, 50, 58, 62, 69, 85, 86, 87, 88, 89, 90, 91, 92, 98, 108, 110, 112, 115, 117, 125, 126, 141, 144, 145, 166–8, 170, 173, 175, 176, 177, 181, 217, 218, 219, 220–1, 222, 224, 226, 233, 245, 246, 249, 250, 251, 260, 285, 286, 287, 288, 291, 293, 295
Thessaly, 15, 18, 19, 28, 31, 33, 141, 156, 166, 176, 177, 239, 249, 250, 253, 291
Thisvi, 213, 241, 264
Thompson, Margaret, 112
Thrace, 15, 16, 17, 109, 141, 156, 198
    theme of, 9, 110, 139, 140, 232, 278
Tiberius II, 35, 49, 54, 88
Tiberius III, 121
Tigani, 99–100, 101, 120, 122, 123, 124, 152, 212
Tinos, island of, 259
Tiryns, 153, 239
Tithorea, 27
titles, 9, 114, 186, 231, 285

Tokatlis, 49
trade, 10, 24, 35, 39, 40, 50, 63, 64, 65, 85, 138–9, 140, 145, 175, 181, 184, 220–3, 289
Traianoupolis, 250, 251
Traquair, Ramsay, 6
Travlos, John, 6
Trikala, 48
Troizen, 116, 126, 250
Tzakonians, 225, 289
tzykanion, 234–5, 263

Vagenetia, 116, 286–7
Vakalopoulos, Apostolos, 7
Valma, 49
Vardar, 145, 221, 251, 289
  fort of, 160n
Varvara, 27, 34
Vasaras, 89
Vasiliev, Alexander, 2
Vasmer, Max, 3, 6
Veroia, 142, 176, 215, 217, 285
  theme of, 178
Via Egnatia, 22, 110, 123, 126, 141, 145, 161n, 218, 221

Vida, Tivadar, 124
villa, 38, 39, 49, 53, 54, 57, 58, 230
villages, 5, 35, 148n, 215, 217–18, 259
Vistonis, lake, 146, 219
Vodena *see* Edessa
Volos, 52, 239
Volvi, lake, 22, 210, 218
Vrya, 184, 215, 218

wells, 57
Willibald, Bishop of Eichstätt, 118–19, 125, 281
woodlands, 210, 212, 224
workshops, 24, 50, 53, 54, 56, 57, 58, 153, 220

Zacha, 90
Zakynthos, 251
Zakythinos, Dionysios A., 3, 68
Zante, 152, 289
Zeiss, Hans, 5
Zemaina, 251, 265
Zogeria, 85, 88
zooarchaeology, 37
Zourtsa, 195

EU representative:
Easy Access System Europe
Mustamäe tee 50, 10621 Tallinn, Estonia
Gpsr.requests@easproject.com

www.ingramcontent.com/pod-product-compliance
Lightning Source LLC
Chambersburg PA
CBHW050323020526
44117CB00031B/1491